INTERPRETING
and TEACHING
AMERICAN HISTORY

INTERPRETING and TEACHING AMERICAN HISTORY

WILLIAM H. CARTWRIGHT
AND RICHARD L. WATSON, JR.
Co-Editors

Thirty-First Yearbook of the

NATIONAL COUNCIL FOR THE SOCIAL STUDIES
A DEPARTMENT OF THE NATIONAL EDUCATION ASSOCIATION
1201 SIXTEENTH STREET, N. W., WASHINGTON 6, D. C.

Price: paperbound, $4.00; clothbound, $5.00

Preface

WE do not come to truly love and respect America by knowing too little about her history but by knowing as much as we can. The scholarship set forth by the distinguished contributors to the chapters of this Yearbook should, if used properly, enable teachers of social studies to be more effective in assisting young people to know their country better.

In the difficult and dangerous years ahead, such knowledge will be needed. It will be needed by our young citizens if they are to be equal to the task of upholding those principles of freedom and justice which is their American heritage, whether it be on the excursion circuits of the tourists, in the prison camps of future enemies, at the conference tables of the diplomats, or in opposition to demagoguery at home.

The National Council for the Social Studies is proud to be able to present this Yearbook to its members and friends. We hope it will be a welcome addition to the libraries of the schools and the professional libraries of history teachers. The Council is grateful to the editors, William Cartwright and Richard Watson, and to the authors who made it possible.

EMLYN JONES, *President*
The National Council for the Social Studies

Foreword

THE editors desire to acknowledge their indebtedness to the many people who have cooperated to make the production of this Yearbook possible. We are particularly grateful to the scholars who have contributed, without remuneration, the chapters to this Yearbook. The biographical section gives the present position and provides a select list of publications of each author. It does not attempt to list the numerous fellowships, awards, and other forms of recognition which the authors have been accorded. The enthusiasm with which they have cooperated in the preparation of the Yearbook testifies to their interest in the improvement of the teaching of history.

Three of the authors have written pamphlets on essentially the same subjects for the Service Center for Teachers of History of the American Historical Association. The editors are grateful to the Service Center and its Director, George Barr Carson, Jr., for permitting the publication of the chapters on the American Revolution and the Progressive Era and a portion of the chapter on the New Deal in almost the same form as they appeared in the Service Center series.

Miss Mary Paige Cubbison, a graduate assistant in the Department of History at Duke University, painstakingly checked the hundreds of footnotes. A part of the editorial work was carried out with the help of a grant from the Research Council of Duke University. Mrs. Carrie G. Grimsley, Editorial Assistant on the staff of the National Council for the Social Studies, gave valuable help with detail work.

The members of the Publications Committee of the National Council, Gertrude Whipple, Howard Anderson, and Harris Dante, read the entire manuscript and made useful suggestions for its improvement.

At the same time that they express their gratitude for the assistance which they have received, the editors should make it clear that they alone are responsible for errors in editorial judgment.

WILLIAM H. CARTWRIGHT
RICHARD L. WATSON, JR.
Co-Editors

THE NATIONAL COUNCIL FOR THE SOCIAL STUDIES

Officers for 1961

The National Council for the Social Studies is the Department of Social Studies of the National Education Association of the United States. It is the professional organization of teachers of social studies. It holds a series of meetings each year and publishes materials of significance to those interested in instruction in this field. Membership in the National Council carries with it a subscription to the Council's official journal, *Social Education*, the monthly magazine for social studies teachers, and the yearbook. In addition, the Council publishes bulletins, pamphlets, and other materials of practical use for teachers of the social studies. Membership dues are seven dollars a year for teachers with salaries over $3600 per year, five dollars for teachers with salaries of $3600 or less. Applications for membership and orders for the purchase of publications should be made to the Executive Secretary, 1201 Sixteenth Street, N.W., Washington 6, D.C.

PRINTED BY UNIVERSAL LITHOGRAPHERS, INC.

BALTIMORE, MARYLAND, U.S.A.

Contents

CHAPTER I

Historical Scholarship and the Teaching of History

William H. Cartwright and Richard L. Watson, Jr.

COOPERATION IN THE IMPROVEMENT OF TEACHING

THE hope is sometimes expressed that all issues which create argument among educators, such as those between teachers of education and teachers in other fields, soon will be resolved. However, is it not preferable to hope that the issues will never be resolved so long as controversy is accompanied by a meeting of minds in working out problems that are of interest to all members of the teaching profession? Fortunately, the professional aim of all teachers, whatever their subject, is the same—the improvement of teaching; and fortunately, too, an increasing number of people in schools and in colleges, both in and out of departments of education, are beginning to understand the position of one another. As a result there have been many efforts in which specialists in education and other subjects have cooperated to improve instruction in elementary and secondary schools; at the same time there has been a corresponding assessment of means to improve teaching in the colleges.

The yearbooks of the National Council for the Social Studies have provided outstanding examples of such collaboration. Not only has it permeated almost all recent yearbooks, but several volumes in the series have been devoted to specific school subjects. Thus, individual yearbooks have treated the study, interpretation, and teaching of geography, citizenship, contemporary affairs, world affairs, world history, American history, the social sciences as a whole, and the relationship of the social studies and science.

NEED FOR NEW INTERPRETATIONS

It has been fourteen years since the appearance of the Seventeenth Yearbook, which was devoted to American history.[1] College teachers of

---

[1] Richard E. Thursfield, ed., *The Study and Teaching of American History* (Washington: National Council for the Social Studies, a department of the National Education Association, 1946).

1

education, historians, and school teachers cooperated under excellent editorial leadership to make that volume an eminent success. It met a pressing need and continues to be extremely useful. Nevertheless, the flood of research and interpretations in both history and pedagogy since 1946 justifies a new treatment of the subject. Such a treatment is also timely because of the substantial changes in ways of living and in relationships among the peoples of the world which have taken place since World War II. With the tragedy of war and the optimism of victory fresh in mind, the editors of the Seventeenth Yearbook could see, as a leading purpose of education, the creating of an atmosphere in which such a tragedy could not happen again. Consequently, they emphasized as a principal aim for the study of history the gaining of an understanding of the need for "one world." It was possible to talk in optimistic terms about a world mobilization of educators for intelligent action designed to create the good citizen. The good citizen was defined as one who "believes in the inherent dignity of man," who is "tolerant, understanding, and humane, and free from the burden of bigotry, prejudice and discrimination"; at the same time, this good citizen would know that "a world of free men can be constructed only by individuals who have pledged themselves to work with the tools of intelligence."

These sentiments are as appropriate as they have ever been, but it would be rash indeed to prophesy today that the forces of reason, toleration, and humaneness can hope to win an early victory. We are still living in an age of loyalty oaths, affidavits, and state legislation which threatens to close schools; we still see student faces screwed up in hate because of attitudes which are clearly the reverse of any notion of the brotherhood of man; and those who talked of "one world" in 1960 are frequently labeled as either naive or hypocritical.

However, the editors of the present Yearbook are in complete agreement with the implicit philosophy behind the aims expressed by the editors of the earlier volume. We believe that history, if properly taught, can lead to a depth of perception which discourages irrational and emotional responses to current issues; the study of history can lead man, as Hans Kohn has said, to "a deeper understanding of himself, of his fellowman, and of the situations in which men are put."[2] Yet we must also recognize that history, if improperly taught, can become a vicious tool. The lessons of history may be debased to demonstrate the

---

[2] Hans Kohn, "A Historian's Creed for our Time," *American Association of University Professors Bulletin*, 39:612; Winter 1953-1954.

superiority of a race, or to sustain myths, or to create devils. From a different point of view, if rote memory is the method, and if the fact is considered the end rather than the means to the end, the teaching of history may result in a dislike for history. On the other hand, an undue de-emphasis of facts and the much-abused date can lead to a lack of precision in thinking which too often is nothing more than sloppiness.

CRITICAL THINKING IN HISTORICAL STUDY

Perhaps with the hazards as well as the value of teaching history in mind, the editors of this Yearbook might take as their text a statement of that distinguished first professor of political economy at Yale, William Graham Sumner. Sumner, pessimistic about any "formula for intellectual security," told new initiates into a chapter of Sigma XI in the year 1905, that "The only security is the constant practice of critical thinking. We ought never to accept fantastic notions of any kind; we ought to test all notions," Sumner went on; "we ought to pursue all propositions until we find out their connection with reality."[3]

We are, of course, quite aware that we are not suggesting any original purpose for the 1961 Yearbook. Indeed, one of the strengths of the series through the years has been that "critical thinking" has appeared as a recurring theme. Some contributors have considered it an ideal objective for education in general; others have put special emphasis on the fundamental need for developing the power of critical thinking as a practical skill. For example, Elmer Ellis, editor of the Seventh Yearbook (1937), hoped, through the encouragement of critical thinking, to provide some guidance to the potential citizen in his appraisal of "Sources of Information about Public Affairs." Howard R. Anderson called the Yearbook which he edited in 1942 *Teaching Critical Thinking in the Social Studies.* Howard Cummings, in the lead-off chapter of the 1950 Yearbook, *The Teaching of Contemporary Affairs,* listed as the first characteristic "of the citizen who is able to contribute to the formation of sound public opinion" an ability to arrive "at his decisions on public issues by a process or reflection of critical thinking." The Twenty-Fourth Yearbook, edited by Helen McCracken Carpenter, contains a chapter on the nature of critical thinking; while the same theme is implicit in Howard Anderson's *Approaches to an Understanding of World Affairs,* the Yearbook for 1954.

[3] Quoted in Ralph H. Gabriel, *The Course of American Democratic Thought* (2nd edition, New York: Ronald, 1956), p. 241.

Surely for the historian, it should be clear that to develop in our students this skill is a prerequisite to any other values that spring from a study of history. Herbert Baxter Adams, whose influence on the teaching of history in this country can hardly be over-estimated, wrote in 1879 that, "It is, perhaps, of as much consequence to teach a young person *how* to study history as to teach him history itself."[4] Every teacher of history should read an address by Learned Hand, one of the twentieth century's most distinguished jurists, in which he said that history was especially well "fitted to admonish us how tentative and provisional are our attainments, intellectual and moral; and how often the deepest convictions of one generation are the rejects of the next." According to Hand, this uncertainty "does not deny the possibility that, as time goes on, we shall accumulate some body of valued conclusions; but it does mean that these we can achieve only by accumulation; that wisdom is to be gained only as we stand upon the shoulders of those who have gone before."[5]

Hand is here asserting that one function of history is to give a student the intellectual capacity to face the world's problems. His argument may be used equally well to meet the complaints of those who say that each generation of historians re-interprets the past to such an extent that the value of any study of history at all is questionable. To them we can answer, as does Learned Hand, that the historian does not throw out the work that his predecessors have done; that, in fact, "wisdom is to be gained only as we stand upon the shoulders of those who have gone before."

The need for periodic re-evaluation of the interpretations of "those who have gone before" justifies such a Yearbook as this one. And furthermore the communication of the process of re-evaluation to the student may well be a teaching technique useful in further enlivening a class. The intelligent student should find the "interpretative" approach to history stimulating. Whether in high school or in college, he likes to feel that he is up-to-date. He likes to have questions raised about conventional interpretations. Nothing does more to promote intellectual alertness than to encourage thoughtful criticism. What can better promote thoughtful criticism than introducing the student to history through the most recent interpretations?

---

[4] G. Stanley Hall, ed., *Methods of Teaching History* (Ginn, Heath, 1885) p. 120.
[5] Learned Hand, "Freedom and the Humanities," speech reprinted in *American Association of University Professors Bulletin,* Winter 1952-1953, p. 525.

The History Teacher and Historical Research

If the primary aim of the Yearbook is to encourage critical thinking through the interpretative approach, another aim of almost equal importance is to bring teachers of social studies in the elementary and secondary schools into somewhat closer contact with those in the colleges and universities. The historical chapters of the Yearbook accomplish this aim in two ways. In the first place they are written by scholars who have specialized in the subject or period covered; and in the second place the chapters not only stress some of the significant interpretations of the period, but specify the scholars responsible for the interpretations.

The usefulness of the article which combines the interpretative and bibliographical approach is beyond question. Even the specialist is today constantly bemoaning the fact that he cannot keep up with the literature of his own limited field. The plight of the teacher of a survey course, in either college or school, is even worse. Books and articles are coming off the presses so rapidly that the best a teacher can do is to modify his notes or plans at a few points every year. Fortunately, the editors of some of the professional journals are taking cognizance of the difficulty of the teachers of general courses and are commissioning articles designed to pull together the recent literature on a particular subject. The *South Atlantic Quarterly,* the *Journal of Modern History,* the English publication *History,* the *Mississippi Valley Historical Review,* the *William and Mary Quarterly,* and the *American Historical Review* are among the journals which have printed useful review articles. A number have been particularly useful for the student of American history. For example, "The Problem of American Intervention, 1917," written by Richard Leopold of the history department at Northwestern University is a penetrating article which anyone teaching the United States' entry into World War I would do well to consult;[6] Edmund Morgan, now at Yale University, specialist on the Stamp Act and recent author of a brief history of the American Revolution, has contributed "Revisions in Need of Revising," a brilliant article on the American Revolution, to the *William and Mary Quarterly;*[7] and Richard Morris of Columbia University has written an equally penetrating article entitled "The Confederation Period and the American Historian."[8] Roy Nichols, now Dean of the Graduate School

---

[6] *Journal of Politics,* 2:405-25; April 1950.

[7] *William and Mary Quarterly,* 14:1 (f.); January 1957.

[8] *Ibid.,* 13:139 (f.); April 1956.

of Arts and Sciences at the University of Pennsylvania, whose book, *The Disruption of American Democracy*, won the Pulitzer prize in 1948, wrote "The Kansas-Nebraska Act: A Century of Historiography."[9] Wayne S. Cole of Iowa State College at Ames wrote a superb analysis of the entry of the United States into World War II;[10] and one of the editors of the present Yearbook surveyed twenty years of books and articles about Woodrow Wilson and some of the writing about Franklin D. Roosevelt.[11]

However, the isolated article, useful though it may be, does not solve the problem of the teachers in the schools, who lack time to keep up with many professional journals. An important aid in meeting their need is the series of pamphlets published by the Service Center for Teachers of History of the American Historical Association. The authors of the pamphlets are experts in their fields, and the subjects chosen are significant. Although the purpose of the series is essentially the same as that of the present Yearbook, the two projects will supplement rather than compete with one another. The authors, and therefore the treatments, in most instances, are different. Further, the comprehensive organization of the Yearbook provides in a single volume an inclusive approach to the history of the United States, together with suggestions for teaching the subject.

ORGANIZATION OF THE YEARBOOK

In considering how best to organize the Yearbook, the editors decided upon an organization fundamentally different from that of 1946. This decision was prompted by an equally fundamental decision to devote at least two-thirds of the book to historical chapters and the remainder of the volume to chapters emphasizing approaches to teaching. With this plan, chapters of respectable length could be provided coinciding with the conventional chronological periods of American history. As a matter of principle, both editors favor a chronological approach on the ground that this approach best indicates the way in which things happen. Topical chapters are used only when the author might be strained to introduce a key interpretation into a chapter based upon a strictly chronological organization.

---

[9] *Mississippi Valley Historical Review*, 43:187 (f.); September 1956.

[10] "American Entry into World War II: A Historiographical Appraisal," *Ibid.*, 43:595-617; March 1957.

[11] Richard L. Watson, Jr., "Woodrow Wilson and His Interpreters, 1947-1957," *Ibid.*, 44:207-36; September 1957. "Franklin D. Roosevelt in Historical Writing," *South Atlantic Quarterly*, 55:104-26; Winter 1958.

One of the minor problems that developed from this organization was the possibility of one chapter's overlapping another. It is obviously impossible to avoid some duplication between topical chapters and chronological ones, but it is almost equally impossible to find a complete chronological breakdown that will confine interpretations drawn from books and articles within a neat chronological framework. Consequently, the editors accepted as inevitable some duplication when it seemed necessary to illuminate the subject of any chapter.

An even more difficult problem faced by the editors and the authors was to decide how much a chapter should be "interpretative" and how much "bibliographical." The editors are quite aware that some may question the decision to permit the chapters to become somewhat heavily weighted on the side of bibliography. The questions may be asked, are the books and articles cited available to the average teacher in the schools, and even if they are available does the teacher have the time to read them. The editors considered these questions carefully. To understand their decision, it should be recognized, first of all, that this Yearbook was not designed to provide a simple narrative of American history based upon the most recent scholarship. If this were the purpose, the teacher need only buy one of the numerous excellent textbooks for college students which are continually being published.[12] However, the purpose was not to provide an easy substitute for a text; the purpose was to introduce students of the social studies to recent interpretations of history through the world of scholarship and at the same time to emphasize the variety of the interpretations by relating them to the scholars responsible for the interpretations. This purpose required the inclusion of substantial bibliographical references. Even so, the references are highly selective. In every case, the authors referred only to the most important articles, and the books actually cited constitute only a small portion of the thousands of volumes on American history which have been published in recent years.

The topics of some chapters lent themselves readily to an interpretative approach; whereas others seemed to require a greater attention to bibliography. In asking distinguished historians to contribute to the Yearbook, the editors believed it necessary to allow the authors considerable freedom to report as they saw fit in accordance with the canons of their profession.

---

[12] See for example, T. Harry Williams, Richard N. Current, and Frank Freidel, *A History of the United States* (2 vols.; New York: Knopf, 1959); Arthur Link, *American Epoch* (New York: Knopf, 1955), soon to be revised.

The approach followed by the historians should encourage the readers of these chapters to add wisely to their own personal libraries. Even more it is to be hoped that the social studies teacher will be in a position to urge the purchase of some of the books for the school library and to recommend books to his students. Even though it may be impossible to read all books cited, it should be recognized that an essential element in the mastery of a subject is a knowledge of the literature of that subject. The authors of the Yearbook's chapters are writing for their fellow students, and certainly the editors would not condone any disposition on the part of these scholars to assume that they need "write down" to their colleagues who teach in the elementary and secondary schools. After all, if the historians were required to do the entire job of simplifying and reorganizing materials for purposes of instruction, there should be no need for highly educated teachers or specialists in pedagogy.

The last six chapters of the Yearbook suggest various approaches to the teaching of history. The relationship of geography to history is so significant that the editors asked a professor of geography to write a practical treatment on the use of geography in the teaching of history. The usefulness and abundance of local resources for teaching American history are so great that a chapter was provided by a specialist in their use. Perhaps the greatest market for books in the United States is for those which are written in the first place for children and adolescents. Many of these deal with American history, and the Yearbook provides a chapter on their use by a professor of library science and a professor of history who have well-earned reputations as authorities on such books.

Chapters XVIII, XIX, and XX were written by persons who were trained in historical scholarship, but who are well-known as experts in teaching social studies at the three levels toward which the chapters are directed. The authors of these chapters had the historians' chapters in hand as they wrote. The extent to which complex interpretations of history can be utilized directly in instruction increases with the maturity of the learner. Much use of these interpretations can be made in the senior high school, less in the junior high school or upper grades, and still less in the middle grades. Indeed, the author of the chapter on teaching American history in the middle grades was constrained to write almost independently of the historical chapters of the Yearbook. But, even in the middle grades, the teacher of history will be more effective as she grasps the deeper meaning of her subject.

FURTHER SUGGESTIONS

In spite of the comprehensive nature of the chapters, there are a few general suggestions which might be of further use to readers. In the first place, one of the most valuable reference works for any student of American history is *The Harvard Guide to American History*.[13] This book has chapters on the nature of history, research and writing, and the sources of history, and, most importantly, contains comprehensive bibliographies of almost every conceivable subject in American history.

There are also several important historical series which every student of American history would find most useful. Of these, perhaps the most important is the New American Nation Series. Historians for years have been indebted to the American Nation Series published by Harper and edited by Albert Bushnell Hart. Although the volumes of this series began to appear around the turn of the twentieth century, some of them are still useful in their field. The first volume of the New American Nation Series, edited by Henry Steele Commager and Richard B. Morris, was published in 1954. New volumes are appearing regularly. About forty volumes are planned. They are brief and readable, are written by scholars of note, and contain excellent bibliographies.[14] Another well-known series, The Chronicles of America, has been brought through World War II with five volumes edited by Allan Nevins and published in 1950 and 1951;[15] and only one or two volumes of a superb ten-volume History of the South (but valuable for others than students of Southern history) remain to be published.[16] In addition, several publishing houses have been experimenting with biographical series. One of these, the Great Lives in Brief, published by Alfred A. Knopf, contains volumes from every field of history; while the Library of American Biography, edited by Oscar Handlin and published by Little, Brown, is devoted only to American subjects. The biographies in both of these series are brief, relatively inexpensive, based upon the most recent scholarship, and written in a way that would appeal not only to teachers but as well to the better students.

Another significant development of the post-war period has been a tremendous increase in the publication of paperback editions. The

---

[13] Oscar Handlin, Arthur M. Schlesinger, et al, eds., *Harvard Guide to American History* (Cambridge: Harvard University, 1955).

[14] The series is published by Harper, and has a textbook edition for students which is considerably less expensive than the trade edition.

[15] The Chronicles of America Series is published by Yale University Press.

[16] Wendell Holmes Stephenson and E. Merton Coulter, eds., *A History of the South* (10 vols.; Louisiana State University).

student of American history can now find in inexpensive bindings old classics, new books specially commissioned, and collections of source materials. For the teacher interested in the "interpretation" approach, one of the most thought-provoking series is the Problems in American Civilization, published by D. C. Heath. The paperbacks in this series are focused on a particular problem upon which "opinion has been sharply divided" such as the Declaration of Independence, Wilson at Versailles, or the New Deal. Each book consists of excerpts of writings which represent different points of view on the subject. Another useful series, available both in hard covers and in paperback, is the Chicago History of American Civilization, edited by Daniel J. Boorstin. Here, perhaps, Edmund S. Morgan's *The Birth of the Republic, 1763-1789* and William E. Leuchtenburg's *The Perils of Prosperity, 1914-1932* are worthy of special mention as small books which combine the best of recent scholarship with an eminently readable style.

The paperbacks in series provide only a small part of the flood of inexpensive books useful for the American historian. It is almost impossible to keep up with all the new titles, but there is at least one reference designed to help the reader in this respect.[17] It is now possible to teach a general course in American history by discarding a hard-cover text completely and using paperbacks drawn either from one or more series or from the many miscellaneous titles.[18]

SUMMARY

The opportunities for the teacher of history today are unprecedented. He faces challenges from those who say that the American educational system is inferior to those of other nations. There are those who demand that history be used as propaganda designed to prove that the past of the United States has been without blemish and that its system is at every point superior to the systems of other lands; on the other hand, there are those who see little good in the study of history at all, and who, in the emotionalism surrounding the production of space

---

[17] *Paperbound Books in Print* published periodically by the R. R. Bowker Company, 62 W. 45th Street, New York 36, N. Y.

[18] For example, one might choose the following: George F. Kennan, *American Diplomacy, 1900-1950* (Mentor); Richard Hofstadter, *The American Political Tradition* (Vintage); Alexis de Tocqueville, *Democracy in America* (2 vols.; Vintage); Paul Angle, ed., *The Lincoln Reader* (Pocketbooks); C. Vann Woodward, *Reunion and Reaction* (A Doubleday Anchor Book); Eric Goldman, *Rendezvous with Destiny* (Vintage); Frederick Lewis Allen, *Only Yesterday* (A Bantam Book).

ships and rockets, can think only of producing scientists and engineers. The teacher of history is capable of meeting these challenges. He should be willing, while standing on the shoulders of those who have gone before, constantly to experiment with new methods designed to impart to his students the enthusiasm to investigate critically the past in order to acquire "a deeper understanding of himself, of his fellowman, and of the situations in which men are put."

Part One: Interpretations

CHAPTER II

The Establishment of the American Colonies

Wesley Frank Craven

INTRODUCTION*

IN 1946, when the Seventeenth Yearbook of the National Council for the Social Studies was published, it was far easier to comment on pre-war trends in the study of American history than to suggest the interpretations that were likely to prevail in the post-war era. No other war in the nation's history had so thoroughly disrupted the normal activities of American scholars as had the Second World War. Most of the "recent works" that could be cited in 1946 had been published before the war, and even the few which had found publication during the course of the war owed their inspiration very largely to pre-war interests. One could only hazard a guess as to the influence that the war itself would have on the continuing problem of interpreting the American past.

THE IMPERIAL SCHOOL
Beer and Andrews

For a generation before the coming of the war, the dominant influence in the interpretation of the earlier chapters in the nation's history belonged to the so-called imperial school of historians. Its leaders were George L. Beer and Charles M. Andrews, two of the ablest historians this country has produced. Beer's sympathetic studies of the British colonial system had been published before the First World War.[1] Andrews had written several significant works during this same

---

* All readers are referred to Louis B. Wright, *New Interpretations of American Colonial History*, Publication No. 16 of the American Historical Association's Service Center for Teachers of History (Washington, D. C., 1959). Its very full listing of recent publications has made it possible to reduce the number cited here.

[1] On the period covered by this essay Beer wrote three volumes: *The Origins of the British Colonial System, 1578-1660* (New York: Macmillan, 1908); and *The Old Colonial System, 1660-1754* (2 vols.; New York: Macmillan, 1912).

12

period of time,[2] but his great four-volume study, *The Colonial Period of American History*, was not published until the 1930's, after the author's retirement from a long and influential teaching career at Yale.[3]

Like Beer, Andrews insisted upon the need to study American colonial history in the full context of Britain's commercial and colonial expansion—hence the designation of the imperial school. "I have been convinced for many years that to place the colonies in their rightful historical setting and so to discover what our colonial history is all about," he wrote in the preface to his final work, "it would be necessary to re-examine the evidence from a vantage point other than that usually taken, to view them not from within, as is commonly done, but from without, with the movement constantly forward, following the natural course of historical development, and disregarding all preconceptions based on later events."[4] Despite its title, Andrews' *magnum opus* is not a history of the colonial period. Instead, it presents in the first three volumes a comprehensive and especially instructive account of the original establishment of the colonies. Close attention is paid to the English background; stress is placed on the continuing interdependence of the English and American sides of the story; and the West Indian settlements, as well as those established on the North American continent, are brought into the discussion. The fourth and final volume is a study of the development of England's colonial policy.

In its origins, the imperial school represented a reaction against the nationalist emphasis that had marked so much of the writings on American history in the nineteenth century, not to mention the even narrower provincialism of a large body of literature devoted to the history of the individual states. At the beginning of a new century, as the nation acquired a new maturity and began to assume new responsibilities in world affairs, the more sophisticated approach of the imperial school had a strong appeal. By the 1930's it was no longer new. It had become instead a generally accepted view.

Overseas Expansion

Fortunately, this new approach to the study of American colonial history had coincided with an awakening interest among English his-

---

[2] Especially his volume in the original American Nation Series entitled *Colonial Self-Government, 1652-1689* (New York: Harper, 1904) ; and *British Committees, Commissions, and Councils of Trade and Plantations, 1622-1675* (Baltimore: Johns Hopkins, 1908) .

[3] New Haven: Yale University, 1934-1938.

[4] *Ibid.*, Vol. I, p. xi.

torians in the story of England's overseas expansion. Fortunately, too, the English historians showed an inclination to begin at the beginning, which is to say with the sixteenth century.[5] Thus, in 1913, James A. Williamson's *Maritime Enterprise, 1485-1558* traced in illuminating detail the background that was needed for an understanding of the great age of Elizabethan adventure.[6] He followed this in 1927 with a biography of Hawkins that rescued one of the more significant figures of that age from the category of freebooting piracy to which tradition had tended to assign him.[7] A decade later Williamson added a comprehensive study of *The Age of Drake*.[8]

The volume on Drake and his contemporaries appeared as one in an especially informative and readable series known as the Pioneer Histories, of which Vincent T. Harlow, author of a history of Barbados in the seventeenth century,[9] and Williamson were the general editors. The purpose of the series was "to provide broad surveys of the great migrations of European peoples—for purposes of trade, conquest, and settlement—into the non-European continents." Among the other volumes were several that had special interest for American students. Arthur P. Newton's *The European Nations in the West Indies, 1493-1688*, skillfully placed the story of this "cockpit of international maritime rivalry" in the context of Europe's diplomatic and military history.[10] Sir William Foster's *England's Quest of Eastern Trade* offered many helpful suggestions as to the relationship between westward adventures and those which sought by eastward routes to tap the wealth of the Orient.[11] Edgar Prestage reviewed the story of *The Portuguese Pioneers*,[12] and Frederick A. Kirkpatrick that of *The Spanish Conquistadores*.[13] J. Bartlet Brebner, a Canadian teaching in the United States, studied together "as a related whole the explorations which first

---

[5] For a time after the publication of Sir John R. Seeley's famous lectures on *The Expansion of England* (London, 1883) the modern empire tended to claim first attention, but soon the trend turned toward more intensive study of the earlier years. See Wesley Frank Craven, "Historical Study of the British Empire," *Journal of Modern History*, 6:40-69; 1934.

[6] Oxford: Clarendon, 1913.

[7] *Sir John Hawkins, the Time and the Man* (Oxford: Clarendon, 1927). In his later *Hawkins of Plymouth* (London: A. and C. Black, 1949), Williamson revised some of his earlier views.

[8] London: A. and C. Black, 1938.

[9] *A History of Barbados, 1625-1685* (Oxford: Clarendon, 1926).

[10] *The European Nations in the West Indies, 1493-1688* (London: A. and C. Black, 1933).

[11] London: A. and C. Black, 1933.

[12] London: A. and C. Black, 1933.

[13] London: A. and C. Black, 1934.

revealed the general character of the North American continent" in *The Explorers of North America, 1492-1806*.[14] All of the contributors to the first volume of the *Cambridge History of the British Empire,* which was published in 1929 and was devoted to the Old Empire, were British scholars except for Charles M. Andrews.[15]

In the work of men who are younger than those previously mentioned there is promise that students of American history can continue to expect significant assistance from Britain. A. L. Rowse, who in 1937 contributed a brilliant biography of Sir Richard Grenville,[16] more recently published *The Expansion of Elizabethan England* as the second volume in his stimulating study of the Elizabethan age and four years later added *The Elizabethans and America*.[17] David B. Quinn followed his two-volume collection of *The Voyages and Colonising Enterprises of Sir Humphrey Gilbert*,[18] which has a lengthy introduction summarizing the latest evidence on this important figure, with a comparably valuable collection on *The Roanoke Voyages, 1584-1590*.[19] His *Raleigh and the British Empire* is especially helpful because of the attention it gives to the Irish interests of so many of the earlier English promoters of adventures to America.[20]

Although American scholars in the present century have been more content than one might have expected, to leave the years preceding the period of settlement in the capable hands of their English colleagues, they have not been wholly inactive in this area of investigation. George B. Parks' *Richard Hakluyt and the English Voyages* is a work of major importance on a figure who deserves to be much better remembered by Americans than he has been.[21] Samuel Eliot Morison, whose brilliant writings on American history have ranged all the way from the fifteenth century to the twentieth, published a capital biography of Columbus in 1942, one re-establishing, after years of debate, the old view that Columbus discovered America while attempting to

[14] London: A. and C. Black, 1933.
[15] Cambridge: Cambridge University, 1929. A useful bibliography is appended. Mention belongs also to the very useful studies in the history of geographical knowledge done by Eva G. R. Taylor: *Tudor Geography, 1485-1583* (London: Methuen, 1930); and *Late Tudor and Early Stuart Geography, 1583-1650* (London: Methuen, 1934).
[16] *Sir Richard Grenville of the Revenge, an Elizabethan Hero* (London: Jonathan Cape, 1937).
[17] London: Macmillan, 1955 and New York: Harper, 1959.
[18] Two vols.; London: The Hakluyt Society, 1940.
[19] London: The Hakluyt Society, 1955.
[20] London: Hodder & Stoughton, 1947.
[21] New York: American Geographical Society, 1928.

reach the Orient.[22] That Columbus was the first European to reach the New World after the Vikings was the point of an earlier monograph by Morison on *Portuguese Voyages to America in the Fifteenth Century*.[23] Louis B. Wright presented in 1943 a helpful study of *Religion and Empire; the Alliance Between Piety and Commerce in English Expansion, 1558-1625*.[24] More recently, Willard M. Wallace wrote an excellent biography of *Sir Walter Raleigh*.[25]

A contemporary of Beer and Andrews who also helped to broaden the scope of studies in the field of American history was Herbert E. Bolton of the University of California. The founder, it might be said, of his own school of Latin-American studies, he vigorously insisted that the colonial period of American history should be studied on a continental scale, with close attention to the stories of the Spanish and French settlements as well as to those established by the English and the Dutch.[26] His *The Spanish Borderlands; a Chronicle of Old Florida and the Southwest* will be remembered by many teachers of American history as one of the more helpful volumes in the Yale Chronicles of America Series.[27] His argument is eloquently presented in a collection of his essays published in 1939 under the title of *Wider Horizons of American History*.[28] Among other specialists in Latin American history, the writings of Clarence H. Haring, Lewis Hanke, and John Tate Lanning are helpful for the period here discussed.[29]

Although Canadian historians have tended to concentrate their attention on the more modern periods of their history, two works by the late Professor Harold A. Innis of the University of Toronto have great interest for students of the earlier chapters in the history of the

---

[22] *Admiral of the Ocean Sea; a Life of Christopher Columbus* (2 vols.; Boston: Little, Brown, 1942). There is also a one-volume edition.

[23] Cambridge: Harvard University, 1940.

[24] Chapel Hill: University of North Carolina, 1943.

[25] Princeton: Princeton University, 1959.

[26] As in his text, with Thomas M. Marshall, on *The Colonization of North America, 1492-1783* (New York: Macmillan, 1936).

[27] New Haven: Yale University, 1921.

[28] New York: D. Appleton-Century, 1939. His last major work was *Coronado on the Turquoise Trail; Knight of Pueblos and Plains* (Albuquerque: University of New Mexico, 1949).

[29] Clarence H. Haring, *The Buccaneers in the West Indies in the XVII Century* (New York: E. P. Dutton, 1910); Clarence H. Haring, *Trade and Navigation between Spain and the Indies in the Time of the Hapsburgs* (Cambridge: Harvard University, 1918); Clarence H. Haring, *The Spanish Empire in America* (New York: Oxford University, 1947); Lewis Hanke, *The Spanish Struggle for Justice in the Conquest of America* (Philadelphia: University of Pennsylvania, 1949); John Tate Lanning, *The Spanish Missions of Georgia* (Chapel Hill: University of North Carolina, 1935).

United States. *The Cod Fisheries; the History of an International Economy,* one of the volumes in the series on The Relations of Canada and the United States sponsored by the Carnegie Endowment for International Peace, is of fundamental importance, especially for students of New England's history.[30] *The Fur Trade of Canada* bears less directly on the history of the English colonies, but it cannot be overlooked.[31] The establishment in 1947 of the *Revue d'Histoire de l'Amérique française,* under the sponsorship of the Institut d'Histoire de l'Amerique française at the University of Montreal, promises a reviving interest in the history of French Canada. For the work that is under way W. J. Eccles' *Frontenac: the Courtier Governor* sets a high standard.[32]

THE AMERICAN COLONIES

Twentieth century students of American history, by following Professor Andrews' injunction to view the colonies "from without" and by taking advantage of the assistance of many scholars not primarily concerned with the history of the United States, have acquired a better understanding of their colonial history in its relationship to the broader story of European expansion. But even while Andrews was writing his *magnum opus,* there were indications that newer historical interests would challenge the leadership enjoyed by the imperial school since the beginning of the century.

Many historians had come to feel that it was time to look more closely at the colonies "from within." To some, it seemed that the imperial school had provided the foundation on which to build a better history of the internal development of the colonies. With others, it was felt that the marked sympathy shown by the imperial school for England's colonial system, as in the tendency both Beer and Andrews showed to discount the adverse effects of imperial policy on the economic life of the colonies, had distorted the true picture. It was also believed that the heavy emphasis on a British orientation of colonial history tended to introduce a misleading distinction between the colonial and national periods of our history, with a consequent loss of feeling for the underlying continuity of the American experience. To Andrews' insistence that American colonial history was colonial before

---

[30] New Haven: Yale University, 1940.
[31] New Haven: Yale University, 1930. A revised edition was published posthumously by the University of Toronto in 1956.
[32] Toronto: McClelland & Stewart, 1959.

it was American came now the answer that it *was*, after all and never-theless, American.[33]

A significant indication of a newer trend in colonial studies came with the publication in 1938, the very year in which Andrews completed his history, of Curtis P. Nettels' *The Roots of American Civilization*.[34] In this unusually informative and suggestive text on the colonial period, Professor Nettels quickly disposed of the European background, the explorations, and the settlement of the colonies in 161 pages, thereby clearing the way for use of more than 500 pages in a study that consistently kept its focus on the American scene. Discussions of imperial policy were approached from the point of view of the colonists, rather than that of London, and the author's judgments were frequently critical of London. A heavy emphasis on the economic factor and the evidences of social conflict reflected the times in which the book was written. So, too, did Lawrence Harper's significant study of *The English Navigation Laws* in 1939.[35] Its inspiration was quite different from that which had guided Beer and Andrews. Harper was interested in the ways in which legislative policy might mold the development of a community. The adverse effects of the Navigation Acts on colonial life were as readily admitted to the discussion as any other.

As was noted at the beginning of this Chapter, the Second World War brought a serious interruption in the work of most American historians. But toward the end of the war Harvard's distinguished philosopher, Ralph Barton Perry, published a book that offered a clue as to one of the interests that would engage the attention of post-war students of American history. The title was *Puritanism and Democracy*,[36] and the book had grown out of a course he formerly taught at Harvard on "American Ideals." That he found the essential elements of the American tradition in the pessimism of Puritanism and the optimism of the Declaration of Independence is not so important, for the purposes at least of this discussion, as that he was concerned with the place of the ideal in American history, or that the seventeenth century Puritan once more became important for all who would understand what has made an American an American.

---

[33] See the preface to his *The Colonial Background of the American Revolution* (New Haven: Yale University, 1924) ; and for a discussion of Andrews and his critics, see Abraham S. Eisenstadt, *Charles McLean Andrews; a Study in American Historical Writing* (New York: Columbia University, 1956) .

[34] New York: F. S. Crofts, 1938.

[35] New York: Columbia University, 1939.

[36] New York: Vanguard, 1944.

The responsibilities and the tensions of the post-war era have encouraged renewed attempts to understand our history in its relationship to the whole course of western civilization. This is especially noticeable in the field of intellectual and cultural history, where the emphasis is on the European heritage and the continuing ties with the main centers of European culture, as in Louis B. Wright's *The Cultural Life of the American Colonies*.[37] But no less marked is the search for the distinctive qualities of America itself, as in Daniel J. Boorstin's stimulating and provocative *The Americans; the Colonial Experience*.[38] A lively post-war debate on the character of the American Revolution has brought a new interest in colonial history, and more particularly in the institutional life of the colonies, for the issues turn very largely on the question of how much change the Revolution wrought in an established way of life. As yet, and as would be expected, the debate has directed more attention to the colonies in the eighteenth century than in the seventeenth,[39] but there are exceptions. Clinton Rossiter's *Seedtime of the Republic; the Origin of the American Tradition of Political Liberty* covers the entire colonial period.[40] Its argument may be suggested simply by citing the title he used for an abbreviated paperback edition in 1956, which was *The First American Revolution*.[41]

New England

In this rediscovery of America, as the newer trend of colonial studies might well be described, the greatest single find has been the New England Puritan. In place of the sharp condemnations which earlier in the century were carried almost to the point of rejecting any claim he might have to a place in the American tradition, rightfully interpreted, one finds now the warmest praise—for his practicality, for his moral stamina, for his intellectual achievement, even for the zest he found in life itself. The turning point came in 1930 with the publica-

---

[37] Louis B. Wright, *The Cultural Life of the American Colonies, 1607-1763* (New York: Harper, 1957).

[38] New York: Random House, 1958.

[39] Where the old standard, Herbert L. Osgood, *The American Colonies in the Seventeenth Century* (3 vols.; New York: Columbia University, 1904-1907) continues to be useful.

[40] New York: Harcourt, Brace, 1953.

[41] Harvest Books, New York: Harcourt, Brace, 1956. Post-war interest in the colonial period owes much to the leadership of the Institute of Early American History and Culture at Williamsburg, which is jointly sponsored by the College of William and Mary and Colonial Williamsburg, Inc. Its *William and Mary Quarterly* is perhaps the liveliest historical journal in the country.

tion by Samuel Eliot Morison of *Builders of the Bay Colony*,[42] just as Massachusetts inaugurated a series of tercentennial celebrations of the founding of New England. In the year which preceded Harvard's tercentenary in 1936, Morison published *The Founding of Harvard College*, a book which brilliantly related the history of the American colonial college to the tradition and practice of the European university.[43] This was quickly followed by two meaty volumes on *Harvard College in the Seventeenth Century*, which set a new standard for writing the history of an American educational institution.[44]

The focus on Harvard fitted well into the current interest in intellectual history, and Perry Miller, also of Harvard, had a special gift for restoring life to the theological issues of the seventeenth century. His *Orthodoxy in Massachusetts, 1630-1650*, published in 1933;[45] *The New England Mind: The Seventeenth Century*, in 1939;[46] and *The New England Mind: From Colony to Province*, in 1953,[47] are three of the more important books that have been published in the field of American history by the present generation of scholars. The subject matter is difficult, and Miller refuses to write it down for the benefit of the uninitiated, but fortunately several of his more significant themes can be followed in a collection of his essays entitled *Errand into the Wilderness*.[48] Miller's *Roger Williams; His Contribution to the American Tradition* carries a warning against any assumption that Williams was a forerunner of Jefferson.[49]

Since the war Alan Simpson has suggested that Morison and Miller may have given too much emphasis to the intellectual content of Puritanism, that the mainsprings of Puritanism were after all spiritual.[50] Edmund Morgan's *The Puritan Dilemma; the Story of John Winthrop* in an appreciative study of Winthrop's statesmanship.[51] Ola E. Winslow's *Meetinghouse Hill, 1630-1783* is a sensitive book done with artistry.[52] Douglas E. Leach has given us in *Flintlock and Toma-*

---

[42] Boston and New York: Houghton Mifflin, 1930.
[43] Cambridge: Harvard University, 1935.
[44] Cambridge: Harvard University, 1936.
[45] Cambridge: Harvard University, 1933.
[46] New York: Macmillan, 1939; reissued by Harvard University in 1954.
[47] Cambridge: Harvard University, 1953.
[48] Cambridge: Harvard University, 1956.
[49] Indianapolis and New York: Bobbs-Merrill, 1953.
[50] *Puritanism in Old and New England* (Chicago: University of Chicago, 1955).
[51] Boston: Little, Brown, 1958.
[52] New York: Macmillan, 1952. More recently she has published *Master Roger Williams, A Biography* (New York: Macmillan, 1957).

hawk an excellent study of New England at the time of King Philip's War.[53] Bernard Bailyn's *The New England Merchants in the Seventeenth Century* is an admirable book which opens up for re-interpretation the whole story of New England's economic relations with London.[54] Though basically an economic study, it is also good social history, and the author is always alert to the location of political power in seventeenth century New England.

The Southern Colonies

The restoration to good repute of Captain John Smith will do for a transition from New England to the southern colonies.[55] The works of Thomas J. Wertenbaker, by emphasizing the middle class origins of the Virginia settlers and the dominance of the small farm in seventeenth century Virginia, have helped to bring studies of that area into the main stream of American history.[56] His inclination to view Nathaniel Bacon, leader of the great rebellion in 1676, as a *Torchbearer of the Revolution*[57] has been vigorously disputed by Wilcomb E. Washburn in *The Governor and the Rebel; A History of Bacon's Rebellion in Virginia*.[58] Washburn insists that the dispute had nothing to do with the issues of the eighteenth century, but rather was a quarrel about Indian affairs. Donnell M. Owings' *His Lordship's Patronage; Offices of Profit in Colonial Maryland* indicates that it was more than the love of power which led gentlemen to seek office in colonial times.[59] Abbot E. Smith's *Colonists in Bondage; White Servitude and Convict Labor in America, 1607-1776* relates chiefly to the life of the southern colonies.[60] Verner Crane's useful study of *The Southern Frontier, 1670-1732*, first published in 1929, has recently been reissued as a paperback.[61] Wesley Frank Craven has drawn upon his earlier studies of

---

[53] New York: Macmillan, 1958.

[54] Cambridge: Harvard University, 1955. George Lee Haskins, *Law and Authority in Early Massachusetts; a Study in Tradition and Design* (New York: Macmillan, 1960) is of comparable significance. Unfortunately, it was published too late for mention above.

[55] Actually, the restoration of Captain Smith's reputation for veracity has been under way since early in the century, but Bradford Smith's *Captain John Smith; His Life & Legend* (Philadelphia: Lippincott, 1953) offers new evidence by Laura P. Striker.

[56] Especially *The Planters of Colonial Virginia* (Princeton: Princeton University, 1922).

[57] Princeton: Princeton University, 1940.

[58] Chapel Hill: University of North Carolina, 1957.

[59] Baltimore: Maryland Historical Society, 1953.

[60] Chapel Hill: University of North Carolina, 1947.

[61] Ann Arbor Books, Ann Arbor: University of Michigan, 1956.

Virginia and Bermuda[62] in writing an over-all account of *The Southern Colonies in the Seventeenth Century.*[63]

The Middle Colonies

One is still too much dependent on older works for the seventeenth century history of the middle colonies. John E. Pomfret has done a very useful study of *The Province of West New Jersey, 1609-1702.*[64] The earlier chapters of Frederick B. Tolles' *Meeting House and Counting House; the Quaker Merchants of Colonial Philadelphia, 1682-1763* are especially illuminating on the story of the Quaker migration.[65] Catherine Owens Peare's *William Penn, A Biography* is a readable and informative biography.[66] Henry H. Kessler and Eugene Rachlis have contributed an excellent book on *Peter Stuyvesant and His New York* which reveals, among more important matters, that his famous wooden leg was the right one.[67] Not to be overlooked are the earlier chapters of Philip L. White's *The Beekmans of New York in Politics and Commerce, 1647-1877.*[68] Julius Goebel, Jr., and T. Raymond Naughton's *Law Enforcement in Colonial New York; a Study in Criminal Procedure, 1664-1776* has broad interest for students of legal institutions.[69]

General Studies

There have been an encouraging number of general studies, leaping over provincial and even sectional bounds. Richard B. Morris' *Studies in the History of American Law; with Special Reference to the Seventeenth and Eighteenth Centuries* is one of the more useful,[70] as is his more recent *Government and Labor in Early America.*[71] Carl Bridenbaugh's *Cities in the Wilderness; the First Century of Urban Life in America, 1652-1742* is full of information.[72] Stella H. Sutherland's *Population Distribution in Colonial America* is frequently useful.[73] Mention belongs also to the earlier chapters of Joseph Dorfman's open-

---

[62] *Dissolution of the Virginia Company* (New York: Oxford University, 1932) and *An Introduction to the History of Bermuda* (Williamsburg, 1938).

[63] *The Southern Colonies in the Seventeenth Century, 1607-1689* (Baton Rouge: Louisiana State University, 1949).

[64] Princeton: Princeton University, 1956.

[65] Chapel Hill: University of North Carolina, 1948.

[66] Philadelphia: Lippincott, 1957.

[67] New York: Random House, 1959.

[68] New York: New York Historical Society, 1956.

[69] New York: The Commonwealth Fund, 1944.

[70] New York: Columbia University, 1930.

[71] New York: Columbia University, 1946.

[72] New York: Ronald Press, 1938; reissued by Alfred A. Knopf in 1955.

[73] New York: Columbia University, 1936.

ing volume on *The Economic Mind in American Civilization, 1606-1865*.[74] Harold R. Shurtleff's *The Log Cabin Myth* should be kept in mind by all teachers of American history at a time when historical restorations seem to be ever more and more popular.[75] In the field of social history the most ambitious effort has been Thomas J. Wertenbaker's trilogy on *The Founding of American Civilization*, where architectural and other such evidences of colonial life are prominently featured.[76] In the general chorus of praise for the New England Puritan, Professor Wertenbaker strikes a discordant note.

CONCLUSION

When recent historical writing on the earliest years of American history is broadly considered, two points deserve emphasis. There has been no inclination to dispute the need, so strongly insisted upon by the older imperial school, for study of the North American colonies in the full context of British and European overseas expansion. Indeed, the modern interest in intellectual and social history has stimulated an even broader attempt to interpret the American story in the light of the total experience of the western world. At the same time, one notes a tendency to argue that some distortion of that story has resulted from the special bias of the imperial school, however sound its basic propositions may have been, and to insist upon the need for fresh attention to the origins of a peculiarly *American* type of civilization. Perhaps we will soon achieve a more balanced synthesis than the nation has at any time heretofore enjoyed.

[74] New York: Viking, 1946.
[75] Cambridge: Harvard University, 1939.
[76] *The Middle Colonies* (New York: Scribner, 1938; *The Puritan Oligarchy* (New York: Scribner, 1947); and *The Old South* (New York: Scribner, 1942).

CHAPTER III

The North American Colonies in the Eighteenth Century, 1688-1763

Clarence L. Ver Steeg

INTRODUCTION

H ISTORIANS have tended to follow cycles, not always clearly defined, in writing about colonial America. At one time the accounts replayed the struggle of selected heroes and villains, success too often being the factor that determined which label would be applied. At another time accounts stressed the impersonal economic forces sweeping men before them as chaff in a hurricane, while still later, and more recently, cultural and intellectual history have received special attention. In each case monographs and more general works have been written, extending the dimensions of historical scholarship. Moreover, scholarship on the colonial period has always fluctuated between studies on indigenous colonial developments and the larger world of British imperial relations.

After more than a century of work, research, writing, and extemporization it might readily be assumed that historians know all they really need to know in order to understand the whole of colonial America, that all the important subject matter has been exhausted. No presumption could be more fallacious. Indeed, the period, 1688-1763, the colonial eighteenth century, illustrates well how fallacious this presumption is.

Two definite factors have made the eighteenth century a relatively unpopular field: First, each time a new cycle of historical writing began, there was a pronounced inclination for the historians of early America to direct their researches and writing either to the early settlements, the trauma of birth and infancy, or to the period of the American Revolution, the charged and often romantic spectacle of a people meeting their foreordained greatness. Second, the colonial

24

eighteenth century, in contrast to the seventeenth century and the Revolution, lacks a unifying theme. This has resulted in a lack of direction, an absence of focus.

A number of well-known historians can be cited to support the first generalization. The remarkable works of Philip Bruce on Virginia, beginning in the 1890's are an excellent example. Representing a cycle of historical investigation in which the internal development of a colony was examined intensively, Bruce published five volumes on Virginia—all covering the seventeenth century.[1] Whether he thought the colonial eighteenth century unworthy of investigation, or whether he viewed it merely as an extension of the seventeenth century is uncertain. Perhaps he succumbed to fatigue. Whatever the explanation, he never made the contribution to an understanding of eighteenth century Virginia that he did to seventeenth century Virginia.

A look at imperial relations confirms these observations. George Louis Beer, a pioneer in investigating British colonial policy, left the period from the 1680's to the 1750's a blank, although it had been his intention to fill in this gap. It is interesting to note, however, that he did write extensively on imperial relations in the period preceding and succeeding the 1690-1750 period.[2] Charles M. Andrews, whose *The Colonial Period of American History*[3] represents the climax of a cycle of institutional studies of the colonial period, also failed to extend his work into the colonial eighteenth century, except for a brief segment of his final volume.

The lack of a unifying theme has greatly hampered the writing of well-directed and meaningful studies on the colonial eighteenth century. With the founding of the colonies, England is, of course, the unifying theme. When the revolutionary movement sweeps everything before it during and after the 1760's, or to use Abigail Adams' apt phrase, "the flame is kindled, and like lightning it catches

---

[1] Philip A. Bruce, *Economic History of Virginia in the Seventeenth Century* (2 vols.; New York and London: Macmillan, 1895); *Institutional History of Virginia in the Seventeenth Century* (2 vols.; New York and London: Putnam, 1910); and *Social Life of Virginia in the Seventeenth Century* (Richmond: Whittet and Shepperson, 1907).

[2] George Louis Beer, *British Colonial Policy, 1754-1765* (New York: Macmillan, 1907); *The Origins of the British Colonial System, 1578-1660* (New York: Macmillan, 1908); *The Old Colonial System, 1660-1754* (2 vols.; New York: Macmillan, 1912). Beer planned four volumes to carry to 1754 but he only completed two volumes, reaching to approximately 1690.

[3] Four vols.; New Haven: Yale University, 1934-1938.

from soul to soul," there is a focus, a central theme. The period from 1690-1763, in contrast, tends to be a no-man's land. Each colony was working out its pattern of life—its political practices, its economic system, its cultural advancement. Each colony acted as a miniature England, understandable only in terms of its own conditions and its own development. There were parallel trends among the colonies, often centering around imperial policy or political experience, but the truth is that the historian's knowledge of the colonial eighteenth century is so scanty and imprecise at points that the generalizations on such broader developments are frequently untrustworthy.

To know intimately the detailed development of each colony over three quarters of a century is a prodigious task that has discouraged thorough investigation and encouraged generalizations, too often inconsequential or misleading. A favorite sage observation has been that the colonies from 1690-to-1763 "grew up and prospered." Of course, this is true just as it is true to announce that between 1900 and 1950 the United States "grew and prospered." But what, in the latter case, of the cataclysmic shock of the First World War and its aftermath, and what of the Great Depression—events that left deep scars upon the American experience? Without knowing about the Great Depression and its results, it would be difficult to explain the current policies and attitude of the national government in economic affairs. Without knowing about the aftermath of the First World War, American foreign policy since 1945 would be inexplicable. So historians, in discussing contemporary America, do not indulge in indiscriminate oversimplifications such as the United States "grew and prospered." Yet we have tried to understand the American Revolution and its results with only the sketchiest knowledge of the three quarters of a century that preceded it.

Despite the historical activity in the colonial period, therefore, the treatment of the period 1688-1763—and especially 1690 to the 1740's and 1750's—too often consisted of disjointed accounts of isolated episodes, or, in some cases, a total lack of information on elementary topics. As this brief chapter will demonstrate, recent studies have begun to alter this pattern. For the most part, however, the cycles in colonial historical writing have often left a wide gap in our knowledge of the colonial period after 1690, and the lack of focus has discouraged an extensive scholarly project to correct this situation.

The first industrious effort to remedy this neglect was undertaken by Herbert Levi Osgood upon the posthumous publication of *The*

American Colonies in the Eighteenth Century.[4] In any essay on new interpretations or in any attempt to outline a factual survey, the point of departure is still Osgood's volumes, the best work for the whole period. By using the colonial wars to divide the period into self-contained units, Osgood's organization of materials is meaningless and often misleading. Moreover, by devoting each chapter to individual colonies throughout most of his work, he failed to produce a genuine synthesis. The weaknesses of Osgood's work, it should be emphasized, are not so much a reflection of his limits as an historian as they are a reflection of the serious shortcomings of the scholarship of the period. It is difficult, if not impossible, to build a meaningful synthesis upon an inadequate base. Historians for the colonial eighteenth century are desperately in need of more solid building blocks.

Fortunately, since the 1940's there has been a renewed interest among historians in strengthening and broadening the investigation of the colonial eighteenth century. Much of the research has stressed provincial and local history, an indispensable prelude to works of larger scope. Until the intra-colonial researches are more complete, general works will not be able to speak with the authority, accuracy, and perception needed to provoke a fresh and illuminating insight into this formative period. The work achieved along the line of central themes or tentative interpretations is less significant than is desirable, but it is to be hoped that a new cycle of historical writing will not distract investigators from the period until this task is more nearly completed.

Recognizing these limitations, let us briefly survey the most recent writing on the colonial eighteenth century. To introduce order where little exists, the discussion will begin with more general works and then emphasize specific categories which have received special attention from historians since the 1940's: imperial relations, colonial self-government, the origins of American science, biographical studies, trade, cultural life, and finally, the search for the distinctive characteristics of eighteenth century colonial society, or to employ a widely used phrase, the origins of the American character.

GENERAL WORKS

Although Osgood remains the point of departure, the next step is to consult regional studies. James Truslow Adams, *Revolutionary*

---

[4] Four vols.; New York: Columbia University, 1924.

New England, 1691-1776[5]—the second volume of a trilogy on New England—continues to be the only book currently in print that serves as a regional study, although Volume II of A History of the South Series to be entitled *The Southern Colonies in the Eighteenth Century, 1689-1763* will soon be completed.[6] It is expected that the volume on the Southern Colonies will incorporate the best results of recent scholarship as well as contribute its own interpretations to the colonial eighteenth century. There is no immediate prospect that a volume comparable to the South series will be available for the Middle Colonies.

In the area of general studies, mention should be made of the New American Nation Series, a projected forty volumes to cover all of American History and directed toward a wider reading audience. The volume specifically devoted to the years 1690-1763 has not yet (by 1960) appeared. Fortunately, however, one volume of this publishing enterprise, Louis B. Wright's *The Cultural Life of the American Colonies, 1607-1763*, embracing, as the title suggests, the whole of the colonial period, not only creatively and succinctly summarizes the best scholarship in this phase of eighteenth century life but also effectively demonstrates what giant strides have been made in cultural and social history in the last two to three decades.[7]

IMPERIAL RELATIONS

Since the early 1940's less attention has been paid to imperial relations, relatively speaking, than to most other phases of early American history. Perhaps, as America's ties to the Atlantic community become stronger in the twentieth century, the relationship between Britain and its colonies of the eighteenth century will gradually receive additional attention. Such attention will be encouraged by a more genuine appreciation of the striking similarities of the eighteenth century experience to that of the twentieth. For an American today, the experience of having events throughout the world affect his life is relatively new, but for his eighteenth century counterpart it was an accepted part of the everyday world. To him the Atlantic community

---

[5] Boston: Atlantic Monthly, 1923. Adams also wrote *Provincial Society, 1690-1763* (New York: Macmillan, 1927), a volume in the *American Life* series edited by A. M. Schlesinger and Dixon R. Fox which stresses social and cultural history.

[6] Wendell H. Stephenson and E. Merton Coulter (editors), *A History of the South* (projected 10 vols.; Baton Rouge: Louisiana State University, 1947—). Seven volumes have appeared. The second volume is being written by the author of this chapter.

[7] New York: Harper, 1957.

was a personal matter, represented by the goods he purchased, the ships at the wharf, and the tutor teaching his child. If, for a moment, the perception of the eighteenth century American became blurred, his newspaper was a constant reminder that the course of events throughout the world had a direct influence upon his well-being.

An exception to the general observations that less study has been devoted to imperial relations is the work of Lawrence Gipson whose magisterial volumes record the events that brought the first British Empire to its apex of power and esteem in the 1750's and the 1760's. Nearing the completion of a dozen volumes on *The British Empire Before the American Revolution,* Gipson sees the problems of the colonies through the eyes of the British—too much so, say Gipson's critics, who find his volumes overly generous in allowing for British shortcomings and too limited in his appreciation of the colonial point of view.[8] Let there be no mistake about it, however, Gipson is erecting an enduring monument to the first British colonial system that will command attention as long as British-colonial relations are studied. These volumes, in a sense, also represent a monument to an earlier age of scholarship on imperial relations, rather than a recent trend. Moreover, the orientation is toward the American Revolution, not the colonial eighteenth century, and it is within this framework that Gipson makes his greatest contribution.

Aside from Gipson's work, only Oliver M. Dickerson's *The Navigation Acts and the American Revolution*[9] has attempted to wrestle with the centuries-old question: Did British colonial policy seriously impair the development of the American colonies? As the title suggests, however, this study does not fill the gap between 1690 and 1750 left by other historians of the British imperial system. For partial answers as to the influence of British policy, historians continue to be dependent upon the work of earlier scholars—Lawrence Harper, Leonard Labaree, and Charles M. Andrews come prominently to mind—who have written on a phase or segment of imperial relations.[10] At present, perhaps the most widely accepted position is that, in the colonial eighteenth century, British policies cost the colonies money,

---

[8] Vols. I-III; Caldwell, Idaho: Caxton Printers, 1936. Vol. IV—; New York: Knopf, 1939—. The first three vols. have been reprinted by Knopf.

[9] Philadelphia: University of Pennsylvania, 1951.

[10] Lawrence A. Harper, *The English Navigation Laws* (New York: Columbia University, 1939); Leonard W. Labaree, *Royal Government in America* (New Haven: Yale University, 1930).

but that British protection and assistance were probably worth the price.

COLONIAL SELF-GOVERNMENT

In contrast to the flagging interest in imperial relations, there has been a brisk revival of studies on the growth and practice of colonial self-government. Not since the late nineteenth century and early twentieth century has the investigation of colonial self-government enjoyed such vogue. The late nineteenth century studies were probably the product of the times, when men feared that democratic government might be crushed under the weight of industrial bigness and power. In a slightly different way, current conditions have undoubtedly influenced historians of the mid-twentieth century. With political democracy a lively issue in domestic politics and with the hot and cold wars placing democracy as practiced in the United States on display for all the world to see, it is natural that scholars should investigate the origins of the nation's faith in self-government and the ability of such a government to withstand the shock of drastically changing conditions. Democratization has been a central theme in American history beginning with the first settlements and reaching to the present, but it is instructive to note that the subject attracts the most attention when the very concept itself is undergoing its severest tests.

A moment of reflection can be of service in approaching the question of self-government in the colonial eighteenth century. Historians of the nineteenth century, at least those whose influence was most pervasive, created the impression that a government of all the people was a feature of the American colonies. Although a careful reading of these historians would quickly have dispelled such a misleading impression, the idea was engraved in the popular mind. "Scientific" historians of the late nineteenth and twentieth centuries, wary of glib generalities, found it easy to puncture such an illusion; for, of course, the evidence was overwhelming that the franchise was restricted and that qualifications were placed upon those who could hold office. It was seriously questioned whether the colonial governments and their successors were truly governments of, by, and for the people. As a result, it became quite the fashion, beginning particularly in the 1920's, to sneer at the autocratic Puritans, to scorn the aristocratic Virginia planters, to question the affluent Quaker merchants, and to indict all others who controlled the powers of government.

In the late 1930's and early 1940's a decided change in intellectual climate gradually began to assert itself in the investigations of the political life of the colonial eighteenth century. Whether it was due to the realization that government can be a dynamic instrument for creating policies that affect all phases of everyday life, or whether it was due to the economic crisis of the 1930's and the world crisis of the late 1930's and the 1940's, in which the government of the people was subjected to a test of survival, can be only a conjecture; but the resulting research on colonial self-government in the eighteenth century has produced a far more sympathetic approach. Using local records to advantage, researchers have demonstrated that there was more political democracy than historians had previously suggested.[11]

It is probable that in shifting from the anti-democratic emphasis of the late 1920's and early 1930's to the democratic emphasis of the 1940's and 1950's, the pendulum, in each case, has swung too far. The question of "how democratic" is a relative one, that is relative to what it is being compared. If political practices between 1690 and 1763 are compared with those in Britain, one might arrive at one conclusion. However, a comparison between the practices of the twentieth century and those of the eighteenth might lead to quite a different conclusion. The scorners of the 1920's and 1930's, whether they intended to or not, leaned toward the use of a twentieth century standard of measurement, while more recent investigations, alert to this particular danger, have sometimes relied too heavily on the externals of eighteenth century politics, neglecting the realities of its political machinery and political pressure.

In any critique of the question, "How 'democratic' were the political practices of the colonial eighteenth century?", it is prudent to make distinctions among four related but separate factors: (1) Who has the right to vote? (2) How does the political machinery operate? (3) Who has the power? (4) What are the key issues and ideas? As of the moment, investigations have led historians to the tentative conclusion that more people had the opportunity to vote than the scorners believed, but that such voters repeatedly placed an elite group in office. Whether this was due to pressure, subtle or overt, or to the recognition of rank and status—for the eighteenth century was certainly not a classless society—is not easy to judge; but these distinctions and these queries will unquestionably figure in future investigations.

---

[11] Robert E. Brown's, *Middle-Class Democracy and the Revolution in Massachusetts, 1691-1780* (Ithaca: Cornell University, 1955) is a good example of recent scholarship along the line of colonial democratization.

ORIGINS OF AMERICAN SCIENCE

The scientific wonders of modern life have also aroused a passionate re-discovery of science in the colonial eighteenth century. This has been a happy wedding of sorts because the eighteenth century was also oriented toward science, the indisputable laws of Newton rather than the relativity theories of Einstein. Indeed, the scholarly devotion to colonial science has been so overwhelming that it has perhaps been exaggerated as an influential force in colonial America.

Although the colonials were genuinely attracted by the mysteries of science, their interest was primarily empirical rather than theoretical in nature, a characteristic that many scholars would attach to American science throughout its history. Generally, the colonial scientists were men of many parts, their experience and knowledge in science more often than not being avocational. Although there is some dispute on this question, the weight of opinions seems to be that the colonial scientists were curious amateurs rather than skilled professionals. It is intriguing, however, that men of such widely different temperaments as Jefferson and Washington were most interested in the practical applications of science—a machine that made possible a reduction in human labor or a fertilizer and schedule of crops that raised production. After the 1730's, as a recent monograph has shown, the scientific curiosity became channeled along institutional lines, with the appearance of science societies, and the like.[12]

BIOGRAPHICAL STUDIES

Individuals preoccupied with science have been subject to the probings of biographers at the same time that there has been a renewed interest in biographical studies generally.[13] In this respect the writing on the colonial eighteenth century is being influenced by a trend affecting historical scholarship in all fields. It would appear that the complexities of the mid-twentieth century world, where men live increasingly in faceless anonymity and where individual effort so often appears thwarted or made futile by unyielding external conditions, have prompted laymen and scholars alike to attempt to

---

[12] Brooke Hindle, *The Pursuit of Science in Revolutionary America, 1735-89* (Chapel Hill: University of North Carolina, 1956). See Whitefield J. Bell, Jr., *Early American Science: Needs and Opportunities for Study* (Williamsburg: Institute of Early American History and Culture, 1955).

[13] An interesting example is that of I. Bernard Cohen in *Benjamin Franklin, his Contribution to the American Tradition* (Indianapolis: Bobbs-Merrill, 1953) and *Franklin and Newton* (Philadelphia: American Philosophical Society, 1956).

rescue the value of the individual from the irresistible sweep of historical forces.

Probably these external forces are no more or less irresistible than in other periods of mankind's history, but people seem better able to recognize their dilemma. Moreover, the profound frustrations of daily living must be met without the comfort of a Calvinist theology that interprets whatever is happening as a manifestation of the Divine Will or the secular faith of the pragmatist that whatever is happening must be. Viewed from a slightly different perspective, secularization, assuredly a modern trend, has often encouraged man to seek his values in the men that have preceded him, to worship at the temple of man, in a sense, rather than at the temple of God. This emphasis on man, too, might help to explain the profusion of biographical studies.

Biographical studies of the colonial eighteenth century have ranged widely. They include the extensive life and times biographies of leaders whose careers reached a climax during or after the American Revolution as well as brief studies of men who figured prominently in the life of their particular colony during the first half of the eighteenth century but who have been neglected because they neither acquired inter-colonial reputations nor lived to be active in the Revolutionary generation. Multi-volume biographies of the famous Virginia quartet —Patrick Henry, George Washington, Thomas Jefferson, and James Madison—amply document the first trend.[14] In the second category there are such attractive recent volumes as those of Frederick B. Tolles' perceptive study on *James Logan and the Culture of Provincial America*[15] and Aubrey C. Land's volume on *The Dulanys of Maryland*.[16] Equally enlightening and often entertaining are the genuinely personal documents, represented best by the publication of the fasci-

---

[14] Robert D. Meade, *Patrick Henry: Patriot in the Making* (Philadelphia: Lippincott, 1957). A second volume is yet to be published. Douglas S. Freeman, *George Washington: A Biography* (7 vols.: New York: Scribner, 1948-1957). The final volume was completed by John A. Carroll and Mary W. Ashworth. Dumas Malone, *Jefferson and His Time* (Boston: Little, Brown, 1948—). Two volumes of an expected four volumes have been published. Irving Brant, *James Madison* (Indianapolis: Bobbs-Merrill, 1941—). Five volumes of an expected six volumes have been published. David J. Mays' discriminating biography of *Edmund Pendleton, 1721-1803* (2 vols.; Cambridge: Harvard University, 1952) has made an outstanding contribution toward understanding the workings of provincial politics.

[15] Boston: Little, Brown, 1957.

[16] *The Dulanys of Maryland: A Biographical Study of Daniel Dulany, the Elder (1685-1753) and Daniel Dulany, the Younger (1722-1797)* (Baltimore: Maryland Historical Society, 1955).

nating secret diaries of William Byrd II of Virginia.[17] Yet biographical study of the colonial eighteenth century lags far behind that of the Revolution.

The biographical approach to the period 1690-1763 will always be bounded by the limited personal materials on most prominent figures. Moreover, it is a period when larger institutional changes are pre-eminent, a period when individuals seem to be somewhat less in evidence. More can be accomplished, however, and it is likely that historians will be increasingly attracted to the idea of doing brief, perceptive biographies of men and women, forgotten except by the scholars thoroughly familiar with the colonial eighteenth century. Such studies will illuminate every important aspect of life, from the prayer book to the counting house, from political practices to the habits of diet and self-medication.

TRADE

Biographical studies of a type have invaded the world of colonial trade. The list of valuable books on merchant families who gained fame and fortune in the colonial eighteenth century is impressive, a choice example being James B. Hedges' *The Browns of Providence Plantations: Colonial Years*.[18] This book represents biography of a special type, deeply influenced by the recent wave of historical scholarship on business leaders and business firms in American history.[19] Actually, the recent studies of mercantile families represent business history applied to the colonial period. The results have given historians a much more precise appreciation of the conduct of trade, the changing conditions of trade, the creation of colonial capital, and other questions central to an understanding of mercantile activity.

Many studies that emphasize a particular phase or region of trade have not yet had their full impact on historical scholarship, because they are dissertations yet to be transformed into books or incorporated into more general works. A happy exception is Arthur P. Middleton's

---

[17] Louis B. Wright and Marion Tinling, eds., *William Byrd of Virginia: The London Diary, 1717-21* (New York: Oxford University, 1958) completes the publication of the known segments of Byrd's Diary.

[18] Cambridge: Harvard University, 1952.

[19] Comparable examples of this trend are: William Threipland Baxter, *The House of Hancock: Business in Boston, 1724-1775* (Cambridge: Harvard University, 1945); Byron Fairchild, *Messers. William Pepperrell: Merchants at Piscataqua* (Ithaca: Cornell University, 1954); and Frederic B. Tolles, *Meeting House and Counting House: The Quaker Merchants of Colonial Pennsylvania, 1682-1763* (Chapel Hill: University of North Carolina, 1948).

Tobacco Coast[20] which made a valuable contribution to the political-economic life of the Chesapeake colonies. It is fair to say that the results of these studies on trade did not drastically modify existing interpretations, but they underscored the complexity and maturation of the colonial economy, on the one hand, and the sensitivity of that economy to the tides of fortune in Britain and to changing conditions of world trade.

CULTURAL LIFE AND THE AMERICAN CHARACTER

The area of the colonial eighteenth century that has attracted the most attention in recent scholarship is that which relates to the "distinctiveness" of the American society. Long pre-occupied with Crèvecoeur's comment "What, then, is the American, this new man?", American scholarship searches anew for the touchstone of America's individuality. It is perhaps a reflection, in times of national crisis, of a compulsion to seek out the fountainhead of the American spirit, particularly its indigenous sources of strength. Whatever the hidden motivation, renewed emphasis has been placed on the development of the American colonies as distinctive societies rather than as append-ages of an older community.

Many of the leading colonial historians have played a part in this investigation—Thomas J. Wertenbaker, Carl Bridenbaugh, Max Savelle, and Louis B. Wright, although the latter has perhaps been somewhat more sensitive to the English cultural seeds. Their respec-tive titles underscore the theme—*The Founding of American Civi-lization: The Middle Colonies*;[21] *Cities in the Wilderness*;[22] *Seeds of Liberty*;[23] and *The First Gentlemen of Virginia*.[24] More recent titles, *Seedtime of the Republic*[25] by Clinton Rossiter and *The Americans: The Colonial Experience*[26] by Daniel Boorstin suggest that, to parody Captain John Paul Jones, we have not yet begun to write.

Of course, the distinctive character of colonial society is an old theme, revived in modern dress. Whereas the earliest historians stressed

---

[20] *Tobacco Coast: A Maritime History of the Chesapeake Bay in the Colonial Era*, George C. Mason, ed., (Newport News: Mariner's Museum, 1953).

[21] New York: Scribner, 1938.

[22] *Cities in the Wilderness: The First Century of Urban Life in America, 1625-1742* (New York: Ronald, 1938; 2nd edition, New York: Knopf, 1955).

[23] New York: Knopf, 1948.

[24] *The First Gentlemen of Virginia: Intellectual Qualities of the Early Colonial Ruling Class* (San Marino, Calif.: The Huntington Library, 1940).

[25] *Seedtime of the Republic; the Origin of the American Tradition of Political Liberty* (New York: Harcourt, Brace, 1953).

[26] New York: Random House, 1958.

political individuality, the modern emphasis has usually been placed upon distinctive cultural and intellectual developments. Even in this area, Moses Coit Tyler's valuable *A History of American Literature during the Colonial Period*,[27] written eighty years ago, forecast the contemporary emphasis on "ideas" and culture. We have not yet given an equivalent stress to distinctiveness in the economic sphere, although the theme is as applicable in this area as in any other; and the investigations of political life, recording colonial political practices and policies, require a new dimension, an added depth, to underscore its individual character. In this respect Charles Sydnor's succinct gem of a book, *Gentlemen Freeholders* points the way.[28]

NEGLECTED SUBJECTS

Certain subjects continue to be neglected, somewhat surprisingly in many cases. Although William W. Sweet surveyed ecclesiastical development in *Religion in Colonial America*,[29] penetrating studies have not appeared. Perhaps science is still warring with religion; as reflected in the researches of the colonial eighteenth century, science at this point is assuredly supreme, despite the numerous subjects in the field of religious history that would reward any investigator. For everyday colonial eighteenth century life, historians must often return to such well-thumbed books as those of Alice Earle, despite the vast number of local records that would enable investigators to tell this particular story with greater precision and understanding.[30] Although a few books on the eighteenth century frontier have appeared since 1940, much remains to be done; and there continues to be a wide gap in scholarly studies of eighteenth century labor, particularly in thorough studies of slavery.[31]

---

[27] *A History of American Literature* (2 vols.; New York: Putnam, 1879, new edition, Ithaca: Cornell University, 1949).

[28] Chapel Hill: University of North Carolina, 1952. Michael Kraus, *The Atlantic Civilization: Eighteenth Century Origins* (Ithaca: Cornell University, 1949) is something of an exception to the general trend.

[29] New York: Scribner, 1942.

[30] Alice Morse Earle, *Home Life in Colonial Days* (New York: Macmillan, 1898). This is only one of several books written by Mrs. Earle touching upon everyday life. Edmund S. Morgan, *Virginians at Home; Family Life in the Eighteenth Century* (Williamsburg: Colonial Williamsburg, Inc., 1952) is a recent book that explores this theme, but there is little scholarly activity along this line of inquiry.

[31] For the frontier, John R. Alden's *John Stuart and the Southern Colonial Frontier . . . 1754-1775* (Ann Arbor: University of Michigan, 1944) is one of the few volumes. See also *American Indian and White Relations to 1830: Needs and Opportunities for Study* (Chapel Hill: University of North Carolina, 1957) edited

An unevenness that is not entirely healthy has appeared in the emphasis upon certain regions. Far more study is being devoted to Virginia in the colonial eighteenth century, for instance, than to any other colony, due, of course, to the activity in and around Colonial Williamsburg. Yet the riches of the South Carolina records are only beginning to be tapped, while the story of New York and Pennsylvania for this period has not been fully told. New Jersey, through the work of John E. Pomfret,[32] begins to receive the attention it merits, but, for New England, historians have relied far too long on J. T. Adams' *Revolutionary New England* which, in many respects, is seriously dated.

Most of all, what is needed is a precise definition of the issues of the colonial eighteenth century which can guide aspiring young researchers and which can help the teacher present a meaningful story of these formative years. What questions should historians attempt to answer for the period 1690-1763? Do materials exist to answer these queries? What approach would yield the best results? These are some of the questions that need to be asked and answered. It is to be hoped that the pre-eminent consideration of defining the issues will command the attention it merits before another Yearbook on new interpretations is written.

by Lyman H. Butterfield, Wilcomb E. Washburn, and William E. Fenton. An exception on labor is Richard B. Morris' *Government and Labor in Early America* (New York: Columbia University, 1946). Abbot Smith's *Colonists in Bondage: White Servitude and Convict Labor in America, 1607-1776* (Chapel Hill: University of North Carolina, 1947) concentrates on the background of servitude labor.

[32] John E. Pomfret's *The Province of West New Jersey, 1607-1702: A History of the Origins of an American Colony* (Princeton: Princeton University, 1956) will have a sequel. David C. Douglas' *English Historical Documents*: Vol. IX, *American Colonial Documents to 1776*, Merrill Jensen, ed., (London: Eyre & Spottiswoode, 1955) is a valuable and solid contribution.

CHAPTER IV

The American Revolution: A Review of Changing Interpretations[1]

Edmund S. Morgan

AMERICANS who lived from 1763 to 1789 witnessed the most remarkable transformation in our history, from empire to republic, from colony to state, from multiplicity to union. Events moved so rapidly in those years that we do not hesitate to use the word "revolution" in talking about them. But everyone who has studied them knows how hard it is to decide what was revolutionary and what was not. What was old and what was new? What *was* the American Revolution?

THE WHIG SCHOOL: BANCROFT AND TREVELYAN

Until the present century the answer most often given to this question was the one formulated by George Bancroft, the first great historian to deal with it.[2] Bancroft, a Jacksonian Democrat, saw American history as the story of liberty: the Revolution was simply the culminating episode in a long series of unsuccessful attempts by England to suppress the freedom that grew naturally on American soil. Bancroft was obliged to agree that liberty had sometimes found a home in England, but he was inclined to think that the best Englishmen—those, that is, who loved freedom best—had made their way to America. Had not the Puritans been driven out by English persecution? And had not the Englishmen who stayed home demonstrated their lack of zeal for liberty by allowing their government to bind the Americans in subjection to an unfair economic system?

---

[1] The editors are grateful to the Service Center for Teachers of History of the American Historical Association for permitting the reprinting of this chapter from their series of pamphlets in almost its original form. Mr. Morgan has made a few changes from the original, principally to account for books which have appeared since the pamphlet was written in 1958.

[2] George Bancroft, *A History of the United States, from the Discovery of the American Continent.* . . . (Boston: Little, Brown, 1834-1875).

38

Bancroft tended to look upon any exertion of English authority in America as a usurpation. He even labelled his chapter on the exploration of Virginia in the sixteenth century with the audacious title, "England takes possession of the United States," English mercantilism, expressed in the Navigation Acts, seemed to him almost an infringement of United States sovereignty, something that Andrew Jackson would never have put up with. By the time one has read through Bancroft's early volumes, the Revolution comes as no surprise. George III is only the last of a bad lot, while the Americans of 1776 are the best of a line of men who first resisted tyranny under the Stuarts.

It is easy today to discover the weaknesses in Bancroft. For him everything was black or white. He abused quotations shamelessly. He chopped truths in half and sometimes offered up the smaller part. But we will err more seriously than he if we disregard him. He did not write in ignorance. Probably no one else has known the original sources for the Revolutionary period as well as he, and he knew them when only a small portion had found their way into print. Even today anyone who has worked through the unpublished Revolutionary manuscripts in some of our great repositories will find it instructive to go to Bancroft and see evidence of his familiarity with them. He simplified, yes, but simplification is the business of the historian; and though he has been proved wrong at many points, no one else has yet been able to bend his bow. No one has yet rewritten the history of the Revolution on the grand scale.

It is perhaps no coincidence that the one historian who came closest to it was an Englishman writing with a similar animus against George III and a similar fondness for old-fashioned political liberty. Sir George Otto Trevelyan was a nineteenth century Whig in search of his Party's eighteenth century forbears. He found them, as he thought, among the men who opposed George III during the disastrous ministry of Lord North. His four volumes on *The American Revolution* show a small band of dedicated men, the Rockingham Whigs, arrayed against a power-hungry king and a corrupt horde of place-hunters. The Whigs do their best to halt the drive toward tyranny, but the king and his cohorts overpower them, until American success and royal failure bring a new dispensation to British politics. Trevelyan, like Bancroft, could slash his way through complex problems and show his readers what appeared to be the heart of the matter. Of all histories of the Revolution his is still the most readable.[3]

---

[3] Sir George O. Trevelyan, *The American Revolution* (4 vols.; New York: Longmans, Green, 1899-1913).

THE IMPERIAL SCHOOL

Even before Trevelyan finished telling his story, a new school of historians had begun to re-examine the assumptions upon which he and Bancroft proceeded. Most of these historians did not directly approach the Revolution itself. Instead, they fastened upon the earlier history of the colonies, which for Bancroft had exhibited the same forces that produced the Revolution. Was the old British Empire, they asked, so bad a thing as Bancroft implied? Were the restrictions placed on the colonists unfair? To both these questions they returned a resounding "No."

The first effective spokesman of this "imperial" school of history was George Louis Beer, a New York tobacco merchant, who had studied history at Columbia. Beer retired from business with a small fortune at the age of thirty-one, in order to devote himself to the study of British colonial policy in the seventeenth and eighteenth centuries. In 1907 he produced his *British Colonial Policy, 1754-1765,* which demonstrated that the behavior of the American colonists during the Seven Years' War was far from commendable, while that of Great Britain was constructive and responsible. The colonists, he thought, offered little loyalty and no gratitude to the country which protected them from the French and Spanish. Once the French menace was destroyed, they moved swiftly toward independence, not in order to preserve civil or political liberty, but because they had nothing further to gain by remaining in the empire. Later events made the Revolution seem a milestone on the road to democracy, but Beer wondered. It was not at all improbable, he thought, "that the political evolution of the next centuries may take such a course that the American Revolution will lose the great significance that is now attached to it, and will appear merely as the temporary separation of two kindred peoples whose inherent similarity was obscured by superficial differences, resulting from dissimilar economic and social conditions."[4]

After this brief glance at the Revolution, Beer moved back to the seventeenth century and wrote *The Origins of the British Colonial System, 1578-1660* and *The Old Colonial System, 1660-1688.*[5] Here he found, as Bancroft had, that much the same forces were at work as

---

[4] George Louis Beer, *British Colonial Policy, 1754-1765* (New York: Macmillan, 1907; reprinted New York: P. Smith, 1933).

[5] George Louis Beer, *The Origins of the British Colonial System, 1578-1660* (New York: Macmillan, 1908; reprinted New York: P. Smith, 1933); *The Old Colonial System, 1660 1754* (2 vols.; New York: Macmillan, 1912; reprinted New York: P. Smith, 1933).

in the later period, but where Bancorft saw tyranny in England and freedom in America, Beer saw statesmanship in England and irresponsibility in America. Beer's historical studies ended when the first World War broke out and he sensed an opportunity to restore the union which the Revolution had interrupted. He worked hard toward this goal during the war and at the peace conference and died in 1920.

Beer's work, in spite of his strong attachment to Anglo-American union, was based on careful scholarship. Both his scrupulousness as a scholar and much of his point of view were carried on by the great colonial historian, Charles McLean Andrews. Andrews, like Beer, gave his attention principally to the period before the Revolution. He trained a generation of scholars to look at colonial history as imperial history. The familiar events of American settlement took on a new meaning when viewed from London instead of Boston or Jamestown. And the students who traversed colonial history under Andrews' guidance arrived at the Revolution with a sympathetic understanding of the problems with which British administrators had to wrestle. The Navigation Acts appeared no longer to be an instrument of economic oppression but rather a sensible means of giving England a return for the protection she furnished to the colonists. The Admiralty Courts ceased to be a tool of tyranny and became useful devices for keeping trade and commerce flowing.

Andrews understood the colonial point of view as well as the English, even where the colonists were at odds with England. His brief monograph on the *Colonial Background of the American Revolution* has nothing of the doctrinaire about it. But he did not attempt a full-scale consideration of the Revolution itself, and his *magnum opus, The Colonial Period of American History,* is primarily concerned with the founding of the colonies. Only in the final volume did he begin to approach the Revolution with a consideration of "England's Commercial and Colonial Policy."[6]

Andrews' students have continued the study of British policy, and among other notable studies they have produced is Leonard W. Labaree's *Royal Government in America,* which discusses at length the friction between royal governors and colonial assemblies.[7] It has re-

---

[6] Charles McLean Andrews, *The Colonial Background of the American Revolution; Four Essays in American Colonial History* (Rev. ed., New Haven: Yale University, 1931); *The Colonial Period of American History* (4 vols.; New Haven: Yale University, 1934-1938).

[7] Leonard W. Labaree, *Royal Government in America; a Study of the British Colonial System before 1783* (New Haven: Yale University, 1930).

mained for another of Andrews' students, Lawrence H. Gipson, to undertake a full-scale consideration, from the imperial point of view, of the events leading up to the Declaration of Independence. In a monumental study, still under way, of *The British Empire before the American Revolution,*[8] Gipson surveyed the condition of the empire in 1750, not neglecting its eastern as well as its western outposts, and then began the long march toward 1776. In the eighth volume he reached the conclusion of the Seven Years' War, which in its imperial phase he renamed "The Great War for the Empire." His view of the conduct of Americans in this war was no higher than that of Beer. The war, as Professor Gipson saw it, was won primarily by English money and English blood, both of which were spilt freely in America. The ninth volume, published in 1956, dealt with the administrative problems presented by the Peace of Paris in 1763. Professor Gipson will not reach the events normally associated with the beginning of the Revolution until the tenth volume, which has not yet appeared.

Thus we still do not have a full, scholarly account of the origins of the Revolution from the imperial point of view. Professor Gipson has, however, supplied us with a preliminary sketch of the subject in his volume of the New American Nation Series, *The Coming of the Revolution, 1763-1775.*[9] Though the treatment is brief, especially for the years after 1767, we can perceive what the interpretation is likely to be: the British government in attempting to tax the colonies was making an equitable claim on a people whose tax burdens were extremely light by comparison with those of Englishmen, and who were the principal beneficiaries of a war in which England's national debt had doubled. In objecting to Parliamentary taxation, the Americans talked much about constitutional principles; but the sincerity of their attachment to those principles, Professor Gipson suggested, may be questioned, especially in the light of their shifting from one argument to another as the situation altered.

POLITICAL THEORY

In stressing the inconstancy of colonial arguments against taxation, Professor Gipson has claimed no more than several historians of American political ideas, none of whom falls properly within the

---

[8] Lawrence H. Gipson, *The British Empire before the American Revolution; Provincial Characteristics and Sectional Tendencies in the Era Preceding the American Crisis* (Vols. 1-3; Caldwell, Ind.: Caxton, vol. 4; New York: Knopf). (Nine volumes published by 1956).

[9] Lawrence H. Gipson, *The Coming of the Revolution, 1763-1775* (New York: Harper, 1954).

imperial, or any other, school of interpretation. Carl Becker, in *The Declaration of Independence* discussed with his usual felicity the American expression of eighteenth century political ideas.[10] He showed the colonists moving through a series of preliminary stages before they reached a total denial of Parliament's authority. At the time of the Stamp Act, he maintained, they objected to internal taxes but admitted the validity of external ones. After Parliament took them at their word and levied the external Townshend duties, they shifted to a denial of all Parliamentary taxes but admitted that Parliament could regulate their trade. By the time of the First Continental Congress they were ready to refuse Parliament any authority over them at all.

Randolph G. Adams in *The Political Ideas of the American Revolution* traced the same progression.[11] Adams was primarily interested in the conception of the British Empire expressed in the last stage of American opposition, that of an empire with several co-ordinate legislatures, linked only by allegiance to a common sovereign. This conception later proved fruitful in keeping the rest of Britain's empire together, and Adams praised the vision of the men who formulated it. But he readily agreed that it was inconsistent with the ideas expressed in the early years of opposition to Parliament. Even Charles Howard McIlwain, who argued in *The American Revolution: A Constitutional Interpretation* for the constitutional validity of this conception of empire, admitted that the colonists did not reach it until they had tried less valid ideas. (McIlwain's contention that the final colonial position was constitutionally valid is questioned by Robert L. Schuyler in *Parliament and the British Empire*.)[12]

The most recent detailed account of the development of Revolutionary political theory is Clinton Rossiter's *Seedtime of the Republic,* which follows Bancroft in seeking the roots of American freedom deep in the colonial past.[13] Rossiter, like Becker and Adams, was sympathetic

---

[10] Carl L. Becker, *The Declaration of Independence, a Study in the History of Political Ideas* (New York: Harcourt, Brace, 1922; reprinted New York: Knopf, 1942).

[11] Randolph G. Adams, *The Political Ideas of the American Revolution; Britannic-American Contributions to the Problem of Imperial Organization, 1765 to 1775* (Durham: Trinity College, 1922; reprinted New York: Barnes and Noble, 1958).

[12] Charles H. McIlwain, *The American Revolution: A Constitutional Interpretation* (New York: Macmillan, 1923); cf. Robert L. Schuyler, *Parliament and the British Empire; Some Constitutional Controversies Concerning Imperial Legislative Jurisdiction* (New York: Columbia University, 1929).

[13] Clinton Rossiter, *Seedtime of the Republic; the Origin of the American Tradition of Political Liberty* (New York: Harcourt, Brace, 1953).

with the Americans, but he too acknowledged that the Americans shifted their ground several times after the controversy began.

It would appear then, that Bancroft's story of English tyranny and American liberty has undergone revision. Historians of political thought have agreed that the Americans were inconsistent or wavering in their devotion to principles, and the imperial historians have found them selfish and narrow by comparison with their English masters.

ENGLISH POLITICS

At the same time, historians in England have been revising the picture of eighteenth century British politics drawn by Sir George Trevelyan and other Whig scholars. The high priest of the new movement is Sir Lewis Namier, and its sacred scriptures are his *Structure of Politics at the Accession of George III* and his *England in the Age of the American Revolution*.[14] These works, which have been the model for many subsequent studies, examine in detail the people elected to George III's first Parliaments and the way they voted. The result is to disband the Whig Party that Trevelyan had created from the followers of Rockingham. There were, Sir Lewis tells us, no political parties in England during the age of the American Revolution: no Whig Party, no Tory Party. The King's Friends were a small and insignificant group who in any case did not always do as the king told them. Small factions, usually the followers of some influential leader, often organized for the purpose of capturing political offices. But a party built on attachment to any set of principles, good or bad, had yet to be born.

In the absence of parties, Sir Lewis said, most members were occupied primarily in the attempt to secure privileges for themselves and for their local constituents. Matters of national concern held little interest for them. In this situation a larger responsibility devolved upon the monarch than previous historians had realized. It was up to him to keep the wheels of the empire turning. The ministers who guided important bills through Parliament were, in more than a nominal sense, *his* ministers. When he told them what to do and pulled strings to secure a majority in the House of Commons, he was not usurping a function that his ancestors had already given up. Rather he was doing what a responsible man in his position had to do. It is not denied that he did a bad job of it. George was a man of mediocre

---

[14] Sir Lewis B. Namier, *England in the Age of the American Revolution* (London: Macmillan, 1930) and *Structure of Politics at the Accession of George III* (London: Macmillan, 1929).

abilities, faced with a task that required genius. He failed, but not, Sir Lewis insisted, because of any native taste for tyranny.

THE SOCIAL VIEW OF THE REVOLUTION

When we compare the new views held by historians of British politics, of the empire, and of political ideas, we find certain inconsistencies. How, for example, can we stress the imperial vision of a government dominated by local interests? Until the new views are reconciled in a new synthesis, we can only speculate on what relative importance to assign them. One thing, however, is clear: they all demand that we re-examine the question as to why there should have been a revolution at all. If the Navigation Acts were fair, if Americans were not initially attached to any particular view of Parliament's authority, if George III was no tyrant, why should the colonists have sought independence? What, again, *was* the Revolution? If Bancroft's answer was wrong, what should we put in its place?

Historians have not neglected this question, and the answer that seems to have pleased them most, at least until recently, was that offered by Carl Becker. In his *History of Political Parties in the Province of New York, 1760-1776*, Becker said that the politics of New York in the Revolutionary period revolved around two questions, home rule and who should rule at home.[15] Everyone knew that the Revolution was fought to gain home rule, in other words, independence. Becker's statement, and the substance of his book, drew attention to a simultaneous conflict among the colonists themselves.

New York was perhaps the best place Becker could have chosen to illustrate his statement. As a later study by Irving Mark *(Agrarian Conflicts in Colonial New York, 1711-1775)* has demonstrated, the government of the colony was dominated before the Revolution by a closely knit local aristocracy.[16] The governor's council, the assembly, the bench, and even the bar were filled with men, or the relatives of men, who held large estates, sometimes running over 100,000 acres, in the Hudson valley and the northern Connecticut valley. Though he did not possess the statistics to demonstrate this fact, Becker believed that the opposition to British taxation in New York was closely linked with a popular opposition to the local ruling class.

---

[15] Carl Becker, *The History of Political Parties in the Province of New York, 1760-1776* (Bulletin of the University of Wisconsin No. 286. History series, Vol. II, No. 1. Madison: University of Wisconsin, 1909; reprinted, 1959).

[16] Irving Mark, *Agrarian Conflicts in Colonial New York, 1711-1775* (New York: Columbia University, 1940).

Initially the big men took the lead in arousing hostility to British taxation (possibly because they saw in it a threat to their own local control). But the riots which occurred over the Stamp Act demonstrated to these aristocrats that they might have more to fear from popular than from British control. They therefore drew back from opposition to England and tried to keep the people acquiescent. Unfortunately for this plan, the Stamp Act troubles had brought forward a group of popular leaders who could not be easily quieted. The provincial assembly, safely in the control of conservative aristocrats, was tame enough, but extra-legal committees kept appearing to carry on hostility to England.

Although the conservatives frequently joined these committees in an effort to retain control, they were eventually faced with the alternative of becoming loyalists or else casting their lot with the popular Revolutionary group. Many of them, John Jay and James Duane for example, did join the Revolution, and retained sufficient leadership to fasten a conservative constitution on the new state. The history of New York during the ensuing decade showed a continuing conflict among the successful Revolutionists, between the members of the former ruling class on the one hand and the small farmers on the other.[17]

Becker did not contend that the Revolution in New York was merely an internal struggle between social classes, nor did he argue that what was true for New York was necessarily true for the other colonies. Succeeding historians have carried his interpretation somewhat further. Arthur Meier Schlesinger in *The Colonial Merchants and the American Revolution* examined the role of the merchants of all the colonies in the troubled twelve years preceding the Declaration of Independence.[18] In the initial opposition to the Sugar Act and the Stamp Act he found the merchants playing a leading role. The Stamp Act riots, however, gave them pause. When the Townshend Acts were passed, they resorted again to nonimportation agreements but took a firm stand against violence. As the lower classes became enthusiastic about nonimportation, the merchants grew less so. After 1770 they did their best to keep the lower classes under control and to prevent outbreaks of hostility to England. Only when the Tea Act threatened to cut them out of the tea business did they again take the lead in opposing Britain. The

---

[17] The story of that conflict during the 1780's is well told in Ernest Wilder Spaulding's *New York in the Critical Period, 1783-1789* (New York: Columbia University, 1932).

[18] Arthur M. Schlesinger, *The Colonial Merchants and the American Revolution, 1763-1776.* (New York: Columbia University, 1918).

results of their opposition were so catastrophic that many quickly drew back, but too late. Professor Schlesinger brought his story to a close with the coming of independence, but in a final chapter he looked ahead toward the war, and the years just after it, to see the merchants and aristocrats still arrayed against the same lower classes who had come into prominence in the Revolutionary agitations.

Both Becker and Schlesinger were writing about particular developments during the Revolution, Becker about politics in New York, Schlesinger about merchants in all the colonies. J. Franklin Jameson undertook to view the entire Revolution as a democratic upheaval, beginning perhaps as a mere political protest against certain acts of Parliament, but fanning out in the same manner as the French and Russian Revolutions, to transform the whole society.[19] "The stream of revolution," said Jameson, "once started, could not be confined within narrow banks, but spread abroad upon the land." And he traced its outflowing in a multitude of social changes, all of them "tending in the direction of a levelling democracy."[20] The abolition of the slave trade and of slavery in many states, the abolition of primogeniture and entail, the confiscation and dispersal of Royalists estates, the reduction in the property qualification for voting, the disestablishment of the Anglican Church—in these and similar developments Jameson saw the ultimate answer to the question of who should rule at home.

The social view of the Revolution, as expressed by Becker, Schlesinger, and Jameson, maximizes the conflicts among the colonists themselves. It thereby tends to minimize the struggle between the colonies and England. We see why the colonists disliked each other, but why they were so angry with England is less clearly revealed.

A possible answer is propaganda. Three important books have discussed the way in which propaganda created popular hostility against the mother country. In *Sam Adams: Pioneer in Propaganda,* John Chester Miller showed how one man led Massachusetts through the events that precipitated revolt.[21] In *Propaganda and the American Revolution,* Philip Davidson showed how other agitators and groups of agitators played on popular passions in all the colonies.[22] And in

---

[19] J. Franklin Jameson, *The American Revolution Considered as a Social Movement* (Princeton: Princeton University, 1926; reprinted Boston: Beacon, 1956).

[20] *Ibid.*, p. 11 and 25.

[21] John C. Miller, *Sam Adams: Pioneer in Propaganda* (Boston: Little, Brown, 1936).

[22] Philip Davidson, *Propaganda and the American Revolution, 1763-1783* (Chapel Hill: University of North Carolina, 1941).

Prelude to Independence, Professor Schlesinger has given us his own exhaustive study of the role of newspapers and their printers.[23] These books all contain valuable information, but the word "propaganda" has lost the magic charm it possessed fifteen or twenty years ago. We are not even sure any more that we know what it means (Can the truth be propaganda or is propaganda always false?). There remains, nevertheless, a feeling that the Revolution, so far as it was a movement for home rule, grew out of the efforts of agitators like Sam Adams and Patrick Henry, who magnified England's sins in order to gain their own particular ends.

THE ECONOMIC AND SOCIAL INTERPRETATION OF THE CONFEDERATION AND THE CONSTITUTION

This is scarcely a complete answer. But neither the imperial nor the social-economic historians, both of whom rely on it, have shown much interest in finding a better one. It has been suggested that the Revolution was the inevitable result of colonial economic growth; but such a thesis has not yet been demonstrated in any extended study of the period. The historians who stress economic and social forces have, in fact, been less concerned with the causes of colonial hostility to England than with the subsequent history of the social divisions which Becker and Schlesinger observed in the years before independence. What happened, they ask, to the old ruling class within the colonies? Were they completely overwhelmed, so that the new American states were governed entirely by revolutionary democrats? Two surveys of the new state governments, one by Allan Nevins and a more recent one by Elisha Douglass, indicate a negative answer.[24] Though the story varied from place to place, the old ruling class was not completely displaced in any state. The new governments may have offered more to the lower classes than the old ones, but the rich and well-born continued to exert a powerful influence.

In the 1780's, then, as in the 1770's, class was arrayed against class, each seeking to dominate the government. Social divisions may be used as a key to the understanding of American history after the Declaration of Independence as well as before.

---

[23] Arthur M. Schlesinger, *Prelude to Independence: The Newspaper War on Britain, 1764-1776* (New York: Knopf, 1958).

[24] Allan Nevins, *The American States during and after the Revolution, 1775-1789* (New York: Macmillan, 1924); Elisha P. Douglass, *Rebels and Democrats: the Struggle for Equal Political Rights and Majority Rule during the American Revolution* (Chapel Hill: University of North Carolina, 1955).

It is in this context that we must read Charles Beard's *An Economic Intepretation of the Constitution* (1913), one of the most influential books ever written on American history.[25] Published shortly after Becker's study, Beard's book, though it did not touch upon the Revolution itself, probably did more than Becker's to persuade historians that the whole Revolutionary period must be viewed in terms of class conflict.

The heart of Beard's book is a person-by-person examination of the fifty-five members of the Constitutional Convention of 1787 (Beard anticipated Namier in this technique of historical investigation). On the basis of Treasury records Beard was able to show that most of these men held public securities which rose in value as a result of the new Constitution. By stiffening both the government and the credit of the United States they made their investments in its funds pay off. They may have operated on the assumption that what was good for them was good for the country, but Beard argued that they had invested in personal, as opposed to real, property; that they designed the Constitution to bolster the security of this kind of property; and that they were able to put it across only because a majority of the population did not vote. Thus, the founding fathers from Beard's study appear as a talented group of capitalist speculators who succeeded in bamboozling the common man into acceptance of a form of government that was calculated to benefit a few uncommon men.

It is not difficult to identify Beard's personal property-holders as the economic descendants, or perhaps the very same men (it was only eleven years from the Declaration of Independence to the Constitutional Convention) as Arthur Schlesinger's merchants or Carl Becker's New York aristocrats. If Beard's view was correct, it would seem that the aristocrats who lost control but not influence in 1776 regained full power in 1789.

This conclusion is spelled out in two studies of the 1780's by Merrill Jensen. In older works the 1780's had been regarded as a dark and gloomy period, when the Americans, successful in war, appeared in danger of foundering on local quarrels and jealousies. The Critical Period, John Fiske had called it in a book of that title, in which he showed the United States falling to pieces, impotent to resist foreign insults, its trade and commerce depressed, all for lack of a real central government.[26] Other historians had recognized that this picture was

---

[25] Charles A. Beard, *An Economic Interpretation of the Constitution of the United States* (Reprint, New York: Macmillan, 1936).

[26] John Fiske, *The Critical Period of American History, 1783-1789* (Boston and New York: Houghton, Mifflin, 1898).

not wholly accurate, but Jensen assaulted it frontally in *The Articles of Confederation* and *The New Nation*.[27]

The Articles of Confederation, Jensen argued, were the political embodiment of the principles of the Declaration of Independence, and the Declaration was the embodiment of the democratic revolution against the local aristocracy as well as against England. Throughout the period of national existence under the Articles, the conservative aristocrats were intriguing to re-establish a centralized authority of the kind that Great Britain had formerly exerted. If the period was critical, it was because these "reluctant revolutionaries" made it so. But actually it was not so bad anyhow. The local tariffs erected by the states were generally directed against foreign countries, not against other members of the Confederation. In diplomacy American failures were the product of European conditions, not of American weakness. Economic prosperity had already begun to return before the Articles were abandoned. What the aristocrats really disliked about the period was its democracy.

Thus from a variety of works we gain a consistent explanation of the entire period from 1763 to 1789. The dominant theme is that of class conflict, the question of who shall rule at home. In the period of agitation preceding independence the masses are aroused to action against a supposed British tyranny but discover some additional and more accessible native tyrannies to exercise their wrath against. With the coming of independence they manage to achieve many reforms in the interest of a broader democracy, but the conservative property-holders and capitalist speculators manage to hang on and finally gain the upper hand with the adoption of the Constitution.

This interpretation, constructed of several different pieces of research, has an attractive symmetry. It makes sense out of the whole period and even points the way to a similar interpretation of the rest of American history as the story of democratic aspirations against upper-class despotism. It looks forward to the Jeffersonian revolution of 1800, Jacksonian democracy, Populism, Progressivisim, the New Deal, all embodiments of the spirit of '76, and to the Federalists, the Whigs, the post-Civil War Republicans, all representing resurgent aristocracy.

---

[27] Merrill Jensen, *The Articles of Confederation; an Interpretation of the Social-Constitutional History of the American Revolution, 1774-1781* (Madison: University of Wisconsin, 1948) and *The New Nation; a History of the United States during the Confederation, 1781-1789* (New York: Knopf, 1950).

CHALLENGES TO EARLIER INTERPRETATIONS

During the first four decades of the twentieth century, when Progressivism and the New Deal commanded the allegiance of most intellectuals, this interpretation was almost irresistible. Charles Beard's *Economic Interpretation of the Constitution* was itself a weapon of Progressivism, directed against a Supreme Court which wielded the Constitution as a club against social legislation. The 1940's and 1950's have witnessed a change. We had the social legislation of the New Deal by this time; and we also had an unparalleled prosperity. Perhaps because this period did not display the lines of class conflict so clearly as did the earlier part of the century, we were able to see less of it in the Revolution than we had once supposed to be there. Or perhaps, after two generations of professional scholarship, we knew enough to form a more accurate appraisal. Whatever the reason, during the fifteen years between 1945 and 1960 a number of studies appeared that began to alter the previous answers to the question of what the Revolution was.

One of the most important of these studies is Oliver M. Dickerson's *The Navigation Acts and the American Revolution*.[28] In the first part of this book the author demonstrated that the Americans did not object to the Navigation Acts or to the mercantilist policies they represented. In this view he continued the familiar attack of the imperial school of historians on Bancroft. In the second part of the book Professor Dickerson addressed himself to the question which so few recent historians have asked: why did the Americans revolt against England?

Professor Dickerson's answer was new. The heart of the trouble, he said, was the American Board of Customs Commissioners established at Boston in 1767. Before that year American customs officers reported directly to a Board of Commissioners in England. With the creation by the Townshend Acts of separate commissioners for America, England gave free rein to a set of men who in less than ten years dissolved the loyalty and mutual interest that had hitherto bound the empire together. Professor Dickerson traced in detail the activities of the American Customs Commisioners and of the officers who operated under their direction. What he found was "customs racketeering," the use of technicalities in the law to trap American merchants and seize their ships (the officers received a third of the proceeds of ships condemned and sold for customs violations). Among those victimized where two

---

[28] Oliver M. Dickerson, *The Navigation Acts and the American Revolution* (Philadelphia: University of Pennsylvania, 1951).

leading figures of the Revolution, John Hancock of Boston and Henry Laurens of Charleston, South Carolina. Behind many of the famous incidents that provoked American hostility to England, including the Boston Massacre and the depredations of the Schooner *Gaspee,* Professor Dickerson saw the guiding hand of the Customs Commissioners.

The Navigation Acts and the American Revolution offers the most important new information about the Revolution produced in the past twenty-five years. The effect of it is to swing attention away from internal conflicts and back toward the question of home rule. It shows that the colonists had genuine grievances against England and may not have been influenced merely by propaganda or by a desire to evade taxes which they ought in equity to have paid. It does not, however, discuss directly the validity or consistency of colonial objections to Parliamentary taxation.

In *The Stamp Act Crisis: Prologue to Revolution,* written in collaboration with Helen M. Morgan, Edmund S. Morgan examined the colonial arguments against the Sugar Act and the Stamp Act and found them more sweeping than has generally been supposed.[29] When England first tried to tax Americans in 1764, they objected on principle to all taxation by Parliament and did not make the distinction between external and internal taxes so often attributed to them. They were not, therefore, guilty of all the inconsistencies with which they have been charged. Their political ideas were not altogether static, but their attachment to principle was greater than twentieth century historians have usually supposed. In a shorter book on the entire period from 1763 to 1789 Morgan tried to describe the American search for principles of freedom and to see these years as a time of extraordinary unification rather than division.[30]

Oscar and Mary Handlin have challenged one of the assumptions of the social-economic interpretation.[31] The point made by the Handlins is that in Massachusetts the divisions found by Schlesinger before 1776 were not continuous with those observable later. The Federalists and anti-Federalists of 1788 did not correspond geographically, socially, or politically with the radicals and conservatives of the 1770's.

---

[29] Edmund S. and Helen M. Morgan, *The Stamp Act Crisis: Prologue to Revolution* (Chapel Hill: University of North Carolina, 1953).

[30] Edmund S. Morgan, *The Birth of the Republic, 1763-89* (Chicago: University of Chicago, 1956). This book was published in cloth and paper editions.

[31] Oscar and Mary F. Handlin, "Radicals and Conservatives in Massachusetts after Independence," *New England Quarterly,* 17:343-55; September 1944.

A more direct assault on the view of the Revolution as a class conflict is that of Robert E. Brown.[32] The interpretation of the Revolution as a social conflict has posited the existence of a large lower-class the members of which were unable to vote because they could not meet the property qualifications. Brown demonstrated that in Massachusetts there was no such class. By producing statistics for a number of representative towns, he showed that the great majority of adult males in Massachusetts enjoyed the right to vote before the Revolution was ever thought of. He likewise showed that, whatever may have been the case in other states, in Massachusetts the farmers of the West enjoyed as full representation in the legislature as the merchants of the East. There was no democratic revolution here, Professor Brown argued, because there was no room for one: Massachusetts was already democratic. Critics answered, with some justice, that the existence of an equitable scheme of representation and of a broad suffrage do not necessarily mean democracy. But the fact remains that the supposed establishment of these conditions, either during the Revolution or later, has frequently been hailed as evidence of the rise of democracy.

It would be dangerous to project Professor Brown's conclusions to all the other colonies, and a separate study of western Massachusetts shows that class conflict played some part in that area of the state if not in the East.[33] But it is equally dangerous to project Carl Becker's findings for New York. Recent studies of Maryland, Pennsylvania, New Jersey, and Rhode Island show unique patterns of political-social events in each state.[34] In Maryland, New Jersey and Rhode Island at least, the patterns do not indicate a social revolution. But before we can form an accurate judgment of the Revolution as a social movement we will need studies covering the period from 1763 to 1789 in every state.

---

[32] Robert E. Brown, *Middle-Class Democracy and the Revolution in Massachusetts, 1691-1780* (Ithaca: Cornell University, 1955).

[33] Robert J. Taylor, *Western Massachusetts in the Revolution* (Providence: Brown University, 1954).

[34] Charles A. Barker, *The Background of the Revolution in Maryland* (New Haven: Yale University, 1940); Philip A. Crowl, *Maryland during and after the Revolution, a Political and Economic Study* (Baltimore: The Johns Hopkins University, 1943); Theodore Thayer, *Pennsylvania Politics and the Growth of Democracy, 1740-1776* (Harrisburg: Pennsylvania Historical and Museum Commission, 1953); Robert L. Brunhouse, *The Counter-Revolution in Pennsylvania, 1776-1790* (Harrisburg: Pennsylvania Historical and Museum Commission, 1953); Richard P. McCormick, *Experiment in Independence: New Jersey in the Critical Period, 1781-1789* (New Brunswick: Rutgers University, 1950); David S. Lovejoy, *Rhode Island Politics and the American Revolution, 1760-1776* (Providence: Brown University, 1958).

Meanwhile Professor Brown attacked the citadel of the social-economic interpretation in another book.[35] This is a meticulous examination of virtually every statement in Beard's *Economic Interpretation of the Constitution.* In spite of the negative tone of the book, it succeeds in showing that Beard's evidence for his economic interpretation will not bear scrutiny. Most of the Treasury records used by Beard date from several years after the Constitutional Convention. Even if we accept them as an accurate index to the holdings of the members of the Convention in 1787, a study of the other properties held by the members indicates that only a small proportion of their capital was invested in public securities and a much larger proportion in land. Brown also shows that the members of the convention proceeded on the assumption (contrary to Beard's) that a majority of the adult males in most states were able to vote. Thus, by indirect evidence, Brown extends his findings for Massachusetts to cover the other states.

Working independently of Brown, Forrest McDonald, in *We the People,* has arrived at similar conclusions.[36] Beard himself had stated that a proper testing of his interpretation would require an examination of members in the various ratifying conventions. McDonald has made such an examination and has also studied the economic history of each state during the Confederation period. The result does not bear out Beard's contentions. In most states there was little correlation between possession of public securities and attitudes toward the Constitution. McDonald accepts the possibility of an economic interpretation of the Constitution, but he shows that it will have to be a far more complex one than that which Beard propounded.

A different kind of attack on Beard's *Economic Interpretation* comes from Cecilia M. Kenyon in an article entitled "Men of Little Faith: The Anti-Federalists on the Nature of Representative Government."[37] It had been Beard's contention that the Constitution was designed by its framers to protect speculative capitalist interests from the power of majority rule and that opposition to the Constitution arose from a

---

[35] Robert E. Brown, *Charles Beard and the Constitution, a Critical Analysis of "An Economic Interpretation of the Constitution"* (Princeton: Princeton University, 1956).

[36] Forrest McDonald, *We The People: The Economic Origins of the Constitution* (Chicago: University of Chicago, 1958). A vigorous criticism of McDonald's findings is Jackson T. Main's, "Charles A. Beard and the Constitution: A Critical Review of Forrest McDonald's *We the People,*" *William and Mary Quarterly,* 3rd Series, 17:86-102; January 1960. McDonald, although admitting minor factual errors, firmly stands by his conclusions. *Ibid.,* 102-10.

[37] *William and Mary Quarterly,* 3rd Series, 12:3-43; January 1955.

democratic impulse to protect majority rule. Professor Kenyon surveyed the arguments offered against ratification of the Constitution and found the anti-Federalists to have been unconcerned by the checks imposed on the majority. Instead, they worried that the checks were not strong enough. They were men of little faith because they did not wish to give any government such extensive power as they feared the national government would have under the Constitution.

There are still other signs of reaction. Frederick Tolles assessed Jameson's findings in the light of subsequent research.[38] Though he saw much that is still valid in them, he concluded that the American Revolution was not so much of a social movement as Jameson had supposed. And Richard B. Morris, in a survey of writings on the Critical Period, aligned himself more with Fiske than with Jensen.[39]

In England, too, the excitement over Sir Lewis Namier's discoveries has begun to subside, and at least one historian has suggested that there may have been something more to eighteenth century politics than the struggle between factions without principle and without party. Herbert Butterfield, in *George III and the Historians*, argues that the exclusive attention given by Namier and his disciples to the structure of politics has blinded them to the outer framework of ideas and principles through which men have always viewed their political actions.[40] The result, he says, has been a loss of perspective, an atomization of history. Butterfield calls for renewed consideration of the larger public issues as the major theme of historical narrative.

It would be wrong to leave the impression that the imperial, the social-economic, or the Namierist interpretation is now finished. Each has made a lasting contribution to our knowledge of the Revolutionary period. Each is still inspiring new studies. But the time has come when we may begin to determine the limits of these interpretations.[41] We should employ the new insights we have gained toward a better understanding of why men behaved as they did in 1776 or 1787, but we must not expand particular insights into a complete explanation. We must continue to ask, for we still do not fully know, what the Revolution was.

[38] Frederick B. Tolles, "The American Revolution Considered as a Social Movement: A Re-evaluation," *American Historical Review*, 60:1-12; October 1954.

[39] Richard B. Morris, "The Confederation Period and the American Historian," *William and Mary Quarterly*, 3rd Series, 13:139-56; April 1956.

[40] Herbert Butterfield, *George III and the Historians* (New York: Macmillan, 1959).

[41] Edmund S. Morgan, "The American Revolution: Revisions in Need of Revising," *William and Mary Quarterly*, 3rd Series, 14:3-15; January 1957.

CHAPTER V

Federalists and Republicans, 1789-1825: Political Developments and Foreign Affairs

Alexander DeConde

INTRODUCTION

THE politics and diplomacy of the Federalist and Republican eras have often attracted historians and since 1940, the starting point for the writings considered in this chapter, that attraction has continued virtually unabated. One reason for the lasting interest in the period covering the first thirty-five years of our national existence under the Constitution of 1787 is that Americans in those years organized their first national political parties, made them work, and laid the foundations of a foreign policy that has been uniquely successful ever since.

Political ideas and developments in those years of the young nation have left such a deep imprint on American history that some scholars have interpreted the whole of the country's history from either the political viewpoint of Thomas Jefferson or of Alexander Hamilton, long acknowledged as the principal founders of the American political system.[1] To this day politicians and statesmen occasionally refer to themselves as either Jeffersonians or Hamiltonians.

Since the Federalist period, covering the years 1789 to 1801, and the Republican period, covering roughly the years 1801 to 1825, are the

---

[1] See in particular Vernon L. Parrington, *Main Currents in American Thought* (3 vols.; New York: Harcourt Brace, 1927-1930) which emphasizes the Jeffersonian tradition in a theme of industrialism *vs.* agrarianism; Charles M. Wiltse, *The Jeffersonian Tradition in American Democracy* (Chapel Hill: University of North Carolina, 1935); and Max Beloff, *Thomas Jefferson and American Democracy* (London: Hodder & Stoughton, 1948). For emphasis on the Hamiltonian view, see the introductory remarks in Louis M. Hacker, *Alexander Hamilton in the American Tradition* (New York: McGraw-Hill, 1957); Broadus Mitchell, *Heritage from Hamilton* (New York: Columbia University, 1957); and Bray Hammond, *Banks and Politics in America, From the Revolution to the Civil War* (Princeton: Princeton University, 1957).

fountainheads of our national politics and foreign policy, historians have interpreted and reinterpreted ideas and developments in those periods while groping for a better understanding of our national growth. Sometimes the "new" interpretations have been merely differences of opinion; sometimes they have been of such significance as to outmode earlier views. Historical writing on the Federalist and Republican eras in the past two decades has not produced any sweeping or startlingly new interpretation. Yet if any one influence has distinguished the recent writings on the politics and diplomacy of our early national years it has been the emphasis which graduate schools and historians have placed on interpretation, analysis, and ideas.

GENERAL STUDIES: MARCUS CUNLIFFE

For purposes of investigation, the historians dealing with the period 1789 to 1825 have usually broken it down into smaller units of time. There is, therefore, no one special history that emphasizes it as a distinct period of American history. However, Marcus Cunliffe, an English student of American history, recently wrote a broad popular synthesis that comes closest of any single volume to developing that period as a whole.[2] In an effort to give the period coherence and pattern, he has emphasized the shaping of the "national character," maintaining that nearly all the main American characteristics could be found in this period. Although Cunliffe told a familiar story, his short book is a readable and coherent condensation of the history of the nation's first half-century. It offers a good introduction to the early national period.

POLITICAL DEVELOPMENTS, 1789-1820
Federalists: General Studies

For the Federalist era, covering the period from 1789 to 1801, John Spencer Bassett's volume in the first American Nation Series, describing the foundations of the American party system and the problems of foreign policy confronting the administrations of Presidents George Washington and John Adams, was for many years the basic general study.[3] Although clear in its story and well-written, it lacks depth and shows a Jeffersonian bias.

---

[2] *The Nation Takes Shape, 1789-1837* (Chicago: University of Chicago, 1959).

[3] *The Federalist System, 1789-1801* (New York: Harper, 1906). After the type for this chapter had been set, the volume covering the Federalist years in the New American Nation Series, John C. Miller, *The Federalist Era, 1789-1801* (New York: Harper, 1960), was published. In presenting a well-written and carefully balanced story, based on the latest scholarship, it supersedes its predecessor and other political surveys of the period.

The other broad synthesis of the Federalist era, written twenty years later by Claude G. Bowers, has an even stronger Jeffersonian bias.[4] Bowers also wrote well, depicting the period as picturesque and dramatic. He succeeded in his goal of reaching the general public, for his book was popular and his interpretation became the one that many literate Americans accepted. He described the period as a continuation of the Revolution that created a democratic republic and presented the political issue between Jefferson and Hamilton as "a clear-cut fight between democracy and aristocracy," with Hamilton on the wrong side.

In contrast, a recent general study of the Federalist era, by Nathan Schachner, is markedly sympathetic to Hamilton and the Federalists.[5] Schachner's volume is larger and broader than those of his predecessors'. Like Bowers, he wrote well and for the general public, emphasized the dramatic and the picturesque, stressed personalities, and made the political battle between Jefferson and Hamilton his main theme. He believed that the key to understanding the period lay in the conflicting philosophies of the political leaders. Although he offered no interpretation which the historian could call new, he advanced the view that out of the clashing politics of the time came a middle course that led the new nation between the extremes of either side in a world dominated by predatory powers.

John Dos Passos, in a well-written portrayal of American statesmen from 1782 to 1802, also tried to reach a popular audience and also emphasized personalities. He related the history of the period in terms of the men who shaped it and presented something of a balance between Jeffersonianism and Hamiltonianism, but he offered no new information or fresh interpretations.[6]

George Washington

Douglas Southall Freeman projected a seven-volume biography of George Washington, completing six volumes before he died.[7] His sixth volume covers Washington's presidential years to 1793[8] and the

---

[4] *Jefferson and Hamilton: The Struggle for Democracy in America* (Boston: Houghton Mifflin, 1925).

[5] *The Founding Fathers* (New York: Putnam, 1954).

[6] *The Men Who Made the Nation* (Garden City, N. Y.: Doubleday, 1957).

[7] *George Washington: A Biography* (6 vols.; New York: Scribner, 1948-1954).

[8] *George Washington: Patriot and President* (New York: Scribner, 1954).

seventh, written by his former assistants, John Alexander Carroll and Mary Ashworth Wells, deals with the years since 1793.[9]

These last two volumes, like the earlier ones, present the history of Washington's times from the President's point of view. As a result, the main interpretation that emerges is that of Washington as an able administrator clearly coming to grips with many problems and mastering them.

Alexander Hamilton

The best one-volume biography of Hamilton has just come from the pen of John C. Miller.[10] Concentrating on Hamilton's political ideas and career, Miller is sympathetic to his subject without abusing Jefferson and Hamilton's other opponents. This is a scholarly, well-written and carefully balanced interpretation of a man who is depicted as paradoxical, a package of contradictions, one who was neither hero nor villain. Hamilton, Miller maintains, was both right and wrong in his political thinking and had vices that were never far removed from his virtues, hence the paradox.

The Adams Administration

Two new studies of John Adams' administration show Adams as having been a more able politician and a President of greater stature than historians have generally portrayed. Manning J. Dauer concentrated in his study on those Federalists who favored Adams rather than Hamilton.[11] He analyzed votes in Congress, Adams' political and economic ideas, and those of his leading associates, to explain the political relationships within the Federalist party. Dauer's interpretation presents the Federalist party as being made up of both commercial and agrarian interests, and argues that Adams, unlike Hamilton, whose policies were designed to benefit the commercial group, gave equal consideration to agriculture. In this respect, Adams' point of view was comparable to that of Jefferson.

---

[9] *George Washington: First in Peace* (New York: Scribner, 1957). For a concise summary of Washington's political views, see Harold W. Bradley, "The Political Thinking of George Washington," *The Journal of Southern History*, 11:469-86; November 1945.

[10] *Alexander Hamilton: Portrait in Paradox* (New York: Harper, 1959). Broadus Mitchell has completed the first volume of an intensive study, *Alexander Hamilton: Youth to Maturity, 1755-1788* (New York: Macmillan, 1957). Nathan Schachner has also written a brief biography of Hamilton in which Hamilton is portrayed in a favorable light, *Alexander Hamilton* (New York: Appleton-Century, 1946).

[11] *The Adams Federalists* (Baltimore: Johns Hopkins, 1953).

The other study, by Stephen G. Kurtz, rather than being a history of the Adams administration is also concerned primarily with the conflict between Adams and Hamilton.[12] According to Kurtz's interpretation, a small group of powerful Federalists under Hamilton's leadership sought to make use of the tensions resulting from the Quasi-War with France for political purposes. They wanted to fasten a militaristic government on the country under Federalist control and destroy the Republican opposition. Thus the role of the army, Kurtz suggested, was the most significant single issue in the four years of Adams' Presidency.

Two other recent studies have concentrated on the politics of civil liberties in the Adams administration. The first, by John C. Miller, is a popular, well-written history of the Alien and Sedition Acts and the prosecutions under them.[13] Miller stressed the sectional roots of the acts, showing that they received overwhelming support from the states north of the Potomac river. He also contended that the social and political climate of America in the early 1950's was similar to that of the late 1790's.

In the first of two volumes to be devoted to the subject, James M. Smith also studied the enactment and enforcement of the Alien and Sedition laws but did not consciously connect them with his own time.[14] He did, however, find modern parellels to them. Smith's is the first thorough scholarly study of the acts, which he saw as part of the evolution of American civil liberties. Those laws, according to his interpretation, helped elevate the Republicans to power and thus contributed to the "Revolution of 1800." Smith's main thesis is that the Federalist party manifestly lacked any deep concern for the liberty of the individual since it was willing to resort to harsh and repressive measures to preserve its political power. It used the largely imaginary danger of a French attack as an excuse to cripple if not destroy the opposing Republican party.

---

[12] *The Presidency of John Adams: The Collapse of Federalism, 1795-1800* (Philadelphia: University of Pennsylvania, 1957). For other views on the same theme see Alexander DeConde, "William Vans Murray and the Diplomacy of Peace: 1797-1800," *Maryland Historical Magazine*, 48:1-26; March 1953. Adrienne Koch, "Hamilton, Adams, and the Pursuit of Power," *Review of Politics*, 16:37-66; January 1954. Marshall Smelser, "The Jacobin Phrenzy: Federalism and the Menace of Liberty, Equality, and Fraternity," *Review of Politics*, 13: 457-82; October 1951.

[13] *Crisis in Freedom: The Alien and Sedition Acts* (Boston: Little, Brown, 1951).

[14] *Freedom's Fetters: The Alien and Sedition Laws and American Civil Liberties* (Ithaca, N. Y.: Cornell University, 1956). See also Marshall Smelser, "George Washington and the Alien and Sedition Acts," *The American Historical Review*, 59:322-34; January 1954.

Richard Hofstadter

Although his treatment of the Federalist and Jeffersonian era covers only a small part of his book—two short essays on Jefferson and Jacksonian democracy—Richard Hofstadter played down the differences between Jeffersonians and Hamiltonians, maintaining that these differences have been overemphasized. He suggested that what the two groups and their political descendants have had in common is more important.[15]

Administrative Techniques and Ideas

Leonard D. White, in two volumes of a four-volume history, covered the politics of the Federalist and Republican eras, but from the special viewpoint of the administrative historian.[16] He emphasized institutions, the men who helped shape them, and their ideas on public administration. In exploring the origin and growth of opinions on public administration, he showed in his first volume how Americans in the Federalist period faced practical problems of government and formulated their administrative ideas. Although White presented no new factual data, his study is valuable to the historian because, through interpretation, he shed new light on administrative problems that helped mold political and diplomatic decisions, the central problems of the era. He concluded that the Federalists had few administrative precedents to follow in building a central administration. Neither the British experience nor their own colonial and state experience offered guides. The new ideas came primarily from Hamilton.

In his second volume White pointed out that the Jeffersonians continued, in most instances, the Federalist practices and accepted the Federalist ideals of public administration.[17] The Jeffersonians did remedy the weaknesses that they found, particularly as revealed by the War of 1812. According to White's interpretation, the political differences between Jefferson and Hamilton were much more profound than their differences in the manner and spirit of conducting public business. Jefferson and his able lieutenant, Albert Gallatin,

---

[15] *The American Political Tradition and the Men Who Made It* (New York: Knopf, 1951).

[16] *The Federalists: A Study in Administrative History* (New York, 1948) and *The Jeffersonians: A Study in Administrative History, 1801-1829* (New York, 1951). The last two volumes are *The Jacksonians: A Study in Administrative History, 1829-1861* (New York, 1954), and *The Republican Era, 1869-1901: A Study in Administrative History* (New York, 1958). All were published by Macmillan.

[17] *The Jeffersonians, Passim.*

inherited a going concern. Twelve years of Federalist rule, White concluded, had been enough to set the patterns of governmental practice that persisted throughout the next thirty.

Before White began his large history, his student, Lynton K. Caldwell, had offered a fresh approach to the political ideologies of Jefferson and Hamilton through a broad interpretation of administrative theory.[18] He advanced the thesis that a great deal in the rivalry between Hamilton and Jefferson grew out of the administrative problem of how to allocate authority among the departments in Washington's government. Caldwell explained that "the fundamental difference between the administrative ideas of Hamilton and Jefferson appears to be in their attitude toward the control of political power. . . . Hamilton stood for responsible government and Jefferson for limited government."

Marshall Smelser, in telling the story of the founding of the United States Navy, also stresses the rivalry between Hamiltonians and Jeffersonians. He explains how Congress decided to provide for and maintain the Navy, and of the political conflicts leading to that decision. By design, he tells little of sea battles, admirals, or administrative quarrels. His is basically a political history built on the theme that the founding of the Navy was a political act. Its main thesis states that the naval establishment grew out of partisan politics and reflected deeply rooted differences between Republicans and Federalists.[19]

Origin of Political Parties

Several new studies have concentrated on the origins of national political parties and in particular on the rise of Jeffersonian democracy. Traditionally, historians have viewed Jefferson's election to the Presidency in 1800 as symbolizing a movement toward greater democracy than prevailed under the Federalist administrations. Jefferson and his followers were certain that they had completed a political revolution, had saved the country from monarchists, and were returning to the original point of view of the founders of the republic. Although many historians have spoken of the "Revolution of 1800," few who have closely examined the politics and events of the Jeffersonian era could find a "revolution."

---

[18] *The Administrative Theories of Hamilton and Jefferson: Their Contribution to Thought on Public Administration* (Chicago: University of Chicago, 1944).

[19] *The Congress Founds the Navy, 1787-1798* (Notre Dame: University of Notre Dame, 1959).

One of the most stimulating recent studies of party origins is made up of three essays written by Joseph E. Charles who questioned the traditional view that Jefferson originated Jeffersonian democracy.[20] "Jefferson," he wrote, "did not create a party: a widespread movement recognized and claimed him as its leader." Charles stressed the roles of Washington, John Adams, Hamilton, and Jefferson in building the national political parties. He viewed the beginnings of the parties as a contest "between two shifting groups of men who, differing upon practical problems as they arose, came to suspect the views and purposes of those in the opposite camp and to regard their own pursuit of power and their determination to defeat their opponents as the supreme consideration." His interpretation reduces the origin of political parties to a mere struggle for power devoid of abstract differences over principle or economics, and is highly critical of Washington and Hamilton.[21]

Two other recent political studies concentrate almost exclusively on the Jeffersonian Republicans. Stuart Gerry Brown, using familiar materials and interpretations, analyzed the basic ideas that bound Jeffersonians together in political action to form the Republican party.[22] Throughout, he showed an undisguised sympathy for Republicans as opposed to Federalists.

Noble E. Cunningham, Jr., studied the growth of the political organization that lay behind Jefferson's election to the Presidency, emphasizing political technique.[23] He did not deal with the broader aspects of the origin and rise of Jeffersonian democracy. He focused his attention on the immediate origins of the Jeffersonian party and the means it used to gain control of the national administration. Like several other recent historians, he questioned the view, advanced by Bowers and earlier writers, that Jefferson personally organized a political party to oppose Hamilton by cementing together local parties in each of the states. The adoption of the Constitution of 1787, he pointed out, marked a sharp change in party development and from that time on party growth was a process of gradual evolution with James Madison playing a significant part. Cunningham's thesis is that

[20] *The Origins of the American Party System: Three Essays* (Williamsburg, Va.: Institute of Early American History and Culture, 1956).

[21] For the economic background, see Charles A. Beard, *Economic Origins of Jeffersonian Democracy* (New York: Macmillan, 1915).

[22] *The First Republicans: Political Philosophy and Public Policy in the Party of Jefferson and Madison* (Syracuse, N. Y.: Syracuse University, 1954).

[23] *The Jeffersonian Republicans: The Formation of Party Organization, 1789-1801* (Chapel Hill: University of North Carolina, 1957).

"the Republican party was a new growth that sprang from the divisions in Congress and the national government; it was a product of national rather than state politics."[24]

Several other historians have given James Madison much more credit than he has received in the past for helping to organize the Republican party. Adrienne Koch, in a history of ideas, analyzed the political doctrines of Jefferson and Madison and concluded that "the political philosophy known simply as 'Jeffersonian Democracy' is actually an amalgam of ideas, which owes very much to James Madison."[25] The growth of Republican political doctrine, she said, was the joint activity of two equals, more so than scholars had previously recognized. Miss Koch's book also presented a revised version of the parts played by Jefferson and Madison in the preparation of the Virginia and Kentucky Resolutions. She showed that, when the second set of those resolutions was under discussion in the summer of 1799, Jefferson brought up the idea of secession as a final recourse in answer to the violations of civil liberties by the federal government; but that he omitted the threat after discussing the issue with Madison.

Irving Brant, in the third volume of his large-scale biography of James Madison, traced in detail Madison's connection with the Republican party and also claimed, with convincing evidence, that Madison made a far greater contribution to the organization of the party than historians have hitherto recognized.[26] Jefferson, according to Brant's interpretation, has received too much credit for the work other political leaders had inaugurated and carried out. Jefferson's retirement from politics, 1794 to 1797, he pointed out, was real rather than apparent. According to his thesis, the crucial test leading to the organization of the Republican party was the fight over the Jay treaty of 1794, and Jefferson, he said, took almost no part in it. Madison, in his view, was "the fusing agent" of the Jeffersonian party. In his fourth volume Brant devoted himself primarily to Madison's diplomacy as Secretary of State during Jefferson's two terms

---

[24] Cunningham also contradicts the view of Eugene P. Link, *Democratic-Republican Societies, 1790-1800* (New York: Columbia University, 1942), that "the democratic societies laid the groundwork for the Republican party."

[25] *Jefferson and Madison: The Great Collaboration* (New York: Knopf, 1950). See also Adrienne Koch, *The Philosophy of Thomas Jefferson* (New York: Columbia University, 1943).

[26] *James Madison: Father of the Constitution, 1787-1800* (Indianapolis, 1950). The other volumes, all published by Bobbs-Merrill, are *James Madison: The Nationalist, 1780-1787* (Indianapolis, 1948); and *James Madison: Secretary of State, 1800-1809* (Indianapolis, 1953).

in the Presidency.[27] Here again Brant magnified Madison's achievements, showing the Secretary of State as a leader rather than as a lieutenant in the formulation of foreign policy. He suggested, for example, that Madison's diplomacy was significantly responsible for Napoleon's decision to sell Louisiana to the United States.

Jefferson Biographies

In spite of the growing emphasis on Madison, Jefferson, of all of the leaders in the Federalist and Jeffersonian eras, has most fascinated the biographers of the past two decades. The leading study is a projected five-volume biography, two volumes of which are completed, by Dumas Malone. [28] In the second volume, covering the years 1784 through 1792, Malone concentrated on foreign affairs, as Jefferson in those years was involved primarily in the diplomacy of the young nation.[29] Malone is partial to Jefferson and hence tried to whittle down Hamilton's stature. According to Malone's interpretation, Jefferson was not as pro-French as historians have generally described him as being. Contrary to the findings of Joseph Charles, George Washington in Malone's study emerges with enhanced stature as a statesman. In his two-volume biography of Jefferson, Nathan Schachner pointed out Jefferson's weaknesses as well as his strong points as a political leader.[30] Schachner's study is essentially factual and does not contain much interpretation.

Biographies of Lesser Figures

Several new biographies of lesser politicians and diplomats include fresh materials and ideas.[31] Particularly significant is the scholarly and meticulous study of Albert Gallatin by Raymond Walters, Jr.

---

[27] *Madison: Secretary of State.*

[28] *Jefferson and His Time* is the title for the full biography but each volume has its own title. The first volume is *Jefferson the Virginian* (Boston: Little, Brown, 1948). See also Nathan Schachner, *Thomas Jefferson: A Biography* (2 vols.; New York: Appleton-Century-Crofts, 1951) and the three volumes of Marie Kimball's biography, *Jefferson: The Road to Glory, 1743 to 1776* (New York, 1943); *Jefferson: The Scene of Europe, 1784 to 1789* (New York, 1950); and *Jefferson: War and Peace, 1776 to 1784* (New York, 1947). All were published by Coward-McCann.

[29] *Jefferson and the Rights of Man* (Boston: Little, Brown, 1951).

[30] *Thomas Jefferson: A Biography* (2 vols.; New York: Appleton-Century-Crofts, 1951).

[31] See in particular John H. Powell, *Richard Rush: Republican Diplomat, 1780-1859* (Philadelphia: University of Pennsylvania, 1942); Raymond Walters, Jr., *Alexander James Dallas: Lawyer, Politician, Financier, 1759-1817* (Philadelphia: University of Pennsylvania, 1943); Frederick B. Tolles, *George Logan of Philadelphia* (New York: Oxford University, 1953); and Blackwell P. Robinson, *William R. Davie* (Chapel Hill: University of North Carolina, 1957).

This study confirms the prevailing view that Gallatin was a master financier, a great politician, and that his contribution to the formation of American foreign policy was second only to that of John Quincy Adams.[32]

The political intrigue of Aaron Burr has long fascinated historians. In 1937 Nathan Schachner's[33] highly sympathetic biography of Burr was published and more recently Thomas P. Abernethy[34] brought together all available material on the conspiracy from 1804 to Burr's trial in 1807. Abernethy suggested that the Burr affair was "only a little less momentous than the acquisition of Louisiana." Abernethy's evidence seems to show that Burr was certainly guilty of a complicated conspiracy against both the United States and Spain.

FOREIGN POLICY TO 1820

A number of recent studies have dealt with foreign policy in the Federalist era. Arthur Burr Darling, in his detailed history of American diplomacy from 1763 to 1803, focused his attention on American efforts to obtain the Mississippi Valley.[35] He followed two main themes: first that no one of the great powers of the time, Great Britain, France, or Spain, wished to see the United States establish itself in the valley; and second, that the men who guided American diplomacy had a vision of empire, and in seeking territorial gains they displayed as much hard political realism as did their European antagonists.

Admitting frankly that he looked upon George Washington as the first and greatest of Americans, Louis M. Sears wrote a diplomatic history that concentrated on Washington's reaction to the French Revolution.[36] That revolution, Sears said, tested Washington's theory and practice as a political thinker and statesman. Sears' theme states that during a time of bitter political cleavage over foreign policy Washington guided American diplomacy with wisdom, that his was a wise and prudent record.

---

[32] *Albert Gallatin: Jeffersonian Financier and Diplomat* (New York: Macmillan, 1957). For the prevailing view, see Henry Adams, *The Life of Albert Gallatin* (Philadelphia: Lippincott, 1879).

[33] *Aaron Burr: A Biography* (New York: Frederick A. Stokes, 1937).

[34] *The Burr Conspiracy* (New York: Oxford University, 1954). For a colorful, readable account of Burr's trial, see Francis F. Beirne, *Shout Treason: The Trial of Aaron Burr* (New York: Hastings House, 1959).

[35] *Our Rising Empire, 1763-1803* (New Haven: Yale University, 1940).

[36] *George Washington and the French Revolution* (Detroit: Wayne State University, 1960).

Alexander DeConde, while emphasizing diplomacy, wrote a synthesis showing the interaction of politics and foreign policy during Washington's administrations.[37] The main theme of his book is the combined influence of diplomacy and domestic politics on the French alliance of 1778. In analyzing the origin of national political parties and foreign policy, he presented the thesis that differences over foreign policy contributed to the formation of political parties because foreign policy was a national issue transcending sectional differences. Harry Ammon advanced a similar idea in his study of the origins of the Republican party in Virginia.[38]

In foreign policy, DeConde challenged the traditional interpretation of the Federalist era as being the "Golden Age" of American diplomacy and "the classic age of American statecraft."[39] He pointed out that the statesmen of the Washington era often played their politics and diplomacy by ear and sometimes placed political advantage above national welfare. In their struggles over foreign policy, the Federalists and Republicans were motivated by their own self-interests. He also contended that the Washington era was not essentially isolationist and that it did not truly set a precedent for isolationism. In his view, Americans differed in their attitudes toward Europe. Some Americans were isolationists, and some wanted their government to take part in the international politics of Europe.

Washington's Farewell Address, frequently cited in isolationist controversy and analyzed by historians, is one of the basic documents in America's diplomatic history. Two recent interpretations deserve brief mention. Albert K. Weinberg questioned the view that Washington's advice has determined the American attitude and policy toward alliances.[40] Weinberg said that "the great rule was created

---

[37] *Entangling Alliance: Politics and Diplomacy under George Washington* (Durham, N. C.: Duke University, 1958). See also Albert H. Bowman, "Jefferson, Hamilton and American Foreign Policy," *Political Science Quarterly*, 71:18-41; March 1956.

[38] "The Formation of the Republican Party in Virginia, 1789-1796," *The Journal of Southern History*, 19:283-310; August 1953.

[39] For some of the other interpretations see Carl L. Becker, "What is Still Living in the Political Philosophy of Thomas Jefferson," *The American Historical Review*, 48:691-706; July 1943; Schachner, *Founding Fathers*, p. vii; George F. Kennan, *Realities of American Foreign Policy* (Princeton: Princeton University, 1954), p. 3-4; and Hans J. Morgenthau, *In Defense of the National Interest: A Critical Examination of American Foreign Policy* (New York: Knopf, 1951), p. 3.

[40] "Washington's 'Great Rule' in Its Historical Evolution" in Eric F. Goldman, ed., *Historiography and Urbanization: Essays in Honor of W. Stull Holt* (Baltimore: Johns Hopkins, 1941), p. 109-38.

not in the Farewell Address alone but in all subsequent American history as well." According to his interpretation, it was "the joint product of Washington and the American people."

Alexander DeConde presented a revision of the traditional view that Washington's Farewell was a wise, timeless, and unbiased warning to the nation against foreign dangers.[41] Its objectives, he said, were "practical, immediate, and partisan." They bore directly on the presidential election of 1796, on the French alliance of 1778, and on the status of Franco-American relations in general.[42]

In the transition from the Federalist to Republican administrations, Bradford Perkins added new information to the history of Anglo-American relations.[43] His thesis is that capable diplomacy, particularly on the part of England, made possible the first Anglo-American rapprochement after the American Revolution. Events after 1805, which destroyed the accord, he blamed on inept English and American diplomacy. With qualification, he attributed most of the fault to the Jeffersonians who later led the nation into the War of 1812.

In another important diplomatic study, Alfred L. Burt challenged a number of existing interpretations of our early relations with Great Britain.[44] His interpretation of the diplomacy leading to the Jay treaty of 1794 differed from that of Samuel F. Bemis' standard work.[45] Burt contended that the United States could not have wrung concessions from Great Britain in her war with France even if John Jay had threatened to bring the Untied States into the Armed Neutrality of the northern European nations and had not been undercut by Alexander Hamilton who told the British his government would not join the Armed Neutrality.

Burt also rejected the traditional American view that Great Britain continued to hold the Northwest posts after 1783, in violation of the peace treaty, because she wanted to continue her monopoly of the fur

---

[41] "Washington's Farewell, the French Alliance, and the Election of 1796," *The Mississippi Valley Historical Review*, 43:641-58; March 1957. See also DeConde, *Entangling Alliance*, p. 461-71.

[42] See also the interpretation of Samuel F. Bemis, "Washington's Farewell Address: A Foreign Policy of Independence," *The American Historical Review*, 39:250-68; January 1934.

[43] *The First Rapprochement: England and the United States, 1795-1805* (Philadelphia: University of Pennsylvania, 1955).

[44] *The United States, Great Britain and British North America from the Revolution to the Establishment of Peace After the War of 1812* (New Haven: Yale University, 1940).

[45] *Jay's Treaty: A Study in Commerce and Diplomacy* (New York: Macmillan, 1923).

trade. He suggested instead that the British held on to the posts indefinitely primarily because they had blundered in neglecting the welfare of the Indians in the peace treaty of 1783 and because of "American "weakness." After the peace, Great Britain tried to rectify the "blunder" by protecting the Indians against the Americans and in so doing retained the posts.

In dealing with the causes of the War of 1812, Burt attempted to revise a revision of an earlier interpretation advanced by Henry Adams.[46] He argued in particular against the thesis of Julian W. Pratt that without the ambitions of aggressive Westerners and their grievances against Great Britain there would have been no war.[47] He re-emphasized, instead, the older interpretation of the war as one for free trade and sailors' rights. "The impressment issue," he said, "was the rock that wrecked the last hope of peace."

In his interpretation of the causes of the war, Burt has illustrated how historical interpretations sometimes work in cycles and how interpretation in history is almost always linked to the subjective appraisal of the historian himself. Warren H. Goodman, in his review of the literature on the causes of the War of 1812, also suggested that the maritime factors deserved more consideration in interpreting the causes of the war than the Pratt thesis gave them.[48]

Diplomatic historians have also revised the interpretations of several events after the Treaty of Ghent. Charles P. Stacey corrected earlier

[46] *History of the United States of America during the Administrations of Jefferson and Madison* (9 vols.; New York: Scribner, 1889-1891). This is still the best broad study of the Jefferson and Madison periods, absorbing history written on a grand scale. Recent findings have revealed some important flaws in Adams' work but it is still considered, by most historians, one of the finest histories written in America. It is particularly strong in its treatment of diplomacy and of domestic politics relating to foreign affairs.

[47] *Expansionists of 1812* (New York: Macmillan, 1925). Mary K. Latimer in "South Carolina—A Protagonist of the War of 1812," *The American Historical Review*, 61:914-29; July 1956, supports Burt's observations and presents evidence that weakens the Pratt thesis. She points out that South Carolina, whose representatives in Congress had significant roles in bringing on the war, favored war for different reasons from those of the Westerners. South Carolina's desire for war stemmed from her hope that war would provide a remedy for her agricultural and commercial distress.

[48] "The Origins of the War of 1812: A Survey of Changing Interpretations," *The Mississipppi Valley Historical Review*, 28:171-86; September 1941. For two new popular accounts of the War of 1812, with stress on the military and naval aspects, see Francis F. Beirne, *The War of 1812* (New York: E. P. Dutton, 1949) and Glenn Tucker, *Poltroons and Patriots: A Popular Account of the War of 1812* (Indianapolis: Bobbs-Merrill, 1954). See also Alec R. Gilpin, *The War of 1812 in the Old Northwest* (East Lansing: Michigan State University, 1958).

interpretations of the significance of the Rush-Bagot Agreement of 1817.[49] He showed that the "undefended border" between the United States and Canada dated from the Washington Treaty of 1871, not from the agreement of 1817 which was limited to naval disarmament on the Great Lakes and Lake Champlain. His evidence shows that the idea of the "unfortified frontier" is founded on legend.[50]

Recent studies have placed the treaty of February 22, 1819, with Spain in a larger context than did past interpretations. Diplomatic historians no longer refer to it merely as the Florida Treaty; they recognize that it was much broader and that it solved other boundary problems in North America.[51] Since the treaty brought the United States to the Pacific Ocean, through Spain's surrender of her claims to Oregon, Samuel F. Bemis has called it the "Transcontinental Treaty." His earlier writings placed the treaty in its larger setting, but he has brought his findings together in his award-winning study of John Quincy Adams, which he called a diplomatic biography.[52] Since the book takes its contours from events in Adams' diplomatic career rather than from personality, it is essentially a detailed history of American foreign relations from 1795 to 1829. It pays scant attention to domestic affairs. Bemis gave Adams considerable credit for the Monroe Doctrine but did not slight the contribution of James Monroe himself. By saying that Adams was "the greatest isolationist of them all," Bemis advanced an interesting new interpretation on nineteenth century isolationists.

THE ERA OF GOOD FEELINGS

Monroe's two terms in the Presidency, a period of one-party government, has been known as the "Era of Good Feelings" during which there was relative calmness in national politics. Paradoxically, historians have also regarded it as a turbulent period when sectional rivalry was destroying national unity. The key to the interpretation

---

[49] "The Myth of the Unguarded Frontier, 1815-1871," *The American Historical Review*, 56: 1-18; October 1950.

[50] The earlier interpretation is summarized in Edgar W. McInnis, *The Unguarded Frontier: A History of American-Canadian Relations* (Garden City, N. Y.: Doubleday, Doran, 1942).

[51] For the latest and best study of the Florida question itself that deals with local problems as well as with the broader issues of diplomacy, see Rembert W. Patrick, *Florida Fiasco: Rampant Rebels on the Georgia-Florida Border, 1810-1815* (Athens Ga.: University of Georgia, 1954).

[52] *John Quincy Adams and the Foundations of American Foreign Policy* (New York: Knopf, 1949).

of the period as an "Era of Good Feelings," Charles S. Sydnor has written, is not the method the Republicans used to make their nominations but the fact that only one party was active nationally.[53] The caucus system, he pointed out, was a more elaborate form of party organization than the occasional meetings of the congressional caucuses. He suggested that the one-party rule contributed to the political events leading to the spread of Jacksonian democracy over the country.[54]

The sectional controversy during the "Era of Good Feelings" is symbolized by the controversy over Missouri statehood. Glover Moore's book is the first comprehensive treatment of the congressional action that led to the three compromises necessary to settle the Missouri question in 1820.[55] The Federalist minority in the North, according to his interpretation, saw in the controversy an opportunity for a new alignment of political parties that would give it a favored position in a common front of the North against the South. Contrary to the usual story, showing the people as reacting with intense feeling to the heated arguments in Congress, Moore pointed out that the people were primarily concerned with the hard times created by a nationwide depression. Politicians and journalists generated most of the heat. Moore concluded that the significance of the Missouri controversy lay in what it clarified and foreshadowed. "It was an epitome of the entire sectional controversy before 1860," he wrote, "containing all the important elements of previous and future antagonisms."

A prize-winning synthesis covering the political transition from Jeffersonian democracy to Jacksonian democracy in the years from 1815 to 1828 was written by an Englishman, George Dangerfield.[56] In his well-written book Dangerfield stressed personalities, politics, and diplomacy. He made a significant contribution in considering

---

[53] "The One-Party Period of American History," *The American Historical Review*, 51:439-51; April 1946.

[54] The best biography of Monroe is William P. Cresson, *James Monroe* (Chapel Hill: University of North Carolina, 1946). See also Charles M. Wiltse, *John C. Calhoun: Nationalist, 1782-1828* (Indianapolis: Bobbs-Merrill, 1944). Recently, Stuart Gerry Brown edited *The Autobiography of James Monroe* (Syracuse: Syracuse University, 1959), which is, in fact, only a large fragment of an unfinished autobiography written after Monroe left the Presidency. It is, in effect, a defense of Monroe's controversial diplomatic career in the middle years of his life.

[55] *The Missouri Controversy, 1819-1821* (Lexington: University of Kentucky, 1953).

[56] *The Era of Good Feelings* (New York: Harcourt, Brace, 1952). See also Harry Ammon, "James Monroe and the Era of Good Feelings," *The Virginia Magazine of History and Biography*, 66:387-98; October 1958. Ammon analyzes Monroe's policies as they related to party trends in the "Era of Good Feelings." He praises Monroe's policies as being skillful.

the Monroe Doctrine against the background of European politics. He argued that the liberal Tories in their movement toward free trade, favored an understanding with the United States as a means of promoting commerce. At this time, however, the nationalism of the American system favored protection. John Quincy Adams rejected British proposals; and hence the Monroe doctrine was formulated.

The generally accepted interpretation is that the Monroe Doctrine was aimed against the Holy Alliance, particularly against France, and Russia's advance in North America. It can be found in a newly revised summary of the researches of Dexter Perkins, the foremost authority on the Monroe Doctrine.[57] Arthur P. Whitaker[58] has suggested a modification of the usual interpretation by de-emphasizing the role of John Quincy Adams and by giving more credit to Monroe; and Gale W. McGee[59] has viewed the Monroe Doctrine as a temporary expedient, "a stopgap measure," designed to hold off European designs on the Americas while the United States negotiated with England over a joint declaration.

An article by Lynn W. Turner recently demolished the legend that James Monroe missed unanimous re-election to the Presidency in 1820 only by the capricious act of one member of the electoral college who "did not want Washington to be robbed of the glory of being the only President who had ever received the unanimous vote of the electors."[60] Turner also pointed out that the nearly unanimous election did not indicate an equally widespread approval of Monroe's administration.

THE ADAMS ADMINISTRATION

In the second volume of his widely acclaimed biography of John Quincy Adams, Samuel F. Bemis devoted less than a third of his pages to Adams' unsuccessful four years as President.[61] Yet he has written the best account of Adams the President. He devoted more space to Adams the man, to his complex character, to his personal life, and gave domestic politics the attention they lacked in the first volume. Adams the President, he said, had visions for a consolidated union of liberty with power.

---

[57] *A History of the Monroe Doctrine* (Rev. ed. Boston: Little, Brown, 1955).

[58] *The United States and the Independence of Latin America, 1800-1830* (Baltimore: Johns Hopkins, 1941).

[59] "The Monroe Doctrine—A Stopgap Measure," *The Mississippi Valley Historical Review,* 38:233-50; September 1951.

[60] "The Electoral Vote against Monroe in 1820—An American Legend," *The Mississippi Valley Historical Review,* 42:250-73; September 1955.

[61] *John Quincy Adams and the Union* (New York: Knopf, 1956).

LOCAL HISTORY

Studies of local and state history have contributed some of the most useful new interpretations to the political history of our early years, primarily because they have often revealed fresh and unique information. Three recent books cover the politics of Pennsylvania for the entire Federalist and Republican era.[62] Harry M. Tinkcom focused on the local responses to the national issues which formed the fabric of Pennsylvania political activity in the Federalist period. He showed how amorphous factions grew into political parties, stressing the thesis that state politics at that time were a reflection of national politics. Picking up where Tinkcom left off, Sanford W. Higginbotham emphasized Pennsylvania's persistent Jeffersonian Republicanism in the years which he studied and advanced the thesis that Pennsylvania was the keystone in the arch of political democracy. Philip S. Klein dealt with the transition from an old to a new political order, showing that Pennsylvania's aristocracy of birth and wealth concentrated on commerce and finance. Since it did not enter politics, as did the aristocracy of the South, Pennsylvania did not attain national influence commensurate with its wealth and population.

John A. Munroe in his study of Federalism in Delaware wrote a synthesis of cultural, social, economic, and political history, with politics forming the main thread.[63] He explained why Federalism remained strong in Delaware while becoming weaker throughout the country. Astute politics, he maintained, is the answer. Delaware Federalists, showing a shrewd leadership the party lacked elsewhere, gave the people the moderately conservative government they desired. James A. Bayard, a Delaware politician who became the leader of the Federalist party after 1800, is the central figure of Morton Borden's recent book.[64] Borden showed that moderation was the key to Delaware's Federalism. In this study of Bayard's congressional career, Borden explained that Bayard was a strong nationalist as well as a

---

[62] Harry M. Tinkcom, *The Republicans and Federalists in Pennsylvania, 1790-1801: A Study in National Stimulus and Local Response* (Harrisburg, Pa.: Pennsylvania Historical and Museum Commission, 1950); Sanford W. Higginbotham, *The Keystone in the Democratic Arch: Pennsylvania Politics, 1800-1816* (Harrisburg, Pa.: Pennsylvania Historical and Museum Commission, 1952); and Philip S. Klein, *Pennsylvania Politics, 1817-1832: A Game Without Rules* (Philadelphia: Historical Society of Pennsylvania, 1940).

[63] *Federalist Delaware, 1775-1815* (New Brunswick, New Jersey: Rutgers University, 1954).

[64] *The Federalism of James A. Bayard* (New York: Columbia University, 1955).

staunch Federalist who often disagreed with the extreme members of his own party.

Starting the central part of his narrative in 1821 and closing it in July, 1824, Harry R. Stevens explored the beginning of party organizations in support of Andrew Jackson in Ohio.[65] He tried to answer one fundamental question: How was a national political party created in Ohio? His thesis says that there was little basic difference between parties in Ohio. Their conduct showed no determining pattern. The local political leaders made use of whatever issues were most likely to appeal to the voters. The fundamental political adhesive in forming a national party, according to Stevens, was the election of a President.

CONCLUSION

From this brief survey we can see that scholars have taken little for granted in their study of the political history of the first thirty-five years of our federal history. As a result, historians know more about our early national politics and diplomacy and understand them better than ever before. New interpretations, the historian's equivalent of hypothesis, and deeper understanding will doubtless continue to come from new generations of scholars. Like others before them, however, they will build on the findings and ideas of those historians who have advanced interpretations such as those discussed in this chapter.

---

[65] *The Early Jackson Party in Ohio* (Durham, N. C.: Duke University, 1957). For a study of early Jacksonian politics in Tennessee that tries to bridge the gap between state and local politics, see Charles G. Sellers, *James K. Polk: Jacksonian, 1795-1843* (Princeton: Princeton University, 1957). David J. Mays, *Edmund Pendleton, 1721-1803: A Biography* (2 vols.; Cambridge: Harvard University, 1952) is a political history of Virginia in the Federalist era as well as a biography.

CHAPTER VI

Jacksonian Democracy, 1825-1849

Harry Stevens

INTRODUCTION

HISTORIANS since the 1880's have been much concerned with the problems of American government in the second quarter of the nineteenth century. For a large number of them the most conspicuous feature was democracy; and for some, who confused the democracy of the period with the Democratic party, the addition of the name of the most prominent early Democratic leader, Andrew Jackson, seemed a necessary, a desirable, and a sufficiently enlightening means of explaining it, so that "Jacksonian democracy" has become a broadly inclusive label for the entire subject. The confusion has led to a great deal of controversy, and along with a good bit of careful, thoughtful work has come even more muddleheadedness. For the reader who is not an expert in the field the results may seem to be that historians do not and perhaps cannot agree, or that they are parading an endless treadmill of historical relativism, where one man's opinion is as good as another's, or that they do not know what they are talking about. The situation is not that bad.

ORIGINS OF JACKSONIAN DEMOCRACY

When the controversy opened, much of it centered around Frederick Jackson Turner's proposition that the elements that made American democracy distinctive originated on the frontier. They included the experience of opening up a new country—chopping down trees and plowing virgin land, and bringing civilization into it—social and political isolation with consequent self-reliance and individualism, freedom of opportunity with rewards for initiative and enterprise, and a pioneer spirit.[1] Since the frontier lay in the West, at the edge

---

[1] Robert E. Riegel, "American Frontier Theory," *Journal of World History,* 3:356-80; No. 2, 1956. Gene M. Gressley, "The Turner Thesis—A Problem in Historiography," *Agricultural History,* 32:227-49; October 1958.

of "free land," the thesis was quickly combined with two other basic ideas; first, that democracy was closely linked with land, farming, and a rural or agrarian society; and second, that the political history of the times could best be understood in terms of sectionalism, sometimes stated as simply as a contest between a democratic West and an aristocratic East.[2]

Within twenty years A. M. Simons and others began to suggest a somewhat more complex origin for Jacksonian democracy, including an infant labor movement in the cities.[3] After thirty years of such work had been done, Louis M. Hacker found a sufficient basis to support the thesis that Jacksonian democracy had its origin not in a conflict of interests between different geographical sections, nor in the frontier experience, but in a conflict between economic classes. It originated not in a comparatively classless rural society in the West but in class-structured cities in the East.[4]

Those divergent explanations had already been summarized in 1930 by Charles A. Beard and Mary R. Beard in *The Rise of American Civilization*.[5] According to Beard, Jacksonian democracy was "a triumphant Farmer-Labor Party." At first the Jackson party was based on a passion for rank and place among various factions rather than on definite issues, but it became (either before or after it triumphed— Beard is not clear) a combination of farmers in the new Western states and laborers and mechanics in some of the Atlantic coast states. After it triumphed, it was concerned with basic economic problems, the tariff, public lands, and the national bank. Geographically it represented a combination of the Northeast and the West. A low-tax-paying franchise gave a broad popular base to the government and paved the way for "Jacobinical democracy." This radical democracy produced four major changes in government: (1) the method of electing a president was altered by taking the choice away from a caucus of Congressmen and giving it to conventions ruled mainly by

---

[2] Ray A. Billington, *The American Frontier*, Publication No. 8, Service Center for Teachers of History (Washington, D. C., 1958).

[3] Algie M. Simons, *Social Forces in American History* (New York: Macmillan, 1911). Frank T. Carlton, "The Workingmen's Party of New York City: 1829-1831," *Political Science Quarterly*, 22:401-15; September 1907. William Trimble, "Diverging Tendencies in the New York Democracy in the Period of the Locofocos," *American Historical Review*, 24:396-421; April 1919.

[4] Louis M. Hacker, "Sections—or Classes?" (a review of Frederick Jackon Turner, *The Significance of Sections in American History*) *Nation*, 137:108-10; 1933.

[5] One-volume edition; New York: Macmillan, 1930.

office-holders and office-seekers;   (2) party organization was developed; (3) the profits and powers of public office became of interest to democracy; and (4) rotation in office was introduced into national politics. Opposed to it was the party of the Whigs (made up of capitalists, the economic interests of manufacturing, commerce, and banking, and, in the South, the wealthy plantation owners) who spoke in favor of the Bank of the United States, "sound money," and a high protective tariff for industry. Their aims had been those of Alexander Hamilton and the Federalists, which the government had adopted after the War of 1812. The Jacksonian Revolution was a revulsion against that Hamiltonian system.

Since 1930 much effort has been devoted to sustaining the Simons-Beard-Hacker thesis that labor supported the Jacksonian Democratic party and to challenging and refuting it. Arthur M. Schlesinger, Jr., in *The Age of Jackson* made the most extensive and persuasive summary in favor of it.[6] The case against it may be represented by Florence Weston's *The Presidential Election of 1828*.[7] According to Weston, Jackson's managers won the adherence of workingmen's parties in Philadelphia, New York, and Baltimore, but they did not do so in Boston, Richmond, or Norfolk. Those contradictory results are reconciled in the thesis that opportunities for demagogues were present in all cities.

Other criticisms of the Simons-Beard-Hacker thesis followed the publication of Schlesinger's widely-acclaimed book. Richard B. Morris showed that President Jackson himself was not sympathetic but hostile to organized labor.[8] Bray Hammond suggested that as far as Jacksonian democracy embodied the interests of an economic class it was the protest of a newly emerging group of business enterprisers against already established business interests.[9] Further attempts to analyze the origins of Jacksonian democracy on the basis of economic interests and classes led rapidly to increasingly complex explanations, both of that party and of the Whig opponents. While Beard saw the Whig party in the South centered in a planting aristocracy, Charles G. Sellers concluded that the Southern Whigs were controlled by

---

[6] Boston: Little, Brown, 1945.

[7] Washington, D. C.: Ruddick, 1938.

[8] Richard B. Morris, "Andrew Jackson, Strikebreaker," *American Historical Review*, 55:54-68; October 1949. Joseph Dorfman, "The Jackson Wage-Earner Thesis," *ibid.*, 54:296-306; January 1949.

[9] Bray Hammond, review of Schlesinger, *The Age of Jackson*, in *Journal of Economic History*, 6:79-84; May 1946.

urban commercial and banking interests.[10] Again, Beard saw the early Jackson party as a combination of diverse factions united only by the personality of their leader and a common desire to hold public office, and the Whig party as an alliance of Southern planters with Northern men firmly and consistently in favor of business interests. In contrast, Marvin Meyers, in *The Jacksonian Persuasion,* asserted that the Whigs were for the most part without unity of interests, attitude, or outlook, and that it was the Jacksonians who had a coherent set of attitudes and plans.[11]

Although many historians tried to analyze the origins of Jacksonian democracy by assuming the existence of economic classes and by linking them with either the Whig or Democratic party, other historians tried to strengthen the thesis of a rural, agricultural, and essentially Western origin. John D. Barnhart, in *The Valley of Democracy,* found that American democracy originated from a fourfold inheritance, the attitudes and institutions of the Old World and Eastern America, the experience of the Revolution, a contest between "aristocrats" and "yeomen," and the experience of crossing the mountains westward. Crossing the mountains led to a struggle in the Ohio Valley (between 1775 and 1818) which added four new elements to the inheritance: (1) self-government in new Western states, (2) democratization (the destruction of the bonds of social caste, government favoritism, and hopeless inequality), (3) the principle of majority rule, and (4) individualism (the belief that all men were worthy of equality, freedom, and a share in government).[12]

The supposition that geographical sections were a basic fact in American history and hence fundamental to any explanation of Jacksonian democracy was shown also by the studies of several Southern historians. Fletcher M. Green demonstrated in *Constitutional Development in the South Atlantic States, 1776-1860* that (apart from the peculiar institution of slavery) democracy was as widespread in the Southeast as in other parts of the country and that it was achieved at as early a date.[13] Avery O. Craven in *The Coming of the Civil War* extended the proposition to social and economic as well as political life, and to the Southwest as well as the Southeast.[14]

[10] Charles G. Sellers, "Who Were the Southern Whigs?" *American Historical Review,* 59:335-46; January 1954.

[11] Stanford: Stanford University, 1957.

[12] *Valley of Democracy: The Frontier versus the Plantation in the Ohio Valley, 1775-1818* (Bloomington: Indiana University, 1953).

[13] Chapel Hill: University of North Carolina, 1930.

[14] New York: Scribner, 1942; 2d ed., Chicago: University of Chicago, 1957.

A few writers, among them Philip S. Klein in *Pennsylvania Politics, 1817-1832*[15] and Harry R. Stevens in *The Early Jackson Party in Ohio*, examined the origins and development of the political forms and behavior that constituted the democracy of the period. Stevens, like others, noted that the dispersion of the people of the country over wide new areas and their reorganization into new states reduced the concentration of political power at the capital, thus creating opportunities for many presidential candidates. Those candidates and their friends, seizing the opportunities, formed the new political parties and other instruments for contesting elections (such as more voter participation, local and state committees, conventions, lists of pledged and united candidates, definition of public questions, and platforms) that came to be called "democracy."[16] A few others, such as Reginald C. McGrane[17] and William S. Hoffmann[18] have called attention to later developments of democracy in the special technique of "the right of instruction."

DEMOCRACY AND THE PUBLIC ISSUES

Attention may be turned from the origins of Jacksonian democracy to the expression and achievements of democracy in relation to public land problems, internal improvements, banking, and government. Earlier writers generalized the land problem in the same terms that had been used by many political leaders of the period after 1824. In each of three or four great geographical sections of the country a large number of men with similar interests and outlook formed an economic interest that was upheld by its spokesmen in Congress, and the conflicting sectional interests in public lands resulted in political battles over land legislation. The West in particular, with a large population of land-hungry and individualistic pioneers, demanded a "liberal" land policy (especially through Democratic Senator Benton) that was presumably democratic.[19] More recently several historians

---

[15] *Pennsylvania Politics, 1817-1832: A Game Without Rules* (Philadelphia: Historical Society of Pennsylvania, 1940).

[16] Durham, N. C.: Duke University, 1957.

[17] Reginald C. McGrane, "Orator Bob and the Right of Instruction," Historical and Philosophical Society of Ohio *Bulletin*, 11:251-73; October 1953.

[18] William S. Hoffmann, "Willie P. Mangum and the Whig Revival of the Doctrine of Instructions," *Journal of Southern History*, 22:338-54; August 1956.

[19] Payson J. Treat, *The National Land System, 1785-1820* (New York: E. B. Treat and Company, 1910); Raynor G. Wellington, *The Political and Sectional Influence of the Public Lands, 1828-1842* (Cambridge, Mass.: Riverside, 1914); George M. Stephenson, *The Political History of the Public Lands, from 1840 to 1862* . . . (Boston: R. G. Badger . . . , 1917).

have maintained that the individual Western settler, whether pioneer freeholder or squatter, was less important in shaping land policy than the land speculator; but no new synthesis for this period comparable to the old sectional interpretation has been presented.

Summarizing' much recent literature on internal improvements Goodrich concludes that government intervention was never a matter of doctrine but of expediency. In the decades before 1850 federal activity was slight because, with the South opposed to national projects for both economic and political reasons, agreement at the top level was difficult to achieve. State and local governments held a more important role. But initiative remained with private enterprise.[20]

The relationship of banking history to Jacksonian democracy and politics has, on the other hand, received a great deal of attention. In addition to a substantial number of monographs (especially on the relationship of state governments and business) a recent broad synthesis with a vast amount of detail is also available. Bray Hammond, studying the Bank of the United States and its adversaries and successors in *Banks and Politics in America from the Revolution to the Civil War,*[21] said that the bank was a victim of the "money power" which used Jackson, states' rights, and agrarian sentiment to destroy it. The bank stood too much in the way of credit expansion to suit popular interests. The bank's adversaries were not farmers but business men. The contest produced a crisis in both the economic and political history of the country deeper than a mere conflict between Biddle and Jackson. The people of the age were led by visions of money-making. Liberty became transformed into *laissez faire*. A violent, aggressive, economic individualism was established. The democracy became greedy, imperialistic, and lawless. Changes opened economic advantages to men who had not previously enjoyed them, yet it allowed wealth to be concentrated in new hands only somewhat more numerous than before, less responsible, and less disciplined. Socially, the Jacksonian revolution meant that a nation of democrats was tired of being governed by gentlemen from Virginia and Massachusetts. They democratized business under a show of agrarian idealism and made the age of Jackson a festival of *laissez faire* "prelusive" to the age of Grant and the robber barons. In politics they were unconventional and skillful. In their assault on the bank they united

---

[20] Carter Goodrich, *Government Promotion of American Canals and Railroads, 1800-1900* (New York: Columbia University, 1960).
[21] Princeton: Princeton University, 1957.

five important elements, Wall Street (New York) jealousy of Chestnut Street (Philadelphia), businessmen's dislike of the federal bank's re-, straint, the politicians' resentment at the bank's interference with states' rights, popular identification of the bank with business aristocracy, and the shift of agrarian antipathy away from banks in general to the federal bank in particular. The result Hammond deemed disastrous, and he observed that the achievements of the Jacksonians were repudiated in the administrations of Lincoln, Wilson, and Franklin Roosevelt.

On the subject of Jacksonian democracy in relation to government and politics the important field of public administration was examined by Leonard D. White in *The Jacksonians: A Study in Administrative History, 1829-1861*.[22] According to White, the new democracy was a combination of rotation in office, wide suffrage, and a democratic spirit. His monumental study thus came around to the same conclusions that have been held (and disputed) ever since the period it treated.[23]

POLITICAL NARRATIVES

Among the numerous political narratives dealing with part or all of the period, almost all have successfully avoided the flat, colorless, and insipid qualities of impartiality and the confusion of being on both sides at once. Many of them tell their stories effectively from a well-defined point of view, and they avoid the dangers involved in attempting to reach a synthesis broader than that demanded by a partisan protagonist. George R. Poage, *Henry Clay and the Whig Party*[24] is friendly to Clay; Oscar D. Lambert, *Presidential Politics in the United States, 1841-1844*[25] and Robert J. Morgan, *A Whig Embattled*[26] are friendly to John Tyler; Hugh R. Fraser, *Democracy in the Making*[27] is sympathetic to Jackson and Tyler, hostile to Clay and Webster; Arthur M. Schlesinger, Jr., *The Age of Jackson* is partial to Jackson and Van Buren. Most recent biographies, many of which are quite well written, are similarly successful.

---

[22] New York: Macmillan, 1954.

[23] Charles G. Sellers, "Andrew Jackson versus the Historians," *Mississippi Valley Historical Review*, 44:615-34; March 1958.

[24] Chapel Hill: University of North Carolina, 1936.

[25] Durham, N. C.: Duke University, 1936.

[26] *A Whig Embattled; the Presidency Under John Tyler* (Lincoln: University of Nebraska, 1954).

[27] *Democracy in the Making; the Jackson-Tyler Era* (Indianapolis: Bobbs-Merrill, 1938).

As the Jackson era came to a close in the 1840's, it was clear that public attention shifted from the questions of the 1830's, public lands, tariff, internal improvements, and the banking system to territorial expansion, slavery, and section conflict. Those subjects are being given consideration in other chapters.[28]

IDEAS AND THE SPIRIT OF JACKSONIAN DEMOCRACY

The ideas and spirit of Jacksonian democracy have been the subjects of investigation and comment by a large number of historians. Vernon L. Parrington, in the second volume of *Main Currents in American Thought*,[29] described the entire period from 1800 to 1860 as one of the romanticization of thought. Two quite different kinds of democracy came into being. One, taught to the South by Calhoun, was "Greek democracy," an agrarian civilization based on slave labor, with a government of decentralized powers. The other, learned through experience by sons of the South who move to the Ohio valley, included the worth of certain Jeffersonian principles, the doctrine of equality, and a preference for managing their own affairs in their own way by appeal to the majority rather than to established authorities. Parrington found the latter democracy "springing up naturally on the frontier," and becoming the common faith first of the West and ultimately of America. Jacksonian democracy was created by "coonskin individualism" but was undermined by the middle-class individualism of "Whiggery." Andrew Jackson was characterized as an agrarian liberal; the equalitarian West that bred him also bred Lincoln, in whom, however, the philosophy of progress displaced the old agrarianism, and a paternalistic nationalism replaced the "vital democratic principle of decentralized powers." The old philosophies of equalitarian democracy and local home rule were at length swept on the rubbish heap. The Civil War carried the ideal of decentralized democracy and individual liberty down to defeat, and American democratic political theory was engulfed in that revolution.

---

[28] See chapters VI and VIII. For a general bibliographical survey of this period, see the "Bibliographical Essay" at the close of G. G. Van Deusen, *The Jacksonian Era, 1828-1848*, cited in n. 34. Study of American foreign relations during this period has been concerned almost entirely with the problems emerging from expansion (Texas, Mexico, and Oregon) and (as far as domestic politics goes) sectionalism, both of which are treated elsewhere in this volume. Otherwise the most significant recent work has dealt with the Canadian boundary and problems rising from the Canadian rebellion of 1837-38. See Albert B. Corey, *The Crisis of 1830-1842 in Canadian-American Relations* (New Haven: Yale University, 1941).

[29] Three vols., New York: Harcourt, Brace, 1927-1930. The volume referred to here is *The Romantic Revolution in America, 1800-1860*.

John William Ward, in *Andrew Jackson, Symbol for an Age*,[30] found the symbolic Jackson a configuration in which the three concepts of Nature, Providence, and Will coincided. These concepts were all oriented in a single direction, and all sanctioned a violently activistic social philosophy. Two years later, Marvin Meyers, in *The Jacksonian Persuasion*, concluded, on the contrary, that Jacksonian democracy was an effort to recall agrarian republican innocence to a society fatally being drawn to the ways of acquisition. This effort was taking place just as agrarianism and commercialism were splitting hopelessly apart. The Jacksonians were trapped by the past. The capitalistic future lay with their opponents. But in spite of the widening rift, long before the end of the Jacksonian period, the attitudes and plans of the two rival groups (Whigs and Democrats) had become almost indistinguishable.

Two distinctive attempts to create a broader interpretation of democracy call for special attention, those of Craven and Nichols. Avery O. Craven undertook to write *The Coming of the Civil War*[31] as a history of American democracy from 1820 to 1860. He placed it in the perspective of three major characteristics of the United States together with rapid growth and expansion and the sharp development of sectionalism. The third characteristic, "democratic and humanitarian stirrings," he found sweeping the nation in every decade, originating partly in the West where the frontier generated new faith in common men and revived old dreams of a more perfect society, and partly in the Old World among those capable of disinterested thinking about war, poverty, and slavery. However, he found the democratic "stirrings" mostly in rural belts, rising from the ills of a re-forming economic and social order. He classified democratic attitudes as either positive or defensive. The positive "waves," which were called Jackson's brand of democracy, were the longings of common men for political equality and plunder and their resentment against the things they did not share or understand, which they termed privilege and aristocracy. They came from the West and South and the lesser coast and back-country people of the Northeast. The defensive expressions of democracy, which he considered more significant, were protests against inequality, and included the efforts to achieve a more perfect social order, peace, temperance, education, and labor rights. Combined with the new fervor of the evangelical

---

[30] New York: Oxford University, 1955.
[31] See note 14.

churches, they produced a fusion in which the fight for democracy and the fight for morality were one and the same.

Roy F. Nichols, while dealing with the 1850's in *The Disruption of American Democracy*,[32] analyzed ten highly influential attitudes in the cultural federalism that had come into existence previously, two he considered pervasive, five divisive, and three cohesive. The latter three, cultivated by those who wished to heal the breaches cut by the divisive attitudes, were nationalism, regionalism, and democracy. The new type of democracy, representative rather than direct, was something that pertained to the states rather than to the federal government directly. It rose from the onward march of universal suffrage, which popularized the idea of majority rule. Later, however, the effort by Northern spokesmen to make such a democracy a cohesive formula was opposed by their Southern antagonists who feared the tyranny of numbers and labored to secure the acceptance of regionalism and the recognition of a minority veto as an alternative to the rule of the majority; and thus it too became divisive.

Richard Hofstadter, attempting to synthesize recent work on Jacksonian politics, concluded in his chapter on Andrew Jackson in *The American Political Tradition*[33] that it was not a simple matter. Jackson himself was both a pioneer and an aristocrat. Many Americans began for the first time to think of politics as having an intimate relation to their welfare. Jackson, the beneficiary of that movement, disapproved of it. The main themes of Jacksonian democracy at the outset were militant nationalism and equal access to public office. Jackson's election was more a result than a cause of the rise of democracy, and the leader swung to the democratic camp after a varied and uneven personal history when the democratic camp swung to him. Thereafter the core of the philosophy of both the regular Jackson leaders and their radical Locofoco school aimed at taking the grip of government-granted privilege off the natural economic order. Its aim was to open every possible pathway to the creative enterprise of the people. It was the classic bourgeois ideal, equality before the law and limiting government to equal protection of its citizens. It was the philosophy of a rising middle class.

One of the few recent works that has risen above the level of partisan apology and beyond confusing what democracy was with what Democrats thought it was is Glyndon G. Van Deusen, *The*

---

[32] New York: Macmillan, 1948.
[33] New York: Knopf, 1948.

Jacksonian Era, 1828-1848.[34] The author found the political parties of the period made up of conflicting interests, sometimes conceived in national terms, often conceived regionally or locally. The leaders strove to keep the parties organized and operating as effective units. Jacksonian democracy joined an appreciation of the common man with an inadequate conception of the economic methods by which liberty and equality might be achieved and maintained. The opponents of Jacksonian democracy had a more realistic appreciation of the needs of a dynamic economy but were handicapped by the absence of either an aristocracy or a rabble to contend with and by an unwillingness or an inability to understand and share the fundamental aspirations of the ordinary American. Yet each party appealed to about half the voters of the country. In summary the entire period was one of intense political strife carried on by two major parties. Their power waxed and waned, but neither ever gained a decided majority over its opponent. The Whigs were the more conservative. Their strength lay with the business class. Their outlook was national. The Democrats were more liberal. They feared a powerful central government, but they failed in their aim of liberty and equality for all because they confused liberty with equality, had little conception of the role of the central government, and were hampered by defective monetary theory. At the national level Democratic policy was largely negative. By the close of the 1840's many of the issues dividing Whigs from Democrats ceased to be national issues, and it was hard to distinguish the principles of one from the other. But democracy in America was a living, working concern; and no significant sentiment existed for the abandonment of the democratic process either as a political system or as a way of life.

CONCLUSIONS

What that democratic process was, either as a political system or as a way of life, remains about as obscure today as it was fifty years ago. The failure of historians to make it more intelligible has been so discouraging to some that they have concluded that it is a matter of personal preference, or that it may depend on what part of the country, or what social or economic class the historian happens to belong to. No real foundation exists for such discouragement. The failure is understandable. Nine reasons for the failure should be mentioned. (1) Too much attention has been devoted to proving or

---

[34] New York: Harper, 1959. This is a volume in the New American Nation Series.

disproving "theses" rather than to studying evidence more broadly to discover what it shows: it has concentrated particularly on the Turner and Simons-Beard-Hacker hypotheses; (2) unnecessarily crude instruments of historical analysis have been used, especially those of regionalism, sectionalism, and economic and social classes, which, no matter how far they are refined, remain too coarse, abstract, and theoretical, too remote from historical reality to afford much opportunity of reaching substantive conclusions; (3) overmuch attention has been given to the search for a single "cause" or all-inclusive explanatory proposition; (4) focus has often been centered on verbalizations rather than on people and events; (5) the assumption has frequently been made that the realities of history may be found in forces, factors, trends, or movements rather than in human beings; (6) use of a colorful adjective or a label has been substituted for analysis and explanation; (7) facile generalizations have been adopted from social science, philosophy, or other non-historical disciplines and applied as explanations rather than questioned; (8) generalizations have been made that are too broad or too simple to be helpful, such as the identification of democracy with a wide franchise, with the spoils system, rotation in office, nominating conventions, and majority rule, with a "democratic spirit" and humanitarianism, or even, in some instances, with the Democratic party; and (9) at times, some writers, perhaps under pressure, have published without the thorough research and careful, deliberate thought that may be expected. But others, as this chapter may have shown, have given real help to their readers in understanding this large portion of their inheritance.

CHAPTER VII

The Background of the Civil War

David M. Potter

INTRODUCTION

THE period from 1830 to 1861 in American history may conceivably have an integral, free-standing significance of its own, apart from the Civil War which followed, but historians have rarely been able to treat this era in any way except as a prelude to the War. Some writers have made half-hearted efforts to read the record of the decades in question without reference to the ensuing crisis, and, accordingly, have pointed out the importance of such developments as the growth of railroads, the rise of industry, the great waves of immigration, the thrust into the Trans-Mississippi region, the technological revolution, and the like, which engaged the attentions and energies of men, sometimes to the exclusion of the slavery controversy. But even the very historians who call attention to these factors usually go on to a treatment which reverts to the growing antagonism between the sections as the central topic of the whole period. The implicit acceptance of this emphasis shows in the fact that no one questioned the aptness of the title *Ordeal of the Union* for a work, by Allan Nevins, which treated American history for the decade 1850-1860 comprehensively in four volumes, without any visible ordeal materializing, until it came as a climax in Volume V. It is singular that in our historical literature, the decades 1763-1773 and 1850-1860 are almost invariably treated simply as preludes to war, while the years before 1917 and 1941 are seldom treated in this way.

Because of the intensity of this focus, a high proportion of the literature on the period from about 1830 to 1861 deals either (a) directly with the question of the causes of the Civil War or (b) with topics which bear indirectly upon the schism between North and South, such as the development of sectionalism in its economic and cultural phases, the institution of slavery, the humanitarian movement in its anti-slavery aspect, the nature of Southern society, both as to social structure and as to intellectual climate, and the specific steps such as the Compromise of 1850, the Dred Scott decision, and so forth, which led toward a final crisis.

This chapter attempts to summarize the developments of the historical literature during the last twenty years (1940-1959) as it relates to these two areas.

THE CAUSES OF THE CIVIL WAR

The last twenty years have witnessed considerable advances in the historical understanding of many of the developments which preceded the Civil War, but it can hardly be said that they have brought us visibly closer to the point at which a jury of historians seems likely to arrive at a verdict which will settle the controversy as to causes. Indeed some of the most fundamental issues in the controversy, namely those turning upon the significance of the slavery question, have been reactivated and seem now to leave the dispute father from settlement than ever.

By 1940, the literature on the Civil War had already been accumulating for eighty years.[1] During these eight decades, interpretation of the War had passed through three major phases. First, during the immediate post-war era, there had been a literature by participants and partisans, designed to justify their own course of conduct and therefore striving either to vindicate or indict. Both sides had appealed to absolute values: if they were partisans of the Union, they had explained the War in terms of slavery and disunion, appealing to the moral absolute of human freedom and national unity; if they were partisans of the South, they had explained it in terms of the secession issue, appealing to the legal absolute inherent in the theory of state sovereignty and to the moral absolute of the right of self-government.

Second, in the period after the wounds of war began to heal, there had been a nationalistic interpretation, well exemplified in the seven-volume history by James Ford Rhodes (1893-1906), which avoided the

---

[1] Efforts to explain the War in historical terms began as early as 1861-62, with interpretations by John L. Motley, George Bancroft, Francis Parkman, and Edward A. Pollard. For general discussion of the historiography of the War, including these writers, see Thomas J. Pressly, *Americans Interpret Their Civil War* (Princeton: Princeton University, 1954) and Howard K. Beale, "What Historians Have Said About the Causes of the Civil War," in Social Science Research Council Bulletin 54, *Theory and Practice in Historical Study* (New York: Social Science Research Council, 1946).

attribution of blame and emphasized the sincerity and high motive of both the Blue and the Gray.[2] Rhodes himself argued unequivocally that slavery was the cause of the War, but he held the nation rather than the South responsible for slavery, and if he blamed the South for secession, he blamed the North for Reconstruction. In such an interpretation the concept of an inevitable or "irrepressible" conflict fitted well, for if the War could not possibly have been prevented, then no one could be blamed for failing to prevent it, and thus no one was guilty. Charles Francis Adams pushed this view to its logical limit in 1902 by declaring that "Everybody, in short, was right; no one wrong."[3]

Third, in the 1920's, after ideas of economic determinism began to prevail widely in American intellectual circles, Charles and Mary Beard had published an immensely influential interpretation of the War in their *The Rise of American Civilization*.[4] Seeing the great contests of history as struggles for power, rather than for principle, and regarding moral and legal arguments as mere rationalizations, the Beards had denied that the South really cared about states rights or the North about slavery. The South had simply used states rights as a tactical device in defending a minority position. The Republicans had simply used the slavery issue to turn public opinion against the South, but in fact the Republicans had not been abolitionists and had done nothing to help the slaves, but had sought only to "contain" the power of the slaveholders by excluding them from the new territories. The War, therefore, had not been a contest over principles but a struggle for power—a clash of economic sections in which freedom did not necessarily combat slavery but industrialism most assuredly combated the planter interests.

These three were, in brief, the major interpretations which had held sway up to 1940. Since 1940, the major tendencies have been: (1) the development of a so-called "revisionist" interpretation which minimized the importance of slavery or any other fundamental factor as a cause of the War and also argued that the War could have been and should have been averted; and (2) a counterattack upon the revisionists by writers who reassert the causative importance of the slavery question.

---

[2] *History of the United States from the Compromise of 1850 to the Final Restoration of Home Rule in the South in 1877* (New York: Macmillan, 1893-1906).

[3] "The Ethics of Secession," an address delivered in 1902 and printed in *Studies Military and Diplomatic, 1775-1865* (New York: Macmillan, 1911), p. 208.

[4] New York: Macmillan, 1927.

The Revisionists

Although sometimes mentioned as if they were a "school," the so-called revisionists have in fact been a number of distinctively independent scholars, working separately, disagreeing on occasion, and united only by their skepticism about the role of slavery as the heart of the sectional issue and their doubt that the conflict was irrepressible.

These doubts are as old as the War itself, but modern revisionism possibly begins with Albert J. Beveridge, Republican Senator from Indiana and biographer of John Marshall. About 1920, Beveridge set out to write a biography of Lincoln. He approached this undertaking with the traditional Republican reverence for an almost superhuman being—the inevitable protagonist of the anti-slavery drama in which there had to be an antagonist or villain, and in which Stephen A. Douglas was inevitably stereotyped for the latter role. But when Beveridge began his research, he found the facts far more complex than the tradition, and when he came to the Lincoln-Douglas debates, he concluded that Douglas had acted with integrity and had represented a very respectable point of view—namely that the question of slavery in the territories was a fictitious issue, not worth a crisis which would endanger the nation. Because the abolitionists had "agitated" this issue in such a way as to precipitate the crisis, Beveridge formed an unfavorable opinion of them and began to think that, without them, there might have been no war—indeed that slavery might in time have disappeared peacebly under the pressure of economic forces.[5]

In 1927, Beveridge died. His life of Lincoln, published in the following year,[6] had been completed only to the year 1858, and we can never know what broad, overall interpretation he would have advanced. But certain of the ideas which he had foreshadowed continued to develop in the decade of the thirties. In 1933, Gilbert H. Barnes published an account of the early abolitionist movement (*The Anti-Slavery Impulse, 1830-1844*)[7] in which he emphasized the neglected figure of Theodore Dwight Weld, and de-emphasized the importance of William Lloyd Garrison, at the same time condemning the fanaticism of the abolitionists in general. During the same year, Gerald W. Johnson of *The Baltimore Sun* published a small interpretive volume on *The Secession of the Southern States*, which stated

---

[5] Claude G. Bowers, *Beveridge and the Progressive Era* (Boston: Houghton Mifflin, 1932), p. 561-79.

[6] *Abraham Lincoln, 1809-1858* (2 vols.; Boston: Houghton Mifflin, 1928).

[7] New York: Appleton-Century.

brilliantly the argument that dogmatic, rigid adherence to "principle" on the part of both anti-slavery zealots like Charles Sumner of Massachusetts and doctrinaire legalists like John C. Calhoun of South Carolina had caused an unnecessary war in which "everybody was wrong and no one was right." Johnson's little book has been neglected,[8] perhaps because he was not a professional historian, but it remains to this day one of the most vigorous and effective statements of a major thesis of revisionism. In 1934, George Fort Milton, editor of *The Chattanooga News*, brought out a full-scale biography of Douglas, based on extensive new manuscripts, and bearing the significant title, *The Eve of Conflict: Stephen A. Douglas and the Needless War*.[9] Like Beveridge, Milton considered Douglas statesmanlike in his effort to play down the territorial issue, and believed that unwise political leadership was responsible for the War.

After these preliminaries, the full tide of the revisionist reaction struck in the late thirties and early forties, primarily as the result of the work of two men—James G. Randall and Avery O. Craven—advancing independently along somewhat parallel lines.

Craven first enunciated his views clearly in an article, "Coming of the War Between the States: An Interpretation," in 1936.[10] He followed this with a brief interpretive volume, *The Repressible Conflict*, in 1939,[11] and with a full scale history of the years from 1830 to 1861 in *The Coming of the Civil War* in 1942.[12] Since then he has continued to develop and to modify his ideas in a number of writings, including notably a volume on *The Growth of Southern Nationalism, 1848-1861* (1953) in the History of the South Series, and a set of interpretive lectures, *Civil War in the Making, 1815-1860* (1959).[13]

Perhaps the crucial feature of Craven's interpretation is his belief that the basic and essential differences between North and South were not great enough to make war necessary. The dissimilarities between the agrarian society of the South and the industrial society of the Northeast were, to be sure, a fertile seed-bed for friction and for misunderstandings, but these misunderstandings were not, on the whole, realistic. The great difference traditionally emphasized is that of

[8] New York: Putnam. It is not mentioned at all in Pressly, *Americans Interpret Their Civil War*, a book-length historiographical survey which deals at length with a number of less important items.

[9] Boston: Houghton Mifflin.

[10] *Journal of Southern History*, 2:303-22; August 1936.

[11] Baton Rouge: Louisiana State University.

[12] New York: Scribner. Second edition, Chicago: University of Chicago, 1957.

[13] Both Baton Rouge: Louisiana State University.

slavery, but Craven argued that the economic condition of the Negro as an unskilled laborer engaged in the cotton culture was much more important in controlling the conditions of his life than his legal status as a chattel. Because of these economic factors the condition of the Negro after emancipation changed very little until the cotton economy itself changed in the 1930's. Craven also emphasized the fact that three-quarters of the Southern whites were not slaveholders and were not directly involved in the slavery complex. North and South did not, in fact, present polar extremes.

But if sectional antagonisms did not arise out of fundamental differences, what did they arise from? Craven believed that they resulted from the creation of false images of each section by the other, and from the charging of these images with a high, unreasoning emotional content. He believed that these stereotypes were to some extent manufactured by irresponsible political agitators, both North and South—that is by the "fire-eating" secessionists and by the abolitionists. In other words, the explanation lies more in psychological attitudes than in objective conditions. From this conclusion, it follows that we should beware of any arbitrary assumption that the conflict was irrepressible (though Craven later concluded that the opposite assumption should also be avoided, since the question really cannot be determined). It follows, too, that slavery should be played down: Craven suggested "the possibility that behind the determination to put slavery on the road to ultimate extinction, there may have lain drives that had little to do with Negro slavery or the American South, as well as others that were the direct product of slavery itself and of the so-called 'Slave Power'." Since, in his opinion, "the great body of Americans were moderate and conservative in their attitudes (and) . . . came to the brink of Civil War reluctantly,"[14] a heavy burden of what may really be called war-guilt rests with the political leaders ("extremists") like Charles Sumner and Barnwell Rhett who played upon public emotions until they brought about a conflict which the circumstances did not require and which neither the Northern nor the Southern majority wanted.

While Craven was developing these themes at the University of Chicago, James G. Randall at the University of Illinois was concurrently working out an interpretation to which he himself applied the term "revisionist." His first clear-cut statement of this interpretation appeared, but was not heavily emphasized, in his *The Civil War*

---

[14] *Civil War in the Making, 1815-1860*, p. viii.

and Reconstruction in 1937.[15] It was more fully elaborated in three important articles, "The Blundering Generation," "The Civil War Restudied," and "When War Came in 1861," all published in 1940.[16] Finally, in *Lincoln, the President: Springfield to Gettysburg* (1915) ,[17] he set forth his views in their fully matured form.

Critics sometimes discuss Craven and Randall as if their views were identical. It is easy to see why this happens, for both men held a number of major ideas in common: that sectional differences were not great enough to necessitate a war; that the crisis resulted more from the whipping-up of emotions than from the impact of realistic issues; that extremists on both sides were responsible for this emotional jag, but that the responsibility of the extremists of the North (i.e., the abolitionists) which had been disregarded by many historians, needed to be emphasized rather more than the responsibility of the extremists of the South (i.e., the fire-eating secessionists) whom historians had blamed excessively; and above all, that the War was both avoidable and unnecessary and that it occurred as the result of a failure of leadership. But within this broad framework of agreement, Craven and Randall each developed distinctive points of emphasis. Where Craven argued that the Civil War in particular ought not to have occurred, Randall showed greater concern with the problem of war as such, and writing at a time when the world was rapidly losing the international peace which World War I and the League of Nations were supposed to have won, he argued that war as such should be prevented, that it is a "fallacy" to believe that "fundamental motives produce war."[18] Indeed, he contended that analysis of the causes of war must fail unless it takes into consideration psychopathic factors.

Because of his greater concern with the general problem of the causation of war, Randall was also more concerned than was Craven to refute the idea of economic determinism in the Beardian sense, as an explanation of war. In some of his best analysis, Randall pointed out that economic determinists have a kind of "heads, I win—tails, you lose" formula. If a people who lack economic diversity make war, their belligerence can be explained in terms of the need for economic

---

[15] Boston: D. C. Heath.

[16] In *Mississippi Valley Historical Review*, 27:3-28; June 1940. *Journal of Southern History*, 6:439-57; November 1940. *Abraham Lincoln Quarterly*, 1:3-42; March 1940. The first and third of these essays were republished with some revision in J. G. Randall, *Lincoln, the Liberal Statesman* (New York: Dodd, Mead, 1947) .

[17] New York: Dodd, Mead.

[18] Randall, *Lincoln, the Liberal Statesman,* p. 88.

self-sufficiency. But if a people with diversity have an internal war, their conflict can be explained in terms of the clash of diverse interests. In either case, the explanation for war stands ready-made. As Randall argued, features of diversity may lead to mutual interdependence rather than to war, and the existence of economic differences creates no presumption that antagonism need follow. Where antagonism exists, it must be explained on specific grounds.[19]

A second respect in which Randall's emphasis differed from Craven's is that where Craven discounted the significance of slavery as an institution, Randall minimized its significance as an issue. One of his most effective arguments was his contention that, while the broad issue of freedom versus slavery may be worth a war, the issue as defined by the opposing forces in 1861 was not that broad, and was not worth a war in the form in which they defined it; for the Republicans in 1861 did not propose to emancipate the slaves, they even agreed in 1861 to guarantee slavery in the existing slave states and to return fugitives to slavery. The one point on which they stuck was that they would not sanction slavery in any of the new territories. But since the climate and the economy of these new regions made them inhospitable to slavery anyway, the territorial question could be viewed as an abstraction—a contest over "an imaginary Negro in an impossible place," and a very inadequate cause for a war. The idea that the territorial issue was a fictitious one was not new—it had been vigorously expressed by James K. Polk—but Randall gave it a new application in his treatment of the causes of war.

A third major expression of revisionism appeared in 1948, when Roy F. Nichols of the University of Pennsylvania published his *The Disruption of American Democracy*.[20] Unlike Craven and Randall, Nichols did not undertake a general interpretation of the sectional crisis as a whole. Instead he set himself to the more specialized study of the impact of sectional antagonisms in shattering a national political party—the Democratic party. His work, which won the Pulitzer Prize, was, therefore, an institutional study of the impact of sectional pressures upon American political machinery. But the findings fitted well with the revisionist thesis, for Nichols showed how the defects of the political system (excessive localism, the need for agitation in order to stimulate voters in the frequent elections, etc.) contributed to the breakdown of a national political organization under the weight of

---

[19] Randall, *Lincoln, the Liberal Statesman*, p. 88.
[20] New York: Macmillan.

sectional pressures. Moreover, Nichols asserted in clear-cut terms his belief that the "hyperemotionalism" of the times made it possible for "irresponsible and blind operators of local political machinery" to exploit the inflammable issues which led to war.

Toward the end of the forties, revisionism had very largely swept the field of Civil War literature. With the partial exception of Allan Nevins' *Ordeal of the Union* (1947), all the major works on the Civil War for a decade had reflected a revisionist view. Revisionism had made its way into the textbooks, and had been taken up by popular writers. It is perhaps symptomatic that, in 1951, William E. Woodward's posthumous history of the War, tentatively entitled: *The Civil War: A National Blunder,* was finally issued under the title, *Years of Madness.*[21]

The Reaction to Revisionism

About nine years after Craven and Randall had sounded the first trumpets of a broad revisionism, Arthur Schlesinger, Jr., in his *The Age of Jackson* (1945) entered a dissenting opinion. In a brief discussion, made in passing, Schlesinger affirmed his belief that "the emotion which moved the North finally to battlefield and bloodshed was moral disgust with slavery." He also denied the Beardian thesis that slavery was resisted because it constituted an obstacle to industrial capitalism; on the contrary, he said, "the aspirations which were first felt to be menaced by the slave power were in actuality democratic aspirations."[22] Four years later, in an article on Randall's contention he returned to the subject for a more extended treatment.[23] Attacking the revisionists for using the claim of objectivity and the concept of automatic progress as devices for avoiding consideration of the moral issue of slavery, Schlesinger argued that the focus of the slavery contest had fallen on the territories, not because industrialists on-the-make were covetous of power in new regions and indifferent to slave hardships in old ones, but because Americans found their moral scruples about slavery in conflict with their civic scruples to obey the Constitution, which protected slavery in the slave states.[24] Therefore,

---

[21] New York: Putnam. These titles are mentioned in Pressly, *Americans Interpret their Civil War*, p. 285.

[22] Boston: Little, Brown. Quotations from p. 432-33.

[23] "The Causes of the Civil War: A Note on Historical Sentimentalism," in *Partisan Review,* 16:469-81; 1949.

[24] The same point of view was also put forward in the same year by David M. Potter in David M. Potter and Thomas G. Manning, *Nationalism and Sectionalism in America, 1775-1877: Select Problems in Historical Interpretation* (New York: Holt, 1949), p. 215-16.

96 INTERPRETING AND TEACHING AMERICAN HISTORY

their powerful impulse against human bondage was deflected from its natural target, slavery in the states, and was sublimated, as it were, into an attack on the peripheral question of slavery in the territories. But despite this displacement of the objective, Schlesinger felt no doubt that the moral question of slavery was basic in precipitating conflict between the sections.

During the same year when Schlesinger published this latter article, Pieter Geyl, an eminent Dutch historian of major stature, also published, in Dutch, a critique of Randall's idea that the War could have been avoided. (A part of this was published in English translation in 1951).[25] Geyl focused his attention especially on Randall's contention that because the majority did not want conflict, war should have been avoidable. He argued that the historical process is not as rational as Randall assumed, and that the issues of sectional disagreement could not be neatly separated from the emotions which they generated, and which ultimately got out of control. His criticism must rank with Schlesinger's as one of the two major rebuttals to the revisionist argument, but other voices have been raised as well. Bernard De Voto assailed the revisionists in two influential articles in *Harper's Magazine*, which were notable for their early date (1946) as well as for their vigorous, hard-hitting tone.[26] In 1950, Oscar Handlin, in a review of Nevins, deplored the practice of equating the abolitionists and the secessionists because both groups were fanatics: "There is surely a difference," he said, "between being a fanatic for freedom and being a fanatic for slavery."[27]

Harry V. Jaffa has provided an important full-scale criticism of much of the revisionist position.[28] Jaffa denied that slavery had reached the geographical limits of its expansion and that the political restriction was redundant. He denied also that Douglas' popular sovereignty and Lincoln's restrictionism would both have come to the same thing, that is freedom in the territories, and that they presented no basic

---

[25] *De Amerikaanse Burgeroorlog en het Probleem der onvermijdelijkheid* ([Mededelingen der Koninklijke Nederlandsche Akademie van Wetenschappen Afd. Letterkunde, Nieuwe Reeks, Deel 12, No. 5] Amsterdam, 1919) , p. 295-340. A translation of part of this article appeared as "The American Civil War and the Problem of Inevitability," *New England Quarterly*, 24:147-68; June 1951. Reprinted in Geyl, *Debates with Historians* (Groningen: J. B. Wolters, 1955), p. 216-35.

[26] Bernard De Voto, "The Easy Chair," *Harper's*, 192:123-26; February 1946. *Ibid.*, 192:234-37; March 1946.

[27] Review of Nevins, *The Emergence of Lincoln*, in *Nation*, 171:512-13; December 2, 1950.

[28] Harry V. Jaffa, *Crisis of the House Divided. An Interpretation of the Issues in the Lincoln-Douglas Debates* (New York: Doubleday, 1959) .

issue. Instead he argued, Douglas was willing to sacrifice the principles of freedom and equality to the principle of majority rule, while Lincoln, though not a doctrinaire equalitarian, wanted "the highest degree of equality for which general [majority] consent could be obtained." Emphasizing this distinction as he did, he dismissed the idea that emotions of the crisis period were "whipped up" or unrealistic. Don E. Fehrenbacher, moreover, showed how genuinely Lincoln feared that the Dred Scott decision was a prelude to steps which would legalize slavery throughout the nation, and how effectively Lincoln himself defined the fundamental incompatibility between his position and Douglas'.[29]

The counterattack upon revisionism has gained a wide following, perhaps because many historians felt dissatisfied with the revisionist version of history, and welcomed a challenge to it. But the critics of revisionism have not been specialists in the Civil War period: Schlesinger is an authority on the Jacksonian and New Deal periods; Geyl on Dutch history; Jaffa is a political scientist. Consequently, they have stated their views in critical essays but, with the exception of Jaffa, have not woven them into the fabric of historical narrative. Craven, Randall, and Nichols, by contrast, have been such diligent researchers and such prolific writers on the developments of the crisis period that many teachers who may disagree with their interpretations nevertheless rely upon their histories for content. With one capital exception, most of the general historical exposition during the last twenty years has been written by revisionists. This exception is Allan Nevins.

Many years ago, Nevins conceived the idea of a large scale history that would treat the entire period of sectional crisis and Civil War from 1850 to 1865. Since James Ford Rhodes, at the turn of the century, published his volumes on the period 1850-1877, no such history had been written by anyone, and certainly none such had been written in the light of modern historical scholarship. Nevins engaged in a vast research enterprise, and in 1947 he published two volumes covering the period 1850-1857; two more in 1950 carried the narrative to 1860; and a fifth in 1959 has covered the outbreak of war and the War itself to the end of 1861.[30]

---

[29] Don E. Fehrenbacher, "The Origins and Purpose of Lincoln's House Divided Speech," *Mississippi Valley Historical Review*, 46:615-43; March 1960.

[30] The titles were *Ordeal of the Union* (2 vols., 1947), *The Emergence of Lincoln* (2 vols., 1950), and *The War for the Union* (1959). All New York: Scribner.

Some critics complain that Nevins did not apply a consistent philosophy in his interpretation of the crisis. At some times he seemed, like the revisionists, to emphasize "the unrealties of passion"; at others the view that "while hysteria was important, we have always to ask what basic reasons made possible the propaganda which aroused it."[31] On the one hand he seemed to agree with the revisionists that "failure of American leadership" contributed to the breakdown of Union, and he even stated a belief that "the War should have been avoidable,"[32] which is by no means the same as saying that it could have been avoided. Also, he rejected the older simplistic idea that slavery as a moral issue was the crux of the controversy, and offered in its stead the view that "the main root of the conflict (and there were minor roots), was the problem of slavery *with its complementary problem of race-adjustment. . . .* It was a war over slavery *and* the future position of the Negro race in North America."[33] But this view, itself, was far from a revisionist position, and Nevins rejected revisionism even more distinctly in his attention to the harsher aspects of slavery and in his condemnation of what he considered the moral obtuseness of Stephen A. Douglas in sponsoring the Kansas-Nebraska Act.

In the light of Nevins' treatment, one might infer that revisionism, like all historical correctives, has served its purpose not by winning adoption of its own categorical views, but by forcing a modification in the conventional themes. Never again can well-trained historians explain the Civil War purely in terms of economic determinism or of the moral crusade against slavery; never again can they dismiss questions of responsibility and failure of leadership with the blanket formula that the conflict was irrepressible. These are lasting consequences of revisionism.

But questions of the role of leadership, the role of psychological factors ("emotions"), and above all, the role of slavery, remain and perhaps will continue to remain the subject of debate. Abraham Lincoln, a master of exact statement, said in his second inaugural, "all know that slavery was somehow the cause of the war." The operative word was "somehow," and it is around this word that historical debate continues to turn.

---

[31] *Ordeal of the Union,* Vol. I, p. ix, and *The Emergence of Lincoln,* Vol. II, p. 470.

[32] *The Emergence of Lincoln,* Vol. II, p. 463, and *Ordeal of the Union,* Vol. I, p. viii.

[33] *The Emergence of Lincoln,* Vol. IV, p. 468-71.

Meanwhile, at the immensely important level of historical exposition, the volumes by Nevins provide a narrative which is unexcelled for its comprehensiveness and detail, and which maintains throughout a high critical excellence in dealing with many thorny problems and a breadth and power of imagination, in showing old content in a new light.

FACTORS CONTRIBUTING TO THE CRISIS OF THE UNION

While general treatments of the coming of the war have formed the main focus of historical interpretation, there has also appeared, during the last twenty years, a remarkably extensive literature on all aspects of the sectional divergencies and sectional antagonisms which came to a crisis in 1860. The emphasis in this literature has shifted from a heavy stress upon the political and economic aspects to a broader treatment which continues to develop further analytical insights into political and economic themes, but which has also ranged out to a more comprehensive consideration of the nature of sectionalism and of the social, cultural, and ideological factors in the sectional cleavage. In reviewing this literature, the following account will divide it into three groups, dealing with (1) sectionalism and the South as a section, (2) the anti-slavery movement, and (3) specific episodes or developments in the mounting sectional crisis from 1820 to 1861.

Sectionalism and the South as a Section

Sectionalism involves the interplay of more or less opposing human groups, geographically set apart but operating within a common political organization. The understanding of sectionalism, therefore, involves an understanding of the forces involved in this adverse relationship. These forces, in the United States between 1830 and 1860, were on the one hand, the development of "the South" as a distinctive, self-conscious entity, to some degree separable from the rest of the Union, and the development outside the South, of an opposition to what the South conceived to be its interests, especially insofar as these interests were identified with the institution of slavery. Historians dispute whether the South was a conscious minority defending itself, or an aggressive slavocracy seeking to dominate the Union. They also disagree as to whether Northern opposition to the South sprang from an idealistic rejection of slavery as such, or from more subtle incompatibilities and more sordid motives of sectional advantage. But no matter how these questions are resolved, an understanding of sectionalism must depend upon an understanding first of what was intrinsic in the identity of the South, and how this intrinsic identity was brought into an adverse relationship with the region outside the South, a region which is less readily recognized as a section because it constituted a majority whose interests could therefore be made to coincide with the national interest.[34]

The importance of sectionalism has been recognized for a long time and some of its aspects were worked out many years ago in studies which still remain standard. For instance, on the institution of slavery, important studies which have not yet become dated were made for Missouri, North Carolina, Georgia, Mississippi, Alabama, Louisiana, and Kentucky.[35] Similarly, on secession, Dwight L. Dumond's general treatment in 1931[36] and a number of state studies of long-standing still remain unsuperseded: South Carolina, Missouri, Alabama, Virginia, Mississippi, Louisiana, and North Carolina.[37] Some of the major themes of Southern history were fully developed by William E. Dodd, who did all his significant work before 1920, and by Ulrich B. Phillips, who died in 1934. Phillips' views on slavery have been sharply challenged by Kenneth M. Stampp, but even

---

[34] Merrill Jensen, ed., *Regionalism in America* (Madison: University of Wisconsin, 1951) contains essays by Fulmer Mood and Vernon Carstensen, p. 5-98, 99-118, on the development of sectional-regional concepts, and an essay by Francis B. Simkins on "The South," p. 147-72.

[35] Harrison A. Trexler, *Slavery in Missouri, 1804-1865* ([Studies in Historical and Political Science, XXXII, No. 2] Baltimore: Johns Hopkins University, 1914) ; Rosser H. Taylor, *Slaveholding in North Carolina: An Economic View* (Chapel Hill: University of North Carolina, 1926) ; Ralph B. Flanders, *Plantation Slavery in Georgia* (Chapel Hill: University of North Carolina, 1933) ; Charles S. Sydnor, *Slavery in Mississippi* (New York: Appleton-Century, 1933) ; Charles S. Davis, *The Cotton Kingdom in Alabama* (Montgomery: Alabama State Department of Archives and History, 1939); Roger W. Shugg, *Origins of Class Struggle in Louisiana* (Baton Rouge: Louisiana State University, 1939) , Chapters 1-5; John Winston Coleman, *Slavery Times in Kentucky* (Chapel Hill: University of North Carolina, 1940).

[36] *The Secession Movement, 1860-1861* (New York: Macmillan) .

[37] Philip M. Hamer, *The Secession Movement in South Carolina, 1847-1852* (Allentown, Pennsylvania: H. R. Haas, 1918); Chauncey S. Boucher, *The Secession and Cooperation Movements in South Carolina, 1848-1852* (St. Louis: Washington University Studies, Vol. V, No. 2, 1918); Walter H. Ryle, *Missouri: Union or Secession* (Nashville: George Peabody College for Teachers, 1931; Clarence P. Denman, *The Secession Movement in Alabama* (Montgomery State Department of Archives and History, 1933) ; Henry T. Shanks, *The Secession Movement in Virginia, 1847-1861* (Richmond Garrett and Massie, 1934); Percy L. Rainwater, *Mississippi, Storm Center of Secession, 1856-1861* (Baton Rouge: Otto Claitor, 1938) ; Willie Malvin Caskey, *Secession and Restoration of Louisiana* (Baton Rouge: Louisiana State University, 1938) ; Joseph Carlyle Sitterson, *The Secession Movement in North Carolina* ([James Sprunt Studies in History and Political Science, Vol. 23, No. 2] Chapel Hill: University of North Carolina, 1939) .

Stampp does not question the fundamental importance of Phillips' studies of *American Negro Slavery* (1918) [38] and of the ante-bellum economy and society (1929).[39] Lewis C. Gray's classic *History of Agriculture in the Southern United States to 1860*,[40] has never been approached as a final and comprehensive treatment of the pre-Civil War agricultural economy.

But without discounting the continuing importance of basic earlier works and interpretations, one can still note vast advances in the past two decades. Nothing illustrates this development more forcibly than the fact that seven volumes of a projected ten-volume History of the South have appeared since 1947. This important enterprise, edited by Wendell H. Stephenson and E. Merton Coulter, has included volumes on *The South in the Revolution, 1763-1789* (1957), by John R. Alden; *The Development of Southern Sectionalism, 1819-1848* (1948), by the late Charles S. Sydnor; and *The Growth of Southern Nationalism, 1848-1861* (1953), by Avery O. Craven.[41] These volumes have done much to throw new light upon the nature of sectionalism. Alden's volume shows the emergence of conflict between North and South at a time when it has been assumed that the only significant sectional cleavage was on an East-West axis between coastal areas and frontier districts. To Alden it seemed justifiable to say that "by the end of the Revolutionary epoch . . . the South had emerged as a section and the Southerners as a people different from Northerners."[42] But these early sectional demarcations tended to disappear during the ascendancy of the Jeffersonian party, and Sydnor regarded the sectional factor as almost negligible as late as 1819. At that time, he wrote, the South still remained an "unawakened" area, where "regional differences had not borne the evil fruit of sectional bitterness" and where "perhaps it is anachronistic to speak of Southerners."[43] Sydnor then proceeded to trace the development of a really deep-seated sectionalism which grew up between the Missouri Controversy and the end of the Mexican War. His way of treating his theme was important in two ways especially. One of these was his emphasis upon the idea that the South was not a region ruled by a high-handed planter aristocracy,

---

[38] New York: Appleton.

[39] *Life and Labor in the Old South* (Boston: Little, Brown), and numerous articles.

[40] Two vols.; (Publication No. 430) Washington: Carnegie Institution of Washington, 1933.

[41] All Baton Rouge: Louisiana State University.

[42] Alden, p. 2.

[43] Sydnor, p. 32.

but one in which democratic political and social forces were steadily increasing their dominance. The political aspects of this democracy have also been developed by Fletcher M. Green, both before and since Sydnor's contribution,[44] and the theme of social democracy has been intensively stressed through a series of census analyses by the late Frank L. Owsley, his wife, and his students, designed to show that plain non-slaveholding farmers occupied an important and respected place in the Southern social structure. These studies, begun before 1940, reached their fullest exposition in Owsley's *Plain Folk of the Old South*,[45] but the length to which he carried the argument had already provoked an adverse critique, closely and lengthily argued, by Fabian Linden in the *Journal of Negro History* in 1946.[46] It is ironical that, after a vast amount of intensive study by many scholars, the essential structure of society in the ante-bellum South still remains in dispute.

The second important feature of Sydnor's work was its tracing of the rise of sectionalism in terms of cultural self-consciousness and psychological feelings of separateness. This concept was, of course, not original with him, but he developed and applied the idea with unusual effectiveness. Avery Craven, in the volume following Sydnor's, also traced the course of sectionalism in terms of psychological reactions to crucial events, such as the Kansas-Nebraska Act, which was used to arouse the North, although Southern opinion seemed relatively indifferent toward it, and John Brown's raid which was crucial in the polarization of Southern feeling.

Along with emphasis upon psychological factors, there has also been a growing attention to the aspects of sectionalism which can be devel-

---

[44] Fletcher M. Green, *Constitutional Development in the South Atlantic States, 1776-1860* (Chapel Hill: University of North Carolina, 1930); "Democracy in the Old South," *Journal of Southern History*, 12:3-23; February 1946.

[45] Frank L. and Harriet C. Owsley, "The Economic Basis of Society in the Late Ante-Bellum South," *Journal of Southern History*, 7:24-45; February 1940, and "The Economic Structure of Rural Tennessee, 1850-1860," *ibid.*, 8:161-82; May 1942. Blanche H. Clark, *The Tennessee Yeoman, 1840-1860* (Nashville: Vanderbilt University, 1942). Harry L. Coles, Jr., "Some Notes on Slaveownership and Landownership in Louisiana, 1850-1860," *Journal of Southern History*, 9:381-94; August 1943. Herbert Weaver, *Mississippi Farmers, 1850-1860* (Nashville: Vanderbilt University, 1945). Frank L. Owsley, *Plain Folk of the Old South* (Baton Rouge: Louisiana State University, 1949).

[46] Fabian Linden, "Economic Democracy in the Slave South: An Appraisal of Some Recent Views," *Journal of Negro History*, 31:140-89; April 1949. James C. Bonner, "Profile of a Late Ante-Bellum Community," *American Historical Review*, 49:663-80; July 1944. Both of these articles present data which indicate an undemocratic social structure.

oped through the study of intellectual history. This is one of the phases of Southern history which has advanced most rapidly. As recently as 1940, probably the best treatments were a section in Parrington's *Main Currents of American Thought*, three chapters in Dodd's *Cotton Kingdom*, and one rather lonely monograph by William S. Jenkins on *Pro-Slavery Thought in the Old South*.[47] In 1940, however, Clement Eaton published his *Freedom of Thought in the Old South*,[48] which traced the transition in the South from the liberalism of the Jeffersonian era to the conservatism of the time of Calhoun. Eaton found Southern defensiveness on the slavery question at the root of this conservative reaction, and he showed this same defensiveness leading to the imposition of an "intellectual blockade" to keep out all liberal or modern ideas. Only a year after Eaton, Joseph C. Robert's *The Road from Monticello* developed another aspect of this conservative theme by tracing the decline of the anti-slavery movement in Virginia.[49] More recently, John Hope Franklin's *The Militant South, 1800-1861* (1956),[50] has shown still another phase of Southern defensiveness—the pugnacious temper of the ante-bellum South.

Study of the social philosophy of the South has centered upon two figures—George Fitzhugh and John C. Calhoun. Fitzhugh adopted the prevailing Southern argument that chattel slavery was less exploitative than "wage slavery," and carried this claim to its logical conclusion by contending that slavery was preferable for white as well as Negro workers.[51] His ideas never won any appreciable acceptance, but they have some significance in showing the implications of the ideal of a status society. This ideal found its leading champion in

---

[47] Vernon Louis Parrington, *Main Currents in American Thought* (3 vols.; Harcourt, Brace, 1927-1930), Vol. II, p. 1-179; William E. Dodd, *The Cotton Kingdom* ([Chronicles of America Series] New Haven: Yale University, 1919), p. 48-117; William S. Jenkins, *Pro-Slavery Thought in the Old South* ([Social Study Series] Chapel Hill: University of North Carolina, 1935).

[48] Durham: Duke University.

[49] *The Road from Monticello: A Study of the Virginia Slavery Debate of 1832* ([Historical Papers of the Trinity College Historical Society, Ser. XXIV] Durham: Duke University, 1941). This study showed that the abolitionist attack on slavery was less instrumental than is commonly supposed in causing the South to swing to the defense of slavery.

[50] Cambridge: Belknap of Harvard University.

[51] Harvey Wish, *George Fitzhugh: Propagandist of the Old South* ([Southern Biography Series] Baton Rouge: Louisiana State University, 1943); Louis Hartz, *The Liberal Tradition in America* (New York: Harcourt, Brace, 1955), Part IV, "The Feudal Dream of the South"; Arnaud B. Leavelle and Thomas I. Cook, "George Fitzhugh and the Theory of American Conservatism," *Journal of Politics*, 7:145-68; May 1945.

Calhoun, who was long regarded as a hair-splitting constitutional theoretician, but who has been appraised more recently as an important social thinker. A significant essay by Richard Hofstadter and an important three-volume biography by Charles M. Wiltse have served particularly to show Calhoun as a defender of the idea of an organic society with a fixed social order.[52]

While these writers have emphasized the conservative factor in Southern thought, others have stressed the importance of romanticism in shaping the Southern mind. Wilbur J. Cash in 1941 wrote a brilliant synthesis which was especially effective in showing how frontier strains of romanticism merged with upper-class chivalric strains in forming a Southern romantic image of life.[53] In 1949, Rollin G. Osterweis published a study showing some of the ways in which the romantic strain entered into the Southern nationalism of the decade before secession.[54] Other studies, in the field of literature, have also pointed up the importance of cultural nationalism as a phase of Southern nationalism. Perhaps the most important of these are Jay B. Hubbell's monumental literary history of the South, a long essay by him on Cultural Nationalism in the South, and a biography of William A. Caruthers, by Curtis Carroll Davis, in which Davis shows how the novels of Caruthers contributed to the South's image of itself as the stronghold of the cavalier tradition.[55]

---

[52] "John C. Calhoun, the Marx of the Master Class" in Richard Hofstadter, *The American Political Tradition and the Men Who Made It* (New York: Knopf, 1948). Charles M. Wiltse, *John C. Calhoun* (3 vols.; Indianapolis: Bobbs-Merrill, 1944-1951). Margaret L. Coit, *John C. Calhoun, American Portrait* (Boston: Houghton Mifflin, 1950). Also see Richard N. Current, "John C. Calhoun, Philosopher of Reaction," *Antioch Review*, 3:223-34; Summer 1943. Ralph H. Gabriel, *The Course of American Democratic Thought* (New York: Ronald, 1940), p. 103-10, "A Footnote on John C. Calhoun." Louis Hartz, "South Carolina vs. the United States," in Daniel Aaron, ed., *America in Crisis* (New York: Knopf, 1952), p. 73-90. August O. Spain, *The Political Theory of John C. Calhoun* (New York: Bookman Associates, 1951). A new edition of *The Papers of John C. Calhoun* has been launched and the first volume, edited by the late Robert Lee Meriwether, appeared in 1959 (Columbia: University of South Carolina, published for South Caroliniana Society). Subsequent volumes will be edited by W. Edwin Hemphill.

[53] *The Mind of the South* (New York: Knopf, 1941).

[54] *Romanticism and Nationalism in the Old South* (New Haven: Yale University).

[55] Jay B. Hubbell, *The South in American Literature, 1607-1900* (Durham: Duke University, 1954); Hubbell, "Literary Nationalism in the Old South" in David K. Jackson, *American Studies in Honor of William Kenneth Boyd* (Durham: Duke University, 1940); Curtis Carroll Davis, *Chronicler of the Cavaliers: a Life of the Virginia Novelist, Dr. William A. Caruthers* (Richmond: Dietz, 1953). Also important in the cultural history of the South is Mary C. Simms Oliphant, Alfred T. Odell, and T. C. Duncan Eaves, eds., *The Letters of William Gilmore Simms* (5 vols.; Columbia: University of South Carolina, 1952-1956).

Although there has been more significant work on these new social and cultural themes than on slavery, secession, politics, and similar favored topics of earlier writers, these traditional areas of study continue to attract a share of able interpreters. The older state monographs on secession have been supplemented by two excellent studies of South Carolina: Harold S. Schultz, *Nationalism and Sectionalism in South Carolina, 1852-1860* (1950),[56] and Charles E. Cauthen, *South Carolina Goes to War, 1860-1865* (1950).[57] Schultz and Cauthen both argue that unionism and disunionism in this strategic Southern state were not co-efficients of love or lack of love for the Union, but that they varied in direct proportion to Southern fears that anti-slavery would dominate the North. That is, Unionism was a contingent value, relative to slavery, not an absolute value, reflecting only the intensity of patriotic feeling.

Also the older literature on the economy of the South has been enriched by the addition of important new studies on rice and sugar.[58] As for the institution of slavery, there have been three more full-scale monographs on slavery in the states of Alabama, Tennessee, and Arkansas,[59] and one of these, Chase C. Mooney's *Slavery in Tennessee,* has broken new ground by its intensive study of how slaveholding was related, statistically, to land tenure and to agricultural production. Also, John Hope Franklin has provided the first satisfactory general history of the Negro in America.[60] But the major development in the historiography of slavery has been Kenneth M. Stampp's *The Peculiar*

---

[56] Durham: Duke University.

[57] (James Sprunt Studies in History and Political Science, Vol. 32.) Chapel Hill: University of North Carolina.

[58] J. H. Easterby, ed., *The South Carolina Rice Plantation as Revealed in the Papers of Robert F. W. Allston* (Chicago: University of Chicago, 1945); J. Carlyle Sitterson, *Sugar Country: The Cane Sugar Industry in the South, 1753-1950* (Lexington: University of Kentucky, 1953). Also, in 1938, Joseph C. Robert published *The Tobacco Kingdom: Plantation, Market, and Factory in Virginia and North Carolina, 1800-1860* (Durham: Duke University). Other important recent works on the Southern economic system are Albert V. House, ed., *Planter Management and Capitalism in Ante-Bellum Georgia: The Journal of Hugh Fraser Grant, Rice-grower* ([Studies in the History of American Agriculture, No. 13] New York: Columbia University, 1954); John Hebron Moore, *Agriculture in Ante-Bellum Mississippi* (New York: Bookman Associates, 1958); Lewis E. Atherton, *The Southern Country Store, 1800-1860* (Baton Rouge: Louisiana State University, 1949).

[59] James B. Sellers, *Slavery in Alabama* (University, Alabama: University of Alabama, 1950); Chase C. Mooney, *Slavery in Tennessee* ([Social Science Series, No. 17] Bloomington: Indiana University, 1957); Orville W. Taylor, *Negro Slavery in Arkansas* (Durham: Duke University, 1958).

[60] *From Slavery to Freedom: A History of American Negroes* (New York: Knopf, 1947; second revised edition, 1956).

Institution, an overall account, with its focus on the question: What was it like to be a slave? Stampp sees the harsh factors looming very large; he also believes that slavery was more profitable than is usually supposed, and that there was no chance that it would have fallen of its own weight, as some Southern historians have claimed.[61] More recently, Stanley M. Elkins, *Slavery, A Problem in American Institutional Life* has appeared.[62] Whereas Stampp tended to treat Negroes as culturally comparable to whites, Elkins made a leading theme of his argument that the conditions of slavery tended to infantilize the Negro, to stunt the development of the Negro personality, and to produce the "Jim Crow" characteristics of the carefree, obsequious, irresponsible Negro. Elkins' treatment is controversial, but deals with profound questions, and is of major importance.

A century after the Civil War, the development of sectional forces has now been examined in immense detail. More than a generation ago, the conflict in the political and constitutional arena over specific sectional issues had already been worked out quite fully. More recently, the cultural and psychological aspects of Southernism have received greater attention. Thus, the most important recent advances have occurred in establishing the character of the section rather than in recounting its conflicts. With all the analysis that has gone into the interpretation of the cultural factors, however, great disagreement still exists as to the extent to which the Old South was democratic or aristocratic in its regime. Doubt also surrounds the question whether cultural affinity or common interests maintained in common defense against the North were primary in creating a sense of Southern unity. On the one hand, there is no doubt that staple-crop agriculture, biracialism, and a status society shaped a distinctive way of life for the South, but on the other, the so-called cultural nationalism of the South had a certain thinness about it which suggests that instead of a real Southern nationalism producing friction with the North, friction with the North may have produced the figment of nationalism. In this sense, it is perhaps unfortunate that the theme of conflict of interest tends to be neglected by cultural historians. Years ago studies

---

[61] Kenneth M. Stampp, *The Peculiar Institution: Slavery in the Ante-Bellum South* (New York: Knopf, 1956). The discovery that slavery was reasonably profitable is not original with Stampp, nor does he claim it to be. Lewis C. Gray and others have recognized the fact since 1930, but Stampp has developed the significance of the profitability of slavery in indicating that the institution could not have been left to extinguish itself.

[62] Chicago: University of Chicago, 1960.

of the commercial conventions which were held in the South, and of the economic aspects of sectionalism showed that the economic grievances of the South, and the growing economic disparities between it and the North were accompanied by expressions of militant Southernism.[63] But, except for a study by Robert R. Russel of the sectional conflict over the building of a Pacific railroad,[64] there has been relatively little analysis of the economic aspects of sectionalism for many years. Far the most significant general economic study of the period of recent date is George R. Taylor's *The Transportation Revolution, 1815-1860*.[65] This volume does a masterly job of depicting the economic transformation which strengthened the links between the northeast and the West at the expense of the South, and indeed it shows the creation of the economic basis for a more consolidated Union. But it pays relatively little attention to the sectional reactions to these developments, or to the effects of differential rates of sectional growth in accentuating sectionalism. Without taking these factors into account, it is difficult to know whether Southernism was primarily generated from the inside by factors and feelings of cultural affinity or induced from the outside by feelings of shared disadvantage and danger.

Humanitarianism and the Anti-Slavery Movement

If the development of a separate South—self-conscious and defensive —formed one side of the sectional coin, the development, outside the South, of opposition to slavery, went far to form the other. This side, too, has come in for considerable historical reinterpretation, especially in two respects: first, the broad nature of the reform movement of which the anti-slavery movement was a part has been more fully

---

[63] The principal studies were Robert Royal Russel, *Economic Aspects of Southern Sectionalism, 1840-1861* ([Studies in the Social Sciences, Vol. XI, Nos. 1 and 2] Urbana: University of Illinois, 1924); John G. Van Deusen, *Economic Bases of Disunion in South Carolina* ([Studies in History, Economics and Public Law, No. 305] New York: Columbia University, 1928) ; John G. Van Deusen, *The Ante-Bellum Southern Commercial Conventions* (Durham: Duke University, 1926); Herbert Wender, *Southern Commercial Conventions, 1837-1859* ([Studies in Historical and Political Science, XLVIII, No. 4] Baltimore Johns Hopkins University, 1930).

[64] Expansion to the Pacific brought with it a prolonged rivalry, partly between sections, partly between commercial centers in the Mississippi Valley, for control of the eastern terminus of an overland route or railroad to the Pacific coast. This rivalry, an important phase of sectional and economic history, is fully analyzed in Robert R. Russel, *Improvement of Communication to the Pacific Coast as an Issue in American Politics, 1783-1864* (Cedar Rapids: Torch, 1948) .

[65] New York: Rinehart, 1951.

investigated, and secondly, a growing number of writers have questioned to what extent abolitionism really represented an altruistic concern for the welfare of the Negroes.

The broader view of the anti-slavery movement gained its first important momentum when Gilbert H. Barnes published *The Anti-Slavery Impulse, 1830-1844* in 1933.[66] This work broke the monopolistic focus upon William Lloyd Garrison as the one standard symbol of abolitionism by showing the great importance of Theodore Dwight Weld and others. At the same time, it shifted attention from New England to the Middle West. It also began to link anti-slavery with other forces by demonstrating the integral relationship of abolitionism with the fervent evangelical religion of which Weld was an apostle. With the Garrisonian mold thus broken, other writers have done much more to explore the social and intellectual origins and relationships of the anti-slavery movement. Illustrative of this tendency are: Alice Felt Tyler, *Freedom's Ferment*, which deals comprehensively with the many-faceted movement of humanitarian reform, within the context of which the anti-slavery movement developed; Thomas E. Drake, *Quakers and Slavery in America*, which focussed attention again on some of the less sensational, less militant aspects of the resistance to slavery; Samuel Flagg Bemis, *John Quincy Adams and the Union*, which told the story of Adams' career as an anti-slavery leader in Congress, and thus showed how broad the anti-slavery movement was in comparison with the abolitionists' campaign for immediate emancipation; and Philip S. Foner, *The Life and Writings of Frederick Douglass*, which emphasizes the role of free Negroes in the abolition movement.[67]

Identification of the anti-slavery movement with the humanitarian movement usually implies a measure of approbation for the abolitionists. But, while this approval has certainly been prominent in part of the literature, there has also been a growing tendency to question the basic motivation of abolitionists, sometimes in modern psychological terms. The abolitionists have, of course, always been condemned by writers who attribute the disruption of the Union to the fanaticism of the anti-slavery crusade. But most of the recent criticism, coming from quite an opposite direction, reflects a belief

---

[66] New York: Appleton-Century.

[67] Tyler, *Freedom's Ferment: Phases of American Social History to 1860* (Minneapolis: University of Minnesota, 1944); Drake ([Yale Historical Publications, Miscellany No. 51] New Haven: Yale University, 1950); Bemis (New York: Knopf, 1956); Foner (4 vols.; New York: International Publishers, 1950-1955).

that the abolitionists were motivated less by a concern for Negro welfare than by a drive to fulfill certain peculiar psychological needs of their own.

This theme was implied in 1949, in Russell B. Nye's *Fettered Freedom*, which argued that the slave system, both in itself and in its zealous defensiveness, constituted a threat to civil liberties and thus provoked the opposition of men who opposed the slave power without necessarily caring about the slave. At almost the same time, Richard Hofstadter described Lincoln as one who owed his success to his skill in finding a way "to win the support of both Negrophobes and anti-slavery men." Hofstadter did not picture the anti-slavery men as being Negrophobes themselves, but Joseph C. Furnas has actually carried the argument to this position in *Goodbye to Uncle Tom*. Furnas castigates the abolitionists for paving the way to the later system of segregation by their acceptance of the idea of the inferiority of the Negro, and he shows very clearly that many abolitionists, although rejecting slavery, nevertheless did "type" the Negro as an inferior. Since his book appeared, Robert F. Durden's biography of *James Shepherd Pike* has shown how the strands of anti-slavery and Negro-phobia were strikingly united in the person of one of the editors of the *New York Tribune*, the most important journalistic organ of the anti-slavery cause.[68]

Meanwhile, David Donald has advanced some generalizations about the abolitionists, based upon a study of the backgrounds of 106 prominent anti-slavery men. He found them, in general, conservative, indifferent to the exploitation of industrial labor, and hostile to Jacksonian democracy. He also suggested that many of them were descendants of New England clerical families who found their leadership challenged by the new industrialism and who turned to reform as a medium through which "their own class" could reassert "its former social dominance . . . an attack upon slavery was their best, if quite unconscious, attack upon the new industrial system.[69]

---

[68] Nye, *Fettered Freedom: Civil Liberties and the Slavery Controversy, 1830-1860* (East Lansing: Michigan State College); Hofstadter, *The American Political Tradition*, p. 112; Furnas, (New York: Sloane, 1956); Durden, *James Shepherd Pike: Republicanism and the American Negro, 1850-1882* (Durham: Duke University, 1957).

[69] David Donald, "Toward a Reconsideration of Abolitionists," in *Lincoln Reconsidered* (New York: Knopf, 1956), p. 19-36. But see also Robert A. Skotheim, "A Note on Historical Method: David Donald's 'Toward a Reconsideration of Abolitionists'," *Journal of Southern History*, 25:356-65; August 1959.

Probably most historians will not agree either that the anti-slavery leaders were predominantly Negrophobes, nor that their crusade was only a vicarious protest against the industrial threat to their own dominance. But in the light of the scholarship of the last two decades, it is hard to escape the conclusion that most of the anti-slavery leaders were not great humanitarians in the broadest sense, and that they failed to perceive the problem of racial adjustment in America, which was the essence of the problem of slavery. Partly because they construed the issue in such limited terms, the problem of the slave was not solved by emancipation but was merely replaced by the problem of the caste-subordinated Negro.[70]

The Mounting Sectional Crisis

Along with a study of the opposing sectional forces, any study of the background of the Civil War must also take account of the long series of developments which marked the increase of sectional tension, mounting steadily until the bonds of union snapped in 1860-1861. These developments include the Missouri Controversy of 1820, the Tariff and Nullification Controversy of 1832, the contest over the annexation of Texas between 1836 and 1844, the struggle over the status of slavery in the territory acquired from Mexico—beginning with the Wilmot Proviso in 1846 and ending with the Compromise of 1850, the resistance in the North to the Fugitive Slave Act, the repeal of the Missouri Compromise by the Kansas-Nebraska Act in 1854, the chronic violence which became known as Bleeding Kansas, the Dred Scott decision, the Lincoln-Douglas debates, John Brown's Raid at Harpers Ferry, the election of Lincoln, the secession of the Lower South, the formation of the Southern Confederacy, and the outbreak of hostilities at Fort Sumter.

All of these events have received intensive study. Some of them were investigated so thoroughly many years ago that little of signifi-

---

[70] In addition to the work on Douglass, mentioned above, there have been several valuable contributions to the literature of the anti-slavery movement in the form of biographies: Ralph V. Harlow, *Gerrit Smith, Philanthropist and Reformer* (New York: Holt, 1939) ; Forrest Wilson, *Crusader in Crinoline: The Life of Harriet Beecher Stowe* (Philadelphia: Lippincott, 1941) ; Frank Freidel, *Francis Lieber, Nineteenth-Century Liberal* (Baton Rouge: Louisiana State University, 1947); Ralph Korngold, *Two Friends of Man: The Story of William Lloyd Garrison and Wendell Phillips* (Boston: Little, Brown, 1950) ; Benjamin P. Thomas, *Theodore Weld: Crusader for Freedom* (New Brunswick: Rutgers University, 1950) ; Russell B. Nye, *William Lloyd Garrison and the Humanitarian Reformers* ([Library of American Biography] Boston: Little, Brown, 1955); Betty L. Fladeland, *James Gillespie Birney: Slaveholder to Abolitionist* (Ithaca: Cornell University, 1955) .

cance has been added in the last score of years; for instance, this is largely true of John Brown's raid. But others have been the objects of new research—sometimes with results that have acquired drastic reinterpretation.

The Missouri Controversy, to begin with, has been re-examined by Glover Moore.[71] In addition to giving a fuller account than was previously available, Moore has shown that the majority of Southern congressmen did not vote for the line 36° 30′ as a boundary to divide the Louisiana Purchase between freedom and slavery. Since there was no acceptance of the settlement by both contesting groups, there was no compromise in the true sense. Hence it was not entirely accurate to say that a "solemn compact" had been violated when the 36° 30′ line was repealed thirty-four years later.

On the sectional rivalries for the period after the Missouri Compromise and before the Compromise of 1850, perhaps the most significant recent treatments have appeared in biographies. These include not only the definitive studies of Calhoun by Wiltse and of J. Q. Adams by Bemis, mentioned above, but also a life of Sam Houston which for the first time treats fully his career after the annexation of Texas, a full-scale study of John Tyler, and thorough, scholarly accounts of Silas Wright, Millard Fillmore, and John Bell. Charles G. Sellers has published the first volume of a life of James K. Polk, dealing with his career up to 1843. There have been two lives of Zachary Taylor, by Brainerd Dyer and by Holman Hamilton (the latter discussed below) and two of Thomas Hart Benton, by William N. Chambers and by Elbert B. Smith, of which the former is more broadly concerned with Benton's times while the latter is more a personal portrait. Biographies of Andrew Stevenson, George Bancroft, William L. Marcy, and John Bigelow are in many instances just as significant historically as the lives of the major figures. On Henry Clay and Daniel Webster, the earlier full-scale biographies by Glyndon G. Van Deusen (1937) and by Claude Fuess (1930), respectively, remain the standard works, but Clement Eaton and Richard Current have written valuable brief, interpretive lives of these two men, and the University of Kentucky Press has announced a definitive edition of the writings of Clay, under the editorship of James F. Hopkins. There has been no good overall biography of Van Buren, though Robert V. Remini has provided a thorough treatment of a

---

[71] *The Missouri Controversy, 1819-1821* (Lexington: University of Kentucky, 1953).

crucial stage of his career between 1821 and 1828.[72] The most recent summing up of the period, and a notably judicious one, is Glyndon G. Van Deusen's history of *The Jacksonian Era, 1828-1848* (1959).[73]

On the expansionist drive to make the United States a transcontinental republic—a drive which brought sectional rivalries into sharp focus—significant new contributions have been limited. One of the most important is Norman A. Graebner's *Empire on the Pacific*, which challenges the long-standing tradition of agrarian expansionism by arguing that the desire of eastern commercial interests to control Pacific coastal ports was an important factor in Manifest Destiny.[74] Next to this in importance, perhaps, is a study by James C. N. Paul of the effects of the expansion question in causing a split, which was later covered up but never healed, between the Polk and the Van Buren wings of the Democratic party at the Baltimore Convention in 1844.[75]

---

[72] Llerena Friend, *Sam Houston, The Great Designer* (Austin: University of Texas, 1954); Oliver P. Chitwood, *John Tyler, Champion of the Old South* (New York: Appleton-Century, 1939); John A. Garraty, *Silas Wright* (New York: Columbia University, 1949); Robert J. Rayback, *Millard Fillmore: Biography of a President* (Buffalo Historical Society, Vol. 40; Buffalo: Stewart, 1959); Joseph Parks, *John Bell of Tennessee* (Baton Rouge: Louisiana State University, 1950); Charles G. Sellers, *James K. Polk, Jacksonian, 1795-1843* (Princeton: Princeton University, 1957); Brainerd Dyer, *Zachary Taylor* ([Southern Biography Series] Baton Rouge: Louisiana State University, 1946); Holman Hamilton, *Zachary Taylor* (2 vols.; Indianapolis: Bobbs-Merrill, 1941-1951); William N. Chambers, *Old Bullion Benton, Senator from the New West: Thomas Hart Benton* ([An Atlantic Monthly Book] Boston: Little, Brown, 1956); Elbert B. Smith, *Magnificent Missourian: The Life of Thomas Hart Benton* (Philadelphia Lippincott, 1958); Francis F. Wayland, *Andrew Stevenson: Democrat and Diplomat, 1785-1857* (Philadelphia: University of Pennsylvania, 1949); Russell B. Nye, *George Bancroft, Brahmin Rebel* (New York: Knopf, 1944); Ivor D. Spencer, *The Victor and the Spoils: A Life of William L. Marcy* (Providence: Brown University, 1959); Margaret A. Clapp, *Forgotten First Citizen: John Bigelow* (Boston: Little, Brown, 1947); Clement Eaton, *Henry Clay and the Art of American Politics* ([Library of American Biography] Boston: Little, Brown, 1957); Richard N. Current, *Daniel Webster and the Rise of National Conservatism* ([Library of American Biography] Boston: Little, Brown, 1955); Robert V. Remini, *Martin Van Buren and the Making of the Democratic Party* (New York: Columbia University, 1959).

[73] (New American Nation Series) New York: Harper.

[74] *Empire on the Pacific: A Study in American Continental Expansion* (New York: Ronald, 1955).

[75] Paul, *Rift in the Democracy* (Philadelphia: University of Pennsylvania, 1951); perhaps the severest critic of the expansionist politics of the Polk administration is Richard R. Stenberg. See, for instance, his "Intrigue for Annexation," *Southwest Review,* 25:58-69; October 1939. A significant footnote to the election of 1844 is provided in Edwin Miles' " 'Fifty-Four Forty or Fight'—an American Political Legend," *Mississippi Valley Historical Review,* 44:291-309; September 1957. Miles shows that the slogan was not used in the campaign and actually "did not gain currency until approximately one year after Polk's inauguration."

All the sectional friction of the 1840's came to a head in the first session of Congress after Zachary Taylor's inauguration, when North and South fought over the question of the status of slavery in the Mexican Cession, and emerged with the compromise of 1850.[76] By 1940, the history of the compromise had already been worked and reworked; historians had recognized the importance of Stephen A. Douglas, rather than Henry Clay, in getting the compromise adopted; and an article by Herbert D. Foster had convinced most historians that disunion was really imminent when the compromise was enacted.[77] But the finality of these conclusions, like the finality of the compromise itself, was advertised prematurely. Since then, Holman Hamilton, in an important series of journal articles and in his biography of Zachary Taylor, has told the story of the compromise anew.[78] His brilliant analysis proves two important facts: first, that there was not a majority supporting the compromise as such, but only a minority which secured adoption by garnering votes alternatively from Northern ranks or from Southern ranks, for specific measures which, in composite, made up the compromise; and second that the interests of the

[76] On the Mexican War itself, rather than its causes, three recent treatments are Bernard De Voto, *The Year of Decision, 1846* (Boston: Little, Brown, 1943) ; Alfred Hoyt Bill, *Rehearsal for Conflict: the War with Mexico, 1846-1848* (New York: Knopf, 1947) ; and Robert Selph Henry, *The Story of the Mexican War* (Indianapolis: Bobbs-Merrill, 1950). On the later stages of filibustering and Southern expansionism during the Pierce administration, there have been no major contributions in the past two decades, but the following have added important information on this phase of "Manifest Destiny": Ollinger Crenshaw, "The Knights of the Golden Circle," in *American Historical Review*, 47:23-50; October 1941. C. A. Bridges, "The Knights of the Golden Circle: A Filibustering Fantasy," *Southwestern Historical Quarterly*, 44:287-302; January 1941. Robert F. Durden, "J. D. B. De Bow: Convolutions of a Slavery Expansionist," *Journal of Southern History*, 17:441-61; November 1951. Basil Rauch, *American Interests in Cuba: 1848-1855* ([Studies in History, Economics and Public Law, No. 537] New York: Columbia University, 1948); and a series of articles in various periodicals by C. Stanley Urban on Southern attitudes and activities in connection with filibustering.

[77] George D. Harmon, "Douglas and the Compromise of 1850" in *Journal of the Illinois State Historical Society*, 21:453-99; January 1929. Milton, *The Eve of Conflict*, p. 75-78. Frank H. Hodder, "The Authorship of the Compromise of 1850," *Mississippi Valley Historical Review*, 22:525-36; March 1936. Herbert D. Foster, "Webster's Seventh of March Speech and the Secession Movement, 1850," *American Historical Review*, 27:245-70; January 1922.

[78] "Democratic Senate Leadership and the Compromise of 1850," *Mississippi Valley Historical Review*, 41:403-18; December 1954. "The 'Cave of the Winds' and the Compromise of 1850," *Journal of Southern History*, 23:331-53; August 1957. "Texas Bonds and Northern Profits: A Study in Compromise, Investment, and Lobby Influence," *Mississippi Valley Historical Review*, 43:579-94; March 1957. For a precise analysis of the provisions on slavery in the Compromise, which have been handled loosely by many historians, see Robert R. Russel, "What Was the Compromise of 1850?" *Journal of Southern History*, 22:292-309; August 1956.

holders of Texas bonds were strategic in securing adoption. Hamilton also advanced an important argument: he contended that the South would not have seceded in 1850, and that Zachary Taylor's unyielding policy was better than compromise. If Hamilton's presentation does not prove this contention, it certainly reopens the question.

Less than four years after the Compromise, the Kansas-Nebraska Act released the sectional furies again. This episode, too, has caused floods of ink to be shed. By 1940, the historical tides in this perennial dispute were running in favor of Stephen A. Douglas. Defenders of Douglas denied that he had been motivated by Presidential ambition, and they stressed the importance of his purpose to open the West, as well as the truly democratic character of his proposal to use the principle of popular sovereignty in settling the status of slavery in the territories.[79] Since 1940, the battle over Douglas has continued. Allan Nevins in *Ordeal of the Union* provided an excellent critique of previous interpretations of Douglas' motives. He himself interpreted Douglas in terms which emphasized his vigor and ability, but pictured him as insincere, coarse, and casuistical.[80] But this verdict gained no more universal acceptance than previous ones, and in 1959, Gerald M. Capers, in a new biography of Douglas, depicted the Little Giant as a true nationalist who has been the historical victim of personal slander at the hands of self-righteous leaders of the anti-slavery movement.[81] Meanwhile James C. Malin has advanced the hypothesis that, in a larger sense, Douglas, with his localistic principle of Popular Sovereignty, was fighting the centralizing forces of industrialization. Malin also contended that developments had made the issue of slavery on the Missouri frontier obsolete and that Douglas was striving to avoid it, but that sectionalists, eager for a fight, forced it into Douglas' bill.[82] A particularly able historiographical article by Roy F. Nichols has further demonstrated how completely Douglas was swept away from his original purpose.[83] Thus, by an irony, Douglas now appears as the key figure in the adoption of the Compromise of 1850, which was

---

[79] Frank H. Hodder, "The Railroad Background of the Kansas-Nebraska Act," *Mississippi Valley Historical Review*, 12:3-22; June 1925. Beveridge, *Abraham Lincoln, 1809-1858* (4 vols.) Vol. III, p. 187. Milton, *Eve of Conflict* (1934), p. 114-54. Craven, *Coming of the Civil War* (1942 ed.), p. 328-32.

[80] *Ordeal of the Union*, Vol. II, p. 11, 101, 102-106, 143-44, 422-23.

[81] *Stephen A. Douglas, Defender of the Union* ([Library of American Biography] Boston: Little, Brown, 1959), p. 72-77, 231.

[82] Malin, *The Nebraska Question, 1852-1854* (Lawrence, Kansas: the author, 1953).

[83] "The Kansas-Nebraska Act: A Century of Historiography," *Mississippi Valley Historical Review*, 43:187-212; September 1956.

traditionally identified with Clay, and not as the real creator of the Kansas-Nebraska Act, with which his name has always been linked.

The strife of Kansas which followed the Kansas-Nebraska Act presents a confused and much controverted story. Recent scholarship suggests that much of the aggressive activity in the new territory resulted from competition for land, and that the settlers were not motivated solely by their opposing convictions on the subject of slavery—a subject which was extremely abstract for most of them.[84] In a literature which often reflects the confusion of the subject itself, two recent works are outstanding for their clarity. Samuel A. Johnson has written a history which for the first time arrives at the truth, lying between pro-slavery accusations and anti-slavery evasions, about the role of the New England Emigrant Aid Society in the Kansas crusade.[85] James C. Malin, in *John Brown and the Legend of Fifty-Six* has applied the rigorous pruning-hook of historical method to the luxuriant growth of unsupported assertion about John Brown in Kansas.[86] The residue of fact which remains presents such startling contrasts to the legend that Malin's study has value, apart from the Kansas question, as a case-study in historical method.

Three years after the Kansas-Nebraska Act, the Supreme Court, in the Dred Scott case, declared that the Missouri Compromise had been null from the beginning. Since the justices held that Scott was not eligible to bring his plea to the court in any case, there was no clear necessity for them to decide about the applicability of the Missouri Compromise to his case. Consequently, historians have wrestled ever since with the question why the justices went out of their way—if they did go out of their way—to rule on this explosive question. Anti-slavery tradition regarded their act simply as another illustration of the aggressiveness of the slavocracy. In 1933, however, F. H. Hodder advanced the argument, widely accepted since then, that two Northern justices, McLean and Curtis, forced the reluctant Southerners to a broad decision by writing dissenting opinions in which they asserted, at length, the constitutionality of the act of 1820.[87] But in 1950,

---

[84]See discussion in Craven, *Coming of the Civil War*, p. 362-65, with citations to Paul Wallace Gates and James C. Malin.

[85] *The Battle Cry of Freedom: The New England Emigrant Aid Company in the Kansas Crusade* (Lawrence: University of Kansas, 1954) .

[86] (Memoirs of the American Philosophical Society, Vol. XVII.) Philadelphia: American Philosophical Society, 1942.

[87] Frank H. Hodder, "Some Phases of the Dred Scott Case," *Mississippi Valley Historical Review*, 16:3-22; June 1929.

Allan Nevins included a close analysis of the Dred Scott case in his *Emergence of Lincoln*. In this critique, he advanced strong proof that the Southern justices were already prepared for a broad decision before McLean and Curtis took their positions. Nevins also showed that while there is no proof of collusion in the decision, as Republicans at the time asserted, there is evidence of marked impropriety in the communication between James Buchanan and the members of the Court before the decision was rendered.[88]

For the period from the Dred Scott decision to the crisis at Fort Sumter, a number of excellent studies have filled out the historical picture without substantially modifying the prevalent interpretations. Paul M. Angle has published an edition of the complete text of the Lincoln-Douglas debates, with admirable editorial background.[89]

On John Brown's raid, no new insight into Brown himself has been as important as Avery Craven's demonstration of the psychological impact of the raid in precipitating Southern sectional feelings, which had never been as "solid" as Southern sectionalists wished and Northern sectionalists feared.[90] On the election of Lincoln, Reinhard H. Luthin, *The First Lincoln Campaign* and Ollinger Crenshaw, *The Slave States in the Presidential Election of 1860* (1945) have superseded an older study by Emerson D. Fite.[91]

On the secession of the Lower South, most of the political record, at least, was worked out more than twenty years ago.[92] On the Northern reaction to secession, however, interest has been fairly lively. Howard C. Perkins' two volumes of *Northern Editorials on Secession*[93] revealed more clearly than ever before the full range and complexity of Northern responses to the issue of disunion. Perkins' materials

[88] *The Emergence of Lincoln*, Vol. I, p. 90-118; Vol. II, p. 473-77.

[89] Angle, ed., *Created Equal? The Complete Lincoln-Douglas Debates of 1858* (Chicago: University of Chicago, 1958).

[90] Craven, *The Growth of Southern Nationalism*, p. 303-11. Joseph C. Furnas, *The Road to Harpers Ferry* (New York: Sloane, 1959) is an account of the anti-slavery movement in general, with especial attention to Brown.

[91] Luthin (Cambridge: Harvard University, 1944); Crenshaw ([Studies in Historical and Political Science, Ser. 63, No. 3] Baltimore: Johns Hopkins University, 1945); Fite, *The Presidential Campaign of 1860* (New York: Macmillan, 1911).

[92] But see the analysis of the personnel of Southern secession conventions by Ralph A. Wooster, in various state periodicals, summarized in his "An Analysis of the Membership of Secession Conventions in the Lower South," *Journal of Southern History*, 24:360-68; August 1958. Also note references to the studies by Schultz and Cauthen, p. 105 above.

[93] New York: Appleton-Century, 1942.

have not yet been adequately used, and attention has focussed on the policy of the Lincoln administration during the secession crisis. Did Lincoln want war with the South? Did he accept it as necessary? Or did he hope to avert it? All three views have been maintained. The first view was ably argued by Charles W. Ramsdell in 1937 and was overstated by a Montgomery attorney, John Shipley Tilley, in 1941, in a demonstrably fallacious way which may have caused a reaction against it.[94] The second was held by Kenneth M. Stampp in *And the War Came* in 1950.[95] The third was argued by David M. Potter in 1942 in a study which contended that Northern rejection of compromise resulted in part from an unrealistic belief that threats of secession were not serious as well as from a completely realistic observation that the South was not united (eight slave states were still in the Union two months after the formation of the Southern Confederacy).[96] Potter argued that Lincoln planned to avoid a showdown, and to await a unionist reaction in the South, but that the unforeseen necessity of feeding Major Anderson's garrison at Fort Sumter frustrated his plan.

In the history of the final stages of the crisis, as in the general record of this entire period, much of the most valuable historical work appears in studies of particular men. This is especially true as regards Abraham Lincoln, whose life has always been a focus for examining the crisis of the Union. There was already a staggeringly large body of literature on Lincoln twenty years ago, but this has now been supplemented by four additional contributions of vital importance. In 1939 Carl Sandburg published his epic account of *The War Years*, a work of great sweep and imagination and, incidentally, the longest biography—together with the earlier *Prairie Years*—of any American.[97] In 1945, James G. Randall published the first two of a four-volume study which, for the first time, gave a full, scholarly account of the problems and policies of Lincoln's Presidency.[98] In 1952, Benjamin P. Thomas published a one-volume biography which was a model of

---

[94] Ramsdell, "Lincoln and Fort Sumter," *Journal of Southern History*, 3:259-88; August 1937. Tilley, *Lincoln Takes Command* (Chapel Hill: University of North Carolina, 1941).

[95] Stampp, *And the War Came: the North and the Secession Crisis* (Baton Rouge: Louisiana State University, 1950).

[96] Potter, *Lincoln and His Party in the Secession Crisis* ([Yale Historical Publications, No. 13.] New Haven: Yale University 1942).

[97] *Abraham Lincoln: The War Years* (4 vols.; New York: Harcourt, Brace, 1939). *Abraham Lincoln: The Prairie Years* (2 vols.; New York: Harcourt, Brace, 1926).

[98] See p. 92-94 above.

historical conciseness and balance.[99] In 1953, the Rutgers University Press issued Roy P. Basler's eight-volume edition of Lincoln's writings —a great advance over the previous edition by Nicolay and Hay which had been far from complete and not entirely accurate.[100] Other biographies for this period include, on the Southern side, Robert D. Meade's study of Judah P. Benjamin, Rudolph von Abele's life of Alexander H. Stephens, and Hudson Strode's uncritical and excessively laudatory life of Jefferson Davis;[101] and on the Northern side, lives of Thurlow Weed and of Horace Greeley by Glyndon G. Van Deusen, of Nathaniel P. Banks by Fred H. Harrington, of Salmon P. Chase and his family by Thomas G. and Marva R. Belden, of Edwin M. Stanton by Fletcher Pratt, of Lewis Cass by Frank B. Woodford, of John Wentworth by Don Edward Fehrenbacher, and a study of Greeley and the Republican party by Jeter A. Iseley.[102]

The literature on all the varied questions which impinge directly or indirectly upon the Civil War is so vast that it almost defies the effort to view it together in any one focus. Perhaps the most pervasive quality which it all has in common is that it continues to be explicitly or implicitly controversial. Not only have historians failed to agree as to whether slavery furnished the basic motive for the war or whether it provided a smoke-screen for concealing the basic motives; they have also disagreed as to the nature of the society of the Old South, the nature of slavery, the motivation and character of the anti-slavery movement, and the interpretation of every link in the chain of sectional clashes which preceded the final crisis. The irony of this disagreement

---

[99] *Abraham Lincoln: A Biography* (New York: Knopf). Two other books which are very important for the historical interpretation of Lincoln are Donald, *Lincoln Reconsidered* (see note 66, above) and Richard N. Current, *The Lincoln Nobody Knows* (New York: McGraw-Hill, 1958).

[100] *The Collected Works of Abraham Lincoln* (New Brunswick: Rutgers University, published for the Abraham Lincoln Association, 8 vols., 1953; index vol., 1955).

[101] Meade, *Judah P. Benjamin, Confederate Statesman* (New York: Oxford University, 1943); Von Abele, *Alexander H. Stephens* (New York: Knopf, 1946); Strode, *Jefferson Davis* (2 vols. completed; New York: Harcourt, Brace, 1955, 1959).

[102] Van Deusen, *Thurlow Weed, Wizard of the Lobby* (Boston: Little, Brown, 1947); Van Deusen, *Horace Greeley, Nineteenth-Century Crusader* (Philadelphia: University of Pennsylvania, 1953); Harrington, *Fighting Politician: Major General N. P. Banks* (Philadelphia: University of Pennsylvania, 1948); the Beldens, *So Fell the Angels* (Boston: Little, Brown, 1956); Pratt, *Stanton, Lincoln's Secretary of War* (New York: Norton, 1953); Woodford, *Lewis Cass, the Last Jeffersonian* (New Brunswick: Rutgers University, 1950); Fehrenbacher, *Chicago Giant: a Biography of "Long John" Wentworth* (Madison, Wis.: American History Research Center, 1957); Iseley, *Horace Greeley and the Republican Party, 1853-1861* ([Studies in History, Vol. 3] Princeton: Princeton University, 1947).

lies in the fact that it persists in the face of vastly increased factual knowledge and constantly intensified scholarly research. The discrepancy, indeed, is great enough to make apparent a reality about history which is seldom so self-evident as it is here: namely that factual mastery of the data alone does not necessarily lead to agreement upon broad questions of historical truth. It certainly narrows the alternatives between which controversy continues to rage, and this narrowing of alternatives is itself an important proof of objective progress. But within the alternatives the determination of truth depends more perhaps upon basic philosophical assumptions which are applied in interpreting the data, than upon the data themselves. Data, in this sense, are but the raw materials for historical interpretation and not the determinants of the interpretive process. This is why the heavily researched field of the coming of the Civil War still remains, and seems likely ever to remain, subject to what we call reinterpretation—by which we mean the application of individual philosophical views to the record of the past.

CHAPTER VIII

Civil War and Reconstruction

Otis A. Singletary

INTRODUCTION

No other period in American history has received anything like the public attention paid to the years from 1861 to 1877. These years were crucial ones in the national experience and the drama of the events during this decade-and-a-half was equalled only by their significance. The war was the great bloodletting of the American people, a momentous event that was followed by a period of political experimentation unique in the nation's history for its temporary derangement of our traditional system of checks and balances and for the aggressiveness with which a reordering of an established society was attempted. The aims and ambitions of the dominant personalities of the era, the subtlety and complexity of the forces at play, and a growing appreciation of the fundamental importance of the period— all help to explain why it has continued to command the attention of layman and scholar alike.[1]

[1] For other analyses of the period see Howard K. Beale, "What Historians Have Said About the Causes of the Civil War," Social Science Research Bulletin 54 *Theory and Practice in Historical Study* (New York: Social Science Research Council, 1946). Hal Bridges, *Civil War and Reconstruction* (Washington: Service Center for Teachers of History, 1957). Clement Eaton, "Recent Trends in the Writing of Southern History," *Louisiana Historical Quarterly*, 38:26-42; April 1955. Thomas J. Pressly, *Americans Interpret Their Civil War* (Princeton: Princeton University, 1954). Otis A. Singletary, *The South in American History* (Washington: Service Center for Teachers of History, 1957). Wendell Holmes Stephenson, "Civil War, Cold War, Modern War: Thirty Volumes in Review," *The Journal of Southern History*, 25:287-305; August 1959. Frank E. Vandiver, "The Civil War: Its Theory and Practice," *The Texas Quarterly*, 2:102-108; Summer 1959. For somewhat older historiographical articles on Reconstruction see Howard K. Beale, "On Rewriting Reconstruction History," *The American Historical Review*, 45:807-27; July 1940. T. Harry Williams, "An Analysis of Some Reconstruction Attitudes," *Journal of Southern History*, 12:469-86; November 1946. For a more recent treatment, see Bernard A. Weisberger, "The Dark and Bloody Ground of Reconstruction Historiography," *Journal of Southern History*, 25:427-47; November 1959.

THE WAR

The War has captured the fancy of the American reading public in a way that no other incident in our history ever has. Almost every literate adult entertains what can only be described as positive views on the causes, conduct, and consequences of the conflict and is perfectly willing to express them with feeling if not always with clarity. Civil War Round Tables have been organized in cities throughout the United States, a Civil War Book Club is doing what appears to be a flourishing business and there is, at this writing, at least one scholarly journal devoted exclusively to Civil War topics.[2] Since the end of the Second World War this interest has steadily increased and even if one leaves altogether out of account the third-rate novels, the grade B movies and the insipid distortions that appear on the television screen with such distressing regularity, there yet remains a tremendous body of material that can properly be classified as serious work, ranging anywhere from such scholarly contributions as E. Merton Coulter's bibliography of travellers in the Confederacy to James Street's light, humorous commentary on the war.[3]

There have been general histories, regional histories, military histories, army and unit histories, campaign and battle histories, and even a few naval histories thrown in for good measure. Biographies of almost all major military and civilian leaders and an annoying number of lesser luminaries have been written or rewritten and any editor of a memoir, autobiography, or other contemporary account—regardless of how insignificant the author or how remote his area of operations— has been assured not only of publication but also of a reasonably good sale. And the end is not yet in sight! As we approach the centennial observances, the flood of published works threatens to all but overwhelm the poor reader.

All of which means that there is at least one thing about writings on the Civil War that all parties can agree upon and that is that it is plentiful! As regards quality, however, no such easy agreement is possible. And since any attempt to evaluate this voluminous mass of printed matter is by its very nature a hazardous undertaking, it should be understood that the following statements are offered not as final

---

[2] *Civil War History* published by the State University of Iowa.

[3] Ellis Merton Coulter, *Travels in the Confederate States: A Bibliography* (Norman: University of Oklahoma, 1948); James Howell Street, *The Civil War: An Unvarnished Account of the Late but Still Lively Hostilities* (New York: Dial, 1953).

judgments but as tentative conclusions—they are simply what appear at this particular time to this particular writer to be defensible generalizations.

1. A surprising amount of recent Civil War history is extremely well written. This literary quality is, perhaps, due in large measure to the fact that much of it has been written by other than trained historians. Journalists such as Bruce Catton and Burke Davis, novelists of the caliber of Clifford Dowdey and Shelby Foote, and poets of the stature of Carl Sandburg and Allen Tate have written about the war with an elegance of style that has appealed to a wider audience than academic historians normally reach. The fact that creditable works have been authored by a mathematician, a railroad executive, a tax consultant, and a professional soldier is further proof that the Civil War has not been the private preserve of the history professors.

2. The "You are there" approach has been tremendously popular. There is *A Confederate Reader* and *A Union Reader* and that old standby *Battles and Leaders* has been reissued in abbreviated form.[4] H. S. Commager's *The Blue and the Gray* is only one of a number of works that tell the story of the war as seen through the eyes of actual participants.[5] Anyone who cares to can lay hands on a volume describing life in the Twentieth Maine or in "Company Aytch" or can compare the recorded experiences of Private Elisha Stockwell of Wisconsin with those of Private John Allen of Mississippi. The ladies of the Confederacy were inveterate diarists and a number of their works, ranging from the highly emotional anti-Yankee denunciations of Kate Stone to the temperate persuasions of Mary B. M. Blackford, the confirmed Unionist from Virginia whose five sons all fought for the Confederacy, have found their way into print.[6]

In addition to these contemporary accounts, a growing number of illustrated histories have been published. David Donald, Fletcher Pratt, and Lamont Buchanan have all authored pictorial histories of

---

[4] Richard Barksdale Harwell, ed., *The Confederate Reader* (New York: Longmans, Green, 1957) , and *The Union Reader* (New York: Longmans, Green, 1958); Roy F. Nichols, ed., *Battles and Leaders of the Civil War* (New York: Yoseloff, 1956) .

[5] Indianapolis: Bobbs-Merrill, 1950.

[6] Sarah Katherine (Stone) Holmes, *Brokenburn: The Journal of Kate Stone, 1861-1868*, edited by John Q. Anderson (Baton Rouge: Louisiana State University, 1955) ; Launcelot M. Blackford, *Mine Eyes Have Seen the Glory: The Story of a Virginia Lady* (Cambridge, Mass.: Harvard University, 1954).

the war.[7] Roy Meredith's album of Matthew Brady photographs of President Lincoln's contemporaries and William F. Dawson's *A Civil War Artist at the Front* containing Edwin Forbes' sketches of the Army of the Potomac are also worthy of note in this connection.[8]

3. There has been no lessening of interest in purely military history. The fashionable pacifism of the thirties has apparently not found ready acceptance in the post-World War II era, for the present generation has shown a predilection for reading about armies and battles that would have seemed downright abnormal twenty-five years ago.

A sizable portion of what is being written about the war is military history; some of it is very good military history. Kenneth P. Williams' multi-volume work is an outstanding contribution as is Shelby Foote's first volume tracing the course of the war through the Battle of Perryville.[9] Bruce Catton's trilogy on the Army of the Potomac is an impressive literary effort and Jay Luvaas' edition of the works of the English soldier-historian, G. F. R. Henderson, makes readily available some outstanding military essays.[10]

Campaign histories have also been quite numerous. The firing on Fort Sumter has been described in great detail by both Roy Meredith and W. A. Swanberg and the Battle of Gettysburg was the subject of three full-length volumes in the year 1958 alone. Other specialized campaign accounts include one on the seige and capture of Vicksburg, one on Grierson's daring raid through the heart of the Confederacy, one on Fredericksburg and one on Sherman's operations in the Carolinas. The last days of the war have been minutely reported by Burke Davis and by Philip Van Doren Stern.[11]

[7] David Donald, *Divided We Fought: A Pictorial History of the War, 1861-1865* (New York: Macmillan, 1952); Fletcher Pratt, *Civil War in Pictures* (New York: Holt, 1955) ; Lamont Buchanan, *A Pictorial History of the Confederacy* (New York: Crown, 1951) .

[8] William Forrest Dawson, ed., *A Civil War Artist at the Front: Edwin Forbes' Life Studies of the Great Army* (New York: Oxford University, 1957).

[9] Kenneth P. Williams, *Lincoln Finds a General: A Military Study of the Civil War* (4 vols.; New York: Macmillan, 1949-1956) ; Shelby Foote, *The Civil War* (New York: Random House, 1958) .

[10] Bruce Catton's three volumes are *Mr. Lincoln's Army* (1951) , *Glory Road* (1952), and *A Stillness at Appomattox* (1953), all published at Garden City, New York, by Doubleday. Henderson's essays are entitled *The Civil War: A Soldier's View*, edited by Jay Luvaas (Chicago: University of Chicago, 1958) .

[11] Roy Meredith, *Storm Over Sumter* (New York: Simon and Schuster, 1957) ; W. A. Swanberg, *First Blood: The Story of Fort Sumter* (New York: Scribner, 1957) ; Clifford Dowdey, *Death of a Nation: The Story of Lee and his Men at Gettysburg* (New York: Knopf, 1958) ; Fairfax Downey, *The Guns at Gettysburg*

Biographies of military commanders have been turned out literally by the dozen with, as expected, Lee and Grant running ahead of the pack. Sherman, Thomas and, strangely enough, Ben Butler have each been the subject of two recent biographies; individual volumes have been published on Sheridan, Hooker, McClellan, Reynolds, Sickles, Banks, and even the little-known Quartermaster General of the Union Army, Montgomery C. Meigs. Among Confederate commanders only Jackson and Hood have enjoyed the distinction of having been redone twice. Biographies of other Confederate officers are so numerous as to defy listing.

The war at sea has had its devotees, though not in such numbers as the war on land. There have been two volumes on Lincoln and the Navy, two on the ironclads, and two about the war on western waters. The details of the cruises of the *Alabama, Shenandoah,* and *Sumter* have been painstakingly traced and along with a creditable biography of Stephen Mallory and a monograph on blockade-running, add up to a noteworthy contribution to Confederate naval history.[12]

But the most significant development in the writing of military history has been the increased emphasis upon a hitherto neglected theater of the war, the trans-Mississippi west. Jay Monaghan's account of the war on the western border, Albert Castel's study of Kansas during the war, Ludwell Johnson's volume on the Red River cam-

---

(New York: McKay, 1958); Frank A. Haskell, *The Battle of Gettysburg* (Boston: Houghton Mifflin, 1958); Peter F. Walker, *Vicksburg: A People at War, 1860-1865* (Chapel Hill: University of North Carolina, 1960); Earl Schenck Miers, *The Web of Victory: Grant at Vicksburg* (New York: Knopf, 1955); D. Alexander Brown, *Grierson's Raid* (Urbana: University of Illinois, 1954); Edward J. Stackpole, *Drama on the Rappahannock: The Fredericksburg Campaign* (Harrisburg, Penna.: Military Service Publishing Company, 1957); John G. Barrett, *Sherman's March Through the Carolinas* (Chapel Hill: University of North Carolina, 1956); Burke Davis, *To Appomattox: Nine April Days* (New York: Rinehart, 1959); Philip Van Doren Stern, *An End to Valor: The Last Days of the Civil War* (Boston: Houghton Mifflin, 1958).

[12] See, for example, Richard Sedgewick West, *Mr. Lincoln's Navy* (New York: Longmans, Green, 1957); R. W. Daly, *How the Merrimac Won: The Strategic Story of the C. S. S. Virginia* (New York: Thomas Y. Crowell, 1957); Harpur Allen Gosnell, *Guns on the Western Waters* (Baton Rouge: Louisiana State University, 1949); Edward Carriagton Boykin, *Ghost Ship of the Confederacy: The Story of the Alabama and her Captain, Raphael Semmes* (New York: Funk & Wagnalls, 1957); James David Horan, *Seek Out and Destroy* (New York: Crown, 1958); Harpur Allen Gosnell, ed., *Rebel Raider: Being An Account of Raphael Semmes's Cruise in the C. S. S. Sumter* (Chapel Hill: University of North Carolina, 1948); Joseph Thomas Durkin, *Stephen R. Mallory: Confederate Navy Chief* (Chapel Hill: University of North Carolina, 1954); Hamilton Cochran, *Blockade Runners of the Confederacy* (Indianapolis: Bobbs-Merrill, 1958); Robert Carse, *Blockade: The Civil War at Sea* (New York: Rinehart, 1958).

paign, and Joseph H. Parks' prizewinning biography of Kirby Smith contribute a great deal of information about that area.[13] There are two other works devoted exclusively to guerilla activities in the west and Kate Stone's diary provides an interesting though partisan view of the problems besetting the civilian in the trans-Mississippi theater.

4. The Civil War boom has been accompanied by a fantastic interest in tangential and peripheral subjects. Since 1945 there have been published four different volumes about railroads in the war, seven volumes by or about newspapermen and the war and at least a half-dozen more devoted to cloak-and-dagger types. Even our minority groups have been represented in the publications race; there have been two volumes on the Negro, one on the Catholics and one on American Jewry during the war.[14] There have been volumes on Civil War medicine, Civil War prisons, and the influence of foreigners on the war, and more than one author has shown a preoccupation with the role of "chance" or "coincidence" in the conflict. There have, in addition, been published studies of Confederate finance, Confederate engineers, Confederate doctors, Confederate music, and the Confederate command system.

Nowhere, however, is the interest in secondary influences more clearly reflected than in the attention given to the persons who moved in the shadows of the major figures of the day. Lincoln's law partner, his wife, and his sons have all been immortalized and an account of the trial that led to the commitment of Mary Todd Lincoln to an insane asylum has been published.[15] Jefferson Davis' wife and William Tecumseh Sherman's son have also been singled out for special attention;[16] one prominent publishing house has reportedly received a manuscript about Lee's horse, Traveller.

[13] Jay Monaghan, *Civil War on the Western Border* (Boston: Little, Brown, 1955); Albert Castel, *A Frontier State at War: Kansas, 1861-65* (Ithaca: published for the American Historical Association by Cornell University, 1958); Ludwell H. Johnson, *Red River Campaign: Politics and Cotton in the Civil War* (Baltimore: Johns Hopkins University, 1958); Joseph H. Parks, *General Edmund Kirby Smith, C.S.A.* (Baton Rouge: Louisiana State University, 1954).
[14] Dudley Taylor Cornish, *The Sable Arm: Negro Troops in the Union Army, 1861-1865* (New York: Longmans, Green, 1956); Benjamin Quarles, *The Negro in the Civil War* (Boston: Little, Brown, 1953); Benjamin J. Blied, *Catholics and the Civil War* (Milwaukee, 1945); Bertram W. Korn, *American Jewry and the Civil War* (Philadelphia: Jewish Publication Society of America, 1951).
[15] James A. Rhodes and Dean Jauchius, *The Trial of Mary Todd Lincoln* (Indianapolis: Bobbs-Merrill, 1959).
[16] Ishbel Ross, *First Lady of the South; the Life of Mrs. Jefferson Davis* (New York: Harper, 1958); Joseph Thomas Durkin, *General Sherman's Son* (New York: Farrar, Straus and Cudahy, 1959).

5. There is fairly general agreement about the internal failures (as distinct from the tremendous pressures that were being applied externally by a powerful adversary) that contributed to a weakening of, and eventually to the defeat of the Confederacy. The failure to mobilize the total resources of the new nation or to maintain a sufficiently high morale on the home front, both resulting from ineffective administration are emphasized by Clement Eaton and E. Merton Coulter.[17] Frank Vandiver has examined the Confederate command system and found it sadly lacking.[18] According to Vandiver, the South's failure to work out an effective system was rooted in the section's traditions. Stubbornly clinging to States Rights theories and insisting upon decentralization in government, the South unwittingly helped to throttle its own cause. Centralization of power is an unavoidable necessity in the waging of modern war and the unwillingness of the Confederacy to yield on this issue made defeat all the more certain. The monumental problems that beset an agrarian nation engaged in the desperate business of trying to fight a modern, industrial war is a theme that is also dealt with by Clifford Dowdey.[19]

6. The Lincoln myth not only survives, it grows. Its tenacity has resulted at least partially from the fact that Mr. Lincoln has been accorded a unique and seemingly impregnable position by students of the period. No other character in our history has been so fortunate as he in having the historians work out a neat formula ("Everything he did was subordinated to his paramount objective—to preserve the Union") that explains away all the contradictions and inconsistencies of his career.

In recent times, the myth has been bolstered by such works as Richard Current's *The Lincoln Nobody Knows*[20] and by the assorted volumes that have been written about his private secretary, his cabinet officials, his generals, his admirals, his navy, his conduct under enemy fire, and his dealings with such various individuals and groups as Anna Ella Carroll, the war governors and, of all people, the Russians.

---

[17] Clement Eaton, *A History of the Southern Confederacy* (New York: Macmillan, 1954) ; E. Merton Coulter, *The Confederate States of America, 1861-1865* (Baton Rouge: Louisiana State University, 1950).

[18] Frank Vandiver, *Rebel Brass: The Confederate Command System* (Baton Rouge: Louisiana State University, 1956).

[19] Clifford Dowdey, *Experiment in Rebellion* (Garden City, N. Y.: Doubleday, 1946) ; *The Land They Fought For: The Story of the South as the Confederacy, 1832-1865* (Garden City, N. Y.: Doubleday, 1955) (Mainstream of America Series).

[20] New York: McGraw-Hill, 1958.

Some of this material is quite good; some of it is hardly worth the paper it is written on.

Among the works on the wartime leader that deserve special mention are James G. Randall's impressive account of the presidential years and Carl Sandburg's fascinating portrait of the man.[21] The one volume biography by Benjamin P. Thomas is a solid piece of work as is T. Harry Williams' study of Lincoln the Commander-in-Chief.[22] The total effect of this Lincoln literature has been to strengthen the man's position as the dominant personality of the period.

7. There is a perceptible strain of nationalism in the recent literature on the Civil War. A few persons, E. Merton Coulter and Clifford Dowdey come immediately to mind, still write from a distinctly sectional point of view but they are swimming against the tide. This current trend is in all probability a reflection of the age in which we live, an age wherein all other activities are to some degree influenced by the Cold War and the conflicting ideologies behind that war, an age in which the overriding need for unity has generated a pressure to minimize the things that divide us now or have done so in the past.

In this nationalist-oriented reinterpretation, Grant has fared handsomely. Bruce Catton has written lyrically of the general's "deep instinct for democracy" and Earl Schenk Miers has labored valiantly to put to rest the traditional view of Grant as a dull plodder who overwhelmed his opponents by sheer force.[23] Simultaneously, efforts have been made to cut Lee down to size. "Humanizing" biographers have attempted to penetrate the myth and reduce Lee to flesh and blood terms and there has been at least one frontal assault on the Confederate commander's reputation. General J. F. C. Fuller, in his evaluation of the generalship of the two men, declares forthrightly in favor of Grant.[24]

[21] James G. Randall, *Lincoln, the President* (4 vols.; New York: Dodd, Mead, 1945-1955). Volume four completed by Richard N. Current. Carl Sandburg, *Abraham Lincoln: The Prairie Years and the War Years* (New York: Harcourt, Brace, 1954).

[22] Benjamin P. Thomas, *Abraham Lincoln: A Biography* (New York: Knopf, 1952); Thomas Harry Williams, *Lincoln and His Generals* (New York: Knopf, 1952).

[23] Bruce Catton, *U. S. Grant and the American Military Tradition* (Boston: Little, Brown, 1954); Bruce Catton, *Grant Moves South* (Boston: Little, Brown, 1960); Earl Schenk Miers, *The Web of Victory: Grant at Vicksburg* (New York: Knopf, 1955).

[24] John Frederick Charles Fuller, *Grant and Lee* (Bloomington, Indiana: Indiana University, 1957).

What is happening to Lee has already happened to his civilian counterpart Jefferson Davis to such a degree that he might justly be called the Forgotten Man in American history. Davis committed not one but two Great American Sins: he tried to destroy the Union and he lost a war. Such a record would alone have made it difficult to salvage much of a reputation for him; being forced by circumstances to live in the glare of Lincoln's success story has made it impossible. Rembert Patrick sketched a balanced and in some ways sympathetic portrait of Davis but he stands practically alone in this respect.[25] The characterization of Davis as a quarrelsome, meddlesome, domineering, obstinate, unyielding tyrant seems to be firmly fixed and nothing less than a first-rate biography of the Confederate president is likely to alter it. Volume two of Hudson Strode's life of Davis could turn out to be a first step in that direction.[26]

8. Civil War historians are beginning to show an increasing interest in interpretation. Overwhelmed by the endless outpourings of Civil War literature, some are beginning to wonder if there is really anything left to say. More than one historian has asked the question (even though in private) if it is not high time we de-emphasized the amassing of progressively less significant material and channeled our energies into the admittedly more difficult business of trying to interpret and understand what we already know.

This search for meaning has already produced some results. Earl Schenck Miers, for example, has devoted a volume to theorizing about the impact of the war on the American conscience and David Donald, in a stimulating collection of essays, asks some serious new questions about some old dogmas.[27] It is not inconceivable that it will be in this very area, in the search for the ultimate meaning of the war in the American experience, that the most significant contribution is yet to be made.

However, it should be noted that, as of 1961, one of the most detailed surveys of the United States during the Civil War, spiced with sharp interpretations, was still in the process of being written.

---

[25] Rembert W. Patrick, *Jefferson Davis and His Cabinet* (Baton Rouge: Louisiana State University, 1944).

[26] Hudson Strode, *Jefferson Davis: American Patriot, 1808-1861* (New York: Harcourt, Brace, 1955), *Jefferson Davis: Confederate President* (1959).

[27] Earl Schenck Miers, *The Great Rebellion: The Emergence of the American Conscience* (Cleveland: World, 1958); David Donald, *Lincoln Reconsidered: Essays on the Civil War Era* (New York: Knopf, 1956).

Already having written four volumes of his *The Ordeal of the Union* on the events leading up to the war, Allan Nevins published in 1959 the first volume on the war itself. The scope of this work is more comprehensive than the great series of James Ford Rhodes. In the first volume on the war, Nevins stressed the magnitude of the war, and pointed out that because of its magnitude, the war brought about fundamental changes in American society.[28]

RECONSTRUCTION

In contrast to the vast amount of material on the Civil War, recent publications on the Reconstruction Period seem to be in short supply. Nor is there, in these works, any discernible pattern. Some authors continue to write in the pro-Southern "Dunning school" tradition while others have added refinements to the later "revisionist" approach. An occasional writer even succeeds in keeping a foot in each door. Hodding Carter, for example, in his popularly written general history of the period entitled *The Angry Scar* points up the achievements and reforms that have had lasting value while at the same time attacking the stupidity and sometimes the hypocrisy of the reformers.[29] The author's conclusion that the North remembers the Reconstruction too little and the South remembers it too much seems to be a pertinent message for our own time.

Two fine little books have been published dealing with special aspects of the immediate post-war period. In *Escape From Reconstruction*, William C. Nunn describes the abortive attempt to establish a Confederate colony in Mexico after the war.[30] A number of those who were ill-equipped or otherwise indisposed to adjust to the unpleasant reality of defeat fled the country. The Mexican experiment was short-lived, however, and most of them returned to the United States after a relatively brief stay south of the border. Whatever else this story might mean, it underscores the fact that in spite of the many differences that were supposed to divide them, Northerners and Southerners were more like each other than they were like anyone else in the world. James H. Croushore and David M. Potter, in their ably-edited version of John William De Forest's *A Union Officer in the Reconstruction*, have made readily available the comments of an

[28] Allan Nevins, *The Ordeal of the Union* (Volume V). *The War for the Union*. Volume I, *The Improvised War, 1861-1862* (New York: Scribner, 1959).

[29] Garden City, New York: Doubleday, 1959.

[30] Fort Worth: Leo Potishman Foundation, Texas Christian University, 1956.

officer in the Freedmen's Bureau who was, in addition to being a keen observer, a professional writer.[31]

A number of biographies of characters who played important roles during the years from 1865 to 1877 have also appeared. Manly Wade Wellman's work on Wade Hampton, Thomas R. Hay's study on Longstreet, Lillian Kibler's volume on the South Carolina Unionist, Benjamin F. Perry, and Joseph F. Wall's life of the tempestuous editor of the Louisville Courier-Journal, Henry Watterson, deserve special mention.[32] Our focus on familiar figures of the period has been sharpened by the publication of works such as Robert S. Holzman's volume on that genial scamp Ben Butler and Ralph Korngold's persuasave defense of Thaddeus Stevens. Andrew Johnson has been the subject of a significant revisionist study by Eric L. McKitrick. McKitrick, although not unsympathetic to the President, concluded that his stubborness and lack of understanding contributed substantially to the failure of Radical Reconstruction. A fresh new character is introduced as the "Prince of Carpetbaggers" in Jonathan Daniels' story of the clever rascal, Milton S. Littlefield, who successfully teamed up with the local folk to become an important figure in North Carolina during Reconstruction.[33]

Perhaps the most significant contribution of recent historians of the post-war period has been made by the handful of scholars who have broken new ground. Frank W. Klingberg, for example, has unearthed some interesting information about claims made by Southern Unionists against the federal government and Harold M. Hyman has looked carefully into the uses of the "loyalty oath" in the Reconstruction process.[34] Jonathan T. Dorris' definitive study of pardon and

[31] New Haven: Yale University, 1948.

[32] Manly Wade Wellman, Giant in Gray: A Biography of Wade Hampton of South Carolina (New York: Scribner, 1949); Donald Bridgman Sanger and Thomas Robson Hay, James Longstreet: Soldier, Politician, Officeholder, and Writer (Baton Rouge: Louisiana State University, 1952); Lillian A. Kibler, Benjamin F. Perry: South Carolina Unionist (Durham, N. C.: Duke University, 1946); Joseph F. Wall, Henry Watterson: Reconstructed Rebel (New York: Oxford University, 1956).

[33] Robert S. Holzman, Stormy Ben Butler (New York: Macmillan, 1954); Ralph Korngold, Thaddeus Stevens: A Being Darkly Wise and Rudely Great (New York: Harcourt, Brace, 1955); Eric L. McKitrick, Andrew Johnson and Reconstruction (Chicago: University of Chicago, 1960); Jonathan Daniels, Prince of Carpetbaggars (Philadelphia: Lippincott, 1958).

[34] Frank W. Klingberg, The Southern Claims Commission (Berkeley: University of California, 1955); Harold M. Hyman, Era of the Oath: Northern Loyalty Tests during the Civil War and Reconstruction (Philadelphia: University of Pennsylvania, 1954).

amnesty under Lincoln and his successor and Joseph B. James' analysis of the factors influencing the framing of the Fourteenth Amendment are both interesting and informative works.[35] Three other noteworthy special studies are George R. Woolfolk's description of the activities and influence of the Northern merchant class, Mary R. Dearing's analysis of the political role of the veterans and Ralph Morrow's account of the attempt by Northern Methodists to recast their Southern brethren in a mold suspiciously resembling their own image.[36]

The effect of Reconstruction upon the Negro and of the Negro upon Reconstruction has been the subject of several recent books. In *The Negro Freedman*, Henderson H. Donald describes the Negro's early attempts to adjust to emancipation and George R. Bentley's history of the Freedmen's Bureau spells out in detail the activities of the agency most directly concerned with facilitating that adjustment.[37] Vernon Wharton's excellent monograph on the Negro in Mississippi and Hampton Jarrell's volume on Wade Hampton's dealings with the Negro in South Carolina are significant additions to the growing list of state studies on the Negro.[38] Otis A. Singletary's volume on the Negro militia movement during Reconstruction is an attempt to identify one of the sources of the racial violence that scarred the period.[39]

One of the really important books on Reconstruction to appear within the last decade is C. Vann Woodward's *Reunion and Reaction*.[40] In this revision of the traditional view about the Compromise

[35] Jonathan T. Dorris, *Pardon and Amnesty under Lincoln and Johnson: The Restoration of the Confederates to their Rights and Privileges, 1861-1898* (Chapel Hill: University of North Carolina, 1953); Joseph B. James, *The Framing of the Fourteenth Amendment* (Urbana: University of Illinois, 1956).

[36] George R. Woolfolk, *The Cotton Regency: The Northern Merchants and Reconstruction, 1865-1880* (New York: Bookman Associates, 1958); Mary R. Dearing, *Veterans in Politics: The Story of the G.A.R.* (Baton Rouge: Louisiana State University, 1952); Ralph E. Morrow, *Northern Methodism and Reconstruction* (East Lansing: Michigan State University, 1956).

[37] Henderson H. Donald, *The Negro Freedman: Life Conditions of the American Negro in the Early Years After Emancipation* (New York: H. Schuman, 1952); George R. Bentley, *A History of the Freedmen's Bureau* (Philadelphia: University of Pennsylvania, 1955).

[38] Vernon L. Wharton, *The Negro in Mississippi, 1865-1890* (Chapel Hill: University of North Carolina, 1947); Hampton M. Jarrell, *Wade Hampton and the Negro: The Road Not Taken* (Columbia, S. C.: University of South Carolina, 1949).

[39] Otis A. Singletary, *Negro Militia and Reconstruction* (Austin: University of Texas, 1957).

[40] Boston: Little, Brown, 1951.

of 1877 and the end of the Reconstruction experiment, Woodward argues that the real bargain was an economic rather than a political one and that it was engineered by a group of ex-Whigs-become-Southern-Democrats who were primarily interested in building railroads and in sharing the bounty of the federal government.

It may well be that the flood of printed matter will diminish in the wake of the oncoming Centennial celebration but it is hardly likely that the period between the inauguration of Lincoln and the inauguration of Hayes will cease to be a primary concern of American historians. This is true because of the intrinsic significance of the era. It is significant, first of all, because of the momentous events it encompassed: the traumatic experience of war, the baffling period of readjustment that followed the war and the remarkably rapid transformation of an essentially agrarian society into what we have come to know as modern, industrial America. It is significant, furthermore, because of its consequences—for out of those years of war and reconstruction arose many of the problems that continue to perplex us in mid-twentieth century America.

CHAPTER IX

Intellectual History to 1900

Arthur Bestor

INTRODUCTION

MAN is a thinking animal. Obviously, however, his thinking is often far from clear or rational. His conduct, moreover, is rarely in complete accord with what he professes his ideas to be. Man is capable of thought, but he is also capable of acting without thought, and even in defiance of thought.

This being so, what is the historian to make of ideas? Is he to take them seriously and try to explain history as partly the consequence of men's thoughts and beliefs? If so, he runs the risk of picturing mankind as more rational than experience shows it to be. Should, then, the historian admit that thought is too feeble a force to affect the course of history, and look elsewhere for causes and explanations? If so, he leaves out of human history the one element that is distinctively human—the power to manage a train of thought, which no beast can do.

Faced by this dilemma, scholars who study intellectual history have made their choice. They are committed, perforce, to the view that ideas do play a role in history. In defending this position, however, they are resisting a current that has flowed strongly in the opposite direction for at least a century. Ever since historians became interested in the economic forces that operate within history, they have grown increasingly skeptical of explanations that assign to ideas a causative role. This skepticism has been a healthy thing for intellectual history. Scholars have had to examine with care their assumptions and their logic. They have purged their pages of loose statements about ideas, such as abounded in earlier historical writings. A present-day intellectual historian is as unlikely to write about disembodied ideas, possessed of a mysterious power to "realize" themselves in historical events, as he is to write about family ghosts and haunted castles.

Intellectual history, like everything else, has a history of its own. And to comprehend what intellectual historians are doing today—

hence to grasp the best way of using their findings—one needs to know something about the way the discipline has developed.

The Problem of Historical Causation

Intellectual history may be new in name and new in certain of its techniques of investigation, but the questions with which it deals are old. Thoughtful men have always asked how—or, more skeptically, whether—ideas affect the course of history. In most ages, however, historians were content to leave this question to philosophers. They took for granted some connection between ideas and events, but they rarely bothered to examine, critically and logically, the nature of the connection. Instead, historians typically concealed the problem by wrapping it up in metaphors. George Bancroft, for example, had much to say about "the idea of freedom," when, in 1858, he wrote about the American Revolution. The "growing energy" of that particular idea, he insisted, "can be traced in the tendency of the ages." The Revolution itself "grew naturally and necessarily out of the series of past events by the formative principle of a living belief."[1]

One cannot be sure whether Bancroft intended his words as a serious statement about historical causation, or whether he was simply embellishing his narrative with Fourth-of-July rhetoric. Be that as it may, his sentences, if taken literally, went far beyond the simple assertion that ideas are historical facts. Bancroft was ascribing to ideas a trans-historical reality. Not only were they said to exist above history and outside it, but they were also supposed to be capable of influencing events directly, by means that lay beyond the reach of historical investigation.

Such a view of the nature and power of ideas may not have been held, in logical completeness, by George Bancroft. It was, however, propounded as the ultimate truth of the matter by the most influential philosopher of the generation preceding Bancroft's, namely Georg Wilhelm Friedrich Hegel. Ever since the time of Plato, of course, philosophers of one stamp of mind have ascribed to ideas a reality superior to that possessed by material objects. Though philosophical idealism of this sort has occasionally colored the thinking of historians, it remained for Hegel to erect the doctrine into a completely thought-out philosophy of history.

"Reason," wrote Hegel, "governs the world, and has consequently governed its history." In other words, "the History of the World

---

[1] George Bancroft, *History of the United States*, vol. VII (Boston: Little, Brown, 1858) , p. 22-23.

begins with its general aim," which is "the realization of the Idea of Spirit." At the outset, of course, this aim is "hidden," "unconscious," "implicit." But as events unfold, one sees clearly that "the whole process of History . . . is directed to rendering this unconscious impulse a conscious one."[2] Hegel, be it observed, was not making the commonplace observation that men often try to put into practice a body of ideas which they have consciously accepted. Hegel was saying much more than this. He was arguing that men, through their actions, are engaged in making effective a body of ideas of which they are totally unaware. Especially is this true of "World-Historical Individuals." Such "Heroes," Hegel taught, act not only for conscious reasons but also and at the same time from an "unconscious impulse," which the philosopher is bound to recognize (given the advantage of hindsight) as nothing more nor less than "the will of the World-Spirit."[3]

Though Hegelianism dominated many fields of thought during the first half of the nineteenth century, history was relatively immune to its influence. To most historians, indeed, Hegel's philosophy of history seemed a *reductio ad absurdum,* and they accordingly rejected the premise—philosophical idealism—on which it was based. The history of ideas almost became a casualty of this reaction, for the very word *idea* took on Hegelian overtones that aroused instant suspicion. Hegel had made ideas all-powerful; the natural reaction was to deny to ideas any influence whatever upon the history of the workaday world.

The opposing position was stated in its most extreme form by Karl Marx, whose own creed of dialectical materialism was (as someone has said) "Hegelianism turned upside down." Material forces, according to Hegel, obey the command of ideas. Not so, said Marx; material forces bring ideas into existence and hence do not obey, but instead command, the processes of the mind. "Men's conceptions, thoughts, spiritual intercourse," asserted Marx, are "the direct emanation of their material conduct." Alterations in methods of production oblige men to alter their methods of thought. "It is not consciousness that determines life, but life that determines consciousness."[4]

Nineteenth century historians might not accept materialism so unreservedly and dogmatically as Marx, but most of them leaned more

---

[2] G. W. F. Hegel (1770-1831), "Introduction to the Philosophy of History" (posthumously published in 1837), trans., J. Sibree, in *Hegel: Selections,* ed., J. Loewenberg (New York: Scribner, 1929), p. 369-70.

[3] *Ibid.,* p. 375-76.

[4] Karl Marx (1818-1883), "The German Ideology" (written 1845-46; posthumously published), trans., Max Eastman in his edition, *Capital, the Communist Manifesto, and Other Writings by Karl Marx* (New York: Modern Library, 1932), p. 9-10.

or less strongly toward it. In their opinion, ideas were usually out-and-out rationalizations, adopted by men and women not to reveal but to disguise (even from themselves) the real motives behind their acts. To the degree that this is true, historians are simply wasting their time when they examine ideas; their proper task is to cut a clean path through ideas, as one would through a thicket of brambles.

Hacking their way through ideas, historians did come upon and exploit many historical causes and forces that had been hidden under a too-luxuriant foliage of words and abstractions. They called attention to innumerable incidents in which more tangible motives to action could be found than the ideological reasons professed by participants. They wrote an exciting brand of history, stimulating in its iconoclasm and immensely suggestive in its indication of new ways to analyze old situations.

Particularly influential were the historians who found the key to events in economic motives and concerns. Undertaking *An Economic Interpretation of the Constitution of the United States,* for example, Charles A. Beard examined the proceedings of the Federal Convention of 1787 in terms not of the political philosophy of the delegates but of their economic interests and attitudes.[5] Another school of interpreters insisted that economic phenomena are themselves determined by even more primordial forces: physiography, climate, and the natural environment generally. The so-called "frontier" interpretation of American history—propounded as an hypothesis by Frederick Jackson Turner but converted into a dogma by some of his followers—amounted, in the last analysis, to the contention that ideas were less powerful than the physical environment in shaping American institutions. "From the conditions of frontier life," concluded Turner in his original paper on the subject, "came intellectual traits of profound importance. . . . These traits have, while softening down, still persisted as survivals in the place of their origin, even when a higher social organization succeeded. The result is that to the frontier the American intellect owes its striking characteristics."[6]

---

[5] Charles A. Beard (1874-1948), *An Economic Interpretation of the Constitution* (New York: Macmillan, 1913). Recent studies have dealt harshly with Beard's thesis, notably: Robert E. Brown, *Charles Beard and the Constitution* (Princeton: Princeton University, 1956), and Forrest McDonald, *We the People: The Economic Origins of the Constitution* (Chicago: University of Chicago, 1958).

[6] Frederick Jackson Turner (1861-1932), "The Significance of the Frontier in American History" (1893), reprinted in George R. Taylor, ed., *The Turner Thesis* (Boston: Heath, 1949), p. 17. The collection cited includes scholarly comments, favorable and unfavorable, on Turner's seminal interpretation.

THE ROLE OF IDEAS

The belief that the "hard facts" of history are to be sought among economic and geographical phenomena is a useful corrective to the view that ideas are transcendent forces resistlessly shaping history. Skepticism is the proper attitude to maintain in the face of extravagant assertions about the primacy of ideas in history. Skepticism is likewise the proper attitude to maintain in the face of extravagant assertions about the primacy of material forces. Under careful scrutiny the "hard facts" of history lose their hardness. Forces may appear to be materialistic, but when they begin to operate in history they are found to be interpenetrated by ideas. To speak of an *economic interest* is to speak not only of something that is economic (and hence in a sense materialistic), but also of something that is an interest (and hence something that exists only in men's minds).

To defend the validity of intellectual history it is only necessary to point out that political parties, business corporations, and the like— the reality of whose influence on history no one dreams of denying— are no more "real" than ideas, if "reality" is supposed to inhere only in tangible physical objects. What is it that entitles us to speak of an aggregation of men and women not as a mere aggregation but as a political party or a corporation or a church or a nation? The answer is: *an idea*—either an idea which the persons concerned have been brought up to share, or an idea they have communicated to one another, or an agreement or contract or law (an idea still) in terms of which they have deliberately united for a particular purpose. To dismiss ideas as unreal and hence unsuitable for historical investigation is to dismiss, in the same breath, virtually all the entities that political and economic historians have been accustomed to study.

Ideas are neither all-powerful nor completely powerless—this is the conclusion to which common sense comes and which present-day intellectual history accepts. To put the matter somewhat differently, so far as history is concerned, ideas are neither above comprehension nor beneath contempt. They are facts to be studied like other historical facts.

The only assumption that the intellectual historian makes is that ideas have consequences in the realm of practical affairs. Ideas are influenced by their historical context and they are, in turn, capable of making a measurable impact upon history. In other words, ideas are historical forces, constantly interacting with other historical forces, in ways that are as open to historical investigation as any other historical phenomena. Such a view imposes an inescapable obligation. By insisting that ideas are *historical* realities, the intellectual historian surrenders the right to treat them as *transcendental* forces, capable of influencing events by means that are hidden and mysterious. The intellectual historian today considers himself bound to examine the impact of an idea upon history in precisely the way that he would examine the impact of any other force, that is to say, in terms of evidence, assessed by critical procedures identical with those used to establish other historical relationships.

Intellectual history, to put the matter briefly, is a branch of history, not a branch of metaphysics.

INTELLECTUAL HISTORY: A DEFINITION

From one point of view, intellectual history is the newest of the fields of history. The phrase is only beginning to appear in the titles of college courses and among the subdivisions of classified bibliographies. Until recently, intellectual history was merely one element in a great miscellany—one tile in a great mosaic—variously described as cultural history, or social history, or the history of civilization. Under the last of these labels the historian G. P. Gooch was able, as late as 1913, to lump together all the approaches to history that diverged from the prevailing political one. In Gooch's magisterial survey of nineteenth century scholarship, economic history and intellectual history (which differ from one another as profoundly as either from political history) found themselves bedfellows, even within the compass of a single paragraph.[7]

A classification that so signally failed to classify could not remain acceptable for long. In an archetype of the present volume, published in 1946, J. Montgomery Gambrill lamented the fact that the term *social history* was already a catch-all, and he did his best to prevent the term *cultural history* from becoming one also. In employing the latter phrase as the title of his chapter, he was careful to limit its scope to "the intellectual and esthetic interests and activities of a people."[8] The dilution of meaning that Gambrill feared was some-

---

[7] George P. Gooch, *History and Historians in the Nineteenth Century* (London: Longmans, Green, 1913), chapter 28, "The History of Civilisation," p. 573-94. A single paragraph on p. 584-85 manages to encompass W. E. H. Lecky's *History of European Morals* and William Cunningham's *Growth of English Industry and Commerce.*

[8] J. Montgomery Gambrill, "Cultural History," in *The Study and Teaching of American History*, ed., Richard E. Thursfield (National Council for the Social Studies, *Seventeenth Yearbook, 1946*; Washington, 1947), p. 156.

thing that could not be checked, and today *intellectual history* is the preferred term for the subject that he discussed—preferred because it is more definite and also because it is less likely to be used as the label for a mere collection of odds and ends.

Intellectual history, to frame a rough-and-ready definition, concerns itself with ideas and their relationship to events. Different historians, of course, give differing emphases to the several elements in this definition. Some are interested mainly in ideas, others mainly in events, and still others mainly in the mechanisms linking the two—that is, the channels through which ideas flow and the agencies by which intellectual effort is fostered. A glance at the work of a few representative writers will illustrate the various approaches that can be made to intellectual history, and the special value of each approach.

CONTRIBUTIONS OF HISTORIANS AND PHILOSOPHERS

Intellectual history obviously lies in the frontier zone where several scholarly fields overlap. It belongs in part to the discipline of history, as its very name makes clear. It also belongs to the discipline of philosophy, for the analysis of ideas has always been the peculiar concern of philosophers. The most effective transmission of ideas probably occurs through literature (if that word is used in its broadest sense), hence students of literature have been equal partners in the enterprise of intellectual history. Scholars in many other fields—scientists concerned with the history of their own fields, sociologists and social psychologists, lawyers and political scientists, art historians, theologians—have all made important contributions. Nevertheless, it is probably fair to say that intellectual history at present is primarily a synthesis of work done by philosophers, specialists in literature, and historians.

In examining mankind and the thoughts of mankind, each of these disciplines takes its start from a different point. They complement one another in highly significant ways, and enrich intellectual history by reason of the differing points of view which they bring to it.

The tradition of history is to look at events. The historian, accordingly, tends to work back from actual happenings to the ideas that influenced them. He finds, as a rule, that the most direct and immediate impact upon events is made not by the great systematic thinkers, concerned with abstract ideas and logical distinctions, but by popularizers and intermediaries—journalists, politicians, and authors of widely-circulated handbooks or widely-read novels. The first step of the historian into the realm of ideas is therefore likely to be an examination of the intellectual content of Congressional debates, of newspaper editorials, of pamphlets, and of popular literature generally, from almanacs to dime novels.

The great contribution of the historian to intellectual history is a sense of immediacy. In his work one sees ideas actually at work, infusing themselves into practical affairs and shaping by direct contact the course of events.

This particular approach to intellectual history finds admirable embodiment in Merle Curti's Growth of American Thought, awarded the Pulitzer Prize on its first appearance. The kind of question that particularly interests Curti is indicated by the titles of the five chapters that together cover the later nineteenth century: "The Delimitation of Supernaturalism," "Evolutionary Thought in a Utilitarian Society," "Professionalization and Popularization of Learning," "Formulas of Protest and Reform," and "The Conservative Defense."[9] Throughout these chapters runs the theme of rapidly developing scientific thought, particularly the evolutionary thought stemming from the work of Charles Darwin. Scientific theory, however, is examined not in its own terms but in terms of its interaction with economic activity and religious life, in terms of the agencies of intellectual life (universities, periodicals, the Chautauqua movement, and the like) through which it was transmitted and diffused, and in terms of the social implications that reformers and conservatives discovered in it. In his preface Curti describes the work as "a social history of American thought." It does not, he says, "purport to provide an exhaustive analysis of the 'interiors' of the ideas and systems of thought chosen for consideration."[10]

Now the "interiors" of ideas—that is to say, their precise content and their logical structure—are of prime concern to the discipline of philosophy. To intellectual history philosophers make an invaluable contribution precisely because they tackle its problems from the other end. Like the historians, they must look carefully at the popularizers who translate philosophical ideas into public opinion. By reason of their training, however, they are better equipped than most historians to understand what actually goes on in the process of popularization. Often an idea is all but completely transformed by the time it enters the consciousness of the general public. Some of its original implications may be over-emphasized, while others

[9] Merle Curti, The Growth of American Thought (2nd ed.; New York: Harper, 1951), chapters 21-25, constituting Part VI of the book.
[10] Ibid., p. vi.

are completely forgotten. Significant logical distinctions may be ignored and confused. False analogies may be drawn. To all these modifications and distortions of ideas philosophers are professionally sensitized, and their critical analyses have clarified intellectual history and strengthened its foundations.

The kind of contribution that philosophy can make is exemplified by Herbert W. Schneider's excellent *History of American Philosophy*. The book gives full attention to the work of professional philosophers, but its range is far wider than that. The author's conviction, firmly stated in his preface, is that "political, economic, theological, and metaphysical principles have been more closely associated in American thought than we have hitherto been led to believe."[11] The difference between his approach and Curti's becomes clear if we compare the five chapters in which he (like Curti) discusses the thought of the late nineteenth century. These chapters are grouped under the general heading "Evolution and Human Progress," and they discuss the impact of Darwinian ideas upon, successively, professional philosophers, biologists, theologians, social scientists, and (finally) those who were developing, in the broadest sense, a new world-outlook—one that Schneider calls "Desperate Naturalism."[12]

The currents of thought circulating through the United States during the later nineteenth century are the common concern of both authors. In Curti we see how these currents affected a multitude of institutions and activities. In Schneider we see how they flowed together to create a pervasive "climate of opinion."

A strikingly different approach to intellectual history is exemplified by the work of the philosopher Arthur O. Lovejoy. To characterize his method of study he always used the term "history of ideas," ascribing to the phrase a very precise meaning, and carefully distinguishing it from the history of philosophy. "The total body of doctrine of any philosopher or school," he wrote, "is almost always a complex and heterogeneous aggregate." The historian of ideas "cuts into the hard-and-fast individual systems and . . . breaks them up into their component elements, into what may be called their unit-ideas." The purpose of doing so is to enable the historian to trace the unit-idea "through more than one—ultimately, indeed, through all—of the provinces of history in which it figures in any important degree, whether those provinces are called philosophy,

---

[11] Herbert W. Schneider, *A History of American Philosophy* (New York: Columbia University, 1946), p. x.

[12] *Ibid.*, chapters 30-34, constituting Part VI.

science, literature, art, religion, or politics."[13] In Lovejoy's most famous book, *The Great Chain of Being,* he takes from Plato the "unit-idea" that the universe is composed of an immense number of beings ranging by infinitesimal gradations from the very lowest to the very highest, and traces the ramifications of this idea of an unbroken "Great Chain of Being" throughout the subsequent thought of the entire Western World, showing how, on the one hand, it finds expression in literature, and, on another hand, provides a controlling assumption for scientific theory.

The "history of ideas," as Lovejoy conceived it, must necessarily overleap the frontiers of nations as it overleaps the boundaries separating the various fields of knowledge. Accordingly, no writing of his can be pinned down within the confines of *American* intellectual history. Nevertheless, many of his articles—including, but not limited to, those collected as *Essays in the History of Ideas*[14]—have a most direct bearing upon the intellectual history of the United States. Not only do they reveal the connections between American thought and the thought of the rest of the world, but they also lay bare the inner nature of many ideas whose implications never fully appear when viewed within a merely national frame.

CONTRIBUTION OF STUDENTS OF LITERATURE

Students of literature have contributed the third major element to modern intellectual history. Literary criticism has, as a general rule, bestowed attention upon the biographical and historical background of a given literary work and upon its philosophical content. The affiliation of literature with intellectual history is thus natural and obvious. But does literary criticism have a distinctive contribution of its own to make? The question calls for a brief discussion.

According to the apostles of the "new criticism," many students of literature have been nothing but historians or philosophers. By devoting themselves to intellectual history, runs the charge, they have abandoned literary criticism entirely. Without taking too exposed a position on this shell-torn battlefield, a mere historian may at least agree with the "new critics" that literary criticism has distinctive tasks to perform that belong to the domain neither of history nor of philosophy. To describe this task as the analysis of form

---

[13] Arthur O. Lovejoy, *The Great Chain of Being: A Study of the History of an Idea* (Cambridge: Harvard University, 1936), p. 3, 15.

[14] Arthur O. Lovejoy, *Essays in the History of Ideas* (Baltimore: Johns Hopkins, 1948). A full bibliography of Lovejoy's writings occupies p. 339-44.

and imagery is to give a definition that is doubtless inadequate but that at least points in the proper direction. "Symbol," "myth," and "irony" are vital words in the vocabulary of criticism. Though they may be transferred to history and philosophy, they hardly belong to the native language of the latter fields. Conversely, philosophical propositions and historical documents can be freely paraphrased, yet Cleanth Brooks argues with great cogency that the ultimate sin against criticism is "the heresy of paraphrase." "Unless one asserts the primacy of the pattern," he writes, "a poem becomes merely a bouquet of intrinsically beautiful items."[15]

The critic's interest in the relationship of an image to the thing for which it stands, his realization that symbols can have a life of their own, his preoccupation with patterns and the way in which they control not merely the form but even the very content of thought—these critical perceptions have begun to have a profound effect upon intellectual history.

To understand the distinctive character of this contribution one cannot do better than turn to Henry Nash Smith's brilliant interpretive study, *Virgin Land*. Its sub-title, *The American West As Symbol and Myth*, is elucidated in the preface. "Myth" and "symbol," the author explains, are essentially synonymous, save that the first is a larger unit than the second. Each term designates "an intellectual construction that fuses concept and emotion into an image." Whether or not such images "accurately reflect empirical fact," they exist, they persist, and, most significantly of all, "they sometimes exert a decided influence on practical affairs."[16]

Henry Nash Smith's book itself is a closely-knit series of illustrations of the latter point. The final section shows, with a wealth of detail, how "the image of an agricultural paradise in the West, embodying group memories of an earlier, a simpler, and, it was believed, a happier state of society, long survived as a force in American thought and politics."[17] So strong was the image that it caused contemporaries to overlook what was happening under their very eyes—the rapid industrialization and urbanization of the West.[18] And it stood in the way of a rational revision of policies that had failed to work,

---

[15] Cleanth Brooks, *The Well Wrought Urn* (New York: Reynal & Hitchcock, 1947), p. 178.

[16] Henry Nash Smith, *Virgin Land: The American West. As Symbol and Myth* (Cambridge: Harvard University, 1950), p. vii.

[17] *Ibid.*, p. 124.

[18] *Ibid.*, p. 159.

such as the homestead system. The crust of a cherished tradition, Smith's study would indicate, is often harder than the "hard facts" of geography and economics. Images can survive in "increasing irrelevance to the facts,"[19] resisting and deflecting forces that some historians have considered indomitable.

PANORAMIC HISTORIES OF AMERICAN THOUGHT

The contributions of these distinctive fields combine to give intellectual history its three-dimensional solidity. Differences in approach were deliberately emphasized in choosing the books already discussed. These contrasts, however, fade into the background as one contemplates the whole field of intellectual history. As participants in a common enterprise, historians produce studies hardly distinguishable from those of philosophers or literary specialists. The methods devised within each field are at the service of all.

Three other historians besides Curti have, in recent years, published full-length histories of American intellectual life. The first of these, Ralph H. Gabriel's *The Course of American Democratic Thought,* has a somewhat closer kinship with the writings of literary scholars than with the work of Curti, including, as it does, separate chapters on Emerson and Thoreau, Melville, and Whitman. Gabriel's primary aim, however, is to describe "climates of opinion," and he does so with even greater directness than Schneider. To note but a single chapter, Gabriel describes, more perceptively than any other historian, the way various intellectual traditions combined to create, during the later nineteenth century, what he calls "The Gospel of Wealth of the Gilded Age."[20]

Stow Persons, in his recent volume entitled *American Minds,* approaches even more closely the tradition of philosophical investigation, with his elaborate analysis of five successive "social minds." This term he defines as "the cluster of ideas and attitudes" that "binds together in an intellectual community those who share its beliefs," and furnishes "a generation of thinkers with a common set of assumptions."[21] In Harvey Wish's two volumes on *Society and Thought in America,* one finds again an approach like Curti's. The sub-title describes the book as being concerned with both social and

---

[19] *Ibid.,* p. 200.

[20] Ralph H. Gabriel, *The Course of American Democratic Thought* (2nd ed.; New York: Ronald, 1956). The chapters mentioned are 4, 6, 11, and 13.

[21] Stow Persons, *American Minds: A History of Ideas* (New York: Holt, 1958), p. vii.

intellectual history, and the author announces his intention of making "broad incursions into economic history."[22]

A dominant tradition of American literary history has been to relate individual writers closely to their geographic, economic, and political backgrounds, and to discuss their works in terms of the ideas contained in them rather more frequently than in terms of purely literary criteria. This was true of Moses Coit Tyler's noted *History of American Literature,* which was, in effect, a pioneer intellectual history of the colonial period.[23] Vernon L. Parrington, in his three-volume *Main Currents in American Thought,* was even more explicit in choosing "to follow the broad path of our political, economic, and social development, rather than the narrower belletristic." His primary concern, he announced, was with "forces that are anterior to literary schools and movements, creating the body of ideas from which literary culture eventually springs." Recognizing that "dead partisanships have a disconcerting way of coming to life again in the pages of their historians," he avowed with refreshing frankness his own point of view: "liberal rather than conservative, Jeffersonian rather than Federalistic."[24]

The great co-operative histories of American literature—most recently the *Literary History of the United States*—continue this tradition of concern for the political, geographical, and economic context. Chapter titles from the last-mentioned work are indicative: "Literary Culture on the Frontier," "The Education of Everyman," "Literature As Business," "Fiction and Social Debate."[25] If co-operative works in literature reflect a concern with history, so co-operative works in history reflect a concern for literature and ideology. Ground was broken by the thirteen-volume *History of American Life,* begun in the late 1920's.[26] Today the New American Nation Series—successor to a great co-operative work of half a century ago—reflects the

[22] Harvey Wish, *Society and Thought in America* (2 vols.; New York: Longmans, Green, 1950-1952), vol. I, p. vii.
[23] Moses Coit Tyler, *A History of American Literature* (2 vols.; New York: Putnam, 1878), vol. I, *1607-1676;* vol. II, *1676-1765.*
[24] Vernon L. Parrington, *Main Currents in American Thought* (3 vols.; New York: Harcourt, Brace, 1927-1930), vol. I, p. iii, i. The third volume was incomplete at the author's death.
[25] *Literary History of the United States,* edited by Robert E. Spiller and others (3 vols.; New York: Macmillan, 1948). The chapters noted are 39, 49, 58, 60. The third volume is devoted entirely to bibliography and is indispensable to the serious student of American intellectual history.
[26] Arthur M. Schlesinger and Dixon Ryan Fox, eds., *A History of American Life* (13 vols.; New York: Macmillan, 1929-1948).

attention given today to the history of ideas as a constituent of general history.[27]

Intellectual history has, of course, many topical subdivisions, because economic thought, science, art, and the like, must often be isolated for systematic historical study. A few books only can be mentioned. Joseph Dorfman's *The Economic Mind in American Civilization*,[28] and Oliver W. Larkin's *Art and Life in America*[29] are works of widely acknowledged importance. Several excellent histories of colleges and universities have appeared, and an admirable interpretation of the history of higher education is to be found in the book (broader in its coverage than the title indicates) by Richard Hofstadter and Walter P. Metzger, *The Development of Academic Freedom in the United States*.[30] The history of science must of necessity be studied on an international scale. A useful bibliographical guide, *History of Science*, by Marie Boas, has been published by the Service Center for Teachers of History, established by the American Historical Association[31]—one of a pamphlet series that every teacher should know.

Literary anthologies and selections of historical documents contain much that is valuable for the historian of ideas. Certain collections lay particular stress upon intellectual history, notably the pamphlet series entitled *Problems in American Civilization*, edited at Amherst College;[32] the co-operative volume of *Problems in American History*, edited by Leopold and Link;[33] and the anthologies of Warfel-Gabriel-Williams[34] and of Thorp-Curti-Baker.[35]

---

[27] Henry Steele Commager and Richard B. Morris, eds., *The New American Nation Series* (New York: Harper, 1954–), in course of publication.

[28] Joseph Dorfman, *The Economic Mind in American Civilization* (5 vols.; New York: Viking, 1946-1959).

[29] Oliver W. Larkin, *Art and Life in America* (New York: Rinehart, 1949).

[30] Richard Hofstadter and Walter P. Metzger, *The Development of Academic Freedom in the United States* (New York: Columbia University, 1955).

[31] Marie Boas, *History of Science* (Washington: Service Center for Teachers of History, American Historical Association, 1958). This admirable bibliographical series already covers more than thirty different historical topics.

[32] *Problems in American Civilization: Readings Selected by the Department of American Studies, Amherst College* (Boston: Heath, 1949–), additions to the series are constantly being made.

[33] Richard W. Leopold and Arthur S. Link, eds., *Problems in American History* (2nd ed.; Englewood Cliffs, N. J.: Prentice-Hall, 1957).

[34] Harry R. Warfel, Ralph Henry Gabriel, and Stanley T. Williams, eds., *The American Mind* (New York: American Book, 1937).

[35] Willard Thorp, Merle Curti, and Carlos Baker, eds., *American Issues* (2 vols.; Philadelphia: Lippincott, 1941).

Every book, pamphlet, or newspaper—indeed, every manuscript letter—is potentially a source to be used in the study of intellectual history. For practical purposes, however, the influential books of the past constitute the key documents. Fortunately, many of these are being reprinted in inexpensive paperback editions. No titles can be listed here, but student and teacher should be constantly aware that no commentary can take the place of the original, and that the original is often no farther away than the drug-store book-rack or the public library.

The most intimate acquaintance with intellectual history in the making is to be derived from the published diaries and letters of men of wide-ranging intellectual interests. Several notable series are in course of publication— the papers of Benjamin Franklin[36] and of Thomas Jefferson,[37] for example—and others, including the papers of the Adams family, will appear shortly. Uniquely valuable for intellectual history is the copiously annotated *Catalogue of the Library of Thomas Jefferson,* edited by E. Millicent Sowerby.[38] For Ralph Waldo Emerson, there is a complete edition of his *Letters* and a ten-volume selection from his *Journals.*[39] Diaries and letters —and biographies that incorporate both types of material—are plentiful for all periods of American history.

Articles on intellectual history are frequent in the standard scholarly journals of all fields. Specially to be noted are the *Journal of the History of Ideas,* the *American Quarterly,* the *William and Mary Quarterly,* and the *New England Quarterly.* The next to the last of these confines its attention to colonial and early national history; the others span all periods of time.

DETAILED STUDIES

Valuable as are the panoramic histories of American thought, painted on canvases of a breadth measured in centuries, the com-

[36] Benjamin Franklin, *Papers,* ed., Leonard W. Labaree and others (New Haven: Yale University, 1959–), to be completed in 40 volumes.

[37] Thomas Jefferson, *Papers,* ed., Julian P. Boyd and others (Princeton: Princeton University, 1950–), to be completed in 50 volumes.

[38] *Catalogue of the Library of Thomas Jefferson,* ed., Emily Millicent Sowerby (Washington: Library of Congress, 1952–), to be completed in 5 volumes.

[39] Ralph Waldo Emerson, *Letters,* edited by Ralph L. Rusk (6 vols.; New York: Columbia University, 1939); *Journals, 1820-1876,* edited by Edward W. Emerson and Waldo Emerson Forbes (10 vols.; Boston: Houghton Mifflin, 1909-1914). The first volume of a new and much more complete edition of *The Journals and Miscellaneous Notebooks of Ralph Waldo Emerson* appeared in 1960. It is edited by William H. Gilman et al. (Cambridge: Belknap of Harvard University, 1960–).

plicated interaction of ideas and events can often be seen more clearly through detailed studies of particular periods and particular movements. From a literature so vast, only a few examples can be chosen. In the paragraphs that follow, certain crucial topics are noted and a brief sampling of significant studies is offered. The selection is necessarily somewhat arbitrary, for limitations of space have excluded many titles equal in value to those that are listed. In particular, biographical studies are inadequately represented, very few articles are listed, and general works that have already been mentioned are excluded, even though they often include chapters on particular topics that are as brilliant or profound as any of the monographs.

Puritanism

Puritanism was obviously a major intellectual force during the colonial period, and historians have always discussed its theology and some of its political implications. In recent years, however, a more subtle and profound investigation has been made of its wide-ranging influence upon all aspects of intellectual life. Especially notable has been the work of Perry Miller, embodied in two volumes on *The New England Mind,* in a biography of Jonathan Edwards, in a monograph on *Orthodoxy in Massachusetts, 1630-1650,* and in various essays collected under the title *Errand into the Wilderness.*[40] Other contributions of major importance include William Haller's *The Rise of Puritanism,*[41] an indispensable study of the English side of the story; Samuel Eliot Morison's *The Intellectual Life of Colonial New England* and his volumes on the history of Harvard;[42] and Edmund S. Morgan's *The Puritan Family* and *The Puritan Dilemma: The Story of John Winthrop.*[43] The extremely varied interpretations of Puritanism that historians have offered are

---

[40] Perry Miller, *The New England Mind: The Seventeenth Century* (New York: Macmillan, 1939); *The New England Mind: From Colony to Province* (Cambridge: Harvard University, 1953); *Jonathan Edwards* (New York: W. Sloane, 1949); *Orthodoxy in Massachusetts, 1630-1650* (Cambridge: Harvard University, 1933); *Errand into the Wilderness* (Cambridge: Belknap of Harvard University, 1956) .

[41] William Haller, *The Rise of Puritanism* (New York: Columbia University, 1938; paperback edition, New York: Harper, 1957).

[42] Samuel Eliot Morison, *The Intellectual Life of Colonial New England* (New York: New York University, 1956; originally published as *The Puritan Pronaos,* 1936); *The Founding of Harvard College* and *Harvard College in the Seventeenth Century* (together 3 vols.; Cambridge: Harvard University, 1935-1936).

[43] Edmund S. Morgan, *The Puritan Family: Essays on Religion and Domestic Relations in Seventeenth-Century New England* (Boston: Boston Public Library, 1944); *The Puritan Dilemma: The Story of John Winthrop* (Boston: Little, Brown, 1958).

displayed by means of brief selections in the Amherst paperback, *Puritanism in Early America,* edited by George M. Waller.[44]

The Middle and Southern Colonies

Intellectual life in the middle and southern colonies, once a seriously neglected topic, has now been studied from several different vantage points, notably by Carl Bridenbaugh in *Cities in the Wilderness, Rebels and Gentlemen,* and *Cities in Revolt;*[45] by Thomas J. Wertenbaker in three volumes on *The Founding of American Civilization;*[46] and by Louis B. Wright in a number of useful volumes, including *The First Gentlemen of Virginia,* and, most recently, *The Cultural Life of the American Colonies.*[47] A comprehensive treatment of colonial intellectual and cultural history is Max Savelle, *Seeds of Liberty.* And Bernard Bailyn, in *Education in the Forming of American Society,* acutely analyzes another subject of particular interest to the readers of this Yearbook.[48]

The Revolution and the Constitution

The Revolution and the establishment of the Constitution have always been studied with one aspect of intellectual history clearly in mind, namely the history of political theory. Even this aspect, however, has been deepened and enlarged by newer studies of the Enlightenment, by both European and American scholars. The impact of scientific thought upon political philosophy has been a particularly rewarding field of study. Exploring this and related matters, Carl Becker produced two books that have already become classics: *The Heavenly City of the Eighteenth-Century Philosophers* and *The*

[44] George M. Waller, ed., *Puritanism in Early America* (Amherst College, Problems in American Civilization; Boston: Heath, 1950), paperback.

[45] Carl Bridenbaugh, *Cities in the Wilderness: The First Century of Urban Life in America, 1625-1742* (New York: Ronald, 1938) ; *Rebels and Gentlemen: Philadelphia in the Age of Franklin,* Jessica Bridenbaugh, co-author (New York: Reynal & Hitchcock, 1942); *Cities in Revolt: Urban Life in America, 1743-1776* (New York: Knopf, 1955).

[46] Thomas J. Wertenbaker, *The Founding of American Civilization* (3 vols.; New York: Scribner, 1938-1947).

[47] Louis B. Wright, *The First Gentlemen of Virginia: Intellectual Qualities of the Early Colonial Ruling Class* (San Marino, Calif.: Huntington Library, 1940); *The Cultural Life of the American Colonies, 1607-1763* (New American Nation Series; New York: Harper, 1957). See also his bibliographical survey, *New Interpretations of American Colonial History* (American Historical Association, Service Center for Teachers of History, Publication No. 16; Washington, 1959).

[48] Max Savelle, *Seeds of Liberty: The Genesis of the American Mind* (New York: Knopf, 1948) ; Bernard Bailyn, *Education in the Forming of American Society* (Chapel Hill: University of North Carolina, 1960).

Declaration of Independence: A Study in the History of Political Ideas.[49] Likewise impressive for their range and subtlety are Edward S. Corwin's essay, *The "Higher Law" Background of American Constitutional Law;*[50] Benjamin F. Wright's *American Interpretations of Natural Law;*[51] Randolph G. Adams' *Political Ideas of the American Revolution,*[52] and Clinton Rossiter's *Seedtime of the Republic.*[53] Though political philosophy is apt to be in the background of any study of the period, its connections with other fields of thought are apparent from the titles of the following excellent special studies: Bernard Faÿ, *The Revolutionary Spirit in France and America;*[54] Zoltán Haraszti, *John Adams & the Prophets of Progress,*[55] a study of Adams' marginal annotations on the books in his library; Arthur M. Schlesinger, *Prelude to Independence: The Newspaper War on Britain;*[56] Daniel J. Boorstin, *The Lost World of Thomas Jefferson;*[57] Brooke Hindle, *The Pursuit of Science in Revolutionary America;*[58] and Allen O. Hansen, *Liberalism and American Education in the Eighteenth Century.*[59]

The Jacksonian Era

The Jacksonian era has attracted relatively more attention from intellectual historians than the earliest years of the nineteenth century. The political developments of the period, long the almost

---

[49] Carl L. Becker, *The Heavenly City of the Eighteenth-Century Philosophers* (New Haven: Yale University, 1932; paperback edition, Yale, 1959); *The Declaration of Independence: A Study in the History of Political Ideas* (New York: Harcourt, Brace, 1922; paperback edition, New York: Vintage, 1958).

[50] Edward S. Corwin, *The "Higher Law" Background of American Constitutional Law* (Ithaca: Great Seal Books, 1955).

[51] Benjamin F. Wright, *American Interpretations of Natural Law* (Cambridge: Harvard University, 1931).

[52] Randolph G. Adams, *Political Ideas of the American Revolution* (Durham, N. C.: Trinity College, 1922; paperback edition, New York: Barnes & Noble, 1958).

[53] Clinton Rossiter, *Seedtime of the Republic: The Origin of the American Tradition of Political Liberty* (New York: Harcourt, Brace, 1953).

[54] Bernard Faÿ, *The Revolutionary Spirit in France and America,* translated by Ramon Guthrie (New York: Harcourt, Brace, 1927).

[55] Zoltán Haraszti, *John Adams & the Prophets of Progress* (Cambridge: Harvard University, 1952).

[56] Arthur M. Schlesinger, *Prelude to Independence: The Newspaper War on Britain, 1764-1776* (New York: Knopf, 1957).

[57] Daniel J. Boorstin, *The Lost World of Thomas Jefferson* (New York: Holt, 1948).

[58] Brooke Hindle, *The Pursuit of Science in Revolutionary America, 1735-1789* (Chapel Hill: Published for the Institute of Early American History and Culture by the University of North Carolina, 1956).

[59] Allen O. Hansen, *Liberalism and American Education in the Eighteenth Century* (New York: Macmillan, 1926).

exclusive concern of historians, have been illuminated from many directions by recent critical studies of the literature and the competing ideologies of the time. In a highly controversial book, *The Age of Jackson*, Arthur M. Schlesinger, Jr.,[60] re-examined the political story in the light of certain of these factors. More recently Marvin Meyers, in *The Jacksonian Persuasion*,[61] has discussed the patterns of ideas of the period. No synthesis, however, as yet weaves together the diverse strands that have been specially investigated in the intellectual history of the period from the 1820's through the 1840's (a span of years longer than can properly be called "the Jacksonian era," yet a period that cannot well be subdivided). Among these special studies, only a few can be mentioned here. These have been chosen primarily to indicate the diversity of the topics that have been covered: Alice Felt Tyler, *Freedom's Ferment: Phases of American Social History to 1860;* Arthur A. Ekirch, *The Idea of Progress in America, 1815-1860;* Carl Bode, *The American Lyceum;* John A. Krout, *The Origins of Prohibition;* Blake McKelvey, *American Prisons;* Arthur Bestor, *Backwoods Utopias;* Ray A. Billington, *The Protestant Crusade;* Timothy L. Smith, *Revivalism and Social Reform in Mid-Nineteenth-Century America;* Albert K. Weinberg, *Manifest Destiny;* George Boas, ed., *Romanticism in America;* F. O. Matthiessen, *American Renaissance: Art and Expression in the Age of Emerson and Whitman;* Marcus L. Hansen, *The Atlantic Migration, 1607-1860;* and Lawrence Cremin, *The American Common School, an Historic Conception.*[62]

---

[60] Arthur M. Schlesinger, Jr., *The Age of Jackson* (Boston: Little, Brown, 1945).

[61] Marvin Meyers, *The Jacksonian Persuasion: Politics and Belief* (Stanford, Calif.: Stanford University, 1957).

[62] Alice Felt Tyler, *Freedom's Ferment: Phases of American Social History to 1860* (Minneapolis: University of Minnesota, 1944); Arthur A. Ekirch, *The Idea of Progress in America, 1815-1860* (New York: Columbia University, 1944); Carl Bode, *The American Lyceum: Town Meeting of the Mind* (New York: Oxford University, 1956); John A. Krout, *The Origins of Prohibition* (New York: Knopf, 1925); Blake McKelvey, *American Prisons: A Study in American Social History Prior to 1915* (Chicago: University of Chicago, 1936); Arthur Bestor, *Backwoods Utopias: The Sectarian and Owenite Phases of Communitarian Socialism in America, 1663-1829* (Philadelphia: University of Pennsylvania, 1950); Ray A. Billington, *The Protestant Crusade, 1800-1860: A Study of the Origins of American Nativism* (New York: Macmillan, 1938); Timothy L. Smith, *Revivalism and Social Reform in Mid-Nineteenth-Century America* (New York: Abingdon, 1957); Albert K. Weinberg, *Manifest Destiny* (Baltimore: Johns Hopkins, 1935); George Boas, ed., *Romanticism in America* (Baltimore: Johns Hopkins, 1940); Francis O. Matthiessen, *American Renaissance: Art and Expression in the Age of Emerson and Whitman* (New York: Oxford University, 1941); Marcus L. Hansen, *The Atlantic Migration, 1607-1860* (Cambridge: Harvard University, 1940); Lawrence Cremin, *The American Common School, an Historic Conception* (New York: Columbia University, 1951).

Slavery, Civil War, Reconstruction

The slavery dispute, the Civil War, and Reconstruction constituted a three-decade-long crisis, the sharpest and gravest through which the nation has gone. Upon it historians have focused a concentrated attention, which may be expected to grow even more intense as the centennial of one event after another approaches and passes by. Political and military affairs will doubtless always receive primary attention, but underlying intellectual forces are being studied in depth. Changing attitudes toward the conflict itself form an important strand in American intellectual history, admirably traced in Thomas J. Pressly's book, *Americans Interpret Their Civil War*,[63] and in Howard K. Beale's review article, "On Rewriting Reconstruction History."[64] From the relatively barren task of assessing blame, historians have turned to a more objective analysis of the relationship between the specific issues in dispute and the deeper currents of intellectual life in the two opposed sections. Gilbert H. Barnes in *The Antislavery Impulse, 1830-1844*,[65] pioneered in exploring the connections between abolition and the religious and reform movements (already discussed) of the earlier period. Many other scholars have followed his lead, placing the anti-slavery movement in its intellectual context and presenting its leaders not as isolated fanatics but as spokesmen for a widely diffused and deeply felt moral sentiment. The views of the opposing side have been similarly examined, with William S. Jenkins analyzing *Pro-Slavery Thought in the Old South*, Clement Eaton looking into *Freedom of Thought in the Old South*, and Rollin G. Osterweis connecting *Romanticism and Nationalism in the Old South*.[66] No major history of recent date has failed to go beyond the debates themselves and to explore the cultural and intellectual roots of the conflict. Alike in this respect, though rather opposite in sympathy and conclusion, are the comprehensive works of Avery Craven, *The Growth of Southern Na-*

---

[63] Thomas J. Pressly, *Americans Interpret Their Civil War* (Princeton: Princeton University, 1954).

[64] Howard K. Beale, "On Rewriting Reconstruction History," *American Historical Review*, 45:807-27; July 1940.

[65] Gilbert H. Barnes, *The Antislavery Impulse, 1830-1844* (New York: Appleton-Century, 1933).

[66] William S. Jenkins, *Pro-Slavery Thought in the Old South* (Chapel Hill: University of North Carolina, 1935); Clement Eaton, *Freedom of Thought in the Old South* (Durham: Duke University, 1940); Rollin G. Osterweis, *Romanticism and Nationalism in the Old South* (New Haven: Yale University, 1949).

tionalism and *The Coming of the Civil War*,[67] and the multi-volume history by Allan Nevins, *Ordeal of the Union, The Emergence of Lincoln,* and *The War for the Union.*[68]

The Last Third of the Nineteenth Century

The last third of the nineteenth century was a period of painful readjustment to new forces, most of them related in one way or another to the growth of scientific knowledge or to the rise of big business (founded partly on the practical application of the new knowledge, or technology). Economic history was, in a sense, born in the midst of this upheaval, and the economic transformations of the period were studied more promptly than the intellectual ones. Recent years, however, have produced a vast literature examining the profound effects of the new intellectual outlook generated by science and technology. Of seminal importance, of course, were the evolutionary ideas presented by Charles Darwin in *The Origin of Species,* which appeared in 1859. The centennial of that publication has called forth numerous studies of the evolutionary theory in all its bearings, generally in a world-wide context that puts them somewhat outside the scope of an essay on *American* intellectual history, arbitrary though that exclusion must be. For the impact of evolution in the United States, basic studies include Richard Hofstadter's *Social Darwinism in American Thought;* the volume on *Evolutionary Thought in America,* edited by Stow Persons; various articles by Bert J. Loewenberg, especially "Darwinism Comes to America"; and Philip Wiener's *Evolution and the Founders of Pragmatism.*[69] Notable studies of the impact of urbanism and industrialism upon the agencies of intellectual life are Arthur M. Schlesinger, *The Rise of the City,* and Henry F. May, *Protestant Churches and Industrial America.*[70] Two interpretive works of the highest importance—both pro-

[67] Avery O. Craven, *The Growth of Southern Nationalism, 1848-1861* ([Vol. VI, "A History of the South"] Baton Rouge: Louisiana State University, 1953) ; *The Coming of the Civil War* (2nd ed.; Chicago: University of Chicago, 1957) .

[68] Allan Nevins, *Ordeal of the Union* (2 vols.; New York: Scribner, 1947); *The Emergence of Lincoln* (2 vols.; New York: Scribner, 1950); *The War for the Union* (New York: Scribner, 1959–).

[69] Richard Hofstadter, *Social Darwinism in American Thought* (Philadelphia: University of Pennsylvania, 1944; paperback edition, rev., Boston: Beacon, 1955); Stow Persons, ed., *Evolutionary Thought in America* (New Haven: Yale University, 1950); Bert James Loewenberg, "Darwinism Comes to America, 1859-1900," *Mississippi Valley Historical Review*, 28:339-68; December 1941. Philip P. Wiener, *Evolution and the Founders of Pragmatism* (Cambridge: Harvard University, 1949).

[70] Arthur M. Schlesinger, *The Rise of the City, 1878-1898* ([A History of American Life, vol. X] New York: Macmillan, 1933) ; Henry F. May, *Protestant Churches and Industrial America* (New York: Harper, 1949).

jecting the story into the twentieth century—deserve the honor of concluding the present catalogue: Morton White's *Social Thought in America,* and Perry Miller's introduction to his paperback anthology entitled *American Thought, Civil War to World War I.*[71]

THE VALUE OF INTELLECTUAL HISTORY

Because ideas are woven into the very fabric of historical development, intellectual history can be made to contribute to the understanding of almost any historical period or event. This, indeed, is the primary reason for including a chapter on intellectual history in the present volume. It is unlikely that courses in intellectual history as such will be offered to any great extent to students of pre-college age. On the other hand, the teaching of general history at any level can be both deepened and illuminated if the ideas that pervade a given historical situation are subjected to the kind of analysis for which intellectual history stands.

It is a commonplace to say that students of history should see events as if through the eyes of contemporaries. It is not enough to pay heed to the visible and tangible surroundings of past events —the costumes worn; the tools, utensils, and weapons used; the means of transportation available. It would obviously be ludicrous to represent George Washington dressed in the clothes of a later era and surrounded by machines that had not yet been invented. In a far deeper sense, it is ludicrous to represent him as using ideas that were never formulated during his lifetime. Only the externals of history are affected if errors are made in picturing the furniture of Washington's *home.* But history is distorted to its very core if errors are made in describing the furniture of Washington's *mind.*

What Washington did, and especially why he did it, are the matters of real concern to us today. To get at the *why* of any action means entering to some degree into the mind of the person involved and understanding the ideas that prompted him to act. The most significant parts of history belong, in substantial part at least, to the domain that intellectual history explores.

All too often the controlling ideas of a given historical period are taken for granted, even by careful students, with the result that present-day meanings are erroneously read back into them. Once it be-

---

[71] Morton White, *Social Thought in America: The Revolt Against Formalism* (paperback edition with new preface and epilogue; Boston: Beacon, 1957); Perry Miller, ed., *American Thought, Civil War to World War I* (New York: Rinehart, 1954), Introduction, p. ix-lii.

comes clear that every idea has a history of its own, that it develops and changes with time, then history reveals itself as a process vastly more dynamic than it previously appeared to be. Events no longer unroll before a changeless backdrop of ideas. Instead, ideas and events are seen to alter together, affecting each other at every turn. Observing this, a student comes to understand that a great controlling idea like *democracy* or *nationalism* is not a static idea, the meaning of which can be looked up, once and for all, in a dictionary. Instead he realizes that the meaning of an idea in any given period (and hence in any given document) must be ascertained by historical investigation, precisely as the outward events of the period are ascertained. A student who has grasped this fact has learned, in the profoundest meaning of the phrase, to think historically.

CHAPTER X

Economic and Social Revolution, 1860-1900

J. Carlyle Sitterson

INTRODUCTION

AMERICAN historians have properly devoted much attention to that great seminal event in American history, the Civil War. They have written many volumes on the ante-bellum period, the war itself, and the Reconstruction Era that followed the war. Perhaps unavoidably the years between Reconstruction and the twentieth century were often regarded as that dreary age between Reconstruction and contemporary America. To be sure, volumes in the old American Nation Series traced, albeit sketchily, the political history of the late nineteenth century, and volumes in the Chronicles of America, intended for the general reader, dealt with many developments in the period. Nevertheless, certainly until as late as the 1920's, little serious and thorough research had been done on the economic and social history of the late nineteenth century which to a large extent provided the foundations for modern America.

A mere mention of the most obvious historical developments of the era—the settlement of the last American West, the revolutionary changes in agriculture, the construction of the transcontinental railroads, the building of the great American industries, the growth of cities with all their attendant urban problems, the rise of the labor movement, and the great migration of immigrants to America—makes clear both the importance and the dramatic character of this period of our history. In the years since 1940, scholars in increasing numbers have been investigating the "dismal era," and, entirely apart from the political and cultural developments of the period, the major social and economic developments mentioned above have all received treatment, varying, of course, in both quality and quantity.

TRANS-MISSISSIPPI WEST

The American West continues to be a fertile field for historical research and retains its irresistible appeal to American readers and television viewers. The ideas of Frederick Jackson Turner—especially the importance of cheap land in the expansion of the frontier, the frontier as a great democratic force, the frontier as a "melting pot" in which immigrants were Americanized, and free land as a "safety valve" for the unemployed and discontented of the urban East—were subjected to sharp attack in the 1930's and 1940's. In contrast, the writing on the Turner thesis during the decade of the 1950's was less acrimonious and was characterized by a desire to probe more deeply into the facts as well as a willingness to construct new generalizations in the light of new evidence.[1] However, the evidence is certainly strong that the unemployed worker in the city knew little or nothing about farming and did not want to farm, and thus had little interest in going West. Moreover, he had no money for a trip West or for establishing himself as a farmer once he had arrived. If the western lands did act as a safety-valve, they did so for the sons of farmers who homesteaded rather than moved to the city to swell the ranks of the urban unemployed.

The most detailed and comprehensive treatment of the West to appear since Robert E. Riegel's *America Moves West*[2] is the well written account by Ray A. Billington and James B. Hedges, *Westward Expansion: a History of the American Frontier*.[3] A provocative and highly controversial application of the Turner thesis on a world basis is Walter P. Webb's *The Great Frontier*.[4] A most original study of the West is Henry Nash Smith's *Virgin Land; The American West as Symbol and Myth*.[5] This is not a study of western history, but rather a brilliant analysis of the manner in which such images of the West of the nineteenth century as westward course of empire, the frontiersman,

---

[1] See, for example, Fred A. Shannon, "The Homestead Act and the Labor Surplus," *American Historical Review*, 42:637-51; July 1936, and Paul Wallace Gates, "The Homestead Law in an Incongruous Land System," *ibid.*, 42:652-81; George W. Pierson, "The Frontier and American Institutions; a Criticism of the Turner Theory," *New England Quarterly*, 15:224-25; June 1942. Fred A. Shannon, "A Post Mortem on the Labor-Safety-Valve-Theory," *Agricultural History*, 19:31-37; January 1945.

[2] Third edition, New York: Holt, 1956. Originally published in 1930.

[3] New York: Macmillan, 1949. It contains an extensive annotated bibliography.

[4] Boston: Houghton Mifflin, 1952.

[5] Cambridge: Harvard University, 1950.

the wild-west hero, and the agrarian Utopia have influenced and shaped the life and character of American society.

Additional evidences that the nineteenth century West as a source of study has by no means been exhausted are contained in the recent works of Robert Taft, Robert G. Athearn, and Earl S. Pomeroy. In his *Artists and Illustrators of the Old West, 1850-1900*,[6] Taft followed the artists through the West and showed the importance of the illustrations as advertisers of the West and as records of the time. Students will find here original material of great value which has generally been neglected by writers on the West. In his readable *Westward the Briton*,[7] Athearn synthesized three hundred travel volumes of British travelers in the Rocky Mountain region from 1865 to 1900. While some were critical of the West and Westerners and others were sympathetic in their comments, all saw the region as a land of limitless opportunity. Pomeroy's *In Search of the Golden West: The Tourist in Western America*[8] is not travel literature but rather a book about travelers as seekers of the Golden West and the transformation they have made in the region as the West itself in time catered to the tourists. Pomeroy traced the tourist industry from the completion of the first transcontinental railroad when the aristocratic Europeans came to see the fabulous West to the organized tours of the twentieth century.

Regional Studies of the West

Our knowledge of the West has been enlarged by a steady stream of regional and state histories as well as additional volumes in the American Lakes Series and the Rivers of America Series. Especially valuable for making the results of historical research on the Pacific Northwest available to the general reader is Oscar O. Winther's *The Great Northwest: A History*.[9] More limited in both time and geographic area but nevertheless suggestive are Paul F. Sharp's comparative study of the Canadian-American frontier region of northern Montana in his *Whoop-Up Country: The Canadian-American West, 1865-1885*[10] and Richard Sheridan's valuable study of economic development in south central Kansas before 1900.[11]

---

[6] New York: Scribner, 1953.
[7] New York: Scribner, 1953.
[8] New York: Knopf, 1957.
[9] New York: Knopf, 1947.
[10] Minneapolis: University of Minnesota, 1955.
[11] *Economic Development in South Central Kansas: Part 1A, An Economic History, 1500-1900* (Lawrence: University of Kansas, 1956).

Bruce Nelson, *Land of the Dacotahs*[12] treats many of the major events in the history of South Dakota, North Dakota, and Montana. Nelson cast James J. Hill in the unaccustomed role of empire "spoiler" as he fostered the development of agriculture in a region not suited to it, rather than the usual one of empire "builder." Paul W. Gates, *Fifty Million Acres: Conflicts over Kansas Land Policy, 1854-1890*[13] shows the conflict between land speculator purchases and squatters which contributed much to the unrest in Kansas and the agrarian uprising in the post-Civil War era. Especially significant are his findings indicating the limited supply of public land available to squatters in Kansas after 1870.

A valuable study of the role of the Mormons in the economic development of Utah, Nevada, and parts of Idaho, Arizona, and Colorado is Leonard J. Arrington's *Great Basin Kingdom: An Economic History of the Latter-Day Saints, 1830-1900.*[14] Readers will be particularly interested in his thesis that the Mormon attitude toward social welfare is closer to the American tradition than is that of the nineteenth century "robber-barons."

Mining

Mining, the early economic activity of the last West, has received comparatively little recent attention. However, special mention should be made of the new edition (1947) of Dan DeQuille (William Wright), *The Big Bonanza: An Authenic Account of the Discovery, History, and Working of the World-Renowned Comstock Lode of Nevada. . . .*[15] Written by William Wright, who prospected in California and Nevada from 1857 to 1862 and was editor of the Virginia City *Enterprise* from 1862 to 1893, this classic on early Nevada mining days is an indispensable source for a knowledge of Comstock mining from the 1850's to the great fire of 1875. In addition, two accounts written in the 1950's

---

[12] Minneapolis: University of Minnesota, 1946.

[13] Ithaca: Cornell University, 1954.

[14] [Studies in Economic History] Cambridge, Mass.: Harvard University, 1958. For a recent account of the Mormon settlement of Utah see Ray B. West, Jr., *Kingdom of the Saints* (New York: Viking, 1957). Other examples of good regional histories are Carl Coke Rister's entertaining account of the Oklahoma Panhandle, *No Man's Land* (Norman: University of Oklahoma, 1948), Erna Fergusson's well-written and informative *New Mexico: A Pageant of Three Peoples* (New York: Knopf, 1951), Dale L. Morgan's *The Great Salt Lake* (Indianapolis: Bobbs-Merrill, 1947), and George and Bliss Hinkle's *Sierra-Nevada Lakes* (Indianapolis: Bobbs-Merrill, 1949).

[15] New York: Knopf, 1947. The first edition appeared in 1876 and has been out of print since 1912. The new edition contains a useful introduction by Oscar Lewis.

are significant. The most important is Clark C. Spence, *British Investments and the American Mining Frontier, 1860-1901*.[16] Spence gave us for the first time not only a comprehensive account of British investment in the West but also an insight into the problems of managing the western mines. Robert G. Cleland, *A History of Phelps Dodge, 1834-1950*[17] is a useful account of the expansion of copper mining and smelting with major emphasis on the period after 1880, even though it is sparsely documented and many of its generalizations are inadequately supported.

Exploration

John Wesley Powell, the great explorer of the Colorado River canyons from Wyoming to Arizona, died in 1902. Yet, it was not until about half a century later that the first full length biography of him appeared, William C. Darrah, *Powell of the Colorado*.[18] Powell's major contributions, exploration of the Colorado and the development of a new concept of the geology of the canyon country based upon his findings, his proposals for reformation of the land acts which eventuated in the establishment of the Bureau of Reclamation, and his important classification of American Indian languages, all received adequate treatment. In a later work, Wallace E. Stegner describes Powell's exploration of the Colorado vividly, but Stegner's account of the remainder of Powell's life is less satisfactory. Indeed, he attributed to Powell far greater influence in the conservation movement than he actually had.[19]

Transportation

Students seeking knowledge of the role of Wells Fargo in opening the West will find two useful accounts. Edward Hungerford, *Wells Fargo: Advancing the American Frontier*[20] and Lucius Beebe and Charles Clegg, *U. S. West: The Saga of Wells Fargo*.[21] Hungerford, who was once an employee of Wells Fargo, avoided the merely romantic and gave an accurate account of the company's business history from 1852, when Wells Fargo was formed as a separate company from

---

[16] Ithaca, N. Y.: Cornell University, published for the American Historical Association, 1958.

[17] New York: Knopf, 1952. See below, William B. Gates, Jr.'s study of Calumet and Hecla.

[18] Princeton: Princeton University, 1951.

[19] *Beyond the Hundredth Meridian: John Wesley Powell and the Second Opening of the West* (Boston: Houghton Mifflin, 1954).

[20] New York: Random House, 1949.

[21] New York: Dutton, 1949.

the American Express Company, to 1948. In contrast, Beebe and Clegg approached the subject with a frankly romantic interest. The result is a heavily illustrated account of Wells Fargo, but telling in a light vein the story of the great deeds of Wells Fargo drivers and messengers, and emphasizing Wells Fargo's part in the latter-day Nevada gold camps of the late 1890's. Although more limited in scope, Agnes W. Spring, *The Cheyenne and Black Hills Stage and Express Routes*[22] is of considerable importance in the early history of transportation in the West because it is the first book to give attention to the Cheyenne gateway and the development of transportation facilities to the mining centers of southwest South Dakota and northeast Wyoming in the decade after 1874.

The Cattle Kingdom

The cowboy and the early cattle kingdom of the great plains have a perennial interest for students of the West. Even before Walter P. Webb had written his influential *The Great Plains* (1931),[23] E. D. Branch,[24] E. E. Dale,[25] and E. S. Osgood,[26] among others, had begun their writing about the cowboy and the range cattle industry. Our knowledge of the cowboy has been enlarged and enriched by a variety of works of the 1950's. Dee Brown, *Trail Driving Days*[27] is largely a pictorial history of cattlemen but an accompanying text adds value to the pictures. Wayne Gard, in *The Chisholm Trail,*[28] used the trail as a theme to tell the larger story of the early cattle industry on the plains. Using reminiscences of many who participated in the great buffalo hunts, Gard also provided the first full account of the destruction of the herds in his *The Great Buffalo Hunt.*[29] Different in approach is Joe B. Frantz and Julian Ernest Choate, Jr., *The American Cowboy: The Myth and the Reality.*[30] Basing their study on the available cowboy literature, the authors treated the cowboy in history, fiction, and

---

[22] [American Trail Series, Vol. VI] Glendale, California: Clark, 1949.

[23] Boston: Ginn, 1931.

[24] Edward Douglas Branch, *The Cowboy and His Interpreters* (N. Y.: Appleton, 1926).

[25] Edward Everett Dale, *The Range Cattle Industry* (Norman: University of Oklahoma, 1930).

[26] Ernest Staples Osgood, *The Day of the Cattleman* (Minneapolis: University of Minnesota, 1929).

[27] New York: Scribner, 1952.

[28] Norman: University of Oklahoma, 1954.

[29] New York: Knopf, 1959. Earlier Edward P. Branch had covered much of this ground in *The Hunting of the Buffalo* (N. Y.: Appleton, 1929).

[30] Norman: University of Oklahoma, 1955.

folklore and tried, without complete success, to separate the cowboy as he was in history from what he has become in myth. Clifford P. Westermeier, ed., *Trailing the Cowboy: His Life and Lore as Told by Frontier Journalists*[31] is especially valuable because it gives us the cowboy as portrayed by contemporary frontier newspapers and magazines. Westermeier correctly dismissed the "typical cowboy" as a fiction and revealed how climate, topography, range conditions, and remoteness from thickly settled areas affected his life, work, play, and in some respects even his character traits. Edward N. Wentworth, *America's Sheep Trails: History, Personalities*[32] gives a complete coverage of the rise and development of the sheep industry in the United States and of the men who developed the industry, with major emphasis on the West and Southwest.

Indians

Since the publication of Clark Wissler's excellent *Indians of the United States*,[33] our knowledge and understanding of the American Indian and the conflict between whites and Indians has been greatly increased by a number of studies by anthropologists and historians. D'Arcy McNickle, *They Came Here First: The Epic of the American Indian*[34] is a popular account, part three of which treats briefly the period in which the Indians have been subject to the authority of the United States. This should be supplemented by Edward E. Dale, *The Indians of the Southwest; A Century of Development Under the United States*[35] which treats the relations of the United States government with the Indians in the areas acquired from Mexico in 1848 and 1853.

Since the appearance in 1932 of the first volume in The Civilization of the American Indian Series, fifty-one volumes have been published by the University of Oklahoma Press largely on the history and culture of particular tribes. Among the tribes of the Southwest, satisfactory studies have been completed on the Navajos, Comanches, Utes, Apaches, and Hopis. Of the central and northern tribes important

---

[31] Caldwell, Idaho: Caxton, 1955.

[32] Ames: Iowa State College, 1948.

[33] New York: Doubleday Doran, 1940.

[34] [The Peoples of America Series] Philadelphia: Lippincott, 1949.

[35] [Civilization of the American Indian Series] Norman: University of Oklahoma, 1949; published in cooperation with the Huntington Library, San Marino, California.

recent studies have been made of the Cheyenne, Utes, Blackfeet, Sioux, the Nez Percés, and the Sac and Fox.[36]

In addition to the works on the various tribes which tell the story of the dramatic episodes in the contest for control of the West, readers will find Robert G. Athearn, *William Tecumseh Sherman and the Settlement of the West*[37] useful in throwing light on the efforts of the army to insure peace in the period from 1865 to 1885 during the rush of settlement into the trans-Mississippi West. Recent thorough studies by Edgar I. Stewart and Stanley Vestal make clear that there is little new to add to our knowledge of the most famous of the Indian-white conflicts, the battle of the Little Big Horn and the destruction of Custer's command.[38]

Settlement

Perceptive studies on the settlement of the trans-Mississippi West continue to throw doubt on the thesis that the West by attracting industrial workers during periods of depression acted as a safety-valve for the East. James P. Shannon, *Catholic Colonization on the Western Frontier*,[39] although concerned primarily with the work of Bishop John Ireland of St. Paul in establishing ten colonies of Catholic farmers in Minnesota between 1875 and 1885, nevertheless provides additional new data on the colonization of the West and the character of early midwestern Catholicism. Shannon pointed out that Catholic colonization did not relieve the crowded slums of the cities, but rather that the Minnesota settlers had been farmers or small businessmen in

---

[36] Laura Thompson, *Culture in Crisis: A Study of the Hopi Indians* (New York: Harper, 1950) ; Ernest Wallace and E. Adamson Hoebel, *The Comanches, Lords of the South Plains* (Norman: University of Oklahoma, 1952) ; Robert Emmitt, *The Last War Trail: The Utes and the Settlement of Colorado* (Norman: University of Oklahoma, 1954) ; Francis Haines, *The Nez Percés: Tribesmen of the Columbia Plateau* (Norman: University of Oklahoma, 1955) ; George E. Hyde, *A Sioux Chronicle* (Norman: University of Oklahoma, 1956) ; George B. Grinnell, *The Fighting Cheyennes* (Norman: University of Oklahoma, 1956) ; Charles L. Sonnichsen, *The Mescalero Apaches* (Norman: University of Oklahoma, 1958) ; William T. Hagan, *The Sac and Fox Indians* (Norman: University of Oklahoma, 1958) ; John C. Ewers, *The Blackfeet: Raiders on the Northwestern Plains* (Norman: University of Oklahoma, 1958).

[37] Norman: University of Oklahoma, 1956.

[38] Edgar I. Stewart, *Custer's Luck* (Norman: University of Oklahoma, 1955) ; Stanley Vestal, *Sitting Bull: Champion of the Sioux, A Biography* (Norman: University of Oklahoma, 1957).

[39] [Yale Publications in American Studies, I] New Haven, Conn.: Yale University, 1957.

Europe or North America who had the capital, character, and desire to farm the prairies.

William Mulder, *Homeward to Zion: The Mormon Migration from Scandinavia*[40] reminds us of the large proportion of the population of Deseret which the Scandinavians formed. Valuable for the information they furnish on Norwegian settlement in the West as well as useful additions to the history of the region are Aagot Raaen, *Grass of the Earth: Immigrant Life in the Dakota Country*[41] and Kenneth O. Björk, *West of the Great Divide: Norwegian Migration to the Pacific Coast, 1857-1893.*[42] A more novel aspect of the settlement of the West is treated in Robert V. Hine, *California's Utopian Colonies.*[43] Utopian experiments found a fertile soil in California, but despite the large number established there they made little lasting impression upon the state.

AGRICULTURE

Historians and economists have long recognized that the late nineteenth century was a difficult one for American agriculture. Indeed, much of the literature on agriculture and agrarian politics has assumed not only that the farmer was the victim of adverse economic, social, and political forces but that political action provided an appropriate means for their remedy. The decline of agricultural prices in the post-Civil War era is well-known, as well as the farmers' efforts to correct this situation by monetary inflation. How American staple crop farmers selling on an export market would have benefited from domestic inflation which would certainly have increased the prices of non-agricultural goods is less clear.

Although no comprehensive treatment of agriculture in the post-Civil War era has appeared since Fred A. Shannon, *The Farmer's Last Frontier,*[44] a number of important studies on hitherto unexplored aspects of American agriculture have been published. Raymond M. Wik, *Steam Power on the American Farm*[45] is the first study to give

---

[40] Minneapolis: University of Minnesota, 1957.

[41] [Publications of the Norwegian-American Historical Association] Northfield, Minnesota: the Association, 1950.

[42] [Publications of the Norwegian-American Historical Association] Northfield, Minnesota: the Association, 1958.

[43] San Marino, California: Huntington Library, 1953.

[44] New York: Farmer and Rinehart, 1945 (Vol. V, *Economic History of the United States*).

[45] Philadelphia: University of Pennsylvania, published for the American Historical Association, 1953.

serious attention to the use of steam power on the farm and consequently bridges the gap in our knowledge of agricultural technology between animal power and gasoline power. Although Wik treated the efforts to use steam power in other agricultural areas, he properly concentrated on the major grain-growing regions during the height of the steam engine boom from 1885 to 1912 when steam power was applied to threshing machines, the harvester-thresher combine, and to a lesser extent to plows.

Allan G. Bogue, *Money at Interest: The Farm Mortgage on the Middle Border*[46] is concerned with the activities of lending agencies during the latter nineteenth century in Illinois, Iowa, Kansas, Nebraska, and Texas. Bogue's contention that the lenders were not as mercenary and predatory as they have been portrayed may well be true, but his study is not sufficiently definitive to establish his case fully. Gerald Carson, *The Old Country Store*[47] is a well-written account of the country store in American life, mainly in the nineteenth century. Although it is impressionistic and makes no attempt at economic analysis or historical thoroughness, it throws some light on the evolution of credit institutions, the competition of peddlers and mail order houses, and the role of the country store in a rural economy.[48]

A comprehensive account of one of the South's agricultural staples is J. Carlyle Sitterson, *Sugar Country: The Cane Sugar Industry in the South, 1753-1950*.[49] Although it does not deal with one of the nation's leading crops, it is especially valuable because it shows the relationship between the economic and social development of a region for two centuries. Nannie May Tilley, *The Bright-Tobacco Industry, 1860-1929*[50] is a full account of the growth, marketing, and manufacture of flue-cured tobacco in the South. Both Tilley and Sitterson deal with several of the important but neglected aspects of American agriculture including capital needs, credit, costs, prices, and profits, as well as the more generally treated questions of expansion in production and changes in technology. Important in this connection, also, is John S. Spratt, *The Road to Spindletop: Economic Change in*

---

[46] Ithaca, New York: Cornell University, 1955.

[47] New York: Oxford University, 1954.

[48] Students of scientific agriculture will find especially useful Thomas Swann Harding, *Two Blades of Grass: A History of Scientific Development in the U. S. Department of Agriculture* (Norman: University of Oklahoma, 1947).

[49] Lexington: University of Kentucky, 1953.

[50] Chapel Hill: University of North Carolina, 1948.

Texas, 1875-1901[51] in which the influence of the scarcity of capital upon the rise of single crop agriculture is clearly demonstrated.

RAILROADS

The construction of the transcontinental railroads, the rebuilding of the southern railroads after the Civil War, and the expansion and integration of the eastern roads into regional systems have long been recognized by historians as basic factors in the economic development of the nation. Nevertheless, despite the many satisfactory studies of particular railroads and various aspects of railroad technology, only in recent years have studies appeared that are sufficiently broad in scope to provide readers with a clear understanding of American transportation development. Indeed, one cannot but be impressed with the high quality of much of the writing in railroad history. The pioneer work of Edward C. Kirkland, *Men, Cities and Transportation: A Study in New England History, 1820-1900*[52] is at once an analysis of the region's transportation problems and a study of the manner in which the New England mind solved them. It does not attempt to cover the same ground already treated in George Pierce Baker, *The Formation of the New England Railroad Systems*,[53] but rather treats selective transportation problems including the coastal trade, highways, inland waterways, and railroads. Less inclusive in scope for the

---

[51] Dallas: Southern Methodist University, 1955. Willard Range, *A Century of Georgia Agriculture, 1850-1950* (Athens: University of Georgia, 1954) is another useful account of agricultural development in a single state. Vincent P. Carosso, *The California Wine Industry, 1830-1895: A Study of the Formative Years* (Berkeley: University of California, 1951) is a valuable state study not only because it is the only satisfactory account of a little known aspect of American agriculture but also because it is more analytical than most other accounts of a staple crop industry. There are a number of southern regional studies of value among which the most valuable book about the post-Civil War South is C. Vann Woodward, *Origins of the New South, 1877-1913* [*A History of the South*, Vol. IX], Baton Rouge: Louisiana State University, 1951. For details, see Chapter XI, p. 188-89. George L. Simpson, Jr., *The Cokers of Carolina: A Social Biography of a Family* (Chapel Hill: University of North Carolina, 1956) traces the role of an important South Carolina family in the social and economic life of the region. Students interested in the economic development of the Tennessee Valley will find Donald Davidson, *The Tennessee: Vol. II, The New River: Civil War to TVA* [*Rivers of America*] (New York: Rinehart, 1948) both interesting and informative. Although the literature on slavery is extensive, only in recent years have satisfactory studies of the Negro in the post-Civil War South begun to appear. For a consideration of this literature, see Chapter XI, p. 191-92.

[52] Two vols., Cambridge: Harvard University, 1948.

[53] *The Formation of the New England Railroad Systems: A Study of Railroad Combination in the Nineteenth Century* (Cambridge: Harvard University, 1937).

South is John F. Stover, *The Railroads of the South, 1865-1900: A Study in Finance and Control.*[54] Stover traced the evolution of the southern railroad systems and pointed out the gradual shift of control of the roads from southern to northern hands. The most satisfactory account of the physical integration of the nation's railroads in the period covered is given in George Rogers Taylor and Irene D. Neu, *The American Railroad Network, 1861-1890.*[55] In addition, our knowledge of railroad competition has been enlarged by a number of useful studies on particular railroads or special aspects of the question.[56] In one of these special studies, Lee Benson contended that the merchants of New York City took a leading role in the early advocacy of railroad regulation and that the role of the western farmers has been overemphasized by historians. However, this thesis, while suggestive, is not entirely convincing.[57]

BUSINESS LEADERSHIP

Among the most important historical writing in the years between 1940 and 1960 were the studies of the business leadership and industrial development of the late nineteenth century. The "predatory

---

[54] Chapel Hill: University of North Carolina, 1955.

[55] [Studies in Economic History published in cooperation with the Committee on Research in Economic History] Cambridge: Harvard University, 1956. Readers will find Stewart Hall Holbrook, *Story of American Railroads* (New York: Crown, 1947) interesting, but the mass of details, much of it apparently unrelated to any central theme, will tend to confuse some.

[56] See, for example: Joseph T. Lambie, *From Mine to Market: The History of Coal Transportation on the Norfolk and Western Railway* ([Business History Series] New York: New York University, 1954) ; Richard C. Overton, *Gulf to Rockies: The Heritage of the Fort Worth and Denver—Colorado and Southern Railways, 1861-1898* [A Northwestern Study in Business History, I] Austin: University of Texas, 1953) ; Julius Grodinsky, *The Iowa Pool: A Study in Railroad Competition, 1870-1884* (Chicago: University of Chicago, 1950) ; Lloyd Lewis and Stanley Pargellis, eds., *Granger Country: A Pictorial and Social History of the Burlington Railroad* (Boston: Little, Brown, 1949) ; George Heckman Burgess and Miles C. Kennedy, *Centennial History of the Pennsylvania Railroad Company, 1846-1946* (Philadelphia: Pennsylvania Railroad Company, 1949); Marvin W. Schlegel, *Ruler of the Reading: The Life of Franklin B. Gowen, 1836-1889* (Harrisburg: Archives Publishing Company of Pennsylvania, 1947) .

[57] Lee Benson, *Merchants, Farmers, and Railroads: Railroad Regulation and New York Politics, 1850-1887* ([Studies in Economic History Published in Cooperation with the Committee on Research in Economic History] Cambridge: Harvard University, 1955) . Louis C. Hunter's excellent *Steamboats on the Western Rivers* ([Studies in Economic History] Cambridge: Harvard University, 1949) is an outstanding work in transportation history but its major emphasis is on an earlier period. Regrettably, there have been almost no thorough studies of public utilities other than railroads during the late nineteenth century.

capitalist" portrayed so vividly in the highly critical literature of the muckraking era[58] changed his coloration only slightly if at all in the pages of biographers and historians writing during the depression thirties.[59] The first important steps in the re-evaluation of American business leadership in the Gilded Age came in the early 1940's. Allan Nevins, Thomas C. Cochran, Edward C. Kirkland, and others, using extensive collections of primary sources and without glossing over the obvious flaws in the picture, emphasized the important contributions made by many of the so-called "robber barons" to the economic development of the nation.[60] Once initiated, this trend has continued without interruption and with only occasional dissent.[61]

Allan Nevins, *Study in Power: John D. Rockefeller, Industrialist and Philanthropist*[62] is a revision of Nevins' earlier work published on Rockefeller in 1940. Five hundred pages shorter, omitting much early family history, and utilizing additional valuable source material unavailable earlier, the revision is a considerably better study than the original. Nevins did not hesitate to criticize Rockefeller and Standard Oil when he thought that the facts justified such treatment, but he insisted that with his genius for planning and organization, Rockefeller made major contributions to the growth of American enterprise, notably in the development of vertical integration in business organization.

Surprisingly, Frederick Lewis Allen, *The Great Pierpont Morgan*[63] is the only well-balanced study available on the elder J. P. Morgan. The lack of significant studies is due largely to the fact that no sub-

---

[58] For example, Henry D. Lloyd, *Wealth Against Commonwealth* (New York: Harper, 1894) ; Ida M. Tarbell, *The History of the Standard Oil Company* (2 vols.; New York: McClure, Phillips, 1904); Gustavus Myers, *History of the Great American Fortunes* (3 vols.; Chicago: C. H. Kerr, 1910) .

[59] For example, John T. Flynn, *God's Gold* (New York: Harcourt, Brace, 1932) ; Matthew Josephson, *The Robber Barons: The Great American Capitalists, 1861-1901* (New York: Harcourt, Brace, 1934) .

[60] For example, Allan Nevins, *John D. Rockefeller: The Heroic Age of American Business* (2 vols.; New York: Scribner, 1940) ; Thomas C. Cochran and William Miller, *The Age of Enterprise: A Social History of Industrial America* (New York: Macmillan, 1942) .

[61] A vigorous dissenter from the new interpretation of Rockefeller is Chester McA. Destler. See, for example, his "Wealth Against Commonwealth, 1894-1944" in *American Historical Review*, 50:49-70; October 1944. See also Matthew Josephson, "Should American History be Rewritten?—No" in *Saturday Review of Literature*, 37:9-10, 44-46; February 6, 1954.

[62] Two vols., New York: Scribner, 1953; a one-volume abridgment by William Greenleaf of *Study in Power* appeared in 1959 (New York: Scribner) .

[63] New York: Harper, 1949.

stantial amount of Morgan material has been available to historians; nor is it known whether such sources exist. As a result, Allen's biography, although well-written, is episodic and fails to give an adequate account of Morgan's contributions to the development of investment banking. The lack of a thorough and scholarly treatment of Morgan is one of the serious deficiencies in our knowledge of the history of this era.

Julius Grodinsky, *Jay Gould: His Business Career, 1867-1892*[64] is a good example of how far revisionism has gone. Grodinsky took the view that despite Gould's admitted callousness toward human tragedy and his indifference to ethical rules, he was a long-range benefactor to the economy because he unleashed a flood of speculative capital and built thousands of miles of railroads.

Especially interesting and valuable are the composite studies of the business leadership of the late 1800's. William Miller, editor, *Men in Business: Essays in the History of Entrepreneurship*[65] contains several essays attacking the "rags to riches" thesis of the rise of American entrepreneurs and emphasizing the well-to-do social origins of American business leaders. Thomas C. Cochran, *Railroad Leaders, 1845-1890: The Business Mind in Action* studies the careers of sixty-one railroad executives and appraises their attitudes toward expansion, innovation, competition, labor, and government control.[66] As would

---

[64] Philadelphia: University of Pennsylvania, 1957. Biographies of a number of less well-known business leaders of the late 1800's furnish interesting case studies in the growth of the American economy during this period. Philip Dorf, *The Builder: A Biography of Ezra Cornell* (New York: Macmillan, 1952) is a sympathetic account of Cornell's career in the telegraph industry and as an educational philanthropist. Richard Lowitt, *A Merchant Prince of the Nineteenth Century: William E. Dodge* (New York: Columbia University, 1954) is an excellent case study in the transition in American business in the middle of the nineteenth century from mercantile to industrial capitalism. Hal Bridges, *Iron Millionaire: Life of Charlemagne Tower* (Philadelphia: University of Pennsylvania, 1952), in addition to being a good study of a businessman of the post-Civil War era, throws considerable light on the development of the Lake Superior iron range. Sidney Walter Martin, *Florida's Flagler* (Athens: University of Georgia, 1949) is a sympathetic treatment of one of the Standard Oil group, with major emphasis upon Flagler's part in the development of Florida.

[65] Cambridge: Harvard University, 1952. For a similar approach to southern business leaders, see J. Carlyle Sitterson "Business Leaders in Post-Civil War North Carolina, 1865-1900," in Sitterson, ed., *Studies in Southern History* (Chapel Hill: University of North Carolina, 1957).

[66] [Studies in Entrepreneurial History] Cambridge: Harvard University, 1953. Alfred D. Chandler, Jr., *Henry Varnum Poor: Business Editor, Analyst, and Reformer* ([Studies in Entrepreneurial History] Cambridge: Harvard University, 1956) is a full account of the railroad editor who was closely associated with the *subjects* of Cochran's study.

perhaps be expected, Cochran found them to be basically conservative, preferring tradition to innovation in business, politics, and society. Cochran's work is important not only for its findings, but also because it points out the type of study needed to understand the entrepreneur of the early industrial age. Unusually provocative is Edward C. Kirkland, *Dream and Thought in the Business Community, 1860-1900*.[67] Kirkland concentrated on what businessmen thought and said but made no effort to measure words by practice. He assumed that businessmen, like other groups, generally meant what they said. The essays treat the businessman's reactions to the hazards of business enterprise and the competitive market, and his thoughts on, among other things, education and government. Kirkland's fundamental thesis is that business thought during this era was a reflection of business insecurity in that fiercely competitive economic era.

Cochran's and Kirkland's studies of the businessman should be supplemented by Clarence E. Bonnett, *History of Employers' Associations in the United States*.[68] Concentrating on the period from 1860 to 1916, Bonnett claims that until the 1890's the employers' associations were anxious to collaborate with unions in limiting production and fixing prices and that the belligerent associations are a twentieth century phenomenon, largely a reaction to the rise of collective bargaining. The real victims of organization, he concludes, have been the non-union workers, the non-association employers, and consumers, all helpless in the face of collusive practices of organized capital and labor.

Business and Industrial History

One of the most important developments in the writing of economic history has been the increasing attention given to business history and to the history of particular industries. In view of the many books on Rockefeller and Standard Oil, it is surprising that Ralph W. and Muriel E. Hidy, *History of Standard Oil Company (New Jersey)*: Vol.

---

[67] Ithaca: Cornell University, 1956. See also the same author's *Business in the Gilded Age: The Conservatives' Balance Sheet* (Madison: University of Wisconsin, 1952). Readers interested in entertaining anecdotes and dramatic incidents in the lives of business leaders of the late nineteenth and early twentieth centuries will find them in Stewart H. Holbrook, *The Age of the Moguls* ([Mainstream of America Series] Garden City, N. Y.: Doubleday, 1953). Unfortunately, they will find little new and in many instances will learn of the merely colorful at the expense of the significant.

[68] New York: Vantage, 1956.

1, *Pioneering in Big Business, 1882-1911*,[69] adds much to our understanding not only of Standard Oil but of the operation and management of the large business enterprise of the industrial age. The Hidys made no attempt to retrace the ground so fully covered by Nevins in his life of Rockefeller. Rather their approach is less personal and more institutional as they attempted to portray an entire system at work—the vertically integrated corporation. Somewhat different in emphasis is Carl Coke Rister, *Oil! Titan of the Southwest*,[70] a comprehensive regional account of the petroleum industry from its beginnings through World War II, emphasizing the period since 1900. In contrast to the Standard Oil studies, it concentrates on the search for and extraction of oil with only incidental treatment of transportation, marketing, refining, industrial relations, and prices and profits. Another important study of a hitherto neglected aspect of the oil industry is Arthur M. Johnson, *The Development of American Petroleum Pipelines: A Study in Private Enterprise and Public Policy, 1862-1906*.[71] Beginning with the early pipelines in western Pennsylvania, Johnson showed their importance to the trunkline railroads and traced the consolidation of the pipelines into great systems. The central theme is the growing conflict between private ownership of the lines and public interest that led finally to state and federal regulation.

One of the most significant aspects of the industrial development of the United States is the relationship between technological advance and entrepreneurial leadership. While many of the earlier studies of the rise of industry have touched upon this problem, none has dealt with it in so thorough a fashion as several recent works. Warren C. Scoville, *Revolution in Glassmaking: Entrepreneurship and Technological Change in the American Industry, 1880-1920*[72] points out

---

[69] New York: Harper, 1955. The later period is comprehensively covered in George S. Gibb and Evelyn H. Knowlton, *History of Standard Oil Company (New Jersey)*; Vol. II, *The Resurgent Years, 1911-1927* (New York: Harper, 1956). Less well-known is the history of Standard Oil of Indiana, told in detail in Paul H. Giddens, *Standard Oil Company (Indiana): Oil Pioneer of the Middle West* (New York: Appleton-Century-Crofts, 1956). Although the story begins in 1889, the body of the study covers the period after 1911.

[70] Norman: University of Oklahoma, 1949. More useful for the earlier period is the excellent general account, Joseph Stanley Clark, *The Oil Century: From the Drake Well to the Conservation Era* (Norman: University of Oklahoma, 1958).

[71] Ithaca: Cornell University, published for the American Historical Association, 1956.

[72] [Studies in Economic History] Cambridge: Harvard University, 1948. More general in scope is Pearce Davis' excellent *The Development of the American Glass Industry* ([Harvard Economic Studies] Cambridge: Harvard University, 1949).

that the glass industry had reached its maximum in handicraft development by 1880, but that thereafter a technological revolution centering in Toledo under the leadership of entrepreneurs such as Edward L. Libby, Michael Owens, and others resulted in an impressive growth in the industry with a corresponding increase in assets and earnings. Harold C. Passer, *The Electrical Manufacturers, 1857-1900: A Study in Competition, Entrepreneurship, Technical Change, and Economic Growth*[73] shows the contribution of the engineer-entrepreneurs, Edison, Westinghouse, Brush, Thomson, Weston, and others, who saw the commercial possibilities in the application of scientific principles to the industry. Passer contended that the free industrial market with the consumer as the judge resulted in the adoption of improved technology. He further claimed that oligopoly does not necessarily destroy competition since mass production creates factors that provide a new form of competition.

In contrast to these accounts of technical progress, David B. Tyler, *The American Clyde: A History of Iron and Steel Shipbuilding on the Delaware from 1840 to World War I*[74] shows how the reluctance of American shipowners, builders, and the navy to abandon wood for iron and steel contributed to the decline of the United States merchant marine. When the American iron shipbuilding industry did arise, it was due largely to the enterprise and energy of the engine builders, foundrymen, and other technical experts. The importance of management and administration to the success of a company is also highlighted in studies of two firms in the textile industry.[75] Human

---

[73] [Studies in Entrepreneurial History] Cambridge: Harvard University, 1953. Arthur A. Bright, Jr., deals with similar aspects of the electric lamp industry throughout its history. *The Electric-Lamp Industry: Technological Change and Economic Development from 1880 to 1947* (New York: Macmillan, 1949). Ralph O. Cummings, *American Ice Harvests: A Historical Study in Technology, 1800-1918* (Berkeley: University of California, 1949), and Oscar E. Anderson, *Refrigeration in America: A History of a New Technology and its Impact* (Princeton: Princeton University, 1953) properly concentrate on the relationship between technological change and economic and social developments.

[74] Newark: University of Delaware, 1958.

[75] Evelyn H. Knowlton, *Pepperell's Progress: History of a Cotton Textile Company, 1844-1945* ([Harvard Studies in Business History, XIII] Cambridge: Harvard University, 1948); John S. Ewing and Nancy P. Morton, *Broadlooms and Business men: A History of the Bigelow-Sanford Carpet Company* ([Harvard Studies in Business History, XVII] Cambridge: Harvard University, 1955). A readable narrative is Samuel E. Morison, *The Ropemakers of Plymouth: A History of the Plymouth Cordage Company, 1824-1949* (Boston: Houghton Mifflin, 1950). Several interesting regional studies of middle western industries throw additional light on the relationship between industrial and financial leaders and the utilization of natural resources: Agnes Larson, *History of the White Pine Industry in Minnesota*

factors, in contrast to economic forces, we are reminded, often spell the difference between success and failure in economic enterprise.

Important additions to our knowledge of producers' goods industries are provided by studies of two textile machinery companies.[76] Both companies shifted from the manufacture of textiles to the manufacture of machinery. Students of the migration of the textile industry will be interested to learn that the New England machinery builders played an important part in the development of cotton manufacturing in the South after the Civil War.

Marshall Field and Company, one of the nation's largest retail stores, is the subject of two recent studies. Lloyd Wendt and Herman Kogan in a volume intended for popular consumption placed major emphasis upon the men who made the policy decisions in the growth of the firm, whereas Robert W. Twyman in a book of real value subordinated personalities to the description and analysis of purshasing, sales, and management policies. Sears, Roebuck has received similar treatment by Emmet and Jeuck.[77]

A thorough study of the cyclical course of American economic development in the post-Civil War era has long been needed. Fortunately, this is now available in Rendigs Fels, *American Business Cycles, 1865-1897*.[78] Combining analysis and description and skillfully utilizing business cycle theory, Fels made a major contribution to our knowledge of the period. Historians may find some of the analysis difficult and the economic terminology at times too technical, but they

(Minneapolis: University of Minnesota, 1949), William B. Gates, Jr., *Michigan Copper and Boston Dollars: An Economic History of the Michigan Copper Mining Industry* [Studies in Economic History] Cambridge: Harvard University, 1951). This is mainly a study of the Calumet and Hecla Copper Company, and Robert F. Fries, *Empire in Pine: The Story of Lumbering in Wisconsin, 1830-1900* (Madison: State Historical Society of Wisconsin, 1951). See also Arthur R. Reynolds, *The David Shaw Lumber Company: A Case Study of the Wisconsin Lumbering Frontier* ([Business History Series, V] New York: New York University, 1957). Unfortunately, satisfactory studies of lumbering in the South and on the West Coast have not yet appeared.

[76] Thomas R. Navin, *The Whitin Machine Works Since 1831: A Textile Machinery Company in an Industrial Village* ([Harvard Studies in Business History, XV] Cambridge: Harvard University, 1950); George S. Gibb, *The Saco-Lowell Shops: Textile Machinery Building in New England, 1813-1849* ([Harvard Studies in Business History, XVI] Cambridge: Harvard University, 1950).

[77] *Give the Lady What She Wants! The Story of Marshall Field & Company* (Chicago: Rand McNally, 1952); *History of Marshall Fiela & Co., 1852-1906* (Philadelphia: University of Pennsylvania, published for the American Historical Association, 1954). Boris Emmet and John E. Jeuck, *Catalogues and Counters: A History of Sears, Roebuck and Company* (Chicago: University of Chicago, 1950).

[78] Chapel Hill: University of North Carolina, 1959.

will be well advised to read it before making further generalizations about the depressions of the late nineteenth century.[79]

URBAN STUDIES

It is not surprising that a nation becoming increasingly urban should be interested in urban developments in its history. Since the appearance of Arthur M. Schlesinger's pioneer work, *The Rise of the City 1878-1898*,[80] historians have studied the rise of towns and cities in all periods of American history; nevertheless, writing in the field of urban history has not yet reached the stage where we may expect satisfactory syntheses of the history of the city in America. However, excellent studies of individual cities are now available. A work begun in the 1930's for example, is Bessie L. Pierce's monumental *A History of Chicago*, the third volume covering the period from the Great Fire of 1871 to the Columbian Exposition of 1893, appeared in 1957.[81] The task of rebuilding the city after the fire unleashed the energy and optimism among the city's leaders necessary to accomplish the remarkable transformation in Chicago during these two decades. From a moderate sized city of 300,000 Chicago emerged in the 1890's as a modern city with a population of more than 1,000,000. Here is the

[79] Unfortunately, little attention in the period, 1940-1960, has been given to the highly important life insurance business, one of the principal means by which savings were channeled into capital investment. Marquis James, *The Metropolitan Life: A Study in Business Growth* (New York: Viking, 1947) is a friendly account based upon full access to the company records. More useful to the serious student, because they deal with capital accumulation and investment, are Harold F. Williamson and Orange A. Smalley, *Northwestern Mutual Life: A Century of Trusteeship* ([Northwestern University Studies in Business History, vol. 4] Evanston, Illinois: Northwestern University, 1957), and Shepard B. Clough, *A Century of American Life Insurance: A History of the Mutual Life Insurance Company of New York, 1843-1943* (New York: Columbia University, 1946). A pioneering essay by Douglass North explores the problem of capital accumulation, but a comprehensive account of the relationship between life insurance and economic expansion during the late nineteenth century is greatly needed. See Douglass C. North, "Capital Accumulation in Life Insurance Between the Civil War and the Investigation of 1905," in William Miller, ed., *Men in Business*. A similar lack exists in the literature on banking during this period. Fritz Redlich, *The Molding of American Banking: Men and Ideas, 1840-1910*, Part II (New York: Hafner, 1951) is useful and opens up an important area of study. David M. Pletcher, *Rails, Mines, and Progress: Seven American Promoters in Mexico, 1867-1911* (Ithaca: Cornell University, published for the American Historical Association, 1958) is a valuable addition to the limited literature on the export of American capital prior to 1900.

[80] *A History of American Life*, Vol. X (New York: Macmillan, 1933).

[81] Vol. III, *The Rise of a Modern City, 1873-1893* (New York: Knopf, 1957). See also the brief but readable Wayne Andrews, *Battle for Chicago* (New York: Harcourt, Brace, 1946).

story of urbanization and industrialization told with a richness of detail rarely present in American historical writing. Of major importance also is Blake McKelvey, *Rochester, the Flower City, 1855-1890*,[82] the second volume in this multi-volume history. Objective and thorough in his research, McKelvey succeeded in writing the history of Rochester without losing sight of the fact that the city's story was a part of a larger, national history.[83]

Three somewhat different types of urban history are those by Lewis Atherton, Arthur Mann, and Constance M. Green. Atherton's *Main Street on the Middle Border*[84] is at once a contrast and a supplement to the histories of the large cities. This readable and well-organized study of the small towns of the Middle West since the Civil War portrays small town life with its preoccupation with the mundane and its aspirations for human betterment, along with its fundamental complacency. Mann's *Yankee Reformers in the Urban Age*[85] questions the Parrington thesis that Boston had little part in the democratic advances of the late nineteenth century.[86] On the contrary, he demonstrates that there was considerable intellectual ferment there and that the reforming Bostonian played an important part in the social advances of that era. An interesting attempt to appraise the history of the city in various periods is Green's *American Cities in the Growth of the Nation*.[87] The author selects several seaboard cities for treatment in the early nineteenth century, several industrial cities of varying sizes in the late nineteenth, and carries several of the newer cities into the twentieth century.

Labor and Immigration

Although the amount of historical writing on labor in recent years has not been as extensive as that on business, industry, and entrepre-

---

[82] ([Rochester Public Library, Kate Gleason Fund Publications, No. 2] Cambridge: Harvard University, 1949) ; vol. III, *Rochester: The Quest for Quality, 1890-1925* (1956).

[83] The following additional studies have greatly enlarged our knowledge of the rise of American cities. Bayrd Still, *Milwaukee: The History of a City* (Madison: State Historical Society of Wisconsin, 1948) ; Constance M. Green, *History of Naugatuck, Connecticut* (New Haven: Yale University, 1949); Hugh Allen, *Rubber's Home Town: The Real-Life Story of Akron* (New York: Stratford House, 1949); Lucile F. Fargo, *Spokane Story* (New York: Columbia University, 1950).

[84] Bloomington: Indiana University, 1954.

[85] Cambridge: Belknap Press of Harvard University, 1954.

[86] Vernon L. Parrington, *Main Currents in American Thought*, Vol. III (New York: Harcourt, Brace, 1930).

[87] New York: de Graff, 1957.

neurship, a number of important studies have appeared. Two strikingly different general studies are Foster R. Dulles, *Labor in America: A History* and Lloyd Ulman, *The Rise of the National Trade Union: The Development and Significance of its Structure, Governing Institutions, and Economic Policies.*[88] The Dulles volume is probably the most interesting history of trade unionism in the United States that has been written. However, it is confined almost entirely to trade unions with little attention to labor in general. Moreover, its emphasis on the narrative approach to the neglect of the analytical limits its usefulness as an interpretation and explanation of the trade union movement. In contrast, the Ulman volume emphasizes analysis so heavily and uses so little description that while it throws considerable light on the forces that led to the rise of the national trade union, it is almost devoid of the human factors in the labor movement. Two studies, one on the A. F. of L.[89] and the other on the Knights of Labor, can be used to supplement those by Dulles and Ulman. That on the Knights, Henry J. Browne's *The Catholic Church and the Knights of Labor*,[90] deals primarily with the period from 1879 to 1891 when Powderly headed the Knights. Based upon extensive sources, it is the best account of the relation of the Knights to the Catholic Church and in addition it contains valuable information on the conflict within the Catholic Church on the economic and social problems of the industrial era.

Two important studies in depth are basic for an understanding of the labor movement. Rendigs Fels, *Wages, Earnings and Employment: N., C., & St. L. Railway, 1866-1896* is one of the few studies that provides quantitative data on wages and employment.[91] As more such studies appear, it will be possible for labor historians to write with more assurance as to the actual economic status of workers during the late nineteenth century. Donald L. McMurry, *The Great Burlington*

---

[88] New York: Crowell, 1949 (The Growth of America Series) ; [Wertheim Publications in Industrial Relations] Cambridge: Harvard University, 1955.

[89] Philip Taft, *The A.F. of L. in the Time of Gompers* (New York: Harper, 1957). Despite its partisan point of view, this account is the most satisfactory one of the Federation.

[90] Washington: Catholic University of America, 1949. Charles A. Madison, *American Labor Leaders: Personalities and Forces in the Labor Movement* (New York: Harper, 1950) is highly critical of the leadership of both Stephens and Powderly in the Knights and of the emphasis of the A.F.L. on craft and business unionism.

[91] Nashville: Vanderbilt University, 1953. Papers of the Institute of Research and Training in the Social Sciences of Vanderbilt University, No. 10.

Strike of 1888: A Case History in Labor Relations[92] is a more important book than its title might indicate. Despite the many works on
labor history, this is the first complete account of a major strike as
seen from the perspective of the participants on both sides.[93]

In an age in which Americans have become conscious of the interdependence of the peoples and cultures of the world, historians have
properly re-examined the interaction of immigrant and "native
American." To the pioneering studies of M. L. Hanson, Carl Wittke,
and others in the 1930's, have been added several volumes of major
importance. Oscar Handlin, *The Uprooted*[94] is a brilliant and sensitive account of the great migration of peoples to this country over two
centuries, based upon a wide variety of published and manuscript
sources. Its theme is succinctly expressed in the title, for Handlin
was concerned with the meaning of this great experience for families
and individuals who were uprooted from their traditional ties and
set down in a new culture. Despite its emphasis upon the urban
immigrants to the neglect of those who settled in the rural areas and
its preoccupation with the depressing aspects of immigration and
assimilation, Handlin's work is a landmark in the field of immigration
literature.

John Higham, *Strangers in the Land: Patterns of American Nativism, 1860-1925*[95] should be read along with Handlin, as the best
account of the anti-foreign spirit in America from 1860 to 1925. The
three major elements in American nativism, anti-Catholicism, the fear
of foreign radicals, and the concept of a superior Anglo-Saxon race,
have long been recognized by historians. Higham's important contribution is that he showed how and why these factors manifest themselves in American history. He pointed out that the anti-foreign
movement of the ante-bellum period disappeared in the age of confidence and expansion that followed the Civil War. Modern nativism
dates from the labor upheavals of the 1880's, the Catholic insistence
upon parochial schools, the acute urban problems, and the rise of a
new nationalism, all in the closing decades of the century.

A number of studies have enlarged our knowledge of particular
immigrant groups. It is not surprising that Rowland T. Berthoff,

---

[92] [Studies in Economic History] Cambridge: Harvard University, 1956.

[93] The story of one of organized labor's most conspicuous failures is told in
Grace H. Stimson, *Rise of the Labor Movement in Los Angeles* ([Publications of
the Institute of Industrial Relations] Berkeley: University of California, 1955).

[94] Boston: Little, Brown (Atlantic Monthly), 1951.

[95] New Brunswick, N. J.: Rutgers University, 1955.

British Immigrants in Industrial America, 1790-1950[96] found that the British immigrants held better-paying jobs than other immigrants and that their cultural background made adjustment easier for them. An important corrective to the overemphasis upon the contract labor act of 1864 as a factor in immigration is Charlotte Erickson, *American Industry and the European Immigrant, 1860-1885.*[97] Contract labor was, in fact, rare in the years after the Civil War. Far more effective in attracting immigrants were the propoganda of steamship and railroad companies and above all the "letters" describing opportunity in America. Colman J. Barry, *The Catholic Church and German Americans*[98] treats the program of German-American Catholic leaders after 1860 to aid the German migrant to America. Barry pointed up the conflict between the emphasis of Catholics of English and Irish descent upon "Americanization" and that of German-Americans on the preservation of German culture. The most comprehensive study of Irish migration to America and the role of the Irish in American social, economic, and political life is Carl F. Wittke, *The Irish in America.*[99]

In concluding a survey of the recent literature on this period of American history, one cannot fail to be impressed with its volume, its richness and variety, the extensiveness of the research, the eagerness of many authors to investigate neglected phases of history, and the willingness of some to correct and reappraise interpretations that have become hallowed by time or prestige.

The teacher of history will be able to find books to illuminate many hitherto unknown points on the West in its various ramifications including mining, transportation, cattle and cowboys, and Indians. Careful analyses of labor problems and immigration now make it possible to investigate many of the questions which should be asked about the development of the labor movement and the position of the immigrant in American society. The teacher may likewise find studies questioning the safety-valve frontier theory and the assumption that

---

[96] Cambridge: Harvard University, 1953. Less satisfactory but useful in enlarging our knowledge of the role of British immigrants in the American labor movement is Clifton K. Yearley, Jr., *Britons in American Labor: A History of the Influence of the United Kingdom Immigrants on American Labor, 1820-1914* ([*Johns Hopkins University Studies in Historical and Political Science*, LXXV, No. 1] Baltimore: Johns Hopkins University, 1957).

[97] [Studies in Economic History published in cooperation with the Committee on Research in Economic History] Cambridge: Harvard University, 1957.

[98] Washington, D. C.: Catholic University of America, 1953 (printed by Bruce Publishing Company, Milwaukee).

[99] Baton Rouge: Louisiana State University, 1956.

interest rates for farmers were unduly high. Important too are the analyses of business practices and institutions which substantially change the notion that entrepreneurs of the late nineteenth century were without exception robber barons. However, no important work of synthesis on the period has yet appeared. What Woodward has done so effectively for the South during the post-Civil War era has been done for no other region, much less for the nation as a whole. Perhaps, the time has now come when the monographic literature is of sufficient quantity and excellence to provide the materials from which a comprehensive account of the foundations of our contemporary age may be written.

CHAPTER XI

Politics in the Gilded Age, 1877-1896

Robert F. Durden

INTRODUCTION

THE name by which the materialistic years after the Civil War are widely known was coined by Mark Twain. Despite the tawdry gilt which did characterize many features of American life, historians have displayed an increasing interest in the period. There are at least two explanations for this: (1) the period was long simply neglected in favor of the more colorful and dramatic eras such as the Civil War; and (2) there has been a growing realization that the 1890's, with all of their political ferment and socio-intellectual unrest, constitute a transitional decade of central importance in understanding contemporary America. In the historical sense the twentieth century was born in the 1890's. Not only did agrarianism make its last great determined bid, but industrialization and urbanization then became recognizable factors of primary importance. The central political questions dealt not with tired and tattered sectional issues, but with the relationship of the government, federal and state, to the economy and to the welfare of society. Recognition of these developments in the Gilded Age clearly justifies and explains historical attention to it.

THE COMPROMISE OF 1877

The final liquidation of the Reconstruction, which came with the settlement of the disputed Hayes-Tilden election, was given a fresh look by C. Vann Woodward in his important revisionist study, *Reunion and Reaction: The Compromise of 1877 and the End of Reconstruction*. Woodward argued convincingly that the famous Wormley Hotel conference, despite its hallowed place in the textbooks, really had little to do with the naming of Hayes as the victor in 1876 and his subsequent removal of the last federal troops from the South. Woodward traced a political and economic agreement which was negotiated, informally and prior to the Wormley meeting, by Republican intimates of Hayes, by a group of ex-Whig Southern Redeemers or Democrats, and by several key businessmen in railways and publishing. With the Northern Democrats and Tilden preaching reform and retrenchment, Southern Democrats were satisfied to recognize Hayes' claim to the disputed electoral votes of Louisiana, South Carolina, and Florida in exchange, among other things, for federal aid to internal improvements in the South. The refusal of Southern Democrats to support a filibuster by outraged Northern Democrats in the House of Representatives assured Hayes' inauguration on schedule. Thus another, albeit long unheralded, sectional compromise in the tradition of 1820 and 1850 had been effected.[1]

Biographies of Hayes and Tilden, as well as of some of the lesser figures, further illumined the Compromise of 1877. Alexander C. Flick wrote a full-length political biography of Tilden which explained the great hold which he had on many Americans, despite his unimpressive oratory and routine writing, as deriving from the strength of his ideas. Tilden not only denounced corruption and sincerely demanded reform in government; he also demonstrated a strong, appealing faith in the capacity of American democratic institutions to meet national needs. Mark D. Hirsch, on the other hand, pictured Tilden as indecisive in times of crisis despite his identification with worthy causes, as ambitious for political power but unable to rise entirely above partisan cunning and personal opportunism, and finally as one whose story "may not be so much one of a lost cause as one of a lost opportunity." In *Rutherford B. Hayes and His America,* Harry Barnard presented a fresh interpretation which emphasized psychological influence in the formative years and re-created a human being rather than concentrated on the presidential years. Barnard saw Hayes as a president, not in the heroic mold, who presided over a "care-taker regime" which prized political morality more than leadership.[2]

---

[1] C. Vann Woodward, *Reunion and Reaction: The Compromise of 1877 and the End of Reconstruction* (Boston: Little, Brown, 1951).

[2] Alexander Clarence Flick, assisted by Gustav S. Lobrano, *Samuel Jones Tilden: A Study in Political Sagacity* (New York: Dodd, Mead, 1939). Mark D. Hirsch, "Samuel J. Tilden: The Story of a Lost Opportunity," *American Historical Review,* 56:788-802; July 1951. Harry Barnard, *Rutherford B. Hayes and His America* (Indianapolis: Bobbs-Merrill, 1954). For another facet of Hayes' career, see Henry L. Swint, "Rutherford B. Hayes, Educator," *Mississippi Valley Historical Review,* 39:45-60; June 1952.

NATIONAL POLITICS

Picking up the political story after the Compromise of 1877, Vincent P. DeSantis argued that Hayes' removal of federal troops from the South constituted, among other things, the first step in a carefully wrought policy to rebuild the Republican party in the South. Because of the sectional and near-minority status of the Republican party, the "solidly" Democratic South presented both challenge and opportunity to the Republicans. Developing the general thesis that Republican lack of success in the South in the twenty years after Reconstruction was not from a lack of effort, DeSantis traced the shifting strategy of Republican leaders. Hayes hoped to conciliate Southern whites, securing their consent to and protection for the constitutional rights of the Negroes, and to lure Whiggish Southerners into the Republican party by a program of federal aid to internal improvements. Garfield waved the bloody shirt in 1880, as Hayes had done in 1876, and recognized the failure of Hayes' Southern policy. Yet, when General William Mahone broke with the dominant Democrats in Virginia and led the successful Readjuster movement, Garfield found it expedient to offer limited Republican cooperation. President Arthur, to the surprise and disgust of Stalwarts who had incorrectly anticipated a revival of Grant's Southern policy, wooed not only the Virginia Readjusters, but also the various other Independent movements which had sprung up all over the South. Yet Arthur's policy failed as Hayes' had, and Harrison's major effort to win back the South centered around the abortive Force Bill of 1890. The agrarian revolt of the 1890's resurrected Republican hopes of profiting from Democratic schisms in the South, and "fusion" of Populists and Republicans became widespread. Yet, despite temporary and limited Republican victories, the Republican party's Southern wing was weaker in 1896 than it had been in 1876. Why? DeSantis concluded that these factors accounted for the failure: factionalism among Southern Republicans, often between the "lily-white" and "black-and-tan" elements; white fears of another Reconstruction; bickering among top Republican strategists over what to do about the South; and, finally, business-minded Republicans had only a tradition and a few token federal jobs to offer Negro voters, whose franchise was increasingly imperiled anyhow, and not even that much for the agrarian mass of Southern white voters.[3]

---

[3] Vincent P. DeSantis, *Republicans Face the Southern Question: The New Departure Years, 1877-1897* ([Studies in Historical and Political Science, LXXVII, No. 1] Baltimore: Johns Hopkins University, 1959).

More general in scope than the DeSantis book and still the best and liveliest survey of national politics in this period is Matthew Josephson's *The Politicos*. Yet many particular phases of political life have been explored since Josephson wrote. Mary R. Dearing, for example, in *Veterans in Politics: The Story of the G. A. R.*, showed how the Grand Army posts "became efficient cogs in the Republican machine" and labored to keep alive the war spirit while simultaneously saving the country from such assorted "evils" as anarchism, immigration, and labor strikes.[4] Leonard D. White published *The Republican Era, 1869-1901*, the fourth and final volume in his important study of administrative history, which deals with more than administration and has helpful chapters on the power struggle between presidents and Congress and on the battle for civil service reform. White insisted that the "official climate altered abruptly when Hayes became President" and continued slowly to improve through Garfield and Cleveland. Only reform, he argued, prevented the almost certain collapse of administration by 1900.[5] Much narrower in scope, Herbert J. Clancy's study of the 1880 election tellingly revealed the politics of personality and patronage surrounding the contest between Generals Garfield and Hancock, and George H. Knoles, analyzing the 1892 campaign, suggested that it was not the McKinley tariff which defeated the Republicans in that year but rather the economic forces underlying Populism and the slowly swelling strength of organized labor.[6]

---

[4] Matthew Josephson, *The Politicos, 1865-1896* (New York: Harcourt, Brace, 1938). Mary Rulkotter Dearing, *Veterans in Politics: The Story of the G. A. R.* (Baton Rouge: Louisiana State University, 1952).

[5] Leonard D. White, with the assistance of Jean Schneider, *The Republican Era, 1869-1901: A Study in Administrative History* (New York: Macmillan, 1958). See also Lyon N. Richardson and Curtis W. Garrison, eds., "George William Curtis, Rutherford B. Hayes, and Civil Service Reform," *Mississippi Valley Historical Review*, 32:235-50; September 1945. The patronage side of the administrative scene received attention in Dorothy G. Fowler, *The Cabinet Politician: The Postmasters General, 1829-1909* (New York: Columbia University, 1943).

[6] Herbert J. Clancy, *The Presidential Election of 1880* (Chicago: Loyola University, 1958). George Harmon Knoles, *The Presidential Campaign and Election of 1892* ([Publications in History, Economics, and Political Science, Vol. V, No. 1] California: Stanford University, 1942). Four additional studies which shed light on this area were: Albert Tangeman Volwiler, ed., *The Correspondence between Benjamin Harrison and James G. Blaine, 1882-1893* (Philadelphia: American Philosophical Society, 1940); Mary Louise Hinsdale, ed., *Garfield-Hinsdale Letters: Correspondence between James Abram Garfield and Burke Aaron Hinsdale* (Ann Arbor: University of Michigan, 1949); Harry J. Sievers, *Benjamin Harrison, Hoosier Statesman* (New York: University Publishers, 1959); and Donald Marquand Dozer, "Benjamin Harrison and the Presidential Campaign of 1892," *American Historical Review*, 54:49-77; October 1948. Dozer argued that Harrison's defeat was not attributable to campaign mismanagement, as is often stated, but to the

GROVER CLEVELAND

Republicans held the presidency through most of the Gilded Age but the one Democratic president, Grover Cleveland, and Cleveland-style Democrats have been given renewed attention and revisionist interpretations in the past decade.[7] Horace S. Merrill, in *Bourbon Leader: Grover Cleveland and the Democratic Party*, did not replace the massive, 1932 biography of Cleveland by Allan Nevins. Yet Merrill, departing rather sharply from Nevins' essentially sympathetic portrayal and defying those historians who deplore as confusing the term "Bourbon," made a central thesis of his argument that there was a clearly defined, cohesive Bourbon wing of the Democratic party which dated from the 1868 convention. Conservative Eastern spokesmen for business interests then gained control of the national party machinery and used it to prevent farmer-laborer control as well as to fight corruption and inefficiency. Merrill further suggested that these Bourbons believed that governmental interference with the natural laws of the economic world was futile, if not wicked, and that taxation had to be kept to a minimum. Among businessmen Merrill found that it was conspicuously anti-tariff railroad operators, merchants, and bankers who became Bourbons and who minded losing elections less than they feared losing control of the party machinery. As for Cleveland himself, in Merrill's book he becomes less splendidly courageous and more dogmatically stubborn, despite his admitted honesty and real administrative ability. In his depression-wracked testing-time during the second term, Cleveland failed to restore confidence and avert economic depression by the repeal of the Sherman Silver Purchase Act; he also

failure or inability of Harrison and his party to respond to the popular new forces appearing in American politics. Malcolm Charles Moos, *The Republicans: A History of Their Party* (New York: Random House, 1956) was the first general history of the party in about a generation, and Wilfred E. Binkley, *American Political Parties: Their Natural History* (New York: Knopf, 1943) included succinct chapters on the late nineteenth century.

[7] Among the biographies that illuminate the politics of the period are: Elizabeth Stevenson, *Henry Adams: A Biography* (New York: Macmillan, 1955); Leon Burr Richardson, *William E. Chandler, Republican* ([American Political Leaders Series] New York: Dodd, Mead, 1940); Charles Roll, *Colonel Dick Thompson: the Persistent Whig* ([Indiana Historical Collections, 30] Indianapolis: Indiana Historical Bureau, 1948); Oscar D. Lambert, *Stephen Benton Elkins* (Pittsburgh: University of Pittsburgh, 1955); Blair Bolles, *Tyrant from Illinois: Uncle Joe Cannon's Experiment with Personal Power* (New York: Norton, 1951); William Rea Gwinn, *Uncle Joe Cannon: Archfoe of Insurgency* (New York: Bookman Associates, 1957); Giraud Chester, *Embattled Maiden: The Life of Anna Dickinson* (New York: Putnam, 1951); and Mary Earhart, *Frances Willard, From Prayers to Politics* (Chicago: University of Chicago, 1944).

split his party wide open and ultimately, according to Merrill, contributed largely to the final collapse of Bourbon dominance in the Democracy. Cleveland had finally "narrowed his role to that of a bold protector of the *status quo.*" Richard Hofstadter, in his widely read and influential *American Political Tradition,* presented much the same interpretation as Merrill but without fully developing, documenting, and illustrating the viewpoint. In his witty chapter on "The Spoilsmen," Hofstadter asserted that, while Cleveland was "the flower of American political culture in the Gilded Age," his limitations were glaring, and "he turned his back on distress more acute than any other president would have had the *sang-froid* to ignore."[8]

LOCAL POLITICS

The temptation to concentrate exclusively on presidents and national politics, Republican or Democratic, is always great, so great that many textbooks have traditionally succumbed to it. Yet as Frederick Jackson Turner long ago proclaimed and indisputably established, much of the reality of American political life is regional or sectional; and behind the facile generalizations about national trends and forces lie the rich complexities and stubbornly different facts and circumstances of American localities. Gratifyingly aware of this, many historians, without losing sight of the broader scene and the larger questions, have turned to subjects which contribute to our understanding of the Northern, urban political scene, the Western urban and agrarian one, and the Southern agrarian, racially-complicated picture.

---

[8] Horace Samuel Merrill, *Bourbon Leader: Grover Cleveland and the Democratic Party* ([*Library of American Biography,* edited by Oscar Handlin] Boston: Little, Brown, 1957). Richard Hofstadter, *The American Political Tradition and the Men Who Made It* (New York: Knopf, 1948; Vintage edition, 1954). Other studies which enriched our knowledge of the Cleveland Democrats were: Festus Paul Sumners, *William L. Wilson and Tariff Reform: A Biography* (New Brunswick: Rutgers University, 1953), and *The Cabinet Diary of William L. Wilson, 1896-1897* (Chapel Hill: University of North Carolina, 1957); Mark David Hirsch, *William C. Whitney: Modern Warwick* ([American Political Leaders Series] New York: Dodd, Mead, 1948) portrayed the rich businessman who dealt influentially in Democratic politics until Bryan's nomination in 1896 drove him back to full-time conspicuous consumption; John R. Lambert, *Arthur Pue Gorman* [of Maryland] ([Southern Biography Series] Baton Rouge: Louisiana State University, 1953); George Thomas Palmer, *A Conscientious Turncoat: The Story of John M. Palmer* [of Kentucky], *1817-1900* (New Haven: Yale University, 1941); Charles Callan Tansill, *The Congressional Career of Thomas Francis Bayard* [of Delaware], *1869-1885* ([Georgetown University Studies in History, No. 1] Washington: Georgetown University, 1946).

Urban

Arthur Mann in *Yankee Reformers in the Urban Age* revised an older view that Boston and its environs in the late nineteenth century were intellectually and politically dead, or at least stultified by the genteel tradition. Bessie Pierce, working for many years on a history of Chicago, provided, among much else in her third volume, a concise, clear story of Chicago politics in the latter decades of the century, and Harold C. Syrett took Brooklyn, when it was the third largest city in the country and a crowded industrial port with many foreign-born elements, to show the contest between shrewd political manipulators and a reformer like Seth Low, who triumphed over the corrupt machine in 1881.[9]

Tammany Hall, always noteworthy in American politics, was presented from an unusual perspective in the capably edited autobiography of George B. McClellan, Jr., the somewhat aristocratic son of a famous father. McClellan—whom a contemporary aptly described as "One New York gentleman to the manner born, who has eaten of the tree of knowledge of Tammany Hall and has had no stomach ache"— served as a Tammany-based Gold Democrat in the House of Representatives in the 1890's and as Mayor of New York in the 1900's. Intelligent and a bit cynical, McClellan described the fantastic New York political world in a candid, amusing fashion.[10]

The Northern Negro

Leslie H. Fishel, Jr., studying the political role of Northern Negroes in the decades after Reconstruction, developed the thesis that the

---

[9] Arthur Mann, *Yankee Reformers in the Urban Age* (Cambridge: Belknap, Harvard University, 1954). For more details, see Chapter XII. Bessie Louise Pierce, *The Rise of a Modern City, 1871-1893*, volume III in a *A History of Chicago* (New York: Knopf, 1957). Harold Coffin Syrett, *The City of Brooklyn, 1865-1898: A Political History* ([Studies in History, Economics, and Public Law, 512] New York: Columbia University, 1944).

[10] Harold C. Syrett, ed., *The Gentleman and the Tiger: The Autobiography of George B. McClellan, Jr.* (Philadelphia: Lippincott, 1956). An earlier power in New York politics was presented in William L. Riordan, *Plunkitt of Tammany Hall* . . . (New York: Knopf, 1948); James E. McGurrin, *Bourke Cockran: A Free Lance in American Politics* (New York: Scribner, 1948) emphasized the oratorical feats of the Tammany Brave whom many Catholics hailed as the "Orator of the Blessed Sacrament." John Tracy Ellis, *The Life of James Cardinal Gibbons, Archbishop of Baltimore, 1834-1921* (2 vols.; Milwaukee: Bruce, 1952) and James H. Moynihan, *The Life of Archbishop John Ireland* (New York: Harper, 1953) treated two distinguished and vastly influential Catholic prelates, while Florence Elizabeth Gibson, *The Attitudes of the New York Irish toward State and National Affairs, 1848-1892* ([Studies in History, Economics, and Public Law, 563] New York: Columbia University, 1951) traced and documented the political activities of the highly vocal New York Irish.

Negro, provided with a perplexing introduction to politics, miscalculated the force and direction of political trends with consequences that were long harmful to the Negro race. Led by Frederick Douglass and others, the Negro, according to Fishel, married himself to the Republican party and too late awoke to a realization that the party had eliminated the ideas and policies which at first had made the association mutually profitable. By the 1880's divorce was out of the question, so the Negro remained tied to a party whose appeal was illusory and whose most attractive qualification was a memory.[11]

Western States

Politics in the Western states has been treated in important, regionally conceived monographs and in numerous biographies. Russell B. Nye in *Midwestern Progressive Politics* declared that the reform movement there originated in the 1870's and possessed a largely indigenous character. On the more conservative side of the political spectrum in its subject matter, *Bourbon Democracy of the Middle West, 1865-1896*, by Horace S. Merrill, traced the techniques, successes, and failures of the wealthy Midwestern Democrats who, according to Merrill, were assigned to "sit on the lid of the farmer and wage earner opposition . . . ."[12] Philip Kinsley's history of the *Chicago Tribune*, in the period when Joseph Medill dominated the highly influential newspaper's life, deals with important aspects of Midwestern politics. Moving farther West, Howard R. Lamar chose the Dakota Territory to make a case study of relationship between physical environment and political behavior; Lamar also emphasized the major roles played by government, especially the federal government, in directing and influencing the territory's development.[13]

---

[11] Leslie H. Fishel, Jr., "The Negro in Northern Politics, 1870-1900," *Mississippi Valley Historical Review*, 42:466-89; December 1955.

[12] Russell Blaine Nye, *Midwestern Progressive Politics: A Historical Study of Its Origin and Development, 1870-1950* (East Lansing: Michigan State College, 1951). For more details, see Chapter XII. Horace Samuel Merrill, *Bourbon Democracy of the Middle West, 1865-1896* (Baton Rouge: Louisiana State University, 1953). Also see Merrill's *William Freeman Vilas: Doctrinaire Democrat* (Madison: State Historical Society of Wisconsin, 1954).

[13] Philip Kinsley, *The Chicago Tribune: Its First Hundred Years*. Volume III, *1880-1900* (Chicago: Chicago Tribune, 1946). Howard Roberts Lamar, *Dakota Territory, 1861-1889: A Study of Frontier Politics* ([Yale Historical Publications] New Haven: Yale University, 1956). Among the useful biographies of Midwestern and Western political leaders were: Elmer Ellis, *Henry Moore Teller, Defender of the West* (Caldwell, Idaho: Caxton, 1941); Edward Younger, *John A. Kasson: Politics and Diplomacy from Lincoln to McKinley* (Iowa City: State Historical Society of Iowa, 1955); Everett Walters, *Joseph Benson Foraker: An Uncompromis-*

The South

There have been more books and articles about the South in the Gilded Age than about the other sections, owing perhaps to the continued distinctness of Southern developments and to the presence of the Negro. Of the many books, the most important was clearly C. Vann Woodward's *Origins of the New South, 1877-1913,* in the *History of the South* series. In addition to synthesizing, Woodward presented many challenging interpretations of his own and, indeed, for the first time brought order into the tangled and neglected area of Southern history after Reconstruction. Discarding the term "Bourbon," Woodward emphasized the continuing and long controlling influence of the business-minded, Whiggish Redeemers, the Democrats, who in 1877 had gained not only "home rule" but also highly coveted economic privileges. Woodward showed, in a manner that startled the myth-loving, that not all corruption in government ended with the Democratic overthrow of Radical rule in the Southern states and that the Redeemers, often acting as agents of Northern capital, promoted the Industrial Revolution in the South out of motives that were hardly disinterested. With the mass of white and Negro Southerners suffering from paralyzing poverty, revolt against the economy-minded and conservative Democrats came with the Farmers' Alliance and the Populists of the 1890's. Woodward, having treated this subject in his earlier (1938) and still valuable biography of Tom Watson, made this the climax of the volume and showed how the agrarians in the South, crushed by the "white supremacy" cries of their shrewd opponents, often turned around to join in the movement to disfranchise the Negro which swept over the South around 1900. Yet, even in the disfranchisement struggle, Woodward suggested that the real issue was not white supremacy but rather which white groups would be supreme. The volume then traced the Southern Progressive movement of the early twentieth century before concluding on the eve of Woodrow Wilson's first inauguration. The reviewer who hailed this volume as

---

ing Republican (Columbus: Ohio History, published for Ohio State Archaeological and Historical Society, 1948) ; Leland Livingston Sage, *William Boyd Allison: A Study in Practical Politics* (Iowa City: State Historical Society of Iowa, 1956) ; James C. Olson, *J. Sterling Morton* (Lincoln: University of Nebraska, 1942) ; Richard Nelson Current, *Pine Logs and Politics: A Life of Philetus Sawyer, 1816-1900* (Madison: State Historical Society of Wisconsin, 1950) ; Oscar Lewis, *Silver Kings: The Lives and Times of Mackay, Fair, Flood, and O'Brien, Lords of the Nevada Comstock Lode* (New York: Knopf, 1947) .

"one of the masterpieces of our historical literature" spoke for many who recognized Woodward's achievement.[14]

Another fresh interpretation of Southern history came in Albert D. Kirwan's *Revolt of the Rednecks* which declared that "the central thread in Mississippi politics [after 1876] is a struggle between economic classes, interspersed with the personal struggle of ambitious men." Kirwan dealt fully with the complicating fact that as white democracy increased in the deep South, anti-Negro feeling and proscriptive legislation increased with it. In addition to describing the demagogic methods of Redneck leaders, such as Vardaman, Kirwan showed their more constructive side in the area of political and economic reforms. Allen J. Going studied the Bourbon period in Alabama, and, while illustrating the extreme laissez-faire attitudes and neglect of education and other services, concluded that the Bourbon Democrats in Alabama "made a contribution in instituting an economical government managed by native Alabamians in whom the public generally had confidence."[15]

Frank B. Williams, Jr., analyzed the political uses of the poll tax in the South for the last three decades of the century, and Allen J. Going found that the Blair bill of the 1880's, which called for federal aid to public schools in proportion to the illiteracy within each state, was of peculiar importance in the South, frequently becoming an issue in state politics during the decade. Going suggested that the Bourbon factions were usually for the Blair plan, while the older, agrarian

---

[14] C. Vann Woodward, *Origins of the New South, 1877-1913* ([Vol. IX, *A History of the South*, edited by Wendell H. Stephenson and E. Merton Coulter] Baton Rouge: Louisiana State University, 1951).

[15] Albert Dennis Kirwan, *Revolt of the Rednecks: Mississippi Politics, 1876-1925* (Lexington: University of Kentucky, 1951). Allen Johnston Going, *Bourbon Democracy in Alabama, 1874-1890* (University, Alabama: University of Alabama, 1951). James Fletcher Doster, *Railroads in Alabama Politics, 1875-1914* ([University of Alabama Studies, 12] University, Alabama: University of Alabama, 1957) supplemented Going's work in several ways. Articles treating various Southern political topics were: Willie D. Halsell, ed., "Republican Factionalism in Mississippi, 1882-1884," *Journal of Southern History*, 7:84-101; February 1941. Willie D. Halsell, "James R. Chalmers and 'Mahoneism' in Mississippi," *ibid.*, 10:37-54; February 1944, and "The Bourbon Period in Mississippi Politics, 1875-1890," *ibid.*, 11:519-37; November 1945. Allen W. Moger, "The Origin of the Democratic Machine in Virginia," *ibid.*, 8:183-209; May 1942. Judson C. Ward, Jr., "The Republican Party in Bourbon Georgia, 1872-1890," *ibid.*, 9:196-209; May 1943. James W. Patton, "The Republican Party in South Carolina, 1876-1895," in Fletcher M. Green, ed., *Essays in Southern History, Presented to Joseph Gregoire de Roulhac Hamilton* ([James Sprunt Studies in History and Political Science, 31] Chapel Hill: University of North Carolina, 1949).

groups opposed it on grounds of its unconstitutionality, extravagance, and the high taxes required.[16]

A number of historians have called attention to the existence of early and various reform impulses in the South. Herbert J. Doherty, Jr., for example, admitted that the race question and a "solid defensive spirit toward all things Southern made criticism exceedingly difficult for native Southerners." Yet Doherty insisted that it was a mistake to assume that the South produced no social critics and muckrakers, even in the Gilded Age. These Southern dissenters, according to Doherty, were often more temperate than their counterparts in other sections and called less for remedial government action than for better understanding and more individual humanity. Among Doherty's examples was George Washington Cable, the novelist, whom Arlin Turner, in a masterly biography, showed to be a social and political writer of great interest. Also stressing the early existence of Southern critics and reformers was Arthur S. Link, while Theodore Saloutos showed the extent and special features of the Southern Granger movement of the 1870's. A. Elizabeth Taylor found the roots of the woman suffrage movement in Texas and Tennessee in the postwar era, and Daniel J. Whitener devoted most of his study of the prohibition movement in North Carolina, and its political ramifications, to the late nineteenth and twentieth centuries.[17]

Among the better Southern biographies which have appeared since 1940, perhaps the most outstanding was Francis B. Simkins' study of "Pitchfork Ben" Tillman, the South Carolina agrarian leader of the 1890's who talked more radically than he acted and displayed the full possibilities of political techniques which further inflamed class and

---

[16] Frank B. Williams, Jr., "The Poll Tax as a Suffrage Requirement in the South, 1870-1901," *Journal of Southern History*, 18:469-96; November 1952. Allen J. Going, "The South and the Blair Education Bill," *Mississippi Valley Historical Review*, 44:267-90; September 1957. Thomas D. Clark, *The Southern Country Editor* (Indianapolis: Bobbs-Merrill, 1948) furnished a social and journalistic backdrop for political developments.

[17] Herbert J. Doherty, Jr., "Voices of Protest from the New South, 1875-1910," *Mississippi Valley Historical Review*, 42:45-66; June 1955. Arlin Turner, *George W. Cable: A Biography* (Durham: Duke University, 1956). Arthur S. Link, "The Progressive Movement in the South, 1870-1914," *North Carolina Historical Review*, 23:172-95; April 1946. Theodore Saloutos, "The Grange in the South, 1870-1877," *Journal of Southern History*, 19:473-87; November 1953. Antoinette Elizabeth Taylor, "The Woman Suffrage Movement in Texas," *ibid.*, 17:194-215; May 1951, and *The Woman Suffrage Movement in Tennessee* (New York: Bookman Associates, 1957). Daniel Jay Whitener, *Prohibition in North Carolina, 1715-1945* ([James E. Sprunt Studies in History and Political Science, 27] Chapel Hill: University of North Carolina, 1945).

racial tensions in Southern society. Raymond B. Nixon published
the first scholarly biography of Henry W. Grady but emphasized
Grady's journalistic interests and achievements more than the economic and political aspects of the vastly influential spokesman and
symbol of the New South. While William B. Hesseltine traced the
postwar careers of a large group of Confederate leaders, finding a
certain degree of continuity between prewar and postwar leadership
which is not always true of conquered provinces, some prominent
ex-Confederates have not found satisfactory political biographers.
Wade Hampton, for example, was the subject for more than one biography but none of them adequately treated Hampton's long and
important postwar political career; Charles E. Cauthen did publish
some family letters which revealed much about Hampton.[18]

The Negro in the South

The plight of the Negro after Reconstruction, a subject long
ignored, has attracted significant attention in a large number of
valuable works. Rayford W. Logan provided perhaps the best survey
in his study of the Negro in the years from 1877 to 1901, a period
Logan labelled "the nadir." He traced the gradual diminution of the
Negro's newly won guarantees, emphasizing the desertion of the
Negroes by Northern liberal spokesmen and pointing out that the road
to sectional reunion was also the road to racial reaction. The best
studies of the Negro's life and role in particular Southern states were
written by Vernon L. Wharton and George B. Tindall, while Emma L.
Thornbrough provided a full-length study of the Negro minority's role
in Indiana, with emphasis on the period down to 1900. In his widely
read *Strange Career of Jim Crow*, C. Vann Woodward emphasized the

[18] Francis Butler Simkins, *Pitchfork Ben Tillman, South Carolinian* ([Southern
Biography Series] Baton Rouge: Louisiana State University, 1944). Raymond
Blalock Nixon, *Henry W. Grady: Spokesman of the New South* (New York: Knopf,
1943). William Best Hesseltine, *Confederate Leaders in the New South* ([Walter
Lynwood Fleming Lectures in Southern History] Baton Rouge: Louisiana State
University, 1950). Charles Edward Cauthen, ed., *Family Letters of the Three Wade
Hamptons, 1782-1901* (Columbia: University of South Carolina, 1953). Joseph
Frazier Wall, *Henry Watterson, Reconstructed Rebel* (New York: Oxford Univer-
sity, 1956) depicted the colorful editor of the Louisville *Courier-Journal*; Aubrey
Lee Brooks, *Walter Clark, Fighting Judge* (Chapel Hill: University of North
Carolina, 1944) dealt with a crusading North Carolina jurist; Robert Crawford
Cotner, *James Stephen Hogg, A Biography* (Austin: University of Texas, 1959)
furnished the first full study of Texas' able and colorful Democratic governor in
the 1890's; and Dewey W. Grantham, Jr., in *Hoke Smith and the Politics of the
New South* ([Southern Biography Series] Baton Rouge: Louisiana State University,
1958) devoted the first third of his study to a Cleveland-style, Georgia Democrat
in the 1880's and 1890's.

relatively recent arrival of the formal, rigid segregation codes in the
Southern states, pointed to the presence of "forgotten alternatives' to
legalized segregation in the years between 1877 and 1900, and presented an impressive array of evidence for the thesis that a "new
reconstruction" was successfully if painfully in process in the South
from about 1945 on.[19]

A well-edited volume of George W. Cable's provocative essays on
racial matters, first written in the 1880's, appeared in 1958 and furnished a striking contrast to the patterns of white-supremacist thought
which Guion G. Johnson traced in her essays. Hampton M. Jarrell
traced the clash in South Carolina between the followers of Wade
Hampton, with their paternalistic racial views, and the anti-Negro
elements who eventually triumphed under the leadership of Tillman;
Jarrell also argued that the famous election of 1876 in South Carolina
was generally peaceful and that the victory for Hampton and the
Democrats derived from a strategic accession of Negro votes rather
than from violence and a display of force.[20]

POPULISM AND REFORM

Just as racial developments reached a climax in the 1890's, so too
did all of the important political trends of the Gilded Age. Com-

---

[19] Rayford W. Logan, *The Negro in American Life and Thought: The Nadir,
1877-1901* (New York: Dial, 1954). Vernon Lane Wharton, *The Negro in Missis-
sippi, 1865-1890* ([James Sprunt Studies in History and Political Science, 28] Chapel
Hill: University of North Carolina, 1947). George B. Tindall, *South Carolina
Negroes, 1877-1900* (Columbia: University of South Carolina, 1952). Emma Lou
Thornbrough, *The Negro in Indiana: A Study of a Minority* ([Indiana Historical
Collections, 37] Indianapolis: Indiana Historical Bureau, 1957). Comer Vann
Woodward, *The Strange Career of Jim Crow* (second edition; New York: Oxford
University, 1957).

[20] George W. Cable, *The Negro Question: A Selection of Writings on Civil
Rights in the South* (edited by Arlin Turner; New York: Doubleday, 1958). Guion
Griffis Johnson, "The Ideology of White Supremacy, 1876-1910," in Fletcher M.
Green, editor, *Essays in Southern History* (Chapel Hill: University of North
Carolina, 1949), and "Southern Paternalism toward Negroes after Emancipation,"
Journal of Southern History, 23:483-509; November 1957. Hampton M. Jarrell,
Wade Hampton and the Negro: The Road Not Taken (Columbia: University of
South Carolina, 1949). The best biography to have appeared was Benjamin
Quarles, *Frederick Douglass* (Washington: Associated Publishers, 1948), while
Basil Joseph Mathews, *Booker T. Washington: Educator and Interracial Interpreter*
(Cambridge: Harvard University, 1948), and Samuel R. Spencer, Jr., *Booker T.
Washington and the Negro's Place in American Life* ([Library of American Biog-
raphy] Boston: Little, Brown, 1955) provided studies of the Negro spokesman who
appeared prominently on the scene in 1895, the year Frederick Douglass died. For
a survey of Negro political ideas, largely as revealed in Negro newspapers, see also
Elsie M. Lewis, "The Political Mind of the Negro, 1865-1900," *Journal of Southern
History*, 21:189-202; May 1955.

placent conservatives in both of the old parties looked on in dismay
as angry agrarians mounted the political barricades and urban workers,
crippled by the deep depression after 1893, threatened to join forces
with the militant farmers. Alan P. Grimes analyzed the influential
views of E. L. Godkin's *Nation* which long smiled benignly on civil
service reform and "good government" in general but anathematized
the economic and political agitation of farmers and laborers.[21]

The turning point came in the momentous Bryan-McKinley campaign of 1896, which brought, not a permanent defeat, but a temporary
even if staggering setback to the forces of reform. In his *Politics,
Reform, and Expansion: 1890-1900*, Harold U. Faulkner synthesized
the more specialized work of many historians, including himself, and
persuasively developed the argument that "the nineties were as truly
a period of reform as the 'progressive' period" of the early twentieth
century. The myth of the "gay nineties" having long ago been
exploded, Faulkner chose to emphasize the restlessness and pioneering
which characterized hosts of Americans who were "intent on reforming many aspects of social, economic, and political life.[22]

With an emphasis and approach quite different from Faulkner's,
Richard Hofstadter devoted more than the first third of his *Age of
Reform* to the agrarian revolt; writing from an urban and highly
challenging point of view, Hofstadter suggested that the mythical
"notion of an innocent and victimized populace colors the whole
history of agrarian controversy;" that the idea of Populism's having
derived from the Western, frontier spirit "is a deceptive inheritance
from the [Frederick Jackson Turner] school;" and that Populism can
best be understood as "another episode in the well-established tradition
of American entrepreneurial radicalism, which goes back at least to
the Jacksonian era." Conceding that Populism was the first important
political movement to attack the problems created by industrialism
and to insist that the federal government has some responsibility for
the common welfare, Hofstadter nevertheless emphasized the provin-

[21] Allan Pendleton Grimes, *The Political Liberalism of the New York Nation,
1865-1932* ([James Sprunt Studies in History and Political Science, 34] Chapel Hill:
University of North Carolina, 1953). A handy volume for research in the period is
Daniel Carl Haskell, *The Nation: Indexes of Titles and Contributors, Volumes
1-105, New York, 1865-1917* (New York: New York Public Library, 1951-53) and,
also useful, Herbert O. Brayer, "Preliminary Guide to Indexed Newspapers in the
United States, 1850-1900," *Mississippi Valley Historical Review*, 33:237-58; September
1946.

[22] Harold U. Faulkner, *Politics, Reform, and Expansion, 1890-1900* in the New
American Nation Series (edited by Henry S. Commager and Richard B. Morris;
New York: Harper, 1959).

cialism, nativism and nationalism, and "tincture of anti-Semitism" which he found in the popular writings and speeches of various agrarian leaders.[23]

Eric Goldman authored a lively history of reform which concentrated on the ideas of reformers, and emphasized his concepts of "patrician" or upper-class reform and of the manner in which "reform Darwinians," snatching evolutionary phrases and ideas away from the conservative "social Darwinists," ended up by assuming that improvements in the environment would automatically bring improved human beings. More exclusively devoted to the Gilded Age than the Goldman volume, Sidney Fine's *Laissez Faire and the General Welfare State* provided a useful and objective summary of the conflicting ideas about the proper role of government, which was the central question that the 1890's bequeathed to the twentieth century. Hans B. Thorelli examined the origination of the federal anti-trust policy and, breaking with the older view, found that Congress, when faced with a novel and complex problem, knew what it was doing and did the best it could with the Sherman Antitrust Law. Thorelli insisted that Congress intended to guarantee the continuance of a private enterprise economy based on competition, that the law as passed provided for flexibility and looked to prohibition and prevention rather than regulatory supervision, and that the three conservative presidents who preceded Theodore Roosevelt were just not intent on using the law effectively.[24]

The best single survey of the agrarian movement of the 1890's is still John D. Hicks' *The Populist Revolt*, which was reprinted in 1955. But, in addition to the challenging interpretations in the above-mentioned histories of American reform, Chester M. Destler emphasized the relationships between urban and rural discontent. Using Henry D. Lloyd, the noted critic of Standard Oil and active Chicago reformer, as his focus, Destler argued that to the Populists, "collectivist methods were simply a legitimate means of restoring free enterprise and small, competitive capitalism." But the Socialist group, whom Lloyd tried unsuccessfully to unite with Populists, "advocated collectivism for its own sake, as a means of overthrowing the free

---

[23] Richard Hofstadter, *The Age of Reform: From Bryan to F. D. R.* (New York: Knopf, 1955).

[24] Eric F. Goldman, *Rendezvous with Destiny: A History of Modern American Reform* (New York: Knopf, 1953). Sidney Fine, *Laissez Faire and the General-Welfare State: A Study of Conflict in American Thought, 1865-1901* ([University of Michigan Publications; History and Political Science, 22] Ann Arbor: University of Michigan, 1956). Hans Birger Thorelli, *The Federal Antitrust Policy: Origination of an American Tradition* (Baltimore: Johns Hopkins University, 1955).

enterprise system" and founded their program on an "alien, materialistic, proletarian philosophy entirely antagonistic to that of American
craftsmen and farmers." Despite the incompatibility of Populism and
Socialism, Destler stressed the inadequacy of the view that would
explain Midwestern radicalism as exclusively agrarian in origin and
showed how Eastern, urban thought and leadership had to be combined with Western, agrarian ideas to form a more typical American
program for reform. Without attempting to suggest new interpretations or uncover new material, Fred A. Shannon combined, for classroom purposes, a brief, but useful, survey of American farmers' movements with illustrative documents; and Carl C. Taylor undertook the
same type survey at greater length, concluding that the "struggles of
farmers arose out of, and have always revolved about, the issues of
prices, markets and credits, and all these struggles combined constitute
the American Farmers' Movement." In a study which relied heavily
on statistical evidence, Susan and M. S. Stedman, Jr., found that
farmer-labor parties have attracted their largest vote when the economy was heading downward but before rock-bottom was reached.
Before that point, the Stedmans suggested, one of the major parties
always managed to absorb most of the potential protest vote.[25]

The urban, industrial aspects of the 1890's were vividly recreated
and dramatized in Ray Ginger's *Altgeld's America*, which had as its
theme the perversion of the Lincoln ideal (of human understanding,
social responsibility, and equality of opportunity) by mushrooming
industrialization and urbanization until a group of reformers launched
their struggle to restore and re-adapt the Emancipator's vision. Centering on Chicago in the 1890's, Ginger brought to life a brilliant
group of reform-minded individuals—Altgeld, Clarence Darrow, Jane
Addams, Eugene Debs, John Dewey, Thorsten Veblen, and Frank
Lloyd Wright—as well as some of their personal and impersonal
antagonists. The same author also published the best biography of

---

[25] John Donald Hicks, *The Populist Revolt* (Minneapolis: University of Minne-
sota, 1931; reprinted in 1955). Chester McArthur Destler, *American Radicalism,
1865-1901: Essays and Documents* (New London: Connecticut College, 1946). Fred
Albert Shannon, *American Farmers' Movement* (Princeton, New Jersey: Van
Nostrand, 1957). Carl C. Taylor, *The Farmers' Movement, 1620-1920* ([American
Sociology Series] New York: American Book, 1953). Murray S. Stedman, Jr., and
Susan W. Stedman, *Discontent at the Polls: A Study of Farmer and Labor Parties,
1827-1948* (New York: Columbia University, 1950). Useful books in this area were
Stuart Noblin, *Leonidas LaFayette Polk: Agrarian Crusader* (Chapel Hill: Uni-
versity of North Carolina, 1949), and Helen G. Edmonds, *The Negro and Fusion
Politics in North Carolina, 1894-1901* (Chapel Hill: University of North Carolina,
1951).

Eugene Debs, the labor leader who rose to fame in the 1890's, and Almont Lindsey objectively analyzed the many-sided and crucial Pullman strike. Especially valuable for both teacher and student in dealing with the Pullman strike was the collection of pro and con views, as well as key primary documents, published as part of the "Amherst College" series. The views of conservatives in the Gilded Age, as in most eras, were not articulated to the same degree as those of the reformers, but Edward C. Kirkland and Chester M. Destler provided insight into the views of strategic businessmen of the period.[26]

BRYAN

William Jennings Bryan, the final great spokesman for reform in the nineteenth century, has yet to receive satisfactory biographical treatment. Meanwhile, his reputation and place in American history wobble insecurely. Richard Hofstadter, in the above-mentioned *American Political Tradition*, presented Bryan as a "circuit-riding evangelist in politics," "a boy who never left home" intellectually, "a provincial politician following a provincial populace in provincial prejudices." James A. Barnes, on the other hand, insisted that the campaign of 1896 must be regarded as one of the most significant in American political history, not only because of matters openly discussed but also because of the fundamental underlying issues concerning the control and uses of federal power. Barnes, defending Bryan against charges made by both contemporaries and historians, attacked as false myths the notions that the silver forces were unorganized and leaderless when the Democratic convention met; that Bryan won the nomination merely through the accident of a speech; that Bryan toured the country during the campaign as an incendiary firebrand; that the issue was between honest and dishonest money; that new sources of gold and other economic developments brought prosperity and stripped Bryan of agrarian votes; and finally that the Bryan campaign was a "crackpot circus." Barnes suggested that Bryan

---

[26] Ray Ginger, *Altgeld's America: The Lincoln Ideal versus Changing Realities* (New York: Funk & Wagnalls, 1958), and *The Bending Cross: A Biography of Eugene Victor Debs* (New Brunswick: Rutgers University, 1949). Almont Lindsey, *The Pullman Strike* (Chicago: University of Chicago, 1942). Colston Estey Warne, ed., *The Pullman Boycott of 1894: The Problem of Federal Intervention* in the *Problems in American Civilization* series (Boston: Heath, 1955). Edward C. Kirkland, *Business in the Gilded Age: The Conservatives' Balance Sheet* ([Knapp Lectures] Madison: University of Wisconsin, 1952). Chester M. Destler, "The Opposition of American Businessmen to Social Control during the Gilded Age," *Mississippi Valley Historical Review*, 39:641-72; March 1953.

was defeated both by a flood of propaganda and by coercion of industrial workers, but William Diamond in an analysis of the 1896 voting found, among other things, that in the more industrialized states Bryan received a greater proportion of votes from the city than from the country.[27] Historians will continue to debate the stature of Bryan and the meaning of the 1896 election, but what is surely beyond controversy is the fact that the slowly accumulating tides of dissent and discontent had risen mightily to threaten, and ultimately to doom, the complacency and ultra-conservatism of the Gilded Age.

---

[27] James A. Barnes, "Myths of the Bryan Campaign," *Mississippi Valley Historical Review*, 34:367-404; December 1947. William Diamond, "Urban and Rural Voting in 1896," *American Historical Review*, 46:281-305; January 1941. Another useful volume in the "Amherst series" is George F. Whicher, ed., *William Jennings Bryan and the Campaign of 1896* in *Problems of American Civilization Series* (Boston: Heath, 1953). A revelant book, Paul W. Glad, *The Trumpet Soundth: William Jennings Bryan and His Democracy, 1896-1912* (Lincoln: University of Nebraska, 1960), has appeared too recently to be considered in this chapter.

CHAPTER XII

The Progressive Era, 1897-1917

George E. Mowry

THE PROGRESSIVE MOVEMENT

Historians designate the widespread political and social reform activities covering the period from the end of the Spanish-American War to or through the First World War as the progressive movement. Starting in Midwest cities and states, it spread geographically to both the east and west coasts and by 1910 was nationwide. Its impulse was felt in the farm communities of Iowa and Wisconsin, in the great urban centers of New York, Cleveland, Chicago, and San Francisco, in purely Southern states like Georgia, and in such widely differentiated commonwealths as Maine and California. Starting on the more local levels, the reform crusade made its way upward in the political structure to the level of the state capitals and then finally to the national government. On the local municipal level the movement comprehended such reform crusades as those of Mayor Seth Low of New York against Tammany, of Tom Johnson and Golden Rule Jones in Cleveland and Toledo, Ohio, the fight against the Union Labor Party machine in San Francisco, and the struggle of the "good government" leagues in Los Angeles. It included also Jacob Riis's work with the immigrants in the New York tenement districts, Jane Addams' creation of Hull House in Chicago, and Judge Ben Lindsay's campaign for the juvenile court in Denver.

The reform crusades of Governors Robert LaFollette in Wisconsin, Albert B. Cummins in Iowa, Charles Evans Hughes in New York, Woodrow Wilson in New Jersey, Hiram Johnson in California, Hoke Smith in Georgia, and Jeff Davis in Arkansas were all varied manifestations of the progressive impulse on the state level. The movement became a national one under President Theodore Roosevelt and extended itself through the administrations of his two successors, the Republican William Howard Taft and the Democrat Woodrow Wilson.

The immediate ends of the progressive movement were as varied as its centers of activity. In the cities its more proximate purposes were the overthrow of boss rule through the institution of such new political devices as the direct primary and the nonpartisan political ticket, and such new schemes of city government as the city manager plan and the commission form. Wider aims included the abolition of franchise politics which under the corrupt bosses had resulted in inefficient, inadequate, and costly city utilities, organized prostitution, a lawless liquor trade, and general corruption and venality. But an even more comprehensive aim of the municipal movement was to make twentieth century America a decent, healthy, and enjoyable place in which to live. The fulfillment of this aim meant the abolition of slums and tenements, the abatement of crime, juvenile delinquency, and disease, the creation of parks, playgrounds, and efficient social services.

On the state level the progressive movement concerned itself also with democratic political devices mentioned above; but it was even more interested in such economic issues as the regulation of railroads and monopolies, the adjustment of tax systems so that corporations would be forced to bear their fair share of the costs of government, and in such diverse causes as civil service, the conservation of natural resources, and the protection of women and children, both at home and at work. Nationally the progressive aspirations ranged through an even wider spectrum of causes, but at the heart of the movement was the central question of what to do with the great interstate organizations of capital and labor, known to the day as trusts and unions. Both types of organizations had vastly augmented their economic power until they were national in scope, and by the first decade of the twentieth century they were engaged in a bitter battle for supremacy. A major question raised by the government was how the corporations and the unions were to be protected from each other, but more important, how the general public and the individual were to be protected from each. The national regulations of railroads, the attempt to dissolve monopolistic corporations, the conservation movement, the setting of tariff rates, the pure food laws, the campaign for an income tax, and the government intervention in labor disputes were all phases of the general query: How were the nation's historic values of individualism and equality to be preserved in the new twentieth century collective world of highly organized industry, highly organized labor, and the highly organized city?

THE OLDER INTERPRETATIONS

Since without change there would be no history, historians have always been fascinated by the question of why and how societies move. Soon after the progressive movement started, historians tried to explain why the nation, apparently devoted to McKinley conservatism, suddenly went on a reforming binge that was to dominate both great political parties at all levels of national life and was to last for almost two decades. Until the end of the Second World War the causes of the progressive movement, as well as its meaning and significance, were largely interpreted by historians writing from a rather distinct political approach and from a middle western viewpoint. Their conclusions were that the progressive movement was little more than an extension of the Populist crusade of the 1880's and 1890's which reached its climax and failed in the defeat of William Jennings Bryan and the Democratic party in 1896. Submerged for a while by the Spanish-American War and imperialism, the argument ran, the Populist spirit broke out again after 1900, and under new Republican leaders was successful in achieving in the new century most of the Populist reform proposals.

As one of the midwestern participants in the progressive crusade, William Allen White, phrased it, the Republican progressives "caught the Populists in swimming and stole all their clothing except the frayed underdrawers of free silver." Because of the movement's assumed origins, according to this older interpretation, progressivism was motivated by the same forces that motivated Populism. It was devoted to the agrarian principles of a provincial, individualistic, equalitarian, but capitalistic democracy; it drew its chief support from the farmer and the small merchant; its enemies were the giant corporations and Eastern financiers who were busy transforming the country into one great factory in which a few industrial and financial bosses held the rest of the nation in poverty and subjection.

When the agricultural Midwest alone was concerned, this older interpretation was not too unsatisfactory. As John D. Hicks in *The Populist Revolt* has pointed out, practically every major Populist-sponsored reform, except that of free silver, was passed in the progressive period.[1] But to the younger generation of postwar scholars it has been obvious that, when this interpretation was applied nationally to the movement, serious questions arose. Why, they asked, should Populist reform have failed during the depression days of the nineties

---

[1] Minneapolis: University of Minnesota, 1931.

and its extension, the progressive movement, have succeeded in the prosperous first decade of the twentieth century? The Populist movement even in the Midwest had been strongest in the western part of the region in the more distressed wheat growing states of Kansas, Nebraska, and the Dakotas, whereas progressivism got its start and waxed stronger in the more prosperous states of Wisconsin and Iowa. The questions arose of why large sections of the middle-class, conservative Republican party that fought the radical Populists so bitterly in 1896 should have accepted such doctrines just ten years later, and why the large cities that had been against Bryan should now accept his agrarian principles. When the leadership of the Populist and the progressive movements were compared, more paradoxes appeared. For, instead of being favorable to Populism, the great majority of progressive leaders had been opposed both to Bryan and to the Populist principles. Progressive Republican leaders usually had been McKinley Republicans in the nineties, progressive Democrats usually anti-Bryanites. Moreover, the progressive crusade was supported by so many wealthy men that it has been sometimes referred to as the millionaires' reform movement. This fact, obviously, was difficult to reconcile with the Populists' well known bias against great wealth.

The vexing questions which the older studies of progressivism left unsatisfied impelled many postwar historians to study the movement more intensively and from a great many more viewpoints than had the preceding generations of scholars. Aiding these newer historians greatly was the expansion of historical research into the new fields of intellectual, cultural, religious, and immigration history. The result was a spate of works on the progressive period which in their total have radically changed the basic historical interpretations of the period.

ALLIED RESEARCH

Aiding the historians more directly centered on progressive politics were a number of scholars working in tangential but closely allied fields. Among the most important of such ancillary works were those produced in the area of what is known generally as intellectual history. Comprehensive and historical in its coverage of the life of the mind is Henry Steele Commager, *The American Mind: An Interpretation of American Thought and Character Since the 1880's.*[2] Although relatively derivative in character, Commager's volume is extremely useful

---

[2] New Haven: Yale University, 1950, 1955.

because of its almost encyclopedic coverage of the early twentieth century intellectual trends in a great diversity of fields. For the intellectual background of progressivism, Morton G. White, *Social Thought in America: The Revolt Against Formalism*[3] should also be consulted. Brilliant and creative, the work attempts to trace the evolution of social thought in America through the examination of the ideas of such seminal minds as those of Justice Holmes, John Dewey, Thorstein Veblen, and Charles Beard. It is especially excellent in estimating the impact of pragmatism and relativism on American thinking in its change away from the old rigid nineteenth century formulations.

The long neglected field of American religion has produced several works of great value to the understanding of the progressive period. Charles H. Hopkins, *The Rise of the Social Gospel in American Protestantism, 1865-1915*[4] and Henry F. May, *Protestant Churches and Industrial America*[5] both chronicle the breakdown of religious fundamentalism and the rise of a secular reforming spirit in American protestantism, a spirit that was so evident in progressivism. Of great worth to the understanding of the racial intergroup tensions characterizing the first decades of the twentieth century and giving progressivism distinctive elements that operated in both the fields of domestic and foreign policy are two recent works on immigration, Oscar Handlin, *The Uprooted: The Epic Study of the Great Migrations that Made the American People*[6] and John Higham, *Strangers in the Land: Patterns of American Nativism, 1860-1925*.[7] Higham's book is particularly useful because it stresses the more recent period and because it throws into sharp focus the increasing fragmentation of the American people in the twentieth century into self-conscious racial groups, a process that seemed to deny the existence of a melting pot. As night is hardly understandable except in terms of day, progressivism is scarcely comprehensible without an examination of its leading ideological competitors. Unfortunately there is still no good work on American conservatism in the twentieth century. But the Socialist movement has been the subject of three recent worthwhile books: Ira Kipnis, *The American Socialist Movement, 1897-1912*;[8] Howard H.

---

[3] New York: Viking, 1949.
[4] New Haven: Yale University, 1940.
[5] New York: Harper, 1949.
[6] (An Atlantic Monthly Press Book) Boston: Little, Brown, 1951.
[7] New Brunswick, N. J.: Rutgers University, 1955.
[8] New York: Columbia University, 1952.

Quint, *The Forging of American Socialism: Origins of the Modern Movement*;[9] and David A. Shannon, *The Socialist Party of America: A History*.[10] Quint's book carries the story only until 1901 but is of interest to the student of progressivism because of its thesis that American socialism rose more in response to American conditions and thought than to the impact of European radical and Marxian doctrines. Shannon's volume, which covers the period from 1901 to 1952, is scholarly and objective but contains little interpretation. Kipnis writes from the viewpoint of the left wing of the party, is very critical of the lack of democracy, the chauvinism, and the race consciousness of the majority, and concludes that the opportunism and the lack of principle of the majority was responsible for the decline of American Socialism.

LOCAL AND STATE STUDIES

Directly centered upon progressivism are a number of recent local and state studies that have contributed greatly to our understanding of the movement. There is still much work to be done before the urban roots of progressivism are dug out of local municipal reform efforts. But Walton Bean, *Boss Ruef's San Francisco: The Story of the Union Labor Party, Big Business, and the Graft Prosecution*[11] makes a brilliant start. Although the book is centered upon the prosecution of Reuf and his boodling Labor party colleagues, it clearly analyzes the forces that combined in San Francisco to challenge the corrupt hold of organized labor and organized big business on the city government. Bean's volume also studies the anatomy of a typical municipal reform movement in this period. As the volume indicates, the reform spirit originated in the indignation of the so-called good element in the city against corrupt politicians for their fraudulent uses of city funds and for their protection of vice at a price. But in San Francisco, as in many other cities, when the reformers pushed their prosecution they learned to their amazement that a corrupt nexus ran from the political boodlers to respectable men of wealth and the great corporations. Not only protection for prostitution and illegal liquor establishments was for sale in San Francisco, but also street car franchises, and contracts for the delivery of gas and water and for the paving of streets and for other municipal activities. When the reform movement sought to prosecute the briber as well as the bribed, a good many of its sup-

---

[9] Columbia: University of South Carolina, 1953.
[10] New York: Macmillan, 1955.
[11] Berkeley: University of California, 1952.

porters, unwilling to attack wealth and respectability, fell away, and eventually became enemies of reform. This so retarded the impetus of reform that only Reuf and a few of his political henchmen were sent to jail. But it also convinced the more obdurate reformers that to obtain their aims they must control the city and state governments. Consequently, they were soon organizing nonpartisan groups whose purpose it was to remove the influence of both labor and corporation, first from the municipal government and then from the State house.

Three recent studies have been made of progressivism at the state level: Winston A. Flint, *The Progressive Movement in Vermont*,[12] Ransom E. Noble, Jr., *New Jersey Progressivism before Wilson*,[13] and George E. Mowry, *The California Progressives*.[14] The Flint study is the more conventional because it deals with progressivism in a rural community and because it lacks interpretation. The works of Noble and Mowry deal for the first time with the rise of progressivism in urban and industrial settings. Among the contributions made by the Noble volume are the findings that the reform movement in New Jersey long antedated the rise of Woodrow Wilson and that the early work of the reformers, most of them Republicans, partially explains Wilson's later successes as governor. In his study of New Jersey, Noble also revealed how closely the great corporate interests and the political control of the state were integrated.

The California Progressives attempts to find out by the statistical method just who the progressives were in terms of their social background, education, occupations, and religious and other affiliations. The California book also contains a chapter on the progressive mind, which consists of a group analysis of progressive philosophy, preconceptions, biases, and beliefs. It concludes that the typical California progressive was of the great unorganized middle class, more often than not a professional person, a self-employed business man, or a journalist, who was distinctly troubled by his loss of social status in face of the growing power of organized labor and organized business. Extremely well-educated and ethically minded, he was generally a Protestant who had lost most of his beliefs in the supernatural. Moreover, he had cast aside the conservative assumption of the nineteenth century that man was relatively unchangeable and fervently believed that with the right environment men could be transformed until they attained a

---

[12] (Studies in Political Science) Washington, D. C.: American Council on Public Affairs, 1941.

[13] (Princeton Studies in History, 2) Princeton: Princeton University, 1946.

[14] (Chronicles of California) Berkeley: University of California, 1951.

stature ethically and morally just a little lower than that of the angels. The volume also stresses the antipathy of the urban progressive toward labor, especially when labor sought to influence or engage in politics.

REGIONAL STUDIES

Since regions in the United States are often characterized by distinct economic, social, and even ideological peculiarities the value of studying a reform movement within the boundaries is obvious. Two fine postwar studies have been made of regions: One of an intellectual region and the other of a geographical nature. Arthur Mann, *Yankee Reformers in the Urban Age*[15] is a study of Boston and its intellectual hinterland. Thus it is far more than the study of a city, since it deals almost entirely with the ideas rather than the political mechanics of reform and since Boston was and is the intellectual capital of New England. After the inundation of the Old Yankee stock in New England by the new immigration and after the drying up of the New England nineteenth century literary outpouring, historians have often assumed that the original home of American Puritanism was no longer a vital factor in the American reform impulse. In his volume Mann amply proved the contrary. Moreover, he indicated for the first time the contributions made to late nineteenth and twentieth century reforms by Jews and Irish-Catholics. Women constituted another group whose contributions to the American reform spirit have been largely overlooked by the historian. In his chapter on "The New and the Newer Women as Reformers," Mann outlined at least some of the characteristic feminine influences that have colored the recent reform history of the nation. But Mann's most important service to the better understanding of the progressive years was to prove once again that "modern liberalism owes its beginning to the city as well as to the farm."

For all the past emphasis upon the Midwest as the place of origin and as the intellectual dynamo of early twentieth century reform, until recently no attempt had been made to study the movement within the confines of the section as a whole. Russel Blaine Nye, *Midwestern Progressive Politics: A Historical Study of Its Origins and Development, 1870-1950*[16] has remedied this neglect. In his excellent volume, based mostly upon printed sources, Nye supported the older interpretation that twentieth century progressivism was "the lineal

---

[15] Cambridge: Harvard University, 1954.
[16] East Lansing: Michigan State College, 1951.

descendant of nineteenth century revolt." To do so he went back and looked at the Grangers, the Greenbackers, and the Populists, and traced their ideas straight to the progressive ideological complex. The book thus makes one of its contributions in offsetting the more un-qualified claims of the urban historians that progressivism was the product of the city and not of the farm. But in his defense of the older view Nye also paid tribute, in a way, to the newer interpretation by studying the rise of reform in the midwestern city and by showing that even the agrarian reformers of the section were deeply influenced by the new theology and the new social sciences. In a chapter entitled "The Capture of the Ivory Tower," Nye proved that, although a good deal of the new intellectual and religious force powering the rise of progressivism was decidedly midwestern in origin, it was not the product of rural or Populist thinking, but came rather from the new Midwest of the city and the factory, from the rising universities, and from the urban pulpit.

BIOGRAPHY

There has always been a large question in the mind of the pro-fessonal historian whether biography should be considered history at all. The authors of biography are often so biased for or against their subjects and they so frequently do their research and writing from the extremely narrow dimensions of the papers and viewpoints of their subjects alone that the result often gravely distorts the period under examination.

Two volumes which are decidedly history and biography at the same time are Arthur S. Link, *Wilson: The Road to the White House* and *Wilson: The New Freedom*.[17] These first two volumes of a projected multi-volume life of Woodrow Wilson make an unusual contribution to the study of recent reform history. Hitherto the only full life of Wilson was the one by Ray Stannard Baker, one of Wilson's contem-poraries and strong admirers. Link's interpretation departs radically from Baker's in his estimate of Wilson both as a person and as a major influence on foreign and domestic policies. Since the author made a consistent effort to relate subject to period, and since his research was extraordinarily comprehensive, these two volumes also contain the best study of the nature of the Democratic party and its evolution from 1908-1916. Link was very critical of Wilson's "mis-

---

[17] Princeton: Princeton University, 1947 and 1956. Volume III of the biography, *Wilson, the Struggle for Neutrality*, was published in 1960.

sionary diplomacy" in Latin America as being unrealistic and impolitic. Thus he agreed with George F. Kennan's interpretation in *American Diplomacy, 1900-1950*.[18] On the other hand, he went to great lengths and many pages to describe Wilson's masterful and adept leadership in steering his major domestic reform measures through an uncertain Congress.

For a long time revisions and corrections to Henry F. Pringle's *Theodore Roosevelt: A Biography*[19] have been sorely needed. Although Pringle's volume is one of the most sparkling and exciting biographies in recent American history, the weight of a growing scholarly opinion is that it slights Roosevelt's achievements during his Presidency and is quite inadequate for the period after 1909. George E. Mowry, *Theodore Roosevelt and the Progressive Movement*[20] and John M. Blum, *The Republican Roosevelt*[21] have helped rectify the situation. Blum stated in his preface that his work is "neither a biography of Roosevelt nor a complete record of his public career, but an interpretation of the purposes and methods of that career." Within the limits Blum set for himself he performed brilliantly. His analysis of Roosevelt's mind is an excellent synthesis of arduous research and imaginative writing. His chapter on Roosevelt's part in the Congressional struggle over the passage of the Hepburn Railroad Rate Act furnishes a picture of Roosevelt's adroit political maneuvering that is unduplicated. Perhaps the most challenging part of Blum's book is the author's argument that Roosevelt was a conservative. The volume by George Mowry emphasizes the period after 1909, on which Pringle is sketchy. It examines the reasons for Roosevelt's decision to run for the Presidency again in 1912 and weighs the result of that decision for the nation and for the Republican party. One of the theses of the volume is that Roosevelt, by establishing the Progressive party in 1912 and then leaving it in 1916, so crippled the progressive strength in the Republican party that it never recovered. Thus Roosevelt, in a way, was responsible for 1920 Republicanism and for the party's debacle in 1932 and afterwards.

One of the most competent and inspired acts of editing that recent years have witnessed, although it is certainly not a biography, is

---

[18] (Charles R. Walgreen Foundation Lectures) Chicago: University of Chicago, 1951.

[19] New York: Harcourt, Brace, 1931. Also available in a Harvest Books, paperback edition.

[20] Madison: University of Wisconsin, 1946.

[21] Cambridge: Harvard University, 1954.

Elting E. Morison and John M. Blum, *The Letters of Theodore Roosevelt*,[22] which contains about one of every five of Roosevelt's own letters. The letters are superbly well selected and carefully annotated. In addition the prefaces and the appendixes contain excellent sketches and articles dealing with various phases of the President's personality and his career.

Among the other recent biographical works which have appeared on major figures, Belle Case La Follette and Fola La Follette, *Robert M. La Follette, June 14, 1855—June 18, 1925*[23] is one of the more important, since no good biography of the Wisconsin Senator had previously existed. Considering the fact that the book was written by La Follette's wife and daughter, the work is reasonably objective in what it presents. It does contain some strange omissions of data and should be supplemented by Robert S. Maxwell, *La Follette and the Rise of the Progressives in Wisconsin*.[24]

Two recent works have appeared about Charles Evans Hughes, another major figure hitherto without an adequate biography. Merlo J. Pusey, *Charles Evans Hughes*[25] is the full length authorized biography. It presents, rather uncritically, few new facts and less interpretation of this rather enigmatic man. Nevertheless, it is of worth for the student of progressivism because of its material on the New York insurance investigation and on the period of Hughes's governorship. Dexter Perkins, *Charles Evans Hughes and American Democratic Statesmanship*[26] is a volume in the new "Library of American Biography" edited by Oscar Handlin. This series should be of especial value to high school teachers and students because of the books' small number of pages and low price, and because the series endeavors to interpret the subjects it covers rather than retail a mass of minute facts about them.

John A. Garraty, *Henry Cabot Lodge: A Biography*[27] is the first scholarly work on one of the most controversial men in recent history. The previous books on Lodge have been highly partisan and have not used the Lodge manuscripts which Garraty examined. Perhaps because the author undertook to present, according to the preface, his "subject's point of view" the volume is not entirely satisfying. It

---

[22] 8 Vols. Cambridge: Harvard University, 1951-1954.
[23] 2 Vols. New York: Macmillan, 1953.
[24] Madison: State Historical Society of Wisconsin, 1956.
[25] 2 Vols. New York: Macmillan, 1951.
[26] Boston: Little, Brown, 1956.
[27] New York: Knopf, 1953.

further bolsters the traditional picture of Lodge and agrees with the view of Thomas A. Bailey that both Lodge and Wilson were responsible for the defeat of the League of Nations.

Richard W. Leopold, *Elihu Root and the Conservative Tradition* is another volume in the new "Library of American Biography."[28] An interpretation rather than a life, it is thoroughly scholarly and critical, and supplies a needed revision to the older and excellent two-volume biography by Philip C. Jessup.[29] Leopold's book more than Jessup's stresses the conservatism of Root and his intimate relations with big business and big finance. It also emphasizes the change in Root's attitudes after 1909 which hurried him along the conservative road and operated to make the rest of his long life relatively unproductive compared to the earlier period of his brilliant achievements in the McKinley and Roosevelt Cabinets.

Since there are no monographic studies specifically on progressivism in the South, one must rely mainly upon biographical material for this subject. Fortunately two excellent studies exist of Southern Populists who continued their rebel ways into the twentieth century. C. Vann Woodward, *Tom Watson, Agrarian Rebel*[30] is a superb account of the Georgia leader of the underpriviledged poor-white farming class. And Francis B. Simkins, *Pitchfork Ben Tillman, South Carolinian*[31] is an equivalent study. Both books indicate how a frustrated reform sentiment may become perverted into something asocial and dangerous for democratic society. When these two books are taken together with A. D. Kirwan, *Revolt of the Rednecks: Mississippi Politics, 1876-1925*,[32] which is not a biography but rather a study of the depressed white classes, a fairly good picture of one aspect of Southern reform is obtained.

Louis Filler, *Crusaders for American Liberalism*[33] and Cornelius C. Regier, *The Era of the Muckrakers*[34] are collective biographical studies of the reforming journalists who did so much in educating the American public to the need for reform. Filler's book is much the

---

[28] Boston: Little, Brown, 1954.
[29] 2 Vols. New York: Dodd, Mead, 1938.
[30] New York: Macmillan, 1938. For a general treatment of the South during much of the Progressive era, see C. Vann Woodward, *Origins of the New South, 1877-1913* (Baton Rouge: Louisiana State University, 1951). This is volume IX in A History of the South edited by Wendell H. Stephenson and E. Merton Coulter.
[31] (Southern Biography Series) Baton Rouge: Louisiana State University, 1944.
[32] Lexington: University of Kentucky, 1951.
[33] Yellow Springs, Ohio: Antioch, 1950.
[34] Chapel Hill: University of North Carolina, 1932.

more readable. But unfortunately neither volume inquires into the birth and development of the reform spirit among this group of rather remarkable men. Elmer Ellis, *Mr. Dooley's America: A Life of Finley Peter Dunne*[35] is more than a brilliant biography of America's leading political humorist and satirist of the time. It relates Mr. Dooley to his time and presents a good analysis of the part of journalists in the reform movement.

Among other biographies of the period in which the teacher should also perhaps be interested are John M. Blum, *Woodrow Wilson and the Politics of Morality*[36] and by the same author, *Joe Tumulty and the Wilson Era.*[37] The Wilson volume is more an interpretation than it is a life and should be consulted and compared with Arthur Link's two volumes already mentioned. Ray Ginger, *The Bending Cross: A Biography of Eugene Victor Debs,*[38] is the best existing biography of the fascinating midwestern socialist who was a curious combination of Christian and Marxist, of European theoretician and American Populist.

THE ECONOMIC APPROACH

The one general book devoted exclusively to the economic institutions and their development in the period is Harold U. Faulkner, *The Decline of Laissez Faire, 1897-1917.*[39] This seventh volume of the "Economic History of the United States Series" is more definitive in its presentation of fact than any other existing work. But for the story of agriculture the student should consult Theodore Saloutos and John D. Hicks, *Agricultural Discontent in the Middle West, 1900-1939*[40] of which only the first half dozen chapters are properly in the progressive period. The volume clearly shows that farmer discontent did not disappear with the relatively better farm prices of the first decade of the twentieth century and thus helps to refute some of the new urban-born assumptions about the nature of progressivism. Sidney Fine, *Laissez Faire and the General-Welfare State: A Study of*

---

[35] New York: Knopf, 1941.

[36] This is in the Library of American Biography Series. Boston: Little, Brown, 1956. See also John A. Garraty, *Woodrow Wilson* (New York: Knopf, 1956), in the Great Lives in Brief Series, and Arthur Clarence Walworth, *Woodrow Wilson* (2 vols.; New York: Longmans, Green, 1958).

[37] Boston: Houghton Mifflin, 1951.

[38] New Brunswick: Rutgers University, 1949.

[39] New York: Rinehart, 1951.

[40] Madison: University of Wisconsin, 1951.

Conflict in American Thought, 1865-1901[41] is a very useful summary of the ideas advanced by both sides of the developing controversy between the partisans of government regulation and the defenders of classical liberal doctrines. Hans B. Thorelli, *The Federal Antitrust Policy: Organization of an American Tradition*[42] is centered specifically on the growth of the antitrust movement up until 1903. Contradicting the prevailing opinion, Thorelli argued that Congress knew exactly what it was doing in passing the Sherman Antitrust Act. He sees the Act as an expression of the traditional American egalitarian spirit.

GENERAL INTERPRETATIONS OF THE PROGRESSIVE MOVEMENT

With the help of monographs at least four rather distinctive interpretations have been published. Eric F. Goldman, *Rendezvous with Destiny: A History of Modern American Reform*[43] does not confine itself to the progressive period alone but rather is a history of reform thought from about 1870 through Franklin Roosevelt's New Deal. For the progressive period and the decades that preceded it, Goldman fairly well-confined himself to an examination of the ideas of representative reform thinkers starting with Henry George and running through the academicians, Franz Boas, Richard Ely, Edward A. Ross, and Thorstein Veblen, the philosophers James and Dewey, the legal scholars, Holmes and Brandeis, J. Allen Smith, and Charles Beard, and such other varied people as Theodore Roosevelt, Herbert Croly, Walter Lippmann, and Woodrow Wilson. Goldman's central thesis hangs on the breakdown of social Darwinist thought in the United States and the substitution for it of what he calls "reform Darwinism." Social Darwinism, of course, had stressed the natural selection of the fittest in society by the process of free competiton, the word "natural" being closely identified with the capitalist market and "free" signifying freedom from government's aid or regulation. Such a society operating without government interference was assumed to be the equivalent of Darwin's world of competitive nature. But Goldman suggested that academicians, theologians, philosophers, and political theorists seized upon Darwin's argument that environment was the crucial factor in the selection of such species and individuals as survived.

---

[41] (University of Michigan Publications in History and Political Science, 22) Ann Arbor: University of Michigan, 1956.

[42] Baltimore: Johns Hopkins University, 1955.

[43] New York: Knopf, 1953. This book is also available in a Vintage paperback edition.

Hence if one changed the environment, one changed the species. By transference of the idea into the world of men, reform Darwinism assumed that by changing man's environment one could change man.

Reform Darwinism, Goldman argued, was the crucial idea in the bundle of new religious, economic, political, and philosophic doctrines that challenged nineteenth century conservatism. Between them the prophets of the new doctrines "broke the links" between the old thought and the law. Thus the author concluded that ideas were the real agents in bringing about the change and reform. But these same ideas which helped to break down the old conservative formulations, Goldman continued, also in the end presented a dilemma to the reformers. For with the old unity and old ethics weakened, the question was continually put: reform to what end? The answer of the advance relativists was, in the words of Walter Lippmann in his *A Preface to Politics*,[44] "find out what men want and give it to them." But since various classes of men wanted various and often contradictory things, the only sure guidepost was one of sheer self-interest.

Richard Hofstadter, *The Age of Reform: From Bryan to F. D. R.*[45] uses an entirely different approach in attempting to explain the growth of the reform spirit. Instead of examining individuals and their ideas, Hofstadter studied social groups and classes and emphasized their feelings, aspirations, and frustrations. His study, he said in the preface, is "primarily a study of political thinking and political moods." A good part of the explanation for the progressive movement he finds in what he calls "the status revolution." During the nineties and into the new century, the author saw the old urban unorganized, educated middle-class group becoming increasingly aware that it was losing its privileged position in American society. This group, which included lawyers, doctors, preachers, editors, and independent businessmen, had long supplied the intellectual, moral, and political leadership of the country. Now its position was assaulted both by the leaders of the great corporations and the rising labor unions. As the power of the corporation and labor union penetrated into most sectors of society the frustration of the members of this old American group became acute. They were the victims, the author writes, "of an upheaval in status" which pertained not so much to their relative economic position but to "the changed pattern in the distribution of deference and power."

---

[44] New York: M. Kennerley, 1913.
[45] New York: Knopf, 1955.

This old American middle-class group was largely Anglo-Saxon by descent. Its anxiety over the rise of the corporations and unions was further increased by the flood of new immigrants pouring into the country from southern and central Europe. Thus the group developed a strong sense of racialism. Moreover, these old Americans had strong ideological ties with the agrarian, democratic, egalitarian doctrines of pre-Civil War days. When they looked at the twentieth century city with its spawn of poverty, crime, and vice they developed a marked guilt complex. "The moral indignation of the age," the author stated, "was by no means directed entirely against others; it was in a great and critical measure directed inward." From this complex of feelings marked by anxiety, frustration, racialism, and guilt, Hofstadter argued, came the "mugwump personality" which in the second generation was to supply the leadership for the new reform crusade.

Two volumes in the New American Nation Series, which will eventually cover the entire history of the country in some forty volumes, also add to the new ideas about progressivism. George E. Mowry, *The Era of Theodore Roosevelt, 1900-1912*[46] covers the Republican era of reform; the other, Arthur S. Link, *Woodrow Wilson and the Progressive Era, 1910-1917* extends over the later period dominated by a Democratic President and Congress. Among other factors responsible for the progressive period, Mowry saw as one of its basic causes the developing conflict in the drift of economic institutions and the findings of the new social sciences. Whereas the dominant economic institutions were producing a society of highly stratified classes sharply differentiated in economic, social, and political circumstances, the findings of the new social sciences pointed unerringly toward the conclusion that men of all colors, creeds, and nations were infinitely more alike than they were different. The conflict produced a reform tension, the release of which was aided by the formulation of a new and revolutionary concept of man as master not only of his environment but also of himself. In attempting to analyze the thinking of progressives, conservatives, and radicals, the author maintained that early twentieth century conservatism and radicalism were both offsprings of nineteenth century mechanistic and determinist thought in which man was more an agent than he was a prime force in history. Progressivism, on the contrary, considered man as a "changemaker" and a creator, a director, rather than a passive receptor of natural and social forces. Following this definition the author challenged the

---

[46] New York: Harper, 1958.

assumption that Theodore Roosevelt was a conservative and placed him in the progressive tradition. The author also emphasized the part played by women in creating a climate for reform. He suggested that the educated, middle-class woman, as a member of the nation's best trained group of underprivileged people, was determined to achieve an equality of status with the male not by descending to his ethical and practical standards but by reforming him up to her own elevated standards.

Arthur S. Link, *Woodrow Wilson and the Progressive Era*[47] analyzes both Roosevelt's New Nationalism and Woodrow Wilson's New Freedom and accounts for the difference between the two programs largely in terms of the strong agrarian influence in the Democratic party. Both the South and Bryan had left a rural mark on Democratic thinking. But Link also showed Wilson's gradual acceptance of the tenets of the New Nationalism. Confronted with the practical problems of office, Wilson, the author indicated, gave up the theoretical program which he had urged in the campaign of 1912 and adopted that of his chief adversary. Link offered a new viewpoint on Wilson's Caribbean policy which he described as "missionary diplomacy." He also noted Wilson's support of the Pan American Pact as an act clearly foreshadowing the League of Nation's Covenant and the Good Neighbor Policy.

CONCLUSION

The varied new ideas and interpretations of the past fifteen years about the origins and nature of the progressive movement rest upon the contributions of many historians. As research on the period goes on and as the period itself recedes into the past, new viewpoints and new interpretations will unquestionably augment, and to a surprising extent eventually replace, those of the past and the present. For history is something that can never be frozen into the mold of fixed convictions. To exist at all it must live, and to live it must change.

---

[47] New York: Harper, 1954.

CHAPTER XIII

The New World Power: 1865-1917

Foster Rhea Dulles

INTRODUCTION

THE years between the close of the Civil War and American entry into World War I marked the rise of the United States to a position of world power. The economic and industrial growth of the nation in the latter half of the nineteenth century provided the foundations for its new role, but the war with Spain in 1898 and the unexpected acquisition of an overseas empire were the dramatic events that suddenly thrust America upon the international stage. While the United States had generally followed a policy of abstention from any direct involvement or political commitments in world affairs prior to 1898, it was henceforth to become increasingly engaged in them and ultimately compelled to abandon altogether its onetime isolationism.

American historical writing has always emphasized this basic shift in the evolution of national policy; it is the familiar theme of general histories and textbooks. In the light of the decisive role that the United States has played upon the world scene since 1945, however, there has been a continuing attempt upon the part of recent historians of foreign policy to re-examine more carefully the background for such important developments and to study more deeply the forces and factors underlying the changes that have taken place in the last sixty years. When foreign affairs were little more than a byproduct of domestic policies, attracting little public interest, the diplomatic record seemed to be enough for students of history; now that they are all-important, there is both far more interest and far greater concern over the significance and meaning of past events in this general foreign policy area.

Historians are asking why the American people embarked upon an imperialistic course in 1898; just how the country became so deeply involved in eastern Asia; what the factors were that led to a more aggressive defense of the Monroe Doctrine; and perhaps most importantly, why the United States went to war against Germany in 1917. These questions are not of merely antiquarian interest; the answers to them may throw a revealing light upon the evolution of policies and attitudes which are today of immense importance.

To a limited degree, this new approach to diplomatic history is reflected in the current revisions of such standard texts as those of Samuel F. Bemis and Thomas A. Bailey, and in such shorter volumes on foreign policy as those by Julius W. Pratt and L. Ethan Ellis.[1] It is more conspicuously present in Robert H. Ferrell's recently published *American Diplomacy: A History*.[2] The stated emphasis in this latter book is upon analysis rather than description, and greater stress is placed upon events in the twentieth century than upon those of preceding years.

Even more indicative of the search for the significant causative factors in the evolution of foreign policy, however, are a number of special studies that may deal with the entire span of our national life, but are very revealing in their interpretations of developments around the turn of the century and in the early 1900's. Thomas A. Bailey and Gabriel Almond attempted to analyze the role of public opinion in policy-making; George A. Kennan and Hans J. Morgenthau critically surveyed the past in terms of what the former has characterized as an unfortunate "legalistic-moralistic approach to international problems" and the latter as a failure fully to understand the "national interest"; Frank Tannenbaum offered a distinctly different point of view in sustaining the validity of the inherent idealism in the American tradition, Edward M. Burns explored the idea of America's sense of

---

[1] Samuel Flagg Bemis, *A Diplomatic History of the United States* (Fourth edition. New York: Holt, 1955) and *A Short History of American Foreign Policy and Diplomacy* (New York: Holt, 1959); Thomas A. Bailey, *A Diplomatic History of the American People* (6th ed., New York: Appleton-Century-Crofts, 1958); Julius W. Pratt, *A History of United States Foreign Policy* (New York: Prentice-Hall, 1955); Lewis Ethan Ellis, *A Short History of American Diplomacy* (New York: Harper, 1951). A more recent volume is Nelson T. Barck, Jr., *The United States in Its World Relations* (New York: McGraw-Hill, 1960). See also Foster Rhea Dulles, *America's Rise to World Power, 1898-1954* (New York: Harper, 1955), a volume in the New American Nation Series; and also William A. Williams, *The Shaping of American Diplomacy* (Chicago: Rand McNally, 1956).

[2] Robert H. Ferrell, *American Diplomacy: A History* (New York: Norton, Inc., 1959). To these general studies may be added the very useful collection of documents: Ruhl J. Bartlett, *The Record of American Diplomacy* (Third edition. New York: Knopf, 1954).

mission, and Dexter Perkins provided an even broader synthesis—albeit in very brief compass—by presenting a cyclical theory of American attitudes toward foreign affairs that embraces the entire span of our national history.[3] Perhaps even more significant is the brilliant study by Robert E. Osgood whose attempt to evaluate the conflicting forces that have governed foreign policy, especially since 1900, is suggested by his title, *Ideals and Self-Interest in America's Foreign Relations: The Great Transformation of the Twentieth Century.*[4]

The diplomatic record is not the primary concern of these writers. Their books are characterized by new evaluations and new interpretations, sometimes highly controversial, which reflect a mid-twentieth century point of view.

CIVIL WAR TO THE 1890's

There are perhaps four major divisions in the time span—1865 to 1917—alloted to this chapter. The first extends from the close of the Civil War to the 1890's, a period that Henry Cabot Lodge once characterized as a time when foreign issues had "but a slight place in American politics, and excite[d] generally only a languid interest." The second revolves about the sudden burst of imperialistic fervor which marked the turn of the century and dramatically witnessed the war with Spain, the annexation of overseas colonies, and the pronouncement of the Open Door policy in China. The third embraces the further extension of American influence and power, primarily under the dynamic leadership of Theodore Roosevelt, during the early 1900's. And the fourth and final period is that which ultimately led to American participation in World War I as the American people embarked on their great crusade to make the world safe for democracy.

The relatively barren years of post-Civil War diplomacy have not inspired very much in the way of fresh interpretation of events or any

---

[3] Thomas A. Bailey, *The Man in the Street: The Impact of American Public Opinion on Foreign Policy* (New York: Macmillan, 1948); Gabriel Abraham Almond, *The American People and Foreign Policy* (New York: Harcourt, Brace, 1950); George Frost Kennan, *American Diplomacy, 1900-1950* (Chicago: University of Chicago, 1951); Hans J. Morgenthau, *In Defense of the National Interest; A Critical Examination of American Foreign Policy* (New York: Knopf, 1951); Frank Tannenbaum, *The American Tradition in Foreign Policy* (Norman: University of Oklahoma, 1955); Edward M. Burns, *The American Idea of Mission: Concepts of National Purpose and Destiny* (New Brunswick: Rutgers University, 1957); and Dexter Perkins, *The American Approach to Foreign Policy* (Cambridge: Harvard University, 1952).

[4] Published in Chicago: University of Chicago, 1953.

outstanding re-evaluation of their significance. The negotiations that led to the purchase of Alaska have long since been carefully studied and while the onetime territory's new status as the forty-ninth state gives them an added interest, it does not change the historical record. The settlement of the *Alabama* claims through the Treaty of Washington, concluded with England in 1871, takes on a fresh significance in the continuing story of ever-closer Anglo-American cooperation, but again the facts generally stand of themselves. So, too, the beginnings of American interest in both Hawaii and Samoa, harbingers of the imperialism of the century's close, are a well-known story through monographs and articles published in earlier years.

The Imperialistic Movement of the 1890's

The situation is quite different, however, when we come to the imperialist movement of the 1890's and the consequences of war with Spain. Between 1940 and 1960, new ingredients as well as fresh interpretations were added to the studies of Albert K. Weinberg, Julius Pratt, and other historians of American foreign policy in this period.[5] The climate of opinion in the 1890's, the interplay of the conflicting forces of "isolationism," "imperialism," and "internationalism," and the role of national leaders, were all reconsidered in the light of the new perspectives of mid-twentieth century. This is not to say that the influence of the generally acknowledged factors making for imperialism have been discounted. The closing of the frontier and the sense of "looking outward," the common belief that a surplus of manufactured goods demanded new outlets for American exports, the impact of European imperialism (what John Hay called a "cosmic tendency"), and the historic sense of American mission continue to be accepted as highly significant if not decisive influences upon American policy. It is now believed, however, that they do not necessarily tell the whole story.

Two factors that are heavily stressed in recent interpretations are the impact of Darwinism on American thinking and the influence of the domestic crisis of the 1890's. Neither idea is, of course, completely new; the change here is perhaps one of emphasis. In his re-evaluation of the 1890's as the beginnings of "the age of reform," for example,

---

[5] Albert K. Weinberg, *Manifest Destiny* (Baltimore: Johns Hopkins, 1935). Julius W. Pratt, *Expansionists of 1898; The Acquisition of Hawaii and the Spanish Islands* (Baltimore: Johns Hopkins, 1936). For this whole question the pamphlet in the Amherst College "Problems in American Civilization" series, *American Imperialism in 1898* (Boston: Heath, 1955), is immensely useful.

Richard Hofstadter amplified his well-known ideas on Social Darwinism to suggest that this application of evolutionary theories to society brought both conservatives and progressives together in support of overseas expansion.[6] The American people came to believe that, in the competition of nations, the future lay with that country which could most successfully extend its ideas and institutions over an ever broader area. They saw the peculiar genius of the Anglo-Saxon people, as particularly exemplified in themselves, thus giving the United States an opportunity it could not afford to ignore. It had no alternative to expansion and in this competition upon which it was fated to enter, who could doubt, as Josiah Strong rhetorically asked at the time, that the result would be the survival of the fittest?

These assumptions of the 1890's, however, have been subject to increasing criticism in the more enlightened climate—as it is thought to be—of the mid-twentieth century. "The new manifest destiny—taking for its philosophy the Darwinian beliefs, giving a novel and unfortunate interpretation to the American idea of the mission of democracy," Robert Ferrell has written in his interpretation of our imperialism, "also encumbered itself with the idea of Anglo-Saxon or Aryan superiority."[7]

It is also the writings of Hofstadter, among others, that have drawn fresh attention to the impact of domestic problems in encouraging the jingoistic, imperialistic spirit that characterized the 1890's. Depression, industrial strife, and farm revolt created what Hofstadter has described as a "psychic crisis" for the American people, and they looked to overseas adventure as a means of escape from seemingly insoluble problems at home.[8] A good deal of evidence is indeed available in contemporary writings showing that political leaders successively felt that a strong stand against Great Britain at the time of the Venezuela crisis in 1895, intervention in Cuba in 1898, and the encouragement of overseas expansion in 1899-1900 would serve to unite the nation and overcome the threat of possible social revolt. One newspaper, for example, declared in 1898 that war for Cuba "looms before us as the only rallying standard of the legions of our own national discontent."[9]

---

[6] Richard Hofstadter, *The Age of Reform, From Bryan to F. D. R.* (New York: Knopf, 1955). See also his chapter, "Manifest Destiny and the Philippines," in Daniel Aaron, ed., *America in Crisis* (New York: Knopf, 1952).

[7] Ferrell, *American Diplomacy*, p. 173.

[8] Hofstadter in Aaron, *America in Crisis*, p. 173 f.

[9] The Chicago *Times Herald*, Quoted in Dulles, *The Imperial Years*, p. 124.

220 INTERPRETING AND TEACHING AMERICAN HISTORY

There has also been further reconsideration in recent historical writing of the role of individuals in encouraging and promoting imperialism. The present author discussed the influence of the imperialist-minded circle in Washington which included such men as Theodore Roosevelt, Henry Cabot Lodge, Whitelaw Reid, Albert Beveridge and especially Captain Alfred T. Mahan. This theme was also developed for later years by Howard K. Beale in his consideration of Roosevelt and his imperialistic friends in his monumental *Theodore Roosevelt and the Rise of America to World Power*.[10]

For the Spanish War itself there is no real replacement for the spirited and readable account that Walter Millis provided in *The Martial Spirit*. That conflict remains in John Hay's often-quoted phrase, the "splendid little war." However, there were published a lively journalistic account of those exciting days and also a new descriptive pictorial record of the war relating largely to military and naval operations.[11]

A number of relatively recent studies deal with the results of the Spanish conflict growing out of its appeal to the emotions of the new manifest destiny. A comprehensive and authoritative general account is that of Julius W. Pratt, whose title—*America's Colonial Experiment: How the United States Gained, Governed, and in Part Gave Away a Colonial Empire*—suggests its author's interpretation of these events.[12] There are also more limited studies of developments in other of the territories taken over in 1898 which record their gradual progress along the road to increasing self-government.[13]

The re-interpretations of the general consequences of overseas expansion parallel in some measure the new diagnoses of why the United States embarked upon an imperialistic course. They are often highly controversial but much of the debate centers about the definition of "imperialism." It is maintained on the one hand that the United States quickly repented of imperialistic adventure, and on the other that it continued upon the path upon which it set out in 1900 under a somewhat different guise. The first interpretation is un-

---

[10] Foster Rhea Dulles, *The Imperial Years* (New York: Crowell, 1956); Howard K. Beale, *Theodore Roosevelt and the Rise of America to World Power* (Baltimore: Johns Hopkins, 1956).

[11] Gregory Mason, *Remember the Maine* (New York: Holt, 1959); Frank Freidel, *The Splendid Little War* (Boston: Little, Brown, 1958).

[12] New York: Prentice-Hall, 1950.

[13] Garel A. Grunder and William E. Livezey, *The Philippines and the United States* (Norman: University of Oklahoma, 1951); Earl S. Pomeroy, *Pacific Outpost: American Strategy in Guam and Micronesia* (Stanford: Stanford University, 1951).

questionably valid if territorial imperialism is meant; the latter may be substantiated if economic pressure or dollar diplomacy is taken as constituting imperialism.[14] In any event, the tone of most writing upon American imperialism, and upon the general concept of "the white man's burden," is increasingly critical. While there is nothing new in this, a mid-twentieth century outlook is obviously reflected in the more severe strictures drawn upon our policy in relation to what were in 1900 considered the inferior peoples—the "lesser breeds without the law"—but what in the 1950's are more sympathetically characterized as the "underdeveloped nations."

THE OPEN DOOR AND CHINA, 1899-1914

Before further considering the new books dealing with this and other general issues that developed in the years between 1900 and 1914, it should be noted that several specialized studies have served to throw new light upon the most immediate result of the nation's new position as a world power; that is, the pronouncement of the Open Door policy in China. The well-known role of William W. Rockhill and Alfred E. Hippisley in initiating our China policy was further explored by Paul Varg.[15] He confirmed both the independent nature of the stand Secretary Hay took in 1899 and 1900, and the interest that both Rockhill and Hippisley had in safeguarding China's independence as well as in promoting American trade and commerce. Although England had originally sought American cooperation in upholding the Open Door, the move we finally made was directed against her as well as against the other Powers. Charles S. Campbell, Jr., on the other hand, provided fresh evidence of the strong influence business interests exerted upon the State Department, thereby making Hay the more receptive to the suggestions that Rockhill made for immediate action to safeguard our Far Eastern commerce.[16]

---

[14] Although the economic implications of our foreign policy in the Caribbean are clear in the very term "dollar diplomacy," it has long since been generally agreed by most historians that this policy was more importantly motivated by strategic needs in the Caribbean and the desire to safeguard the approaches to the Panama Canal. See for example Ferrell, *American Diplomacy*, p. 250; Bemis, *American Foreign Policy and Diplomacy*, p. 318.

[15] Paul A. Varg, *Open Door Diplomat: The Life of W. W. Rockhill* (Urbana: University of Illinois, 1952).

[16] Charles S. Campbell, Jr., *Special Business Interests and the Open Door Policy* (New Haven: Yale University, 1951). See also in connection with this and other developments at the turn of the century, the same author's valuable monograph, *Anglo-American Understanding, 1898-1903* (Baltimore: Johns Hopkins, 1957).

As to the success of the Open Door policy current interpretations tend to become increasingly dubious of the value of Hay's diplomacy. They often reflect, however, a curious ambivalence which is again the mark of a mid-twentieth century point of view and of current arguments over "realism" and "idealism" as motivating forces in the determination of policy.

George F. Kennan largely discounted the Open Door policy in his brilliant *American Diplomacy*. He made the point that Hay had no real conception of the realities of world politics and accepted the concept of the Open Door largely because it had a high-minded and idealistic ring. His policy had no practical results and never commanded the support that could have made it effective. Yet in spite of its ineffectiveness, Kennan wrote, nothing could shake the public belief that "a tremendous blow had been struck for the triumph of American principles in international society—an American blow for an American idea."[17]

Another interpretation of these developments is that the Open Door policy was a highly limited proposition when it was first announced, did not succeed (as even Hay acknowledged) in attaining its objectives, launched the United States upon an erratic course of successive advances and retreats in defense of our interests in eastern Asia which seemed very inconclusive, but finally fastened upon the American mind a deep conviction that the United States was committed to the defense of Chinese independence.[18] From this point of view, as Japan became after the Russo-Japanese war of 1904-1905 the most dangerous challenger to the Open Door and Chinese territorial integrity, the policy of 1899-1900 led directly to the crisis of Pearl Harbor forty-one years later. It may all have been a mistake; its ultimate consequences were nevertheless momentous.

There are also a number of new monographs, carrying forward the story of American relations with China during the period up to World War I, which shed additional light on the policies of Roosevelt, Taft, and Woodrow Wilson.[19] They tend to emphasize the economic

---

[17] Kennan, *American Diplomacy*, p. 36-37.

[18] Hay admitted to Japan in 1901 that the United States was not in any way prepared to enforce its views on the Open Door, but such later developments as the Washington conference agreements in 1921-1922 and the Stimson Doctrine of 1932 helped to build up this idea of an American guarantee of China's territorial independence. On this latter concept see Ferrell, *American Diplomacy*, p. 227.

[19] See Charles Vevier, *The United States and China: 1906-1913* (New Brunswick: Rutgers University, 1955); Tien-yi Li, *Woodrow Wilson's China Policy, 1913-1917* (New York: [University of Kansas City] Twayne Publishers, 1952); Roy W. Curry,

aspects of the issues that centered about the Manchurian railways, loans and investments in China, and American membership in the Chinese Consortium. The broader aspects of such developments are dealt with in a highly controversial and also very provocative study by William A. Williams which he titles *The Tragedy of American Diplomacy*.[20] This is a general analysis of American policy during the first half of the twentieth century but its major point is that John Hay's notes initiated what Williams describes as "open door imperialism." This has been the basis, it is maintained, for the continuing foreign policy of the United States ever since 1900, not only in eastern Asia but on a worldwide basis. The economic interpretation is heavily overweighted but the book is nevertheless very stimulating.

ROOSEVELT AND TAFT, 1899-1914

The most important new study dealing with foreign affairs in the period from 1900 to the eve of World War I is undoubtedly Howard K. Beale's volume on Theodore Roosevelt's policies, to which reference has already been made. While it slights some aspects of the diplomacy of this period, no one has dealt more thoroughly or more authoritatively with these years when Roosevelt so largely directed the nation's world role.

Beale clearly brought out—with highly informative detail—Roosevelt's broad conception of the part he believed that the United States should play in international affairs, his understanding of the realities of Great Power politics, his skillful diplomacy, and his flair for personal negotiations through his intimates in Washington and in foreign capitals. He emphasized the President's concern in seeking a close understanding with Great Britain (where he was so ably assisted by John Hay), curbing the rising power of an imperialist-minded Germany, and building up the position of the United States in both eastern Asia and Latin America. His careful research serves to give greater credence to the story Roosevelt later told of his threat to Germany at the time of the Venezuela episode in 1902, so generally questioned by previous historians, and it also sustains the importance of the role that the United States played under Roosevelt's direction at the Algeciras Conference in 1906. Beale also demonstrated that,

---

Woodrow Wilson and Far Eastern Policy, 1913-1921 (New York: Bookman Associates, 1957) ; and Russell H. Fifield, *Woodrow Wilson and the Far East* (New York: Crowell, 1952).

[20] Published in Cleveland: World, 1959.

for all the President's delight in wielding the big stick, he worked zealously for peace, especially in relations with Japan.

Beale's conclusions upon Roosevelt's final role in the evolution of American foreign policy are nevertheless highly critical. He was convinced that Roosevelt never freed himself from his early imperialistic ambitions and continued to have a highly prejudiced attitude toward the peoples of eastern Asia and Latin America which entirely failed to take into account—especially in the case of the Chinese—their revolutionary aspirations and their potentialities for future self-development. In these circumstances his policies were doomed to failure, according to Beale; the course upon which he helped to launch the United States was in the long run highly dangerous to American interests.

While the factual material in this book is immensely valuable, these final conclusions appear to judge Roosevelt by the standards of the 1950's rather than those of the President's own day. They are based upon the ultimate consequences of policies which Roosevelt may have initiated or at least importantly forwarded, but which underwent many shifts and changes at the hands of his successors and over which he rather obviously had no control. It nevertheless remains important to be reminded of the extent to which Roosevelt shared the intolerant racial attitudes that so generally characterized his era, largely accounting for his failure—as that of most of his countrymen—to understand the significance of the rising nationalism of the peoples of Asia.

Roosevelt's part in determining national policy also comes under review in one of the best books dealing with this period as a whole: George E. Mowry's *The Era of Theodore Roosevelt, 1900-1912*.[21] The author's brief treatment of Foreign Affairs emphasizes the President's search for peace and stability in eastern Asia, the new interpretation given to the Monroe Doctrine through Roosevelt's Corollary, and the efforts made to help in maintaining European affairs on an even keel. "In forsaking the principle of isolation and in steadfastly supporting the Anglo-French entente," Mowry wrote in evaluating the final phase of Roosevelt's foreign policy, "the American policy makers at Algeciras were reaching out to the future when twice the power of the New World was to move to redress the balance of the Old."[22]

---

[21] Published as one of the volumes in the New American Nation Series, (New York: Harper, 1958).

[22] Mowry, p. 196.

The policies of William Howard Taft, which were based primarily upon his concepts of "dollar diplomacy," have not been subjected to re-evaluation comparable to that extended to Roosevelt's policies. They were not very successful; they were not too important. Several books (as previously noted) carry forward the discussion of policy in eastern Asia; a number of others deal with Latin America. They do not significantly change our general understanding of this particular period.

THE WILSON ERA

The Woodrow Wilson era, as might well be expected, has inspired a great deal more reconsideration both in general terms and in more particular reference to foreign policy. The most notable contributions here have been those of Arthur S. Link. He embarked on a multi-volume biography of Wilson, contributed a distinctive volume covering the period from 1910 to 1917 to the New American Nation Series, and wrote a shorter study of Wilson's role as a diplomat.[23] There was an apparent change in his evaluation of Wilson as his studies progressed: a highly critical note gave way to a more sympathetic approach.

Link characterized Wilson's policy toward Latin America in the days before World War I as "missionary diplomacy." He heavily stressed in this connection the President's determination to impose upon revolutionary Mexico standards of constitutionalism and democracy that would conform to American tradition, and the consequent dilemma in which he found himself when Mexico failed to follow his counsel and advice. Link was highly critical at this point, finding evidence of a vast gap between promise and performance in Wilsonian diplomacy, and he gave short shrift to the President's idealism. However, as he moved on to further discussion of the Wilson of war days, Link was more willing to accept the sincerity of the President's basic goals and the inner logic of the course that he followed from 1914 to 1917.

The shifts and changes in historical interpretation of the reasons for American entry into World War I, indeed, provide in themselves a topic of fascinating interest. It has long since been agreed by writers

---

[23] Arthur S. Link, *Wilson, the New Freedom* (Princeton: Princeton University, 1956); *Wilson, the Struggle for Neutrality, 1914-1915* (Princeton: Princeton University, 1960); *Woodrow Wilson and the Progressive Era: 1910-1917* (New York: Harper, 1954); *Wilson the Diplomatist: A Look at His Major Foreign Policies* (Baltimore: Johns Hopkins, 1957).

on this period that the immediate cause for American intervention was Germany's adoption of unrestricted submarine warfare, an interpretation first and most significantly developed in the various books of Charles Seymour. None of the newer books dealing with this issue dispute the general verdict. Where interpretations constantly differ is in the emphasis given to the various factors that led the United States to maintain a position—its insistence upon the right to continue unhampered economic aid to the Allies—which finally led to the German attacks upon American shipping.[24]

A first school, stemming largely from contemporary opinion in 1917-1919, stressed the idea that America was prepared to support the Allies because they were fighting for freedom and democracy: this country could not stand aside when the principles for which it also stood were so gravely menaced by monarchical Germany. We entered the war, as Wilson was to declare, the disinterested champions of right. The interpretation in the 1930's was quite different. A number of historians of that decade of disillusionment emphasized the economic factors, stating that the United States too rigidly insisted on its right to trade and then went to war because of the pressure brought to bear by bankers and munitions makers who were concerned only with loans and profits. A decade or so later, when the country was again at war with Germany, a further shift in historical views gave a new importance to the concept that the American people were primarily concerned in 1917—as they were in 1941—with national security. They were prepared to do whatever had to be done to assure an Allied victory not because of either idealistic or economic pressures, but because of an intuitive conviction that a Germany triumphant in Europe would ultimately challenge the United States.[25]

---

[24] Two surveys of this literature are Richard W. Leopold, "The Problem of American Intervention, 1917: An Historical Retrospect," *World Politics*, 2:405-25; April 1950, and Richard L. Watson, Jr., "Woodrow Wilson and His Interpreters, 1945-1957," *Mississippi Valley Historical Review*, 44:207-36; September 1957.

[25] An early study of why the United States entered World War I is Charles Seymour, *Woodrow Wilson and the World War* . . . (New Haven: Yale University, 1921), which was followed by his *American Diplomacy during the World War* (Baltimore: Johns Hopkins, 1934) ; and *American Neutrality, 1914-1917* . . . (New Haven: Yale University, 1935) ; a leading revisionist account is Charles Callan Tansill, *America Goes to War* (Boston: Little, Brown, 1938) ; Walter Lippmann emphasizes the security theme in *U. S. Foreign Policy: Shield of the Republic* (Boston: Little, Brown, 1943); and a more recent book stressing the balance of power concept is Edward Henry Buehrig, *Woodrow Wilson and the Balance of Power* (Bloomington: University of Indiana, 1955) .

These varied interpretations reflect in turn the prevailing climate of opinion at the time they were written. The more recent writers on this phase of American history attempted to view the issues involved with more perspective. They tried to weigh the underlying causes for hostilities with greater objectivity and without letting themselves be more influenced than is inescapable from the currents of contemporary opinion.

The three major texts on American diplomacy, the books by Bemis, Bailey, and Ferrell to which reference has already been made, seek to evaluate the events of 1917 in terms of both new research and the perspective of mid-twentieth century. Bemis continued in his newly revised edition to emphasize the diplomatic record in the struggle to maintain neutrality. Since Wilson early (1915) took the position that the United States would hold Germany to a strict accountability for any interference with its shipping, the latter's resumption of unrestricted submarine warfare "forced" the United States into war. Bemis recognized the importance of the underlying factors in the situation— the mounting sympathy for the Allies, heightened through their highly effective propaganda, and the economic ties promoted by war loans and an expanding trade—but he declared that it was the submarine which served as the final reagent which precipitated actual hostilities.[26]

Bailey discussed more fully the broad, general aspects of the situation as it had developed by 1917, and acknowledged that propagandists, bankers and munitions makers "no doubt had some influence" in shaping the policies that finally goaded the Germans into unrestricted submarine warfare. However, it remained his conclusion, as that of Bemis, that "in the final analysis America fought because she was attacked—the war was 'thrust' upon her."[27]

In his newer book, which is something quite different from a revision of earlier accounts, Ferrell concluded his discussion on American entry into the war on another note. He discussed somewhat more carefully the inter-relation among the contributing factors that helped to make up the American mind, and sought to analyze the relative importance of the idealistic, economic, and political aspects of the question. Our final entry into war, Ferrell then concluded, was basically an emotional decision. "The American people, to the entire disbelief of contem-

---

[26] Bemis, *A Short History of American Foreign Policy and Diplomacy*, p. 403.
[27] Bailey, *A Diplomatic History of the American People*, p. 593-94.

porary foreign observers and to the disbelief of their own children of the next generation," he wrote, "were willing to take a stand in the world for principle. Americans in the long months of neutrality, from 1914 to 1917, had come to feel that their principles were being challenged."[28]

From the point of view of President Wilson's own position, recent biographical studies have sought to examine more closely what his actual attitude may have been and what brought about his final decision for war. The most thorough and comprehensive work along these lines is that of Link who deals with the problem in the several books already noted but most succinctly in his study *Wilson the Diplomatist*.[29] It was Link's conviction that though Wilson accepted the paramount need to defend the nation's rights as a neutral, his constant effort was to avoid American entry into war. This attitude may have involved the President in a fundamental contradiction, as may now be seen so easily, but he continued to hope that somehow the conflict would be resolved with the United States left as the great mediating nation—associated with neither group of powers—in the ultimate peace-making. Link, who has undoubetdly examined the Wilson papers more carefully than any other historian, concluded that the President decided upon war only when "the assault upon American lives and property was so overwhelming and so flagrant that the only possible way to cope with it was to claim the status of a belligerent in order to strike at the sources of German power."[30] He recognized at once both the idealistic and the realistic aspects of Wilson's policy, and the extent to which he finally became the prisoner of circumstances beyond his control. For it could hardly be expected in the light of public opinion as it had developed by 1917, Link pointed out, that the nation would retreat before the challenge of unrestricted submarine warfare.

Approaching the same issue from another angle, Link further suggested that it was in the face of all Wilson's efforts to bring about peace among the warring powers that Germany's leaders rejected

---

[28] Ferrell, *American Diplomacy*, p. 289.

[29] Other biographical studies of Wilson recently published are Arthur Clarence Walworth, *Woodrow Wilson* (2 vols.; New York: Longmans, Green, 1958) and the penetrating essay of John Arthur Garraty, *Woodrow Wilson* (New York: Knopf, 1956). The latter historian is also the author of *Henry Cabot Lodge, A Biography* (New York: Knopf, 1953). An interesting volume of five Wilson essays published to mark the centennial of his birth is Edward H. Buehrig, ed., *Wilson's Foreign Policy in Perspective* (Bloomington: University of Indiana, 1957).

[30] Link, *Wilson the Diplomatist*, p. 87.

American friendship and cooperation and "chose deliberately to bring the United States into war." This decision was based upon the thesis that Germany could win a total victory before American power could become effective on the field of battle and consequently, Link concluded, "the German military and naval chieftains decisively willed American participation, precisely because their plans, essential for victory and domination, made American participation inevitable."[31]

The most comprehensive study of this entire question, going much deeper than the limits of space allow either the general historians or the Wilson biographers, is a volume by Ernest May.[32] It has the benefit of documents and research studies that represent the accumulated knowledge of forty years, but a striking thing about this excellent and authoritative book is that in its general lines it confirms the analysis of the diplomatic record first made in the books by Charles Seymour published in the 1930's. Access to heretofore unavailable German documents has not led him to change this phase of the story.

On the inter-relation between political, economic, and idealistic factors making for war, May tended to give greater emphasis to the moral implications of the situation than most of the earlier historians and generally supported the conclusions of Ferrell. He had great sympathy for the difficulties which Wilson faced and strongly defended his general policy. "Wilson's mixed firmness and patience," he wrote, "offered the only hope in the long run of keeping the peace, and he held to that policy with persistence, foresight and courage." May also paid sincere tribute in his final conclusion to what he considered Wilson's willingness in his dedicated search for world peace to risk immediate interests for the sake of his ultimate dream. May characterized the President's attitude in this respect as "sublime realism."[33]

These somewhat varied interpretations of the events of 1914-1917 suggest that there can be no final evaluation of the causes of American entry into World War I that will be wholly satisfactory to every student of history. Accepting unrestricted submarine warfare as the immediate cause, or the final precipitating agent, the relative weight of the underlying factors in the situation still remain subject to dispute. Where present-day historians would be in complete agree-

---

[31] Link, *American Epoch* (New York: Knopf, 1955), p. 196.

[32] Ernest R. May, *The World War and American Isolation, 1914-1917* (Cambridge: Harvard University, 1959). See also Samuel R. Spencer, Jr., *Decision for War 1917* . . . (Rindge, New Hampshire: R. R. Smith, 1953) and particularly Link, *Wilson, the Struggle for Neutrality.*

[33] May, p. 436-37.

ment, however, is that any attempted over-simplification of such a complex issue, such as the theory of the responsibility of the bankers and munitions makers which was so popular in the 1930's, cannot be reconciled with the actual course of events and tends to falsify the record.

CONCLUSION

The issues in dispute over American foreign policy in 1917 clearly involve an evaluation of the prevailing climate of public opinion, the impact of various social forces and pressure groups, and the influence of national leaders. The same thing may be said of the questions raised in respect to the imperialism of 1898 and the policies subsequently followed in eastern Asia and Latin America. The fact that such considerations are in the forefront of current interest in the study of foreign policy is a measure of the change that has come over the writing of diplomatic history in the past two decades. Such writing is far more concerned than in the past, let it be repeated, with ideas; it has taken on some of the coloration of intellectual history.

The general recognition that the underlying forces which have governed diplomacy are more important than the diplomatic record itself, and that economic, social, and intellectual factors must be more carefully examined, is thus in itself of very real significance. It reflects the immensely enhanced role of foreign policy in today's troubled world and is the natural consequence of our reaction to the position of world leadership in which the United States presently finds itself.

CHAPTER XIV

Prosperity Decade, 1917-1928

Richard Lowitt

INTRODUCTION

PROSPERITY Decade, 1917-1928, seemingly was a period of marked unanimity in the business cycle, in politics, and in the public mood. Prosperity was supposed to be everyman's lot, while conservatism dominated the political scene and spilled over into American life as well. The country supposedly tired of international turmoil and domestic reform lapsed into what Warren G. Harding called "normalcy"—smug complacency, extreme nationalism, and isolationism. Along with the antics of flappers and their raccoon-coated beaux, bigotry, intolerance, and corruption gave evidence that the humane and liberal aspects of the previous period had lost their vigor.

Though characterized by unanimity, Prosperity Decade actually began in a cataclysmic way with America's entry into World War I and ended in an even more cataclysmic way with the Great Depression. But between these two events American life, according to some interpretations, followed the patterns suggested above. Others have lampooned it, a la Scott Fitzgerald, for its Puritanism (a term that was defined with little relationship to its original meaning), its materialism, its infatuation with fads and fashions, its lawlessness, and its concern with the superficial or ridiculous which merely served to accentuate its drabness.

Such, briefly, have been the standard interpretations of the period. And recent scholarship has not entirely changed them. Rather it has explored areas not previously examined, probed deeply into other events, and projected theories or concepts placing the period in the mainstream of American life. Perhaps, the most significant function of recent scholarship has been to show that Prosperity Decade was not a period which could be set apart and examined of and for itself. We now understand clearly that its roots can be found in the Progressive Era and even before, and that some of the problems Americans faced then would continue—what to do about the Soviet Union, the phrenetic antics of our disillusioned youth, and the farm problem, to cite but three. While such an approach may seem obvious, a good portion of the literature on the topic until recently treated it as a separate unit.

Finally, the period is still to close to the present for it to be broadly reinterpreted in the way, for example, that the American Revolution has been. Rather recent scholarship is enabling us to get a fuller picture with various gradations and shadings so that our understanding is becoming more complete. In the future, as more manuscript material is made available and as the army of recent American historians bring forth the fruit of their labors, our knowledge and understanding will become more complete. In certain areas, newer interpretations are already evident. Historians now are coming to view the period as one marked by severe tensions and contradictions, characteristic of a time of transition. Rural America, so to speak, breathed its last gasps. Its values and traditions were being replaced by those of an urbanized, mechanized, secular, and superficially sophisticated nation. This change in outlook was characterized by the reluctance or incapacity of Americans to come to terms with or even recognize the new realties of life in the United States: a stronger state, the dominance of the city, secularization and the collapse of religious sanctions, the end of laissez faire, the responsibility of world leadership, the decline of individualism. The period, in short, represented, according to William E. Leuchtenburg, "the first serious attempt of Americans to make their peace with the twentieth century."[1] It saw a continuing effort to adjust capitalism in America to a concept of democracy formulated in the eighteenth century to meet the needs of a rural republic. That the concept of democracy had to be recast was only beginning to be widely appreciated. The fact that Americans did not succeed in this effort should not surprise us.

Prior to 1940 many of the prominent participants of Prosperity Decade penned accounts of their activities or those of the organization, group or movement in which they participated. Other accounts have been published since then. Historians were slow to investigate some of the areas covered by these personal accounts. Much of the literature of the 1940's and 1950's reflects the concern of Americans with contemporary issues. This type of concern was particularly evident in the realm of foreign affairs, but it also was apparent in the interest in

---

[1] William E. Leuchtenburg, *The Perils of Prosperity, 1914-1932* (Chicago: University of Chicago, 1958). A brief but brilliant interpretative account.

minority groups, the role of business and labor on the national scene and the course of American liberalism.

WARTIME MOBILIZATION

Frederick Logan Paxson was the only historian who attempted to examine comprehensively America at war.[2] His work is thorough but dull reading. The literature on this general topic, however, is chiefly monographic or is concerned with other themes than that of wartime mobilization.

With regard to the military aspects, Frederick Palmer carefully delineated General Pershing's struggle to maintain an independent American Army in France.[3] In contrast, the American Navy, chiefly engaged in convoying men and material, had to function within the Allied chain of command. Admiral Sims, who commanded the United States naval forces operating in European waters, served his country well from the vantage point of a London office.[4] There is a good biography of Enoch A. Crowder, who devised and administered the Selective Service System.[5] Another phase of World War I was probed by I. B. Holley, Jr., who showed the inability of the United States Air Service to adapt technological advances to military techniques.[6] Aspects

---

[2] Frederick Logan Paxson, *American Democracy and the World War: America at War, 1917-1918* (Boston: Houghton Mifflin, 1939).

[3] Frederick Palmer, *John J. Pershing, General of the Armies* (Harrisburg, Pa.: Military Service Publishing Company, 1948). For experiences of Americans involved in the War, see William Matthews and Dixon Wecter, *Our Soldiers Speak, 1775-1918* (Boston: Little, Brown, 1943) and Emmet Crozier, *American Reporters on the Western Front, 1914-1918* (New York: Oxford University, 1959). See also Foster Rhea Dulles, *The American Red Cross, A History* (New York: Harper, 1950).

[4] Elting E. Morison, *Admiral Sims and the Modern American Navy* (Boston: Houghton Mifflin, 1942).

[5] David A. Lockmiller, *Enoch H. Crowder: Soldier, Lawyer, and Statesman* (Columbia, Mo.: University of Missouri, 1955).

[6] Irving Brinton Holley, Jr., *Ideas and Weapons* (New Haven: Yale University, 1953). Bernard Baruch's famous 1921 report summarizing work of the War Industries Board is found in the documentary volume, ed., Richard H. Hippelheuser, *American Industry in the War* (New York: Prentice-Hall, 1941). See also George P. Adams, Jr., *Wartime Price Control* (Washington: American Council on Public Affairs, 1942) and Herbert Stein, *Government Price Policy in the United States during the World War* (Williamstown, Mass.: Williams College, 1939). The discussion in Margaret L. Coit, *Mr. Baruch* (Boston: Houghton Mifflin, 1957), the only full-scale biography to make use of his papers, though well-written is at best superficial and at times contradictory. Probably the best brief discussion can be found in an article by Randall B. Kester, "The War Industries Board, 1917-1918," *American Political Science Review*, 34:655-84; August 1940. The second volume of Bernard M. Baruch's Memoirs, which includes a discussion of the War Industries Board is *Baruch: The Public Years* (New York: Holt, 1960).

of the work of the War Department were recorded by Louis B. Wehle who helped to establish labor boards, formulate labor policies, and negotiate construction contracts. Shortly after the war, he tried to revive foreign trade through the War Finance Corporation. During the war, Wehle became impressed with the high qualities of two of his associates, Food Administrator, Herbert Hoover and Assistant Secretary of the Navy, Franklin D. Roosevelt.[7]

Jonathan Daniels, in a perspicacious study,[8] examined relations between his father, Secretary of the Navy Josephus Daniels and the sophisticated, young Assistant Secretary, Franklin Delano Roosevelt. At the outset Roosevelt thought Daniels naive and virtually incompetent but came, by the end of the war, to have great respect for his chief. Frank Freidel, the first writer to probe carefully the relationship between Franklin D. Roosevelt and Daniels, has presented a picture of life in wartime Washington as well as an account of an important department of government during the War.[9] Moreover, the Secretary of the Navy reported his own experiences as a member of the Wilson cabinet and discussed his close relations, almost paternalistic, with his assistant. Writing from the point of view of a Southerner and a Democrat, Daniels' devotion to Wilson and his policies is evident.[10]

The wartime career of Herbert Hoover was portrayed in several volumes which are either of an autobiographical or an authorized nature, since the ex-President refused to open his papers to all qualified scholars. In the first volume of his memoirs,[11] the former Food Administrator and Post-War Relief Administrator recounted his experiences in these jobs. He also wrote introductions to a detailed and virtually official history of the Food Administration and to a volume of documents examining American relief in Europe.[12]

The effort for national unity during wartime has been examined in many volumes, some of which reflect the nation's continuing concern

---

[7] Louis B. Wehle, *Hidden Threads of History: Wilson Through Roosevelt* (New York: Macmillan, 1953).

[8] *The End of Innocence* (Philadelphia: Lippincott, 1954).

[9] Frank B. Freidel, *Franklin D. Roosevelt: The Apprenticeship* (Boston: Little, Brown, 1952).

[10] Josephus Daniels, *The Wilson Era: Years of War and After, 1917-1923* (Chapel Hill: University of North Carolina, 1946).

[11] *Years of Adventure, 1874-1920* (New York: Macmillan, 1951).

[12] William C. Mullendore, *History of the United States Food Administration, 1917-1919* (Stanford: Stanford University, 1941). Suda Lorena Bane and Ralph Haswell Lutz, eds., *Organization of American Relief in Europe, 1918-1919* (Stanford: Stanford University, 1943).

with this problem. Lewis Paul Todd's study[13] shows how the schools stimulated patriotism, furthered military training and otherwise aided the war effort. He concluded that the federal government did education at least as much harm as good during these years when the school system became an integral part of the drive toward national conformity.

How the drive for conformity in wartime affected the American people has been investigated more thoroughly from the individual viewpoint than from its administrative side. Censorship was carefully examined in a volume, *Censorship, 1917*, by James R. Mock.[14] He amply showed that, while the primary purpose of censorship was to prevent the leak of military information, the secondary purpose was to control public opinion in the United States. In general, Mock concludes, the record of courts in distinguishing between essential control and individual liberty was good as contrasted with that of volunteer boards and local patriots.[15] Ray Ginger movingly described Eugene Debs' loss of civil liberties for violating the Espionage Act of 1917.[16] Debs, a Socialist and an opponent of the war, would later run for the Presidency from his Atlanta prison cell. While Debs was well treated by his jailers, H. C. Peterson and Gilbert C. Fite[17] showed that oppression and brutality were prevalent under the leadership of an idealistic President in a nation engaged in a war to make the world safe for democracy. The Non-Partisan League, an organization mainly interested in agricultural reform, likewise became involved in the question of supporting the war. Beginning in 1915, it sought vigorous state action to remedy the farmers' ills. Successful primarily in North Dakota, it collapsed by 1921, a victim of war and postwar hysteria,

---

[13] *Wartime Relations of the Federal Government and the Public Schools, 1917-1918* (New York: Columbia University, 1945). For the Committee on Public Information, see George Creel, *Rebel at Large* (New York: Putnam, 1947) and James R. Mock and Cedric Larson, *Words That Won the War* (Princeton: Princeton University, 1939).

[14] Princeton: Princeton University, 1941. The classic account of wartime restrictions on civil liberties is Zechariah Chafee, Jr., *Free Speech in the United States* (Cambridge: Harvard University, 1941). See also Carl Brent Swisher, "Civil Liberties in War Time," *Political Science Quarterly*, 55:321-47; September 1940.

[15] See also for a personal account, Ralph Chaplin, *Wobbly: The Rough-and-Tumble Story of an American Radical* (Chicago: University of Chicago, 1948).

[16] Ray Ginger, *The Bending Cross: A Biography of Eugene Victor Debs* (New Brunswick: Rutgers University, 1949).

[17] Horace C. Peterson and Gilbert C. Fite, *Opponents of War, 1917-1918* (Madison: University of Wisconsin, 1957).

normalcy, and mismanagement.[18] Despite the nation's commitment to the war effort, Seward Livermore concluded that other factors besides Wilson's appeal for a Democratic Congress in order to win the peace played a role in the elections of 1918.[19] Most of the factors pertained to sectional economic matters, particularly farm prices, and had little to do directly with patriotism and the conduct of the war.

The conduct of American diplomacy during wartime is a subject that has attracted growing attention in the last two decades. The standard work of Charles Seymour on this subject was reprinted in 1942.[20] In the same year, Thomas A. Bailey, one of the outstanding diplomatic historians, scrutinized America's belligerent policy toward neutrals and noted "the conclusion is inescapable that the Washington government did not violate international law in a sweeping and ruthless fashion, and that its record on the whole is creditable."[21]

Russia, during the Bolshevik Revolution, has received the attention of historians eager to probe relations between what were to be the two major power centers in the world. George Frost Kennan, a former ambassador to Russia, has already published [as of 1960] two volumes of a projected trilogy entitled, *Soviet-American Relations: 1917-1920*. From these volumes one gets a picture of the complexities, irrationalities, and administrative tangles usually present in the formation of policy. The focus in the first volume is on a four-month period beginning late in 1917, wherein the Americans in Petrograd are the major themes examined.[22] Raymond Robins, who served as an informal liaison between the Bolsheviks and the State Department, is the central figure. Kennan tended to be critical of Robins on the grounds that professional diplomats should have handled such matters,

---

[18] Robert L. Morlan, *Political Prairie Fire: The Non-Partisan League, 1915-1922* (Minneapolis: University of Minnesota, 1955). Samuel P. Huntington probes the league as a pressure group in "Election Tactics of the Nonpartisan League," *Mississippi Valley Historical Review*, 36:613-32; March 1950. See also Theodore Saloutos, "Rise of the Nonpartisan League in North Dakota, 1915-1917," and "The Expansion and Decline of the Nonpartisan League," both in *Agricultural History*, 20:43-61; January 1946, and 20:235-52; October 1946.

[19] Seward W. Livermore, "The Sectional Issue in the 1918 Congressional Election," *Mississippi Valley Historical Review*, 35:29-60; June 1948.

[20] Charles Seymour, *American Diplomacy During the World War* (Baltimore: Johns Hopkins, 1934).

[21] Thomas A. Bailey, *The Policy of the United States toward the Neutrals: 1917-1918* (Baltimore: Johns Hopkins, 1942). Relations with a single country are examined in Laurence Martin, *Peace without Victory: Woodrow Wilson and the British Liberals* (New Haven: Yale University, 1958).

[22] George F. Kennan, *Russia Leaves the War* (Princeton: Princeton University, 1956).

and that it was absurd to have considered dealing with Lenin and the Bolsheviks. On the other hand, William A. Williams in *American-Russian Relations, 1781-1947*, a volume which focuses on the Russian Revolution, found that American diplomats in Russia had a much less clear perception of the situation than those who were not connected with the Department of State.[23]

In his second volume Kennan carried the story to the end of World War I[24] when American intervention was under way in Northern Russia and Siberia. He concluded that Wilson intervened in Northern Russia because of Anglo-French pressure, and that the Czech question led him to send troops into Siberia. In this volume, too, Kennan's sympathy toward the State Department men in Russia is abundantly evident as is his ignoring of Wilsonian understanding and idealism as a factor in policy making. In contradistinction to Kennan's views Betty Miller Unterberger, in an excellent monograph,[25] *America's Siberian Expedition, 1918-1920*, concluded that the desire to forestall Japanese intervention and to preserve the Open Door were the basic reasons for the American expedition to Siberia. She further observed that American intervention in Northern Russia "was not primarily to initiate a war against Bolshevism, but to bring about a renewal of the Russian threat against Eastern Germany."[26]

THE PEACE AND DEMOBILIZATION

Peacemaking in 1919 became the subject of renewed historical interest in the 1940's and 1950's owing to the breakdown of the peace in 1939 and the effort to maintain it since 1945. Moreover, in recent years some writers have called for a more realistic approach to world politics. In part this controversy has led some scholars to re-evaluate Wilson's diplomacy and his role at the Versailles Peace Conference.

Focusing directly on the American scene Ruhl J. Bartlett wrote the history of The League to Enforce Peace, the principal private group

---

[23] New York: Rinehart, 1952. Sister Anne Vincent Meiburger critically examines the role of Raymond Robins in *Efforts of Raymond Robins Toward the Recognition of Soviet Russia and the Outlawry of War* (Washington, D.C.: Catholic University, 1958).

[24] Kennan, *The Decision to Intervene* (Princeton: Princeton University, 1958).

[25] Durham: Duke University, 1956.

[26] The National Archives published a *Handbook of Federal World War Agencies and Their Records, 1917-1921* (Washington: United States Government Printing Office, 1943). The organization, functions, and records of over 2300 federal agencies are described. See also Lester J. Cappon, "The Collection of World War I Materials in the States," *American Historical Review*, 48:733-45; July 1943.

favoring an international organization.[27] While Wilson adopted the League's principles and successfully presented them at Versailles, virtually every prominent Republican in the organization dropped them in favor of partisanship and failed to give effective support to the League of Nations. Although he largely accepted Wilson's program as desirable, Thomas A. Bailey, in the first of his significant studies on Wilson and the peace settlement,[28] focused his attention on the Versailles Peace Conference with the idea of noting Wilson's tactical errors. In his sequel, Bailey probed the failure of the Versailles Peace Treaty in the United States Senate.[29] He blamed Wilson for his stubbornness about reservations but nevertheless observed that "blind partisanship, as much as any other single factor, ruined the League of Nations in the United States." Though Bailey recognized the existence of isolationist sentiment, he did not see it as a direct cause of the treaty's defeat. While critical of Henry Cabot Lodge, he claimed that Lodge's ultimate responsibility was to keep his party together in the treaty fight while Wilson's was to get it approved. Thus in the final analysis Bailey believed that Woodrow Wilson prevented American ratification of the Versailles Peace Treaty and the League Covenant.

More critical of Henry Cabot Lodge is Karl Shriftgiesser, a competent journalist, who apparently believed that the real memorial to this particular Gentleman from Massachusetts was the catastrophe of the second World War.[30] John A. Garraty in a splendid scholarly biography, concluded that Lodge let his partisanship and hatred for the President make him jointly responsible with Wilson for the failure to ratify the Treaty of Versailles.[31]

One of the most important evaluations of the Peace Treaty and the role of Woodrow Wilson was presented by Paul Birdsall in *Versailles*

---

[27] *The League to Enforce Peace* (Chapel Hill: University of North Carolina, 1944). Richard W. Leopold in *Elihu Root and the Conservative Tradition* (Boston: Little, Brown, 1954) devotes two chapters of his interpretative brief biography to the relations of Root, a leading member of the League to Enforce Peace, and Wilson during the War and on the League question.

[28] Thomas A. Bailey, *Woodrow Wilson and the Lost Peace* (New York: Macmillan, 1944).

[29] Thomas A. Bailey, *Woodrow Wilson and the Great Betrayal* (New York: Macmillan, 1945). In a popular study, *The Killing of the Peace* (New York: Viking, 1945), Alan M. Cranston concluded that a small Republican minority led by Lodge was responsible for the treaty's failure.

[30] Karl Schriftgiesser, *The Gentleman from Massachusetts: Henry Cabot Lodge* (Boston: Little, Brown, 1944).

[31] *Henry Cabot Lodge* (New York: Knopf, 1953).

Twenty Years After.[32] The treaty's settlements, he claimed, represented
"the closest approximation to an ethnographic map of Europe that
has been achieved." Wilson's failures are ascribed to Europe's "reactionary nationalisms," to partisan pressures, and to several of his
colleagues (Colonel House in particular) who gave him inadequate
support. Wilson emerges from Birdsall's pages as "the only statesman
of stature at Paris." In 1946 a young French scholar, Étienne Mantoux,
indirectly came to Wilson's defense by attacking one of Wilson's earliest critics, John Maynard Keynes, whose volume, *The Economic
Consequences of The Peace*, was published in the United States in
1920. Whereas Keynes suggested that Wilson was "bamboozled" at
Paris because of his lack of economic comprehension, Mantoux argued
that Keynes had been mistaken and the Keynes' attack had actually
encouraged American isolationism. Instead of criticizing Wilson's
economics, Mantoux found fault with his rejection of power politics,
his insistence on the creation of small indefensible states, and his re-
liance upon a League of Nations.[33]

In the years following World War II, several younger scholars
published monographs on aspects of Wilson's work at Versailles. All
reached conclusions favorable to Wilson as a diplomat with either a
clear comprehension of the realities or a general understanding of
the particular situation with which they are concerned, be it the
issue of French security,[34] the rebirth of Poland[35] or the Shantung
question.[36] Moreover, John L. Snell in a series of significant articles
presented evidence that the President despite his "idealistic internationalism" was an effective diplomat. His propaganda appeals,
Snell believed, loosened the ties binding Germany together and thereby

---

[32] New York: Reynal & Hitchcock, 1941.

[33] Étienne Mantoux, *The Carthaginian Peace or the Economic Consequences of
Mr. Keynes* (London: Oxford University, 1946).

[34] Louis A. R. Yates, *United States and French Security, 1917-1921: A Study in
American Diplomatic History* (New York: Twayne, 1957).

[35] Louis L. Gerson, *Woodrow Wilson and the Rebirth of Poland, 1914-1920: A
Study in the Influence on American Foreign Policy of Minority Groups of Foreign
Origin* (New Haven: Yale University, 1953). Gerson concludes that "a united,
independent and free Polish nation could not have been resurrected without the
intervention of the United States and Woodrow Wilson."

[36] Russell H. Fifield, *Woodrow Wilson and the Far East: The Diplomacy of the
Shantung Question* (New York: Crowell, 1952). Fifield argues that Wilson was
fearful lest the Japanese refuse to sign the Peace Treaty if they were not given
satisfaction in Shantung, Wilson reluctantly agreeing, nevertheless managed to
hedge Japanese control with stipulations.

"hastened the victory which guaranteed an Allied interpretation of their semantics."[37]

The two decades after 1940 also brought forth probably the last personal accounts of individuals who participated in one way or another in the making of the peace.[38] Ray Stannard Baker presented a valuable personal account in *American Chronicle*.[39] Baker went to Europe during the war on a mission for the State Department and was then put in charge of press relations for the American delegation at Paris. He later prepared the authorized multi-volume biography of Woodrow Wilson. Herbert Hoover's *The Ordeal of Woodrow Wilson*[40] is valuable possibly more for what it reveals about its author than its subject. Throughout the book he revealed his admiration for Wilson and his struggle to establish a new foundation for the conduct of international relations. Hoover concluded that Wilson's failures were of relatively slight significance compared with the "lasting upsurging toward freedom and the world organization for enduring peace which Woodrow Wilson brought to a distraught world."

Thus most writers in the 1940's and 1950's who probed aspects of Wilsonian diplomacy during the peacemaking period were favorably impressed by it. Wilson, though an idealist who sought a new world order based on moral right and justice rather than power, emerges from most of these writings as an individual with a realistic understanding of the problems he faced. The critics of Wilsonian diplomacy, mostly individuals manifestly concerned with the current situation, have usually presented their views in bold interpretative essay form rather than in painstaking, factual monographs.[41]

On the American scene, the problem of reconverting the economy and returning the society to a peacetime basis is one that has not

---

[37] See especially, "Wilson's Peace Program and German Socialism, January-March 1918," *Mississippi Valley Historical Review*, 38:187-214; September 1951. Rayford W. Logan examines another aspect of the peace settlement in *The Senate and the Versailles Mandate System* (Washington, D. C.: Minorities Publishers, 1945).

[38] See, for example, Stephen Bonsal, *Unfinished Business* (New York: Doubleday, Doran, 1944) and *Suitors and Suppliants* (New York: Prentice-Hall, 1946); Thomas W. Lamont, *Across World Frontiers* (New York: Harcourt, Brace, 1951); Philip Mason Burnett, *Reparation at the Paris Peace Conference from the Standpoint of the American Delegation* (2 vols.; New York: Columbia University for the Carnegie Endowment for International Peace, 1940).

[39] New York: Scribner, 1945.

[40] New York: McGraw-Hill, 1958.

[41] See, for example, George F. Kennan, *American Diplomacy, 1900-1950* (Chicago: University of Chicago, 1951); Robert E. Osgood, *Ideals and Self-Interest in America's Foreign Relations* (Chicago: University of Chicago, 1953). Osgood's volume is probably the most carefully developed of the legal-moralistic critiques.

aroused great interest among scholars. And the one area that has aroused interest, the attack on radicalism, reflects the concern of the American people with this topic in the "cold war" that followed World War II.

During this war James R. Mock and Evangeline Thurber published a volume examining the vast number of reconstruction programs that appeared after November 11, 1918. They revealed the gap between plan and performance and described the shifting climate of opinion between the emotional idealism of war and the sobering realities of peace.[42] But Frederick Logan Paxson wrote the only detailed history of the post-war years.[43] His canvass is a broad one revealing, for example, that Americans in 1919 were more concerned with sports, the Red Scare, the steel strike, and other labor disputes than with the fate of the League of Nations. Paxson saw a continuity of outlook from the end of Wilson's administration on into the Harding period. William E. Leuchtenburg partially disagreed with this position.[44] He believed that under Harding the issues shifted somewhat. The attack on radicals and labor disturbances died down. Eugene Victor Debs was released from Atlanta penitentiary and a program of welfare capitalism was launched. An idealistic interest in foreign affairs abated and an extreme nationalism manifesting itself, for example, in immigration restriction, the KKK, and high tariffs, replaced it.

An aspect of the national hysteria pervading the nation in 1919-1920 was competently discussed by Robert K. Murray in *Red Scare*.[45] Admitting a limited danger to internal security, Murray showed how enemies of organized labor capitalized on prejudice, hatred, and fear to resist the demands of the revitalized labor movement. The "national

---

[42] Mock and Thurber, *Report on Demobilization* (Norman: University of Oklahoma Press, 1944). In *When Johnny Comes Marching Home* (Boston: Houghton Mifflin, 1944), Dixon Wecter discussed the return of the doughboys. See also E. Jay Howenstine, Jr., "Demobilization after the First World War," *Quarterly Journal of Economics*, 58:91-105; November 1943. "Public Works Program after World War I," *Journal of Political Economy*, 51:523-37; December 1943. "Public Works Policy in the Twenties," *Social Research*, 13:479-500; December 1946.

[43] Frederick Logan Paxson, *American Democracy and the World War: Post-War Years: Normalcy, 1918-1923* (Boston: Houghton Mifflin, 1948).

[44] Leuchtenburg, *The Perils of Prosperity, 1914-1932*.

[45] Minneapolis: University of Minnesota, 1955. David Shannon discussed Socialist victims of the Red Scare in *The Socialist Party of America: A History* (New York: Macmillan, 1955). Whether or not to support the war effort created a grave schism in the Socialist party. See Oscar Ameringer's autobiography, *If You Don't Weaken* (New York: Holt, 1940) ; see also Paul H. Anderson, *The Attitude of American Leftist Leaders toward the Russian Revolution* (Notre Dame: University of Notre Dame, 1942).

psychoneurosis" was short-lived, however, and the hysteria was dissolved in the excitement of the 1920 campaign.

As might be expected in a period of cold war with the Soviet Union, the origins and development of American Communism have received attention. Daniel Bell wrote a brilliant essay on this subject,[46] while Theodore Draper provided a definitive analysis in two volumes.[47] Draper showed how the American movement emerged out of left-wing Socialism, and especially how the interplay between this tradition and Bolshevik authority as exercised through the Comintern made for a fundamental tension within the American movement, partly reflected in the conflict that arose between the proponents of reform and those of revolution. This conflict was related to the ethnic composition of the members; native Americans were usually more interested in practical reform and achieving a mass appeal while immigrant members favored a more doctrinaire approach.

The author focusing on the relation of American Communism to Soviet Russia was able to exhume the confidential minutes of many top committees so that his work has authenticity and insight previously unobtainable. These volumes, particularly the second, reveal that the American movement developed not in response to any American need but solely in accordance with the will of the Comintern in Moscow.

FOREIGN POLICIES IN THE 1920's

The study of foreign policies of the United States during the 1920's has benefited from the growing interest in American diplomacy as well as from the increasing availablity of the personal papers of many of the participants and the opening to scholarly use of official records by the Department of State. The study of American diplomacy during this decade raises the question of isolation versus internationalism. Some historians with an internationalist bias have claimed that the nation's failure to live up to the commitments and responsibilities befitting a newly recognized world power had as much to do with the failure to maintain the peace during the following decade as any other factor. And controversy has risen as to just how isolationist were the 1920's. This discussion has merged with a debate of longer standing; namely, how does one define the term and who were the

---

[46] Daniel Bell, "Marxian Socialism in the United States," in Donald D. Egbert and Stow Persons, eds., *Socialism and American Life*, Volume I (Princeton: Princeton University, 1952).

[47] *The Roots of American Communism* (New York: Viking, 1957) and *American Communism and Soviet Russia* (New York: Viking, 1960).

isolationists. In all, a significant literature on American foreign policy during this decade of prosperity has already arisen.

Allan Nevins provided a brief but satisfactory survey of American foreign policy during this decade.[48] He wrote from a liberal, internationalist, and Wilsonian point of view. He believed in collective security and free trade and viewed the Senate's rejection of the Versailles Peace Treaty as a major factor in the losing of the peace. Dexter Perkins, one of the nation's recognized authorities in diplomatic history, by and large agreed with Nevins' point of view. Though Perkins wrote no monograph devoted exclusively to this decade, he published several stimulating surveys of recent American foreign policy.[49]

Selig Adler wrote a general study of American isolationism.[50] Focusing on the years from 1914 to 1956, his greatest emphasis is on the decade following World War I. Adler emphasized the role of hyphenates, political influences, and the shifting views of liberals and conservatives. He wrote from a liberal internationalist point of view and the cumulative effect is damning to the isolationist position. On the other hand William G. Carleton probed this phenomenon from a regional viewpoint by examining isolationism and the Middle West.[51] Reviewing the fight over the peace treaty and the League of Nations, Carleton observed that it was not a conflict between "isolationism and participationism" but more nearly a fight between those who would participate as nationalists or as internationalists. Moreover, in examining the Senate "irreconcilable" vote, he noted that the majority of these votes came from areas other than the Middle West and that a senator from Nebraska (Gilbert M. Hitchcock) led the League forces while a senator from Massachusetts (Henry Cabot Lodge) rallied the opposition.

George L. Grassmuck corroborated some of Carleton's generalizations.[52] He focused on the two decades prior to Pearl Harbor. Most of the issues he discussed were relevant to the 1920's. Grassmuck concluded that the record of Middle-Western congressmen was not

---

[48] Allan Nevins, *The United States in a Chaotic World: a Chronicle of International Affairs, 1918-1933* (New Haven: Yale University, 1950).

[49] See for example, Dexter Perkins, *America and Two Wars* (Boston: Little, Brown, 1944).

[50] Selig Adler, *The Isolationist Impulse* (New York: Abelard-Shuman, 1957).

[51] William G. Carleton, "Isolationism and the Middle West," *Mississippi Valley Historical Review*, 33:377-90; December 1946.

[52] George L. Grassmuck, *Sectional Biases in Congress on Foreign Policy* (Baltimore: Johns Hopkins, 1951).

intensely isolationist. Indeed it compared favorably with that of members from the Northeast on the question, for example, of joining international organizations.

While scholars have been probing, usually critically, this American phenomenon, it has remained for a younger historian to characterize isolationism during the 1920's as "a legend." William A. Williams argued that the foreign relations of the United States during this decade "were marked by express and extended involvement with and intervention in the affairs of other nations of the world."[53] However, Foster Rhea Dulles, accepting Williams' evidence, nevertheless, disagreed with his premise.[54] Dulles pointed out that America's numerous international contacts were characterized by no binding political commitments, and that the United States during the twenties rejected the collective security approach previously suggested by the internationalists. While controversy over isolationism still rages in scholarly circles, our understanding of the problem has increased.

The diplomacy of Charles Evans Hughes, probably the most distinguished member of Harding's cabinet, was favorably analyzed in detail by his official biographer, Merlo Pusey[55] and in brief by a more interpretative one, Dexter Perkins.[56] Perkins wrote, and Pusey would agree, that Hughes' work as Secretary of State marked him as "one of the most eminent Secretaries" in our history, despite the fact that there were no lasting achievements to his credit. The Washington Conference in 1922 which came to some agreement on problems of naval arms limitations and Far Eastern security represents Hughes' greatest accomplishment.

John Chalmers Vinson in *The Parchment Peace*[57] examined the Senate's part in the Washington Conference. By presenting primarily the arguments on the Four-Power Treaty affecting the Open Door in the Far East, Vinson revealed the divergence as to how diplomacy was to be conducted: whether by adhering to collective security or by

---

[53] The article by William A. Williams, "The Legend of Isolationism in the 1920's," published in 1954, is available in his collection of documents and articles, *The Shaping of American Diplomacy* (Chicago: Rand, McNally, 1956).

[54] Foster Rhea Dulles, *America's Rise to World Power, 1898-1954* (New York: Harper, 1955).

[55] Merlo J. Pusey, *Charles Evans Hughes*, Volume II (New York: Macmillan, 1951).

[56] Dexter Perkins, *Charles Evans Hughes and American Democratic Statesmanship* (Boston: Little, Brown, 1956).

[57] Athens: University of Georgia, 1955.

resorting to moral pressures to curb international lawlessness. The Four-Power Treaty did not bind the United States to any commitment but at the same time it guaranteed the security of the Philippines, abrogated the Anglo-Japanese alliance, and seemingly answered the universal demand for peace. Its acceptance by the Senate insured the success of the Washington Conference and illustrated the relationship between idealism and irresponsibility. The parchment peace, in the author's words, was "a peace conceived in the hope that pledges and public opinion unaided by international organizations and military force could meet the problems of a world power."

While Vinson probed one aspect of the Washington Conference, C. L. Hoag studied the role of American public opinion in supporting the conference and its conclusions.[58] "It is conceivable," claimed the author, "that the conference might not have been called had not an overwhelming national opinion expressed its desire so effectively." Hoag particularly noted the role of women, recently enfranchised, in supporting public opinion favorable to the conference. An important volume examining another phase of the conference is that of Harold and Margaret Sprout.[59] Stressing the role of the navy as an instrument of national policy, they discussed the varying points of view in the Navy Department as to the future role of sea power, and they noted the force of public opinion, quickly reflected by politicians, in favor of disarmament. In short, they presented an excellent study of naval policy and world affairs from 1918 to 1922 and viewed the Washington Conference as a groping toward a new order of sea power, taking into account the new conditions of warfare.[60]

Another important aspect of the 1920's, that of foreign economic policy, indicates that despite sentiment to the contrary businessmen were extending their activities overseas. In a suggestive set of essays, *The Diplomacy of the Dollar: First Era, 1919-1932*, Herbert Feis explored the ideas, interests, and attitudes which developed into government policies favoring economic penetration overseas. This analysis

---

[58] Charles Leonard Hoag, *Preface to Preparedness: The Washington Disarmament Conference and Public Opinion* (Washington, D. C.: American Council on Public Affairs, 1941).

[59] Harold and Margaret Sprout, *Toward a New Order of Sea Power* (Princeton: Princeton University, 1940).

[60] See also Merze Tate, *The United States and Armaments* (Cambridge: Harvard University, 1948); George T. Davis, *A Navy Second to None* (New York: Harcourt, Brace, 1940).

is followed by brief accounts of efforts to apply these policies to particular areas.[61]

Little work has been done on American relations with particular countries for this decade.[62] However, in an important book, Dorothy Borg presented a comprehensive analysis of the effect on American policy of the tangled situation in China during those years when the Kuomintang sought to consolidate the revolution started by Sun Yat Sen under the emerging leadership of Chiang Kai-Shek.[63] Another set of problems affecting Sino-American relations emanated from earlier contacts with China, such as revision of customs and extra-territorial status. The missionary impact as well as that of the press and of Congress in determining American policy is also considered.

One significant achievement of American diplomacy during the twenties, the Pact of Paris, has been studied in detail. The role of S. O. Levinson in the movement to outlaw war was assayed by J. O. Stoner.[64] He argued that without the work of Levinson in arousing pacifist sentiment and in persuading Senator Borah to take a leading role, the Kellog-Briand Pact to outlaw war as an instrument of national policy would never have been achieved. While Stoner concerned himself with the genesis of the treaty, Robert H. Ferrell in a penetrating volume, *Peace in Their Time*,[65] examined its diplomacy. He concluded that the peace pact "was the result of some very shrewd diplomacy and some very unsophisticated popular enthusiasm for peace." While members of the State Department regarded Briand's

---

[61] Herbert Feis, *The Diplomacy of the Dollar: First Era, 1919-1932* (Baltimore: Johns Hopkins, 1950). See also William A. Brown, Jr., *The International Gold Standard Reinterpreted, 1914-1934* (New York: National Bureau of Economic Research, 1940); Siegfried Stern, *The United States in International Banking* (New York: Columbia University, 1951); and Asher Isaacs, *International Trade, Tariff, and Commercial Policies* (Chicago: R. O. Irwin, 1948). John A. De Novo, "The Movement for an Aggressive American Oil Policy Abroad, 1918-1920," *American Historical Review*, 61:854-76; July 1956.

[62] However see Robert L. Daniel, "The Armenian Question and American-Turkish Relations, 1914-1927," *Mississippi Valley Historical Review*, 46:252-75; September 1959. Meno Lovenstein, *American Opinion of Soviet Russia* (Washington: American Council on Public Affairs, 1941); and Robert Browder, *The Origins of Soviet-American Diplomacy* (Princeton: Princeton University, 1953).

[63] *American Policy and the Chinese Revolution, 1925-1928* (New York: Macmillan, 1947).

[64] John Edgar Stoner, *S. O. Levinson and the Pact of Paris* (Chicago: University of Chicago, 1943).

[65] New Haven: Yale University, 1952.

proposal (which, incidentally, Nicholas Murray Butler, president of Columbia University, claimed that he first suggested to Briand) as a negative military alliance to outlaw war between the United States and France, the groups favoring the outlawry of war made it difficult for the American diplomats to reject the proposal. To resolve this dilemma the State Department suggested a multilateral plan which proclaimed the virtue of opposing war without assuming the responsibility of a specific commitment.

John Chalmers Vinson examined the role of the Chairman of the Senate Foreign Relations Committee, William E. Borah, in this movement.[66] Borah, like the State Department, desired to extend Briand's proposal from a bilateral to a multilateral arrangement. Once this was achieved, the Senator, assured that the treaty did not obligate the United States in any way, guided it through a lengthy Senate debate. The author, while focusing on the Kellog-Briand Pact, surveyed Borah's career from 1917 to 1931. He concluded that "few men of his time . . . played as important or colorful a part in the war on war." But he noted that Borah's career in the realm of foreign affairs, be it in his opposition to the League of Nations or the World Court,[67] was predicated on the belief that the United States should not be obligated to the use of force to live up to any assumed international responsibility.

DOMESTIC POLICIES IN THE 1920's

The politics of the 1920's mirrored many of the profound changes that had been occurring in American life. Most notably, as Samuel Lubell demonstrated in *The Future of American Politics*,[68] it revealed the emergence of a new frontier—the urbanized, industrialized, new American civilization inhabited by immigrants and Negroes. Recent scholarship has started to reveal the dimensions of this change either by probing unexplored areas of American life or by reinterpreting known segments within this newer framework.

---

[66] John Chalmers Vinson, *William E. Borah and the Outlawry of War* (Athens: University of Georgia, 1957).

[67] Denna Frank Fleming in his volume, *The United States and the World Court* (Garden City: Doubleday, Doran, 1945) sees William E. Borah as one of the chief villains preventing American acceptance of the Court.

[68] New York: Harper, 1952. In a provocative essay, Samuel J. Eldersveld discussed "The Influence of Metropolitan Party Pluralities in Presidential Elections Since 1920," *American Political Science Review*, 43:1189-1206; December 1949.

The fate of the progressive movement, for example, has been challenged by Arthur S. Link.[69] He saw the progressive movement as far from dead during the 1920's, a fate usually ascribed to it. Rather than conduct a post-mortem, Link found the movement still flourishing on lower political levels where it was always most effective. He noted the emergence of new problems to which progressives had to adjust. And rather than eulogize it for its previous performance, Link called for further investigation of progressivism in the 1920's.

There are several volumes that survey the decade of the 1920's with some emphasis on political phases. Aside from William E. Leuchtenburg's splendid study, Harold U. Faulkner wrote the best balanced book,[70] relating clearly and dispassionately the national descent into normalcy. Writing from a liberal bias, Faulkner viewed the decade as one of confusion in which the propagation of myths and symbols associated with prosperity and laissez faire served to conceal, at least partially, the prevalence of corruption in political life as well as corporate domination of a badly balanced economy.

While the survey literature has not been large, the literature focusing on the Republican triumverate of the 1920's and their policies has been abundant. Turning first to Warren G. Harding and what former muckraker Samuel Hopkins Adams has called *The Incredible Era*,[71] there are several valuable accounts of the 1920 campaign. Wesley Bagby probed the nomination of Harding. More than any other historian he tried to examine what actually occurred in the famous "smoke filled room" in Chicago's Blackstone Hotel.[72] He also revealed the dying hope on the part of some devoted Democrats that Wilson himself might lead the party in the solemn referendum campaign of 1920.[73] William T. Hutchinson showed that Frank O. Lowden, usually

---

[69] Arthur S. Link, "What Happened to the Progressive Movement in the 1920's?" *American Historical Review*, 64:833-51; July 1959. Previously Eric F. Goldman in *Rendezvous with Destiny: A History of Modern American Reform* (New York: Knopf, 1952) pointed out the confusion prevalent in the progressive camp during the 1920's. Confusion as to what was the liberal position toward labor, war, peace, isolationism, immigration, etc., was further complicated by the intrusion of foreign ideologies.

[70] *From Versailles to the New Deal* (New Haven: Yale University, 1950). John D. Hicks, *Republican Ascendancy, 1921-1933* (New York: Harper, 1960) in the New American Nation Series is the most up-to-date and comprehensive one volume survey of Prosperity Decade.

[71] Boston: Houghton Mifflin, 1939.

[72] Wesley M. Bagby, "The 'Smoke Filled Room' and the Nomination of Warren G. Harding," *Mississippi Valley Historical Review*, 41:657-74; March 1955.

[73] Wesley M. Bagby, "Woodrow Wilson, a Third Term, and the Solemn Referendum," *American Historical Review*, 60:567-75; April 1955.

regarded as a leading Republican contender in 1920, actually had very little strength at the Chicago convention.[74]

The Democratic side of the 1920 campaign was discussed by the party's nominee, James M. Cox.[75] Cox, who as wartime Governor of Ohio prohibited the teaching of German in the state's public schools, claimed that he was a devoted friend of the League of Nations before he became a candidate, whereas some historians had claimed that his devotion was acquired in 1920. There are already several volumes examining the career of the Democratic vice-presidential candidate, Franklin D. Roosevelt, before his emergence as a leading national figure. Frank Freidel noted that the nominee campaigned in 1920 as a devoted friend of the League, something that he did not do in 1924 or in 1928 though still claiming to be an ardent Wilsonian.[76] While stressing his subject's personal ordeal during the 1920's, Freidel's volume nevertheless reveals much of the ordeal of the Democratic party for the same period.

While Freidel is confining himself to a biography, one of his Harvard colleagues, Arthur Schlesinger, Jr., is endeavoring to portray The Age of Roosevelt. Schlesinger in his first volume, *The Crisis of the Old Order*, relied heavily on published accounts.[77] Utilizing an Emersonian phrase, "Every revolution was first a thought in one man's mind," he surveyed the 1920's in all its aspects before placing his protagonist in it. Though he wrote brilliantly in a style that enables readers to experience the mood of the past, Schlesinger essentially summarized and interpreted while Freidel presented new information. Moreover, Schlesinger was a dedicated advocate of his chief subject and the Democratic party, reserving favorable comments for them while piercing the Republicans and their business allies with virtually all of his penetrating barbs. Daniel R. Fusfeld wrote the only monograph on the future president covering the decade of the twenties.[78] Fusfeld showed that prior to his election in 1932 Roosevelt had obtained through reading and broad experience a sound modern education and that he was far from being an economic neophyte when he entered the White House.

---

[74] William T. Hutchinson, *Lowden of Illinois* (2 vols.; Chicago: University of Chicago, 1957).

[75] *Journey Through My Years* (New York: Simon and Schuster, 1946).

[76] Frank B. Freidel, *The Ordeal* (Boston: Little, Brown, 1954).

[77] Boston: Houghton Mifflin, 1957.

[78] Daniel R. Fusfeld, *The Economic Thought of Franklin D. Roosevelt and the Origins of the New Deal* (New York: Columbia University, 1956).

An astute observer of American presidents was William Allen White who came to respect and admire some, but who sought to understand the motives and forces impelling them to act as they did. Though his captivating autobiography mentions the Harding administration it does not go beyond 1923.[79] Fortunately White was blessed with an able biographer in Walter Johnson who examined White's role as a friend and adviser to Republican leaders during the 1920's.[80] Johnson pointed out that White was a regular Republican on election day though he was an unsparing critic of his party's policies throughout the 1920's. Johnson revealed the dimensions of this deception when he noted that White, by his acquiescence in the corporate interests' controlling his party, helped to delude middle class, small town, progressive Republicans into believing that they had a powerful voice in their party.

Aspects of the campaign of 1924 are discussed by Fola M. LaFollette in a study of her father, Robert M. LaFollette who headed a third party movement.[81] She was interested in presenting her father's viewpoint, getting it on the record. For example, she made clear that the Wisconsin senator was by no means an opponent of world collaboration. Moreover, he realized as early as 1924 that it would be impossible for liberals to work with Communists for purposes of achieving reform. Kenneth C. McKay in *The Progressive Movement of 1924*[82] presented a study of LaFollette's role in the 1924 campaign. Farmer and labor groups plus urban liberals and the Socialists all worked together to support LaFollette who polled some five million votes, more than any other third party candidate in American history.[83]

In one of the most important political studies focusing primarily on Prosperity Decade, J. Joseph Hutmacher explored the evolution

---

[79] William Allen White, *Autobiography* (New York: Macmillan, 1946).

[80] Walter Johnson, *William Allen White's America* (New York: Holt, 1947).

[81] Belle Case LaFollette and Fola LaFollette, *Robert M. LaFollette* (New York: Macmillan, 1953).

[82] New York: Columbia University, 1947.

[83] See also Edward N. Doan, *The LaFollettes and the Wisconsin Idea* (New York: Rinehart, 1947). For other studies of individuals prominent in governmental and political circles, see Harry Barnard's *Independent Man: The Life of Senator James Couzens* (New York: Scribner, 1958); Morton Keller's *In Defense of Yesterday: James M. Beck and the Politics of Conservatism, 1861-1936* (New York: Coward-McCann, 1958); and George Wharton Pepper's autobiography, *Philadelphia Lawyer* (New York: Lippincott, 1944); Howard Zinn, *La Guardia in Congress* (Ithaca: Cornell University, 1960); and Arthur Mann's first portion of a multi-volume biography *La Guardia: A Fighter against his Time, 1882-1933* (Philadelphia: Lippincott, 1959).

of the modern Democratic coalition in the Bay State.[84] He focused on David I. Walsh and his role in welding this urban-immigrant coalition, although he did not ignore other figures, such as James M. Curley.[85] Hutmacher showed how Massachusetts Democrats were alienated from the national party by its stand on such social issues as prohibition and immigration. However, the fact that "Coolidge prosperity" did not prevail in the Bay State led to the embarrassment and defeat of the Republican party. At the end of the decade when national attention focused on economic rather than on social issues, Massachusetts Democrats, who ardently supported Alfred E. Smith, no longer felt alienated from their party.

Some significant literature is available concerning Alfred E. Smith and the election of 1928, when America's urban voters largely cast their ballots for the New York Governor. Edmond A. Moore examined the campaign within the campaign; namely, the religious issue revolving around the fact that Smith was a Roman Catholic.[86] He concluded that "anti-Catholicism was indeed the silent issue . . . very much more significant than the somewhat meagre news or editorial space assigned to it would indicate." Moore also noted that the religious issue was interwoven with that of prohibition, nativism, snobbery, and similar social themes. And he stated that any Democrat would have had a difficult time defeating Hoover and "Republican prosperity."

Oscar Handlin, who has done much to make historians aware of the urban-immigrant contribution and role in American life, contributed an interpretative, impressionistic biography.[87] Though considering the many sociological factors involved in the 1928 campaign, Handlin did not consider the economic factor of prosperity. Nor did he examine the weaknesses within the Democratic fold as an issue affecting the outcome of the election. An inkling of them, some due primarily to Smith's tactics, is suggested in Freidel's Franklin D. Roosevelt biography.

[84] J. Joseph Hutmacher, *Massachusetts People and Politics, 1919-1933* (Cambridge: Belknap of Harvard University, 1959).

[85] See also Dorothy G. Wayman, *David I. Walsh, Citizen-Patriot* (Milwaukee: Bruce, 1952); and Joseph F. Dinneen, *The Purple Shamrock* (New York: Norton, 1949).

[86] Edmund A. Moore, *A Catholic Runs for President: The Campaign of 1928* (New York: Ronald, 1956). For a discussion of the 1928 Democratic campaign in a Southern state, see Richard L. Watson, Jr., "A Political Leader Bolts: F. M. Simmons in the Presidental Election of 1928," *North Carolina Historical Review*, 37:516-43; October 1960.

[87] *Al Smith and His America* (Boston: Little, Brown, 1958).

The agricultural issue in the election was discussed by Gilbert C. Fite.[88] He claimed that the 1928 campaign projected farm problems into sharper focus than at any time since 1896. Many farm leaders, disgusted with Republican inability to come to grips with the agricultural issue, voted Democratic, while Republican majorities in most farm states were sharply reduced.[89] Herbert Hoover gives his own account of the campaign as well as of his "happy years of constructive work" as Secretary of Commerce in the second volume of his memoirs.[90] Though marred by self-jusification and critical of most of his colleagues in governmental circles, Hoover's volume reveals much about his work of aiding the business community during Prosperity Decade.

Another institution that reflects domestic policies is the Supreme Court. During the 1920's the Court continued the trend toward judicial activism in social and economic policy. In the area of civil rights and civil liberties it practiced judicial self-restraint though a vigorous dissenting minority of the Court wished to reverse the pattern. A good portion of the recent literature on the Supreme Court is sympathetic to this dissenting minority. Alpheus Thomas Mason, who has devoted much attention to the Court, accepts the minority position. In a recent volume, *The Supreme Court from Taft to Warren*,[91] he surveyed the principal decisions of the Court and the ideas of its leading spokesmen. Mason's chief contributions, however, are his comprehensive biographies of Stone and Brandeis.[92] In his biography of Louis D. Brandeis, Mason emphasized his subject's career before 1933.[93] Since Brandeis was interested in a wide range of social and economic matters, a study of his decisions or dissents provides an insight into the thought of the Court as well as into American life.[94] Brandeis and Holmes are the subjects of a study by Samuel J. Konefsky who observed that, while

---

[88] Gilbert C. Fite, "The Agricultural Issue in the Campaign of 1928," *Mississippi Valley Historical Review*, 37:653-72; March 1951.

[89] See also Cyril Clemens and Athern P. Daggett, "Coolidge's 'I Do Not Choose to Run': Granite or Putty?" *New England Quarterly*, 18:147-63; June 1945.

[90] *The Cabinet and the Presidency, 1920-1933* (New York: Macmillan, 1952).

[91] Baton Rouge: Louisiana State University, 1958.

[92] Alpheus T. Mason, *Harlan Fiske Stone: Pillar of the Law* (New York: Viking, 1956).

[93] Alpheus T. Mason, *Brandeis, A Free Man's Life* (New York: Viking, 1946).

[94] Alexander M. Bickel, *The Unpublished Opinions of Mr. Justice Brandeis* (Cambridge: Belknap of Harvard University, 1957). Other significant books on the dissenters are Francis B. Biddle, *Mr. Justice Holmes* (New York: Scribner, 1942); Max Lerner, ed., *The Mind and Faith of Justice Holmes* (Boston: Little, Brown, 1943); Mark DeWolfe Howe, ed., *Holmes-Laski Letters. . . . 1916-1935* (2 vols.; Cambridge: Harvard University, 1953); *Holmes-Pollock Letters. . . .* (Cambridge: Harvard University, 1941).

Holmes' gospel was one of judicial self-restraint, Brandeis' contributions lay more in his "adapting law and its techniques to the stark realities of life in the twentieth century."[95]

Further insights into the Supreme Court during this decade are derived from Henry F. Pringle's *The Life and Times of William Howard Taft*.[96] The second volume focuses on Taft's tenure as Chief Justice from 1921 to 1930. Pringle asserted that Taft emphasized and expanded the national powers while construing strictly that of the states. On labor issues he took a middle of the road position. Moreover, Pringle claimed that Taft's attitude toward monopoly regulation and interstate commerce entitled him to rank as a liberal jurist. No such rank could be assigned to Justice Sutherland in a fine biography by Joel F. Paschal.[97] Sutherland, who served on the Court from 1922 to 1938, was an able and eloquent spokesman for the individual or the corporation against both state and federal restraint.

Another area of domestic policy where scholarly work remains to be done is the prohibition experiment. Herbert Asbury, a "popular" historical writer, has written a caustic history of prohibition.[98] He believed it to have been a stupendous mistake based on "the great illusion" that temperance can be compelled by legislation. He made clear that such legislation can lead to corruption, crime, and ultimate chaos. One of the leading proponents of prohibition, Methodist Bishop James Cannon, Jr., is the subject of an exposé by Virginius Dabney, a newspaper editor who bitterly opposed Cannon during the 1920's.[99] A better balanced portrait is presented by Richard L. Watson, Jr., who edited Cannon's autobiography.[100] Though Cannon drafted his life story only as far as the 1928 campaign, a picture of his work in the prohibition movement is available. Cannon was a spokesman for rural America—anti-urban and anti-Catholic in his views. He is credited with playing an important role in breaking "the Solid South" because of his opposition to Alfred E. Smith in 1928.

---

[95] Samuel J. Konefsky, *The Legacy of Holmes and Brandeis: A Study in the Influence of Ideas* (New York: Macmillan, 1956).

[96] New York: Farrar & Rinehart, 1939.

[97] Joel F. Paschal, *Mr. Justice Sutherland* (Princeton: Princeton University, 1951).

[98] Herbert Asbury, *The Great Illusion: An Informal History of Prohibition* (Garden City: Doubleday, 1950). Asbury also wrote a brilliant essay, "The Noble Experiment of Izzy and Moe," for Isabel Leighton, ed., *The Aspirin Age, 1919-1941* (New York, Simon and Schuster, 1949).

[99] Virginius Dabney, *Dry Messiah: The Life of Bishop Cannon* (New York: Knopf, 1949).

[100] Richard L. Watson, Jr., ed., *Bishop Cannon's Own Story* (Durham: Duke University, 1955).

Though prohibition attracted public attention, a more crucial issue, conservation, was also being debated in the legislative halls. Only when corruption was shown to be involved did it command widespread public notice. Otherwise, only directly involved groups were vitally concerned with it. The Teapot Dome scandal commanded national attention; the Muscle Shoals controversy aroused interested groups. Morris R. Werner and John Starr in a recent volume, *Teapot Dome*,[101] have unraveled this sordid tale from available published records. The authors are competent writers, but a comprehensive account of the scandal and its relation to the 1920's is still needed. J. Leonard Bates and Burl Noggle, perhaps, may give this comprehensive account. Noggle has probed the origins of the investigation,[102] and Bates has examined the role of Josephus Daniels in creating the naval oil reserves.[103] He also surveyed the origins of the conservation movement in the twentieth century.[104] And most pertinent, he wrote of "The Teapot Dome Scandal and the Election of 1924" pointing out that too many prominent Democrats were spattered with oil for the party to make the scandal a campaign issue.[105]

During the Muscle Shoals controversy, George W. Norris became the leading advocate of federal ownership and development of hydro-electric power as a phase of the multi-purpose development of the Tennessee River Valley.[106] While Norris battled for federal owner-ship in the Senate of the United States, a personal friend, Judson King, provided him with the specific information necessary to wage the struggle. King also tried to present the public ownership point of view to a wide audience in his work as Executive Director of the National Popular Government League. Dispassionately and with scholarly apparatus King examined this struggle in *The Conservation Fight, from Theodore Roosevelt to the Tennessee Valley Authority*.[107]

[101] New York: Viking, 1959.

[102] Burl Noggle, "The Origins of the Teapot Dome Investigation," *Mississippi Valley Historical Review*, 44:237-66; September 1957. Fola LaFollette in her biography, *Robert M. LaFollette*, revealed the latter's role in originating the investigation.

[103] J. Leonard Bates, "Josephus Daniels and the Naval Oil Reserve," *United States Naval Institute Proceedings*, 79:171-79; February 1953.

[104] Bates, "Fulfilling American Democracy: The Conservation Movement, 1907 to 1921," *Mississippi Valley Historical Review*, 44:29-57; June 1957.

[105] Bates, "The Teapot Dome Scandal and the Election of 1924," *American Historical Review*, 60:303-22; January 1955.

[106] See his autobiography, *Fighting Liberal* (New York: Macmillan, 1945).

[107] Washington: Public Affairs, 1959. Another aspect of the conservation movement was examined by Paul L. Kleinsorge in *The Boulder Canyon Project* (Stanford: Stanford University, 1941). This project, completed during the administration of

Agriculture and Agricultural Policies

One obvious failure in the domestic policies of the government was in agriculture, where wartime prosperity quickly gave way to mounting costs and declining prices. Murray R. Benedict, a distinguished agricultural economist, surveyed the entire problem in *Farm Policies of the United States, 1790-1950*.[108] Fully three-fifths of this volume is devoted to the period following the first World War. The wealth of detail presented by Benedict helps to reveal the variety and complexity of the agricultural economy.[109] An even greater attention to detail was manifested by James H. Shideler in an important monograph, *Farm Crisis, 1919-1923*.[110] Focusing on this brief period, Shideler was able to analyze the disruption of the traditional, individualistic pattern of production and marketing by economic forces beyond the control of individual farmers. In their groping for solutions, first by self-help, then by cooperation, and finally by political action the farm interests "led a movement away from laissez faire to government participation in business affairs, one of the great economic changes of the twentieth century."

The Farm Bureau, the most powerful farm organization of the time, is discussed in two volumes, one by a leader in it and the other by a scholar. Orville M. Kile had been associated with the Farm Bureau from 1919 through the following three decades, chiefly in striving to promote the legislative interests of its members who represent the more conservative and wealthier farmers.[111] Grant McConnell saw the American Farm Bureau Federation as one of the architects of agricultural policy in the 1920's, allied with the agricultural colleges and the Department of Agriculture.[112] The final result,

---

Herbert Hoover, was the first major multi-purpose conservation work in the nation. See also E. Louise Peffer, *The Closing of the Public Domain: Disposal and Reservation Policies, 1900-1950* (Stanford: Stanford University, 1951) ; and Robert Shankland, *Steve Mather of the National Parks* (New York: Knopf, 1951).

[108] New York: Twentieth Century Fund, 1953.

[109] See also Chester C. Davis, "The Development of Agricultural Policy Since the End of the World War," *Farmers in a Changing World: Yearbook of Agriculture* (Washington: United States Government Printing Office, 1940). While Benedict reviews the farm problem from a conservative point of view, Davis was an active leader in New Deal farm policies.

[110] Berkeley: University of California, 1957. See also Theodore Saloutos and John D. Hicks, *Agricultural Discontent in the Middle West, 1900-1939* (Madison: University of Wisconsin, 1951).

[111] Orville Merton Kile, *The Farm Bureau Through Three Decades* (Baltimore: Waverly, 1948).

[112] Grant McConnell, *The Decline of Agrarian Democracy* (Berkeley: University of California, 1953).

McConnell said, was that the individual farmer had little to say in the formulation of policies ostensibly devised in his interest. In short, McConnell explained that more than a decade before the American farmer was subsidized by the New Deal, his individuality had been taken from him by a powerful political pressure organization acting in his name but without any direct responsibility to him.

Several biographical studies are available delineating the work of prominent individuals as they faced up to the farm problem. Gilbert C. Fite wrote a first-rate biography, *George Peek and the Fight for Farm Parity*.[113] Seeking to attain for agriculture the governmental protection that industry had long commanded, Peek is a seminal figure in developing the concept of parity, whereby the farmer with government aid would receive a fair price for his produce. Frank O. Lowden, who sought the Republican nomination in 1920, emerged as an important agricultural spokesman in the 1920's.[114] Like other prominent leaders, Lowden came to realize that agriculture without governmental intervention would operate at a perilous disadvantage. The Wallaces of Iowa, who agreed with this concept, provided two prominent agricultural leaders. Henry C. Wallace was Secretary of Agriculture under Warren G. Harding while his son, Henry A. Wallace, editing a distinguished farm journal, at times disagreed with his father's views. Editor Wallace during this decade shifted his ideas as well as his politics and eventually emerged as a Democratic farm leader.[115]

LABOR AND LABOR POLICIES

In any evaluation of the performance of the American economy, the condition of labor must be considered as an important factor. Though strikes were few after 1919, the lot of many laboring men was not enviable. Both Foster Rhea Dulles[116] and Joseph C. Rayback[117] devoted some attention to their plight in their general histories of labor, while Marguerite Green has examined *The National Civic*

---

[113] Norman: University of Oklahoma, 1954.

[114] William T. Hutchinson, *Lowden of Illinois: The Life of Frank O. Lowden*, volume 2 (Chicago: University of Chicago, 1957). See also Darwin N. Kelley, "The McNary-Haugen Bills, 1924-1928," *Agricultural History*, 14:170-80; October 1940, for an account of the most popular solution to the farm problem propounded during the twenties.

[115] Russell Lord, *The Wallaces of Iowa* (Boston: Houghton Mifflin, 1947).

[116] Foster Rhea Dulles, *Labor in America: A History* (New York: Crowell, 1949).

[117] Joseph G. Rayback, *A History of American Labor* (New York: Macmillan, 1959).

Federation and the American Labor Movement, 1900-1925.[118] After the first World War this organization, which had pioneered in promoting harmony between capital and labor, fell victim to the Red Scare and thereafter waged a campaign against radicalism. Indeed it became so reactionary that its former widespread influence quickly disappeared.

The American Federation of Labor, which dominated the organized labor movement in the early twentieth century, experienced trying times during the 1920's. Its outstanding leader, Samuel Gompers, died in 1924; its membership declined; it could do little to combat the appeal of welfare capitalism and it made no widespread appeal to the growing armies of unskilled workers. Philip Taft in his comprehensive study of the organization devoted space to these and other important issues confronting it in the last years of Gompers' tenure and immediately thereafter.[119] Jean Trepp McKelvey and Milton J. Nadworny independently showed how the A. F. of L., which originally was hostile to the idea of scientific management, came during the 1920's to embrace it.[120] Many cooperative schemes involving both union and management were introduced and the A. F. of L. actually hired a management consultant. However, the Great Depression brought an end to these efforts at union-management cooperation and the A. F. of L.'s flirtation with the principles of scientific management.

The portrait of American labor is further developed by an examination of the career of its outstanding leaders. John L. Lewis emerged as an outstanding figure at this time. By the time his active union career, which saw him come into prominence as head of the United Mine Workers in 1919, came to an end in 1960, he was the subject of two biographies:[121] one hostile, the other friendly. Another labor leader, who rose to national prominence after Prosperity Decade, was Sidney Hillman. During this period he made the Amalgamated Clothing Workers Union one of the most responsible and respected in the nation. His career was sympathetically examined by Matthew

---

[118] Washington: Catholic University, 1956.

[119] Philip Taft, *The A. F. of L. in the Time of Gompers* (1957), and *The A. F. of L. from the Death of Gompers to the Merger* (1959), both New York: Harper.

[120] Jean Trepp McKelvey, *AFL Attitudes Toward Production, 1900-1932* (Ithaca: Cornell University, 1952). Milton J. Nadworny, *Scientific Management and the Unions, 1900-1932* (Cambridge: Harvard University, 1955).

[121] James A. Wechsler, *Labor Baron: A Portrait of John L. Lewis* (New York: Morrow, 1944) is hostile; Saul D. Alinsky, *John L. Lewis: An Unauthorized Biography* (New York: Putnam, 1949) is friendly.

Josephson.[122] And the career of another most outstanding leader whom American labor has produced was examined by Hyman G. Weintraub in a recent volume, *Andrew Furuseth: Emancipator of the Seamen.*[123] Furuseth won his greatest victory with the enactment of the Seamen's Act in 1915, but he served the cause of maritime labor well until his death at the end of the 1920's.[124]

BUSINESS AND ECONOMIC THOUGHT

Flux and ferment is evident when one shifts from an analysis of labor to a discussion of business. Frederick Lewis Allen superficially but suggestively surveyed this theme in his volume, *The Big Change: America Transforms Itself, 1900-1950,*[125] while Thomas G. Cochran probed it with care in *The American Business System: A Historical Perspective, 1900-1955.*[126] Viewing business as a social institution for creating and distributing goods and services for profit, Cochran regarded the Great Depression as the end of an era in which the idea of a self-regulating economy prevailed. Taking advantage of technical studies in the social sciences, he analyzed "bigness and the managerial system" which he believed to be the fundamental business development of the twentieth century.[127] On the other hand, George H. Soule is concerned exclusively with the period of this chapter. In *Prosperity Decade: From War to Depression, 1917-1929*[128] he presented an excellent economic history with the emphasis on business performance. Relying heavily on the publications of the National Bureau of Economic Research, Soule presented much of his information in terms of statistical aggregates.

While Soule was concerned with more technical economic analysis, Joseph Dorfman published a scholarly history of economic thought and its influence, or lack of influence, on the course of events.[129] By

---

[122] *Sidney Hillman: Statesman of American Labor* (Garden City: Doubleday, 1952). See also Max D. Danish, *The World of David Dubinsky* (Cleveland: World, 1957); Benjamin Stolberg, *Tailor's Progress* (Garden City: Doubleday, Doran, 1944); Robert A. Christie, *Empire in Wood: A History of the Carpenters' Union* (Ithaca: Cornell University, 1956).

[123] Berkeley: University of California, 1959.

[124] Although relatively few volumes in the field of labor history pertain entirely to the 1920's, much material on the period can be gleaned from studies surveying particular aspects of labor. For a select list of studies on this subject, see "Specialized Studies in the History of Labor" appended to this chapter.

[125] New York: Harper, 1952.

[126] Cambridge: Harvard University, 1957.

[127] *Ibid.*

[128] New York: Rinehart, 1947.

[129] Joseph Dorfman, *The Economic Mind in American Civilization;* Volumes IV and V, *1918-1933* (New York: Viking, 1959).

and large, economic thought of the time held that government could do little to affect the course of events. Indeed most economists, like most Americans, held a deep and pervasive belief in the automatic functioning of free enterprise. Dorfman revealed that this concept was challenged briefly during and immediately after World War I and more effectively after 1929. In another penetrating volume, James W. Prothro showed that businessmen did not differ from more formal economists in their views.[130] Examining the reports of the United States Chamber of Commerce and the National Association of Manufacturers during the 1920's Prothro revealed the arrogant complacency of businessmen about their ability to direct the operation of the economy and to provide responsible community leadership. The volumes of Dorfman and Prothro together indicate that ideas widely held by many prominent and responsible Americans would render them of little or no service when Prosperity Decade abruptly came to an end. Since they had no comprehension of the background of the depression, they would have few valid ideas of how to cope with it.[131]

RELIGION

Finally, in examining the period of the 1920's, much can be learned of the mood as well as of the tensions and values inherent in American life by surveying recent literature focusing on American religion. Herbert W. Schneider provided an excellent account of *Religion in 20th Century America*.[132] He observed that churches have responded to the economic and technological changes of the twentieth century primarily in material and institutional terms. The social and secular dimensions of religious experience were substituted for personal and subjective salvation. Working within this framework, Paul Carter examined *The Decline and Revival of the Social Gospel: Social and Political Liberalism in American Protestant Churches, 1920-1940*.[133] He traced the decline of the movement during the 1920's blaming it on the concern of the churches with prohibition, fundamentalism, the prestige of business, and rising secularism, all of which made difficult vigorous religious criticism of the social order. On the other hand Carter noted the few remaining evidences of the Social Gospel move-

---

[130] James W. Prothro, *The Dollar Decade* (Baton Rouge: Louisiana State University, 1954).

[131] Numerous excellent monographs and biographies have been written on industries and businessmen of this period. For examples, see "Specialized Studies in the History of Business and Industry" appended to this chapter.

[132] Cambridge: Harvard University, 1952.

[133] Ithaca: Cornell University, 1956.

ment during the period—the stand on the steel strike, the interest in world peace, and the growth of the ecumenical movement. Working in the same period as Carter and indeed complementing his work, Robert Moats Miller surveyed *American Protestantism and Social Issues, 1919-1939*.[134] The churches and the social order, labor, race relations, civil liberties, world peace, all are carefully examined through information gleaned in part from the official records, documents, and publications of thirteen Protestant denominations.

Several significant studies of individuals contribute to an understanding of American religious life. William C. McLoughlin examined the career of the decade's most famous evangelist, Billy Sunday. An Iowa farm boy and former major league baseball player, Sunday conducted more than three hundred revivals, spoke to more than one hundred million people, and converted more than a million—most of whom were urban dwellers.[135] The author portrayed Sunday as a political and religious conservative and claims that the ebb of evangelism coincided with the decline of laissez faire capitalism. The fundamentalism that Billy Sunday expounded is carefully examined by Norman F. Furniss in *The Fundamentalist Controversy, 1918-1931*.[136] Furniss claimed that the movement was a menace to intellectual freedom and that it cannot be identified with any geographic area but flourished in communities or among groups unaffected by the spread of knowledge and enlightenment. The Scopes Trial, the outstanding fundamentalist controversy of the decade, was the subject of a penetrating volume by Ray Ginger.[137] The author probed beneath the evolutionary argument in the trial and revealed more basic issues related to a democratic way of life, such as problems of leadership, majority rule, popular education, and the role of experts. Besides the debate between modern science and old-time religion, forceful and incompatible personalities vied with one another at Dayton. Ginger brought before his readers the drama of the conflict as well as the issues. Though merciless in his criticism of Bryan, he reserved some bitter barbs for Clarence Darrow and revealed how individual personalities can expound as well as distort issues and ideas.

The individual search for spiritual vitality and moral power during Prosperity Decade is revealed in several volumes pertaining to different

---

[134] Chapel Hill: University of North Carolina, 1958.
[135] William G. McLoughlin, Jr., *Billy Sunday Was His Real Name* (Chicago: University of Chicago, 1955).
[136] New Haven: Yale University, 1954.
[137] Ray Ginger, *Six Days or Forever? Tennessee v. John Thomas Scopes* (Boston: Beacon, 1958).

religions.[138] Harry Emerson Fosdick recounted his remarkable career in *The Living of These Days*[139] and Reinhold Niebuhr in a recently reprinted volume related his experience as a parish priest in an urban area in *Leaves From The Notebook of a Tamed Cynic*.[140] While Fosdick wrote from the viewpoint of a religious liberal, Niebuhr analyzed the views and values of the period, as observed from his vantage point of parish priest of a fundamentalist sect in Detroit, from a more orthodox position. And in doing so he wrote one of the best volumes available for presenting a reader an insight and understanding of Prosperity Decade.

One of the reasons why Niebuhr's volume is so penetrating is that the author does not reflect the optimism of religious liberals, businessmen, political leaders, and other prominent spokesmen of the decade. This optimism came to an end with the onset of the Great Depression which crystallized the tensions of Prosperity Decade and brought to the forefront voices, themes, and ideas which though evident during the 1917-1929 period were not in the main channels of American life at that time.[141]

SPECIALIZED STUDIES IN THE HISTORY OF LABOR

David Brody, *Steel Workers in America: The Nonunion Era* (Cambridge: Harvard University, 1960); Herbert J. Lahne, *The Cotton Mill Worker* (New York: Farrar & Rinehart, 1944); Murray Ross, *Stars and Strikes* (New York: Columbia University, 1941); Leonard A. Lecht, *Experience under Railway Labor Legislation* (New York: Columbia University, 1955); Paul M. Angle's *Bloody Williamson: A Chapter in American Lawlessness* (New York: Knopf, 1952); Domenico Gagliardo, *The Kansas Industrial Court: An Experiment in Compulsory Arbitration* (Lawrence, Kans.: University of Kansas, 1941). Several authors comment upon other aspects of the labor movement and its relationship to government: Elias Lieberman, *Unions Before the Bar* (New York:

---

[138] Stephen S. Wise wrote in *Challenging Years* (New York: Putnam, 1949) of his efforts to bring Judaism more in tune with the realities of American life. Elizabeth H. Emerson in her biography of *Walter C. Woodward, Friend on the Frontier* (Richmond, Ind.: The Walter C. Woodward Memorial Comm., 1952) examined the career of a prominent Quaker liberal.

[139] New York: Harper, 1956.

[140] Hamden, Conn.: Shoestring, 1956.

[141] Another important issue upon which there is a growing literature available is that of immigration. See, for example, Robert A. Divine, *American Immigration Policy, 1924-1952* (New Haven: Yale University, 1957). John Higham, *Strangers in the Land: Patterns of American Nativism, 1860-1925* (New Brunswick: Rutgers University, 1955). Barbara Miller Solomon, *Ancestors and Immigrants: A Changing New England Tradition* (Cambridge: Harvard University, 1956). Charles Reznikoff, ed., *Louis Marshall, Champion of Liberty: Selected Papers and Addresses* (2 vols.; Philadelphia: Jewish Publication Society of America, 1957).

Harper, 1950); Charles Oscar Gregory, *Labor and the Law* (New York: Norton, 1946); Louis Waldman, *Labor Lawyer* (New York: Dutton, 1945); John Lombardi, *Labor's Voice in the Cabinet* (New York: Columbia University, 1942); Mary Anderson, *Woman at Work* (Minneapolis: University of Minnesota, 1951).

SPECIALIZED STUDIES IN THE HISTORY OF THE NEGRO

The role of the Negro in the labor movement has not yet been thoroughly studied, although several recent works deal with the subject. See John Hope Franklin, *From Slavery to Freedom* (Rev. ed.; New York: Knopf, 1956) and Gunnar Myrdal, *An American Dilemma* (New York: Harper, 1944). Other aspects of Negro life have received more attention. See Edmund David Cronon, *Black Moses: The Story of Marcus Garvey and the Universal Negro Improvement Association* (Madison: University of Wisconsin, 1955); Francis L. Broderick, *W. E. B. DuBois: Negro Leader in a Time of Crisis* (Stanford: Stanford University, 1959); William Hardin Hughes and Frederick D. Patterson, eds., *Robert Russa Moton of Hampton and Tuskegee* (Chapel Hill: University of North Carolina, 1956); Catherine Owens Peare, *Mary McLeod Bethune* (New York: Vanguard, 1951); [Margaret] Rackham Holt, *George Washington Carver: An American Biography* (Garden City: Doubleday, Doran, 1943); Langston Hughes, *The Big Sea* (New York: Knopf, 1940); Walter F. White, *A Man Called White* (New York: Viking, 1948).

Still another facet of Negro history is examined in the following books: Robert L. Jack, *History of the National Association for the Advancement of Colored People* (Boston: Meador, 1943); Mary White Ovington, *The Walls Came Tumbling Down* (New York: Harcourt, Brace, 1947); Bernard H. Nelson, *The Fourteenth Amendment and the Negro Since 1920* (Washington, D. C.: Catholic University, 1946); Elbert Lee Tatum, *The Changed Political Thought of the Negro, 1915-1940* (New York: Exposition, 1951).

SPECIALIZED STUDIES IN THE HISTORY OF INDUSTRY AND BUSINESS

Mabel Newcomer, *The Big Business Executive: The Factors That Made Him, 1900-1950* (New York: Columbia, 1955); William Haynes, *American Chemical Industry* (6 vols.; New York: Van Nostrand, 1945-1954); Oscar Edward Anderson, *Refrigeration in America* (Princeton: Published for the University of Cincinnati by Princeton University, 1953); George S. Gibb and Evelyn Knowlton, *The Resurgent Years, 1911-1927: History of Standard Oil Company (New Jersey)* (New York: Harper, 1956); Paul H. Giddens, *Standard Oil Company (Indiana): Oil Pioneer of the Middle West* (New York: Appleton-Century-Crofts, 1955); William L. Connelly, *The Oil Business as I Saw It: Half A Century with Sinclair* (Norman: University of Oklahoma, 1954); Carl Coke Rister, *Oil! Titan of the Southwest* (Norman: University of Oklahoma, 1949); John Joseph Mathews, *Life and Death of an Oil Man: The Career of E. W. Marland* (Norman: University of Oklahoma, 1951).

Gertrude G. Schroeder, *The Growth of Major Steel Companies, 1900-1950* (Baltimore: Johns Hopkins, 1953); Tom Mercer Girdler and Boyden

Sparkes, *Boot Straps* (New York: Scribner, 1943); Thomas C. Cochran, *The Pabst Brewing Company: The History of an American Business* (New York: New York University, 1948); Roscoe Carlyle Buley, *The American Life Convention, 1906-1952* (New York: Appleton-Century-Crofts, 1953); Otis A. Pease, *The Responsibilities of American Advertising: Private Control and Public Influence, 1920-1940* (New Haven: Yale University, 1958); Alfred P. Sloan, Jr., and Boyden Sparkes, *Adventures of a White-Collar Man* (New York: Doubleday, Doran, 1941); Walter P. Chrysler and Boyden Sparkes, *Life of an American Workman* (New York: Dodd, Mead, 1950).

John B. Rae, *American Automobile Manufacturers: The First Forty Years* (Philadelphia: Chilton Company, Book Division, 1959); Allan Nevins and Frank Ernest Hill, *Ford: Expansion and Challenge, 1915-1933* (New York: Scribner, 1957); Keith T. Sward, *The Legend of Henry Ford* (New York: Rinehart, 1948); Garet Garett, *The Wild Wheel* (New York: Phaeton, 1952); Harry H. Bennett and Paul Marcus, *We Never Called Him Henry* (New York: Fawcett, 1951); Alfred Lief, *Harvey Firestone: Free Man of Enterprise* (New York: McGraw-Hill, 1951); Jane W. Fisher, *Fabulous Hoosier: A Study of American Achievement* (New York: R. M. McBride, 1947); Edward A. Kennedy, *The Automobile Industry: The Coming of Age of Capitalism's Favorite Child* (New York: Reynal & Hitchcock, 1941); Frederick Logan Paxson, "The Highway Movement, 1916-1935," *American Historical Review*, 51:236-53; January 1946. Charles Lee Dearing, *American Highway Policy* (Washington, D. C.: Brookings Institution, 1941); David L. Cohn, *Combustion on Wheels: An Informal History of the Automobile Age* (Boston: Houghton Mifflin, 1944); Reginald M. Cleveland and S. T. Williamson, *The Road is Yours* (New York: Greystone, 1951); Lloyd B. Morris, *Not So Long Ago* (New York: Random, 1949); Thor Hultgren, *American Transportation in Prosperity and Depression* (New York: National Bureau of Economic Research, 1948); William N. Leonard, *Railroad Consolidation under the Transportation Act of 1920* (New York: Columbia University, 1946); James H. Lemly, *The Gulf, Mobile and Ohio* (Homewood, Ill.: R. D. Irwin, 1953); Donald Richberg, *My Hero* (New York: Putnam, 1954); Claude M. Fuess, *Joseph B. Eastman: Servant of the People* (New York: Columbia University, 1952).

Henry Ladd Smith, *Airways: The History of Commercial Aviation in the United States* (New York: Knopf, 1942); Elspeth E. Freudenthal, *The Aviation Business: From Kitty Hawk to Wall Street* (New York: Vanguard, 1940); Archibald D. Turnbull and Clifford L. Lord, *History of United States Naval Aviation* (New Haven: Yale University, 1949); Emile H. Gauvreau and Lester Cohen, *Billy Mitchell: Founder of Our Air Force and Prophet without Honor* (New York: Dutton, 1942); Roger Burlingame, *General Billy Mitchell* ([They Made America Series] New York: McGraw-Hill, 1952); Charles A. Lindbergh, *The Spirit of St. Louis* (New York: Scribner, 1953); Kenneth S. Davis, *The Hero: Charles A. Lindbergh and the American Dream* (Garden City: Doubleday, 1959).

CHAPTER XV

The New Deal, 1929-1941

Frank Freidel

INTRODUCTION

ALTHOUGH the Great Depression and the New Deal are only two or three decades in the past, already they are one of the most written-about phases of American history. The problem facing the teacher is not one of finding materials, but of sorting and sifting from the enormous bulk those writings which will be of use to him in preparing for his classes, and those most readable for various levels of students. There are books that are lively and polemical, others dull and still polemical, and happily a surprising number that are both highly readable and of substantial historic merit. Some of the best historical writing of recent years, firmly anchored on the vast collections of documentary materials already available, has analyzed the depression and the Roosevelt administration.

As a starting-point beyond secondary school textbooks, teachers may wish to examine some of the more recent one-volume and two-volume college level surveys of United States history and especially some of the histories of the United States in the twentieth century. These, although they vary in their individual interpretations, are for the most part full, clear, and factually reliable in their treatment of the years 1929-1941. They also contain useful selective bibliographies. The most original and extensive of the textbook accounts of the United States during this century is Arthur S. Link, *American Epoch*[1] which contains a full account of the Hoover and Roosevelt administrations. An excellent popular interpretation of American presidents from 1929 is Walter Johnson, *1600 Pennsylvania Avenue.*[2]

---

[1] New York: Knopf, 1955.
[2] Boston: Little, Brown, 1960.

THE DEPRESSION AND HOOVER

Several surveys cover the depression through the Hoover and Roosevelt administrations. Broadus Mitchell, *Depression Decade, From New Era through New Deal, 1929-1941*[3] is a rather lengthy economic history of moderate reading difficulty, critical both of Hoover's outmoded, overoptimistic ways of dealing with the depression, and of Roosevelt's nimble shifts among varying economic policies. It deals topically with relief, banking and currency, agriculture, and the like. The author's viewpoint emerges in the final chapter of the analysis "War to the Rescue." Dixon Wecter, *The Age of the Great Depression, 1929-1941* is a vivid, readable social history.[4] Wecter was more favorable toward New Deal economics than Mitchell, but demonstrated no grasp of it. He gathered a wide variety of materials on American life during the depression, occasionally expressing value judgments (as on Hollywood) which were not well considered. The merit of his account is the remarkable way in which he succeeded in conveying to his readers how people felt during the depression, and how they reacted to the New Deal.

The first volume of Arthur M. Schlesinger, Jr., *The Age of Roosevelt,* subtitled *The Crisis of the Old Order, 1919-1933,* covers from the end of the first World War to the inauguration of Roosevelt.[5] In its trenchant, lively analysis of the failures of the economic and political system leading to the depression, and the inability of the Hoover administration to find workable solutions, it takes the view that the "old order" was bankrupt. This volume makes the case against the business leadership, the Republican party, and the Hoover administration during these years. The case for them appears with even greater vehemence, but in a ponderous and uninviting style in the third volume of *The Memoirs of Herbert Hoover,* subtitled *The Great Depression, 1929-1941.*[6] Hoover deplored the stock speculation and weaknesses of the banking system which should have been remedied at home, but viewed the depression as basically an economic hurricane which struck from abroad. His own policies, which in retrospect he affirmed as sound, he believed were bringing a measure of recovery by the summer of 1932 which would have continued except for the

---

[3] New York: Rinehart, 1947.
[4] New York: Macmillan, 1948.
[5] Boston: Houghton Mifflin, 1957.
[6] New York: Macmillan, 1952.

accession of Roosevelt and the Democratic party. The last section of his book is a detailed critique of the New Deal along these lines:

> The effort to crossbreed some features of Fascism and Socialism with our American free system speedily developed in the Roosevelt administration. The result was that America failed to keep pace with world recovery. Instead we continued with subnormal levels of lessened productivity, high unemployment, and costly relief measures until our man power and industries were absorbed by the war eight years later, in 1941. [p. vii]

An economist, John K. Galbraith, in *The Great Crash, 1929* explained in a brief, interesting, and easily understandable fashion why the 1929 stock market crash occurred, and why it triggered such an acute depression and deflation.[7] Galbraith saw the causes of the depression as complex and difficult to avoid. Two lively, clear accounts of the twenties, culminating with a summary of the causes of the depression and Hoover's efforts to counter it, are William E. Leuchtenburg, *The Perils of Prosperity, 1914-32* and John D. Hicks, *Republican Ascendancy, 1921-1933*.[8]

The most detailed, relatively dispassionate account of the Hoover administration is Harris G. Warren, *Herbert Hoover and the Great Depression*.[9] Unfortunately, Warren did not have access to the Hoover papers, which are closed to most scholars, and did not use other manuscript collections. Consequently Warren's study contributes little new; his viewpoint is favorable. A forthcoming study of the Hoover administration by Edgar E. Robinson is based on extensive research in manuscript and archival material. Biographies of Hoover published in the forties and fifties were popular in content, and in tone have ranged from friendly to adulatory. They add little beyond his own *Memoirs*,[10] although a brilliant critical sketch of Hoover is

---

[7] Boston: Houghton Mifflin, 1955.

[8] Chicago: University of Chicago, 1958 and New York: Harper, 1960. The Hicks volume is in the New American Nation Series.

[9] New York: Oxford, 1959.

[10] For an interesting account of Hoover's life until he became President, and a disappointingly dull account of the Presidency (other than depression problems), see *Years of Adventure, 1874-1920* and *The Cabinet and the Presidency, 1920-1933*, which are the first and second volumes of Hoover *Memoirs* (3 vols.; New York: Macmillan, 1951-1952). A more detailed reminiscence of the first World War is Hoover, *The Ordeal of Woodrow Wilson* (New York: McGraw-Hill, 1958). Several scurrilous and untrustworthy so-called exposés of Hoover's early career appeared in 1932, the most notorious being John Hamill, *The Strange Career of Mr. Hoover under Two Flags* (New York: Faro, 1931). In contrast, recent biographies have tended to be adulatory: Eugene Lyons, *Our Unknown Ex-President* (Garden City: Doubleday, 1948), reissued with new material as *The Herbert Hoover Story* (1959);

to be found in Richard Hofstadter, *The American Political Tradition.*[11]

PRESIDENT ROOSEVELT AND THE NEW DEAL: GENERAL TREATMENTS

Among the many books on President Roosevelt and the New Deal, there are a number of distinct merit, based on sound research and written in an effective fashion. These present a variety of challenging viewpoints. The first of these studies was Basil Rauch, *The History of the New Deal, 1933-1938,*[12] written before the manuscript collections were open and based upon *The Public Papers and Addresses of Franklin D. Roosevelt* and the *New York Times,* with a dash of the reminiscences of Raymond Moley and James A. Farley. It set much of the factual pattern for later treatments of the New Deal, and propounds the important thesis that about 1935 there had been a shift from a first rather conservative New Deal emphasizing recovery, to a second, more radical New Deal concentrating upon reform.

David Hinshaw, *Herbert Hoover, American Quaker* (New York: Farrar, Straus, 1950); and Harold Wolfe, *Herbert Hoover: Public Servant and Leader of the Loyal Opposition* ([A Banner Book] New York: Exposition, 1956). William Starr Myers, ed., *The State Papers and Other Public Writings of Herbert Hoover* (2 vols.; Garden City: Doubleday, Doran, 1934) is the basic compilation. Many of the key documents are quoted in William Starr Myers and Walter S. Newton, *The Hoover Administration: A Documented Narrative* (New York: Scribner, 1936). Hoover has expressed his beliefs in *American Individualism* (Garden City: Doubleday, Page, 1922), *The Challenge to Liberty* (New York: Scribner, 1934), and in seven volumes of collected speeches covering the years 1933 to 1955, under the general title, *Addresses Upon the American Road* (1938-1955). Since this chapter has been written, an outstanding biography of Henry L. Stimson has appeared, Elting Morison, *Turmoil and Tradition; a Study of the Life and Times of Henry L. Stimson.* (Boston: Haughton Mifflin, 1960).

[11] New York: Knopf, 1948. This book is conveniently available in a paperback edition.

[12] New York: Creative Age, 1944. General accounts of the social and intellectual history of the thirties are to be found in Dixon Wecter, *The Age of the Great Depression, 1929-1941* (New York: Macmillan, 1948); Frederick Lewis Allen, *Since Yesterday: The Nineteen-Thirties in America, September 3, 1929—September 3, 1939* (New York: Harper, 1940); Charles and Mary Beard, *America in Midpassage* (2 vols.; New York: Macmillan, 1939); Leo Gurko, *The Angry Decade* (New York: Dodd, Mead, 1947); and Milton Crane, ed., *The Roosevelt Era* (New York: Boni and Gaer, 1947).

The more important documentary collections on Roosevelt and the New Deal are: Samuel I. Rosenman, ed., *The Public Papers and Addresses of Franklin D. Roosevelt* (13 vols.; New York: Random House, 1938-1950) which contains almost encyclopedic summaries of the work of most New Deal agencies and effects of various pieces of legislation; Edgar B. Nixon, ed., *Franklin D. Roosevelt and Conservation, 1911-1945* (2 vols.; Hyde Park: Franklin D. Roosevelt Library, 1957); and Elliott Roosevelt, ed., *F. D. R.: His Personal Letters* (New York: Duell, Sloan and Pearce, 1947-1950) an edited selection by no means complete.

A simple, brief survey is Denis W. Brogan, *The Era of Franklin D. Roosevelt,* which has the merit of being written from an English point of view.[13] A more technical English survey of lasting validity is *The New Deal, An Analysis and Appraisal.*[14] A lucid American survey, excellent for high school students, is Dexter Perkins, *The New Age of Franklin Roosevelt, 1932-45.*[15] Perkins, rather deemphasizing the role of Roosevelt, examines broadly the forces creating the New Deal. He feels that the New Deal failed because it fell between two stools:

It could not restore business confidence; neither could it launch an audacious and far-reaching program of deficit finance. As a consequence, it failed to solve the fundamental problem of unemployment until the conditions of war placed that problem in a new setting. [p. 80]

Out of a careful gathering of evidence, Edgar E. Robinson in *The Roosevelt Leadership, 1933-1945,*[16] came to conservative constitutionalist conclusions. This is the most formidable of the evaluations from the right, far more serious in tone and reasoning than John T. Flynn's bombastic *The Roosevelt Myth.*[17] According to Robinson the effect of the New Deal on American thinking was this:

Within the nation in these twelve years was developed a distrust of the basic democracy of the republic, as well as a social philosophy that included within its practices, if not in its pronouncements, many of the primary leveling objectives of communism. A whole generation of youth was cut off from the past by an eloquent proponent of revolutionary change. [p. 376]

And the effect upon the role of government in the economy:

Roosevelt's leadership resulted in fundamental changes in the government itself: in tremendous concentration of power in the Executive; in building up a vast system of bureaucratic control of private business; and by adding direct economic support of the citizen to the careful adjustment of conflicting economic interests in a free enterprise system. [p. 400]

Richard Hofstadter in the concluding chapter of *The Age of Reform*[18] (a book primarily concerned with Populism and Progressivism) also sees in the New Deal a sharp break from earlier traditions,

---

[13] (Chronicles of America Series, Vol. 52) New Haven: Yale University, 1950.

[14] By the Editors of *The Economist.* New York: Knopf, 1937.

[15] (The Chicago History of American Civilization) Chicago: University of Chicago, 1957.

[16] Philadelphia: Lippincott, 1955. This book contains a valuable 69-page annotated bibliography on Roosevelt and the New Deal.

[17] New York: Devin-Adair, 1948.

[18] New York: Knopf, 1955.

but views with favor what Robinson sees with horror: "If the state was believed neutral in the days of T. R. because its leaders claimed to sanction favors for no one, the state under F.D.R. could be called neutral only in the sense that it offered favors to everyone." In other words, the second Roosevelt moved in a time of depression from a concept of equal rights for all to one of equal privileges for all. Hofstadter points to the large role of organized labor, the interest in regulating rather than smashing big business, and the political alliances with urban bosses, all in contrast to the policies of Progressives.[19]

As its title would imply, Mario Einaudi, *The Roosevelt Revolution* also regarded the New Deal as having wrought vast and permanent changes.[20] Einaudi looked upon these with unreserved enthusiasm, and took issue with Robinson's gloomy views. Students will not find his chapters on Roosevelt and the New Deal as readable as the comparable surveys by Perkins and Brogan, but will find much meat in the introductory "Europe's Image of America," and the concluding commentary, up-dating Tocqueville in the light of the changes first brought about by the New Deal.

Biographical Treatments

Deservedly, the most widely read of the biographies of Roosevelt is the dramatic *Roosevelt: The Lion and the Fox* by James MacGregor Burns, which takes its title from Machiavelli's dictum that the prince must be a fox to recognize traps, and a lion to frighten wolves.[21] Examining Roosevelt and the New Deal from a Keynesian viewpoint, Burns devoted nearly half his book to Roosevelt's second term, which he pronounced a failure. (A brief epilogue covers the war years.) Some of Burns' views are: Congress in 1934-1936 was ready to go further left than the President would move; when he finally went in that direction it was in response to repudiation from the right. His landslide re-election in 1936 created unmanageable Democratic majorities in Congress. These contributed less to his defeat in the abortive effort to increase the number of justices on the Supreme Court than did Roosevelt's tricky tactics. These were made doubly unnecessary, first by the new willingness of the Supreme Court to validate New Deal legislation, second and most important, because Roosevelt could have obtained the objectives the Supreme Court earlier blocked

---

[19] Arthur Link takes the opposite viewpoint that the New Deal was no more than the enactment of an enlarged Progressive program. *American Epoch*, p. 381.
[20] New York: Harcourt, Brace, 1959.
[21] New York: Harcourt, Brace, 1956.

through heavy spending. Burns considered the spending power of the President the tool with which the depression could have been ended, and Roosevelt's cutbacks in 1937, the cause of the recession. Finally, because Roosevelt did not start early enough to build a liberal party, he suffered new humiliation and defeat when he tried to purge conservative Democrats in the 1938 congressional primaries. In all these and most other things, Burns saw Roosevelt as the fox rather than the lion. Not until the summer of 1940 with England at bay, did Roosevelt conclude the leonine "destroyers-for-bases" deal.

In the second volume of *The Age of Roosevelt*, entitled *The Coming of the New Deal* which covers only 1933 and 1934, Schlesinger presented a favorable interpretation of President Roosevelt and the early New Deal, from a viewpoint of modern economics and liberal politics.[22] Differing from the first volume, which by comparison was a sweeping survey and predominantly intellectual history, *The Coming of the New Deal* topically analyzes in concrete detail the establishment and functioning of the early New Deal policies toward agriculture, industry, finance, relief, natural resources, and labor, and explores Roosevelt's presidential leadership. Behind Schlesinger's smooth-flowing style and vivid anecdotal approach is the exhaustive research in both printed and manuscript materials, and innumerable interviews with participants with which he buttressed his conclusions. Judging recovery agencies like the Agricultural Adjustments Administration and the National Recovery Administration by the economic standards of the end of the fifties rather than the beginning of the thirties, he found much merit in them. He saw in the early New Deal much of the spirit of reform, and much substantial accomplishment. This favorable viewpoint is by no means uncritical. In his analysis of the NRA, Schlesinger pointed out:

> NRA always contained the possibility of becoming a conspiracy of organized business and (in certain industries) of organized labor against the public —a profit-wage conspiracy against the consumer. Under such pressures, NRA tended to promote scarcity and hold back recovery. To this degree, the conventional critique of NRA seems justified. . . . But . . . the economic

---

[22] Boston: Houghton Mifflin, 1959. Since this chapter has been written, Schlesinger's third volume has appeared, surpassing in brilliance even the previous two. This volume consists of four parts: the first part discusses the various radical movements of the early 1930's; the second analyzes the shift from the first to the second New Deal and rather substantially modifies earlier interpretations of this shift; the third considers the crisis of the Constitution and Supreme Court; and the fourth describes the election of 1936. Arthur M. Schlesinger, Jr., *The Age of Roosevelt*. Volume III, *The Politics of Upheaval* (Boston: Houghton Mifflin, 1960).

philosophy of NRA was by no means so mistaken as its conventional critics have assumed. . . . The real cure . . . was to strengthen government, labor, and consumer representation in the process of code-making. . . . [p. 172]

. . . . . .

The more enduring achievements of NRA lay not in the economic but in the social field. Here NRA accomplished a fantastic series of reforms, any one of which would have staggered the nation a few years earlier. It established the principle of maximum hours and minimum wages on a national basis. It abolished child labor. It dealt a fatal blow to sweatshops. It made collective bargaining a national policy and thereby transformed the position of organized labor. It gave new status to the consumer. It stamped out a noxious collection of unfair trade practices. It set new standards of economic decency in American life—standards which could not be rolled back, whatever happened to NRA. In doing these things, it accomplished in a few months what reformers had dreamed about for a half a century. [p. 174-75]

As for Roosevelt's leadership, Schlesinger believed that

while he often played at being Machiavelli, he was not really Machiavellian. . . . The rather simplehearted idealism which lay so near the core of Roosevelt's personality could not indefinitely support the experiments in smart-aleckness and trickiness. [p. 557]

An affirmation of the rather simple, humane base of thinking from which Roosevelt embarked into the complicated politics of the New Deal is to be found in Rexford G. Tugwell, *The Democratic Roosevelt*.[23] Tugwell, an ardent, advanced New Dealer, for a while one of Roosevelt's closest advisers, used his own on-the-spot observations and his shrewd afterthoughts. His early chapters analyzing the formation of Roosevelt's character are full of remarkable insights. The section on the first four years of the New Deal, when the President often engaged in complex courses of action, and did not go so far or fast as Tugwell wished, is written in a spirit of affectionate disillusion. The account of events after Tugwell had left Washington at the end of 1936, is less useful.

A projected six-volume biography by Frank Freidel, in the three volumes thus far in print, brings Roosevelt to his election as President in 1932. *The Apprenticeship* covers the period to the end of the first World War; *The Ordeal* to Roosevelt's election as Governor of New York, with emphasis upon his polio attack; and *The Triumph*, the governorship and campaign of 1932.[24]

[23] Garden City: Doubleday, 1957.
[24] Boston: Little, Brown, 1952, 1954, and 1956.

There is an excellent sketch of Roosevelt, rich in insights, in Hofstadter, *The American Political Tradition*. Recent serious studies of Roosevelt have outdated most of the popular biographies. One exception is John Gunther, *Roosevelt in Retrospect, A Profile in History*, a skillful piece of reporting.[25] Despite minor factual errors, it successfully catches the image of the man and the President. A fine campaign biography, Ernest K. Lindley, *Franklin D. Roosevelt, A Career in Progressive Democracy* is still worth reading as a portrait of Roosevelt as he appeared before he became President.[26]

There are two scholarly monographs on Roosevelt before he became President, both based on the Roosevelt papers. David R. Fusfeld, *The Economic Thought of Franklin D. Roosevelt and the Origins of the New Deal* gives a detailed account of Roosevelt's training in the political and economic climate of the Progressive era.[27] It takes a view (at variance with that in Freidel, *The Apprenticeship*) that Roosevelt emerged from his economic courses at Groton and Harvard with a fixed and enduring economic philosophy. In a chapter on Roosevelt's views in 1920, Fusfeld relies heavily upon a memorandum probably not the work of Roosevelt or anyone on his staff. Bernard Bellush, *Franklin D. Roosevelt as Governor of New York* is a definitive administrative history, topically arranged.[28]

Memoirs and Diaries

Much of the character of Roosevelt and the flavor of the New Deal emerges in the memoirs and diaries of participants. These, of course, must be used with some caution since, while they can be remarkable for the insights and the freshness of the inside stories they convey,

---

[25] New York: Harper, 1950.

[26] Indianapolis: Bobbs-Merrill, 1931. Among the popular biographies are the dramatic but superficial Alden Hatch, *Franklin D. Roosevelt: An Informal Biography* (New York: Holt, 1947); Gerald W. Johnson, *Roosevelt: Dictator or Democrat?* (New York: Harper, 1941), an able defense; John T. Flynn, *Country Squire in the White House* (New York: Doubleday, Doran, 1940), a clever attack; Emil Ludwig, *Roosevelt: A Study in Fortune and Power* (New York: Viking, 1938), a misleading psychological study; and Bernard Fay, *Roosevelt and His America* (Boston: Little, Brown, 1933), hasty and laudatory.

[27] (Columbia Studies in the Social Sciences, No. 586) New York: Columbia University, 1956.

[28] (Columbia Studies in the Social Sciences, No. 585) New York: Columbia University, 1955. A popular book based partly on research and partly on memory, is Jonathan Daniels, *The End of Innocence* (Philadelphia: Lippincott, 1954) covering Roosevelt's years as Assistant Secretary of the Navy in the Wilson administration. Three attractive books on Roosevelt's personal life are: Olin Dows, *Franklin Roosevelt at Hyde Park* (New York: American Artists, 1949); Clara and Hardy Steeholm, *The House at Hyde Park* (New York: Viking, 1950); and Turnley Walker, *Roosevelt and the Warm Springs Story* (New York: Wyn, 1953).

they are also occasionally dangerous in their omissions and distortions. Partly their shortcomings are due to the strong emotions and imperfect memories of the writers, partly to the remarkable way in which President Roosevelt managed to convince any number of people associated with him that they were prime-movers in his enterprises. On the whole these memoirs and diaries are accurate enough, but can present only the facets of the President and his program that were seen by the individual viewer. For some the view was broad, for others rather narrow.

The most intimate of the memoirs, remarkable for their candor, are Eleanor Roosevelt's two volumes, *This Is My Story* covering up to the White House, and *This I Remember* on the years when her husband was President.[29] From these a moving portrait emerges of Roosevelt as his affectionate, perceptive wife saw him. Unfortunately Mrs. Roosevelt does not always tell as much as a reader would wish about her own major role as a New Deal figure.[30] A pleasant sketch of Roosevelt by one of his sons is James Roosevelt and Sidney Shalett, *Affectionately, F.D.R.*[31]

The finest of the memoirs is Frances Perkins, *The Roosevelt I Knew*, striking in its insight, broad in its view, and friendly but realistic.[32] Miss Perkins, who was Secretary of Labor, also includes much interesting information on the formation of Social Security and the problems of labor. Equally accurate, and full of detail, is Raymond Moley, *After Seven Years*, which is indispensable on the early New Deal.[33] Moley, who had been the key braintruster, left the New Deal as it moved toward the left in 1936. His incisive analysis of Roosevelt's shortcomings, as he saw them, is clearly a description of other aspects of the same man that Miss Perkins writes about. An unreservedly friendly memoir, describing in detail how Roosevelt prepared his speeches and talked with his intimates, is Samuel I. Rosenman, *Working with Roosevelt.*[34]

---

[29] New York: Harper, 1937 and 1949.

[30] Popular biographies of Mrs. Roosevelt are Ruby A. Black, *Eleanor Roosevelt, A Biography* (New York: Duell, Sloan and Pearce, 1940) and Alfred Steinberg, *Mrs. R.: The Life of Eleanor Roosevelt* (New York: Putnam, 1958).

[31] New York: Harcourt, Brace, 1959.

[32] New York: Viking, 1946.

[33] New York: Harper, 1939.

[34] New York: Harper, 1952. Among the personal reminiscences touching upon Roosevelt in the White House are: Ross T. McIntire and George Creel, *White House Physician* (New York: Putnam, 1946) on Roosevelt's health; Grace G. Tully, *F. D. R., My Boss* (New York: Scribner, 1949) by the President's secretary; and A. Merriman Smith, *Thank You, Mr. President* (New York: Harper, 1946) by a White House correspondent.

Among the New Deal diaries, that of Secretary of the Interior Harold L. Ickes created the greatest sensation upon its publication. Ickes, who had entitled his memoir, *The Autobiography of a Curmudgeon*[35] lives up to his self-image in the far-ranging, gossipy, splenetic pages of *The Secret Diary of Harold L. Ickes*, covering 1933-1941.[36] The diary gives Ickes' viewpoint of the inner workings of the Department of the Interior, of feuds with Harry L. Hopkins, Henry Wallace, and other key New Dealers, and of dealings with President Roosevelt, members of Congress, and a host of Washington figures. Much of the information is valuable, most of it is one-sided, and some of it misleading.

In contrast, readers are not likely to go astray in the carefully organized, clear narrative of John M. Blum, *From the Morgenthau Diaries: Years of Crisis, 1928-1938*.[37] Out of the enormous bulk of the manuscript diaries, Blum wove a detailed account of Secretary of the Treasury Morgenthau's relations with the President and conduct of the business of the Treasury Department. The book contains numerous word-for-word exchanges of conversation between Roosevelt and Morgenthau, from which the reader can picture vividly how Roosevelt worked and relaxed. More than this, it contains invaluable scholarly analyses of the New Deal policies on gold and silver purchases, the debt, taxation, the recession of 1937-1938, and international finance. Although the lucid presentation of these complex matters is the work of Blum, the conclusions are those of Morgenthau. He emerges in these pages as an able administrator, committed to social reforms and humanitarianism, but determined to obtain them within relatively narrow budgetary limits. The theories of Lord Keynes and the New Deal economists never won Morgenthau away from his fruitless aspiration to achieve a balanced budget. An earlier, relatively brief study of one thread of Treasury policy, also based on the Morgenthau diaries, is Allan Seymour Everest, *Morgenthau, the New Deal and Silver*.[38] A contemporary monograph is G. Griffith Johnson, Jr., *The Treasury and Monetary Policy, 1933-1938*.[39]

Marriner Eccles, who as head of the Federal Reserve advocated Keynesian economic policies at variance with those of Secretary

---

[35] New York: Reynal & Hitchcock, 1943.
[36] 3 vols.; New York: Simon and Schuster, 1953-1954.
[37] Boston: Houghton Mifflin, 1959.
[38] New York: King's Crown, 1950.
[39] (Harvard Political Studies) Cambridge: Harvard University, 1939. Analyses of the New Deal utilizing the new economics.

Morgenthau, presents his viewpoints and an account of Federal Reserve activities in his memoirs, *Beckoning Frontiers*.[40] Jesse Jones, who was proud of the conservative fashion in which he ran the Reconstruction Finance Corporation, quotes extensively from documents in Jesse H. Jones and Edward Angly, *Fifty Billion Dollars, My Thirteen Years with the RFC, 1932-1945*.[41] A popular biography covering much of the same material is Bascom N. Timmons, *Jesse H. Jones, The Man and the Statesman*.[42]

Monographs on the New Deal

There is a surprising lack of scholarly monographs on the history of most of the New Deal agencies. The reader often will have to turn to more general works like Schlesinger's *Coming of the New Deal*, or to memoirs and contemporary writings. On the National Recovery Administration, General Hugh S. Johnson's colorful memoir, *The Blue Eagle from Egg to Earth* is still useful although it gives only Johnson's view of the questions over which sharp differences arose.[43] Donald Richberg, with whom he contended, and who succeeded him, presented his contemporary view of the NRA in *The Rainbow* and his afterthoughts in *My Hero*, a facetiously titled autobiography.[44] Leverett S. Lyon et al., *The National Recovery Administration, An Analysis and Appraisal* is a contemporary technical study by Brookings Institution economists.[45]

A compendious survey of agricultural policy during the New Deal is to be found in Murray R. Benedict, *Farm Policies of the United States*.[46] For a readable, anecdotal account, with sketches of some of the policy-makers, see Russell Lord, *The Wallaces of Iowa*, which devotes nearly three hundred pages to the New Deal years.[47] Equally readable, but a scathing attack, is Dwight Macdonald, *Henry Wallace, The Man and the Myth*.[48] A broad, non-technical contemporary survey is Donald C. Blaisdell, *Government and Agriculture, The*

---

[40] *Beckoning Frontiers: Public and Personal Recollections*, ed., Sidney Hyman (New York: Knopf, 1951).

[41] New York: Macmillan, 1951.

[42] New York: Holt, 1956.

[43] Garden City: Doubleday, Doran, 1935.

[44] Garden City: Doubleday, Doran, 1936 and New York: Putnam, 1954.

[45] (Institute of Economics, Publication No. 60) Washington: The Brookings Institution, 1935.

[46] *Farm Policies of the United States, 1790-1950: A Study of their Origins and Development* (New York: Twentieth Century Fund, 1953).

[47] Boston: Houghton Mifflin, 1947.

[48] New York: Vanguard, 1948.

Growth of Federal Farm Aid.[49] More specialized studies are a Brookings Institution monograph, Edwin G. Nourse, Joseph S. Davis, and John D. Black, *Three Years of the Agricultural Adjustment Administration,*[50] and a conservative evaluation, Joseph S. Davis, *On Agricultural Policy, 1926-1938.*[51] Secretary Wallace eloquently states his views in *New Frontiers* and *Democracy Reborn.*[52] Paul K. Conkin, *Tomorrow a New World: The New Deal Community Program* analyzes both the nineteenth century ideological antecedents and the rise and decline during the New Deal of the back-to-land movement and related schools of social and economic planning. These reached their height in the Resettlement Administration and the Farm Security Administration.[53]

The Tennessee Valley Authority, attracting continuing attention within the United States and throughout the world, has been one of the most written-about phases of the New Deal. The standard survey, clear and understandable although a bit dull, is David E. Lilienthal, *TVA: Democracy on the March.*[54] One of the most thought-provoking of the scholarly monographs is Philip Selznick, *TVA and the Grass Roots, A Study in the Sociology of Formal Organization* which analyzes the decentralization of the TVA, and its consequences.[55] An earlier monograph is Charles H. Pritchett, *The Tennessee Valley Authority: A Study in Public Administration.*[56] On the vital role of Senator George W. Norris in fostering TVA, see his autobiography, *Fighting Liberal,* and a forthcoming biography by Richard Lowitt.[57]

New Deal labor policy and the growth of unions in the thirties has also been the subject of extensive writing. Milton Derber and Edwin Young, editors, *Labor and the New Deal* is an indispensable collection of essays, relating New Deal developments to the main stream of labor history, contemporary problems, and subsequent policies.[58] The study

---

[49] (American Government in Action Series, ed., Phillips Bradley) New York: Farrar and Rinehart, 1940.

[50] (Institute of Economics) Washington: The Brookings Institution, 1937.

[51] (Miscellaneous Publications No. 9) Stanford University: Food Research Institute, 1939.

[52] New York: Reynal & Hitchcock, 1934 and 1944.

[53] Ithaca: Cornell University, 1960.

[54] New York: Harper, 1944.

[55] (Publications in Culture and Society, Vol. 3) Berkeley: University of California, 1949.

[56] Chapel Hill: University of North Carolina, 1943.

[57] New York: Macmillan, 1945.

[58] Madison: University of Wisconsin, 1957.

covers the political relationship between the New Deal and organized labor, the effect of the Wagner Act, the split in the labor movement, and the enactment of protective labor legislation and social security. It also contains a bibliography of several hundred books and articles. There are good brief summaries of the New Deal period in Joseph G. Rayback, *A History of American Labor*[59] and Foster Rhea Dulles, *Labor in America*.[60] One of the most significant monographs is Irving Bernstein, *The New Deal Collective Bargaining Policy*[61] which established that President Roosevelt preferred a paternalistic middle course toward unions, and accepted the Wagner Bill with its strong collective bargaining guarantees only when driven to do so by political necessity. A specialized study on the work of the National Labor Relations Board is Harry A. Millis and Emily C. Brown, *From the Wagner Act to Taft-Hartley*.[62]

Historical studies are yet to appear on the federal relief programs and the establishment of Social Security.[63] However, a forthcoming monograph by C. F. Charles analyzes Harry Hopkins' administration of federal relief; there is a brief account in Robert Sherwood, *Roosevelt and Hopkins*;[64] and Hopkins describes his work in *Spending to Save*.[65] Two valuable monographs on the Works Progress Administration are Arthur W. MacMahon et al., *The Administration of Federal Work Relief*, and John K. Galbraith and G. G. Johnson, Jr.,

[59] New York: Macmillan, 1959.

[60] (Growth of America Series) New York: Crowell, 1949.

[61] (Institute of Industrial Relations) Berkeley: University of California, 1950.

[62] Chicago: University of Chicago, 1950. Among the readable popular books are Saul David Alinsky, *John L. Lewis, An Unauthorized Biography* (New York: Putnam, 1949); Herbert Harris, *Labor's Civil War* (New York: Knopf, 1940); Irving Howe and B. J. Widick, *The UAW and Walter Reuther* (New York: Random House, 1949); Benjamin S. Stolberg, *The Story of the CIO* (New York: Viking, 1938); and Samuel Yellen, *American Labor Struggles* (New York: Harcourt, Brace, 1936).

[63] On the impact of the depression in city and country, see David Shannon, *The Great Depression* (Englewood Cliffs: Prentice-Hall, 1960), a collection of documents; Ruth S. Cavan and Katherine H. Ranck, *The Family and the Depression, A Study of One Hundred Chicago Families* ([Social Science Studies, No. XXXV] Chicago: University of Chicago, 1938); Robert S. and Helen Merrell Lynd, *Middletown in Transition* (New York: Harcourt, Brace, 1937); Louise V. Armstrong, *We Too are the People* (Boston: Little, Brown, 1938); Thomas Jackson Woofter, Jr., and Ellen Winston, *Seven Lean Years* (Chapel Hill: University of North Carolina, 1939) on the rural South; Vance Johnson, *Heaven's Tableland: the Dust Bowl Story* (New York: Farrar, Straus, 1947) ; and Marie D. Lane and Francis Steegmuller, *America on Relief* (New York: Harcourt, Brace, 1938).

[64] New York: Harper, 1948.

[65] New York: Norton, 1936.

Economic Effects of Federal Public Works Expenditures, 1933-1938.[66] The background of Social Security is brilliantly described in Perkins, *The Roosevelt I Knew.* A contemporary analysis is Paul H. Douglas, *Social Security in the United States,*[67] and a later overview, Grace Abbott, *From Relief to Social Security.*[68]

Politics during the New Deal are surveyed in Harold F. Gosnell, *Champion Campaigner: Franklin D. Roosevelt.*[69] The election of 1932 is analyzed in Roy V. Peel and Thomas C. Donnelly, *The 1932 Campaign, an Analysis*[70] and Frank Freidel, *Franklin D. Roosevelt: The Triumph.* A brilliant and readable exposition of the functioning of the Democratic political machinery from the primary campaigns of 1932 through the election of 1936 is James A. Farley, *Behind the Ballots,* which is more useful than his later bitter *Jim Farley's Story.*[71] Charles Michelson, *The Ghost Talks* is the memoir of the Democratic press agent.[72] The positions on the New Deal of three of Roosevelt's presidential opponents can be found in Herbert Hoover, *The Challenge to Liberty,*[73] Alfred M. Landon, *America at the Crossroads,*[74] and the definitive D. B. Johnson, *The Republican Party and Wendell Willkie.*[75] Progressive, Socialistic, and "lunatic fringe" movements culminating in William Lemke's Union party candidacy in 1936 are the subject of Donald R. McCoy, *Angry Voices: Left-Of-Center Politics in the New Deal Era.*[76] The threat from the left was represented most colorfully by Huey Long, the subject of a forthcoming biography

---

[66] (Social Science Research Council, Studies in Administration, Vol. 12) Chicago: Public Administration Service, 1941; and Washington: National Resources Planning Board, Government Printing Office, 1940.

[67] New York: McGraw-Hill, 1936.

[68] Chicago: University of Chicago, 1941. A popular account of the Public Works Administration is Harold L. Ickes, *Back to Work: the Story of PWA* (New York: Macmillan, 1935). On the Civilian Conservation Corps, see Alfred C. Oliver, Jr., and Harold M. Dudley, *This New America* (New York: Longmans, Green, 1937). The National Youth Administration is sketched in Betty and Ernest K. Lindley, *A New Deal for Youth; the Story of the National Youth Administration* (New York: Viking, 1938).

[69] New York: Macmillan, 1952.

[70] New York: Farrar & Rinehart, 1935.

[71] New York: Harcourt, Brace, 1938; and New York: Whittlesey House, 1948.

[72] New York: Putnam, 1944.

[73] New York: Scribner, 1934.

[74] New York: Dodge, 1936.

[75] Urbana: University of Illinois, 1960. See also Mary E. Dillon, *Wendell Willkie, 1892-1944* (Philadelphia: Lippincott, 1952).

[76] Lawrence: University of Kansas, 1958.

by T. Harry Williams, and of several popular studies and novels.[77] The Townsend old-age movement is analyzed in Twentieth Century Fund, *The Townsend Crusade*[78] and a contemporary piece of reporting, Richard L. Neuberger and Kelley Loe, *An Army of the Aged.*[79] An indispensable interpretation of radicalism during the thirties is Murray Kempton, *Part of Our Time.*[80] A perceptive collection of vignettes of political leaders is Raymond Moley, *27 Masters of Politics.*[81] As yet there are only autobiographies or popular biographies of Congressional leaders, as, for example, a biography of the Vice President, Bascom N. Timmons, *Garner of Texas,*[82] and the autobiography of a leading Senator, James F. Byrnes, *All in One Lifetime.*[83] Edgar E. Robinson, *They Voted for Roosevelt* is a compendium and analysis of presidential election statistics from 1932 through 1944.[84]

The controversy over enlarging the Supreme Court has been explored in detail both in contemporary and later books. A distinguished piece of reporting is Joseph Alsop and Turner Catledge, *The 168 Days.*[85] A significant favorable study is Robert H. Jackson, *The Struggle for Judicial Supremacy;*[86] a disapproving account, Merlo J. Pusey, *The Supreme Court Crisis.*[87] There is a clear summary and evaluation in Dexter Perkins, *Charles Evans Hughes and American Democratic Statesmanship.*[88] A thorough analysis of the constitutional changes wrought by the Supreme Court beginning in 1937 is Charles H. Pritchett, *The Roosevelt Court, . . . 1937-1947.*[89] Thomas H. Greer, *What Roosevelt Thought* is a compendious topical analysis.[90] A clever exposition of some facets of New Deal thought is Thurman W.

---

[77] See Allan P. Sindler, *Huey Long's Louisiana: State Politics, 1920-1952* (Baltimore: Johns Hopkins, 1956) and Harnett T. Kane, *Louisiana Hayride: The American Rehearsal for Dictatorship, 1928-1940* (New York: Morrow, 1941).

[78] New York: Twentieth Century Fund, 1936.

[79] Caldwell, Idaho: Caxton, 1936.

[80] New York: Simon and Schuster, 1955.

[81] (A Newsweek Book) New York: Funk & Wagnalls, 1949.

[82] New York: Harper, 1948.

[83] New York: Harper, 1958.

[84] Stanford: Stanford University, 1947.

[85] Garden City: Doubleday, Doran, 1938.

[86] New York: Knopf, 1941.

[87] New York: Macmillan, 1937.

[88] (Library of American Biography) Boston: Little, Brown, 1956.

[89] New York: Macmillan, 1948.

[90] East Lansing: Michigan State University, 1958.

Arnold, *The Folklore of Capitalism*.[91] Arnold discusses the new anti-trust policies in *The Bottlenecks of Business*.[92]

CONCLUSION

From the beginning of the New Deal to the end, Roosevelt functioned with a fair degree of consistency.[93] He heartily favored humanitarian welfare legislation and government policing of the economy, so long as these did not dangerously unbalance the budget. He preferred government cooperation with business to warfare with it.

Many of the New Dealers went far beyond Roosevelt in their views, and sometimes saw in his reluctance to support them, betrayal rather than a greater degree of conservatism. They had valid grievances some of the time when Roosevelt stuck to a middle course and seemed to them to be compromising away everything for which they thought he stood, in order to hold his motley political coalitions together. It is a serious moral question whether he compromised more than necessary, and whether at times he compromised his principles. It has been charged that his second four years in the White House represented a failure in political leadership.

In terms of gaining immediate political objectives, like the fiasco of the Court fight, and the abortive "purge" in the 1938 primaries, this is undoubtedly true. In terms of the long-range New Deal program, the reverse is the case. These were years of piece-meal unspectacular consolidation of the earlier spectacular changes. It was many years before historians could say with certainty that these changes were permanent. By 1948 various public opinion samplings indicated that an overwhelming majority of those queried, even though Republican in voting habits, favored such things as social security and the TVA. The election of a Republican president in 1952 did not signify a popular repudiation of these programs. In the years after 1952 they were accepted, and in some instances even expanded, by the Republican administration. The only serious debate over them concerned degree, in which the Republicans were more cautious than the Democrats. The New Deal changes have even come for the most part to be accepted by the business community, although the United

---

[91] New Haven: Yale University, 1937.

[92] New York: Reynal & Hitchcock, 1940.

[93] The editors are grateful to the Service Center for the Teachers of History for permitting them to use the last two pages of Mr. Freidel's pamphlet, *The New Deal in Historical Perspective* (1959) as the concluding paragraphs for his chapter in the Yearbook.

States Chamber of Commerce now issues manifestoes against federal aid to education with all the fervor it once directed against Roosevelt's proposals. The fact is that the business community in part bases its plans for the future upon some things that began as New Deal reforms. It takes for granted such factors as the "built-in stabilizers" in the social security system—something, incidentally, that Roosevelt pointed out at the time the legislation went into effect.

In January 1939 Roosevelt, concerned about the threat of world war, called to a halt his domestic reform program. What he said then, concerning the world crisis of 1939, is remarkably applicable to the United States more than two decades later:

> We have now passed the period of internal conflict in the launching of our program of social reform. Our full energies may now be released to invigorate the processes of recovery in order to preserve our reforms, and to give every man and woman who wants to work a real job at a living wage.
>
> But time is of paramount importance. The deadline of danger from within and from without is not within our control. The hour-glass may be in the hands of other nations. Our own hour-glass tells us that we are off on a race to make democracy work, so that we may be efficient in peace and therefore secure in national defense.

CHAPTER XVI

The United States in World Affairs, 1929-1941

Wayne S. Cole

INTRODUCTION

AMERICA's role in world affairs from 1929 through 1941 was the product of both domestic and world influences. On the domestic side, the Great Depression and the efforts of Americans to cope with their economic difficulties exerted fundamental influences on United States foreign policies. On the world scene, peace and security were undermined by the depression and shattered by the aggression of militarist Japan, Mussolini's Fascist Italy, and Hitler's Nazi Germany. Under the impact of both internal and external forces, the American people and their leaders groped for policies that would satisfy their domestic needs and desires and at the same time protect national peace and securtiy. In a period that was characterized by unusual diversity of thought and freedom of expression, Americans and their leaders earnestly advanced and passionately debated varied theories on the proper role for the United States in world affairs. This labyrinth of forces and controversies culminated with United States involvement in World War II when the Japanese attacked Pearl Harbor on December 7, 1941.

The pre-war controversies over the wisdom or lack of wisdom of various alternatives for American foreign policy are continued today in the scholarly writing of historians. The so-called "revisionist" historians are the academic counterparts of the pre-war "noninterventionists." They believe that the United States need not and should not have entered World War II. They criticize the policies followed before Pearl Harbor and believe that alternative courses of action might have had better results for the United States and the world. The so-called "internationalist" historians are the academic successors to pre-war spokesmen for collective security and aid to Britain. They are critical of pre-war "isolationists" and, in general, view American

282

foreign policies under President Franklin D. Roosevelt with sympathy. The majority of professional historians with views on this subject tends to adhere to variations of the "internationalist" point of view. All of the general textbooks on American diplomatic history are useful for studying this period. Though the approaches in these volumes vary, none of them is written from a revisionist point of view.[1]

For purposes of convenience in examining the more specialized accounts of American foreign affairs, the period from 1929 through 1941 may be divided arbitrarily into three shorter chronological periods: The Hoover-Stimson era, 1929-1933; the New Deal era, 1933-1938; and the period immediately preceding American entry into World War II, 1939-1941. Of these three, the last period has been the subject of more research and publication on American foreign affairs than the other two combined. American diplomacy during the New Deal era has been more neglected, in terms of scholarly publication, than either of the other two periods.

THE HOOVER-STIMSON ERA, 1929-1933

The administration of Herbert Hoover was absorbed primarily with domestic considerations—particularly the problem of the Great Depression. It proved, however, to be an important period in foreign affairs as well. President Hoover and his Secretary of State, Henry L. Stimson, undertook the beginnings of a "good neighbor" policy toward Latin America. They grappled with the problem of armament limitations at the London Naval Conference of 1930 and the World Disarmament Conference beginning in 1932. They attempted to meet the challenge of the Great Depression on a world scale through a moratorium on intergovernmental debts and by sharing in planning the London Economic Conference that met shortly after Hoover left office. Most spectacular of all, Hoover and Stimson were confronted with Japanese aggression in Manchuria and Shanghai—the first major

---

[1] Thomas A. Bailey, *A Diplomatic History of the American People* (Sixth edition; New York: Appleton-Century-Crofts, 1958); Samuel Flagg Bemis, *A Diplomatic History of the United States* (Fourth edition; New York: Holt, 1955) ; Robert H. Ferrell, *American Diplomacy: A History* (New York: Norton, 1959); Julius W. Pratt, *A History of United States Foreign Policy* (New York: Prentice-Hall, 1955); and Richard W. Van Alstyne, *American Diplomacy in Action* (Revised edition; Stanford: Stanford University, 1947). See also, Foster Rhea Dulles, *America's Rise to World Power, 1898-1954* ([The New American Nation Series] New York: Harper, 1955). More sympathetic with the revisionist interpretation is the collection of documents and provocative essays compiled and edited by William Appleman Williams, *The Shaping of American Diplomacy: Readings and Documents in American Foreign Relations, 1750-1955* (Chicago: Rand McNally, 1956).

acts of military aggression in the train of events leading to World War II. Included among the histories of foreign affairs during the Hoover administration are memoirs and official accounts, a revisionist study, and internationalist volumes.

The Foreign Policies of Herbert Hoover, 1929-1933, by William Starr Myers[2] has the earmarks of "official history." Though Myers had access to Hoover's papers, he used them uncritically. He minimized the role of Stimson and could find no significant shortcomings in Hoover's conduct of American foreign affairs. Stimson's memoir, *On Active Service in Peace and War*, (written with McGeorge Bundy) [3] like all memoirs puts its author in a favorable light. But it deals frankly with many touchy issues—including the differences between Stimson and Hoover. Hoover's memoir also treats this subject candidly.[4] The differences in views between the President and his Secretary of State were most clearly highlighted in the Far Eastern crises. Both memoirs agree that it was Hoover who suggested using nonrecognition to indicate American moral disapproval of Japanese aggression in violation of treaties. Both Hoover and Stimson, however, emphasize that the President insisted on limiting American action to nonrecognition, while Stimson favored additional steps against Japan —including economic sanctions. Stimson considered nonrecognition "insufficient" by itself; while Hoover "held that 'economic sanctions' meant war when applied to any large nation." Since Hoover's views prevailed at the time, it is understandable that Stimson in his memoir complained of "the timidity of statesmanship" during the Hoover administration, while Hoover found little to criticize.[5]

A revisionist interpretation of American foreign affairs during this period is advanced by Richard N. Current in *Secretary Stimson: A Study in Statecraft*. This is an analysis of Henry L. Stimson's views and role in American foreign affairs—including his performance as Secretary of War under Taft and Franklin D. Roosevelt, and as

[2] William Starr Myers, *The Foreign Policies of Herbert Hoover, 1929-1933* (New York: Scribner, 1940).

[3] Henry L. Stimson and McGeorge Bundy, *On Active Service in Peace and War* (New York: Harper, 1948). Since this chapter has been written, an outstanding biography of Henry L. Stimson has appeared, Elting Morison, *Turmoil and Tradition; a Study of the Life and Times of Henry L. Stimson* (Boston: Houghton Mifflin, 1960).

[4] Herbert C. Hoover, *Memoirs: The Cabinet and the Presidency, 1920-1933* (New York: Macmillan, 1952).

[5] Stimson and Bundy, *On Active Service*, p. 196-200, 243-45, 258-63, 280-81; and *The Cabinet and the Presidency*, p. 366-79.

Secretary of State under Hoover. Current was critical of Stimson and his "peace through force" approach. In dealing with American foreign policies during the Manchurian crisis, Current found sufficient difference between the views of the President and his Secretary of State to distinguish between the "Hoover Doctrine" and the "Stimson Doctrine." Current, whose sympathies clearly lay with the Hoover approach, wrote: "Nonrecognition itself could be called the Hoover-Stimson Doctrine, since Hoover had suggested and Stimson had formulated it. It could be considered as a final and sufficient measure, a substitute for economic pressure or military force, a policy looking toward conciliation and peace and relying on the moral power of public opinion for its effect. That was the Hoover Doctrine. Or nonrecognition could be viewed not as an alternative but as a preliminary to economic and military sanctions, a way of drawing sharp the issue between the United States (along with the League of Nations) and Japan, a means of laying down the ideological basis for eventual war. That was the Stimson Doctrine."[6] And according to Current, Stimson had no difficulty winning Franklin D. Roosevelt to his view in 1933.

In addition, there are volumes on foreign affairs during the Hoover administration written from an "internationalist" frame of reference. In his well-researched monograph, *Herbert Hoover's Latin-American Policy*, Alexander DeConde demonstrated that Hoover's "good-neighbor policy did much to bring the Americas closer together; it contributed to the elimination of some of the 'sore spots' in inter-American relations; it helped to overcome some of the fears and hates aroused by the policies of previous administrations; and it laid the foundation for a Latin-American policy that paid rich dividends in the crisis of World War II."[7] The most complete general study of American diplomacy during the Hoover administration is *American Diplomacy in the Great Depression*, by Robert H. Ferrell. This volume is based on extensive research and deals with all major American diplomatic events of the period. Except for America's Latin American policies, Ferrell considered most American diplomacy under Hoover and Stimson ineffective and unsuccessful. He stressed four broad explanations for the deficiences. First, Ferrell blamed the Great Depression that "palsied the hands of American statesmen." Second, he considered

---

[6] Richard N. Current, *Secretary Stimson: A Study in Statecraft* (New Brunswick: Rutgers University, 1954), p. 113.

[7] Alexander DeConde, *Herbert Hoover's Latin-American Policy* ([Books in World Politics] Stanford: Stanford University, 1951), p. 127.

the diplomatic assumptions and policies of American leaders "inadequate" in those years. Third, Ferrell found part of the explanation for the failure of American diplomacy in the qualities of American leaders. Ferrell was particularly critical of Stimson's legalistic and moralistic approach to world affairs. He described the differences between Hoover and his Secretary of State, but he found Stimson to have been less consistent and less vigorous in support of the use of sanctions against aggressors than Current did. Ferrell believed that Hoover and Stimson "agreed far more than they disagreed, and it was only in the latter 1930's that they began to differ radically over issues of foreign policy." Ferrell also minimized Stimson's influence on Roosevelt in 1933. And finally, Ferrell concluded that American diplomacy during the Hoover administration was ineffective partly because the magnitude of world events and problems was too great to be controlled effectively by the statesmen.[8]

THE NEW DEAL ERA, 1933-1938

From 1933 to 1938 the American people and the Franklin D. Roosevelt administration were absorbed primarily with the task of coping with the Great Depression. Most Americans and Congressmen were determined that the United States should never again become involved in "Europe's wars." This determination found expression in the enactment of a series of self-denying Neutrality Acts.

Just as Americans in the New Deal era were preoccupied with domestic matters, so, too, historians studying those years have dealt largely with domestic developments. The political studies and the histories of the New Deal that were analyzed in the preceding chapter contain much data relating directly or indirectly to foreign relations. But there is a striking dearth of specialized studies of the history of American foreign affairs in the New Deal era.

Edward O. Guerrant provided a useful survey of United States-Latin American policies in his book, *Roosevelt's Good Neighbor Policy*. Guerrant described the steps taken by the Roosevelt administration to win the friendship of the Latin American states and to secure their cooperation in protecting the security of the Western

[8] Robert H. Ferrell, *American Diplomacy in the Great Depression: Hoover-Stimson Foreign Policy, 1929-1933* ([Yale Historical Publications, No. 17] New Haven: Yale University, 1957), p. 169n, 278-82. This book includes an exceptionally valuable bibliographical chapter on the literature and sources for foreign affairs in the Hoover administration.

Hemisphere against the Axis threat. He concluded that the "United States has never had a foreign policy toward any area that was more successful than the Good Neighbor Policy was from 1933 to 1945."[9]

Two useful accounts focused directly on American foreign affairs in the New Deal period that represent the two major schools of interpretation are Cordell Hull's *Memoirs* and *American Foreign Policy in the Making, 1932-1940*, by Charles A. Beard. These two works advance conflicting interpretations of American foreign policy during the New Deal.

Cordell Hull served as Secretary of State from the beginning of the Roosevelt administration in 1933 until 1944—longer than any other man in American history. His two-volume memoir is a detailed and valuable account of most major American diplomatic developments during the Roosevelt administration. In dealing with the New Deal years and the rise of the Axis challenge, Hull advanced the thesis that he and the President tried to preserve peace and security through internationalism, but that they were forced to move more slowly than they wished because of the isolationist temper of the American people and Congress. Hull emphasized that "Congress was slower on many occasions than the Executive in seeing the dangers looming to world peace and in taking appropriate steps to meet them."[10]

Critical of Roosevelt's foreign policies, Charles A. Beard was a pre-war "continentalist" and a prominent post-war "revisionist" historian. In *American Foreign Policy in the Making, 1932-1940*, Beard contended that, contrary to Hull's thesis, the Roosevelt administration's public foreign policy statements from 1932 to 1940 were not, for the most part, appeals for internationalism and collective security. Instead, Beard found that, except for the Quarantine Speech in 1937, the administration in public repeatedly spoke out in "isolationist" or non-interventionist terms.[11]

---

[9] Edward O. Guerrant, *Roosevelt's Good Neighbor Policy* ([School of Inter-American Affairs, Study No. 5] Albuquerque: University of New Mexico, 1950), p. 212.

[10] *The Memoirs of Cordell Hull* (2 vols.; New York: Macmillan, 1948), Vol. I, p. 176-77, 211, 389-94. For additional interpretations on economic aspects of American foreign affairs in these years, see: Herbert Feis, *Seen from E. A.: Three International Episodes* (New York: Knopf, 1947); and Roland N. Stromberg, "American Business and the Approach of War, 1935-1941," *Journal of Economic History*, 13:58-78; Winter 1953.

[11] Charles A. Beard, *American Foreign Policy in the Making, 1932-1940* (New Haven: Yale University, 1946).

AMERICAN ENTRY INTO WORLD WAR II, 1939-1941

Internationalists

Both "internationalists" and "revisionists" are well represented among the many books and articles on American foreign affairs in the months and years immediately preceding the Japanese attack on Pearl Harbor. Among the early internationalist accounts are *This Is Pearl,* by Walter Millis,[12] and *Roosevelt from Munich to Pearl Harbor,* by Basil Rauch.[13] Robert E. Sherwood used the files of Harry Hopkins as the basis for his Pulitzer-prize-winning *Roosevelt and Hopkins,* published in 1948.[14] Herbert Feis's study of American relations with Japan, entitled *The Road to Pearl Harbor,* was based on more extensive research than earlier volumes on that subject.[15] The culmination of the internationalist interpretation came with the publication in 1952 and 1953 of the two-volume work by William L. Langer and S. Everett Gleason under the general title of *The World Crisis and American Foreign Policy.*[16] These volumes were based on unusually extensive research. The last book in the 1950's written from this same general point of view, and probably the most balanced in its judgments, is *The Passing of American Neutrality, 1937-1941,* by Donald F. Drummond, published in 1955.[17] Though there are variations among these internationalist analyses, it is possible to suggest the main outlines of their interpretation.

Internationalist writers, looking back to the days before Pearl Harbor, viewed the Axis powers as extremely serious threats to American security and interests. They pointed to the strength and speed of the Axis forces which by the middle of 1940 had rolled over

---

[12] Walter Millis, *This Is Pearl! The United States and Japan—1941* (New York: Morrow, 1947). The remainder of this chapter is a slightly condensed version of p. 603-10 of this writer's more detailed article on this subject: Wayne S. Cole, "American Entry into World War II: A Historiographical Appraisal," *Mississippi Valley Historical Review,* 43:595-617; March 1957.

[13] Basil Rauch, *Roosevelt: From Munich to Pearl Harbor* (New York: Creative Age, 1950).

[14] Robert E. Sherwood, *Roosevelt and Hopkins: An Intimate History* (New York: Harper, 1948).

[15] Herbert Feis, *The Road to Pearl Harbor: The Coming of the War Between the United States and Japan* (Princeton: Princeton University, 1950).

[16] William L. Langer and S. Everett Gleason, *The Challenge to Isolation, 1937-1940* (New York: Published for the Council on Foreign Relations by Harper, 1952) ; and William L. Langer and S. Everett Gleason, *The Undeclared War, 1940-1941* (New York: Published for the Council on Foreign Relations by Harper, 1953).

[17] Donald F. Drummond, *The Passing of American Neutrality, 1937-1941* ([Publications in History and Political Science, Vol. 20] Ann Arbor: University of Michigan, 1955).

Austria, Czechoslovakia, Poland, Denmark, Norway, the Netherlands, Luxemburg, Belgium, and France. Britain alone was successfully resisting Nazi assaults on her home islands. Most authorities at the time expected the Soviet Union to fall quickly after Hitler's *Blitzkrieg* was turned against Russia on June 22, 1941. Axis successes in North Africa raised fears that control of that continent might prove a steppingstone to the Western Hemisphere. In the meantime, Japan took advantage of the European crises to step up her aggressive campaigns in Asia. According to the internationalist interpretation, the President hoped to prevent the United States from becoming involved in the hostilities—provided that could be accomplished without sacrificing American security, vital interests, and principles.

In general, internationalist writers followed the administration view that the defeat of Nazi Germany and Fascist Italy was essential to American peace and security. Like the Roosevelt administration, most of these writers tended to rule out a negotiated peace as a possible acceptable alternative in Europe—particularly after the fall of France. President Roosevelt hoped that his policy of extending aid short of war to the victims of Axis aggression in Europe would prevent the defeat of Great Britain, contribute to the essential defeat of the Axis powers, and thereby enable the United States to maintain both its peace and its security. Among the many steps taken by the Roosevelt administration to aid the victims of aggression in Europe were repeal of the arms embargo, the destroyer deal, Lend-Lease, the Atlantic patrol system, the shoot-on-sight policy, arming of American merchant ships, and permitting the use of those ships to transport goods directly to England.

According to the internationalist interpretation, Roosevelt and Hull wanted to prevent war between the United States and Japan—in part because such a war would interfere with the main task of defeating Hitler. They believed that the best way to preserve American peace and security in the Pacific was to take steps short of war to check Japanese aggression. Among American actions of this sort were the "moral embargo," the termination of the commercial treaty with Japan, various forms of aid to Chiang Kai-shek, keeping the American fleet at Pearl Harbor, and freezing Japanese assets in the United States. The United States was eager to seek a peaceful settlement with Japan —provided such a settlement would not jeopardize American security and principles, and provided it would not require the United States to abandon China, Britain, France, and the Netherlands in the Pacific.

As it became increasingly apparent that compromise was impossible on terms acceptable to both countries, the Roosevelt administration tried to delay war to gain time for military preparations.

With regard to the European theater as well as the Pacific, there were distinct variations in the views of administration leaders before Pearl Harbor about implementing American policies and presenting them to the American people. Cordell Hull generally favored limiting action to steps short of war and he explained each step in terms of peace, security, and international morality. Henry L. Stimson, Frank Knox, and others were critical of this indirect and step-at-a-time approach. They early came to believe that aid short of war would not be sufficient to insure the defeat of the Axis and they urged the President to take more vigorous action against the aggressors. Stimson believed that the American people would support the President in a declaration of war even before Pearl Harbor. Though of a different temperament, President Roosevelt, like Hull, was fearful of arousing effective public opposition to his policies and adhered to the step-at-a-time, short-of-war approach.[18]

Internationalist interpretations tend to reflect these variations in attitudes among pre-war interventionists. Feis treated Hull with considerable respect. Rauch's interpretation is similar to that advanced by Hull, though the hero in Rauch's book is definitely President Roosevelt. Millis and Sherwood generally believed that in view of conditions then existing, President Roosevelt's decisions and methods on foreign policy matters were wise and sound at most crucial points before Pearl Harbor. Langer and Gleason were sympathetic with the more direct and vigorous approach urged by Stimson—particularly as applied to the European theater. They believed that Roosevelt over-estimated the strength of the opposition to his policies.[19]

---

[18] For example, see Stimson and Bundy, On Active Service, p. 365-76; Sherwood, Roosevelt and Hopkins, p. 132-35; Langer and Gleason, Challenge to Isolation, p. 5-9; and Langer and Gleason, Undeclared War, p. 457-58. For an interesting analysis of the influence of public opinion on American foreign policy, see: Thomas A. Bailey, The Man in the Street: The Impact of American Public Opinion on Foreign Policy (New York: Macmillan, 1948). See also: Walter Johnson, The Battle Against Isolation (Chicago: University of Chicago, 1944), a study of the interventionist Committee to Defend America by Aiding the Allies; and Wayne S. Cole, America First: The Battle Against Intervention, 1940-1941 (Madison: University of Wisconsin, 1953), a study of the non-interventionist America First Committee.

[19] Millis, This Is Pearl, p. x-xi; Rauch, Roosevelt from Munich to Pearl Harbor, p. 3-6, 22-23, 495-96; Sherwood, Roosevelt and Hopkins, p. 133, 151; Langer and Gleason, Challenge to Isolation, p. 5-6; and Langer and Gleason, Undeclared War, p. 195-97, 441-44.

Writers of the internationalist school found the fundamental causes for American involvement in the war in developments in other parts of the world—beyond the American power to control by 1941. They did not find the explanation within the United States—except in so far as non-interventionist opposition inhibited administration actions that might have prevented the war from beginning or from reaching such a critical stage. Nearly all internationalist historians were highly critical of the opponents of Roosevelt's foreign policies. They all denied that President Roosevelt wanted to get the United States into war. They were convinced that the Japanese attack on Pearl Harbor was a genuine surprise to the members of the Roosevelt administration. In so far as there was any American responsibility for the disaster at Pearl Harbor most internationalist writers blamed the military commanders in Hawaii—Admiral Husband E. Kimmel and General Walter C. Short. None of them believed that there were any alternatives available to President Roosevelt by 1940-1941 that could have prevented American involvement in World War II without sacrificing American security and principles.[20]

Revisionists

Among the early revisionist volumes are *Pearl Harbor*, by George Morgenstern,[21] *President Roosevelt and the Coming of the War, 1941,* by Charles A. Beard,[22] and *America's Second Crusade*, by William Henry Chamberlin.[23] Charles Callan Tansill, after extensive research, published his *Back Door to War* in 1952.[24] Harry Elmer Barnes edited a volume called *Perpetual War for Perpetual Peace* that included essays written by most major revisionists.[25]

---

[20] For example, see Millis, *This Is Pearl*, p. x-xi; Langer and Gleason, *Undeclared War*, p. 936-37; and Rauch, *Roosevelt from Munich to Pearl Harbor*, p. 467-93. For a convenient, brief collection of key documents relating to the attack on Pearl Harbor, see: Hans Louis Trefousse, ed., *What Happened at Pearl Harbor? Documents Pertaining to the Japanese Attack of December 7, 1941, and Its Background* (New York: Twayne, 1958).

[21] George Morgenstern, *Pearl Harbor: The Story of the Secret War* (New York: Devin-Adair, 1947).

[22] Charles A. Beard, *President Roosevelt and the Coming of the War, 1941* (New Haven: Yale University, 1948).

[23] William Henry Chamberlin, *America's Second Crusade* (Chicago: Regnery, 1950).

[24] Charles Callan Tansill, *Back Door to War: The Roosevelt Foreign Policy, 1933-1941* (Chicago: Regnery, 1952).

[25] Harry Elmer Barnes, ed., *Perpetual War for Perpetual Peace: A Critical Examination of the Foreign Policy of Franklin Delano Roosevelt and its Aftermath* (Caldwell, Idaho: Caxton, 1953).

In striking contrast to the internationalist interpretation, the revisionists minimized or rejected the idea that the Axis powers constituted a threat to American security. They pointed out that Hitler had no concrete plans for attacking the Western Hemisphere. They portrayed the Japanese attack on Pearl Harbor as an action provoked by American restrictions that threatened Japanese security and vital interests. In so far as revisionists conceded the reality of an Axis threat to the United States, they believed it was caused largely by American shortsighted and provocative policies. Like non-interventionists before Pearl Harbor, the revisionists maintained that the issue was not primarily security but instead was war or peace. And revisionists held that the United States Government had the power to choose for itself whether it would or would not enter the war. Thus, in contrast to internationalists, the revisionists found the explanation for American entry into World War II primarily within the United States rather than in the actions of nations in other parts of the world. In seeking the explanation within the United States, they focused their attention almost exclusively upon administration and military leaders —and particularly upon President Roosevelt.

Revisionists interpreted Roosevelt's steps to aid Britain short of war as actually steps *to* war. Opinions of revisionists varied on the question of whether Roosevelt deliberately meant these as steps to war. In any event, they contended, these actions did not provoke Hitler into war against the United States; and the shooting incidents that occurred in the Atlantic did not arouse American enthusiasm for entering the European war.

Instead, according to most revisionist writers, the Roosevelt administration got the United States into war through the Asiatic "back door" by provoking Japanese attack on Pearl Harbor.[26] This maneuver was accomplished by increasing pressures on Japan while refusing any compromise that the Japanese could accept. The decisive economic pressure in 1941 was exerted through the curtailment of oil shipments, and the key issue on which compromise proved impossible was China. The freezing of Japanese assets in the United States on July 26, 1941, accompanied by parallel action by the British and Dutch, cut Japan off from her essential oil supplies. The President rejected Premier Konoye's proposal for a personal meeting between the

---

[26] Morgenstern, *Pearl Harbor*, p. 283-84; Beard, *President Roosevelt and the Coming of the War*, p. 564-66; Tansill, *Back Door to War*, p. 615-16; and Barnes, ed., *Perpetual War for Perpetual Peace*, p. 220-21.

two leaders. Then, Secretary of State Hull, after objections from China
and Britain, abandoned the idea of proposing a *modus vivendi*. Instead, on November 26, Hull submitted a ten-point program to Japan
—including the demand that the Japanese withdraw from China and
Indo-China. This proposal (which revisionists generally call an
"ultimatum") was so extreme that Hull knew in advance that Japan
would not accept it. According to most revisionists these and other
actions by the Roosevelt administration (out of either design or
blunder) provoked war with Japan. The United States confronted
Japan with the alternatives of backing down or fighting. With oil
reserves falling dangerously low, and believing that their vital interests
and security were at stake, the Japanese chose to fight.[27]

Through all of this, according to the revisionists, President Roosevelt deceived the American people concerning his policies and objectives in foreign affairs. Revisionists maintained that Roosevelt
publicly committed his administration to a policy of peace while
secretly leading the nation to war—a war that these writers considered
contrary to national interests and contrary to the desires of 80 per
cent of the American people. The most famous expression of this
thesis is in Beard's last book and particularly in his final chapter.[28]

Most revisionists insisted that administration and military leaders
in Washington gave inadequate, ambiguous, and belated warnings to
the commanders in Hawaii and withheld essential information from
them. According to their contention, officials in Washington had
sufficient information—including that obtained by breaking the Japanese secret diplomatic code—to anticipate an early Japanese attack.
After Pearl Harbor, they say, the administration attempted unjustly
to make General Short and Admiral Kimmel, the commanders in
Hawaii, scapegoats for the tragedy. Instead of blaming the commanders
in Hawaii, the revisionists placed the main responsibility upon civilian
and military leaders in Washington—including Stimson, Knox, and
particularly President Roosevelt. On this, as on other phases of the
subject, some revisionists, including Beard and Current, wrote in
more restrained and qualified terms than either Tansill or Barnes.

Finally, the revisionists insisted that the Roosevelt foreign policies
failed to serve American national interests. If, as Roosevelt and Hull
contended, American aid to the victims of aggression was designed to

[27] For example, see Barnes, ed., *Perpetual War for Perpetual Peace*, p. 299-307,
327-86.
[28] Beard, *President Roosevelt and the Coming of the War*, p. 573-91.

keep America out of war, these policies obviously failed. If the Roosevelt policies were designed to protect American security, they were, according to revisionists, of questionable success. By helping to crush Germany and Japan the United States removed two major barriers to Soviet expansion and created power vacuums and chaos that contributed to the rise of the Soviet Union to world power and to the resultant explosive cold war situation. China, which was considered too vital to compromise in 1941, fell into Communist hands— in part, some revisionists said, because of Roosevelt's policies before and during World War II. Revisionists maintained in general that American involvement left the United States less secure, more burdened by debts and taxes, more laden with the necessity of maintaining huge armed forces than ever before in American history.[29]

An excellent recent revisionist study is Paul W. Schroeder's *The Axis Alliance and Japanese-American Relations, 1941*. Schroeder's interpretation differs at many points from that of most revisionists. For example, he rejected the Tansill-Barnes idea that Roosevelt deliberately provoked war with Japan, and he probably would reject the non-interventionist approach toward the European war. Schroeder wrote from the "realist" point of view expressed earlier by Hans Morgenthau and George Kennan. Schroeder contended that United States policies toward Japan underwent an important shift in July, 1941. He wrote:

Until July . . . the United States consistently sought to attain two limited objectives in the Far East, those of splitting the Axis and of stopping Japan's advance southward. Both aims were in accordance with America's broad strategic interests; both were reasonable, attainable goals. Through a combination of favorable circumstances and forceful American action, the United States reached the position where the achievement of these two goals was within sight. At this very moment, on the verge of a major diplomatic victory, the United States abandoned her original goals and concentrated on a third, the liberation of China. This last aim was not in accord with American strategic interests, was not a limited objective, and, most important, was completely incapable of being achieved by peaceful means and doubtful of attainment even by war. Through her single-minded pursuit of this unattainable goal, the United States forfeited the diplomatic victory which she had already virtually won.

Schroeder believed that "American policy from the end of July to December was a grave mistake." He did not, however, place the blame primarily on President Roosevelt. Instead, Schroeder was particularly

---

[29] Barnes, ed., *Perpetual War for Perpetual Peace*, p. viii-ix, 69, 502-42.

critical of Secretary Hull and also suggested that the responsibility for our policies was "shared by the whole nation, with causes that were deeply organic. Behind it was not sinister design or warlike intent, but a sincere and uncompromising adherence to moral principles and liberal doctrines." Schroeder believed that in 1941 there "existed the possibility of a *modus vivendi*, an agreement settling some issues and leaving others in abeyance." He concluded that such "an agreement, limited and temporary in nature, would have involved no sacrifice of principle for either nation, yet would have removed the immediate danger of war.[30]

The continuing interpretative controversies among scholars suggest that historical knowledge and understanding of the background of American entry into World War II are still (as they always will be) incomplete and imperfect. Historians, however, are continuing their research in the endless quest for truth. And their accomplishments thus far are sufficient to give meaning and significance to this exciting and important phase of American history.

---

[30] Paul W. Schroeder, *The Axis Alliance and Japanese-American Relations, 1941* (Ithaca, New York: Published for the American Historical Association by Cornell University, 1958), p. 202-16.

CHAPTER XVII

World War II and Its Aftermath[1]

Hugh G. Cleland

INTRODUCTION

THE problems of writing about very recent history are so obvious as to require little elaboration. It is too soon to know whether policies which are still being pursued will succeed or fail. To pick an example at random, it may be that if the cold war is eventually thawed, Yalta agreements, much despised by some, will one day be generally considered the beginning of wisdom!

Another major problem of recent history is one of dimension. It is now impossible to study the United States without taking into account developments not simply in Europe, but in Iraq, Laos, or other parts of the world. At home, there are more states in the union and more people in the nation; abroad, new nations are born almost every year. Communication technology has shrunk the world, but it has multiplied the raw materials of the historian. In addition to more books, there are now the radio, television, and the tape recorder. At the same time, much source material for recent history is still classified, and often there is no source material at all when modern statesmen, instead of writing letters, make long distance calls, for which no record may be available for the historian.

The actual conduct of the war has produced and will continue to produce a mountain of historical literature almost as staggering as the mountain of material consumed in the conflict. There are multivolume official or semi-official histories being published by the armed forces,[2] but many of these are so voluminous and detailed that the

---

[1] I am greatly indebted to Professor Leland D. Baldwin, once my teacher and now my colleague, for many of the insights and syntheses in this chapter. Errors and shortcomings, however, and interpretations are the responsibility of the author alone.

[2] U. S. Dept. of the Army, Office of Military History, *United States Army in World War II* (99 vols. planned. Washington, D. C.: U.S.G.P.O., 1947–): Samuel Eliot Morison, *History of United States Naval Operations in World War II* (14 vols. planned. Boston: Little, Brown, 1947–); Wesley Frank Craven and James L. Cate, *The Army Air Forces in World War II* (7 vols.; Chicago: University of Chicago, 1948-1958).

secondary teacher (or the average college teacher) will find them more useful for reference purposes than for general reading.[3] Furthermore, competent academicians faced serious problems in writing official histories. They developed a high degree of skepticism about the accuracy of official communiqués. Some commanders were so conscious that the eye of posterity was on them that they rigorously censored historical accounts or confined them to the tactical picture; some bluntly stated that the process of the formation of strategy and the flaws in the execution of important movements were no business of the historians— or they confined this knowledge to a writer who could be trusted to write only what the general wished. Probably the best illustrations of this on the American side were the inaccuracy of the communiqués in the Southwest Pacific theater and the way in which the theater commander, General Douglas MacArthur, reserved key documents for the use of his own chief of intelligence, General Charles A. Willoughby.[4]

Turning from official accounts to memoirs (and almost every surviving commander on both sides has published a set), the historian meets even more frustration. Anyone who seeks to learn about what went on while strategy was being hewn out and policies were being formed must glean his material from a hundred sources. American commanders were frequently famed for their blunt speaking, but their memoirs as finally edited and published are for the most part models of discretion. Even Patton and Bradley[5] became almost reticent as far as important disclosures were concerned.

Eisenhower in his book, *Crusade in Europe*,[6] is bland. In vain does one look for any clue that he realized that his commanders were deliberately disobeying his orders when they pushed on toward the Rhine instead of waiting for Montgomery to cross first.[7] Bitter wrangles with Montgomery are glossed over, presumably for the sake of Anglo-

---

[3] Among the serviceable short accounts are Fletcher Pratt, *War for the World* (New Haven: Yale University, 1950); Thomas Dodson Stamps and Vincent Esposito, eds., *A Military History of World War II* (2 vols. and atlas. West Point: United States Military Academy, 1953); J. F. C. Fuller, *The Second World War* (New York: Duell, Sloan and Pearce, 1949); and B. H. Liddell Hart, *Strategy: The Indirect Approach* (New York: Praeger, 1954).

[4] Charles A. Willoughby and John Chamberlain, *MacArthur, 1941-1951: Victory in the Pacific* (New York: McGraw-Hill, 1954).

[5] George S. Patton, *War as I Knew It* (Boston: Houghton Mifflin, 1947); Omar N. Bradley, *A Soldier's Story* (New York: Holt, 1951).

[6] Dwight D. Eisenhower, *Crusade in Europe* (Garden City, New York: Doubleday, 1948).

[7] Ralph Ingersoll, *Top Secret* (New York: Harcourt, Brace, 1946), p. 299-300.

American comity.[8] There has developed (at least in some quarters) a belief that the big problems were easily worked out by compatible allies and that victory came smoothly and according to plan, and it may be that General George Marshall, when he refused to write his memoirs, was concerned with helping to bury the memory of allied rivalries and mistakes.[9]

THE WAR IN THE WEST

One wartime decision is now clear and has been proved wise. This was the Anglo-American strategy of concentrating on the defeat of Hitler first, even if this meant "short rations" for a period in the Pacific.[10] Hitler had conquered a contiguous area which was highly developed industrially. Given time to consolidate and rationalize the vast workshop that is Europe, he might well have been impregnable. Then, too, unless the Soviet ally was aided, Russia might have been defeated or even might have switched to the German side. Japan, on the other hand, had seized industrially undeveloped areas scattered over thousands of miles of ocean. It would take her much longer to create an integrated wartime economy of her far-flung spoils. And in the Asian theater the only ally of consequence was China, which was much less effective than was Russia in the European theater and therefore was given less consideration.

Likewise, the need for the North African campaign was more or less obvious. A direct assault on Western Europe in 1942 was out of the question because American production of trained troops, supplies, and shipping was still too low. An attack on the outer edge of Axis power in North Africa, however, was possible and would remove the threat to Suez and again open the Mediterranean to allied shipping.[11]

After the successful seizure of North Africa, however, controversy arose as to the next step, and that still rings. Basically, the controversy was between Britain and America. Britain felt that her "experience" was as valuable a contribution to the partnership as America's eco-

---

[8] For interallied friction, see Omar Bradley's *A Soldier's Story*, p. 517-18 and Alan Moorehead, *Montgomery: A Biography* (New York: Coward-McCann, 1946), p. 206-207.

[9] William Frye, *Marshall: Citizen Soldier* (Indianapolis: Bobbs-Merrill, 1947) is good on Marshall as an administrator but skips lightly over Pearl Harbor.

[10] *The War Reports of . . . Marshall . . ., Arnold . . ., and . . . King*, foreword by Walter Millis (Philadelphia: Lippincott, 1947); Louis Morton, "Germany First: The Basic Concept of Allied Strategy in World War II," in Kent Roberts Greenfield, ed., *Command Decisions* (New York: Harcourt, Brace, 1959), p. 3-38.

[11] Leo J. Meyer, "The Decision to Invade North Africa," *Command Decisions*, p. 120-53.

nomic and military power. She therefore sought to reserve for herself the guiding voice in political and politico-military affairs. In this effort Churchill maintained the strictest discipline among his subordinates, insisting that they preserve a common front in presenting the case against the Americans.

The American leaders were irked by these British attitudes. Roosevelt was aware that the British government regarded the Anglo-American partnership as a way of saving the British Empire and knew that Churchill had no vision of any future which would be different in kind from the imperialist past. Further, Churchill was anxious to avoid the enormous British loss of life which had taken place in World War I. Americans suspected that he therefore postponed as long as he could a direct cross-channel invasion.[12] It is impossible not to sympathize with the British position. They had been bled by World War I; so now they undoubtedly preferred to sacrifice as little as possible and to do what they could toward political and economic restoration after the war. Americans, on the other hand, prided themselves upon their single-minded pursuit of victory, upon their determination to win the war with the least expenditure of blood and time. They were anxious to "get on with it" without giving much thought to the shape of the post-war world or the relationship between military action and post-war diplomacy.[13]

With victory in North Africa clearly in sight, Roosevelt and Churchill met at Casablanca in January of 1943 and agreed that the next objective should be Sicily. The conquest of that island would further contribute to clearing the Mediterranean for Allied shipping. The successful invasion of Sicily in July led to Mussolini's being ousted as premier and, shortly afterwards, an offer on the part of Italy to surrender.[14] This opportunity enticed the allies to attack Italy itself, at first with the limited aim of capturing the southern part of the peninsula so as to use the excellent airfields at Foggia as bomber bases. Early in September of 1943 the invasion of southern Italy began. The value to the Allies of the long, slow, and costly Italian campaign remains one of the question marks of the war.[15]

---

[12] Rexford G. Tugwell, *The Democratic Roosevelt* (Garden City, New York: Doubleday, 1957), p. 591-92, 607-608.

[13] Robert E. Sherwood, *Roosevelt and Hopkins: An Intimate History* (New York: Harper, 1948), p. 536-38; Hanson W. Baldwin, *Great Mistakes of the War* (New York: Harper, 1950), p. 1-3.

[14] Eisenhower, *Crusade in Europe,* chapters nine and ten.

[15] Mark W. Clark, *Calculated Risk* (New York: Harper, 1950) .

Anglo-American bickering continued when the assault was finally made on western Europe in June, 1944. The British regarded Eisenhower's appointment to the supreme command as a sop to American self-esteem and tried to rig the situation so as to confine him largely to the management of supplies. There was a tendency among some of the initiated to regard him as a "military politician" rather than as a man of character, impartiality, and military ability.[16] Eisenhower allowed Montgomery to continue arguing about strategy long after he had closed Bradley's and Devers' mouths, and Americans, perhaps wrongly, saw this as insubordination on Montgomery's part.[17] Any move that Eisenhower or any of his commanders made was subject to an interpretation which would ruffle the self-love of one nation or another. Some Americans thought he deferred too much to Montgomery.[18] Britishers thought that he did not listen enough to Montgomery;[19] and De Gaulle,[20] touchy about French honor, found fault with almost all he did. If he tried to placate all sides, he was accused of violating sound military principles by his compromises. If he tried to look at things from a military view, he was assailed for ignoring political factors. Without denying a modicum of truth in both charges, it is only fair to point out that any Supreme Commander who did not act as Eisenhower did might have seen his authority dissolve under him with a consequent danger to the war effort.[21]

Regardless of Eisenhower's military competence, it seems probable that he shared with other American commanders a certain haste to win the war, and that this haste was encouraged by the sanguine attitude of the Roosevelt circle toward Russia. Americans tended to regard speed as military realism. Britishers tried to point out that such a policy would only pose fresh problems after the war; that true realism would recognize that war is an extension of politics and must be waged with an eye to post-war political aims.[22]

Another difficult question of interpretation is that of the effectiveness of the bomber war against Germany. Air power enthusiasts argued that "victory through air power" almost unaided was possible.

[16] Alan Moorehead, Montgomery, p. 205.
[17] Omar Bradley, A Soldier's Story, p. 418, 422.
[18] Ralph Ingersoll, Top Secret, p. 264-65.
[19] Chester Wilmot, The Struggle for Europe (New York: Harper, 1952), p. 489.
[20] Charles De Gaulle, War Memoirs, trans. Jonathan Griffin (2 vols.; New York: Viking, 1955-1959).
[21] Walter Bedell Smith, Eisenhower's Six Great Decisions: Europe, 1944-1945 (New York: Longmans, Green, 1956).
[22] Hanson W. Baldwin, Great Mistakes of the War, p. 1-5.

Their plans were not fully accepted, but a major production and training effort did result in what was eventually almost continuous bombing of Germany.

The German economy did come close to collapse in the closing months of the war, but it is hard to sort out the reasons. The allied blockade and measures of economic warfare (such as buying Swedish ball bearing production so the Germans could not) were very effective. Also, German industrial mobilization was, contrary to American public opinion, not very good—in fact poorer than that of Britain and the United States. Bombing was not particularly successful in interrupting German production, as it turned out, but was successful in destroying communication and transportation centers behind the German army and thus contributing mightily to its defeat.[23]

THE PACIFIC THEATER

In the Pacific the United States had almost complete control of military operations, although Australia provided important forces. In the first anguished months after Pearl Harbor, the Japanese forces hurtled south and west until they controlled, by the spring of 1942, all of Southeast Asia, including a treasure house of raw materials. From that moment on the war became, for the Japanese, a defensive one. Japan held a huge perimeter running from the borders of India eastward to the islands north of Australia, and then north through the island clusters of the central Pacific to the Aleutian chain off the coast of Alaska. Japan's job was to defend this perimeter until her conquests could be integrated into her wartime economy. The task of the Allies was to contain and then crash through this perimeter.[24]

In May, 1942, the Japanese were inching their forces between the United States and Australia by occupying eastern New Guinea and the Solomon Island chain. In the Battle of the Coral Sea and in the Solomons Campaign, the Japanese were turned back beginning in May, 1942. In June, 1942 the Japanese were defeated at sea in the Battle of Midway and lost most of their aircraft carriers. This loss was perhaps the turning point of the war, for air power proved to be much more decisive in the Pacific than it was in the European theater. The role of air power was in fact so significant in the Pacific that the carrier replaced the battleship as the kingpin of naval warfare.

---

[23] See the three reports of the United States Strategic Bombing Survey.

[24] For a concise account of the Pacific War, see J. F. C. Fuller, *The Decisive Battles of the Western World* (3 vols.; London: Eyre & Spottiswoode, 1954-1956), Vol. II, chapters twelve and sixteen.

With the Japanese contained, the problem was to break through their perimeter so as to be able (1) to interdict Japanese shipping bringing raw materials to the home islands, and (2) to get close enough to Japan proper to bomb her and eventually to invade her.

There was considerable rivalry between the army and the navy as to how this should be done and who should do it. The problem was solved by dividing the task. The Central Pacific Theater was put under the over-all command of Admiral Chester Nimitz. Forces under him, including army units, pierced the Japanese ocean frontier by storming the Gilbert, Marshall, and Mariana groups of islands. From the Marianas, taken in June, 1944, it was possible to bomb the home islands. In the meantime, General MacArthur commanded in the Southwest Pacific Theater.[25] Land, naval, and air forces under him fought westward in a series of leapfrogging, sea-borne attacks along the northern coast of New Guinea toward the Philippines, which were attacked in October, 1944. The Japanese navy attempted to intercept the forces attacking the Philippines and came very close to succeeding. By the time the battle was over, however, Japanese sea power was all but destroyed.

It is not fair to insist that the makers of strategy in the Pacific War should have acted on the lines which hindsight now indicates, but it is at least worth while to indicate what those lines might have been. Present knowledge would show that the navy's approach was more nearly right than the army's, and that the strategy of island-hopping was the shortest and cheapest road to Tokyo. The key to victory on the periphery of the Japanese Empire was the destruction of Japanese air and sea power and the consequent ability to interdict supply and leave Japanese island garrisons to be starved out. No more islands needed to be invaded than were necessary for use as American bases. In the same way the key to victory over the Japanese home islands was the destruction of the country's remaining air and sea power and the interdiction of its railway and interisland transportation.[26] The question is could these aims have been accomplished by the navy and marines with some assistance from specially trained army, air, and infantry without the expenditure of effort in support of MacArthur's campaign in the Southwest Pacific?

---

[25] See Frazier Hunt, *MacArthur and the War Against Japan* (New York: Scribner, 1945).

[26] See Jerome B. Cohen, *Japan's Economy in War and Reconstruction* (Minneapolis: University of Minnesota, 1949).

Indeed, the collapse of Japan's economy raises several rather awesome questions. Could the war have been ended sooner than it was, on roughly the same terms as were finally reached? There is evidence that it could have been.[27] Historians do not yet know all they would like to know about early Japanese peace overtures. Even more solemn is the possibility that the use of the atomic bomb was unnecessary from a military point of view.[28] This much we do know—American intelligence about and understanding of Japan was woefully poor throughout the war—otherwise the United States would never have encouraged Russia's entry into the Pacific War. At the same time, it must be recognized that the United States was never in a position to prevent Russia's entry.

WAR DIPLOMACY

Events in the sphere of diplomacy are, like the military record, still incomplete and clouded. For example, one looks in vain in Churchill's surging rhetoric for more than occasional tantalizing glimpses behind the scenes.[29] What was the true story of the relations between Roosevelt and Churchill and thus between America and Britain? Why did Churchill agree to the iniquitous Morgenthau Plan for post-war Germany?[30] Did Churchill agree wholeheartedly to the Casablanca demand for unconditional surrender? (Certainly the unconditional surrender doctrine was one of the most controversial aspects of Allied policy.)[31] Was the American refusal to invade the Balkans unrealistic in light of the political impossibility of stationing American troops there indefinitely to hold back the Russians? Did Bradley foul up at the Bulge, and did Montgomery save the day? Were Roosevelt and Churchill convinced that Stalin would keep the commitments made at Yalta?[32] Was Churchill justified in abandoning Mihailovic and sup-

---

[27] See Robert J. Butow, *Japan's Decision to Surrender* (Stanford: Stanford University, 1954).

[28] Michael Amrine, *The Great Decision: The Secret History of the Atomic Bomb* (New York: Putnam, 1959).

[29] Sir Winston Churchill, *The Second World War* (6 vols.; Boston: Houghton Mifflin, 1948-1953).

[30] Henry Morgenthau, Jr., *Germany Is Our Problem* (New York: Harper, 1945).

[31] Paul Kecskemeti, *Strategic Surrender: The Politics of Victory and Defeat* (Stanford: Stanford University, 1958) discusses the surrender of the three Axis forces.

[32] On Yalta, see Herbert Feis, *Churchill-Roosevelt-Stalin: The War They Waged and the Peace They Sought* (Princeton: Princeton University, 1957); John L. Snell, ed., *The Meaning of Yalta: Big Three Diplomacy and the New Balance of Power* (Baton Rouge: Louisiana State University, 1956); William H. McNeill, *America, Britain, and Russia: Their Cooperation and Conflict, 1941-1946* (New York: Oxford University, 1953) ; and *Foreign Relations of the United States: Diplomatic Papers: The Conferences at Malta and Yalta, 1945* (Washington: Department of State, 1955).

porting Tito? What made Churchill browbeat the Polish government-in-exile into joining Stalin's puppet "Lublin" government?[33] In short, did Churchill, like Roosevelt, fail to anticipate the resurgence of Russian imperialism, and if not, why did he so disastrously misinterpret the facts of Allied power, talk so boastfully of Anglo-Russian friendship, and fail to apprise the West of the perils of the period ahead?

Indeed one is confronted by evidence that he was fundamentally responsible for the later disasters to democracy in Asia. As an old imperialist he had no desire to see a strong native government in China, and did what he dared to prevent the American reinforcement of Chiang Kai-shek. As it was he delayed the reconquest of Burma, and thus delayed the regaining of the Burma Road.[34] The truth is that if one studies Churchill closely, the man does not emerge with quite the aura of infallibility that is popularly supposed to surround him.

The official position of the United States was to favor the end of imperialism, and with rare prescience it warned its allies that their more advanced possessions must be given freedom or autonomy if post-war chaos was to be averted.[35] Still, in its urgency it laid itself open to the accusation of jeopardizing stability, an argument welcomed by imperialists like Churchill. Roosevelt's intention was to replace the balance of power by a collective security system administered by the United Nations.[36] Success depended upon Russian cooperation which even then was uncertain.

Relations between Roosevelt, Stalin, and Churchill present a difficult problem of interpretation. During the war, it would seem that Churchill regarded Stalin as essentially a new Czar who had nationalized Communism and was concerned only with the historic aims of Russian imperialism: domination of Poland; hegemony over the eastern Balkans, Port Arthur, Dairen and the South Manchurian Railroad; predominance in Iran, and so on. Churchill dealt with Stalin

[33] Edward J. Rozek, *Allied Wartime Diplomacy: A Pattern in Poland* (New York: Wiley, 1958).

[34] Winston Churchill, *The Hinge of Fate* (Boston: Houghton Mifflin, 1950), p. 133-35; Sherwood, *Roosevelt and Hopkins*, p. 716, 772-74; Henry L. Stimson and McGeorge Bundy, *On Active Service in War and Peace* (New York: Harper, 1948), p. 528-29, 533-34.

[35] Rexford G. Tugwell, *The Democratic Roosevelt*, p. 591-92; Robert Sherwood, *Roosevelt and Hopkins*, p. 718.

[36] Richard W. Van Alstyne, *American Crisis Diplomacy: The Quest for Collective Security, 1918-1952* (Stanford: Stanford University, 1952). On Congressional aspects of foreign policy, see H. Bradford Westerfield, *Foreign Policy and Party Politics: Pearl Harbor to Korea* (New Haven: Yale University, 1955).

in allotting spheres of influence as if he were a Victorian statesman dealing with a Romanoff.[37]

In great part, Roosevelt followed Churchill's lead. In part, also, he seemed to feel that Stalin could be managed with the same sort of give and take, you-scratch-my-back-and-I'll-scratch-yours kind of compromise so familiar to American domestic politics and therefore to Roosevelt. In a psychological sense he seems to have looked upon Stalin as a juvenile delinquent who could be reformed by good treatment and a show of trust.[38] One should also remember that during the war the American Communist party—at the time "patriotic" and almost respectable as friends of a brave ally—was at the height of its influence. The public opinion generated in support of continued Russian-American friendship was something to be reckoned with. Nor was it generated by Communists alone, for many clearly non-Communist public figures and average citizens as well subscribed to the view. Roosevelt was by no means unaware of the growing truculence and bad faith of Russia, but he apparently hoped that a combination of psychiatric therapy and the celebrated Roosevelt charm would convert Stalin to democracy and gain favorable concessions from him.

There is not the space here to enter upon a detailed analysis of the agreements made at Yalta[39] and upon whether Stalin meant to abide by them. Few critics realize that Chiang got what he wanted at the time and fulsomely expressed his gratitude, and that even Herbert Hoover proclaimed that "it will offer great hope to the world."[40] Indeed it is almost impossible to get anyone to recall calmly the actual state of public and even of expert opinion during 1944 and 1945.

THE HOME FRONT

In a sense, the domestic scene during the war presents an even more difficult task for historians than the military operations.[41] Fiscal policy, production figures, and manpower statistics are not as exciting—or as

---

[37] Winston Churchill, *Triumph and Tragedy* (Boston: Houghton Mifflin, 1953), p. 227-28.

[38] Baldwin, *Great Mistakes of the War*, p. 4-9.

[39] See note 32 on Yalta.

[40] United States State Department, *United States Relations with China* (Washington: Department of State, 1949), p. 120-21; John Snell, et. al., *The Meaning of Yalta*, p. 189.

[41] Critical of the administration is Edgar E. Robinson, *The Roosevelt Leadership, 1933-1945* (Philadelphia: Lippincott, 1955). More balanced are Denis W. Brogan, *The Era of Franklin D. Roosevelt* (New Haven: Yale University, 1950); and Dexter Perkins, *The New Age of Franklin Roosevelt, 1932-1945* (Chicago: University of Chicago, 1957). On Congress, see Roland Young, *Congressional Politics in the Second World War* (New York: Columbia University, 1956).

easy to describe meaningfully—as the surge of combat.[42] Certainly the United States achieved a miracle of production—plant capacity during the war was increased 50 per cent and the standard of living was the highest in United States history to that time—despite war production and the fact that seventeen million of the best members of the labor force were in the armed services. Is this a tribute to free enterprise[43] —or an example of what can be achieved under government rationing, priorities, and financial aid—in short, under what was almost a planned economy?

The role of industry and labor also presents knotty problems of interpretation. One can point out that wages were frozen and workers tied to their jobs while profits soared. But one can also point out that overtime pay swelled wages to new highs, and that government aid helped labor unions to establish themselves in industries and geographic areas where they had been excluded before.[44] Did "production win the war" and was the victory primarily a laurel to industry, or did industry drag its feet until cost-plus contracts, subsidies, and government-provided facilities bribed capital into being patriotic?[45]

POST-WAR FOREIGN AFFAIRS

The biggest "defeat" that the United States suffered in the war— or in this century—came not during the war but afterwards, when China went Communist. Most historians agree, however, that China was not "lost" for the simple reason that the United States never "had" China and probably did all she could to prevent the Communist triumph. Now that partisan charges have subsided it becomes clear that most of the accusations made against Chiang Kai-shek were true, and that American policy suffered from general ignorance about Asia rather than from treason or "softness" toward Communism.[46]

---

[42] But try Elliot Janeway, *The Struggle for Survival: A Chronicle of Economic Mobilization in World War II* (New Haven: Yale University, 1951).

[43] This point of view is taken very dogmatically in Francis Walton, *Miracle of World War II: How American Industry Made Victory Possible* (New York: Macmillan, 1956) .

[44] Joel I. Seidman, *American Labor from Defense to Reconversion* (Chicago: University of Chicago, 1953). On Agriculture, see Walter W. Wilcox, *The Farmer in the Second World War* (Ames: Iowa State College, 1947).

[45] Tugwell, *The Democratic Roosevelt*, p. 523-24.

[46] Herbert Feis, *The China Tangle: The American Effort in China from Pearl Harbor to the Marshall Mission* (Princeton: Princeton University, 1953); Charles F. Romanus and Riley Sunderland, *Stilwell's Mission to China* (Washington: Office of Chief of Military History, Dept. of Army, 1953); *Foreign Relations of the United States: Diplomatic Papers, 1942: China* (Washington: Department of State, 1956); Charles Wertenbaker, "The China Lobby," *The Reporter*, 6:4-24; April 15, 1952 and 4:5-22; April 29, 1952.

Nevertheless, it is for his actions in foreign affairs that President Truman will be longest remembered. The end of the war saw only two great powers remaining, and much of the rest of the world in ferment or even near chaos.[47] It seems probable that Communism would have spread at least to the English Channel had it not been for the Truman Doctrine, the Marshall Plan,[48] and finally NATO. That there were errors, crudities, and shortcomings[49] in the forging of this policy is certain, and the nature, extent, and gravity of these mistakes will concern historians for many years to come.[50] But the Truman foreign policy became by 1960 a firm bi-partisan affair, defended as vigorously by Eisenhower as by Truman before him.

We cannot speak with much assurance of the causes of the Korean War, for it was started by another nation, and we did not capture the records and personnel of the government which initiated the war as we did in the case of Japan and Germany. We cannot be sure whether the Communists thought we would stay out of Korea or hoped we would come in.[51]

One reason for the United States' prompt entry into Korea probably lies in our policy towards Europe—that is, the construction of the NATO alliance.[52] Europe feared that we would again retreat into isolation and leave her alone with the bear. Many have felt that Hitler might have been stopped if the democracies had not dallied in the thirties. Truman was acting on such an assumption when he served notice on the new aggressive force that the non-Communist world could not be chipped away a bit at a time.[53]

---

[47] On the Truman years in general, see Herbert Agar, *The Price of Power: America Since 1945* (Chicago: University of Chicago, 1957); and Eric F. Goldman, *The Crucial Decade: America, 1945-1955* (New York: Knopf, 1956).

[48] Harry B. Price, *The Marshall Plan and Its Meaning* (Cornell: Cornell University, 1955).

[49] Chester Bowles, *American Politics in a Revolutionary World* (Cambridge: Harvard University, 1956); Jonathan B. Bingham, *Shirt Sleeve Diplomacy: Point 4 in Action* (New York: John Day, 1954).

[50] On a key aspect of United States foreign policy, see Filmer Stuart C. Northrop, *European Union and United States Foreign Policy* (New York: Macmillan, 1954).

[51] See Robert T. Oliver, *Why War Came in Korea* (New York: Fordham University, 1950); and *Syngman Rhee* (New York: Dodd, Mead, 1954), but keep in mind that the author is registered with the State Department as an agent of the South Korean Government.

[52] Leland M. Goodrich, *Korea: A Study of U. S. Policy in the United Nations* (New York: Council on Foreign Relations, 1956).

[53] On military operations, see T. Dodson Stamps and Vincent Esposito, *Operations in Korea* (West Point: U. S. Military Academy, 1952); Matthew B. Ridgway and Harold H. Martin, *Soldier* (New York: Harper, 1956). On other aspects, see William H. Vatcher, *Panmunjom: The Story of the Korean Military Armistice*

Whatever Truman's motivation, he did not succeed in overcoming the unpopularity of the war in the United States.[54] And two of the leading personalities of the war—Syngman Rhee and General Mac-Arthur—made his task much harder.[55] Indeed so difficult did the relations between Truman and MacArthur become that in April 1951 the latter was relieved of his command. Already MacArthur's military reputation had suffered as a result of the drive to the Yalu and the unexpected Chinese entry into the war. Here as in so much else in Asia in the World War II period, bad intelligence lay at the heart of the problem.[56]

It was the tension of the peace that was not a peace and then the Korean War which was not a war in the usual sense—not a war to be "won"—which gave rise to the nightmare of McCarthyism in the last years of Truman and the first years of Eisenhower. There was real evidence of Communist espionage in the field of atomic energy and considerable reason to believe that individual Communists had had influence in the State and Treasury Departments—though not as known Communists.[57] McCarthy charged much more than this, however—that Communists, working through a pliable Democratic party, actually guided national policy. The charges would hardly have been listened to in normal times, but many Americans were ready to strike out angrily at the domestic representatives—or imagined representatives—of the overseas power which was at the root of much of the troubles of the times and which was out of reach.

The unpopularity of the Korean War and the charges of McCarthy combined with the popularity of the Republican candidate finally unseated the Democrats in 1952. The new President ended the Korean War on terms certainly no better than Truman could have obtained and presently found that McCarthy—like all demagogues—was the

---

Negotiations (New York: Praeger, 1958); Edward Hunter, *Brainwashing: The Story of Men Who Defied it* (New York: Farrar, Straus and Cudahy, 1956); and William L. White, *The Captives of Korea* (New York: Scribner, 1957).

[54] Norman A. Graebner, *The New Isolationism: A Study in Politics and Foreign Policy Since 1950* (New York: Ronald, 1956).

[55] Richard H. Rovere and Arthur M. Schlesinger, Jr., *The General and the President, and the Future of American Foreign Policy* (New York: Farrar, Straus and Young, 1951).

[56] Edwin O. Reischauer, *Wanted: An Asian Policy* (New York: Knopf, 1955). Two inexpensive paperbacks are very useful for this entire period. They are John Hampden Jackson, *The World in the Postwar Decade, 1945-1955* (Cambridge: Houghton Mifflin, 1956); and Hans W. Gatzke, *The Present in Perspective* (Chicago: Rand McNally, 1957).

[57] Nathaniel Weyl, *The Battle Against Disloyalty* (New York: Crowell, 1951); and Oliver R. Pilat, *The Atom Spies* (New York: Putnam, 1952).

enemy of *whoever* was in power. When McCarthy set out to demoralize the army as he had demoralized the State Department, it was the conservatives in the Senate who finally rose to begin his precipitous political decline.[58]

Eisenhower, like every Republican presidential nominee since Landon, had been the candidate of the "modern" eastern wing of the party.[59] Once in office, however, his differences with the Old Guard proved to be mostly in the area of foreign policy. Plagued by illness through much of his tenure of office, the President turned over much of his authority to advisors drawn from the conservative upper echelons of business and finance.[60] Until his illness and death in 1959, John Foster Dulles was the gray eminence of the Eisenhower regime. Dulles' successes and failures as the real leader of the western alliance await study.[61]

DOMESTIC AFFAIRS AFTER THE WAR

Turning to the post-war domestic scene, most historians would agree that Truman was a better president than his political background and Senate record would have led one to expect. Beyond that, it is difficult to get a concensus.[62] Truman advocated in his Fair Deal program a continuatior of the war-interrupted New Deal, and little domestic legislation that departed significantly from New Deal precedent was enacted.[63] It has become clear that in the post-war period there are three parties in the United States rather than two—at least in Congress. The third party is made up of most of the Southern

---

[58] Friendly to McCarthy is William F. Buckley, *McCarthy and His Enemies* (Chicago: Regnery, 1954); critical is Richard H. Rovere, *Senator Joe McCarthy* (New York: Harcourt, Brace, 1959).

[59] On his leading opponent for the nomination, see William Smith White, *The Taft Story* (New York: Harper, 1954).

[60] Marquis Childs, *Eisenhower: Captive Hero* (New York: Harcourt, Brace, 1958) is critical; Merlo J. Pusey, *Eisenhower, the President* (New York: Macmillan, 1956) is friendly. See also Richard Rovere, *The Eisenhower Years* (New York: Farrar, Straus and Cudahy, 1956) for the years 1952 to 1956. On Eisenhower's two-time opponent, see Kenneth S. Davis, *A Prophet in His Own Country: The Triumphs and Defeats of Adlai E. Stevenson* (Garden City: Doubleday, 1957). On Nixon, see Earl Mazo, *Richard Nixon* (New York: Harper, 1959).

[61] Kenneth Ingram, *History of the Cold War* (London: D. Finlayson, 1955).

[62] Jonathan Daniels, *The Man of Independence* (Philadelphia: Lippincott, 1950) is friendly.

[63] Wilbur Hillman, *Views of Harry S. Truman* (New York: Farrar, Straus and Young, 1952). For example, extension of Social Security, Fair Labor Standards, Federal Housing, Farm Price Supports, and Reciprocal Trade was secured; but Federal Medical Insurance, Federal Aid to Education, and Civil Rights legislation failed.

Democrats; and a coalition between them and the Republicans blocked the Fair Deal and has controlled every Congress since the war, regardless of who was nominally in control.

Another emerging trend is the breaking down of old political loyalties in many regions of the nation. Democrats now have carried regions in New England and the Mid-West which only Franklin Roosevelt, and sometimes not even he, could carry. On the other hand, the Republicans have made perceptible gains in the more and more urban and industrialized South, and twice President Eisenhower carried once-solid states of the old Confederacy.[64]

On the economic and social scene historians have to depend heavily on the sociologists, economists, and psychologists. Present day muckrakers come from the academy rather than from among the journalists. The most trenchant critic of contemporary America is the Columbia sociologist, C. Wright Mills, who has studied in turn the nation's labor leadership, the new middle class of the white collar world, and lastly the interlocking "power elite" of the military leaders, the business tycoons, and the top political leaders.[65] William H. Whyte, Jr., an editor of *Fortune*, has attacked conformity in business and social life and called for a return to American individualism.[66] Harvard economist John K. Galbraith has posed the curious but real and pressing problems of affluence.[67]

American labor has had a tumultuous history since the war. The real effects of the Taft-Hartley Act are yet to be assayed, but certainly the CIO's purge of the Communists within its ranks in 1949 began the swift slide of the American Communist party towards total oblivion.[68] It was apprehension over the effect of the first Republican president in twenty years which led to the reunification of the AFL and CIO in 1955.[69]

---

[64] The most important writer on this topic is Samuel Lubell. See his *The Future of American Politics* (New York: Harper, 1952), and *Revolt of the Moderates* (New York: Harper, 1956).

[65] Charles Wright Mills, *The New Men of Power: America's Labor Leaders* (New York: Harcourt, Brace, 1948); *White Collar: The American Middle Classes* (New York: Oxford University, 1951); and *The Power Elite* (New York: Oxford University, 1956).

[66] William H. Whyte, Jr., *The Organization Man* (New York: Simon and Schuster, 1956).

[67] John Kenneth Galbraith, *The Affluent Society* (Boston: Houghton Mifflin, 1958).

[68] Max M. Kampelman, *The Communist Party vs. the C.I.O.* (New York: Praeger, 1957).

[69] Arthur J. Goldberg, *AFL-CIO: Labor United* (New York: McGraw-Hill, 1956).

The real social revolution in the post-World War II America has been in the area of race relations.[70] Interesting has been the action of the Supreme Court which—in all candidness—has legislated in this field which Congress hardly touched effectively until the Civil Rights Acts of 1957 and 1960. Also to be noted are the very real signs of a growing political consciousness not simply among the urban Negro middle class[71] in the North but in the submerged and hitherto mute Negro masses of the Deep South, well exemplified in the successful Montgomery bus boycott.[72]

The population explosion[73] of recent years has concealed in part the fabulous economic growth of the period. Agricultural productivity per man hour, for example, has *doubled* since 1940 and continues to rise. Industrial expansion has been almost as striking.[74] Awaiting study by historians is the school "crisis," the problem of juvenile delinquency, and the effect of television. Finally the historian of science will face, in describing World War II and after, a truly awesome task.

---

[70] C. Vann Woodward, *The Strange Career of Jim Crow* (New York: Oxford University, 1955).

[71] E. Franklin Frazier, *Black Bourgeoisie* (Glencoe, Ill.: Free Press, 1957).

[72] Martin Luther King, *Stride Toward Freedom: The Montgomery Story* (New York: Harper, 1958).

[73] Editors of *Fortune, The Exploding Metropolis* (Garden City: Doubleday, 1958).

[74] Adolph A. Berle, Jr., *The 20th Century Capitalist Revolution* (New York: Harcourt, Brace, 1954); Frederick Pollock, *Automation: A Study of Its Economic and Social Consequences*, trans. W. O. Henderson and W. H. Chaloner (New York: Praeger, 1957).

CHAPTER XVIII

Ideas and Culture in the Twentieth Century

Ralph Gabriel

BACKGROUND

FOUR major changes in American civilization took place in the years between 1865, when the Civil War ended, and 1917, when the United States entered World War I. An industrial revolution transformed what had been an agricultural-commercial civilization into a developed industrial culture. A rapidly evolving technology, together with the development of the limited-liability corporation, brought about the revolution. The existence of vast natural resources made possible the emergence of the United States in the front rank of industrial nations. Cities grew swiftly and the percentage of the population living in urban areas greatly increased. Historians have called the transformation an urban revolution. Into the cities crowded immigrants who came sometimes at the rate of a million persons a year. The immigrant flood had begun before the Civil War and in the early decades had originated primarily in northern and western Europe. After about 1885 the greater part of the newcomers came from nations in southern and eastern Europe. The outbreak of World War I in 1914 stopped the flow and American legislation after the close of that conflict kept the stream to minimal size. So great had been the total volume of migrants to the New World that immigration brought about a major ethnic change in the population of the United States. The fourth basic modification in American civilization had to do with education. In this area change occurred at three levels. Americans had developed the elementary public school before the Civil War. After that conflict laws requiring attendance of children at school appeared on the statute books of most of the states. At the level of secondary education the public high school, which had originated before 1861, had appeared by 1917 in practically all important communities. The years between the two wars saw the emergence of true universities in which graduate and professional schools took their places beside undergraduate colleges. Some of these universities grew out of the independent liberal arts colleges that had originated in colonial times or in the first half of the nineteenth century. Others sprang from great endowments given by private donors. Still others, destined to become the most important from the point of view of student enrollment, were developed, in some cases out of pre-war institutions, by the separate states and supported by taxation. By World War I the list of American universities included institutions of the first order of excellence. In their libraries and classrooms they conserved and transmitted the great tradition of western civilization. In their research they added significantly to the body of knowledge of all branches of learning.[1]

AMERICAN THOUGHT IN THE TWENTIETH CENTURY

Developments in the natural sciences provided the spear point of change not only in American thought in the twentieth century but in American life. From the eighteenth century onward America had felt the influence of developing European science. Newtonian physics was early established in American colleges. Darwinian evolution after the middle of the nineteenth century profoundly affected not only the biological sciences in the rising universities but made an important impact on social thought as well. Some nineteenth century scientists had made major contributions to basic science. One, Josiah Willard Gibbs, leaving his American contemporaries behind, had prepared the way for certain aspects of twentieth century science. European scientists discovered and acclaimed the importance of Gibbs' work, a fact which suggested that science in the New World had not yet achieved a development equal to that in the Old. In the application of scientific knowledge to technology, nineteenth century Americans, however, achieved pre-eminence.

The advance of the natural sciences to a central position in American civilization together with the popular recognition of the fact is the most striking phenomenon in American thought in the twentieth century. After World War I three different types of organizations carried on the quest for new scientific knowledge and the application

---

[1] For general works on American culture and ideas, see Merle E. Curti, *The Growth of American Thought* (New York: Harper, 1943); Ralph Henry Gabriel, *The Course of American Democratic Thought* (Second edition; New York: Ronald, 1956); Stow Persons, *American Minds; A History of Ideas* (New York: Holt, 1958); Henry Steele Commager, *The American Mind* (New Haven: Yale University, 1950) .

of that knowledge to individual and social living. The universities provided the laboratories in which investigators were preoccupied primarily with basic science. The freedom of the scientist who worked in a university setting not only gave him opportunity but endowed his post with a high prestige. Before World War I the federal government had supported the physical and biological sciences in such agencies as the United States Geological Survey and the research bureaus of the Department of Agriculture. In World War II the government mobilized the scientists of the nation into the Organization of Research and Development (OSRD), the Manhatten Project, and a wide variety of other undertakings to further the war effort. The Manhattan Project ushered in the atomic age and the atom bomb dramatized the relation of science to the national security. The Atomic Energy Commission, created just after the war, furthered and directed atomic research so costly that only the federal government could supply the funds. Some of this research was farmed out to universities or to institutions, such as Brookhaven on Long Island, created by groups of universities. Formal recognition of the basic role of science came after the war, with the establishment of the National Science Foundation. This agency utilized the large appropriations made available to it to further the training of scientists primarily in the universities and to support basic research in non-governmental laboratories. With the dawn of the Space Age the National Aeronautics and Space Administration organized the work in science and engineering required for the conquest of outer space. Industry provided the third agency for the development of science, pure and applied. Industrial laboratories appeared after World War I and grew swiftly in significance. The mid-twentieth century profusion of plastics and electronic devices suggests some of the results when industry turned seriously to scientific research and to the exploration of the possibilities of applying scientific knowledge to the creation of useful goods. While most of the research carried forward in industrial laboratories was motivated by the particular interests of the concern, some of the largest companies financed, to a limited degree, work in pure science.

By the middle of the twentieth century, what had always been true became clearer to all intelligent citizens; namely, that American civilization (as all civilization) rests on a body of knowledge. Of this body, accumulated scientific and technological knowledge was a most important part. The events of the century demonstrated that change in this underlying accumulation of knowledge is one of the principal causes for change in society. With almost bewildering swiftness the automobile, the airplane, the radio, television, plastics, synthetic fibers, and the atomic and hydrogen bombs wrought modifications in American ways of living. These changes in society provide the background for the phenomenon of the social sciences.[2]

In their origins economics, anthropology, sociology and psychology ante-dated the twentieth century. But in the years after 1900 these disciplines underwent their great development. They represent a sustained effort to apply rationality, central to science, to the solution of the problems involved in understanding personality and society. The universities provided the centers for the development of the social sciences. But government, both federal and state, utilized increasingly the services of men and women trained in one or another of the fields. By the middle of the century these sciences had accumulated an impressive body of knowledge of their own. The influence of various aspects of this on the life of the people is suggested by the guidance that psychology has given to parents in child rearing and to teachers in dealing with their pupils. Economics has provided for government guidelines in taking measures to combat recessions. The Supreme Court in 1954 leaned heavily on the findings of psychological investigations in reaching its decision with regard to segregation in the schools. The social sciences represent an attempt on the part of the American people to provide means by which they may deal intelligently with social change.

Acceptance of social change as a normal aspect of life characterizes American thought. From the first English settlements along the Atlantic, change has characterized American life. American democracy was founded on the practice of rational discussion informed as far as possible by the finding of facts. An empirical approach to the solution of problems became basic to the American outlook. In the early twentieth century this emphasis on experimentalism received formal intellectual expression in a philosophy formulated by William James and John Dewey and given the name pragmatism. Pragmatism means experimentation and the judging of the experiment by its results. John Dewey called his version of pragmatism "instrumentalism." He meant by the term the formulation of specific goals (ideas) which then became energizing centers for creative activity. He thought of ideas

---

[2] Important references on the impact of the natural sciences and technology are: John W. Oliver, *History of American Technology* (New York: Ronald, 1956); A. Hunter Dupree, *Science in the Federal Government* (Cambridge: Belknap of Harvard University, 1957); Bernard Jaffe, *Men of Science in America* (Revised edition; New York: Simon and Schuster, 1958); Bernard Barber, *Science and the Social Order* (Glencoe, Ill.: Free Press, 1952).

as the instruments by the use of which society could be purposefully changed. The development of the social sciences in the twentieth century gave increasingly more accurate tools for the measurement of the results of all kinds of social undertakings. But the social sciences, due partly to the complexity of the field in which they worked, lacked the precision of the physical sciences. Difficulties, however, only spurred the practitioners to continuous and determined efforts. In twentieth century United States the social sciences, when all are considered, achieved a development and usefulness surpassing that in any other nation.[3]

If science has provided a central theme for American thought in the twentieth century, so also has the traditional American idea of individualism. Thomas Jefferson set forth in the Declaration of Independence the doctrine of the unalienable rights of the individual person. Later the framers of the Constitution spelled out some of these in the Bill of Rights and by so doing transformed them into civil rights. The frontier experience of Americans in the seventeenth, eighteenth, and nineteenth centuries fostered the development of the self-reliant and responsible individual. In American society an open class system took form in which achievement and personal quality, rather than inherited position, determined the place of the individual in society. This old set of values and attitudes carried over into the twentieth century where they affected and were affected by a social scene undergoing accelerating change. In the complex industrial society evolving since 1900, individualism has undergone some modification.

Since the colonial period one expression of the freedom of Americans had been their habit of forming free associations for the worship of God. Long before the middle of the nineteenth century all American churches were such associations. The free churches continued into the twentieth century. In the latter period, however, the number and variety of free associations proliferated. The labor union, the parent-teachers association, the Young Republican and Young Democratic clubs, the Anti-Saloon League of the years before World War I, the League of Nations Association after the war, the League of Women

---

[3] For an encyclopedic treatment of twentieth century United States including chapters which show the impact of the social sciences, see Max Lerner, *America as a Civilization; Life and Thought in the United States Today* (New York: Simon and Schuster, 1957). For a brilliant interpretation of American history which shows how the behaviorial sciences can be useful to the historian, see David Potter, *People of Plenty; Economic Abundance and the American Character* (Chicago: University of Chicago, 1954). Potter's book is available in a paperback edition.

Voters, Alcoholics Anonymous, not to prolong the list, suggest the variety of organizations with which the mid-twentieth century American identified himself. In the complex urban and industrial society of those years, the free individual expressed himself more and more in and through the group. Normally he belonged to several groups. The net effect of these associations was to increase the range of the freedom of the individual.

After World War I Americans suddenly found themselves confronting an external challenge to the philosophy and practice of individual freedom. Totalitarian dictatorships appeared in the 1920's in communist Russia and in fascist Italy. In the next decade the Nazis in Germany launched an ideological campaign both at home and abroad against the idea of the free individual. Totalitarian Italy, Germany, and Russia proposed and established the dominance of the state over the individual. The success of Mussolini and of Hitler in regimenting their respective populations surprised Americans, trained in the school of freedom. The imperial expansion of both Italy and Germany in the 1930's served as warning to the citizens of the Western Republic of the seriousness of the threat to their fundamental beliefs. The spectacular rise of Hitler, in particular, also tended to focus the attention of anxious Americans on the Nazis and to make them less aware of the threat posed by Russian totalitarianism. An additional cause of the relatively less apprehension of the Soviets in the 1930's lay in the fact that many Americans in that decade were confused by the upsidedown language deliberately developed by communism and had difficulty understanding the realities behind such Russian words as "democratic" and "republic."

The three-fold challenge from Europe to democratic philosophy called forth in the 1930's an urgent re-examination by Americans of the philosophy behind their institutions. The external attack caught the United States unprepared. The American philosophy of pragmatism had emphasized action and had denigrated theory. Most Americans did not have the training to use ideas with precision and had no comprehension of how ideas can be used as weapons. Walter Lippmann, Horace Kallen, William E. Hocking, and Ralph Barton Perry were only a few of those who attempted to meet the varying ideologies from Europe on purely intellectual grounds. These men began the creation of a body of literature dealing with American democratic values and institutions that was to grow vastly during World War II and in the troubled years that followed it. Out of the ferment of the 1930's came a new appraisal of Thomas Jefferson and, as a result, his advance, as a symbol of our democratic faith, to a position equal to that long held by Washington and Lincoln. The Jefferson nickle, like the Lincoln penny a universal coin, kept the image of the author of the Declaration of Independence constantly before all Americans. The Jefferson memorial at Washington erected during World War II, expressed in material form the new veneration.[4]

The 1930's, in which Americans were increasingly aware of Hitler and of his philosophy of the omnipotent state directed by a führer, was the period of the Great Depression. The decade opened with the failure of multitudes of private businesses and the menacing rise of unemployment. The capitalistic system carried on in America appeared to many persons to have failed. The New Deal sought to check what seemed to be the decline of capitalism by clothing the federal government with new powers for dealing with the economy. The Supreme Court, after striking down two major measures, readjusted its philosophy to the needs of a new day. It sustained in 1937 the National Labor Relations Act and by so doing accepted the interpretation that the Constitution empowers Congress to regulate, if it sees fit, all aspects of the economy. Prior to the New Deal the Court had defined interstate commerce as transportation and communication and had limited the regulatory powers of Congress under the interstate commerce clause to that area. The agencies of the federal government grew to meet the new responsibilities and also to provide relief for the unemployed and the aged. A welfare state began to appear.

By the 1930's aged persons had become a higher percentage of the population than ever before in the nation's history. Several causes combined to bring about this situation. The most important, however, were the advance of science of medicine in the conquest of disease, the evolution by governments at all levels of measures for the protection of public health, and advances in the biological sciences in the understanding of nutrition. Between 1900 and 1950 the individual expectancy of life increased significantly. In the complex industrial

[4] For select references on democratic values, see Louis Hartz, *The Liberal Tradition in America: An Interpretation of American Political Thought Since the Revolution* (New York: Harcourt, Brace, 1955) ; Clinton L. Rossiter, *Conservatism in America* (New York: Knopf, 1955); Walter Lippmann, *Essays in the Public Philosophy* (Boston: Little, Brown, 1955). Lippmann's book is in a paperback edition. Horace M. Kallen, *Individualism; An American Way of Life* (New York: Liveright, 1933); *The Education of Free Men* (New York: Farrar, Straus, 1949); *Cultural Pluralism and the American Idea* ([Albert M. Greenfield Center for Human Relations, Studies, No. 1] Philadelphia: University of Pennsylvania, 1956); William E. Hocking, *The Lasting Elements of Individualism* (New Haven: Yale University, 1937); Ralph Barton Perry, *Characteristically American* (New York: Knopf, 1949).

economy of the twentieth century the burden of caring for the aged had to be lifted from the shoulders of the younger generation where it had rested in the old agricultural civilization of the eighteenth and early nineteenth centuries. The Social Security System resulted. Social security represented the adjustment of the old philosophy of the free and responsible individual to the conditions of a new age. When dislocation in the economy prevented a man or woman from getting work, the individual could not be held personally responsible. The development of unemployment insurance resulted. Another insurance plan backed by government provided annuities to retired persons. By so doing it gave them an independence in their later years which such persons had often not had in the earlier centuries when their support devolved upon their children. The over-all effect of the new insurance plans instituted by government was to reinforce the freedom of the individual in a complex society and economy. The welfare state was an extension of the use of the group—this time a group as large as the nation—to further the ability of the individual person to live a full life and to express with a maximum of freedom his own personality. The welfare state, as developed in the United States in the 1930's and after, differed fundamentally from the leviathan state, pursuing its ends through the discipline of naked force, that Stalin, Mussolini, and Hitler brought into being before World War II.

The measures of the New Deal, however, accelerated the development of big government that was already under way. Increasing international tensions culminating in World War II continued this process. After World War II the dangers of the cold war caused further enlargement of government activities as the competition in armament with the Soviet Union went forward in an atomic age. Big government in Communist Russia, in Fascist Italy, and in Nazi Germany had swallowed up the individual and had made him a pawn of the state. In the United States big government both aided and posed problems for the individual. For the most part these had to do with maintaining a balance between liberty and authority in times of tension.[5]

Hardly had World War I ended, when the Supreme Court faced the questions as to how far the individual should be permitted to go in advocacy of radical or revolutionary doctrines. At a time when government was burgeoning, the Court moved to protect the indi-

---

[5] Mario Einaudi, *The Roosevelt Revolution* (New York: Harcourt, Brace, 1959) traces the long-range effects of the New Deal. For other references on the New Deal, see Chapter XV.

vidual. In the 1920's and 1930's the Justices implemented the Bill of Rights as never before in the nation's history. In particular the fundamental rights established by the First Amendment—the right of the citizen to worship as he chooses, the right to assemble in peaceable meetings and the right to freedom of speech—were erected by the Court as a bulwark for the defense of the citizen. The Court, moreover, subsumed these under the Fourteenth Amendment which sets limits to the actions by the states. Before World War II the test proposed by Justice Oliver Wendell Holmes for determining the limits of free speech had received judicial acceptance. Holmes insisted that only when the advocacy of ideas constitutes a "present and immediate danger" to the state can such advocacy legally be suppressed. While the decisions of those decades upheld essential governmental authority, civil rights, particularly that of religious liberty, were emphasized and protected.

After World War II, when the United States faced the challenge of Soviet Russia and the cold war strategy of infiltration and subversion, the Supreme Court approved the conviction and imprisonment of the leading officers of the Communist party in the United States under the Smith Act, our first peacetime sedition act since 1798. They had been convicted of conspiracy to over-throw the government of the United States by force. The discovery of espionage activities during and after World War II, particularly the transfer to the Russians of information concerning nuclear energy, brought into being far-reaching security regulations affecting not only government officials but private persons whose work required them to deal with classified information. The Communist effort to over-run South Korea, that began in 1950, created an atmosphere in which Senator Joseph McCarthy of Wisconsin with, for a time, much public support could take the lead in witch-hunting forays that seriously damaged the State Department and impaired morale not only in other governmental agencies but in schools and colleges.

The rights of no witness before the McCarthy Committee were sacred. After McCarthy had overplayed his hand and had been censured by the Senate, public apprehension relaxed somewhat. The sudden and menacing rise of McCarthyism not only in the federal government but in some states, called forth a literature in the press, in magazines of discussion, and in books in which the problem of the relation between liberty and authority was subjected to searching analysis. The necessity of not permitting a continuing cold war with a totalitarian power to negate the traditional American liberties of the individual was made clear. Of these writings Elmer Davis' witty *But We Were Born Free* was the most widely read. As the result of a better popular understanding of the issues involved in dealing with radicalism, decisions by the Supreme Court in the late 1950's which buttressed the rights of individuals in facing committees of Congress or accusation of being security risks on the part of government agencies met with wide approval. In an age of continuing international tension, Americans were learning to live with the cold war. They rejected totalitarian methods and managed to maintain a reasonable balance between the freedom of the individual and the authority of the state charged with the responsibility of the common defense.[6]

In the twentieth century American minority groups, ethnic and religious, suffered, particularly in the earlier years, from greater or lesser disadvantages. The ruthless degradation and destruction of German Jews in the 1930's together with Nazi affirmation of "Aryan" supremacy tended to remind Americans of their own minority problems. The fact that World War II became for the United States a struggle for survival not only of the nation but of the democratic principles on which it was founded forced Americans to take thought of discrepancies between profession and practice in the actual functioning of democratic ideals and values in their society. After the war, responsibilities of the United States, growing out of a new world leadership against the out-thrust of imperial communism, brought into an international perspective our Negro problem. The logic of the philosophy of unalienable rights set forth in the Declaration of Independence provided, however, the most potent force in the shaping of mid-century American thought concerning minorities. The Declaration's affirmation of the right to life, to liberty, and to the pursuit of happiness became, perhaps more than ever before, the conscience of the American people. The Supreme Court's segregation decision in 1954 and the Civil Rights Acts of 1957 and 1960 were the outgrowth of a better understanding on the part of the American people of the sinister im-

---

[6] For the problem of civil liberties and McCarthyism, see Elmer Davis, *But We Were Born Free* (Indianapolis: Bobbs-Merrill, 1954); Richard H. Rovere, *Senator Joe McCarthy* (New York: Harcourt, Brace, 1959); Zechariah Chafee, *The Blessing of Liberty* (Philadelphia: Lippincott, 1956); John W. Caughey, *In Clear and Present Danger: The Crucial State of our Freedoms* (Chicago: University of Chicago, 1958); Charles Herman Pritchett, *The Roosevelt Court: A Study in Judicial Politics and Values, 1937-1947* (New York: Macmillan, 1948) and *Civil Liberties and the Vinson Court* (Chicago: University of Chicago, 1954); Alpheus T. Mason, *The Supreme Court from Taft to Warren* (Baton Rouge: Louisiana State University, 1958).

plications of minority status. The decision and the Acts represented a determination to give reality to the traditional ideal of equality of opportunity. In these three actions, which followed some earlier decisions of the Supreme Court negating Jim Crow laws and legislation by certain states designed to disfranchize the Negro, the American people through the federal government came to grips with the most difficult of all social problems.[7]

This initiative of the federal government was in harmony with a trend that had become important in the New Deal; namely, to increase the powers of the central government, particularly in dealing with the economy. Though the functions of state governments had increased by absolute standards, the states had declined relatively when compared to what had happened to the national government. The action of the Supreme Court in the matter of segregation in the schools re-awakened the issue of States rights in a form reminiscent of the time of Calhoun. Americans again gave thought to their federal system and to the meaning of the Tenth Amendment which stated that the "powers not delegated to the United States by the Constitution, nor prohibited by it to the states, are reserved to the states respectively, or to the people." The new discussions of federalism, however, took place against a national and international backdrop vastly different from that before which John C. Calhoun spoke his lines.

LITERATURE IN THE TWENTIETH CENTURY

As the century opened, Darwinism moved triumphantly in American thought.[8] Its application in social ideas took many forms. Literate Americans looked upon Darwinism as the new science. In medicine scientific inquiry brought Walter Reed and his company of investigators to the conquest of that ancient scourge Yellow Fever in the first decade of the century. In the same decade the Wright brothers

---

[7] For the Negro and civil rights see *ibid*; also Gunnar Myrdal, *An American Dilemma: The Negro Problem and Modern Democracy* (2 vols.; New York: Harper, 1944); C. Vann Woodward, *The Strange Career of Jim Crow* (Revised edition; New York; Oxford University, 1957). Woodward's book is in a paperback edition. Margaret Just Butcher, *The Negro in American Culture* (New York: Knopf, 1956); Donald R. Green and Warren E. Gauerke, "If the Schools Are Closed: A Critical Analysis of the Private School Plan," (Southern Regional Council Report, 1959); John Hope Franklin, *From Slavery To Freedom* (Second and revised edition; New York: Knopf, 1956).

[8] Richard Hofstadter, *Social Darwinism in American Thought* (Revised edition; Boston: Beacon, 1955). This is a paperback edition [Beacon Paperbacks, No. 16].

learned to escape from the earth into the air. Among educated people science was held in high regard.

The literature of the period reflected the popular mood at least in so far as it paid deference to science. Mark Twain, nearing the end of his life, had long since replaced the forbidding Calvinism of his youth with an almost equally forbidding scientific determinism. The change, far from freeing his spirit, had landed him in black pessimism. The science he knew suggested no meaning for human life, no freedom for the human will. A number of younger writers— Jack London, Frank Norris and Theodore Dreiser—portrayed human life with a naturalism akin to that of Clemens. In the case of Stephen Crane (who did not outlive the 1890's) and the young Dreiser, naturalism was influenced and reinforced by the probings of Emile Zola into the unsavory areas of human life. In *Sister Carrie* before World War I, Dreiser challenged the older Genteel Tradition and proposed a naturalistic explanation of human behavior. A Darwinian naturalism —evolution results from the struggle for existence and the survival of the fittest—permeated the pages of London. Norris in *The Octopus* celebrated the vast impersonal forces that control human destiny. For Henry Adams the dynamo provided the symbol of the modern world. He saw man, driven by the tumultuous forces he had released from nature, as one who grasps a live wire that makes him writhe but which he cannot let go. The transcendentalist approach to nature of Emerson and Thoreau seemed, in the opening decades of the twentieth century, far away.

The transcendentalists were part of the first great period of literary creation in American history. That period came in the nineteenth century as American civilization was beginning to move beyond agriculture and commerce and into the industrial age. A second great creative period came in the decades between World War I and World War II. The fiction of Dreiser, Hemingway, Wolfe, and Faulkner; the poetry of Frost, Eliot, and Pound; and the dramas of O'Neil not only reflected various aspects of the life and thought of the Republic but pioneered in new literary forms. These men were only the more significant in a larger company of writers. Moreover—under the leadership of Eliot, Irving Babbitt, and Paul Elmer More—literary criticism achieved a stature that made it an aspect of literature itself. The vigor and the creative innovations of American literature in this period made a profound impression throughout the British Commonwealth of Nations and on the continent of Europe. Eliot and Pound became ex-patriates as Henry James had been before them. Hemingway and several of his contemporaries had derived inspiration from Gertrude Stein in France. The second great flowering of American literature transcended a national setting. It displayed a cosmopolitanism together with the influence of literary movements in the Old World that kept it from being an isolated nationalistic phenomenon and made it a genuine and important aspect of the literature of western civilization.[9]

ARCHITECTURE

As the twentieth century opened, architecture in the United States was bound to traditional forms. Gothic continued to predominate in ecclesiastical architecture, although in New England the Georgian churches of the eighteenth century provided the models and in California builders borrowed ideas from the Spanish missions. Ralph Adams Cram created the halls of the United States Military Academy at West Point with Gothic forms. The dominant tradition, however, was classical. The spectacular ensemble of buildings at the Chicago World's Fair in 1893 had used classical forms, save for H. H. Richardson's Transportation Building. From the point of view of fixing taste for the next half century the Fair was a tremendous success. Classical facades became the almost unvarying style for banks. Columns, porticos, and rotundas proliferated on college campuses. In academic building, however, Gothic contended for supremacy with the classical. The classical style dominated the rebuilding of the National Capitol which occurred in the first quarter of the century. American architecture in general was traditional, imitative, derivative.

Traditional forms, however, could not contain wholly the dynamism of American society. Louis Sullivan pioneered in creating the skyscraper that in time came to be almost as representative of America as the turkey. Frank Lloyd Wright, pupil of Sullivan, with his refusal to be bound by tradition and his emphasis on materials, on adaptation to environment, and on function became the first great leader, not only in America, but in Europe of a new and vastly varied architecture. In fact Wright's influence came to America by way of Europe where his ideas were first accepted. By the middle of the twentieth

[9] Robert Spiller, et al., *Literary History of the United States* (3 vols.; New York: Macmillan, 1948); Willard Thorp, *American Writing in the Twentieth Century* (Cambridge: Harvard University, 1959); Walter B. Rideout, *The Radical Novel in the United States, 1900-1954: Some Inter-relations of Literature and Society* (Cambridge: Harvard University, 1956); Alfred Kazin, *On Native Grounds: An Interpretation of Modern American Prose Literature* (New York: Reynal & Hitchcock, 1942). Kazin's book is in a paperback edition (1956).

century, American building reflected a spirit of freedom, a capacity for innovation, and a variety appropriate to the dynamism of a great civilization. While Wright still lived, younger men, some of them migrants from the Old World, struck out in many directions. They sought the Holy Grail of architecture not in some traditional style or combination of styles but in experimentation, in the adaptation of form to ends, and in the vision of new possibilities for beauty. Because the present inevitably grows out of the past, these builders did not abandon tradition. In situations where traditional forms seemed best to achieve the end desired, they used the classical, the Gothic, the Georgian, the Spanish, and other styles. But the slavery to tradition that characterized the opening of the century had ended. In the buildings rising in the 1950's, the alert observer could discover the strength of the ties binding the modern United States with its own past and with that of western civilization, the fact of a two-way traffic in ideas across the Atlantic, and an emergence of an architecture as unique in spirit as American life.[10]

THE FINE ARTS

A common stereotype of America found in Europe and even Asia is the concept of American civilization as one dominated by the machine whose cultural crowning glory is the assembly line. A favorite cliché in France is that Americans are barbarous. The caricature grows out of ignorance and is often fostered by envy or outright hostility. The Department of State makes continuous efforts to combat the negative and distorted images that circulate abroad. Its task is made more difficult by the fact that Europeans and Asiatics can afford to come to America only in relatively small numbers to see the United States at first hand. But the Department has met this situation with an increasingly effective program of exchange of persons. In addition the Department has sent abroad symphony orchestras, individual singers (Marian Anderson), an opera (*Porgy and Bess*), drama (*J. B.* and *The Skin of our Teeth*), jazz artists (Louis Armstrong) and exhibitions of painting and sculpture. One of its most important successful undertakings is libraries of information about America in a great many important cities. The American exhibit at the Brussels Fair of 1958

---

[10] Lewis Mumford, *Roots of Contemporary American Architecture* (New York: Reinhold, 1952) ; Lewis Mumford, *From the Ground Up* (New York: Harcourt, Brace, 1956); James Marston Fitch, *American Building: The Forces that Shape It* (Boston: Houghton Mifflin, 1948); Christopher Tunnard and Henry H. Reed, *American Skyline: The Growth and Form of our Cities and Towns* (Boston: Houghton Mifflin, 1955).

and the extensive American display at Moscow in 1959 presented American art in all its forms along with the products of material culture. The resources upon which the American government can call in the middle of the twentieth century suggest the magnitude of the development in the arts since 1900.

Museums have played a major role in the evolution of understanding and appreciation of art among the American people. Important art museums, such as the Metropolitan Museum in New York City, came into being in the second half of the nineteenth century. Since 1900 museums have proliferated. The wealth of the Republic has made it possible for Americans to acquire a significant fraction of the great art of the Western tradition. In the middle of the twentieth century some of these art treasures were in the possession of private collectors, but museums made the great bulk of these imports open to the public. These institutions could not equal in artistic wealth those of Paris, Rome, or Florence. However, it was true that no historian could study thoroughly any important aspect of the heritage of European art without visiting American museums. The museums contain an even more significant proportion of oriental art, from Japan to India. In them, in addition, he could find the long history of art in the United States.

Into the American museums trooped millions of persons—school children sent on particular assignments, adults to enjoy the general collections. Museum directors put on view an almost continuous succession of special shows. Many museums made available reproductions primarily to distribute good art as widely as possible among the people. The contrast between the art available to the American public in the 1850's and the 1950's is one of the striking and important transformations in American history.

Parallel with that change went the development of art instruction in the schools. It appeared in the grammar and secondary schools. In the middle of the twentieth century courses in the history and the appreciation of art had achieved an important place in the curricula of the liberal arts colleges. Professional schools of art and design took their places beside those of law and medicine.

In sculpture and painting the twentieth century saw a development similar to that in architecture. Traditional representational art continued to express the American scene and American life and aspirations. In the field of representational art an evolving photography made outstanding contributions. Partly because of this fact, a growing company of painters and sculptors abandoned tradition and, pioneering on many fronts, sought beauty in shapes, patterns, and colors that represented nothing but themselves. The "modern" art of the mid-twentieth century made, particularly at the Brussels Fair in 1958, a significant impact on the art world of Europe. In its own way it represented American creative energy under liberty. It provided, moreover, a striking contrast with the representational "realism" enforced by the government on Soviet art.

The story of music in the twentieth century had many parallels with that of painting. The pioneering orchestras of the middle of the nineteenth century inaugurated a movement that put an orchestra in every important city. Through these and many other musical organizations, Americans achieved distinguished performance of music. At the same time out of different corners of the nation came an indigenous music —jazz, blues, swing—the creation originally of the Negro who had in the nineteenth century added the spirituals to the folk music of America. Professional schools of music gave training in performance and composition. Beside the popular music appeared a serious music in which tradition and innovation blended. Indigenous music entered the theatre to produce such musicals as "Oklahoma" and "My Fair Lady." The mass acceptance of hi-fi and stereophonic recordings, a phenomenon of the middle decades of the century, brought music of superior quality into American homes. In 1851, when Stephen Foster wrote "Old Folks at Home" for the minstrel stage, Americans were just beginning to emerge from what, by comparison with Italy, France or Germany, was a musical desert. A century later music had become a part of almost every aspect of American life.[11]

In this twentieth century of growth and change and war, the American people expressed themselves as never before through the arts. Mass communication brought art to the great audience. In fluid America, whose people were a blend of many ethnic strains and where social classes had uncertain boundaries, an art that expressed the emotions and tastes of the masses of the people found expression in music, in the cinema, and later in the entertainments of television. This art of the people took its place beside the elite art derived from the

---

[11] Some references on the fine arts in the United States are Oliver W. Larkin, *Art and Life in America* (New York: Rinehart, 1949); John I. H. Baur, *Revolution and Tradition in Modern American Art* ([Library of Congress Series in American Civilization] Cambridge: Harvard University, 1951); Alan S. Downer, *Fifty Years of American Drama, 1900-1956* (Chicago: Regnery, 1951); Bernard Rosenberg and David M. White, eds., *Mass Culture: The Popular Arts in America* (Glencoe, Ill.: Free Press, 1957) ; Marshall W. Stearns, *The Story of Jazz* (New York: Oxford University, 1956).

artistic tradition of the West. But there was as little clash between the two as between American social classes. Partisans of elite art enjoyed the musicals and followed the comments on life made by the comic strips of the daily press. The so-called masses in great numbers visited the museums of traditional and of modern art and supported the orchestras of their public schools and their cities. The phenomenon of the art festival appeared where musical programs were performed in the open in a city park, and near-by art of all kinds was displayed under canvass. In this mingling of the arts of the appeal to the elite and to the great audience, both fine creation and mediocre performance stood side by side. But the more significant aspect of the middle of the twentieth century could be found in the fact that Americans not only viewed and listened to art but also, as amateurs and professionals (painters, actors, craftsmen and musicians), practiced art as never before in the history of the nation.

CHAPTER XIX

American History in the Middle Grades

W. Linwood Chase

INTRODUCTION

MANY critics of education believe that history and geography lost their significance in the elementary curriculum when they were no longer found under those designations. Social studies meant to them an unpalatable mess of undistinguishable content watered down by the inclusion of social activities that had little relation to honest, substantive material. They did not distinguish between social studies as a subject matter area and social education which requires the development of personal competencies in human relationships. Unfortunately, there are too many elementary classroom teachers who also fail to make these distinctions. Even at the middle grade level there must be concern for the learning of content. It is beyond the scope of this chapter to outline a curriculum and a teaching program which properly places social studies in relation to the rest of social education.

The literature dealing with curriculum contains words of warning concerning the place of history in the elementary school. Alilunas says:

Let us face the issue squarely. The pedagogical problem is not that children study too little history in the elementary school grades but rather that they study too much history too soon in their lives. . . . The plain fact is that children do not have a "natural interest" in the past. Their "natural interest" is in the present, in themselves, and in the world around them as they perceive it. . . . School history is dry and meaningless to children, not so much because of the poor teaching of history, but because children would rather face their own everyday life-adjustment problems. Their own social life is real and meaningful. History is not direct and real to them. History is an indirect experience, and it requires cognitive qualities which cannot be expected psychologically of children. . . . A program of social education which is built around children's everyday living problems would seem to be a great deal more desirable than a program which, in the name of school

329

history, compels children to parrot meaningless dates and phrases at too early an age.[1]

Preston presents a different viewpoint,

History that consists in surveying vast spans of time in a single school term with emphasis on the sequence of events has little justification in the elementary school. Where sufficient time is allowed, however, for the learner to linger and become immersed in the detail of a period—the character of the people, customs, dress, language, literature, art, science, games, and education —history becomes one of the most fruitful sources of social studies content.[2]

Alilunas believes, as do others, that children have no real interest in history. Allen takes a different approach.

Children's interests are likewise the subject of re-evaluation. It is perhaps a truism that interest is not merely something children have but something that can be built with proper materials and effective teaching. But, if this has been taken for granted, it has not always been acted upon.[3]

HISTORY WITHOUT SCHOOLING[4]

Alilunas says children "do not have a natural interest in the past" but "in the world around them as they perceive it." But, let us suppose that no history of any kind were taught either formally or informally in the elementary school. Let us suppose further that all adults completely shunned any discussion with children in the area of learning commonly designated as history. Such suppositions serve only to highlight two important but sometimes dormant observations. One, that evidences of the past are always present and form the basis of much that is important in relationships between adults and children. And two, that the curiosities, interests, and needs of children lead to a penetration of the past, regardless of adult controls.

Traditionally, American schools have long sought to develop instructional programs in the field of history which would have meaning for children and at the same time transmit to each younger generation the factual information considered important by each preceding generation. Yet, the same schools bent over backwards in supplying and insisting upon a quantity and quality of historical information which was far too difficult for elementary school children. Intentions

---

[1] Leo J. Alilunas, "History for Children—Too Much Too Soon," *Elementary School Journal*, 52:215-20; December 1951. (*passim*)

[2] Ralph C. Preston, *Teaching Social Studies in the Elementary Schools* (New York: Rinehart, revised, 1958), p. 41.

[3] Jack Allen, "Social Studies for America's Children," *Phi Delta Kappan*, 40: 280; April 1959.

[4] Portions of this section have been adapted from an earlier article by this writer: "History for Today's Children," *The Packet* (Boston: Heath, October 1946).

were good but, as in other subject areas, an understanding of the problems of child growth and development was limited. A review of elementary history textbooks of the nineteenth century astounds us today because of the amount of detail, and yet quite possibly over-telling was better than no telling.

In the everyday living of boys and girls their ordinary experiences cause them to raise questions which require answers involving aspects of history. True, many questions seem rather superficial in nature, but others are so searching that they require complete discussion or direction to the sources where answers can be found at the maturity level of the inquirer.

There are many experiences that children may have today quite apart from school which reach into the field of history:

1. *They compare and contrast ways of living.* If their parents, grandparents, relatives, or neighbors came to settle in this country, with Old World traditions, songs, books, attitudes, and ways of living, questions are apt to arise that necessitate the exploration of historical backgrounds.

2. *They listen to tales of the past.* No elementary school child today remembers *the first* automobile or *the first* airplane. But grand-father's vivid accounts of how they looked and operated give the child some meaningful comparisons between the past and the present.

3. *They observe or take part in the celebration of national and local holidays.* All holidays, even those religiously and politically inspired, have historical meanings. The Cub Scout who marches on July 4, the boy on the sidewalk who on November 11 watches the parade of the veterans of foreign wars, or the child who observes the re-enactment of Texas' Independence Day returns to school with an added bit of knowledge and often great curiosity and interest.

4. *They possess relics of a past era.* A doll made in another coun-try or dressed in the costume of a different time; a music box from Austria; great-great-grandfather's handmade knife which had skinned many a Maine bear; a sea chest of clipper ship days; these are step-pingstones along the path of history.

5. *They notice place names.* Place names sometimes intrigue chil-dren. Places have been named for famous men, for local characters, for local events, for features of local topography, and for places from which the original settlers came. Other names show the influence of various national groups, and many are original Indian names.

6. *Monuments and markers.* "On this site stood . . .," "In this house . . .," "Appeal to the Great Spirit of . . .," lists of heroes on

plaques in public squares—such inscriptions are found at highway crossroads, in community centers, and in city parks all over the country. Though many of these have existed for a long time, it is within comparatively recent years that historical and civic organizations have shown increased interest in marking historical places or symbolizing historical events.

7. *They use maps.* Maps tell stories to those who know how to read them and raise questions that history can answer. To children maps are records of adventure, as they learn some of the stories behind the wavy black lines, the dots, and the many other symbols used.

8. *They collect.* Children collect everything from baseball players on bubblegum cards to old coins, stamps, autographs, and pictures of flags or ships. Collecting interests are extremely varied, but many have far greater meaning when historically oriented by the child himself and by others in response to the child's questions.

9. *They talk with elderly neighbors.* Their reminiscences of how things used to be and how they became what they are now appeal tremendously to many children.

10. *They read.* During the past fifteen years the number of books written for children based on events in history or life in the past has increased markedly. Wide reading of such books makes a considerable difference in historical sophistication.

11. *They travel.* Modern transportation has made known to them a world with far wider horizons than was known to children two decades ago. Some of them have not only read about but actually have seen pueblo houses in New Mexico; Japanese cherry trees along the Potomac Basin; Pilgrim Village and *Mayflower II* in Plymouth, Massachusetts.

12. *They have relatives or friends in the armed services.* As long as any of the veterans who went to the most distant corners of the globe in World War II, or in more recent assignments overseas, continue to live, their children and their children's children will hear stories that will whet their desires for further knowledge—knowledge that can come from the fields of history and geography.

13. *They view television.* In spite of the legitimate criticism that can be made of television fare there is no question that it presents some history if one can separate the wheat from the chaff. At least it must be considered a source of non-school materials.

CHILDREN'S QUESTIONS

A child's questions indicate to some degree his needs and his interests. A number of research studies on children's questions have implications for those who plan the curriculum of the elementary school. In a study done in 1952 under the direction of the writer, 4,740 children in the fourth, fifth, and sixth grades were told:

> If someone had the time and knew enough to answer all of your questions, what questions would you ask? Perhaps you have seen something, heard something, read something, or just thought about something which made you wish someone could answer questions for you about those things. On your papers write down all those questions you would like to have answered.[5]

The directions were carefully written so that there would be no danger of cueing into the social studies. Yet 49.23 per cent of the 54,389 questions asked were classified in the area of social studies. A greater per cent of the boys' questions (51.59) than the girls' questions (46.94) were in this area.

The social studies questions were classified in eleven categories. A recent re-examination of the study indicated that six of those categories could be considered in the field of history; that is, the answers to most of the questions would be found in historical writing or in reference material that would be classified as historical. These categories were: man as a social being; American history and government; communication; travel and transportation; inventions; and war. The questions classified as historical in these six categories comprised 54.37 per cent of all the social studies questions in grade four, 63.06 per cent in grade five, and 66.66 per cent in grade six. In terms of all questions asked, the historical questions were 28.23 per cent of the total questions asked in the fourth grade, 31.23 per cent in the fifth grade, and 31.00 per cent in the sixth grade.

TIME RELATIONSHIPS

The more the writer has carried on research in the field of time relationships the less willing he is to accept earlier findings which would defer teaching definitive history and time relationships until increasing age has given increased maturity to children. Presumably the earlier assumption must have been based on the premise that teaching was done en masse with uniform assignments and uniform recitations. If individual differences are taken into account, as necessary in teaching history as in teaching arithmetic or spelling, one would find many middle grade children perfectly capable of ordering events chronologically and developing an historical time sense.

Alilunas apparently questions whether the elementary school pupil can grasp time relationships. He warns that:

---

[5] Edythe T. Clark, and others, "What Children Want to Know About Their World" (Unpublished Ed. M. Thesis, Boston University School of Education, 1952).

Wesley, Johnson, and other specialists in the teaching of history have recognized that history without time relationships is impossible. Yet, the sense of chronology which deals with events in sequence and which is so indispensable to the study of the past comes late with children. . . . Most children are eleven years old before they have a full understanding of reckoning time, and most of them do not have any sense of chronology before they are in grade 6. They are sixteen years old before they catch up with adults in their understanding of time words and dates, and it is not until they are in gradę 12 that they acquire a satisfactory perspective in being able to number events in chronological order. Maturation, not specific training in time concepts, brings about time sense.[6]

The present writer finds that, although Henry Johnson insisted on the value and necessity of developing a time sense in history, he wrote:

Placing facts in the distant past is, it is urged, a useless exercise anywhere in the elementary school. It can mean to children only "a long time ago." But that is about what it means to many adults. . . . It by no means follows that the time sense is beyond cultivation. It can and should be cultivated, and the cultivation can and should begin in the first grade.[7]

Davis has recently reported on an experiment in teaching time zones to fourth, fifth, and sixth grade children. He writes,

Time and space concepts are two which have been greatly affected by the deferment doctrine. The experiment indicates that instruction about time zones is profitable earlier than was formerly thought possible. These results raise serious questions concerning social studies theory which advocates deferment of these concepts. If this study is indicative of possible findings in other areas of concept development, the deferment theory may have to be modified radically. Much additional experimentation must be conducted in order that curriculum workers may have substantial and realistic evidence with which to make decisions about what should be included in the instructional program and when it is to be taught.[8]

Davis believes that a child is capable of greater depth of learning and greater understanding of concepts than is frequently asserted. According to him,

A child will not learn the most intricate subtleties of most concepts, but he may be able to learn something about them. That his understanding may be incomplete is no cause for complaint and no justification for deferment. There is reason, however, for serious attention to be given to the level of

---

[6] Alilunas, "History for Children," p. 218-19.

[7] Henry Johnson, *Teaching of History* (New York: Macmillan, revised, 1940), p. 101.

[8] O. L. Davis, Jr., "Children Can Learn Complex Concepts," *Educational Leadership*, 17:170-75; December 1959.

meaning he has attained and for careful selection of experiences which will stimulate his continued growth. Rigid assignment of concepts to particular grade levels probably is impossible and certainly undesirable. Provision should be made for opportunities for the sequential development of concepts throughout the curriculum. Continuity and not "complete" mastery, is an essential element of all instructional plans.

A concern for time relationships should begin in the primary grades. A frequency count of a million and a half running words in reading materials in grades one, two, and three was made by Janes to determine the time concepts having the greatest frequency. They are listed in order of frequency.[9]

Grade 1	Grade 2	Grade 3
then	then	then
now	when	when
day	day	day
soon	now	time
time	time	now
morning	soon	soon
when	morning	as
again	again	again
birthday	night	night
night	never	morning
old	before	year
year	once	before
winter	after	never
once	winter	last
first	as	winter
spring	sometime	after
tomorrow	old	once
after	last	while
by and by	until	until
	summer	week
	year	old
	today	first
	always	minute
	spring	summer
	while	always
	minute	sometime
	week	today
	long	long
	tomorrow	still
		spring

---

[9] Ada J. Janes, et al., "A Study of Time Concepts Found in Primary Reading Materials" (Unpublished Ed. M. Thesis, Boston University School of Education, 1950).

Studies at Boston University of the spontaneous speaking vocabulary of children in the primary grades show a remarkably close resemblance to the above lists although the words are not in exactly the same order.

If primary teachers would enrich these words when met in reading in the same way they enrich unfamiliar words for permanent retention, they would be laying the groundwork for the foundation of time concepts and time relationships. There is nothing to be lost and much to be gained by this attention. Furthermore, at every opportunity teachers should develop in their pupils the habit of looking for time relationships through the words and phrases that express them. It is quite possible that one of the reasons time relationships have not been better understood is the neglect of concern for them.

In 1952, Callahan constructed a test in time relationships. It consisted of 24 questions in four categories.[10]

Six questions were concerned with putting in chronological order past events or artifacts, related to each other or to a given present event or artifact. For example:

Item 21. The correct time can be learned at any time by calling the telephone operator. Since early days, men have reckoned time in many ways. Some of the ways of telling time are listed below. Number them, from the earliest method to the most modern method.

    .... shadow stick
    .... clock
    .... sundial
    .... sun and moon
    .... hourglass

Six questions were concerned with putting in chronological order past events or artifacts, unrelated to each other, but related to a given present event or artifact.

Item 9. The Statue of Liberty stands in New York harbor as a symbol of freedom of the American people. Through the years, many people have done things which helped us to become a free nation, and allowed us to remain free. Number them, in order of the time that they occurred.

    .... The United States and its allies were victorious in their war against the dictator nations.
    .... The Pilgrims left England so that they could have freedom of worship.

[10] Mary G. Callahan, "The Construction and Evaluation of a Test in Time Relationships for Grades V, VI, VII, and VIII" (Unpublished Ed. M. Thesis, Boston University School of Education, 1952).

.... Lincoln signed the Emancipation Proclamation.

.... Paul Revere rode to Concord and Lexington to warn the people that the British were coming.

.... The Declaration of Independence was signed.

Six questions were concerned with putting in chronological order past events or artifacts, related to each other, without a present event or artifact being given.

Item 7. Ever since the colonies declared their independence, American generals have led their armies to victory in many wars. Number the names of the generals listed below, in order of the time they commanded armies as generals.

.... Ulysses S. Grant

.... Andrew Jackson

.... John Pershing

.... George Washington

.... Douglas MacArthur

Six questions were concerned with putting in chronological order past events or artifacts, unrelated to each other, without a present event or artifact being given.

Item 10. Here is another set of newspaper headlines of events that have happened in history. Put 1 in front of the event that happened first, number 2 in front of the event that happened next, and so on through number 5.

.... LAFAYETTE COMES TO AID OF WASHINGTON

.... EISENHOWER CHOSEN LEADER OF NATO FORCES

.... BELL INVENTS THE TELEPHONE

.... FULTON'S FOLLY REACHES ALBANY

.... ATOMIC TESTS AT BIKINI SUCCESSFUL

The 24 questions were taken at random from the four categories to make up the sequence of items in the test.

In May of 1960 this test was given again to all the 192 children in the fifth grade and all the 200 children in the sixth grade in a Massachusetts town. Since the score on such a test should stem from the correspondence, or lack of it, between the correct order and the order presented for evaluation, no deviation gave an item a score of 5, and a deviation of 2 a score of 4. Obviously, in sequence items there can never be just one item out of place. But, it must be noted that a deviation of 2 means that the order of only two out of five items was exchanged by the pupil and that the remaining three items were in proper sequence and in correct relationship to the other two. Therefore, in this report, the quality of understanding of time relationships is determined by the per cent of scores of 5 and 4 out of the total possibilities in the 24 items of the test.

Per Cent of Success in Ordering Chronological Events
of 192 Fifth Grade Pupils and 200 Sixth Grade Pupils

	Grade 5	Grade 6
Total grade group	34.7	37.5
Upper 27%	56.7	61.8
Lower 27%	16.9	19.1

Since there was a difference in success among the individual items, the data were further examined in relation to success in the four categories of the 24 items. There was unevenness in success on the six questions in each category but the over-all picture is presented below.

Per Cent of Success in Ordering Chronological Events of 192 Fifth Grade Pupils and 200 Sixth Grade Pupils According to Certain Categories

	Grade 5			Grade 6		
	Total	Upper 27%	Lower 27%	Total	Upper 27%	Lower 27%
Related past events to present event	44	61	27	53	76	33
Unrelated past events to present event	39	65	15	40	63	24
Related past events without present event	24	45	11	27	49	11
Unrelated past events without present event	31	54	12	30	57	8

Certain conclusions can be drawn from the data, although not all of them can be taken from those presented above:

1. Boys in the fifth grade scored higher in 17 of the 24 questions than the girls.

2. In the sixth grade, boys were higher than the girls in 19 and were the same in one other.

3. Sixth grade boys were better in 16 of the 24 questions than the fifth grade and were the same in one.

4. Sixth grade girls were better in 15 of the 24 questions than fifth grade girls.

5. Boys and girls together in both grades scored higher in the two categories when they were required to put in chronological order past events or artifacts, related and unrelated to each other, but related to a given present event or artifact, than in the two categories where past events or artifacts were not related to a present event or artifact.

The percentage of success reported in this time relationship is not necessarily indicative of the desirability of developing this aspect of learning as a major task in teaching history in the middle grades. On the other hand, probability that a large percentage of children may not yet be ready for emphasis on time relationships should not mean that such teaching ought to be deferred for all. If the focus of the school should be on instructional service to the individual child, we cannot conscientiously evade the responsibility of developing time relationships with some children in the middle grades, and doing so as fast as they are capable of learning. There are no definite quantities of time relationships instruction that are to be allocated to definite grades—going just so far in a particular grade and no further. It is quite likely that some fifth grade youngsters will be further developed in this aspect of learning than some seventh graders.

Who says a ten-year-old cannot learn and understand with some degree of accuracy the passage of time in history? To a ten-year-old, time in history can be long, long ago when there were no white men in our country. Time in history can be the first men crossing the Atlantic to our eastern shores, and other discoverers and explorers followed by more explorers. It can be the settlers coming after the explorers, leaving old homes in old lands and making new homes in new lands. It can be wars that must be fought which changed people's ways of thinking about themselves, and inventions which changed people's ways of living. It can mean that one hundred years ago was a time when his great-grandfather was living, and that two hundred years were only three generations further back. It can mean that when cities like New York, Detroit, and San Francisco began there were only a few houses in the new settlements, and that year by year they grew larger. It can mean the town in which he lives has birthdays and once it was one year old.

History for boys and girls need not be mere memorization of isolated facts or a conglomeration of meaningless dates and ideas. Much of the history of our country can be thrilling and exciting. True, the teacher has to work at it to make it that way for boys and girls. Almost, conversely, one has to work at it in some fashion to make it dull and unpalatable.

AIMS AND OBJECTIVES FOR STUDYING HISTORY

Cooper says history for the elementary child may be provided in different kinds of frameworks, but some sort of framework is necessary. Social studies may be organized within a geographical framework, a historical framework, or some combination of the two. He says that history can teach elementary school pupils such things as the following:[11]

---

[11] Kenneth S. Cooper, George Peabody College for Teachers, in a talk before the National Council for the Social Studies, Pittsburgh, 1957.

1. *Who they are.* Knowledge of the past, formal or informal, is an essential part of self-discovery. A pupil comes to understand that he is an American only as he learns who Americans are. He discovers who Americans are through a knowledge of what Americans have done. Self-identification does not stop here. The pupil can know himself only if he also knows something of others. The child must know there *are* and *have been* other peoples who have achieved important things.

2. *Acts have consequences.* To understand this, we must see human activities in time. What is happening is partly the result of what has happened. Chronology as such is not a proper study in the elementary schools, but human activity in time is, because only in this way can the abstract idea that acts have consequences be made specific and understandable. The great value of history lies in this fact: it clothes the abstractions of thought in the specific reality of human actions.

3. *A respect for human achievement.* A large part of the appreciation of any thing depends upon knowing the story behind it. The alphabet does not strike us as a remarkable matter until we understand how writing developed. Our enthusiasm for what man has done depends directly upon knowing what he has done.

4. *How we learn.* Nothing has been more deadly in the teaching of history than the idea that history is a complete and unquestioned body of facts. The student needs to learn how we learn about man and so come to understand the limits of our knowledge. History affords many opportunities to show how we came to know what we do. It also gives many chances to indicate the limits of our knowledge. As pupils come to understand this, they will also come to understand that the mere fact that a thing is printed in a newspaper or broadcast on television does not make it so.

Lists of aims for studying history in the elementary school should tell us the kinds of growth and development to be promoted or achieved through instruction. They must be based on the maturity level of children and be within their range of intellectual achievement.

In the listing or classification of aims there is no end. Courses of study and literature on the teaching of history abound with objectives ranging from two or three main classifications to scores itemized in great detail. This writer suggests thinking of objectives for the teaching of history in two categories: (a) those concerned with growth and development in the appreciations, attitudes, and understandings already well established and generally accepted as concrete and achievable by the majority of workers and writers in the field of teaching history in the elementary school, and (b) those concerned with growth and development in functional skills and habits necessary in using and understanding materials that will continuously contribute to the further building of appreciations, attitudes, and understandings.

Among the appreciations, attitudes, and understandings, now quite generally accepted as aims, are the following:

1. To learn the historical method of establishing facts (how we know what we know)
2. To appreciate the contributions of the past
3. To provide some perspective for looking at the modern world
4. To be aware of the nature of one's social environment
5. To understand the interdependence of peoples
6. To comprehend historical allusions in everyday reading
7. To understand that the past has had a great influence on our present patterns of living
8. To develop intelligent patriotism
9. To understand that continuity and change characterize progress
10. To understand that change is an inevitable part of life
11. To acquire a lasting interest in history
12. To develop a sense of time, and relationship between time and place
13. To have the vicarious experience of reliving the events of history
14. To understand that history was made by common folk as well as those of high degree
15. To use facts constructively in creative thinking
16. To understand something of the motives which led people to act as they did
17. To develop belief and action in democracy as a way of life
18. To understand that history is being made continuously
19. To realize the magnitude of the changes in the world in the last few years.

To develop the skills and habits that should contribute continuously to the further building of appreciations, attitudes, and understandings, we should consider such aims as:

1. To read content material with understanding
2. To read history with feeling
3. To identify and organize major and minor ideas for outlining and summarizing
4. To secure and use information from many sources
5. To read pictures, maps, globes, graphs, charts, etc., for information
6. To express ideas orally and in writing
7. To plan, carry out, and evaluate activities
8. To develop ability in associational reading where one combines his own experiences and purposes with the material read, criticizes the selection, finds illustrations of or exceptions to the author's statements, suggests further research or classroom activities, or in other ways responds independently of the subject matter.

MAKING HISTORY COME ALIVE

History is a "live" subject, a story of men and women and children and the ways in which they have lived. Events that happened four thousand, one thousand, five hundred, one hundred years ago; what people did in our grandfather's time, last year, yesterday, all have had their influence on the way we are living today.

To a ten-year-old, history can be tramping the wilderness with Daniel Boone, raising the flag with the Marines at Iwo Jima, living with seventy-five others 'tween decks on the *Mayflower* in the long voyage across the Atlantic, riding with Paul Revere through the night to Concord town, and floating down the Mississippi with Pere Marquette. It can be an Indian watching the *Santa Maria* and her sister ships drop anchor, climbing the heights of Darien with Balboa, surveying with Washington in virgin territory, imprisonment by Indians with Captain John Smith, and traveling under the North Pole in a nuclear-powered submarine. It can be seeing new homes rise one by one in Jamestown, tasting buffalo meat on the trek by covered wagon across the western plains, smelling exploding gunpowder in many a French and Indian battle, feeling cold water rise to one's armpits in Arnold's march to Quebec, and hearing the great peal of the Liberty Bell on that First Fourth of July.

This is history for our boys and girls if we make it that way.

The memorization of names and dates, causes of wars, and provisions of treaties can be exceedingly dull. Rich associations built around the principal events of history can make the past seem exciting and always very real, and give it enough dramatic detail so that there comes full realization that the people in history books once walked and talked and played and worked. History study that is dull makes children say, "So what? What difference does all that make to me?" History study that satisfies the needs and interests and the natural desire of children to know why things are as they are makes them say, "History isn't like studying at all; it is like going on a new adventure every day."

The clues to making history attractive are (1) making the objectives clear and meaningful; (2) providing a variety of learning activities (reading, discussion, trips, drill, dramatics, and so on); (3) emphasizing matters of personal interest to children, such as accounts of colorful personalities, home life, schools, details of work, games, folklore, and other details that create a feeling for the times; (4) emphasizing biography . . .; (5) bringing history "home" by making the most of local history, including examples of early architecture, heirlooms, dates on buildings, recollections of old-timers, historical roadside markers, and the like . . .; and (6) restricting the content of a unit to one period in history so that through this concentration children may have ample opportunity to discover how people lived.[12]

HISTORY FOR THE ELEMENTARY TEACHER

The training of the elementary teacher for instruction in the self-contained classroom often means that the teacher has too little basic course material in the social sciences which provides only a meagre acquaintance with important facts and concepts in that area. According to Hunnicutt and Grambs:

> Typically, the elementary social studies teacher has had only a limited collegiate education in the social sciences. Two or three introductory courses in sociology, geography, economics, history, or political science are probably the extent of his college-level social science. Some general education programs include a broad survey course that gives an overview of world history and United States history, plus some of the material from the other social sciences. Does this equip the elementary school teacher to do the kind of social studies teaching called for by writers about the modern school curriculum?[13]

If we are realistic we know that comparatively few elementary in-service teachers read history beyond the kinds of materials used by the children of the grade levels at which they teach. Yet, in the light of their general social science background and the fact that present historians are continually bringing their critical and interpretive powers to the task of re-examining all the remains that have come down from the past, there is a real need for the elementary teacher to do some planned reading in history even though he is not a specialist in the subject. With all the other pressures on the elementary teacher that exist this observation is easier for an outsider to make than for a teacher to follow.

However, we have in this Yearbook some material written by historians right at hand for the middle grade teacher. First, he can read those chapters which are directly applicable to the areas being taught in American history at his grade level. Second, he can read further in those chapter references, made by the historian, which appeal to him. Third, he can read other chapters not of immediate concern in his present curriculum which will enrich his total concepts in American history. Fourth, he can lay out a program of reading, guided by the references of the historians, if he is concerned about up-grading his historical scholarship.

---

[12] Preston, *Teaching Social Studies in the Elementary Schools*, p. 245.

[13] C. W. Hunnicutt, and Jean D. Grambs, "The Social Studies Under Fire," *Elementary School Journal*, 56:215; January 1956.

CHAPTER XX

American History in the Upper Grades and Junior High School

I. James Quillen

INTRODUCTION

A NATION's history is the record of its existence, and history is both a product and creator of national experiences. A nation's view of its own image is shaped largely by the common traditions it has developed. Narratives of struggle and crisis, heroes and heroism, courage and idealism, and problems and achievements help give the citizens of a nation common ideals, a sense of being a part of a common cause, and of having a common destiny. In highly developed contemporary cultures, national history is written and taught to the young. It is transmitted in part by parents, the mass media, cultural leaders, and by art, music, and literature, but its systematic transmission is largely the responsibility of the school.

HISTORY IN THE SCHOOL PROGRAM

American history became a subject of study in American schools as soon as independence was won. The political leaders of the new republic recognized the value of education in the development of a free society, and the particular value of history in this respect was recognized early. An American history textbook for use in the schools was published the year the Constitution was written.[1] The war of 1812 greatly stimulated American nationalism and patriotism, and by 1815, six different American history textbooks had been published in some twenty-three editions.[2]

---

[1] William H. Cartwright, "Evolution of American History in the Curriculum," in Richard E. Thursfield, ed., *The Study and Teaching of American History*, Seventeenth Yearbook of the National Council for the Social Studies (Washington, D. C.: The Council, 1947), p. 18.

[2] *Ibid.*, p. 19.

344

There is some question as to the grade placement of American history when it was first taught in the schools, but the evidence available indicates that the subject was taught first in the upper elementary grades, the level assigned for discussion in this chapter. Later other cycles of study were developed for the middle grades of the elementary school and for the senior high school.

Today the typical high school graduate has studied American history at least three times—in (1) the middle grades; (2) the upper grades and the junior high school; and (3) the senior high school. The three grade levels at which American history is most frequently offered are the fifth, the eighth, and the eleventh. Sometimes the cycles of American history at each of the three levels consist of two or three years each.[3] As Richard Gross and William Badger pointed out, "In Grade VIII the student usually is introduced to his second course in American history. There is greater unanimity throughout the United States on the desirability of this eighth grade offering than is true of any other social studies course or emphasis at any other grade level."[4]

It is evident that enough American history is taught. The problems are in the quality of the articulation of the various cycles, the selection of content, the materials of instruction, and the effectiveness of the teacher. Gross states:

Students resist courses in American history because: (1) there is too much overlap between the junior and senior high-school American history courses; (2) courses are stigmatized as required and comprise the largest-sized classes in the academic field; (3) there is resulting lack of time for individualized assignments and attention; (4) integration with courses offered at the same level is lacking; (5) interest in history is stifled by the catalogic names, dates, wars, and events that also too often characterize the preceding year's work in European backgrounds or world history; (6) the facts of United States history are taught as prime ends in themselves via a non-selective, birds-eye approach; (7) there is failure to select materials and experiences which are currently important and functional, and which would help to make history real, and thereby interesting to the student; (8) ill-prepared or uninterested teachers are often assigned to instruct the course; (9) discontent often develops in pupils as the result of the intangible but important factor of teacher personality; (10) there is general discontent with the larger school

[3] Edgar Wesley, Director, *American History in Schools and Colleges* (New York: Macmillan, 1944), p. 25-39.

[4] Richard E. Gross and William V. Badger, "Social Studies," in Chester W. Harris, ed., *Encyclopedia of Educational Research*, Third edition (New York: Macmillan, 1960), p. 1301.

environment; and (11) personal problems and/or conditions in home, community, nation and world are reflected in pupil attitude and effort.[5]

Some people would disagree with the point of view implied in a few of these complaints. However, no one who believes in the value of American history as a school subject can fail to be concerned about a number of them. The chapters written by the historians in this Yearbook can be helpful in dealing with several of these problems. The remainder of this chapter is concerned with how this can be done in the upper grades and the junior high school; for convenience, the American history course at this level will hereafter be referred to as the eighth grade course.

Many teachers believe that repetition is the major problem in the teaching of history in American schools. This is not so much of a problem at the eighth grade level as it is in the senior high school course because the content of the middle grades and eighth grade courses is fairly sharply differentiated. But the eighth grade and senior high school courses often cover the total chronology of American history, with much the same basic content. As a result a senior high school student taking American history often feels that he is repeating something he already has had, and hence, may lack interest in a further study of the subject. This attitude is, indeed, most unfortunate because a deep and abiding interest in the nation's history should be one of the most important outcomes of a high school education.

REASONS FOR STUDYING AMERICAN HISTORY

Many values have been advanced for the study of American history in the schools.[6] Those that are discussed here as most important for the eighth grade course are: (1) building citizenship; (2) understanding the present; (3) providing perspective and balance; (4) developing appreciation and contributing to the wholesome use of leisure; (5) improving critical thinking ability; (6) developing international understanding; and (7) relating and adding meaning to other school subjects. These values, of course, apply to all the courses in American history taught in the school, as well as to the eighth grade course.

---

[5] Richard E. Gross, Leslie D. Zeleny, and Associates, *Educating Citizens for Democracy* (New York: Oxford, 1958), p. 163.

[6] Wesley, *American History in Schools and Colleges*, p. 14-15; Lewis Paul Todd, "Opportunities for American History," in Thursfield, *Study and Teaching of American History*, p. 3-16; and Gross, Zeleny, and Associates, *Educating Citizens for Democracy*, p. 166-68.

Building Citizenship

The value of American history in the development of good citizens is one of the reasons it is so frequently taught in the schools. Through history a student comes to know his nation's ideals and traditions, the nature of its government, and the responsibilities of its citizens. In one sense, history is the door through which an individual can enter the edifice of his nation's culture. Without a knowledge of history, patriotism has no roots and loyalty no bonds tying it to the past. National history has often been distorted for the purpose of developing loyalty and patriotism. However, the firmest loyalty and love of country are built on a foundation of truth; and the more accurately an American understands the history of his country, the more intelligently he can serve it and assume his responsibilities as a citizen of a free society.

Understanding the Present

A knowledge of the past is necessary to any real understanding of the present. The past lives in the present. Our habits, language, clothing, homes, tools, public buildings, ideas, and skills are largely a heritage from the past. Without a knowledge of history a human being has little understanding of the things that surround him or the forces that bear on him in the present, and no firm basis upon which to predict the probable future. The present is, at best, elusive. What we consider the present consists largely of past memories and future hopes. Hence, history adds insight to vision and understanding to perception. As James Mill wrote over a hundred years ago, "It is only by our ideas of the past, that we have any power of anticipating the future. And if we had no power of anticipating the future, we should have no principle of action, but the physical impulses, which we have in common with the brutes."[7]

Providing Perspective and Balance

In times of conflict and difficulty, the individual is likely to be tempted by panaceas that are dangerous to the continuance of freedom. Rome had its bread and circuses, and millions of twentieth century humans have turned their backs on freedom to follow modern dictators who promise "pie in the sky." A knowledge of history can provide perspective and balance in considering contemporary problems and the promises of political leaders. A knowledge of the persistence of many major problems for centuries or milennia, of

---

[7] James Mill, *Analysis of the Phenomena of the Human Mind* (London: Baldwin and Cradock, 1829), vol. I, p. 87.

the human tragedy that has followed the unthinking acceptance of panaceas, and of the tremendous progress that the United States has made in many areas during its short history, can arm the citizen against those who promise easy solutions to complex and persistent problems.

Improving Thought

Providing perspective and balance is an example of the contribution of history to the improvement of critical thinking and problem solving. A study of history gives insight into concepts and information that can be woven into generalizations to use in thinking about new situations and in solving problems. The method of history itself is of great value here—the search for truth, the open yet judicious mind, the collecting and weighing of evidence, the balancing of divergent views, the organization of information into meaningful patterns, the search for clarity in understanding and expression— these are experiences to develop the intellect and give power to thought.

Developing Appreciation

Good history is also often good literature, and to develop a love for history is to gain an appreciation of good writing. Hence, the study of history can raise the level of appreciation and taste in the individual and provide resources for the wholesome use of his leisure. The current interest in historical fiction, biography, and history itself—particularly that about the Civil War—provides evidence that Americans in quite large numbers have developed an interest in history as literature and spend at least a part of their leisure in reading it.

Windows to the World

American history, narrowly conceived, can produce ethnocentrism and chauvinism. On the other hand, it can build international understanding and appreciation. American history is a part of world history. The discovery and settlement of America were a part of the expansion of European culture which began in the mid-fifteenth century; until the Revolution the Thirteen Colonies were a part of the British Empire; the ideas in the Declaration of Independence and the Constitution came, in part, from the eighteenth century Enlightenment in Western Europe; and the French and Indian Wars, the Revolution, and the War of 1812 were part of larger world conflicts and movements. Immigrants have come to the United States from all parts of the world. Many other examples of America's continued involvement in world affairs could be given. A study of American history can, thus, open windows to an understanding of world interdependence and help develop an appreciation of the contributions of other peoples to the American heritage and way of life.

Relation to Other Subjects

It is not surprising that American history has been a center for the correlation and fusion of subject matter from many areas, particularly in the junior high school. This is because history is concerned with the totality of things. In American history, students can learn about art, music, geography, literature, and science in their proper context as a part of the tapestry of civilization. They can read, write, and speak about interesting and challenging subjects. This richness, however, offers danger as well as opportunity. The attempt to tell the whole story can lead to superficiality and distortion. But a sensitivity to the relatedness of the subject matter and skills included in the school's program of study can add meaning and vitality to the study of American history as well as other subjects, regardless of the curricular organization of the school.

PARTICULAR EMPHASES IN THE EIGHTH GRADE AMERICAN HISTORY COURSE

The eighth grade American history course can contribute significantly to all of the purposes discussed above. However, this course, in many American schools, has a particular responsibility in developing an understanding of American institutions, building citizenship, developing an appreciation of the richness of American culture, developing an understanding of our American neighbors in the Western Hemisphere, and helping to build a mastery of basic social skills.

The eighth grade course in American history has the responsibility to go beyond the emphasis on ways of living stressed in the primary and middle grades and to develop an understanding of how Americans have established institutions better to serve their common needs. In the study of American history, the attempt to develop this understanding leads to a stress on the development of American government, economic and recreational institutions, and the development of education. These studies relate directly to the building of citizenship, which is another major responsibility of the seventh, eighth, and ninth grades. Through a study of his nation's history, the young American can begin to understand his own role in a free society—to understand that institutions are made by and for men and that in a democratic republic each citizen has a responsibility to do his part in making political and other institutions effective means for serving the good life. American history demonstrates that democratic citizenship is an active process that involves duties and responsibilities as well as rights and liberties.

In the junior high school, youths are exploring their own potentialities and building interests in order to select and later develop resources for work and leisure. American history can do much to further this exploration of ability and interest. The richness of the American pageant dramatizes the contribution of men and women with a wide variety of backgrounds and a wide range of talents. As indicated earlier, the place of art, music, and literature in American civilization can lead to. an appreciation of and interest in these carriers of culture and can lead to a deeper study and appreciation of them in regular courses in these subjects.

Finally, the upper elementary and junior high school grades carry a heavy responsibility in skill building. In contemporary civilization, the individual who cannot read, write, speak, and think effectively is severely handicapped. The American history course at this school level should pay particular attention to these and other skills, including locating information, map reading, note taking, the organization and interpretation of information, and the like. These skills may be developed by direct teaching, by the proper use of textbooks which stress skill building, and by the use of a wide range of materials in the classroom laboratory, the school library, and in the community generally. History textbooks for the eighth grade can make skill building an integral part of the teaching and learning activities. If such a program is not provided in the textbook, the teachers of eighth grade American history in a school system should develop their own program. What is done in the American history class should, of course, be related to and built upon what is done in skill development in other courses, particularly in courses in the skills themselves and in English courses.

ORGANIZATION AND CONTENT

As indicated earlier, American history was probably introduced into the curriculum of American schools in the upper grades. Hence, the current upper grades and junior high school course itself has a long history. Practically all pupils in American schools study American history in the seventh or eighth grades and some in both. A study made by Howard Anderson for the U.S. Office of Education showed that in 1946-1947 more than 90 per cent of the schools in the sample studied required a year of United States history in grades seven and eight.[8]

The content and organization of the upper grades American history course has changed considerably over the years. Before the Civil War, the early colonial period and wars, especially the Revolution, were stressed. Wars were studied by battles and politics by presidential administrations. There was little attention paid to social and economic history. For a considerable period, there was little differentiation between the upper grades and high school courses in American history—sometimes the same textbook was used in both courses. By 1920 the two courses had been differentiated somewhat with more attention to social and economic factors in the upper grades course and a larger percentage of time being given to the colonial period and the period before the Civil War generally.[9] Anderson found that in 1946-1947, "The median junior high school allots 26-30 per cent of the total time for instruction to the period of United States history before 1789, and 36-40 per cent to the period after 1865. The median senior high allots about 10 per cent more of the total time for instruction to the recent period, and 5 per cent less to each of the other two periods."[10] It is obvious from these data that the median differences between the junior and senior high school courses in allocation of emphasis to broad periods of time were not great. Moreover, Anderson found that practices in this regard varied greatly from school to school. In a number of schools the study of government was combined with the study of American history. In these schools, generally, special attention was given to the Constitution and the governmental structure that was based on it; and in some of them, time was devoted to state and local government as well.[11] It is unfortunate that a more recent study of practices in the teaching of American history at the various grade levels is not available.

The Committee on American History in Schools and Colleges recommended that the emphasis in the junior high school American

[8] Howard R. Anderson, *Teaching of United States History in Public Schools*, Office of Education Bulletin 1949, No. 7 (Washington, D. C.: Superintendent of Documents, U.S. Government Printing Office, 1949), p. 19.

[9] For a detailed analysis, see Dorothy Meredith, "Changing Content of American History Courses," in Thursfield, *Study and Teaching of American History*, p. 35-57. This account has been drawn on here.

[10] Anderson, *Teaching of United States History*, p. 20.

[11] *Ibid.*, p. 20.

history course be on the building of the nation, and that about two-thirds of the time be devoted to the period between 1776 and 1876, with the middle grades course stressing the period before 1789 and the senior high school course the period after 1865.[12] The topics recommended for the junior high school course were:

1. *The American Revolution:* As the outgrowth of colonial development, with attention to outstanding military events, the government during the war, the Articles of Confederation, and the Constitution.

2. *The Rise of Industrial Northeast, Plantation South, and Free-Farm West:* With attention to the geographic and economic factors which promoted sectionalism; sectionalism *versus* national interests.

3. *Territorial Development, the Struggle over New States, and the Civil War:* With attention to the use and influence of public lands, and to the strengthening of national unity.

4. *The Development of Waterways, Highways, Railways, and Airways, and of Domestic and International Trade:* With attention to pertinent inventions, trade routes, and the social effects of the cargoes carried.

5. *Recreation, Sport, and Social Life:* The rise of typical American games, and of resorts and vacation trips, of social clubs and organizations, of theaters, music, movies, and other commercialized amusements.

6. *The Rise and Influence of Major Communication Industries:* Postal service, press, telegraph, telephone, and radio; with attention to pertinent inventions, the industrial organization of these agencies and their cultural power.[13]

The skills to be emphasized were: (1) the interpretation of pictures, charts, diagrams and cartoons; (2) the use of maps; (3) making simple outlines; (4) locating information in reading materials; (5) making and evaluating generalizations; (6) summarizing; and (7) vocabulary building.[14]

While the author knows of no recent study comparable to that made by Anderson, the emphasis in widely used textbooks seems to indicate that eighth grade American history courses today follow the report of the Committee on American History in Schools and Colleges, to the extent that they devote relatively more time to the period before 1876, with special reference to the discovery and settlement of the Americas, colonial life, the Revolutionary War, the Constitution, the westward movement, the growth of sectionalism, and the Civil War.[15] Attention is also given to American neighbors to the North and South. Political, social, and emonomic, and sometimes

---

[12] Wesley, *American History in Schools and Colleges,* p. 70-71.

[13] *Ibid.,* p. 77.

[14] *Ibid.,* p. 78-79.

[15] Leo J. Alilunas and William Chazanof, "Trends in Eighth Grade American History Textbooks," *The Social Studies,* 50:214-16; No. 2, November 1959.

cultural, factors are stressed. William H. Cartwright has come to similar conclusions. In writing about the American history course in the junior high school as compared with the senior high school course, he states, "In general, it may be said that the junior high school course is a simpler and briefer treatment and that it gives relatively more attention to the period before 1865. It also usually places more emphasis than the senior high school on social and economic history."[16]

The course may be organized chronologically, topically, or by a combination of both. A few teachers use the problems approach, although this approach is used more often in the senior high school, and not very frequently in the teaching of American history there. In discussing the organization of the junior high school course, Cartwright says,

While schools organize their United States history courses in many different ways, three general types of organization prevail. One of these is to treat events more or less chronologically from the beginning to the end. Another is to organize them into topics, such as political development, economic development, social development, the westward movement, and international affairs. A third, and apparently growing, scheme is to follow the course of affairs chronologically to 1865, the year ending the War Between the States, and to use a topical arrangement for the period since that time.[17]

One way of organizing the junior high school course is to include the following:

1. Discovery, exploration, and settlement
2. Colonial life
3. The Revolution
4. The Constitution
5. Establishing the national government
6. The westward movement
7. Growing sectionalism
8. The War Between the States and its aftermath
9. The rise of industry
10. Transportation and communication
11. Education and the use of leisure
12. Improving health
13. Becoming a world power
14. Facing new problems
15. Neighbors to the North and South
16. American democratic ideals

---

[16] William H. Cartwright and Arthur C. Bining, *The Teaching of History in the United States* (Mexico, D.F.: Instituto Pan-Americano de Geografia e Historia, 1950), p. 24. Cartwright wrote the section on "The Teaching of History in the Schools of the United States"; for other recent references on content in American history courses see Gross and Badger, "Social Studies," p. 1302-1303.

[17] Cartwright and Bining, *The Teaching of History in the United States*, p. 24.

This organization is chronological to the end of the Reconstruction Period, and then it is largely topical. The course also can be organized by units. These might include: I. Colonial Ways of Living; II. Independence and Federation; III. A New Nation; IV. Frontier Life; V. Sectionalism and the War Between the States; VI. National Unity and Welfare; VII. Assuming World Responsibilities; and VIII. Facing the Problems of the Modern Age.

One of the most important problems in the teaching of American history in the elementary and secondary schools is the differentiation of content and emphasis between the three levels of offerings in the same school. As indicated earlier, it is particularly difficult to differentiate between the courses as usually offered in the junior and the senior high school. The middle grades course tends to stress biography and vivid narrative and usually does not attempt a systematic chronological treatment of the whole span of American history. However, both the junior and senior high school courses do attempt a relatively comprehensive treatment. Typically all that can be said about the difference between the usual eighth and eleventh grade courses is that the eighth grade course is "a simpler and briefer treatment" with more emphasis on social and economic topics and the period before 1865 or 1876. Perhaps greater differentiation could be secured if the eighth grade stressed a narrative account of the political, social, and economic development of the United States; while the eleventh grade course stressed the cultural and intellectual development—the history of ideas—and an interpretation of the meaning of American history. This approach, however, would be too advanced for a large proportion of high school youth and would overlap seriously with the usual college course. Local and state courses of study should pay careful attention to the problem of repetition between the eighth grade American history course and that taught in the senior high school. Some repetition for the purpose of reinforcement is desirable, but each course should have a clearly different emphasis and should contain substantially new content and materials. The relationship between junior and senior high school courses in American history and the general American history course taught in college also needs to be carefully examined. With the steadily growing proportion of youth graduating from high school and going on to college, it is becoming increasingly imperative for American history courses to form a planned sequence from the elementary school through the college.

USE OF HISTORIANS' CHAPTERS

The chapters by the distinguished historians in this Yearbook will be useful to both curriculum specialists and teachers.

Curriculum Specialists

One of the problems faced by curriculum directors in the field of American history is to give leadership to the selection of the content that is of most importance in developing an understanding of American culture and values. Comprehensiveness, balance, and articulation are difficult to achieve. The school program needs to provide full coverage of the basic content required to develop and understand American life. However, more emphasis should be given to the more important content and skills than to the relatively less important. Finally, the program should be developmental. The content of the upper grades and junior high school course in American history should utilize the knowledge acquired and skills developed in the middle grades course and provide for further development of understanding and competence in the senior high school course.

The content of this Yearbook shows the importance of viewing American history not only in its own total context, but also as a part of the history of western civilization, and of an increasingly interdependent world. The significance of intellectual and cultural factors in an understanding of American history is evident. Several chapters—particularly Chapter IX by Arthur Bestor—demonstrate the interrelationship of philosophy, literature, and history. The whole volume can be helpful to the curriculum director in gaining a clearer insight into the range of possibilities in American history for curricular organization. The richness of the content available, as shown by the helpful annotated bibliographies, should enable curriculum leaders to define more clearly the responsibilities of American history courses at each of the levels it is taught, and to reduce the repetition that is now so prevalent.

Curriculum directors will also find the chapters by historians useful in the preparation of teaching and resource units, in building up professional libraries for teachers, and in the selection of books for classroom and school libraries. One of the most urgent needs in the in-service education of teachers and the acceleration of learning for talented students is to make readily accessible to both teachers and students reading materials which represent the best in scholarship in the academic disciplines.

Use by Teachers

The greatest use of the Yearbook will be by teachers. The typical eighth grade teacher is responsible for several subjects, and yet effective teaching requires both a breadth and depth of knowledge in the subjects taught. The pamphlet series of the Service Center for Teachers of History of the American Historical Association has provided an excellent aid to teachers in keeping abreast of trends in scholarship in American history. This Yearbook, within the covers of a single volume, provides a comprehensive and detailed guide to the best recent publications in American history. A teacher with some background in American history can select from references cited in the Yearbook a few key works that will be helpful in providing knowledge in the areas where the teacher has particular concern and responsibility.

A teacher of upper grades and junior high school American history can use the knowledge acquired from the Yearbook in the following ways:

Planning the course. A knowledge of the most recent advances in scholarship in American history can enable a teacher to get a clearer understanding of what topics and content are most appropriate for the eighth grade course. It can also provide a basis for cooperation between teachers of American history at all levels and a clearer assignment of responsibility to each level. After the topics and content for the eighth grade are determined, the teacher can use the knowledge gained from the Yearbook in preparing resource and teaching units. If resource units are used in the school system, groups of teachers might work together on particular units. In this case, there could be some division of responsibility in reading monographic materials and deciding on what content is most appropriate. Assistance might be requested from teachers with special competence in literature, art, and music to enrich the units with suggestions in these areas.

Selecting textbooks. Teachers can use the knowledge gained from recent historical scholarship in the selection of textbooks. There is a tendency for American history textbooks used in the schools to lag behind the most recent advances in scholarship. Carr, Wesley, and Murra, while stating that scholarly accuracy in textbooks has increased, point out that, "one thorough investigation found serious lags between the first announcement of a new discovery or viewpoint in American history and its incorporation in American history textbooks."[18] Some delay in the incorporation of new viewpoints in text-books is no doubt desirable to provide for their careful testing; but this does not account for the persistence of inaccuracies, stereotypes, and discredited generalizations. Teachers need a depth of historical knowledge to decide which textbooks contain solid and accurate content, and interpretations that are substantiated by research. Too often textbooks are selected on the basis of their eye-appeal and the quality of their binding and paper. These things are important, but more important is the accuracy, comprehensiveness, balance, and over-all quality of the content in relation to the objectives of the course. Teachers can also use the many leads to good books in American history in choosing books for their own personal libraries and for classroom and school libraries.

The teaching process. If pupil-teacher planning is used, both a depth and breadth of knowledge of basic content are particularly important. The extent to which pupils can share effectively in the selection, organization, and interpretation of content depends not only on their maturity and capacity for self-direction, but even more on the knowledge of the teacher. If the teacher of a junior high school class in American history where pupil-teacher planning is being used does not have adequate knowledge, the result is almost certain to be superficiality in learning or worse. The quality of the instruction in American history is directly related to the knowledge possessed by the teacher, and the less the dependence on a single textbook, the greater is the importance of the teacher's knowledge. But even where a good textbook is used, the teacher needs a depth of knowledge and understanding to interpret accurately and clearly the concepts and generalizations presented, to stimulate students to gain as great a depth of knowledge as they are capable of acquiring, and to correct inaccuracies, misconceptions, and untenable interpretations that may be advanced by students in class discussions, oral reports, or written papers.

Brighter students can be stimulated to do reflective thinking by considering areas in historical interpretations where there is a lack of agreement among scholars. For example, Wesley Craven, in Chapter II of this Yearbook, refers to the "lively post-war debate on the character of the American Revolution" in which "the issues turn very largely on the question of how much change the Revolution wrought

---

[18] Edwin R. Carr, Edgar B. Wesley, and Wilbur F. Murra, "Social Studies," Walter S. Monroe, ed., *Encyclopedia of Educational Research*, Revised edition (New York: Macmillan, 1950), p. 1231; for other references to studies of American history textbooks see Gross and Badger, "Social Studies," p. 1309.

in an established way of life."[19] The answer to this question has considerable significance for the interpretation of both the late colonial period and the period that followed the Revolution. If the teacher can make pupils aware that historians are debating the significance of the Revolution as an instrument of social change, a powerful stimulant to critical thinking is added. In Chapter III, Clarence Ver Steeg, in discussing colonial self-government in the eighteenth century, says that, "Using local records to advantage, researchers have demonstrated that there was more political democracy than historians had previously suggested."[20] This conclusion will raise questions about statements found in a number of history textbooks, and if a teacher can make pupils aware of it, they again will be more likely to give thought to the factual support behind historical generalizations and to begin to understand more clearly the historical continuities in the development of American democracy.

Another important example of differences in historical interpretation is found in Chapter VII, where David Potter describes the different interpretations of the causes of the Civil War. In speaking of the literature on the War, he writes, "Perhaps the most pervasive quality which it all has in common is that it continues to be explicitly or implicitly controversial. Not only have historians failed to agree as to whether slavery furnished the basic motive for the war or whether it provided a smoke-screen for concealing the basic motives; they have also disagreed as to the nature of the society of the Old South, the nature of slavery, the motivation and character of the anti-slavery movement, and the interpretation of every link in the chain of sectional clashes which preceded the final crisis. The irony of this disagreement lies in the fact that it persists in the face of vastly increased factual knowledge and constantly intensified scholarly research."[21] The teacher can use this as an illustration of the complexity of historical interpretation. It can be pointed out that significant historical events usually have multiple rather than single causes, and that value factors are often present in the formation of historical conclusions, even when factual information is abundant.

It is not contended here that bright eighth grade students can contribute to the solution of complex problems in historiography. It is contended, however, that students at this level can recognize that

---

[19] Chapter II, p. 19.
[20] Chapter III, p. 31.
[21] Chapter VII, p. 118-19.

problems in the historical interpretation of important events do exist, and that such recognition will begin to lay a foundation for objectivity and critical-mindedness which can be developed further as maturity and knowledge increase in later years in high school and college. Some eighth grade students can balance evidence pro and con on a historical issue and at least arrive at a rational explanation of why they hold a particular conclusion.

Meeting individual differences. As all teachers know, the range of individual differences in the eighth grade, as well as in other grades, is great. Some students can be motivated to develop a high level of historical understanding and competence in problem solving. Other students will have difficulty in comprehending simple historical narratives. What is not always recognized, however, is that a depth of knowledge is required in teaching both gifted and retarded students. Some textbook authors and teachers have assumed that the best approach to a slow learner is to provide him with a skeleton-like summary of the same material that is studied in richer detail by students who are more intellectually able. In fact, a summary of a historical event or period is more difficult to understand and requires more background and insight for authentic interpretation than does a more detailed account.

What is needed by slower learners is a more careful selection of the topics and concepts they are to study, so that these can be reduced to a minimum, and then even more enrichment by abundant concrete detail on the fewer topics and concepts studied. As Henry Johnson points out in his classic book on the teaching of history in elementary and secondary schools,

Any kind of history is elementary if it is presented in the form of concrete examples—material remains, physical representations of material remains and of actions, verbal description and narration rich in material for imagery, mental states directly and obviously related to things which can be clearly imaged. Elementary history, whatever its content, is history brought within the sensory experience of children. Any other history is advanced. History presented in the form of generalities is advanced history. . . . A fact presented in one way is elementary; the same fact presented in another way is advanced.[22]

The content in the chapters by historians in this Yearbook will help teachers in the selection of content for both gifted and slow

[22] Henry Johnson, *Teaching of History,* Revised edition (New York: Macmillan, 1940), p. 103.

students. Some textbook publishers are now beginning to publish textbooks with the same basic organization on different ability levels so that they can be used together in the same class or in different classes where grouping on the basis of ability is practiced.

Keeping abreast of historical scholarship. One of the major problems of a classroom teacher is to keep informed of the advances in scholarship in his field. This problem is particularly acute for the history teacher because new knowledge is being accumulated so rapidly—both as a result of the rapidity of cultural change and the discovery of new information and the development of new interpretations of events long past. In order to keep abreast of his field, the history teacher in the schools needs to make careful selections of the most helpful monographs and general works and to develop a planned reading and study program. Both the pamphlets of the Service Center for Teachers of History, mentioned earlier, and this Yearbook will be helpful in this connection. Other sources of help are the reviews in *Social Education,* the *Saturday Review,* the Sunday *New York Times* Book Review Section, and the scholarly historical journals, such as, *The American Historical Review.*

In teaching recent history in the eighth grade, it is important to have a clear frame of reference in order to interpret the meaning of events which are complex and, as yet, not well evaluated. Chapter XVIII on "Intellectual and Cultural Developments, 1900—" by Ralph H. Gabriel will be helpful to teachers in this connection. Mr. Gabriel points out that,

By the middle of the twentieth century what had always been true became clearer to all intelligent citizens, namely that American civilization (as all civilizations) rests on a body of knowledge. Of this body accumulated scientific and technological knowledge was a most important part. The events of the century demonstrated that change in this underlying accumulation of knowledge is one of the principal causes for change in society. With almost bewildering swiftness the automobile, the airplane, the radio, television, plastics, synthetic fibers, and the atomic and hydrogen bombs wrought modifications in American ways of living. These changes in society provide the background of the phenomenon of the social sciences.[23]

If junior high school youth can grasp this fact through the study of American history, perhaps they will be motivated to strive to develop an understanding of the scientific knowledge that underlies American culture and, further, to develop the competence required to extend that knowledge as citizens of a free society.

---

[23] Chapter XVIII, p. 314-15.

Conclusion

In conclusion, the main contribution of this Yearbook to the teacher of American history in the upper grades and the junior high school is to provide an excellent guide to an increase of knowledge concerning recent advances in scholarship. This knowledge is basic to significant improvements in teaching. Intelligence, personality, a knowledge of content, effective methods, and a knowledge of individual growth and development are all important in the making of a good teacher, but basic to everything else in a good teacher is a thorough knowledge of what is being taught.

CHAPTER XXI

American History in the Senior High School

John H. Haefner

INTRODUCTION

"STUDY theory," said a German bee-keeper, "or remain forever a bungler in practice." The Thirty-First Yearbook lends itself appropriately to a paraphrase of this maxim: Refresh yourself at the spring of scholarship, or remain forever an uninspired teacher; for the nature, plan, and content of the Yearbook make it enormously useful to the teacher of history who takes his teaching and his obligations to scholarship seriously. It refurbishes his affection for historical study, provides him with a labor-saving means of keeping abreast of historical research and materials appearing in the last two decades, and stimulates his "teaching imagination" as to ways in which he can revitalize his instruction.

The Yearbook carries subtler overtones and implications as well. The 1950's were a decade of virulent criticism of public education in the United States, marked by some thoughtful appraisal of educational philosophy and practice, but unfortunately accompanied also by some injudicious name-calling and witless vituperation. In the long run, it appears, this criticism will have beneficent effects on our public schools, but there have also been some deleterious concomitants. Since the late 1930's a growing chasm has separated the scholars from the secondary school teachers. The events of the 1950's did little to bridge the gap. The Thirty-First Yearbook makes a significant step toward better communication between scholars and teachers.

The first seventeen chapters are convincing evidence that historians are concerned with historical instruction in the schools, and, to a degree, are aware of some of the difficulties encountered by teachers in keeping up with historical research and incorporating its findings into the classes they teach. No one can read these chapters without being convinced that historians are reaching out friendly hands to teachers by giving freely of their time and talent to make these chapters possible. This kind of constructive cooperation augurs well indeed for improving the quality of instruction in our high schools.

There is help—both explicit and implicit—for each teacher, supervisor, and administrator who wants to improve instruction. The implications of the Yearbook for the secondary school seem to group themselves into suggestions for the teacher and implications for the social studies curriculum.

IMPLICATIONS FOR THE TEACHER . . .

. . . As a Student of History

One of the services which the Yearbook performs is to identify some of the neglected areas of research. Professor Craven points out that colonial history should be studied on a continental scale, and that close attention should be given to South American settlement. Looking at colonial history "from within," increased emphasis needs to be placed on the economic effects of imperial action on the colonies. In Chapter III Professor Ver Steeg enumerates the neglected subjects in eighteenth century colonial research, notably research relating to religious developments, everyday colonial life, the frontier, the role of labor, and of regions other than Virginia and Williamsburg. Professor Morgan in Chapter IV suggests that social, economic, and political developments in every colony were sufficiently different in the period from 1763 to 1789, that classroom treatment of this era would be more meaningful if additional research were available.

Indeed, the first three chapters suggest that our perspective on the early period of American history needs correction and our classroom treatment some modification. It is somewhat difficult to realize that the years from 1607 to 1783 and those from 1783 to 1959 represent equal spans of 176 years. Since the gestation period of our nation is as long as its post-natal life, any inclination to curtail unduly the study of colonial history raises significant questions. In a similar vein, it is easy to overlook the fact that there was a lapse of 126 years between the founding of Jamestown and the founding of Georgia. Recognition of this time differential brings into sharper focus the individual characteristics which the colonies exhibited.

In Chapter XI Professor Durden points out to teachers, both as teachers and as students of history, that among scholars there is "a growing realization that the 1890's, with all of their political ferment and socio-intellectual unrest, constitute a transitional decade of central importance in understanding contemporary America."[1] His own excellent treatment of the years 1877-1896 in the body of the chapter, together with the bibliography in the footnotes, provides a base from which teachers can enlarge their understanding of the period.

Classroom teachers know from experience that their students seek interpretation of the facts of history which will make history more meaningful and understandable to them. In attempting to provide this, teachers are perplexed to discover through their own study that scholarly attempts to synthesize and interpret an era or period are scarce. They will be cheered by the fact that a recurring theme throughout the Yearbook is the recognition by the historians that historical research is raising and seeking to answer new questions, and that scholars are increasingly recognizing their obligation to go beyond the amassing of facts and attempt to find sound interpretations.

"Civil War historians," writes Professor Singletary in Chapter VIII, "are beginning to show an increasing interest in interpretation. . . . More than one historian has asked the question (even though in private) if it is not high time we de-emphasized the amassing of progressively less significant material and channelled our energies into the admittedly more difficult business of trying to interpret and understand what we already know."[2] Similarly, after reviewing recent books dealing with diplomatic history in the period 1865-1917, Professor Dulles in Chapter XIII concludes: "The diplomatic record is not the primary concern of these writers. Their books are characterised by new evaluations and interpretations, sometimes highly controversial, which reflects a mid-twentieth century point of view."[3]

Both for their own use in studying history, and for use with able high school students, teachers welcome interpretation by scholars, however controversial, as means by which they can hone their own minds and the minds of their students.

The Yearbook provides very concrete help to teachers pursuing advanced degrees and searching for thesis topics. The "neglected areas" of research suggested by Professors Craven, Ver Steeg, and Morgan in their three chapters certainly suggest topics for masters theses. Indeed, Professor Ver Steeg in Chapter III declares that "the cycles in colonial historical writing have often left a wide gap in our knowledge of the colonial period after 1690,"[4] thus suggest-

---

[1] Chapter XI, p. 180.
[2] Chapter VIII, p. 128.
[3] Chapter XIII, p. 217.
[4] Chapter III, p. 26.

ing a broad area in which a thesis topic may be sought. In Chapter VII, Professor Potter indicates that the economic aspects of sectionalism in the ante-bellum period have not been thoroughly studied. Little attention has been paid, he points out, to the sectional reactions to economic developments which linked the northeast and West at the expense of the South, or to the effects of differing rates of sectional growth on the increase in sectionalism. Professor Freidel in Chapter XV contends that, while the New Deal is one of the most-written-about aspects of recent American history, scholarly attention has been somewhat uneven. "There is a surprising lack of scholarly monographs on the history of most of the New Deal agencies,"[5] he writes, and points out that the federal relief programs and the establishment of social security are also in need of further study. Professor Bestor's excellent Chapter IX on intellectual history implies that teachers would find courses on this aspect of historical study immensely useful in their teaching, and also suggests areas in which additional study is needed. Throughout the Yearbook, the teacher planning additional study and research in history, will find himself confronted with useful suggestions for his pursuit of knowledge.

...As a Teacher of History

By indicating neglected areas, by stressing the new concern for synthesis and interpretation, and by suggesting areas and topics for study and research, the Thirty-First Yearbook proves to be provocative for teachers as students of history. But it is a veritable mine of help to the teacher as a teacher of history, with many different veins and strata.

To reassess his purposes and methods. It is scarcely any wonder that, with over-size classes, several different courses to teach, and multitudinous extra-curricular duties, many classroom teachers begin to feel uncertain and insecure about their history instruction. Many a teacher, confronted with unwilling students, begins to doubt the efficacy of his methods, and, more significant, the real purpose of historical instruction. To them this Yearbook brings solid words of encouragement.

Implicitly and explicitly, a central theme runs through the first seventeen chapters. It is that a major outcome of instruction in American history ought to be the development of reflective thought. It ought to be, even for high school students, a first step in the search for truth. Reflective thought and the search for truth, of course, can

---

[5] Chapter XV, p. 275.

only be based on the solid foundation of historical fact, but the amassing of facts, *per se*, the historians point out, does not yield understanding or even agreement in all cases. Historians do not agree, Professor Potter points out in Chapter VII, whether slavery was a basic cause for the War Between the States, or merely a smoke-screen for more fundamental motives. He continues:

> The irony of this disagreement lies in the fact that it persists in the face of vastly increased factual knowledge and constantly intensified scholarly research. The discrepancy, indeed, is great enough to make apparent a reality about history which is seldom so self-evident as it is here: namely that factual mastery of the data alone does not necessarily lead to agreement upon broad questions of historical truth. It certainly narrows the alternatives between which controversy continues to rage, and this narrowing of alternatives is itself an important proof of objective progress. But within the alternatives the determination of truth depends more perhaps upon basic philosophical assumptions which are applied in interpreting the data, than upon the data themselves. Data, in this sense, are but the raw materials for historical interpretation and not the determinants of the interpretive process.[6]

Certainly with a large number of his students, if not all, the high school history teacher's goal is more than the mastery of facts. However stumbling and artless their approach, students must be helped to make a start in assessing, analyzing, and interpreting historical data. At the same time, the chapters imply that, while such a goal for history instruction is infinitely more challenging and significant for high school students, it is also infinitely more difficult and beset with risks. No one makes this more clear than Professor Bestor in his Chapter IX on intellectual history. While students of history should be encouraged to seek causes in history through an understanding of the controlling ideas of the time, he asserts, there is also real danger in letting the inadequately informed play too loosely with ideas or encouraging the immature in an unbridled assessment of their impact.

This larger vision of the purposes of historical instruction, teachers are reminded, can be implemented in part by familiarizing students with some aspects of the historical method of inquiry and by the increased use of primary source materials. While the Yearbook chapters do not give systematic attention to these problems of pedagogy, there are useful hints scattered throughout. Professor Potter suggests in Chapter VII that the confused and controversial accounts of Kansas following the Kansas-Nebraska Act make this an especially useful period for acquainting students with some facets of historiography.

---

[6] Chapter VII, p. 118-19.

He suggests a specific resource helpful to teachers in doing this. "James C. Malin, in *John Brown and the Legend of '56*," he reports, "has applied the rigorous pruning-hook of historical method to the luxuriant growth of unsupported assertion about John Brown in Kansas. The residue of fact which remains presents such startling contrasts to the legend that Malin's study has value, apart from the Kansas question, as a case-study in historical method."[7]

Many of the chapters, in reviewing the literature, indicate the accessibility of primary source materials, with the implication that certainly the better students in high school should make considerable use of them. "Every book, pamphlet, or newspaper—indeed, every manuscript letter—is potentially a source to be used in the study of intellectual history," says Professor Bestor in Chapter IX. He points out that paperback books are an evermore plentiful and inexpensive source, and that ". . . student and teacher should be constantly aware that no commentary can take the place of the original, and that the original is often no farther away than the drug-store book-rack or the public library."[8] Professor Singletary, in Chapter VIII, reports that there are any number of first-hand accounts, military unit histories, and innumerable diaries for the period of the Civil War and the Reconstruction. The number of picture histories of the war is also on the increase. Most recently, Mr. Willard Archie of *Living History, Incorporated*, Shenandoah, Iowa, is undertaking the reissuance of *Harper's Weekly*, exactly as it appeared in the original. At a subscription price of $12 for fifty-two issues, Mr. Archie's venture supports the contention of the Yearbook that prohibitive cost is no longer a major factor in preventing the use of original sources in at least some periods of American history.

Professor Cole, also, in dealing with the period 1929-1941, makes note in Chapter XVI of the fact that original sources are plentiful and accessible, and that interpretations of the period vary widely. Under such conditions, teachers might well choose to develop a unit which would stress certain aspects of the historical method, including the use of primary sources, and internal and external criticism. Intellectual and cultural developments in America from 1900, summarized by Professor Gabriel in Chapter XVIII, might well be employed in the same way. Indeed, with a group of able youngsters, the chapter itself might be closely examined for the underlying premises involved, and,

---

[7] Chapter VII, p. 115.
[8] Chapter IX, p. 147.

with the help of some of the materials suggested, a search for evidence might be undertaken to support his conclusions. Certainly the Yearbook as a whole encourages the teacher to try new approaches in developing reflective thought and some skill in historical methods of inquiry through the use of historical materials.

To re-emphasize fundamental concepts. Although they are never exhortatory in nature, the Yearbook chapters carry the clear implication that there are certain basic concepts about the nature of history and historical study which should properly receive greater emphasis in high school teaching. While some of these have already been enumerated, several others deserve mention.

Fully a third of the chapters lay considerable stress on the fact that historians may differ widely in their interpretation of historical facts and periods, and that this results in a good deal of revision in historical writing. Professor Morgan outlines clearly in Chapter IV the differing interpretations of the causes and nature of the American Revolution, and even sub-titles it "A Review of Changing Interpretations." Professor Potter's incisive summary of the background for the Civil War in Chapter VII reveals that the literature passed through three distinct phases prior to 1940, and that since that date a revisionist interpretation, which minimizes slavery as an important cause of the struggle, has gained prominence. Still more recently, a counterattack on the revisionists by other scholars reaffirms the position that slavery was the basic cause. "It is ironical," concludes Professor Potter, "that, after a vast amount of intensive study by many scholars, the essential structure of society in the ante-bellum South still remains in dispute."[9]

Professor Stevens points out in Chapter VI that Jacksonian democracy from 1825 to 1849 is a difficult and highly controversial period of history which is not clearly understood or agreed upon even by historians. Teachers, therefore, must be cautious of indoctrinating the generalizations of the particular textbook they are using. Professor Sitterson, dealing with the economic and social revolution in the period 1860-1900 in Chapter X, reports that "The 'predatory capitalist' portrayed so vividly in the highly critical literature of the muckraking era" began receiving different treatment at the hands of scholars who "emphasized the important contributions made by many of the so-called 'robber barons' to the economic development of the nation."[10]

---

[9] Chapter VII, p. 102.
[10] Chapter X, p. 167-68.

As final examples of the importance of revisionism in the decades from 1940 to 1960, Professors Dulles in Chapter XIII and Cole in Chapter XVI both call attention to the fact that considerable difference of opinion has arisen regarding the entry of America into the first and second world wars.

Revisionism in historical writing carries two mandates for the high school teacher. The first is that he must somehow communicate to his students that history, once written, is not eternal and unchanging. "For history," as Professor Mowry says so cogently, "is something that can never be frozen into the mold of fixed convictions. To exist at all it must live, and to live it must change."[11]

The second mandate to the teacher is that he must tread with special caution in those areas where revisionist writing is most prolific. He must be cognizant of varying interpretations himself, and he must counteract the indoctrination of a single point of view, should his textbook be guilty of this approach. At the same time, revisionism in history provides the imaginative teacher with unparalleled opportunities for developing reflective thought.

A second basic idea for teaching which the historical chapters suggest is that secondary school students are not too young or immature to learn that history is written by human beings influenced by the times in which they live. Even the beginning student of history should keep his "weather eye" cocked for the tenor of the times in which a given historian wrote. In characterizing the literature about the Civil War and Reconstruction, Professor Singletary in Chapter VIII notes that, among other things, recent works show a noticeable strain of nationalism. "This current trend," he remarks, "is in all probability a reflection of the age in which we live, an age wherein all other activities are to some degree influenced by the cold war and the conflicting ideologies behind that war, an age in which the overriding need for unity has generated a pressure to minimize the things that divide us now or have done so in the past."[12] The shifts and changes in interpretation as to why America entered World War I, insists Professor Dulles in Chapter XIII, are due to the "prevailing climate of opinion at the time they were written."[13] And in Chapter V, Professor DeConde, in speaking of the causes of the war of 1812, makes the point that "historical interpretations sometimes work in cycles and . . .

---

[11] Chapter XII, p. 214.
[12] Chapter VIII, p. 127.
[13] Chapter XIII, p. 227.

interpretation in history is almost always linked to the subjective appraisal of the historian himself."[14]

The challenge to the teacher is to communicate to students a discernment for history which lies between the Charybdis of blind acceptance of everything the book says, on the one hand, and the Scylla of cynicism, on the other, which believes with Henry Ford that "History is the bunk." If large numbers of students seem to take one extreme position or the other, teachers should look to their methods of instruction. A fresh approach might well be to take the topics in the three chapters quoted and use them as vehicles for dealing with history as reflecting the time in which it is written, and historians as human beings affected by their "Zeitgeist."

Part One of the Yearbook adds a third to the list of fundamental ideas which the teacher must seek to develop with his students. It is neither new nor revolutionary, but it is crucial to the development of reflective thought through historical study. Historical events of importance, these chapters aver, are almost always the result of multiple causation, and great controlling ideas in history, like democracy and nationalism, are many-faceted. This proves to be a difficult concept for students to learn, and an easy one for teachers to forget. Professor Stevens' perceptive discussion of the Jacksonian period in Chapter VI closes with the observation that the meaning of Jacksonian democracy still remains obscure. He lists nine reasons why this should be true—a list which teachers might well edit and paste in their lesson plan book as a daily reminder of the pit-falls a teacher of history encounters. Number three in Stevens' list is pertinent here: " . . . overmuch attention has been given," he says, "to the search for a single 'cause' or all-inclusive explanatory proposition."[15] The rise of the common man cannot be explained in one easy lesson or in terms of one simple cause. Professor Bestor is persuasive in Chapter IX when he points out that a major value in the study of intellectual history is to help students to discover "the furniture of men's minds" and the dynamic nature of ideas of the past and present. He concludes:

All too often the controlling ideas of a given historical period are taken for granted, even by careful students, with the result that present-day meanings are erroneously read back into them. Once it becomes clear that every idea has a history of its own, that it develops and changes with time, then history reveals itself as a process vastly more dynamic than it previously appeared to be. Events no longer unroll before a changeless backdrop of

[14] Chapter V, p. 69.
[15] Chapter VI, p. 86.

ideas. Instead, ideas and events are seen to alter together, affecting each other at every turn. Observing this, a student comes to understand that a great controlling idea like *democracy* or *nationalism* is not a static idea, the meaning of which can be looked up, once and for all, in a dictionary. Instead he realizes that the meaning of an idea in any given period (and hence in any given document) must be ascertained by historical investigation, precisely as the outward events of the period are ascertained. A student who has grasped this fact has learned, in the profoundest meaning of the phrase, to think historically.[16]

If it is agreed that a major purpose of history is to help students think reflectively and historically, then Part One of the Yearbook has much to say to the history teacher. Recognition of the role of revision in the writing of history, the forces which help to account for a historian's interpretation, and the multi-faceted nature of history, historical events, and ideas are basic to this goal. The first seventeen chapters provide the careful reader with numerous suggestions for suitable materials that can be used to implement these basic ideas in the classroom.

To capitalize the values of biography. Perhaps the single most noticeable feature of the chapters in Part One is the emphasis placed on biographical materials by the authors. Every chapter contains reference to biographies, and at least ten deal extensively with biography either in the text or the footnotes, or both. This attention to biography as a source for historical understanding marks something of a break with the past, for, as Professor Mowry properly points out in Chapter XII, "There has always been a large question in the mind of the professional historian whether biography should be considered history at all."[17] But the changed status of biographical materials does not appear due to mere happenstance, for Professor Ver Steeg, writing of the eighteenth century colonial period in Chapter III says:

Individuals preoccupied with science have been subject to the probings of biographers, together with renewed interest in biographical studies generally. In this respect the writing on the colonial eighteenth century is being influenced by a trend affecting historical scholarship in all fields. It would appear that the complexities of the mid-twentieth century world, where men live increasingly in faceless anonymity and where individual effort so often appears thwarted or made futile by unyielding external conditions, have prompted laymen and scholars alike to attempt to rescue the value of the individual from the irresistible sweep of historical forces.[18]

---

[16] Chapter IX, p. 154-55.
[17] Chapter XII, p. 206.
[18] Chapter III, p. 32-33.

Nor is this the only reason. It is Professor Potter's judgment in Chapter VII that "On the sectional rivalries for the period after the Missouri Compromise and before the Compromise of 1850, perhaps the most significant recent treatments have appeared in biographies" and "In the history of the final stages of the crisis, as in the general record of this entire period, much of the most valuable historical work appears in studies of particular men."[19] Professor Mowry adds still another explanation for the increased stature of biography. In referring to the new Library of American Biography Series edited by Oscar Handlin, he comments that "This Series should be of especial value to high school teachers and students because of the books' small number of pages and slight price, and because *the Series endeavors to interpret the subjects it covers rather than retail a mass of minute facts about them.*"[20] Quite obviously, not all biography is good reading or good history, and Professor Freidel points this out in Chapter XV when commenting on the abundance of biographical and autobiographical materials available relating to the New Deal. His convictions on the value of biography are strong enough, however, so that he has undertaken to write a six-volume biography of Franklin D. Roosevelt, of which three volumes are already in print.

Certainly the Yearbook makes it clear that high school teachers should make extensive use of biographical and autobiographical works, not only in their own study of history but equally so in their teaching. Teachers might profitably, for example, go through the first seventeen chapters, noting the references to biographies, and develop a "reading list" for themselves. Such a list would suggest the best works available for the whole sweep of American history. The same list would serve as reference for the abler students. Unfortunately, really good biographies for less mature readers are not as abundant, though particularly readable ones are usually identified by the authors of the several chapters. Biographies lend themselves to a variety of uses in the classroom. They can be read by individual students for enrichment of the period under study. Two biographies by different authors but about the same person can be used as an exercise in the development of certain skills in reflective thinking and in getting students to develop a more critical attitude toward the author's use of his source material. A panel consisting of students who had read different treatments of the same historical personage should prove provocative and

---

[19] Chapter VII, p. 111 and 117, *passim.*
[20] Chapter XII, p. 208. Italics inserted.

informative to the entire class. An imaginative teacher might experiment through teaching an entire period in history by having the students read biographies of the men and women who played leading roles. The historical context could be provided through selected readings in the textbook and through "bridge" lectures by the teacher which related the person to the times. The extensive biographical references in Professor Lowitt's Chapter XIV on the "Prosperity Decade —1917-1928" would make it relatively easy to try this approach. Finally, historical biography has real promise for schools seriously attempting to provide for the academically interested and able. "Independent readings" or even an advanced seminar course could be centered around the intensive reading and extensive discussion of selected biographical works. Such a course would add great depth of understanding to students already well-founded in the history of their country.

The blessing of the historians, the inherent human interest of books about people, and the ready availability in most communities— all these factors argue strongly that the greatly augmented use of carefully selected biographies will benefit high school teachers, students, and historical instruction generally.

To maximize the use of investigative papers. Although it is nowhere explicitly suggested in Part One, it can be inferred that the authors of the first seventeen chapters would heartily endorse the increased use of student-written investigative papers in high school. Their insistence, already referred to, that the ability to think historically ought to be a major outgrowth of historical study, supports the inference. But more concrete evidence is scattered throughout the chapters, for the careful reader will find a substantial number of ideas for specific topics for student investigation. To be sure, many of these could be handled only by very mature students, and some, because of the location of materials, could be done only in certain regions of the country. But the hints provided by the authors serve as springboards for resourceful teachers.

In Chapter III, Professor Ver Steeg suggests some areas of eighteenth century colonial history which are neglected. Among those he enumerates are aspects of everyday colonial life, and regions other than Virginia and Williamsburg, notably South Carolina, New York, Pennsylvania, and New Jersey. History classes in those parts of the country could certainly find topics and original materials with which to work. Population studies, local customs and folk-sayings, land holdings, and movements into and out of the local community are only a few that come to mind.

The changing tides of interpretation of various aspects of the American Revolution, as portrayed in Chapter IV by Professor Morgan, suggest that able students could trace these patterns through a series of investigative papers using the works of the chief revisionists. Comparing the Bancroft-Trevelyan view of the Revolution with that of Beer, Andrews, Larabee, and Gipson would be a highly meaningful assignment for good students and would be valuable for an entire class if reported to them. A similar project, which high school students might find more intriguing because of the nature of the controversy, would be to collate Beard's *An Economic Interpretation of the Constitution* with Robert E. Brown's *Middle-Class Democracy and the Revolution in Massachusetts* and his *Charles Beard and the Constitution*.

Professor Steven's Chapter VI on "Jacksonian Democracy, 1825-1849" furnishes additional ideas. He makes the point that Jacksonian democracy, like Eve, has many faces, and that we need to know more about some of these, particularly as they applied in some regions and localities. For history classes in the eastern half of the United States, particularly, a series of investigative papers on highly limited, local topics centering around some aspects of Jacksonian democracy would be feasible. Confining themselves to the local community or county, titles such as these come to mind:

"Labor Support of the Jacksonian Democratic Party"
"Early Settlers in This Area and Their Political Affiliation"
"Evidences of Democracy in This Area of the Southeast, 1825-1841"
"Land Speculation in Our County, 1825-1841"
"Banking Operations in Our Community during the Period of Jacksonian Democracy"
"Limitations on Suffrage in Our Community, 1825-1849"

Other teachers will find additional suggestions in the chapter.

Professors Potter and Singletary in Chapters VII and VIII both point out the vastly increased interest in all phases of the Civil War in recent years on the part of laymen and professional historians alike. The extensive efforts to mark the centennial of the War Between the States in all parts of the United States are making available great amounts of material, some of it new, not only in national publications but in local newspapers as well. Substantial papers by high school students should result. In communities where library resources make this feasible, investigative papers on editorial reaction to Southern secession would be of great interest, as Professor Potter suggests. Inasmuch as authentic reproductions of *Harper's Weekly* are now readily available investigations utilizing this important resource are possible.[21]

The final four chapters of Part One deal with the United States since World War I. Each author makes clear, both through the text and the footnotes, that this is a period rich with primary and secondary sources from which investigative papers can be developed. Many communities, large and small, have magazine and newspaper files on which students can draw for knowledge of this period. The analysis of the literature about the New Deal contained in Professor Freidel's Chapter XV, for example, suggests that sharply circumscribed papers by students on some aspects of the depression and New Deal would have merit. Students might profitably study their local communities for the effects of the depression on the local economy including bank failures and unemployment, might analyze shifts in voting in the locality, or might tell the story of the NRA as revealed by local newspapers. The chapters by Professors Cole XVI, Cleland XVII, and Gabriel XVIII are no less productive of proposals for worthwhile topics.

There is increasing consensus among those concerned with quality education that students must be encouraged to write more. But it is important that they write, not merely for the sake of writing, but to write about something of value. The history classroom provides a matchless opportunity to encourage good writing. Indeed, the investigative paper in history has three special merits: (1) it challenges the individual student, particularly the able, to a meaningful task; (2) it exercises his skill in organization and written communication; and (3) it provides an opportunity for him to develop his ability to deal with historical materials and to think reflectively. Both the tone and the treatment in Part One of the Yearbook encourage teachers to maximize their use of the investigative paper.

To stimulate wide student reading. The attitude of teachers toward the exclusive use of the textbook as a means of instruction is reminiscent of the story told on Calvin Coolidge. Upon returning home from church Coolidge reported to his wife that the minister preached about sin. When Mrs. Coolidge asked what he had said about sin, Coolidge

---

[21] See p. 367.

is supposed to have replied, "He was agin it." So, too, are teachers "agin" depending wholly on textbooks for assignments, or limiting student reading to the covers of a single book. The solution to the problem is well-known: get students to read widely. But actual *practice* in the classroom is uncomfortably similar to the remark credited to Mark Twain (in all likelihood incorrectly): "Everybody talks about the weather but nobody does anything about it." There are few aspects of teaching in which theory and practice are as far apart as they are in the matter of getting students to read widely.

The problem is not lack of materials. No one has put it more succinctly than Professor Freidel in Chapter XV.

> The problem facing the teacher is not one of finding materials, but of sorting and sifting from the enormous bulk those writings which will be of use to him in preparing for his classes, and those most readable for various levels of students. There are books that are lively and polemical, others dull and still polemical, and happily a surprising number that are both highly readable and of substantial historic merit.[22]

Even if it had no other virtues, the Thirty-First Yearbook would have repaid the effort which went into it by "sorting and sifting," as it does so excellently, the vast resources in American history which have become available in the past two decades. To have this done for them by eminent scholars is an incalcuable boon to history teachers everywhere.

The bibliographies accompanying each chapter have many different uses. Many of the authors deal at length with the varying interpretations and viewpoints which have developed about the historical periods which they are summarizing. Teachers can use the bibliographies in these chapters to make sure that the collections in their school libraries do not reflect only a single interpretation. New viewpoints toward the American Revolution (Chapter IV), toward the nature of Jacksonian Democracy (Chapter VI), toward the causes of the Civil War (Chapter VII), toward the role of big business in the period from 1860 to 1900 (Chapter X), and toward the reasons for America's entry into World Wars I and II (Chapters XIII, XVI, and XVII) are only a few examples. Using these chapters as guides, teachers can take steps to assure balance in materials available to them as teachers and to their students.

A high proportion of the references cited, of course, are suitable only for the teacher, or for the teacher and only the most able students.

---

[22] Chapter XV, p. 264.

Yet most of the authors seem aware of the problem of finding readable accounts for average students. Professor DeConde, for example, makes the point in Chapter V that the period from 1789 to 1825 has much popularly written material, most of which would be useful for average students. Professor Potter's bibliography in Chapter VII is especially valuable for locating materials during the Civil War Centennial. Professor Singletary's Chapter VIII stresses the fact that the Civil War period has much well-written material about the war and that there has been ". . . a fantastic interest in tangential and peripheral subjects" such as cloak-and-dagger stories, prisons, newspapermen in the war, and the like. Average students would be likely to find these of particular interest. The bibliography of Chapter VIII can also be used to measure the school library in terms of contemporary accounts and illustrated histories of the Civil War. Professor Sitterson's Chapter X reports the period from 1860 to 1900 as rich in readable materials. Stegner's *Beyond the Hundreth Meridian*, Beebe and Clegg's *U.S. West: The Saga of Wells Fargo*, McNickle's *They Came Here First: The Epic of the American Indian*, and Frederick Lewis Allen's, *The Great Pierpont Morgan* are only a few examples of books which many high school students would read and enjoy. Professor Freidel's bibliography in Chapter XV substantiates his assertion, quoted above, that the period from 1929 to 1941 is marked by a surprising number of books which are both highly readable and historically sound.

The careful reader will note that there is some duplication and repetition of titles from chapter to chapter. This repetition is of the greatest possible assistance to teachers. In effect, it makes it possible for them to draw up a "most recommended" list with which to confront the school administration and librarian, and to request that these titles be given priority in acquisition. This priority list can then be followed by another and more extensive collection for further purchase. While it should not be necessary for teachers to resort to such tactics to get the teaching materials they need, experience dictates that strategy of this kind pays dividends.

Certainly the "sorting and sifting" provided by the historians makes an enormous contribution to the problem of stimulating students to read widely. Two difficult aspects remain to be solved by the classroom teacher: (1) how to get the selected books purchased and into the library; and (2) how to get students to read them after they are available. But these are not insoluble problems, and competent and energetic teachers will find ways of meeting them.

To stimulate study by the teacher. Few problems which plague social studies teachers are more frustrating than the attempt to "keep up with the field." It is difficult enough in a single area such as history; it becomes Herculean when the teacher's obligations to all the social sciences are considered. *Any* help which can be provided is welcome, and the Yearbook certainly gives aid and comfort in the field of American history.

The chapters in Part One make it possible for the teacher to undertake a planned and purposeful program of professional reading. Every teacher's reading list, of course, will be individual and tailored to his needs, interests, and the "low spots" in his knowledge and understanding. It might be drawn up on the basis of a single book from each of the topics dealt with in the first seventeen chapters. It might represent a more intensive concentration in a single area or period of time. Or it might be selected on the basis of the annotations provided by the authors. In all likelihood most teachers would draw up a list amalgamating all three of these approaches. Even when the factor of applicability to student use is added, it is difficult to keep the list manageable. What teacher would not teach better for having read Smith's *Virgin Land: The American West as Symbol and Myth* ("brilliant interpretive study")[23]; Dulles, *Labor in America: A History* ("the most interesting history of trade unionism in the United States that has been written")[24]; Handlin's, *The Uprooted* ("brilliant and sensitive account of the great migration of peoples to this country")[25]; Josephson's, *The Politicos* ("still the best and liveliest survey of national politics in this period")[26]; Ellis' *Mr. Dooley's America: A Life of Finley Peter Dunne* ("more than a brilliant biography of America's leading political humorist and satirist of the time")[27]; Wecter's *Age of the Great Depression, 1929-1941* ("vivid, readable social history")[28]; Blum's *From the Morgenthau Diaries: Years of Crisis, 1928-1938* ("carefully organized, clear narrative")[29]; or Potter's *People of Plenty: Economic Abundance and the American Character* ("a brilliant interpretation of American history")[30] It would be easy to make a hundred

---

[23] Chapter IX, p. 143.
[24] Chapter X, p. 176.
[25] *Ibid.,* p. 177.
[26] Chapter XI, p. 183.
[27] Chapter XII, p. 210.
[28] Chapter XV, p. 265.
[29] *Ibid.,* p. 274.
[30] Chapter XVIII, footnote 3 on p. 316.

such reading lists—all different—to guide a teacher's study and to add depth to his instruction.

The chapters provide other suggestions. The bibliography for Chapter IX contains many suggestions for the teacher whose education has not sufficiently emphasized intellectual history. Acquiring a better balance of knowledge and understanding in those areas of American history where interpretations of scholars differ most is both difficult and imperative for the teacher. The summaries provided by the chapters, when followed by wider reading in the materials suggested in the bibliographies, are invaluable road maps for the teacher. Noteworthy examples of such chapters in Part One include Chapter IV on the American Revolution, Chapters VII and VIII on the factors leading up to the Civil War and the changing views of the basic causes of the war, Chapter XIII on America's entry into World War I and Chapter XVII on our participation in World War II.

Not least among the contributions of these chapters to the on-going study of teachers are the excellent and authoritative capsule summaries of complex and difficult materials which many of them contain. Professor Mowry's trenchant resumé of the Progressive movement in Chapter XII, Professor Lowitt's excellent review of the "Prosperity Decade" in Chapter XIV, and Professor Gabriel's discerning survey in Chapter XVIII of intellectual and cultural developments in America from the turn of the century are only three examples. Starting from the bird's-eye view in the chapter, the teacher can read with greater meaning and understanding the materials listed in the footnotes and bibliographies.

No one knows better than the social studies teacher himself that he has "home work" to do. To be effective it must be done regularly and conscientiously. The Thirty-First Yearbook provides him with the assignment and with a superb "study guide" with which to do it.

IMPLICATIONS FOR THE AMERICAN HISTORY COURSE AND THE SOCIAL STUDIES CURRICULUM

The Thirty-First Yearbook was designed by the editors, and the chapters written by the historians, with one over-riding objective in mind: to serve as inspiration, incentive, and aid to the classroom teacher of history. The preceding pages indicate, at least in part, the marked success of the volume in achieving its goal. Indeed, some care has been taken to document from specific chapters a few of the uses to which the teacher can put the Yearbook.

The volume also has broader and more far-reaching implications. In all likelihood, there will be somewhat less agreement on what these are, because inevitably they involve the values and viewpoints of the individual who attempts to enumerate them. Nor is it as readily possible to cite chapter and page in their support. Instead, these broader allusions involve the spirit, tone, and impact of the chapters as a whole and reveal themselves only through hints, inklings, cues, and clues. Most of them center on the existing course in American history in the high school and on aspects of the social studies curriculum.

A Two-Year Sequence in American History

As Professor Quillen points out in Chapter XX, most of our schools treat American history at three different levels: the middle grades, the junior high school, and the senior high school. Perceptive teachers have long been disturbed by the fact that both the junior and senior high school courses attempt a comprehensive treatment and that duplication and repetition in them is serious.

The scope of the first seventeen chapters, individually and collectively, lends impressive support to the idea that a two-year sequence in American history is desirable—more likely a necessity—if students are to derive meaning from it and understanding of it. Every chapter makes it perfectly evident that the history of our country is not a simple and uncomplicated story, the details of which are agreed upon by all. Quite the contrary. And even experienced teachers, upon reading Part One, will be forced to confess that what they know and have read about American history is not as great as what is to be known and to be read about it. The treatment in each chapter implies that the bones of history must be clothed with the flesh and blood of illuminating detail if students are to realize its value and develop love for it. Providing the "flesh and blood" requires time, and time must be found for it. A two-year sequence seems a sensible solution.

There is also some indication that a natural breaking-point for such a two-year course would be at the end of the Civil War or the period of Reconstruction. In commenting on the continuing interest in this period, Professor Singletary, in Chapter VIII, says, "It is significant, furthermore, because of its consequences—for out of those years of war and Reconstruction arose many of the problems that continue to perplex us in mid-twentieth century America."[31] Some

---

[31] Chapter VIII, p. 132.

schools have already put this idea into practice, offering an eighth grade course which is primarily dramatic, narrative, and chronological in nature. This is followed with an eleventh grade course organized around post-Reconstruction problems which have persisted to the present time. It would also be possible to offer American history in a sequential two-year block in grades eight and nine, for example, with elective courses in grades eleven and twelve which would review American civilization in depth with the needs of the academically able and the college preparatory students especially in mind. Whatever the solution devised by a particular school, a two-year offering in American history merits serious consideration.

Emphasis on Intellectual History

The radical changes which have occurred in the teaching of United States history in the past century are dramatized by the nature of the textbooks. School history books of the late nineteenth century were almost entirely political in their emphasis. Indeed, in some each chapter consisted of a descriptive account of a four-year presidential period, devastatingly dull in treatment for adolescents, and unnecessarily drab in physical appearance. Today's textbooks are birds of different feathers. The most fundamental difference is the vastly increased amount of *history* which they contain, social, economic, and cultural as well as political. And, as a bonus, they are highly attractive to young learners in terms of physical appearance, and in the use of charts, graphs, pictures, and source materials as learning aids. Improvement in the teaching of history has tended to follow improvement in the textbooks.

The Yearbook calls attention to the need for giving increased emphasis to still another dimension of history—the history of ideas. As is to be expected, it is Professor Bestor's Chapter IX which makes this suggestion most explicitly, but it is implicit in most of the others, and especially in Chapters IV, VI, X, XII, XIV, and XVIII. "Ideas," says Bestor, "are neither above comprehension nor beneath contempt. . . . ideas are historical forces, constantly interacting with other historical forces, in ways that are as open to historical investigation as any other historical phenomena."[32] What he does not add is that many teachers have observed the quickening of interest, the "straightening up" in the desks when class discussion turns to the history, manifestation, and impact of historical ideas. Particularly for better students, ideas have a reality and significance which other aspects of history

---

[32] Chapter IX, p. 137-38, *passim*.

do not always have. Part One of the Yearbook carries the thought that teachers ought to incorporate more emphasis on intellectual history in the courses they teach.

The summary of the development of intellectual history in Chapter IX suggests that, because of the newness of this field, many teachers have had little opportunity to study and read intellectual history. The bibliographies in the various chapters make it possible for the teacher to fill this gap. So far as instruction is concerned, the implication is not so much that new units within the existing course are needed, though this has interesting possibilities, but rather that the teacher add depth to his present treatment by stressing ideas as historical forces, by demonstrating their interaction with other forces, and by encouraging his students to investigate them as historical phenomena.

A Unit on the Local Region or Section

". . . much of the reality of American political life," says Professor Durden in Chapter XI, "is regional or sectional; and behind the facile generalizations about national trends and forces lie the rich complexities and stubbornly different facts and circumstances of American localities."[33] In a similar vein, Professor Mowry's Chapter XII observes that regions "are often characterized by distinct economic, social, and even ideological peculiarities."[34] Professor Durden goes on to enumerate various materials to increase understanding of the Northern, urban political scene, the Western urban and agrarian scene, and the South as an agrarian society much complicated by racial tensions. Professor Mowry reviews two books published since 1950, one of which deals with Boston as an "intellectual region," and a second which examines progressivism in the midwest region. Professor Sitterson devotes a section of Chapter X to regional studies of the West.

There is a suggestion here for teachers. Hounded by "too much material in too little time," teachers are the first to recognize that they must resort, all too often, to broad generalizations. Yet within existing courses, it is manifestly impossible to treat each topic with the depth it deserves. A solution worth trying, Chapters XI and XII suggest, is to insert a unit which treats some region with greater detail. In most instances, the region in which the school is located

---

[33] Chapter XI, p. 185.
[34] Chapter XII, p. 205.

would seem to be the best choice. Not all the facets of the region need be studied. It might well be a highly limited study, such as the origins and development of the progressive movement in the region for a given period of time.

Such an experiment would not be without its difficulties. Materials for student use would be somewhat difficult to come by. Student interest might not be as high, though it could be made to be if materials were available and the instructor sufficiently enthusiastic. Motivation could be enhanced by centering student research papers, such as those suggested previously, on the study of the region. Properly planned, such a regional unit could focus on important historical skills and familiarize students with many significant primary sources. Whatever promises to help resolve the perennial problem of "depth within breadth" in the American history course is worth trying experimentally, no matter how difficult.

Rearrangement of Topics

Good teachers are always looking for fresh approaches to familiar materials. This appears to be as important for creating a good learning situation as it is for stimulating the intellectual activity of the teacher. Several of the chapters in Part One suggest the possibility of placing topics in a new setting.

The title and content of Chapter X, for example, exemplify a somewhat different approach to the period 1860-1900 than is followed in many textbooks. Professor Sitterson not only views the period as revolutionary from the standpoint of the changes which occurred, but also provides a list of fourteen topics which comprise the major movements of the era. Planning a new unit along these lines might prove stimulating to teacher and students alike.

Professor Lowitt's Chapter XIV provides a second illustration on the "Prosperity Decade, 1917-1928." Even when this period is studied (and many teachers do not get to it), it is likely to be treated as a series of kaleidoscopic topics. Professor Lowitt identifies eight areas needed to study this complex decade: wartime mobilization, peace and demobilization, foreign policies, domestic policies, agriculture and agricultural policies, labor and labor policies, business and economic thought, and religion. If even a small portion of the materials noted by Professor Lowitt were available, a unit planned along these lines, with additional emphasis on the cultural phenomena of the time, would almost certainly be provocative and stimulating.

Courses for the Academically Able

If Part One of the Yearbook has any important limitation, it is that so high a percentage of its implications for high school teaching center around the academically able. This is not at all surprising in view of the assignment given the historians who wrote the chapters. Probing in depth in historical study, which is clearly the theme of the first seventeen chapters, presents exceptionally difficult problems when the teacher is dealing with average and below average students. It would be folly to deny this. The need for providing a higher quality of social studies instruction for the academically able is so urgent, however, that if the Yearbook did nothing but stimulate this it would have justified its existence. Fortunately, as indicated above, it has broader implications.

The utility of Part One for schools where honors courses, advanced placement courses, and accelerated classes are already in existence is so obvious that no further elaboration is required. It is a gold mine of stimulation and ideas for the teachers of such courses.

There are also helpful clues for schools planning to establish advanced work in the social studies, and for those casting about for additional courses that might be offered. Certainly an elective course in intellectual history would be one possibility. An independent reading course employing biographies as the unifying strand would be another. A seminar centered upon the areas where historical revision has been most pronounced would be still another. These are but a few illustrations, and imaginative teachers will see additional alternatives.

Still another idea would merit discussion by social studies departments which are reappraising their course offerings. As has been mentioned earlier, a two-year sequence in American history might be offered in grades eight and nine. This would assure that students not completing high school would have had the opportunity to develop understanding of their country's history, and love for it. In the senior high school, however, provision would need to be made for the college bound students beset with entrance examinations, and for those who have a natural affinity for the study of history. This need might be met by offering two sequential elective courses, in grades eleven and twelve, under the general title of "Problems in American Civilization." It would be the purpose of these courses to review American history and development, with special emphasis on depth in treatment and on the development of historical skills and abilities.

Second Thoughts on Integrated Courses

As noted earlier, a recurring concern in the chapters of the volume centers about the fact that historians, in spite of vastly increased amounts of detailed research, have found it difficult, or even impossible, to arrive at any kind of synthesis for many periods of American history. Professor Ver Steeg's Chapter III deplores the lack of a unifying theme for the colonial eighteenth century, in spite of massive research. Professor Durden in Chapter XI singles out a single book as one of the few attempts to synthesize the specialized work of many historians on the politics of the Gilded Age. Professor Lowitt, as shown in Chapter XIV, feels that the period 1917-1928 is greatly in need of a synthesis which historical research to date has not produced. One of the noteworthy aspects of this Yearbook is the frank recognition by the historians that American historical research has been successful in amassing facts but less successful in interpretation and synthesis.

This acknowledgment by the scholars provides food for thought and discussion by teachers and curriculum consultants. The premise underlying the core curriculum and various attempts at integrated social studies courses seems to be that a synthesis within history and between the social sciences is in existence. The problem of the teacher in integrated courses is to communicate this synthesis to students. The tone of Part One of the Yearbook calls this premise into question. It is clear that synthesis even in the restricted area of American history has not been achieved. It is legitimate to infer that synthesis between the social sciences is even less an accomplished fact.

The validity of courses which assume that junior and senior high school teachers can do what dedicated scholars have been unable to accomplish needs to be evaluated and questioned. Confronted with such a task, teachers can hardly be castigated for falling prey to oversimplification and easy generalization. This is certainly not true of all teachers nor of all core curriculum or integrated courses. But the unvoiced queries of Part One provoke sober thoughts about the current trend toward integration in the social studies curriculum.

Reminder to Textbook Authors and Publishers

The hints for the improvement of instruction which this Yearbook contains are not confined to teachers nor to the American history course and the social studies curriculum. It has never been a secret that a distressing lag exists between historical research and interpretation and the treatment which students study in their textbooks. With tactful subtlety the first seventeen chapters suggest that textbook authors and publishers could do much to narrow this gap.

Illustrations of this are too numerous to do more than to sample them. Professor Morgan makes it plain in Chapter IV that high school texts should contain a better treatment of the American Revolution and that present generalizations contained in most of them require modification. In his brilliant Chapter XIII on America as a new world power in the period from 1865-1917, Professor Dulles summarizes with great clarity the changing evaluations of America's entry into World War I. He concludes that no interpretation would suit all scholars but that all would agree that "any attempted oversimplification of such a complex issue . . . cannot be reconciled with the actual course of events and tends to falsify the record."[35] There are still far too many textbooks of which this criticism would be true. In Chapter XVI Professor Cole voices a similar sentiment, except that he is concerned with textbook treatment of America's entry into the second World War.

None of the foregoing is meant to imply that all or even most of the recent American history texts for high schools are inaccurate and obsolete. Quite the contrary. One of the noteworthy characteristics of the good textbooks today is the tremendous amount of scholarly effort and verification which have gone into them. The import of the Yearbook is a challenge to textbook authors and publishers to make a concerted and renewed effort to reduce the breadth of their generalizations and to treat more fully the work of some of the "revisionist" historians.

Note to College Professors of History

To a considerable degree, high school teachers of history are what they are because of the instruction in history they have had in college. If they communicate love of history to their students, it is in part because their college professors infected them. If they seek to place the facts of history into a meaningful setting, it is partly because their college mentors did so for them. By the same token, some of the limitations of secondary school teachers come in a direct line of descent from their college instruction.

What the Thirty-First Yearbook has to say to the high school teacher it says also, at least in part, to the professor who teaches history classes in which prospective teachers are enrolled. He, too, must bring his venerated lecture notes up-to-date in the light of recent

---

[35] Chapter XIII, p. 230.

historical research. He, too, must reassess his purposes and methods, re-emphasize fundamental concepts, capitalize on the values of biography, maximize the use of investigative papers, and stimulate wide reading by his students. And he must never forget that many of his best "customers" will be, not research historians with impressive publication lists, but high school classroom teachers who will be more effective teachers because they have been under his instruction.

What is the worth of this Yearbook? It is a storehouse of stimulation and help for the high school teacher of history who cares enough about excellence in education to seek to improve the quality of his own instruction. But it is also more. It is an immensely encouraging example of how the channels of communication between scholars and teachers can be re-opened in a cooperative effort to improve the quality of social education.

CHAPTER XXII

Use of Geography in Teaching American History

John W. Morris

INTRODUCTION

THE history of the United States, as does all history, encompasses the unifying elements of time. Geography, on the other hand, provides the unifying elements of space. The actions of mankind, be they American, Asiatic or European, take place in both time and space. Frequently, especially in the past, spacial characteristics have had a far greater influence upon the outcome of man's activities than has time. The historian must realize, however, that land, like time, changes from age to age; thus, the particular influences of and within a specific area vary with time. Man has been largely responsible for these variations of influence in space by his technological advancements. He can, for instance, conquer space much easier today than he did 500, 200, or even 25 years ago. One must, then, study American history in the light of man's interrelationship with the space in which he lived *at the specific time the event occurred.*

The natural environment has played an intricate role in the development of the United States. In teaching American history it would be unthinkable to disregard the geographical factors that were involved in the formation of the nation, for the geography of yesterday may be an important causative factor in the history of today. Failure to teach such relationships may result not only in an injustice to the student but in his ultimate disinterest and apathy.

GEOGRAPHICAL FACTORS

American history has been greatly affected by numerous local geographical factors. These factors, when correctly related by the teacher and understood by the student, will help explain the causes for certain reactions that may in turn answer the perplexing "why" of many historical problems. In most instances the American pioneer

388

had definite reasons for what he was attempting to do even though those reasons may have been based upon incorrect ideas. Since the settlers lived close to the earth much of their thinking was based upon conditions within their immediate environment. Students will recall their American history much better if they know the geographical setting in which the historical events took place. Such events need to be located and the setting visualized not as it would be seen today but as the people living at the specific time under discussion saw it.

Location

The first geographical factor to be considered in any history lesson is where the event took place. Often the location greatly influenced and, in some situations, even determined the outcome. The location of an event should be as specific as possible. To say that some historic action took place or is located in New York, California, or some other state, or that it occurred in the Great Lakes Area or New England has little meaning. There are so many variations in topography, water-forms, resources, and climate in areas as large as these that general locations have little significance.

Places, like dates, if they are to be useful and correct, should be as accurate as possible. Numerous examples of the importance of location in American history can be given. The Hudson River Valley and Lake Champlain Lowland, because of their location, served as the principal route of travel between the population centers of New York and Montreal; thus, they could be expected to play an important role in both the American Revolution and the War of 1812. St. Louis became an important French post because of its location near the confluence of the Missouri and Mississippi rivers. Presque Isle is an excellent example of the changing importance of location. Perry selected this point for the building of his lake fleet because the narrow, curving peninsula protected a good harbor from attack. Also nearby there were large forests from which ships could be made. To help the student understand that this location was a very satisfactory one, the teacher must carry the student back to the geography and technology of 1812. Ships were small, made of wood, and propelled by wind; armaments were small, and the frontier along the southern shore of Lake Erie was forested, swampy, and generally unpopulated.

If the student knows specific locations he will not be confused by similar names such as Cumberland Gap, Cumberland Road, and Cumberland River. Specific knowledge of the why of location at a specific time can add much to the interest of a history lesson.

Climate

One of the most influential of the geographical factors upon history, and probably the least understood, is climate. It was not so much what man knew about climatic conditions, but rather his misconceptions and lack of knowledge that influenced the course of history in several parts of the nation. Numerous early explorers and travelers identified the Great Plains as the Great American Desert. Settlers in the central parts of Kansas, Nebraska, Texas, Oklahoma, and the Dakotas often considered the area ideal farming country because they migrated to it during a wet rather than a dry cycle. By tracing the movement of the American people westward one immediately notices a distinct difference in population density east and west of the 95th meridian. From about this longitude the people practically "jumped" across the plains, mountains, and plateaus to the West Coast not because of soil, topography, or natural resources, but because of climate. Since technology and science have given many clues to the weather of this previously believed unhabitable area, people are now learning how to adjust and make it productive. Cotton and slavery and much of the resulting history are definitely related to the climate of the southeastern quarter of the United States.

The teachers of American history must be certain that their students understand the basic concepts of the climate of the United States as it is today. Too many popular textbooks of American history are not up to date on the topic. The old idea of a "temperate-zone" climate, which is still referred to, is very inaccurate and has long been obsolete. In general the United States is divided into seven large climatic regions, each having its own characteristics, but at the same time each grades gradually into the other. The amount of yearly rainfall, the yearly distribution of that rainfall, the temperature extremes as well as the averages, the length of the frost-free period, wind velocities and directions, and the formation and movement of pressure areas are but a few of the elements to be considered. In addition it must be kept constantly before the students that these items are influenced by, sometimes governed by, the world weather conditions in the tropic or polar areas. The air-age history of the nation that is being written today is definitely influenced by the various climates of the nation and the world.

Topography

The roughness or smoothness of the landscape, the barrier effects of the mountains, the direction of river flow, and the hardness of rock all had a tremendous influence upon the historical development of the United States. During the colonial period, when river navigation furnished the chief means of transportation, the differences in rock structure that caused rapids and falls at the Fall Line limited the distance inland that a ship could travel. As a result, where this topographic change occurred, a series of settlements was formed. Many, such as Washington and Richmond, have played important roles in the history of the nation. The Appalachian Barrier largely confined the British Colonists to the Coastal Plain and the Piedmont Plateau. Travel through and across the barrier was largely determined by the direction of valleys and the location of its wind and water gaps. The Wilderness Road and the Cumberland Gap were formed by nature, not by man. The downstream course of the Tennessee, Cumberland, and Ohio rivers carried migrants downhill to the Mississippi, and the upstream course of the Missouri, Platte, Arkansas, and other western rivers guided them into and through the western mountains. The courses of such western trails as the Oregon, Santa Fe, and California were largely determined by springs, stream valleys, and mountain passes, sometimes in spite of the adverse influence of hostile climate and Indians. One of the principal reasons for the Gadsden Purchase was the desire to acquire a more favorable topography for transportation routes. One of the most significant devices for adding color to an event is to describe the physical environment in which it occurred. Poets and novelists have been inspired by the beauty of American deserts, lakes, rivers, and mountains that were both assets and liabilities to the American frontier life. Why not students of history?

The student must be made aware that the influence of topography upon the historical development of the nation has diminished with each succeeding generation. Once a trail through the Appalachian Barrier was discovered, and a road of sorts hewn out of the rocks and through the forests, wagons replaced pack animals and travel became easier. With the development of steamboats, railroads, automobiles, and airplanes, with increasing technical knowledge, the movement of people became easier and faster and the geographical influence of topography upon the development of the nation decreased. Today hills are cut down and moved, swamps are drained or filled, and the course of rivers changed to aid man in his progress. Thus, the teacher must present the idea of change in space as well as in time.

Natural Resources

One factor which helps to make the United States a great nation is the vast amount of natural resources found within its borders. Productive soil, great coniferous and deciduous forests, vast quantities of mineral fuels (coal, petroleum, natural gas) easily accessible in great amounts, the primary metallic minerals (iron, copper, lead, zinc, uranium), and enormous quantities of fresh water when combined with intelligent usage make for a progressive, industrial nation. The uneven distribution of these resources has created many problems. Not always has the history of resource use been an intelligent one. Forest fires, sometimes deliberately started, destroyed millions of board feet of lumber; the polution of streams and smaller bodies of water caused many mill sites to be abandoned. Extravagant and wasteful mining methods caused the loss of millions of dollars worth of essential minerals. A study of the history if the Conservation Movement will point up the necessity of man and nature working together.

The agricultural history of the United States is a turbulent one. For many decades the governing bodies of the nation were dominantly rural in composition. Their lack of knowledge about soils and climate, plus the idea that all farming should be like that in the wetter eastern third of the nation, resulted in a series of Homestead Laws that were entirely unsatisfactory. As a result of these laws and of incompetent farming methods, much of the good American topsoil was either washed or blown away. Today's problems of over-production, the lack of markets, and the numerous misunderstandings of rural problems are making the national agricultural history a political nightmare. To understand clearly why some crops dominate in certain areas, history needs to explain more than just the habits of mankind. Shortly after the different areas of Oklahoma were opened for settlement the farmers from the various parts of the nation found that they had to adjust their practices and crops to the soil and climatic conditions in which they were living. The cotton grower settling in the northern part of the state found the growing season too short and the soils of poor quality for cotton production. The wheat farmer in the southeastern part of the state found the soil and climate both too wet for wheat. Eventually the settlers recognized the situation and adjusted accordingly.

As the resources of the nation decrease, the United States becomes more dependent upon the rest of the world. The uneven geographical distribution of natural resources could cause a final world war to gain control of them, or it could bring about world peace through an understanding of national interdependence.

MAPS

The principal tool of the geographer is the map. It is an important tool of the historian as well and should be the chief visual aid of the teacher of history. There are very few lessons in American history that can be taught properly without at least one map before the students and most lessons require several maps or combinations of maps. Topic after topic has a geographical basis so significant that without a map the data lack meaning. Throughout the study of the periods of exploration and colonization the map is necessary to an understanding of the facts of history. Without the map the story of a military campaign consists of a series of arbitrary details. Similarly, the study of such topics as territorial growth, the Missouri Compromise, the growth of slavery, the development of the West, the problems of distribution, or the American participation in world wars is unintelligible without a familiarity with maps. Each student, at the beginning of the course, should learn to read maps with as much care as he reads his textbooks. Among the facts that he must keep constantly in mind are (1) that longitude lines always extend in a north-south direction regardless of their location on the map, (2) that latitude lines always extend in an east-west direction whether straight or curved on the map, (3) that any direction, sometimes even several different directions, may appear at the top or side of a map, (4) that map scales must be studied and used. A careful study of a good map is the next best thing to visiting a historical locality in person.

Most maps of the United States and North America are made on a projection that has a conic base. Have the students note that on such a projection the latitude lines are curved and that the longitude lines are not parallel to each other. Even though the state of Maine may be nearer the top of the map than any other state, by following latitude lines across the map it will be noted that parts of Washington, Idaho, Montana, North Dakota, Minnesota, Wisconsin, and Michigan all extend farther north than does Maine. Have the students follow across the nation along the 45th parallel, the northern boundary of the state of New York, and they can immediately note how much of the United States is north of the Empire State. Follow along the 25th parallel to check the southern extent of Florida and Texas. The same type of exercise may be done for various longitude lines. By so doing the student can be shown graphically that Reno, even though far inland, is west of Los Angeles, or that most of South

America is east of Philadelphia. When a map of North America showing the 49 continental states in their correct relative positions is used, the latitude lines are going to be so curved that West, North, and East, will all be at the top of the map. Longitude lines will be so angled that both South and West will appear on the left and South and East on the right side of the map. Thus, it is absolutely necessary that the student be taught enough geography to be able to read and interpret maps if he is to understand historical events and places in their correct relationship to each other.

Equipment in a history classroom is just as important and essential to the proper conduct of that class as is equipment for a class in physics, chemistry, or home economics. History classrooms need to be equipped with physical, historical, political, and blackboard outline maps as well as a large globe. The maps must be large enough to be seen easily at the back of the room. They should also be made in such a manner that they will be interesting to look at and conducive to study. Numerous small outline maps can profitably be used by each student. In addition to the maps there should be a large historical atlas for class use, and it should be as accessible as an unabridged dictionary. Smaller individual student atlases will aid the student in his daily preparation.

Physical Maps

A large colored plastic relief model, or a shaded and colored relief-like map of the United States should hang in each American history classroom. These maps show the topography and drainage of the country plus certain cultural developments and place locations as they exist today. With few minor exceptions, such as present-day utilization of the Black Swamp area and the formation of large man-made lakes along the Tennessee, Colorado, and other rivers, the maps present the surface features accurately enough for all the various phases of American history on the high school level. The teacher must certainly remind the students, however, that the cultural features and political boundaries shown on the map have developed during different periods of time and have changed from time to time and place to place. Relief maps will be especially helpful in showing the routes followed by various trails, the development of transportation systems, the determination of natural boundaries, as well as the distribution of landforms, agricultural areas, industrial regions, and population. If much attention is to be given to wars and battles, the physical map will furnish the best base for discussions.

Climatic maps that show the distribution of rainfall and variations in temperature conditions can also be used to advantage. By comparing the climatic and relief maps many questions about the historical development of an area can be more easily answered.

One very successful teacher of American history always starts his classes with a detailed study of the physical characteristics of the Atlantic Ocean and the 48 contiguous states. The map of the Atlantic area is used to illustrate relative latitudinal positions of the Caribbean Islands and various parts of the North American continent with that of Spain, Portugal, France, England and the Netherlands. Also the location of the trade winds and the prevailing westerly wind belt along with the direction of flow of the equatorial currents, Gulf Stream, and North Atlantic Drift are pointed out. Brief explanations of the causes that make these features move in the direction they do are made. The chief purpose of the study of the physical map of the United States is to show the relative location of one area to the other, and to teach the names and something about the topography of the more important physical regions. By so doing the student becomes familiar with such locations as the Fall Line, Piedmont, Break of the Plains, and Nashville Basin, and begins to understand something of the importance such places have had in the development of the nation. Only after the "stage has been set" does the teacher introduce the "characters." He then tries to present to the class the continuously changing geographic landscapes as the history of the nation develops.

Historical Maps

For the most efficient teaching of American history a large number of simplified historical maps should be available. These maps, which show the activities during a specific period of time, present the situation as it actually was. For example, a historical map for the period just prior to the Civil War will show the states and territories as they existed at that time. No state of West Virginia will be shown, but the area will be included as a part of Virginia. Numerous territories west of the Mississippi River will be indicated and the student can easily note the difference between political boundaries of the past and present. Such maps will also indicate the more important cities or places for the period under consideration. Many textbooks contain several historical maps that can be used if large ones are not available.

Political Maps

All too often the classrooms are equipped with only a poor quality political map of the nation prior to the admission of Alaska and Hawaii. To be sure, these maps are better than none at all, but the teacher must use them with caution. Often the teacher must remind the student that the political map, as he is viewing it, developed over a century and a half of time and that it is still subject to change. Although it will probably not happen, two or more states could combine, states can adjust boundaries, and Texas has the right to divide itself into five separate states. Students must also be made to realize that although the boundaries shown on the map separate the states politically, they do not change the climate, physical features, agricultural production, or other activties of mankind in adjoining states. In fact the only way one can tell that he is going from one state to another is by signs that man has erected.

Blackboard Maps

One of the most useful of all maps is the blackboard outline map. Such maps usually have the boundaries of the states drawn in as they exist today. On some the rivers are shown in a different shade of black so that their correct location can be easily determined. The teacher, by using various colors of chalk, may use such a map to illustrate many different situations. Thus, it is very easy and quite effective to show with different colors the continuous progress of a specific development; for example, the addition of territory to the original area of the United States. The lands added by the Louisiana Purchase can be shaded yellow, those acquired through the treaty with England in 1818 could be colored pink, and so on for the acquisition of Florida, the annexation of Texas, and of other territories. It is on such a map as this that the teacher can, with a little practice, combine the physical, historical, and political factors for any specific period so that the students may visualize not only the where but gain an understanding of the "why" of history.

Outline Maps

There are many kinds and types of outline maps that may aid the student in his understanding of American history. Too frequently, however, teachers use maps that have only the state boundaries designated. And, probably, these are the least useful of all the outline maps that are available. If the outline map used for student work is to have real value, and leave the correct impressions, it should have the more important physical features—rivers, lakes, mountains—as well as the state boundaries clearly shown. Several of the larger map companies now have such maps available for the continents and the United States. The cost is no more than that of the more commonly used maps.

Many teachers now have their students buy a copy of the map by Lobeck, "Physiographic Diagram of the United States," or the map by Raisz, "Landforms of the United States." These maps have the relief features clearly shown by shading or hachure markings, all the important rivers indicated, the latitudes and longitudes identified, and the present state boundaries marked. The Raisz map has place names on it, but because of its slightly larger size, it is more difficult for the student to handle. With these maps locations can be accurately placed and the relation of the place or area to its surroundings more easily understood. With maps like these before them the students can study and discuss the various additions of territory to the United States, and the location and settlement of boundary disputes as illustrated by the Webster-Ashburton Treaty. They can draw on the map such important trails as the Santa Fe, Oregon, Old Spanish, and others. As they develop the trails along the changing landforms, under varying climatic conditions, through different vegetation areas, with the transportation available at the time, a realization of the meaning of the term "pioneer spirit" and a pride in the achievements of the frontiersmen develops. Not only do the students understand the when, where, and what of American history but they also better understand the why.

Conclusion

Geography can ably assist the teacher of American history if given the opportunity, for no subject is absolutely independent in the material it presents. As mathematics is a tool for the explanation of certain aspects of physics, and the knowledge of languages is an aid to the understanding of literature, so is geography the instrument by which many phases of history can be made more intelligible and interesting to high school students. Correlation and integration of material from two or more academic fields need not mean the loss of identity of either, but should strengthen and supplement the material being presented. In all probability incidental correlation was used by the first good teacher, and it has been utilized by good teachers to varying degrees ever since.

CHAPTER XXIII

Making History Live Through Reading

Helen McCracken Carpenter and Mary Virginia Gaver

THERE has never been a more auspicious time for the teaching of American history than exists today. Each generation, looking at the threats and insecurities of its age, has considered the teaching of American history one remedy for contemporary ills. To us, living in a world with horizons spreading out to encompass the solar system, the need to preserve a nation proud of its past and confident of its future seems more imperative than ever before. Yet who is to say that the race into space is any greater challenge than the problem of national independence or the threat of national division faced by our forefathers? Our time is not unique in a sense of need, for that has been continuous. The sixties are especially propitious in opportunity. Never before has the teacher had the benefit of so many favorable factors for making American history live.

THE MEANS ARE AT HAND

Ours is an era increasingly conscious of its past. This characteristic became discernible as the twentieth century moved into its second quarter and the years since have witnessed a quickening interest in Americana. Like the history of many inventions, the idea of the restored community took root simultaneously in more than one place in the mid-twenties. Decorah, Iowa, began the reconstruction of a frontier village as the Williamsburg Restoration was yielding its first fruits. Today there are over thirty restored communities east of the Mississippi alone. In addition, the reconstruction of single historical sites dot our land from Fort Mackinac on the north to The Alamo on the south—from the Spanish missions along the Pacific to Fort Sumter and the Saugus Ironworks on the Atlantic Coast. It is a rare teacher in this age of rapid transportation who does not have access to some restorations of our past.

The long list of pageants and celebrations presented each summer across our land, commemorating historic events of the locality, further attest our consciousness of the nation's development. The opening of Freedomland indicates that this interest is sufficient to make the re-creation of dramatic events commercially profitable.

Congress, too, recognized the importance of preserving important primary sources when it authorized the establishment of the National Archives and, more recently, of libraries for the papers of each President beginning with Mr. Truman.

Further evidence of the popular appeal of historical themes is to be found in statistics on book production. In the decade between 1946 and 1957, the number of titles in history and the sister area of geography increased more than one hundred fifty per cent. No other fields except agriculture and science, exhibited so marked a rise.[1] In children's book publishing, during the same decade, science showed the greatest gain in number of titles, followed in turn by biography and then history and geography.[2] The phenomenal popular reception accorded *American Heritage, The Magazine of History*, since 1954 has pertinency in this connection also.

In addition to the numerous advantages accruing from a dawning awareness of our nation's heritage, the teacher has available today better and more varied materials prepared for school use than ever before. The format of the modern textbook with its use of multiple color, photographic illustrations and devices to intrigue the listless would fulfill Noah Webster's most ecstatic dreams. Nor would this scholarly propagandist for American history be likely to contend that his classic *American Selections* met the needs of its age as well as the content of contemporary texts serves the needs of today. To dramatize, illustrate, and supplement the written word the new medium of recordings exists in abundance and variety. In the past decade the production of both documentary and dramatic sound films has increased at an encouraging rate. The availability of some television programs dealing with historical subjects on film is a fortuitous development for the teacher. The appearance during the fifties of plastic maps and globes molded to contour can help make the geographical setting of events more meaningful. The production of inexpensive facsimiles of official papers, letters, money, and correspondence is

---

[1] Robert W. Frase, "Economic Development in Publishing," *Library Trends*, 7:8; No. 1, July 1958.

[2] Rachael W. De Angelo, "Children's Book Publishing," *Library Trends*, 7:229; No. 1, July 1958.

growing apace and providing the teacher with a new kind of *realia*. As might be expected, in each of these different media more items are being produced dealing with the growth of the United States than with the development of non-American nations.

The teacher of history is fortunate likewise these days not only that knowledge within the field is extending, as the figures on book publishing indicate, but also that means exist for keeping abreast of the findings of research. The authorization of this Yearbook and its organization devoting three-fourths of the allotted length to interpretation of trends in content is in itself evidence of this point.

READING IS GAINING GROUND

Another source of optimism for the teacher, at least at the secondary level where reading constitutes the chief avenue of learning, is heartening evidence that teen-agers are reading more books and more difficult books than in decades past. A recent survey of seventy-three school and university libraries and state library commissions across the United States reveals a teen-age rush to adult books. In New York City, for example, the 13 to 18 year-olds account for a fourth to a half of the book circulation of adult departments in the branches of the public library. In Reading, Pennsylvania, where population increased little in the two decades between 1938 and 1958, book circulation to young people increased substantially, with a rise in non-fiction from 49,000 to 92,000 and for fiction from 68,500 to 91,250. In Lincoln, Nebraska, population during the 1950's rose thirty per cent but book circulation climbed one hundred per cent. Increased borrowing by teen-agers constituted a noticeable trend.[3] Although statistics are not available to prove it conclusively, librarians assert that works of non-fiction are beginning to outstrip those of fiction in popularity among young people.[4]

The efforts of those outside the academic field to aid in the promotion of reading among children and youth is an encouraging sign of the times which redounds to the benefit of all teachers, including those in American history. The decision of *This Week* magazine to undertake a quarterly feature beginning in September 1960, reporting data from high schools and public libraries under the heading "What Young Americans Are Reading" both reflects the upsurge in reading and also serves to stimulate further book consumption among teen-

---

[3] *Publisher's Weekly*, 178:19; No. 4, July 25, 1960.
[4] *New York Herald Tribune*, July 10, 1960.

agers. The current community service project of the United States Junior Chamber of Commerce, "Good Reading for Youth," focused on children from five to fifteen is a substantial undertaking with benefits accruing to the 3800 communities which have local chapters. The project includes surveys of the availability of books and knowledge about them, the dissemination of good reading lists, a film on the importance of reading and a traveling book exhibit of four hundred titles. The project is being co-sponsored by the Pilgrim Book Society and will have the assistance of professional librarians.

Recent trends in books for children and young adults both mirror and bring to focus these developments in our society. The teacher, hoping to initiate or to keep pace with a reading boom among students, needs to be aware of the trends. The 1950's witnessed the revival and phenomenal growth of publishers' series. Some observers consider this the major trend in children's publishing since World War II although it is not limited to children's books. Series books as developed during the past decade meet uniform standards in format, are written by different authors on different but often related subjects, and are issued by the same publisher under a series name. The practice of publishing books in series received renewed impetus in 1950 with the appearance of the first volumes in the Landmark Books of Random House. Sales of this series alone have totalled more than ten million copies.[5] It is the sole source of selections for the Junior Book-of-the-Month Club. The series field is, however, increasingly competitive. By 1952, ninety-three series were identifiable from the presses of thirty-six publishers. Early in 1958 the number had risen to 148 series from fifty-four publishers[6] and new ones continue to appear. Most of the series books are non-fiction, with American history and heroes serving more frequently than any other emphasis for subject material. The focus of the Landmark Books is entirely that. Other examples of series in which aspects of Americana receive prominent if not total attention include *The Real Books* of Garden City Press; *The First Books* by Watts; *The Signature Books* by Grosset and Dunlap; *The American Heritage Books* by American Book; *The Strength-of-Union Series* by Scribner; and *The American Heritage Junior Library Books* from the Golden Press. The trend is discernible likewise in material for young adults as *Great Lives in Brief* by Knopf,

---

[5] Rachael W. De Angelo, "Children's Book Publishing," *Library Trends*, 7:229; No. 1, July 1958.
[6] *Ibid.*

the *American Heritage Series* from the Sagamore Press and the *Rivers of America Series* issued by Rinehart indicate. Clearly the series has become a marketing device. As such it has resulted, unfortunately, in production and consumption that is not always discriminating. A series mark is no guarantee of uniform quality. Within each of the series now deluging the market, wide variations can be noted in accuracy, readability, and appeal among the volumes. Hence no series should be accepted *in toto* without evaluation of specific titles. A particular trademark on books does not assure a standard brand as it does in groceries or household appliances.

Another trend, related to the growth of series books and yet independent of it also, is the explosion in junior biography. Again the majority of the titles treat figures in the development of America so a harvest awaits the teacher willing to make the effort necessary to garner it. Some of the boom in junior biography results from the development of history series. A number of the well-known series contain volumes of biography, such as *George Washington Carver* by Anne Terry White in Landmark Books; *The Real Book About George Washington Carver* by Harold Coy in the series of Garden City and *The Story of George Washington Carver* by Arna Bontemps from the Signature Series. Various publishers of juveniles have series which are entirely biographical. Examples include Abingdon's *Makers of America*; Putnam's *Lives to Remember*; Houghton's *Piper Books*; and Bobbs-Merrill's *Childhood of Famous Americans*. The same need to judge each title in a series individually applies equally to biography as to other works. In addition to the production of biographical books within series, many publishers issue titles independent of series. The following serve as illustrations: from offerings of Crowell, *Restless Johnny, The Story of Johnny Appleseed* by Ruth L. Holberg; *Peter Zenger, Fighter for Freedom* by Tom Galt; and *Tom Paine, Freedom's Apostle* written by Leo Gurko. The biographies of Jean Lee Latham represent books published individually by Harper—*Young Man in a Hurry*; *The Story of Cyrus W. Field*; *On Stage, Mr. Jefferson*; and *Carry On, Mr. Bowditch*. The individual books cited in this paragraph illustrate two developments in the selection of biographical subjects. The marked increase in number of titles has not resulted in a corresponding expansion of lives presented. All too frequently the same persons are treated again and again. The materials on George Washington Carver above illustrate this point. For statesmen such as Washington, Lincoln, and Franklin the concentration is even greater.

At the same time some efforts are being exerted to portray figures not previously studied. The titles of Crowell and Harper suggest this development. Despite the bulge in juvenile biography, many Americans who contributed to our national development still await the researches of children's authors. An area scarcely touched, for example, is the industrial one for figures in management and labor alike.

Another trend which has occasioned some difference of opinion is the increasing appearance of adult books simplified for young people. The changes take various forms. One is directed toward purification for young minds, as illustrated in the abridgment of Guthrie's *The Big Sky*. Another approach to simplification is the cutting of long descriptive passages and verbiage to highlight the main thought as in the young people's edition of Douglas Southall Freeman's *America's Robert E. Lee*. Yet another avenue is to use an earlier published book as inspiration for the creation of a new work as Alice Dalgliesh has done in *Ride the Wind*, based on Lindbergh's *The Spirit of St. Louis*. To those who look askance at any tampering with a work, none of these methods will result in a satisfactory version. On the other side of the question are a goodly number who feel that simplification, done with skill and respect for the integrity of the original, can bring valuable works within the comprehension of many who are unlikely to enjoy the primary version. In this connection the "Harvard Report" observes:

> There is a need for versions of the great works cleared of unnecessary and unrewarding obstacles and made by abridgment and reflective editing more accessible to general readers. . . . Great books are being read increasingly in abridgments. If these are not made by scholars, they will be made by relatively incompetent hands. Only the scholar knows enough to distinguish the parts of Homer, Plato, the Old Testament, Bacon, Dante, Shakespeare, or Tolstoy which are essential to their value for contemporary general readers from the parts which concern only the special student. But the scholar, by his training, his competitive position, above all his professional ideal, is as a rule unconcerned with this problem. . . . How far this process of clarification or simplification should be carried is, of course, in every instance the prime question. Nothing but a fine awareness both of the material and of the reader's resources will answer it.[7]

It would be hard to minimize the influence of the reading bonanza resulting from a final trend in books for young people. The rise of the paperback has brought change in book publishing, in mass mer-

---

[7] Harvard University Committee on General Education, *General Education in a Free Society* (Cambridge, Massachusetts: Harvard University, 1945), p. 114.

chandising, in libraries, in classrooms, and everywhere a reader may consume a book. The statistics on paperback production tell a remarkable success story. Publication figures first became significant in the annual analysis made by *Publisher's Weekly* for book titles published in 1953. In that year four publishers moved into the group of largest houses on the basis of an increase in paperback titles alone. The number of publishers and paperbound titles each increased steadily until 1958, when figures seem to have levelled at a high peak. An encouraging development accompanying this increase is the appearance of standard works of quality. No longer does the paperback necessarily connote a tawdry story or crude thriller. It has become the means of making the best in writing widely available at a reasonable price. Although there are only about five hundred good, adequately stocked bookstores for the dissemination of knowledge in hard cover editions, the paperback rack has found space in more than 100,000 outlets frequented by Americans as they go about their daily lives. Another advantage of this kind of book packaging is its use in making available works that are out of print in hard cover editions. Examples of interest to the teacher of American history are Margaret Leech's *Reveille in Washington*; Thomas J. Wertenbaker's *Puritan Oligarchy*; and Henry Adams' *The United States in 1800*. Accepted now by the staunchest supporters of hardback collections among teachers and librarians, the little paperback book, like the little car, has become a familiar object on the American scene.

GUIDES FOR BOOK SELECTION ABOUND

The mushrooming popularity of paperbacks highlights a factor which must ever be kept in mind; namely, that easy access to books begets the reading of them. It follows, then, that one of the primary responsibilities of the teacher intent upon making history live through books is to insure the availability of them in the school and the community. Book selection should be a cooperative endeavor of teacher and school librarian. On such a team the librarian is the generalist, possessing knowledge of general and specialized bibliographies and of the basic materials in American history, together with the techniques for judging editions and evaluating series. The teacher brings to the task a thorough knowledge of the subject matter content of American history and the particular needs at the grade level concerned. Together the teacher and the school librarian can build a collection of materials suited to the needs of the school and its students.

Whatever academic level the school serves, its library should contain special reference tools in the field of American history, and a balanced selection of trade books providing fiction, biography, and factual materials related to the field, as well as an organized pamphlet and periodical collection.

Basic guides most useful for accomplishing this purpose are described in the paragraphs which follow. The numbers given in parentheses refer to order of listing at the end of this chapter. Bibliographies selected for recommendation are those considered to be the most inclusive, up-to-date and likely to continue in print, on materials in American history for grades five through fourteen. No regional bibliographies are included.

General Guides

Since specialized bibliographies, limited by both subject area and grade level, seldom provide an over-all coverage, general aids in book selection such as the volumes in the "Standard Catalog Series" are necessary basic tools. Most important in this series are the *Children's Catalog* (7) for grades one through eight, the *Standard Catalog for High School Libraries* (19) covering grades seven through twelve, and the *Standard Catalog for Public Libraries* (20) listing best titles, of non-fiction only, for adult use. Recommendations for each volume are selected by a committee of consultants working with the age level of concern in each bibliography. Pertinent sections for the teacher of American history are 917.3 to 917.98 covering the geography of the United States and of individual states; 920 and 92 for biography; and 973 to 979.8 for the history of the United States and of individual states. Annotations aid in the identification of content. For many years these works have been considered the most authoritative guides for book selection. Recently, however, with the expansion of the school curriculum and increasing attention to the needs of the gifted, the first two titles are proving adequate only for basic collections but not for extensive supplementary references.

Therefore, the teacher who needs a wider choice of titles for depth or breadth of subject matter might turn profitably to a new annual bibliography, *Subject Guide to Books in Print* (21). The most recent edition will list most books, exclusive of fiction and texts, currently in print in the United States, by subject. Teachers of the middle grades should note that juvenile non-fiction is listed in one of two ways: either under a special sub-heading (e.g., "Frontier and Pioneer

Life—Juvenile Literature") or by grade level (e.g., "gr. 4-6") after the title. The teacher will find useful also a desk copy of the inexpensive *Paperbound Books in Print* (17) issued quarterly as well as a copy of *Textbooks in Print* (23).

The imposing title of Hoffman's *Readers' Adviser and Bookman's Manual* (13) does not suggest its usefulness to teachers. This compact book provides a selective guide to the best adult literature in print by noting the important works of some 2000 authors with annotations and critical quotations. Of particular importance is the fact that the ninth edition features in the chapter on "American History," the newest titles on the Civil War. Other relevant chapters are those on "Travel and Adventure" and "Biography and Autobiography." For handy desk use, this guide is more comprehensive than Larrabee (15).

Specialized Guides

The true scholar-teacher will have recourse also to the various specialized bibliographies now available. The most important ones for grades five through fourteen are grouped below in three categories.

Factual materials. A new publication from the Library of Congress is a real boon for teachers at the senior high school or junior college level. The compilers of *A Guide to the Study of the United States of America* (25) "aimed to gather together in one publication a series of bibliographical studies of development in the United States." The basis of selection has been the value and timeliness of each book, with a terminal date of 1955, although some sections list titles published to 1958. The wide scope of this tool is indicated by such chapter headings as "Literature," "Local History," "Entertainment" and "Constitutional Government."

Mention was made in Chapter I of the materials available from the Service Center for Teachers of the American Historical Association. Representative examples of the inexpensive monographs designed to bring teachers up-to-date on research in particular phases are *The American Frontier* by Ray Billington; *New Interpretations of American Colonial History* by Louis B. Wright; and *United States History, A Bridge to the World of Ideas* by William Burlie Brown. Another title in this series, *Key to the Past* (10) is entirely bibliographical, listing general and specialized works and biography on American history (p. 30-59) for the pre-college reader.

Teachers in secondary schools and junior colleges need constantly at hand *The Harvard Guide to American History* edited by Handlin (12) which is even more definitive than its predecessor, the old *Guide* by Channing, Hart and Turner now long out of print. The emphasis on scholarly works makes the *Harvard Guide* a rewarding tool for leads to material for advanced placement classes. For the same grade levels, *American Panorama* (15) likewise has utility. Its contents are interesting and unique in that the titles consist of books selected by the Carnegie Corporation to be sent as gifts to libraries in British Commonwealth countries to interpret "presentday American civilization and its origins." One-page essays by such authorities as Carl Carmer and Jacques Barzun give perspective on each book. A desk copy of either Carr's *Guide to Reading for Social Studies Teachers* (6) or Clarke's *Research Materials in the Social Sciences* (8) is essential. Carr annotates seventy-two books on United States history (p. 59-76) selected on the basis of scholarship, utility, recency, and readability. Clarke's work was designed to replace Louis Kaplan's standard research manual. It is more limited in scope but more up-to-date than Carr.

Biography is an essential part of the American history collection at all grade levels. The basic guide is the *Biography Index* (3) which indicates materials published since January, 1946. This comprehensive guide lists not only whole books, but also articles from books and from 1500 magazines and includes such kinds of information as obituaries, pictorial works, genealogies and imaginative works about real people. A symbol denotes juvenile titles.

Historical fiction. Guides to this kind of material are useful to the teacher and much in demand by students. Nevertheless, coverage is inadequate for the grade levels of concern in this chapter. Logasa's *Historical Fiction* has been widely used but is inaccurate in the information supplied on both the citation and the scope of titles included. In addition, it recommends uncritically many titles of doubtful historical value. Its utility is impaired further by the large proportion of titles which have long been out of print. Examples of inaccurate classifications are as follows: listing of a story of Nathaniel Bowditch under 1760-1776, when his dates were 1773-1838; recommendation of *The Courage of Sarah Noble*, a fine story of an eight-year-old written at third to fourth grade reading level, for the junior high school; placement of Jones' biographical novel of Eli Terry under 1670-1776 when Terry's dates were 1772-1852. Finally, many annotations are so short as to be not only inadequate but actually misleading. For these reasons, Logasa is not recommended.

These criticisms illustrate the difficulties in providing a tool which is accurate, up-to-date and adequately annotated. One is needed especially for the middle and junior high school grades. Teachers of these grades must in the meantime use the *Children's Catalog* (7) and *Standard Catalog for High School Libraries* (19) supplemented by three specialized lists which can be recommended. Baker's *Stories About Negro Life for Children* (2) lists books of all kinds which are deemed to "give an unbiased, accurate well-rounded picture of Negro life in all parts of the world." Ladley's *Selective, Annotated Bibliography* (14) and Carpenter's *Gateways to American History* (5) list materials for special needs in teaching American history. Carpenter's bibliography has long been out of print but a complete revision is in press. Since titles are selected for slow learners in junior high school, the listings are useful also at the elementary school level.

Tooze and Krone's *Literature and Music as Resources for Social Studies* (24) lists books for grades five to nine (p. 126-43). In spite of the fact that it is difficult to use and now somewhat dated, the book is reported to be of real usefulness to teachers in schools where librarians have built collections of the titles recommended by this bibliography.

Historical fiction at the secondary and junior college level is more adequately listed in available selection aids. The most inclusive title is the *Fiction Catalog* (11) a part of the "Standard Catalog Series." Novels can be identified in this tool under headings as specific as "Frontenac" and "Mormons" as well as under more general headings, such as "Frontier and Pioneer Life" or "United States—18th Century—Revolution." Titles recommended for ages fourteen to twenty are marked by "Y"; annotations describing the content are given only under the author of each title. For a more selective, inexpensive list, Coan and Lillard's *America in Fiction* (10) can be strongly recommended. Designed to serve young people in the eleventh and twelfth grades and adults, it is selective and representative rather than exhaustive. Ahlers' *Enriching American History* (1) is inexpensive and has proved useful and accurate. Carlsen and Alm's *Social Understanding Through Literature* (4) is another excellent publication of the National Council for the Social Studies which is being revised. Although this work focuses chiefly on literature dealing with modern social problems in this country, many of the titles are pertinent for a course in American history which is presented chronologically.

Supplementary materials. Supplementary aids such as magazines and government documents are listed for teachers of United States history in a variety of guides. For identification of periodicals useful in studying American history two reference works are recommended.

Teachers should consult the list of magazines indexed in each work for information on what is available. The *Subject Index to Children's Magazines* (22) lists forty-two periodicals published for children, of which five are junior historical magazines, seven are classroom news magazines, and three are classroom geography publications. For secondary grades and junior college, the *Readers' Guide to Periodical Literature* (18) provides comparable help in building a periodical collection. The school library should have available also for the teacher a set of the indexes to the *National Geographic Magazine* (16). Articles in this periodical on geography, local historical shrines, and such subjects as the new states of Hawaii and Alaska are appropriate for use at all grade levels.

Finally, no teacher of United States history should ignore the value of government documents. The How To Do It pamphlet published by the National Council (26) supplies helpful information on the location of such materials. The single most useful series of lists for the teacher, which can be secured free from the U. S. Superintendent of Documents, is the *Price List Series.* These are leaflets which appear annually and list selected titles on a variety of subjects. Most useful in this connection are those on American history (Price List #50), Foreign Relations (Price List #65), Geography and Exploration (Price List #35), and Political Science (Price List #54).

CRITERIA HELP IDENTIFY QUALITY

In providing a wealth of reading resources, familiarity with the guides to available materials, however, it not enough. A knowledge of the characteristics of literature in its various forms is necessary also. Everyone concerned in getting the "right book for the right child" in American history—teacher, librarian *and* student—needs to be aware of the qualities which make fiction truly historical. This involves an understanding of the relationship between history, historical facts, and fiction. It requires the ability to discriminate between the journalistic approach which allows the reader to witness historical happenings and that of the master novelist who communicates a sense of living them. The balance between fidelity to history as an objective record and to the novel as a literary art form is a delicate one and the qualities which indicate achievement of it need to be kept in mind. Another fascinating and useful hybrid is the biographical novel, a newcomer to the literary stage in the last thirty years. Here the characteristics which distinguish history, fiction and biography must be understood for discriminating selection. Born of the union of biography and fiction as parents, with history for the grandparent, this approach, if true to standards of documentation and honesty in interpretation of data, can make history live more vividly than the purely biographical presentation. Both biography and poetry offer contributions to the enrichment of teaching if selection is made based on an understanding of the unique attributes of each.

In addition to knowledge of the characteristics which mark the best works in these various literary forms, the teacher should know the qualities which make each most appealing to students at the different levels of the school system. For example, in the junior high school grades, biography is the most popular which describes acts of daring and courage, excitement, humor and human interest. For older young people, an appealing form is the personal narrative of adventure of which there has been a goodly number recently.

Obviously, criteria for judging the form, content, and appeal of materials for reading enrichment in American history would be appropriate for inclusion in this chapter but space limitations necessitate their omission. Readers seeking help on these matters will find useful several series of articles appearing in *Social Education*, the official magazine of the National Council for the Social Studies.[8] Perhaps the single volume which is the most recent, succinct, and comprehensive on characteristics and use of different forms of literature is by Dwight L. Burton.[9] Application to the teaching of the social studies, including history, is made at many points throughout the book.

Quite apart from the need for criteria for judging material according to high standards of quality as a piece of literature is the importance of having a policy for the selection of resources of a controversial nature. This is true for reading matter whether it be fictional or factual. The need to use materials presenting all phases of American life or all points of view on an issue is accepted, at least verbally, by most teachers of history. However, forces in the community often are blamed by educators for thwarting freedom in the choice of reading matter and topics for consideration. Yet a recent investigation using schools in California has found that it is more often the teacher's and

---

[8] See articles on local biography by Ralph A. Brown in the issues from February through May 1952; on historical fiction by Morris Gall in the issues of April 1953, February 1, 1955, and December 1956; on biography by Ralph A. and Marian R. Brown in issues for January, February, April, November, and December 1954 and for May 1955. John A. Garraty's article on writing biography, November 1955, has pertinency also.

[9] *Literature Study in the High Schools* (New York: Holt, 1959), 291 p.

the librarian's failure to acquire needed materials which results in so-called censorship than it is in the intervention of community pressures.[10] Nothing is more important or useful in the education of citizens than the fair and balanced consideration of controversial issues and materials. The path to the avoidance of difficulties does not lie in fearful inactivity but rather in strong joint leadership by teachers and librarians in the formulation and adoption by the school administration and the faculty of a clear statement of policy in these matters.

MOTIVATION DETERMINES USE

Various avenues to the motivation of reading are suggested at the beginning of this chapter. Each teacher must find for himself the method best suited to his own personality, the resources of the school and community, and the nature of his students. Both teachers and students should realize that historical fiction and biography, newspapers and other periodicals, primary sources, reference books, and specialized factual accounts can make an important contribution and should be an integral part of classwork. The prominence given to books in class discussions will help promote wide reading.

Pupils should be encouraged to bring to class the materials most helpful to them on the topic for consideration, and to paticipate with books open, making reference to authors' interpretations where pertinent, and reading to the class appropriate illustrative bits. Class time given occasionally to discussion of books which various pupils are enjoying and can recommend to others is rewarding. Book talks by the teacher or the librarian at the beginning of a unit stimulate interest and provide guidance. Early in a unit, class periods devoted entirely to reading in the classroom or the library help focus attention on the importance of that activity and also enable the teacher to give needed help.

The accessibility of reading materials contributes to frequency of use. Teachers hope that, in making pupils aware of books, the library habit in school and outside will be established. Once students have become book conscious, deriving pleasure as well as information from printed materials, they will read, and stimulate each other to read more. The "learning-sharing-together" spirit is the most pleasant of all classroom feelings and is fostered better through a wide reading program than by any other method. Many students read little because

---

[10] Marjorie Fiske, *Book Selection and Censorship: A Study of School and Public Libraries in California* (Berkeley, Calfornia: University of California, 1959), Chapter 5.

they are not required to do much. The classwork must be conducted in such a way that the students will have to read a variety of books to get what they need.

Successful use depends not only on motivation but also on skill development. Nothing dampens a reading program faster than student frustration in locating and interpreting material. Skills involved include facility in the use of the card catalog and classification system in a library, together with the ability to use basic reference tools such as the dictionary, encyclopedia, and periodical indexes. Competence in the use of specialized reference materials such as the *Dictionary of American History,* the *Dictionary of American Biography,* and historical atlases also is necessary. Important, too, is skill in recognizing the kinds of resources most likely to yield information. In building a program for the development of these skills, it is mutually advantageous for the teacher and the librarian to cooperate.

Success in creating a classroom atmosphere conducive to wide reading depends on the teachers' own reading attitudes, interests, and habits. He must know books, read them, love them, and talk about them. His enthusiasm will do much to spread the book germ in his own classes, and conceivably in the school. The comment of MacKinlay Kantor on the task of the historical novelist has pertinence for the teacher who would make history live for his students.

. . . he who would bring the past quivering to life, cannot buy his paints at the nearest shop and spread them quickly upon his palette. He must bruise the petals of rare flowers found in unfrequented spots, and mix them with the gum that oozes from equally lonely trees. He must climb distant and dangerous cliffs in order to scrape up his ochre. He must go far into the Sahara of libraries, to shoot the lonely camel whose hair, and only whose hair, will be fit to make his brush.

All patriotism and all pride demand that he shall make a molten sacrifice of his eyes and his fingers. The past lies buried deep and cannot be torn from its immurement without pain.

Go and live in that other time, before you would tell of it. This has been done, it can be done, it will be done again.[11]

BIBLIOGRAPHIES RECOMMENDED

1. Ahlers, Eleanor E., ed., *Enriching American History; An Annotated Bibliography of Fiction and Biography for High School,* Curriculum Bulletin No. 178 (Eugene, Oregon: School of Education, University of Oregon, 1956), 49 p. Mimeo.

---

[11] "The Historical Novel" in *Three Views of the Novel* (Washington, D. C.: Superintendent of Documents, U.S. Government Printing Office, 1957), p. 41.

2. Baker, Augusta, *Stories About Negro Life for Children* (New York: New York Public Library, 1957), 24 p.

3. *Biography Index; A Cumulative Index to Biographical Material in Books and Magazines*, January 1946—date (New York: H. W. Wilson Company, 1949—date).

4. Carlsen, G. Robert and Alm, Richard S., *Social Understanding Through Literature; A Bibliography for Secondary Schools* (Washington, D. C.: National Council for the Social Studies, a department of the National Education Association, 1954), 111 p.

5. Carpenter, Helen McCracken, *Gateways to American History; An Annotated Graded List of Books for Slow Learners in Junior High School* (New York: H. W. Wilson Company, 1942), 255 p. (o.p.; rev. ed. in press).

6. Carr, Edwin R., *Guide to Reading for Social Studies Teachers*, Bulletin No. 26 (Washington, D. C.: National Council for the Social Studies, a department of the National Education Association, 1951), 154 p.

7. *Children's Catalog; A Classified Catalog of 3,204 Children's Books Recommended for Public and School Libraries With an Author, Title and Subject Index* (9th ed.; New York: H. W. Wilson Company, 1956), supplements to date.

8. Clarke, Jack Alden, comp., *Research Materials in the Social Sciences* (Madison, Wisconsin: University of Wisconsin, 1959), 42 p.

9. Coan, Otis W. and Lillard, Richard G., eds., *America in Fiction; An Annotated List of Novels That Interpret Aspects of Life in the United States* (4th ed.; Stanford, California: Stanford University, 1956), 200 p.

10. Faissler, Margareta, *Key to the Past; Some History Books for Pre-College Readers* (2nd ed., Washington, D. C.: Service Center for Teachers of History, American Historical Association, 1959), 77 p.

11. *Fiction Catalog, 1950 Edition; A Subject, Author and Title List of 3,400 Works of Fiction in the English Language With Annotations* (New York: H. W. Wilson Company, 1951), supplements to date.

12. Handlin, Oscar, et al., *Harvard Guide to American History* (Cambridge, Massachusetts: Belknap, 1954), 689 p.

13. Hoffman, Hester R., *The Reader's Adviser and Bookman's Manual; Formerly "The Bookman's Manual"* (9th ed.; New York: R. R. Bowker Company, 1960), 1117 p.

14. Ladley, Winifred C., ed., *Selective, Annotated Bibliography of Books Published 1945-1957 to be Used in a Social Studies Program Concerning the United States, at the Intermediate Level*, Curriculum Bulletin No. 188 (Eugene, Oregon: School of Education, University of Oregon, 1958), 58 p. Mimeo.

15. Larrabee, Eric, ed., *American Panorama; Esseys by Fifteen American Critics on 350 Books Past and Present Which Portray the U. S. A. in its Many Aspects* (New York: New York University, 1957), 436 p.

16. National Geographic Magazine, *Cumulative Index, 1899-1956* (2 vols.; Washington, D. C.: National Geographic Society, 1932-1957).

17. *Paperbound Books in Print;* An Index to . . . Actively Available Inexpensive Reprints and Originals (New York: R. R. Bowker Company, 1955–date), quarterly.

18 *Readers' Guide to Periodical Literature,* 1901–date (New York: H. W. Wilson Company, 1901–date).

19. *Standard Catalog for High School Libraries, Seventh Edition; A Selected Catalog of 3,585 Books* (New York: H. W. Wilson Company, 1957), supplements to date.

20. *Standard Catalog for Public Libraries, Fourth Edition, 1958; A Classified Annotated List of 7,610 Non-Fiction Books Recommended for Public and College Libraries, With a Full Analytical Index* (New York: H. W. Wilson Company, 1959), supplements to date.

21. *Subject Guide to Books in Print; An Index to the Publisher's Trade List Annual* (New York: R. R. Bowker Company, 1957–date), annual.

22. *Subject Index to Children's Magazines,* vol. 1, 1948–date. (Order from Meribah Hazen, 301 Palomino Lane, Madison 5, Wisconsin.)

23. *Textbooks in Print* (New York: R. R. Bowker Company), annual.

24. Tooze, Ruth and Krone, Beatrice Parham, *Literature and Music are Resources for Social Studies* (Englewood Cliffs, New Jersey: Prentice-Hall, 1955), 457 p.

25. U. S. Library of Congress, *A Guide to the Study of the United States of America; Representative Books Reflecting the Development of American Life and Thought,* prepared under the direction of Roy P. Basler by Donald H. Mugridge and Blanche P. McCrum (Washington, D. C.: General Reference and Bibliography Department, Library of Congress, 1960), 1193 p.

26. Wronski, Stanley P., *How to Locate Useful Government Publications,* How To Do It Series No. 11 (Washington, D. C.: National Council for the Social Studies, a department of the National Education Association, 1952), 7 p. Temporarily o.p.

CHAPTER XXIV

Local Resources for Teaching American History

William G. Tyrrell

INTRODUCTION

THE study of American history can be facilitated greatly by wise use of local resources. Utilization of these resources is stimulated by the celebration of anniversaries of great events.

Ceremonies commemorating the one hundredth anniversary of the Civil War, beginning in January 1961, focused new attention on five momentous years in our history. In addition to re-enactments of exciting events on battlefields, the Civil War Centennial planned also to examine with greater care than ever before the impact of the war on existing institutions and communities throughout the nation. Anniversary programs emphasized the need to search out new materials and sources of information in order to enlarge understanding of the war and its influence on the course of history. Collectors have had a field day adding to their stocks of wartime mementoes and memorabilia. Scholars seeking new light on the war and its implications have been confronted with numerous first-hand accounts. Letters and diaries, scribbled in pencil or scrawled in ink that is fading into illegibility a century later, tell the experiences of young men of courage of earlier generations. Their observations about the routine of camp life, the uncertain anticipation of conflict, and the horrors and bravery on the battlefields are personal, intimate commentaries on an epoch of history.

Carefully folded and tightly-bound collections of letters and the well-worn pages of notebook diaries are available in profusion. Shelves of local historical societies, library collections, and manuscript repositories contain many of these original sources of information about the Civil War. For individual soldiers and sailors and their families, as well as for the entire nation, the war was a great turning point. It is not surprising, therefore, that documentary materials along with the souvenirs have been preserved in quantity. Emphasis on aspects of history shifts, and today's historian complains that there has not been preserved a comparable quantity of documentary materials that relate to experience on the homefront or that tell about social, economic, and cultural developments during the war. The current Centennial is giving attention to this need and should expand knowledge about the entire scope of the war.

The decade following the Civil War produced additional local sources for the study of American history. In the 1870's a corps of veterans was available to serve as salesmen for a flood of county histories. In addition, the Centennial Celebration in that decade of one hundred years of independence greatly stimulated the publication of local history. There had been occasional histories of counties before the 1870's, but they were on a much smaller scale. Those that appeared in the last decades of the nineteenth century and into the first years of the twentieth century were designed to be far more impressive. The new examples were all very much the same with garish gilt decorations and steel engraved portraits of leading citizens or line cuts of farmsteads of the area. The county histories stressed the beginnings of settlement and the organization of local institutions. In addition to geological and geographical descriptions, many quarto-sized volumes reproduced original land grants, letters from early visitors, and lists of local officials, clergymen, lawyers, and veterans. The compilers also gave ardent attention to churches, the press, and "bench and bar" of the region.

Authors of county histories were well-meaning individuals with affection for their neighborhood and devotion and enthusiasm for collecting information about community history. Their efforts resulted in preserving a quantity of information that is not readily available elsewhere, and historians must be grateful to their antiquarian pursuits. At their best, however, the books are exceedingly weak in historical synthesis and interpretation. Later generations have described these county histories as "mug books." Each title had an added section or volume of illustrated biographies to swell the importance of the local subscribers. It was the cash payments by the subscribers that financed publication of the histories, and the biographical sketches were written in the most laudatory style. Approbation prevailed throughout the volumes, and criticism never soiled their pages. The authors, however, stressed the role of individuals in the community and supplied a biographical, personalized approach to history.

Primary sources of information about historic events, particularly those connected with military and naval history, an emphasis on individuals as creators of history—all of these are characteristics of local sources of history.

ADVANTAGES OF LOCAL SOURCES

Almost every community contains a wide variety of historical source materials. These local sources afford an unmatched opportunity for revealing to students the processes of history and its methodology. Quantities of material are available for demonstrating the significance of primary sources as the basis for historical knowledge. Here, too, are actual materials that require critical evaluation. Local manuscript materials can also be used to display the existence of differences of opinion and to show that historians may sometimes never reach a complete and final decision about the past. Local documentary sources are extremely valuable for explaining historical analysis and synthesis, and these same sources cannot be surpassed for making clear the prevalence of both change and continuity in history. Familiar references in the community can be employed as devices for teaching chronology. The use of the familiar to explain the remote is, of course, an accepted teaching method, and local sources facilitate this important approach to instruction.

Moreover, national history is based to a large extent on generalizations formed from the study of the sources of history in localities. The community and all its resources supply a closeup view of history. More frequent and careful examination of local sources will thus help to illuminate subjects in national history. Every community has in it materials for explaining and for making concrete and realistic countless historic topics. All communities, it is apparent, have not had identical historical experiences, but each rural village or industrial city, seacoast port or plantation settlement supplies complete, convenient, and authentic materials for explaining the influence of environment on history.

Community sources of history make it possible to enrich the study of American history by introducing local references to educational developments, religious changes, and accomplishments in the arts and technology—topics that cannot usually be fitted into the syllabus. With imagination, based on the full utilization of local sources, teachers of

American history can devise many activities in and out of the class-room to encourage historical research as well as individual expression in recreating history. Depending on the individual's interest and skills, these projects may be used to translate historical expression into words, pictures, models, maps, clothing, food, or many other devices according to the student's abilities.

Libraries, historical societies, government offices, museums and local individuals preserve the raw materials of history. Not every community, unfortunately, has been so conscious of its past as to pre-serve adequately its historical materials. But most communities, both large and small, do possess documentary evidence that tells of its beginning and development, its problems and accomplishments, and that also helps to explain the ideas and concepts which we consider to be part of our history. In smaller places, historical materials may still have to be searched for and collected; in the larger, the quantity may be overwhelming. But all places provide challenges in seeking out the solution to some problem of the past.

RECORDS OF INDIVIDUALS

Letters, journals, and diaries, as already mentioned, are significant sources of history. They are available in every community. Informa-tion in such sources may relate to the unusual and exceptional rather than to day-by-day, normal happenings that constitute a legitimate record of history. The rambling letters of a school boy to his pal, the secret diary of a school girl, the carefully noted record of the daily activities of the local blacksmith, storekeeper, clergyman, or doctor provide a wealth of details about the past and place historical develop-ments in a new perspective.

One problem for the person planning to use local materials is that letters with information about community life are usually mailed to some other area. In the same way, the community receives letters from other spots. Correspondence from the soldier on duty in some distant post and from the adventurous youth in search of wealth in western minefields contain references about completely different areas. But these documents do relate to a part of the community experience, and the fact that they came from a local resident can re-enforce or re-awaken interest in some subjects that would appear to have only remote relations to the immediate surroundings.

Too often, the old is preserved on account of its age without evalua-tion of its historical content. Wartime material, for example, exists in quantity and frequently with a duplication of details. At the same time, there is a need for authentic documentary evidence about other experiences of individuals. This need is particularly acute for the recent decades of the 1920's and 1930's. Locating and using any such local sources that are at all comprehensive in scope would supply information about the period and would be appropriate for evaluating evidence and for making judgments about historical interpretations of the decades.

RECORDS OF ORGANIZATIONS

Records of community organizations are among the primary sources that are most useful in the study of history. Business records—ledgers, journals, daybooks, and budgets—document economic history. These materials explain the scope of business organizations: they indicate how the concern operated, how much it paid for goods and services, and how much it received for its products. The records of a local grist mill or those of a new electronics plant are helpful materials for explaining changes in economic life. They document revolutions in production along with developments in such related fields as financial resources, labor supply, union organizations, and marketing and distribution.

School and church records also reveal modifications and adjustments in many features of life. Churches have declined, merged, or disappeared; their responsibilities and activities have altered. Records that throw light on these changes are enlightening sources for part of our social history. Churches with a strong central organization have preserved source materials more carefully than those that adhere to looser, local control. School documents recount the existence of a one-room school house and its replacement by a central school. School materials also indicate curriculum changes, new concepts of education, and attitudes towards the school in the community. Such sources are pertinent and understandable for discussing historical change and for displaying contrasts between past and present.

Many private and public organizations have records which illuminate many aspects of local history. The establishment of a local agricultural society, fire department, or civic improvement league represents a milestone in many communities. The lyceum, temperance society, and veterans association are other local groups that have contributed additional sources of historical information. These groups provide many challenging experiences in seeking out information, evaluating it, and determining the effectiveness of the organization in the community.

Local offices of government contain historical materials with a close relationship to several subjects in history. Minute books specify in detail, chronologically, administrative actions and decisions and local laws and ordinances. These basic sources of information trace the expansion of functions and responsibilities that is a characteristic of every level of government. Annual and special reports are additional sources of information about governmental affairs. Government offices have long given careful attention to preserving records about the sale and transfer of public and private real property; along with assessment rolls and official maps and surveys, these materials are the substances for showing changes in community structure. Census records and vital statistics, after their preservation came to be formally required in the late nineteenth century, combine a personal approach to history with statistical data. They both verify and measure population changes and sources. Judicial records are significant for studying legal concepts and shifts in moral standards.

Many government offices suffer from gaps in their records because of the loss or destruction of documents. Also unfortunate is the fact that records do not always explain why decisions were made nor indicate the conflict and arguments that were involved in reaching a particular decision. These conditions remind the historian that he cannot be satisfied with one source of information but must search in many places for material on which to base his own interpretations. In recent years, many decisions have been made by telephone calls, and these impermanent conversations provide no evidence for the historical record. At the same time, government offices acquire such a quantity of materials in correspondence, routine records, and reports that research is now much more difficult. The person who plans to use government records should know what materials are available and in which office they are located. Public officials are busy people, but when approached properly they can furnish invaluable sources of information, with bearing on political history and on many other developments in the past.

PRINTED SOURCES

Local newspapers are obvious printed sources of history. The daily or weekly paper provides convenient insight into most features of community life. News columns highlight events of interest and importance along with the trivial, but the latter can also be used advantageously by the resourceful teacher. Editorial pages, letters to the editor, and cartoons reveal individual points of view, and, if used cautiously, may serve as a guide to community attitudes. Every student, however, should be warned against generalizing about public opinion without adequate evidence. Advertisements illustrate and express changes in style and taste as well as in price levels.

Anyone who has used newspapers as sources of history soon becomes aware of the problems they present. Inaccurate reporting and printing mean that they must be checked against other sources. Rarely does a local newspaper have any sort of index. The person doing the research, therefore, can use considerable time turning and examining pages unless he knows the approximate date of the item for which he is searching. Moreover, because of its quality, paper deteriorates rapidly thus adding to the difficulty of use; and, indeed, frequent use may completely shred the pages of 50-year-old newspapers. Microfilm copies or other photo-duplication processes can be investigated as solutions to this problem. But when many newspaper pages are filled with identical materials supplied by press services and newspaper syndicates it may not seem worth the expense to preserve all papers.

Other printed sources of information are the local histories. Although these are secondary sources, many contain varying amounts of primary materials. Histories of local organizations and institutions may be only pamphlet size, but their contents relate specifically to broader developments in social, economic, or political history. Gazetteers, directories, and almanacs afford splendid opportunities for becoming familiar with innovations in the community and its activities. If the community is not large enough to have its own published directory, the telephone book, in the last half century, at least, can help to document changes in occupations and other local pursuits. Many communities have published specialized periodicals to promote some special cause. Those for temperance and agrarian reform have been especially conspicuous and relate directly to social and economic history.

Guide books and travelers' accounts are frequently the earliest descriptions of natural surroundings and the infant community. In a similar category is the promotional literature of land companies and, at a later time, of local chambers of commerce. Local resources such as these furnish experience in evaluating sources. The traveler's report may be overly critical, while that of the real estate promoter is probably extravagantly enthusiastic and uncritical. Students need to know how to read critically and to determine the existence of bias. Materials of this sort aid invaluably in these processes of learning.

Catalogs, brochures, and prospectuses contain information about a new business or school and are rich sources for showing historical innovations. Broadsides, timetables, business cards, and programs are further examples of ephemera that exist in every community and which can be used to illustrate and make more realistic many classroom discussions.

Non-Written Sources

Non-written materials are additional local sources of historical information. Examples of this sort are the traditional attitudes and beliefs that are widely accepted throughout the community. In spite of their importance, they might be ignored as historical sources. Nevertheless, the feelings they express have considerable relevancy in historical developments. Traditional songs, for example, may express, in a colorful and vital way, pertinent beliefs about some subject, person, or event of the past. Celebrations and festivals by groups in the community can be related to similar affairs of others. Connecting these events to an international background can be especially beneficial in many sections of the study of history.

Another example of the non-written source is the memory of individuals. Many elderly men and women have observed or even taken part in community changes during the years of a long life. Most will never write down their reminiscences, but they can be used as sources of information. The interview is an accepted method of obtaining information, and students can benefit from meeting and questioning individuals and from seeking to determine the validity of their statements. Tape recorders facilitate and encourage the utilization of this source. As in all examples of historical investigation, students must have basic ideas about the sort of information they hope to obtain and guidance in effective and tactful ways of obtaining it.

Visual Materials

Pictures, prints, paintings, engravings, and photographs supply visual records of the past. Oils, watercolors, lithographs, or colored photographs, show the appearance of buildings, scenery, persons, and events in history. Illustrations on broadsides, advertisements, and sheet music also furnish views of history. Pictorial materials supply realistic impressions that may be closer contacts with history than narrative accounts. As more and more information comes from pictures, students must know how to interpret and explain the value of the material. They should be able to recognize different levels of quality in reproducing reality in pictorial representations. They should also recognize artistic conventions and be familiar with perspective and the point of view of the person making the scene. As in any historical material, the person using it should verify its authenticity by attempting to find out when, where, why, and by whom it was created.

Individuals or classes can prepare their own pictorial records of transformations in the physical appearance of the community. Amateur photographers and embryo artists have countless local historic subjects for their lens or brush. A class-made motion picture, play, or pageant involves careful research in historical backgrounds and contributes to experiences in both verbal and visual expression.

Maps, as symbols of reality, can be effectively explained by relating the map to the actual area it represents. Maps of city blocks, of highway surveys, or of rural residents in a county atlas of the mid-nineteenth century can be used to acquire a necessary skill. Other maps of physical surroundings, land use, and economic activities are essential for exhibiting transformations in the local environment.

Charts and graphs are similar devices for interpreting reality, and students need to know the basis for these symbols. By collecting, evaluating, and interpreting historical data students will acquire skills in preparing and using these materials. Population changes, land values, and costs of living are some subjects that lend themselves to graphic interpretation.

REALISTIC MATERIALS

The local community preserves in many ways realistic evidences of the past. The preserved, restored, or reconstructed building with its period furnishings and equipment makes it possible to walk directly into the past. An increasing interest in historical preservation, at the present time, affords notable contributions to contemporary education. Student visitors to historic sites can relive the past by actually seeing how their ancestors lived, worked, played, worshipped, and also fought.

Museums preserve other real objects that tell about the past. A simple tool can, in a clearcut way, indicate differences between handcraftsmanship and machine production. A display of candlemolds, whale oil vessels, kerosene lamps, gas fixtures, incandescent bulbs, and flourescent tubes explains shifts in household duties, technological improvements, and industrial expansion. The museum, however, should not merely be a storage place for a miscellaneous collection of antiquated objects. It should, instead, preserve and arrange its materials in a simple and attractive way so that the clothing, furniture, or equipment from the past will be aids to learning and will also stimulate further learning.

The use of local resources implies that the community itself, and not just the classroom, can provide a wealth of educational experiences. The visit, field trip, or more extensive journey relates evidences of the past to class activities in American history.

THE GRADED USE OF LOCAL RESOURCES

Community sources are appropriate for teaching American history on all grade levels. Realistic items out of the past combined with documentary details about history constitute essential classroom assets. Lower grades widely utilize the realistic, but, as the grade level increases, the emphasis shifts to the application of greater quantities of documentary evidence.

In Elementary School

Elementary classes use materials that relate to the original inhabitants and first settlers. Indians and pioneers and the beginnings of community life draw heavily on local sources. Aboriginal life is a colorful and attractive topic of study but too much time may be devoted to it. And, unfortunately, this study may also result in the collection and preservation of miscellaneous bits and pieces of arrowheads, which, by themselves, do not furnish information about Indian life. More valuable would be the incorporation of the methods and contributions of archeologists to learning about pre-history. Archeologists, however, prefer that untrained persons do not attempt any archeological investigations.

Pioneer life embraces household surroundings with a study of food, clothing, and shelter. The use of realia here supplies the basis for contrasting familiar objects at different times. Familiar names in the community may also be observed by a visit to a local cemetery in order to indicate the progression of generations and the start for acquiring concepts of chronological order. Personal references on all levels are useful, but school students have little interest in genealogy as such. By the full use of appropriate local materials, however, elementary classes may plan many imaginative projects with educational value.

In Junior High School

On the junior high school level, American history classes explore the development of institutions, particularly those that relate to political and economic life. These classes cry out for the use of local materials—both realistic and documentary. The tools and equipment that individuals used in their mills, farms, factories, or stores supply concrete evidence for showing how people made a living. Services, professions, and transportation are additional parts of the changing economy; these endeavors also contributed a variety of physical remains for teaching purposes. Graphic materials indicate political innovations and the issues that were involved in election disputes. The transformation of these institutions and their impact on community developments are traced in maps and pictures and in an examination of the houses, buildings, streets, roads, waterways, fields, and forests of the surrounding environment.

Primary source materials are also of great value in these classes. Original observations and first-hand reports of local events and experiences add excitement to the study of history. Such letters, journals, and official records supply the rudiments for documentary interpretation and analysis.

In Senior High School

The stress on ideas in the secondary school study of American history implies that much attention will be given to verbal materials and the abstract. Words and ideas go together with documents, but, at the same time, there are numerous occasions for making use of pictorial and graphic references in order to explain and also stimulate an interest in these topics of history. The greatest potential in these years, however, is to expose students to the methodology of history. Local documentary collections and other resources furnish frequent opportunities for critically evaluating source materials, for weighing evidence, for analyzing related materials, and for formulating generalizations from the accumulated data.

Research possibilities are limitless and may be planned according to the student's ability and interests. Some of these activities may stress visual interpretation and the expression of historical information by mechanical or artistic skills, as in pictures, models, or dioramas. For many others, however, their activities must stress the exploitation of verbal sources in interpreting some phase of history. Local sources make possible the convenient attainment of these goals.

On all levels and for all abilities, local resources contribute to the development of many necessary skills and to acquiring information and ideas about both past and present that are essential for sound, effective citizens.

Contributors' Who's Who

BESTOR, ARTHUR, Professor of History at the University of Illinois, is the author of several historical works, including *Backwoods Utopias* (1950) and *Education and Reform at New Harmony* (1948), and is co-author of several others, including *Three Presidents and Their Books* (1955) and *The Heritage of the Middle West* (1958). He has written on educational questions in two books, *Education Wastelands* (1953) and *The Restoration of Learning* (1955), and in a number of articles, most recently, "History, Social Studies, and Citizenship," in the *Proceedings* of the American Philosophical Society (1960). In 1956-1957 he was Harmsworth Professor of American History at Oxford.

CARPENTER, HELEN McCRACKEN, is Professor of History at Trenton State College. She has taught in several other colleges and universities and in public school. She is a Past President of NCSS and was editor of its Twenty-Fourth Yearbook, *Skills in the Social Studies*. She has contributed many articles to educational journals and is the author of *Leads to Listening* for Enrichment Records, based on Landmark Books. She is well known as an author of textbooks in the social studies and of *Gateways to American History*.

CARTWRIGHT, WILLIAM H., is Chairman of the Department of Education at Duke University. He is a Past President of NCSS, NEASST, and the Southern Council on Teacher Education. He has been Chairman of the NEA Committee on International Relations and is a member of the Committee on Teaching of the AHA. He is a textbook author in American history and has written various articles and books on education and history, including *The Teaching of History in the United States* (with Arthur C. Bining).

CHASE, W. LINWOOD, is Professor in the Boston University School of Education where he was Dean for many years. He has had wide experience in elementary education. He is a Past President of NCSS and of the National Junior Town Meeting League. He was a delegate to the World Conference on Education in Oslo in 1954 and to the White House Conference on Education in 1955. He has been consultant on elementary education to many school systems and is the author of elementary school textbooks in the social studies and of many articles.

CLELAND, HUGH G., is Assistant Professor of History at the University of Pittsburgh. Among his writings are *George Washington in the Ohio Valley* (1956). He is currently working on a senior high school textbook. His interest in recent history stems partly from his service with the Eighth Army in the Pacific during World War II and partly from research in the history of the CIO.

COLE, WAYNE S., is Professor of History at Iowa State University of Science and Technology. Among his writings on American foreign relations are *America First: The Battle Against Intervention, 1940-1941* and "American Entry into World War II; A Historiographical Appraisal," *Mississippi Valley Historical Review,* 43:595-617; March 1957. He is currently engaged in a study of Gerald P. Nye, former senator from North Dakota.

CRAVEN, WESLEY FRANK, is Edwards Professor of American History at Princeton University. He is the author of books and numerous articles on the Colonial period of American history, including *The Southern Colonies in the Seventeenth Century* (1949), a volume of the History of the South Series. He edited with James Lee Cate, *The Army Air Forces in World War II* (1948-1958), in seven volumes. He is presently working on a volume for the New American Nation Series on the colonies in the second half of the seventeenth century.

DeCONDE, ALEXANDER, is Associate Professor of American History at the University of Michigan. His writings include *Herbert Hoover's Latin American Policy* (1951) and *Entangling Alliance: Politics and Diplomacy under George Washington* (1958). He was also editor of and contributor to *Isolation and Security: Ideas and Interests in Twentieth Century American Foreign Policy* (1957).

DULLES, FOSTER RHEA, is Professor of American History at the Ohio State University. He has written numerous books on American history. Among those recently published are *The United States Since 1865*, a volume in the History of the Modern World Series sponsored by the University of Michigan, *America's Rise to World Power, 1898-1954* (1954) in the New American Nation Series, and *Labor in America* (revised 1960).

DURDEN, ROBERT F., is Assistant Professor of American History at Duke University. Among his writings are *James Shepherd Pike: Republicanism and the American Negro, 1850-1882* (1957), and "James S. Pike: President Lincoln's Minister to the Netherlands," *New England Quarterly,* 29:341-64; September 1956. He is currently working on a biography of Marion Butler, populist senator from North Carolina.

FREIDEL, FRANK B., JR., is Professor of History at Harvard University. Among his writings are *The Splendid Little War* (1958), and the first three volumes of a multi-volume life of Franklin D. Roosevelt, *The Apprenticeship* (1952), *The Ordeal* (1954), and *The Triumph* (1956), which carry the life of Roosevelt up to 1932. He has also written college textbooks on United States history. In 1955-1956, he was Harmsworth Professor of American History at Oxford University.

GABRIEL, RALPH HENRY, is Sterling Professor Emeritus of History at Yale University. For the past three years he has been serving as Professor of

American Civilization in the School of International Service at the American University, Washington, D. C. He is the author of a textbook which has been widely used in the public schools; he edited *The Pageant of America*, a multi-volume pictorial history of American life; and he has published *The Course of American Democratic Thought* (revised in 1956), *Religion and Learning at Yale: The Church of Christ in the College and University, 1757-1957* (1958), and many other writings on American intellectual history.

GAVER, MARY VIRGINIA, is Professor in the Graduate School of Library Service at Rutgers University. She has taught library science at several colleges and universities in the United States and at the University of Tehran, and has been a public school librarian. She is a Past President of the Library Education Division of the American Library Association, the New Jersey Library Association, and the American Association of School Librarians. She is the author of numerous professional articles and books, including *Every Child Needs a School Library*.

HAEFNER, JOHN H., is Professor of Social Studies Education at the State University of Iowa and Head of Social Studies in University High School. He is a Past President of NCSS and has contributed to several of its yearbooks and to *Social Education*, as well as to other journals in both education and the social sciences. He is a textbook author and has aided in the development of testing instruments in various social studies areas. He was a member of the social studies team sent to the American zone of occupation in Western Germany following World War II.

LOWITT, RICHARD, is Associate Professor of History at Connecticut College. Among his writings are *A Merchant Prince of the Nineteenth Century: William E. Dodge* (1954), and "Norris and Nebraska, 1885-1890," *Nebraska History*, 39:23-39; March 1958. He is currently engaged in writing a biography of George Norris, the late U. S. senator from Nebraska, and has completed a chapter on Theodore Roosevelt in a book scheduled for publication in 1961.

MORGAN, EDMUND S., is Professor of American History at Yale University. He is the author of numerous articles and books on colonial America, including *The Stamp Act Crisis: Prologue to Revolution* (1953), written in collaboration with Helen M. Morgan; *The Birth of the Republic 1763-1789* (1956) in the Chicago History of American Civilization Series; and *The Puritan Dilemma: The Story of John Winthrop* (1958) in the Library of American Biography series.

MORRIS, JOHN W., is Professor of Geography at the University of Oklahoma. He has taught social studies in junior and senior high school. He is a Past President of the National Council for Geographic Education and has been Chairman of its Publication Committee. He is a member of the Oklahoma State Social Studies Curriculum Committee and has served as consultant to numerous state and city social studies groups. He is editor of a series of junior high school state geography textbooks and co-author of *World Geography*, a college textbook.

MOWRY, GEORGE, is Professor of History and Dean, Division of Social Sciences, at the University of California, Los Angeles. He is presently serving as Harmsworth Professor, Queens College, Oxford University. Among his writings are *Theodore Roosevelt and the Progressive Movement* (1946), *The California Progressives* (1951), and *The Era of Theodore Roosevelt, 1900-1912* in the New American Nation Series.

POTTER, DAVID M., is William Robertson Coe Professor of American History at Yale University. His writings cover a wide range of American history. He contributed the chapter on the period 1829-1861 to Volume X (1960) of the *New Cambridge Modern History*. He is also the author of *Lincoln and His Party in the Secession Crisis* (1942) and edited with Thomas G. Manning, *Nationalism and Sectionalism in America, 1776-1877* (1949). He is now writing the forthcoming volume on the period 1848-1861 in the New American Nation Series. In 1947-1948 he was Harmsworth Professor of American History at Oxford University.

QUILLEN, I. JAMES, is Dean of the School of Education at Stanford University. He received his Master's and Doctor of Philosophy degrees in American history from Yale University. He was Co-Director of the Stanford Social Education Investigation. He is a Past President of NCSS. He has served as an official of the UNESCO Secretariat in Paris and as Chairman of the Committee on International Relations of the NEA. He is author and co-author of a number of textbooks and other works, including *Education for Social Competence.*

SINGLETARY, OTIS A., is Professor of History and Assistant to the President at the University of Texas. He is the author of *Negro Militia and Reconstruction* (1957) and *The Mexican War* (1960). He has also written the pamphlet, *The South in American History* (1957) for the Service Center for the Teachers of History Series as well as articles in professional journals.

SITTERSON, J. CARLYLE, is Professor of History and Dean of the College of Arts and Sciences at the University of North Carolina. He is on the Board of Editors of the *Journal of Southern History*. Among his writings are *The Secession Movement in North Carolina* (1939), *Sugar Country: The Cane Sugar Industry in the South* (1953), (as co-author), *Industrial Mobilization for War* (1947), and *American Society and the Changing World* (1942).

STEVENS, HARRY R., is Associate Professor of History at Ohio University. He is the author of books and articles on American history including *The Early Jackson Party in Ohio* (1957), "Henry Clay, the Bank, and the West in 1824," *The American Historical Review*, 60:843-48; July 1955, and *The Middle West* (1958), in the Service Center for Teachers of History Series.

TYRRELL, WILLIAM G., Historian in the Division of Archives and History of the New York State Education Department, is responsible for planning and coordinating local history programs throughout the state. He is co-author of *How to Use Local History*, a frequent contributor to *Social Education* and other periodicals. He was editor of Curriculum Series Number Eight, *Social Studies in the College.*

Ver Steeg, Clarence L., is Professor of History at Northwestern University. He is the author of several books, numerous articles, and a recently published high school text. His *Robert Morris, Revolutionary Financier* (1954), was awarded the Albert J. Beveridge Prize by the American Historical Association. He is currently engaged in writing a volume on *The Southern Colonies in the Eighteenth Century, 1689-1763* in the History of the South Series.

Watson, Richard L., Jr., is Professor of History and Chairman of the Department at Duke University. He is presently serving on the Board of Editors of the *Mississippi Valley Historical Review*. Among his publications are (as editor) *Bishop Cannon's Own Story* (1955), seven chapters in the multivolume *The Army Air Forces in World War II*, and "Woodrow Wilson and his Interpreters," *Mississippi Valley Historical Review*, 44:207-36; September 1957.

SELECTED PUBLICATIONS
OF THE NATIONAL COUNCIL FOR THE SOCIAL STUDIES
1201 Sixteenth St., N.W., Washington 6, D. C.

Yearbooks

Thirtieth Yearbook (1960), *Citizenship and a Free Society: Education for the Future*, Franklin Patterson, editor. $4.00; clothbound $5.00.

Twenty-Ninth Yearbook (1959), *New Viewpoints in Geography*, Preston E. James, editor. $4.00; clothbound $5.00.

Twenty-Eighth Yearbook (1958), *New Viewpoints in the Social Sciences*, Roy A., Price, editor. $4.00; clothbound $5.00.

Twenty-Seventh Yearbook (1956-57), *Science and the Social Studies*, Howard H. Cummings, editor. $4.00; clothbound $5.00.

Twenty-Sixth Yearbook (1955), *Improving the Social Studies Curriculum*, Ruth Ellsworth and Ole Sand, co-editors. $3.50; clothbound $4.00.

Twenty-Fifth Yearbook (1954), *Approaches to an Understanding of World Affairs*, Howard R. Anderson, editor. $3.50; clothbound $4.00.

Twenty-Fourth Yearbook (1953), *Skills in Social Studies*, Helen McCracken Carpenter, editor. $3.00; clothbound $3.50.

Twenty-Third Yearbook (1952), *The Teacher of the Social Studies*, Jack Allen, editor. $3.00; clothbound $3.50.

Twentieth Yearbook (1949), *Improving the Teaching of World History*, Edith West, editor. $2.50; clothbound $3.00.

Bulletins

Bulletin No. 31 (1959), *World History Book List for High Schools: A Selection for Supplementary Reading*, prepared by The World History Bibliography Committee, Alice W. Spieseke, *Chairman*, $1.25.

Bulletin No. 15 (rev. ed. 1957), *Selected Items for the Testing of Study Skills and Critical Thinking*, by Horace T. Morse and George H. McCune. $1.50.

Bulletin No. 9 (rev. ed. 1960), *Selected Test Items in World History*, by H. R. Anderson and E. F. Lindquist. Revised by David K. Heenan. $1.50.

Bulletin No. 6 (rev. ed. 1957), *Selected Test Items in American History*, by H. R. Anderson and E. F. Lindquist. Revised by Harriet Stull. $1.25.

Curriculum Series

Number Ten (1958), *The Social Education of the Academically Talented*, Ruth Wood Gavian, editor. $2.00.

Number Nine (rev. ed. 1960), *The Problems Approach and the Social Studies*, G. L. Fersh, R. E. Gross, and R. H. Muessig, co-editors. $2.00.

Number Seven (1953), *Social Studies in the Senior High School: Programs for Grades Ten, Eleven, and Twelve*, Eunice Johns, editor. $2.00.

Number Six (1957), *Social Studies for the Junior High School: Programs for Grades Seven, Eight, and Nine*, Julian C. Aldrich, editor. $2.00.

Number Five (new ed. 1960), *Social Studies for the Middle Grades: Answering Teachers' Questions*, C. W. Hunnicutt, editor. $2.25.

Number Four (1956), *Social Education of Young Children: Kindergarten and Primary Grades*, Mary Willcockson, editor. $2.00.

Orders which amount to $2.00 or less must be accompanied by cash.

Carriage charges will be prepaid on cash orders, but orders not accompanied by cash will be billed with carriage charges included.

A complete publications list sent free on request.